# Wide Acclaim For Miriam Weinstein's
# MAKING A DIFFERENCE
# COLLEGE & GRADUATE GUIDE

"Buy this book. It's the bible for students who seek higher education for higher purposes - one of the most practical and insightful college selection resources today."
Marcy Hamilton, College Counselor, CA

"Profiles hidden gem colleges that most students should know about but rarely do. It is *the* college guide for idealistic students, and fills a tremendous need"
Marty Nemko, College Counselor; Host, *School & Career Talk*, NPR, SF

"Commitment to community and caring about both our human and physical environments should be critical components of a student's educational experience. We feel fortunate to be considered with other colleges that emphasize consciousness about and responsibility for the future of our world."
Richard H. Shaw Jr., Dean of Admissions, Yale University

"Our nation is fortunate that so many of its youth seek to contribute to a more just and sustainable future. And fortunate, as well, are the students, parents, and college counselors who get this book. The institutions profiled within offer academic preparation that enables students to promote social justice and environmental protection. And the guide is not only idealistic, but also pragmatically career-oriented so that students can go on to make a difference in the context of a decent job."
Richard Clugston, Exec. Director, Center for Respect of Life & Environment

"Until the emergence of *Making A Difference College Guide*, high school students who care about the world blindly faced a bewildering array of questionable college options, but not anymore. Even thumbing through this book, you'll wonder how any intelligent student, parent, or guidance counselor could do without it."     *Green Teacher Magazine*

"So many students are being directed into corporate and business life which is soulless and will not serve their future. This extremely important book, however, could help them assist in saving the Planet."
Dr. Helen Caldicott

"What an amazing feat this guide has accomplished! First it harnesses the idealism of today's college bound youth, next it points them to relevant, value-based education, often filled with service programs - whether in local communities or abroad, and then tops it off with practical yet meaningful career-oriented studies!"
Youth Service America

"Weinstein targets those students who are dissatisfied with the prospects of a traditional, passive, and one-dimensional approach to higher education. Interesting, informative and well-written, this book can make a difference for us all."
*Journal of College Admission*

MORE. . . .

# Wide Acclaim For Miriam Weinstein's
# MAKING A DIFFERENCE
# COLLEGE & GRADUATE GUIDE

"I highly recommend this guide for students who care about the Earth."
David Brower, Founder, Earth Island Institute & Friends of the Earth

"We are very excited that there is a guide to college whose basis is service to others and community concerns. This Guide is particularly rewarding. With our college's emphasis on service to others we are proud to be included."
Wallace Ayres, Ass't. Director of Admissions, Swarthmore College

"The sign of a good book reviewer is the ability to rave enthusiastically about the book, and tell the reader everything about it in just a few words. This guide is very difficult to rave about in just a few words. It makes me want to go back to college!"
*Subud Youth*

"I'm honored to have the chance to extol the virtues of this book. It's about time a college guide addressed the really important issues in education today. This Guide profiles a unique cross-spectrum of schools offering a rich, empowering and relevant education."
Steven Antonoff, *The College Finder*

"An excellent resource. It can help students find institutions that will deepen both their understanding of human problem-solving and their social commitment to a better world, and help ensure that they make the most of their college education."
T. Stanton, Ph.D., Director- Haas Center for Public Service, Stanford University

"Until I read this guide, I had no interest in going to college. Now I've picked out a school which I am actually eager to attend."    Daniel Palmer, CA

"As a parent, I am grateful for this book, and urge all concerned parents to buy a copy. This book changes lives. I was so excited by the opportunities in this guide, I bought five more copies for my son's classmates."    Julie Palmer, CA

"Like no other resource on the market. The colleges in the guide include the schools of choice for most of the young people with whom I have worked and is particularly strong for students who want a non-traditional major or who seek to be involved in high quality community service, who are creative and/or who do not look forward to four years of listening to professors lecture. As a college counselor, *Making A Difference* is my best reference. In the last three years, I have directed over three-hundred young people to the colleges in the Guide and have found the schools to be remarkably responsive to their students needs. When I send a student to one of these colleges, I know s/he will have a life-affecting and satisfying collegiate experience."
Nicole Shepherd-Boothman, City Year-Americorps, R.I.

# Wide Acclaim For Miriam Weinstein's
# MAKING A DIFFERENCE
# COLLEGE & GRADUATE GUIDE

"*Making A Difference College Guide* is distinctive in that its criteria focus on what should be the fundamental purpose of our campuses: launching students, with heart and mind, to enhance life for present and future generations. The Guide's value-centered approach to college selection fulfills a much needed demand."

Doug Orr, President, Warren Wilson College

"Deserves to be on the shelf of every career counselor in the country."
*Career Planning & Adult Development Network Newsletter*

"Lights the path to a values-based education."     *College Bound*

"Through I*EARN Global Telecommunications Network, high school students collaborate internationally on projects that make a meaningful difference in the health and welfare of the planet and its people. Afterwards, students are hungry to build on their experience and commitment in both college and career. Ms. Weinstein's book is the first resource to which we point them."

Edwin H. Gragert, Ph.D. Executive Director, I*EARN

"Thanks for making this book available. It is exactly like the kind of information I've been killing myself trying to track down in the library."     Ed Lawson, VA

"The Exxon oil spill, the vanishing rain forests, and the starving children in Rwanda all made you want to throw out your homework and pitch in. But first you had to finish high school. Now it's time for college, and with this guide's help in finding socially aware colleges, you may actually get that chance to help save the world."
*Detroit Free Press*

"Three of our children have found wonderful colleges through this guide that we would have never known about otherwise. Our children are inspired, and as parents, we are most grateful."     Richard & Marie Mermin, CA

"Most college students attend massive state universities because their peers and elders consider it the only option. This guide allowed me to find a smaller, more alternative college with a friendly atmosphere, a family-like structure and wonderful professors who enjoy their occupation. Ms. Weinstein's book led me to the path of a higher education."
Amy Mermin, CA

"Recommended. In spirit the Guide resembles the *Whole Earth Catalog*."
*American Library Association Booklist*

*How wonderful it is that nobody need wait a single moment
before starting to improve the world.*
Anne Frank

*Anyone can be great, because anyone can serve.*
Martin Luther King Jr.

*It's better to light a candle than to curse the darkness.*
Eleanor Roosevelt

*When I was young, I was quite idealistic. We had the freedom
in those days to be idealistic and not necessarily to have to
produce immediate results.... But the reality is, you don't have the
time, the world doesn't have the time, for the sort of idealism
my generation enjoyed. You have to be so much more practical
than we had to be at your age. You must look at your idealism
and not compromise it. And yet, you must also be wise enough and
smart enough and patient enough to know how to go by steps....*
Theresa Heinz, Chairman, Heinz Family Fdn.
Remarks delivered to the Campus Earth Summit

*To be free is to be able to enjoy the fruits of life in a
just, caring, and compassionate community.*
Abraham Heschel

*Religions are too pious, the corporations too plundering, the
government too subservient to provide any adequate remedy. In
this situation, the university has a special role... to reorient
the human community toward a greater awareness that the human
exists with the single great community of the planet Earth.*
Thomas Berry
Remarks to Education for a Just and Sustainable Future Conference

**SIXTH EDITION**

# MAKING A DIFFERENCE

## COLLEGE & GRADUATE GUIDE

MIRIAM WEINSTEIN

SageWorks Press

Copyright © 1999 by Miriam Weinstein
SageWorks Press
POB 441
Fairfax, CA 94978
(800) 218-GAIA

*College Report Card, How To Test Drive A College* © 1993 by Martin Nemko
*What is Education For?* © 1994 by David Orr

Publisher's Cataloging-in-Publication
(Provided by Quality Books, Inc.)


Weinstein, Miriam (Miriam H.)
    Making a difference college & graduate guide :
outstanding colleges to help you make a better world
/ Miriam Weinstein. -- 6th ed.
    p. cm
    Includes bibliographical references and indexes.
    ISBN: 0-9634618-4-2



    1. Universities and colleges--United States--
Directories.  2. Universities and colleges--United
States--Sociological aspects--Directories.  3.
Vocational guidance.  I. Title

L901.W45 1999                378.73
                             QB198-1666

Printed on recycled paper with soy based ink

Printed in the United States of America

Individual copies: $18.00 plus $2.50 postage and handling. Discounts available
for quantity orders. We encourage orders by youth groups, non-profits, service-
learning organizations, grassroots and religious groups working to make a better world.
For information please call or write to the address above.

*For my children,*
*Radha, Elam, Pascal, Mira*
*and to native peoples struggling to maintain*
*their cultures and their land base.*

# ACKNOWLEDGMENTS

First, this acknowledgement would not be complete without the sincerest appreciation to Marty Nemko, who has generously given me his time and mentoring. Thanks to my childhood neighborhood - The Amalgamated - a hotbed of social consciousness, and to my beloved friend Joanne Lukomnik who dragged me along on so many picket lines and demonstrations. Helen Gibbs, thank you and Bob for your friendship and listening to my many complaints! Thanks to Aftab Choudhary for his calm generosity, and to Barry Gordon for his practical wisdom. I am particularly indebted to the gracious educators and many prominent organizations for contributing introductory essays. I appreciate the permission from the Peace Corps to include their Master's Internationalist and Fellows Programs. I am especially grateful for the enthusiastic reception, cooperation, and faith I've received from the colleges and programs profiled in the guide, and for the valuable service they render.

I've received valuable feedback for the sixth edition from a superlative board of advisors: Anthony Cortese of Second Nature; Rick Clugston of Association of University Leaders for a Sustainable Future; Robert Hackett of the Bonner Foundation; Professor David Orr of Oberlin; Professor Milly Henry of New College of California; author and career counselor Marty Nemko; Pam Boylan of Campus Compact and Stephen Antonoff, author and career counselor.

Lastly, heartfelt gratitude to Mother Earth who sustains us all.

# CONTENTS

## MAKING A DIFFERENCE COLLEGES

## MAKING A DIFFERENCE GRADUATE PROGRAMS

## RESOURCES & INDEXES

# PREFACE

## WALTER H. CORSON
### GLOBAL TOMORROW COALITION

Daily we see mounting social and environmental problems that threaten our communities and the survival of our global life-support systems. These problems underscore the need for an education that sheds light on the underlying causes of issues such as poverty, unemployment, and crime; and ecological concerns such as environmental pollution and natural resource depletion.

Miriam Weinstein's *Making A Difference College Guide* moves well beyond the traditional guides and highlights a wide range of innovative, programs and courses that provide practical, problem-solving approaches to some of the great issues of our time - issues that may ultimately imperil our future survival.

The book features colleges and universities that, through their development of programs and selection of faculty, demonstrate a concern for social responsibility, the quality of life, and the future of humankind. Most entries contain a description of the institution's philosophy and its approach to social and environmental concerns, and provide summaries of key programs designed to "make a difference."

The *Guide* highlights innovative programs at more traditional universities such as Tufts, Michigan, and Oregon; at well-known colleges such as Oberlin, St. Olaf, and Swarthmore, at less-known but valuable institutions such as Warren Wilson, Earlham and Prescott, and tiny but unique programs such as the Institute for Social Ecology, and the School for International Training.

A wide range of practical programs leading to good employment opportunities are covered in areas such as forestry, applied environmental technology, environmental engineering, natural resource management, community health, and social work.

The publication is obviously a labor of love; Miriam Weinstein is committed to promoting critical values needed for the twenty-first century such as environmental protection, conflict resolution, and social equity. *Making A Difference College Guide* reveals educational programs that will help students make the planet a better place for themselves and for future generations.

Walter Corson is a Senior Associate at Global Tomorrow Coalition, a not-for-profit alliance of nearly 100 U.S. organizations, institutions, corporations, and individuals committed to acting today to assure a more sustainable, equitable, and humane global future.

# INTRODUCTION

You know why you chose this college guide, now let me tell you how I got to write it. I didn't decide to write this book, this book picked me. This book picked me because I was committed to healing the Earth, to healing people. I'm not an expert on education. I'm not a college counselor. I'm a mother of four, armed with an "empowering" education from one of the colleges in this guide, who, like you, cares deeply about life on earth. Back in 1988, while doing a college search with my eldest child, I scoured the college guides and the viewbooks, and wondered if we were living on the same troubled planet! I figured there had to be more out there. The good news is the answer is yes, there are colleges committed to the environment, social change and service. Some of the colleges which offer a relevant, values-based education are true hidden treasures, and others are among the nation's most prestigious.

Parents, whether you support your students decision to use his/her education to make a difference, or if you're uncertain about the idea, I urge you to at least read the essays by seminal thinkers Jeremy Rifkin -- *Rethinking the Mission of American Education* and David Orr -- *What Is Education For?* along with Stephen Rockefeller's *Walking in Beauty*. You'll find lots of informative and thought provoking ideas in their and the other introductory materials in this section.

And to you, college seekers, do you feel your life has a purpose, to make a difference? Do you ask yourself what kind of meaningful work awaits you? Maybe you want to become a lawyer working to prevent logging of the last ancient forests in North America or a policy planner helping to decide how to best protect the water supply and still meet the needs of farmers and wildlife. Maybe you'd like to help inner city kids make it through college. Perhaps you'll do that by becoming wealthy, and having money to donate. Maybe you'll write about indigenous cultures, and help protect them and their knowledge. Maybe you don't have a clue, you just know you want to make a difference. But you correctly sense that the right college education can be a significant factor.

For you then, choosing a college involves very different questions. In addition to the usual "Will I get a good name education?" "How's the football?" "Will I get a high paying job?" your questions are also: "Will this college help me discover my calling?" "Will this college provide me with the tools to make a better world?" and "Does this college support my values?" Use this book to find a college where you're not strange because you want to make a better world, where one-third or even 100% of the students are actively involved in community service. You'll also discover that most colleges in this guide are committed to and actively engaged in helping solve our world's complex and pressing needs, both in and out of the classroom.

When considering a college, of course you'll look at academic caliber, location, majors and courses, and accessibility of professors. But also learn if it has an ethic of service, concerns for peace and social justice, an environmental focus, and how these concerns are brought into the classroom and the world. Then ask yourself - will this college give me what I need in order to fulfill my purpose? The nearly 100 profiled herein can give you the skills, tools, self-trust, and connections you'll need. Read the profiles and find which colleges are most consistent with your values and goals. Pick out several that pique your interest. Then seriously start checking the colleges out to see if they are really a good fit for you. Use Martin Nemko's *College Report Card* to evaluate a college's fit. Take advantage of *How To Test Drive A College* to learn how to conduct an educated armchair tour that can be as valuable as a real tour.

The spectrum of colleges profiled in this guide is truly unique. There are colleges dedicated to peace and social justice (i.e. Quaker and Mennonite,) strongly environmental colleges (i.e. Northland and Unity,) and a Buddhist college (Naropa). There are work colleges (Berea, Goddard and Warren Wilson,) and international colleges (Friends World) and travel programs (i.e. Audubon, Geocommons and International Honors.) You'll find two small colleges on islands at opposite ends of the country (College of the Atlantic and Sheldon Jackson.) At "60's colleges" such as Evergreen or Hampshire you can take courses taught by teams of teachers from different disciplines, or design you own major incorporating your own interests in your own particular way, or take service-learning courses. Many offer a holistic approach to education.

What else is different? At these distinctive campuses you'll find opportunities to learn while doing service. Imagine working in a health clinic in a remote part of Nepal, assisting migrant laborers in the South, teaching sustainable agriculture in Central America, or building water cisterns at a school in the African countryside. You might help monitor a local river for pollution, save a threatened species such as the peregrine falcon, or sail on a clipper ship to study marine mammals. You might design affordable housing or erect an ecological straw bale building. You can spend study in rainforests, student teach at Native American reservations, tutor inner city kids, or have a say in local development plans. This is the kind of education your parents would likely have died for! But if your parents are worried that this doesn't sound sufficiently academic, put their fears to rest. Educators have come to consider this the most effective kind of learning, and it's blossoming in middle and high schools, colleges and universities nationwide. In fact, college students who are out of the ivory tower get experience, the opportunity to try out their career interests, and valuable contacts which often turn into a job offer upon graduation.

From the smallest hidden-gem college to the prestigious Ivy Leagues, every school in this guide has something valuable to offer you. Many socially committed colleges are small, undergraduate-centered, and have approachable faculty who care more about teaching than research. Smaller colleges can usually be more flexible, responsive and quicker to change. They generally have fewer students per class, resulting in more personal attention. Universities, on the other hand, offer a mind-boggling array of majors, star professors, greater opportunities to participate in advanced research, vast resources, and often a more diverse student body.

While some schools in this guide characterize themselves as only moderately, or even non-selective in their admissions process, be aware that selectivity is a function of the number of applications received as well as academic difficulty. It is not not always a direct reflection of a quality undergraduate education. It doesn't matter how prestigious or selective a college is, what matters is if it is the *right* college for *you*. This is why I have removed the selectivity classifications this year.

As you read this guide, you'll notice its emphasis on meaningful career-oriented studies. The more specialized your area of study, the easier it is to initially find work. Experts are quick to note, however, liberal arts students often find greater flexibility in career opportunities over the years. And although studies such as social work, peace, urban planning, and natural resources are the ones listed herein, students who major in traditional liberal arts such as literature gain critical thinking skills beneficial to an many careers, and often specialize further in graduate school.

Many parents fear that making a difference means a life of poverty, but these fears are unfounded. The *Making A Difference Careers* section lists hundreds of pathways corresponding to the myriad studies noted in this guide, some of which have both good pay and tremendous demand for graduates. Job opportunities in the non-profit sector are also growing rapidly.

We all know that nowadays a college degree doesn't guarantee a secure, interesting or high paying job. It's also true that if you're looking to make a better world, and if you are persistent in seeking it out, there is a meaningful career waiting for you. Even if you won't be able to measure your wealth in dollars, you will have the immeasurable gains that come from a life of integrity, and the joy of improving lives and of caring for the earth.

Then of course, there's finances. If you are low or even moderate income, take the time to learn the ins and outs of financial aid; the benefits might be more substantial than you realize. If you need aid, apply early. While the largest aid is government and college based, learn to seek out scholarships which aren't need based. Many of the colleges in this guide offer scholarships for students engaged in community service. You can learn about these scholarships in *Making A Difference Scholarship Guide*. If at the end, finances don't add up, one possible strategy is to attend a community college for the first two years, and then transfer into the college of your choice as a junior. If graduate school is in your plans, another way to shave expenses is to look for a 3/2 program, where you can obtain a master's degree after your fifth year. Whatever your family's income, do not assume you can't attend any particular college based on it's sticker price. With school grants, even an expensive private college education may be much more affordable than you realize. So, once again, even if your income is upper middle-class, depending upon your age, income, asset level, and number of children, your family may be eligible for grant aid.

As for the profiles and course listings, a few notes. *Making A Difference Studies* listed after the profiles are a small selection of those offered at any individual institution. Likewise, for courses - what I have listed is only a sample. Most often the studies listed are majors, but an occasional interesting minor makes an appearance here and there. Also, the courses listed may not be currently offered. One college was upset when I listed it as having vegetarian meals thinking prospective students would believe they'd be served nothing but lettuce. The vegetarian meals designation means the college *claims* to have nutritious vegetarian meals available *in addition* to the regular fare. I make no promises, however, about the caliber of the cooking!

Lastly, I have chosen to let the schools speak for themselves. I have neither the expertise nor the desire to rank or judge them beyond their fitness for inclusion in this guide. The absence of a school you are interested in could be due to several things: 1) I'm unfamiliar with it; 2) they didn't meet enough of my criteria; or 3) they didn't respond to my requests for information. For this edition I assembled a terrific board of advisors to help evaluate the colleges, and I am sincerely grateful for their input.

Two requests. If you're eighteen, and you haven't registered to vote, do so today. If you're not eighteen, please make registering to vote an act of celebration on your birthday. Decide which party's legislation could make the world a better place. Learn about third parties such as the Green Party. Local elections can be crucial arenas as well, so every opportunity you get, use your vote. If you opt out of participatory democracy, don't complain about what comes down the pike.

Secondly, if you're not already volunteering, now is the best time to start. Check with your church or synagogue, the local volunteer center, or your favorite environmental group. Volunteer with friends and family too!

Both for you and the world, the choices before you are pivotal. I applaud your wish to stand up and be counted. Use this book to choose a college as an important step on your way to contributing to a better world. My sincere gratitude is extended to you for joining with the many caring and often courageous people across the planet who are working to make a difference.

# RETHINKING THE MISSION OF AMERICAN EDUCATION

## JEREMY RIFKIN

The shift from the Industrial Age to the Information Age is transforming our civilization. Vast economic, social, and political changes are already underway. Preparing students for a radically different world in the 21st century requires a reaffirmation of the principles of democracy and community that have served as a beacon in the first two centuries of the American experience. Our schools, colleges and universities can play a key role in fostering a more civil society.

Corporate downsizing, the increasing automation of the manufacturing and service sectors, the shift from mass to elite workforces, growing job insecurity, the widening gap between rich and poor, continued racial tensions, escalating crime, new patterns of immigration, an aging population, and the globalization of the economy are creating a host of new uncertainties and challenges for the American economy.

At the same time, government, at every level, is being fundamentally transformed. The "welfare state" is being pared down and entitlement programs are shrinking. The social net is being streamlined and overhauled and government subsidies of various kinds are being reduced or eliminated.

The new economic and political realities stir us to look once again to America's civil society for help and guidance as we have on so many occasions in the past when our country found itself in the midst of profound change. While historians are quick to credit the market economy and democratic form of government with America's greatness, the civil society- the Third Sector- has played an equally significant role in defining the American way of life.

The nation's hospitals, social service organizations, religious institutions, fraternal orders, women's clubs, youth organizations, civil rights groups, groups, animal welfare organizations, theaters, orchestras, art galleries, libraries, museums, civic associations, community development organizations, neighborhood advisory councils, volunteer fire departments and civilian security patrols are all institutions of the Third Sector.

Today, more than 1,400,000 nonprofit organizations are serving the needs and helping fulfill the dreams of millions of Americans. The civil society is the bonding force, the social glue that unites the many diverse interests of the American people into a cohesive social identity. If there is a single defining characteristic that sums up the unique qualities of being an American, it would be our capacity to join together in civic associations to serve one another.

America's Third Sector will need to play a far more expansive role in the coming century as an arena for job creation and social service provider. The civic sector must also become a more organized social and cultural force in every community, working with, and, at times, pressuring the market and government sectors to meet the needs of workers, families and neighborhoods. Thinking of society as three sectors that work together to create a productive and caring society opens up new possibilities for reconceptualizing the social contract and the kind of education we give our young people.

**Broadening The Mission Of American Education**

Weaving a seamless web between school and community needs to be made an urgent priority if we are to meet the growing challenges of the coming century. A quiet revolution, to bring school and community closer together, has been spreading through the nation's schools and colleges over the past ten years. The effort is designed to create that seamless web. "Civil education" is based on the premise that a primary purpose of schooling is to help young people develop the skills and acquire the values necessary for civic life. Advancing the goals of a civil education requires that educators look to the non-profit sector in addition to the marketplace and government, to inform curriculum development, pedagogy, and the organization of schooling.

Civil education is gaining ground in schools around the country. Many school systems have established service learning activities which integrate service within the curriculum and/or enable students to earn credit for their involvement in neighborhood non-profit organizations, service oriented businesses, and other Third Sector enterprises. Some schools have established character education and citizen education programs to promote civic values. A growing number of schools have begun to recognize the power of connecting civil society and course curriculum. The civil society furnishes ample material for broadening and deepening the school experience across a range of academic studies. All of these initiatives are designed to create a seamless web between school and community.

At a time when teachers, parents, and communities are becoming more concerned about the growing sense of alienation, detachment, and aimlessness of the nation's students, civil education is an important development. Civil education engenders a sense of personal responsibility and accountability, fosters self esteem and leadership, and most of all, allows the feeling of empathy to grow and flourish.

Civil education can give a student a sense of place and belonging, as well as add personal meaning to his or her life. Civil education also provides a much needed alternative frame of reference for a generation increasingly immersed in the simulated worlds of the new telecommunications revolution. Television, computers, and now cyberspace, are becoming an ever more pervasive force in the lives of our students. The new Information Age media technologies offer an array of innovative teaching tools and learning environments for American students. Still, a growing number of educators worry that children growing up in front of the computer screen and TV set are at risk of being less exposed to the kind of authentic real world experiences that are such a necessary part of normal social education and child development. Civil education, combined with the appropriate use of the new Information Age technologies, can act as an antidote to the increasingly isolated world of simulation and virtual reality children experience.

We believe that civil education needs to be incorporated into the heart of the school experience. Learning that occurs through active student participation in service and other aspects of civil life benefits the student, as well as the community. Students learn best by doing. At the same time, weaving the rich 200-year historical legacy and values of the Third Sector into a broad range of curricula, provides a context and framework for children to understand the importance of service learning in the community and the central role that the civil society plays in the life of the country. Learning about the heroes and heroines and the many organizations, movements and causes that have helped forge America's civil society, offers historical role models for children to emulate and a positive vision to help guide their personal journeys in life. Weaving a seamless web between school and community can enhance academic performance and provide a more meaningful educational experience for American students. A civil education also benefits the community itself. Millions of young people reaching out with helping hands to friends and neighbors can enrich the civic life of communities across the country.

As we enter the Information Age, we face the very real challenge of redirecting the course of American education so that our young people will be ready to wrestle with both the demands of the new global economy and the austere new realities facing government. We need to bear in mind that the strength of the market and the effectiveness of our democratic form of government have always depended, in the final analysis, on the vitality of America's civil sector. It is the wellspring of our spirit as a people. Shifting the social paradigm from a two sector to a three sector focus and strengthening the role of the civil society, making it once again the center of American life, is essential if we are to renew our social covenant in the new century. Preparing the next generation for a life-long commitment to the civil society is, perhaps, the single most important challenge facing educators and the American K-12 and collegiate systems as we make the transition into a new era and a new economic epoch in history.

Jeremy Rifkin is the author of *The End of Work: The Decline of the Global Labor Force and the Dawn of the Post Market Era* (Tarcher/Putnam). He is also co-chair of The Partnering Initiative on Education and Civil Society, whose mission is to prepare students for a lifelong commitment to the values of the civil society.

# WHAT IS EDUCATION FOR?
## DAVID W. ORR

*If humans are to flourish on this planet, education, whose dominant focus has been human culture, must clearly place culture within the larger context of nature. Here, David Orr, Professor of Environmental Studies at Oberlin College in Ohio, speaks to the myths that drive modern education and suggests a set of principles that might replace them.*

If today is a typical day on planet Earth, we will lose 116 square miles of rainforest or about an acre a second. We will lose another 72 square miles to encroaching deserts, the results of human mismanagement and overpopulation. We will lose 40 - 100 species, and no one knows whether the number is 40 or 100. Today the human population will increase by 250,000. And today we will add 2,700 tons of chlorofluorocarbons to the atmosphere and 15 million tons of carbon. Tonite the Earth will be a little hotter, its waters more acidic, and the fabric of life more threadbare. By the year's end the numbers are staggering: the total loss of rainforest will equal an area the size of the state of Washington; expanding deserts will equal an area the size of the state of West Virginia; and the global population will have risen by more than 90,000,000. By the year 2000 perhaps as many as 20% of the life forms on the planet in the year 1900 will be extinct.

The truth is that many things on which our future health and prosperity depend are in dire jeopardy; climate stability, the resilience and productivity of natural systems, the beauty of the natural world, and biological diversity.

It is worth noting that this is not the work of ignorant people. It is rather largely the results of work by people with B.A.s, B.S.s, M.B.A.s and Ph.D.s. Elie Wiesel recently made the same point in a speech to the Global Forum in Moscow, saying that the designers and perpetrators of Auschwitz, Dachau, and the Buchenwald were the heirs of Kant and Goethe. In most respects the Germans were the best educated people on Earth, but their education did not serve as an adequate barrier to barbarity. What was wrong with their education? In Wiesel's words: "It emphasized theories instead of values, concepts rather than human beings, abstraction rather than consciousness, answers instead of questions, ideology and efficiency rather than conscience."[1]

I believe that the same could be said for our education. Toward the natural world it too emphasizes theories, not values, abstraction rather than consciousness, neat answers instead of questions, and technical efficiency over conscience. It is a matter of no small consequence that the only people who have lived sustainably on the planet for any length of time could not read, or like the Amish do not make a fetish of reading. My point is simply that education is no guarantee of decency, prudence, or wisdom. This is not an argument for ignorance, but rather a statement that the world of education must now be measured against the standards of decency and human survival -- the issues now looming so large before us in the decade of the 1990's and beyond. It is not education that will save us, but education of a certain kind.

What went wrong with contemporary culture and with education? We can find insight in literature including Christopher Marlowe's Faust who trades his soul for knowledge and power, Mary Shelley's Dr. Frankenstein who refuses to take responsibility for his creation, and Herman Melville's Captain Ahab who says "All my means are sane, my motive and my object mad." In these characters we encounter the essence of the modern drive to dominate nature.

Historically, Francis Bacon's proposed union between knowledge and power foreshadowed the contemporary alliance between government, business, and knowledge that has wrought so much mischief. Galileo's separation of the intellect foreshadowed the dominance of the analytical mind over that part given to creativity, humor, and wholeness. And in Descartes' epistemology one finds the roots of the radical separation of self and object. Together these three laid the foundations for modern education, foundations that now are enshrined in myths that we have come to accept without question. Let me suggest six.

First there is the myth that ignorance is a solvable problem. Ignorance is not a solvable problem; it is rather an inescapable part of the human condition. We cannot comprehend the world in its entirety. The advance of knowledge always carries with it the advance of some form of ignorance. For example, in 1929 ignorance of what chlorofluorocarbons would do to the stratospheric ozone and climate stability was of no importance, since they had not been invented. But after Thomas Midgley, Jr. discovered CFCs in 1930, what had been trivial ignorance became a life-threatening gap in human understanding of the biosphere. Not until the early 1970s did anyone think to ask "what does this substance do to what?" In 1986 we discovered that CFCs had created a hole in the ozone over the South Pole the size of the lower 48 states, and by 1990 a serious general thinning of ozone worldwide. With the discovery of CFC's, knowledge increased, but like the circumference of an expanding circle, ignorance grew as well.

A second myth is that, with enough knowledge and technology, we can manage planet Earth. Higher education has been largely shaped by the drive to extend human domination to its fullest. In this mission human intelligence may have taken the wrong road. Nonetheless, managing the planet has a nice ring to it. It appeals to our fascination with digital readouts, computers, buttons, and dials. But the complexity of Earth and its life systems can never be safely managed. The ecology of the top inch of topsoil is still largely unknown, as is its relationship to the large systems of the biosphere. What might be managed, however, is us: human desires, economies, politics, and communities. But our attention is caught by those things that avoid the hard choices implied by politics, morality, ethics, and common sense. It makes far better sense to reshape ourselves to fit a finite planet than to attempt to reshape the planet to fit our infinite wants.

9

A third myth is that knowledge is increasing and, by implication, so is human goodness. There is an information explosion going on, by which I mean a rapid increase in data, words, and paper. But this explosion should not be mistaken for an increase in knowledge and wisdom, which cannot be measured so easily. What can be said truthfully is that some knowledge is increasing, while other kinds of knowledge is being lost. For example, David Ehrenfeld has pointed out that biology departments no longer hire faculty in such areas as systematics, taxonomy, or ornithology. In other words, important knowledge is being lost because of the recent overemphasis on molecular biology and genetic engineering, which are more lucrative but not more important areas of inquiry. Despite all of our advances in some areas, we still do not have anything like the science of land health that Aldo Leopold called for half a century ago.

It is not just knowledge in certain areas that we're losing, but vernacular knowledge as well, by which I mean the knowledge that people have of their places. In Barry Lopez's words: "It is the chilling nature of modern society to find an ignorance of geography, local or national, as excusable as an ignorance of hand tools, and to find the commitment of people to their home places only momentarily entertaining, and finally naive.... (I am) forced to the realization that something strange, if not dangerous, is afoot. Year by year the number of people with firsthand experience in the land dwindles. Rural populations continue to shift to the cities. In the wake of this loss of personal and local knowledge, the knowledge from which a real geography is derived, the knowledge on which a country must ultimately stand, has come something hard to define but I think sinister and unsettling." 2

The modern university does not consider this kind of knowledge worth knowing except to record it as an oddity "'folk culture." Instead it conceived its mission as that of adding to what is called the "fund of human knowledge" through research. And what can be said of research? Historian Page Smith offers one answer: "The vast majority of so-called research turned out in the modern university is essentially worthless. It does not in the main result in greater health or happiness among the general populace or any particular segment of it. It is busywork on a vast, almost incomprehensible scale. It is dispiriting, it depresses the whole scholarly enterprise, and most important of all, it deprives the student of what he or she deserves - the thoughtful and considered attention of a teacher deeply and unequivocally committed to teaching." 3

In the confusion of data with knowledge is a deeper mistake that learning will make us better people. But learning, as Loren Eiseley once said, "is endless and in itself it will never make us ethical men."4 Ultimately, it may be the knowledge of the good that is most threatened by all of our other advances. All things considered, it is possible that we are becoming more ignorant of the things we must know to live well and sustainably on the Earth.

In thinking about the kinds of knowledge and the kinds of research that we will need to build a sustainable society, there is a distinction to be made between intelligence and cleverness. Intelligence is long term and aims toward wholeness. Cleverness is mostly short term and tends to break reality into bits and pieces. Cleverness is personified by the functionally rational technician armed with know-how and methods, but without a clue about the higher ends to which technique should be subservient. The goal of education should be to connect intelligence, with its emphasis on whole systems and the long term, with cleverness, which is being smart about details.

A fourth myth of higher education is that we can adequately restore that which we have dismantled. I am referring to the modern curriculum. We have fragmented the world into bits and pieces called disciplines, hermetically sealed from other disciplines. As a result most students graduate without any broad, integrated sense of the unity of things. The consequences for their personhood and for the planet are large. For example, we routinely produce economists who lack the most rudimentary knowledge of ecology. This explains why our national accounting systems do not subtract the costs of biotic impoverishment, soil erosion, and poisons in our air and water from gross national product. We add the price of the sale of a bushel of wheat to GNP while forgetting to subtract the three bushels of topsoil lost in its production. As a result of incomplete education, we've fooled ourselves into thinking that we're much richer than we are. The same point could be made about other hermetically sealed disciplines.

Fifth, there is a myth that the purpose of education is that of giving you the means for upward mobility and success. Thomas Merton once identified this as the "mass production of people literally unfit for anything except to take part in an elaborate and completely artificial charade."[5] The plain fact is that the planet does not need more successful people. But it does desperately need more peacemakers, healers, restorers, storytellers, and lovers. It needs people who live well in their places. It needs people of moral courage willing to join the fight to make the world habitable and humane. These have little to do with success as our culture has defined it.

Finally, there is a myth that our culture represents the pinnacle of human achievement. This myth represents cultural arrogance of the worst sort, and a gross misreading of history and anthropology. Recently this view has taken the form that we won the cold war. Communism failed because it produced too little at too high a cost. But capitalism has also failed because it produces too much, shares too little, at too high a cost to our children and grandchildren. Communism failed as an aesthetic morality. Capitalism has failed because it destroys morality altogether. This is not the happy world that advertisers and politicians describe. We have built a world of sybaritic wealth for a few and Calcutta poverty for a growing underclass. At its worst it is a world of crack on the streets, insensate violence, and desperate poverty. The fact is that we live in a disintegrating culture. In the words of Ron Miller, editor of *Holistic Review*: "Our culture does not nourish that which is best or noblest in the human spirit. It does not cultivate vision, imagination, or aesthetic or spiritual sensitivity. It does not encourage gentleness, generosity, caring, or compassion. Increasingly in the last twentieth century, the economic-technocratic-statist world view has become of a monstrous destroyer of what is loving and life-affirming in the human soul."[6]

Measured against the agenda of human survival, how might we rethink education? Let me suggest six principles.

First, all education is environmental education. By what is included or excluded we teach students that they are part of or apart from the natural world. To teach economics, for example, without relevance to the laws of thermodynamics or those of ecology is to teach a fundamentally important ecological lesson: that physics and ecology have nothing to do with the economy. It just happens to be dead wrong. The same is true throughout all of the curriculum.

A second principle comes from the Greek concept of Paideia: the goal of education is not a mastery of subject matter, but mastery of one's person. Subject matter is simply the tool. Much one would use a hammer and chisel to carve a block of marble, one uses ideas and knowledge to forge one's own personhood. For the most part we labor under a confusion of ends and means, that the goal of education is to stuff all kind of facts, techniques, methods, and information into the student's mind, regardless of how and with what effect it will be used. The Greeks knew better.

Third, I would like to propose that knowledge carries with it the responsibility to see that it is well used in the world. The results of a great deal of contemporary research bear resemblance to those foreshadowed by Mary Shelley: monsters of technology and its byproducts for which no one takes responsibility or is even expected to take responsibility. Whose responsibility is Love Canal? Chernobyl? Ozone depletion? The Valdez oil spill? Each of these tragedies was possible because of knowledge created for which no one was ultimately responsible. This may finally come to be seen for what I think it is: a problem of scale. Knowledge of how to do vast and risky things has far outrun our ability to responsibly use it. Some of it cannot be used responsibly, which is to say safely and to consistently good purposes.

Fourth, we cannot say that we know something until we understand the effects of this knowledge on real people and their communities. I grew up near Youngstown, Ohio, which was largely destroyed by corporate decisions to "dis-invest" in the economy of the region. In this case M.B.A.s, educated in the tools of leveraged buyouts, tax breaks, and capital mobility have done what no invading army could do -- they destroyed an American city with total impunity on behalf of something called the "bottom line." But the bottom line for society includes other costs, those of unemployment, crime, alcoholism, child abuse, lost savings, and wrecked lives. In this instance what was taught in the business schools and economics departments did not include the value of good communities. or the human costs of a narrow destructive economic rationality that valued efficiency and economic abstractions above people and community.

My fifth principle has to do with the power of example over words. Students hear about global responsibility while being educated in institutions that often spend their budgets and invest their endowments in the most irresponsible things. The lessons being taught are those of hypocrisy and ultimately despair. Students learn, without anyone ever saying it, that they are helpless to overcome the frightening gap between ideals and reality. What is desperately needed are faculty and administrators who provide role models of integrity, care, thoughtfulness, and institutions capable of embodying ideals wholly and completely in all of their operations.

Finally, I would like to propose that the way learning occurs is as important as the content of particular courses. Process is important for learning. Lecture courses tend to induce passivity. Indoor classes create the illusion that learning only occurs inside four walls isolated from what students call, without apparent irony, the "real world." Dissecting frogs in biology teaches lessons about nature that no one would verbally profess. Campus architecture is crystallized pedagogy that often reinforces passivity, monologue, and artificiality. My point is simply that students that are being taught in various and subtle ways beyond the content of courses (the tacit curriculum).

If education is to be measured against the standard of sustainability, what can be done? I would like to propose four things. First, I would like to propose a dialogue in every educational institution about the substance and process of education. Are graduates better planetary citizens or are they, in Wendell Berry's words, "itinerant professional vandals?" Does the institution contribute to the development of sustainable regional economy, or in the name of efficiency, to the processes of destruction?

My second suggestion is to use campus resource flows (food, energy, water, materials, and waste) as part of curriculum. Faculty and students together might study the wells, mines, farms, feed-lots, and forests that supply the campus, as well as the dumps, smokestacks, and outfall pipes at the other end. The purpose is both pedagogic, using real things to teach stewardship, and practical, to change the way the particular institution spends its operational budget. One result would be to engage the creative energy of students in finding ways to shift the institutional buying power to support better alternatives that do less environmental damage, reduce use of toxic substances, promote energy efficiency and of solar energy, help to build a sustainable regional economy, cut long-term costs, and provide an example to other institutions. Study results should be woven into the curriculum as interdisciplinary courses, seminars. lectures, and research.

My third suggestion is to examine institutional investments. Is the endowment invested according to the Valdez Principles? Is it invested in companies doing things that the world needs done and in a responsible manner? Can some part of it be invested locally to help leverage energy efficiency and the evolution of a sustainable economy in the surrounding region? The research necessary to answer such questions might also form the basis of courses that focus on the development of sustainable local and regional economies.

Finally, every educational institution should set a goal of ecological literacy for all of its students. No student should graduate from any educational institution without a basic comprehension of: (1) the laws of thermodynamics; (2) the basic principles of ecology; (3) carrying capacity; (4) energetics; (5) least-cost, end-use analysis; (6) how to live well in a place; (7) limits of technology; (8) sustainable agriculture and forestry; (9) appropriate scale; (10) steady-state economics and (11) environmental philosophy and ethics. Collectively these imply the capacity to distinguish between health and disease, development and growth, sufficient and efficient, optimum and maximum, and "should do" from "can do."

As Aldo Leopold asked in a similar context: "If education does not teach us these things, then what is education for?"

David Orr, Professor of Environmental Studies at Oberlin College is the co-founder of the Meadowcreek Project, a nonprofit environmental organization in Arkansas and author of *Ecological Literacy: Education and the Transition to a Postmodern World*. This essay is from his book *Earth in Mind* published by Island Press. The Campus Blueprint for a Sustainable Future crafted by delegates from 111 U.S. colleges and universities at the Campus Earth Summit in 1995 included many of the principles advocated here by Professor Orr.

# AMERICORPS:
## GOOD FOR YOUR COUNTRY, GOOD FOR YOUR CAREER
### CORPORATION FOR NATIONAL SERVICE

If you're reading this book, chances are you want more than a quality college education. You also want to change the world -- or at least make a difference. What if there was a way you could earn money for college, gain real life skills and get a leg up in the admissions process -- all while solving problems and making a difference in your community?

Well, now there is. It's called AmeriCorps, the domestic Peace Corps. Created by Congress and President Clinton in 1993, AmeriCorps has already offered more than 100,000 Americans this simple bargain: if you give a hand to your country, you'll get a hand up for your education. Just like the G.I.Bill for military service, those who serve in AmeriCorps earn money for college in exchange for serving their country. This year 40,000 men and women will take AmeriCorps' pledge to "get things done for America -- to make our people safer, smarter and healthier." Working through national and local nonprofits, members will tutor and mentor children, build Habitat for Humanity homes, fight crime, run afterschool programs, restore parks and streams, help the Red Cross rebuild after floods and hurricanes and do countless other things to improve our lives and bring people together.

As an AmeriCorps member, you will receive a living allowance and health insurance. After completing a year of full-time service, you'll receive an education award worth $4,725. This award can be used to pay off student loans or to finance college, graduate school or vocational training.

At a time of rising college costs, AmeriCorps' education award is helping thousands of young Americans achieve their dream of a college degree. Equally important, AmeriCorps is helping communities across America solve their toughest social problems. We live in a time of great prosperity, but our country continues to face profound challenges that need our attention -- from hunger and homelessness and environmental degradation to city streets plagued by crime and children who can't read. At a time of shrinking government, we need citizens to do more, and young people have the time, energy and talents to lead the way.

## A Life-Changing Experience

You know that a college education will help you make a difference later in life. But do you want to wait? What about starting right now, before college, by giving a year of service in AmeriCorps? Not only will you learn new skills and feel the satisfaction of helping others, you will gain valuable insights to help decide what college to attend and what career to pursue.

Beyond the skills and real life experience, AmeriCorps can change your life in another more subtle way -- by raising your self-confidence and aspirations. Consider the path of Marilyn Concepcion of Providence, RI. In 1993, Marilyn was a high school dropout working on an assembly line. Then she joined the City Year AmeriCorps program, where she helped renovate a community center and taught English to elementary students. AmeriCorps helped Marilyn discover gifts she didn't know she had, and boosted her self-esteem. She applied to Brown University, where she's now studying to be a pediatrician.

At age 19, Kristen Woolf didn't know what she wanted to study in college -- or how to pay for it. For Kristen, AmeriCorps was just the answer. She joined AmeriCorps and worked with young people in an afterschool program in Austin, Texas. She enjoyed the experience so much that she signed up for another year as an AmeriCorps Leader. With nearly $10,000 in college money and two years of real world experience, Kristen was ready to go to school. She's now a sophomore at Southwest Texas State University pursuing a degree in social work.

After four years of high school, some students want to take a break before plunging into full-time academics. Beyond helping others, they want an adventure -- the chance to meet new people, experience new things and visit parts of the country they've never been before. All AmeriCorps programs offer this, but one in particular -- the National Civilian Community Corps (NCCC) -- is ideally suited to this type of student.

The NCCC is a 10-month residential service program for men and women ages 18-24. It takes its inspiration from the Depression-era Civilian Conservation Corps, which put millions of young people to work restoring our natural environment. AmeriCorps NCCC retains this focus on the environment, but recognizes that our nation's challenges today are more diverse. NCCC members work in teams on a variety of projects -- building trails, restoring streams and parks, building low-income housing, tutoring children, and providing disaster relief. Members live together on closed military bases and are often sent on 'spikes' to other parts of the country to work on special projects.

With no required skills necessary, AmeriCorps NCCC teaches members what they need to get the job done. Just ask NCCC member Lisa Melkert. After renovating a Denver inner-city school and repairing a school for the deaf in Indianapolis, Lisa attended an AmeriCorps crash course on the IRS tax system. Trained and armed with a lap top, she visited local senior centers providing free tax services for low-income senior citizens. Several NCCC teams are trained by the U.S. Forest Service in forest fire suppression. One member said, "My favorite part of the NCCC so far was the time we got called out to Idaho to put out forest fires. Who ever thought I could do that?"

15

For parents worried about paying for college, the AmeriCorps education award can be a big help. And a growing number of colleges and universities are offering to match the $4,725 education award with their own scholarship aid. But AmeriCorps can offer more than financial help. The qualities AmeriCorps promotes -- creativity, teamwork, initiative, problem-solving -- are just what college admissions officers are looking for in a prospective student. Of course GPA and SAT scores are the first thing any college will look at. But increasingly colleges are looking for well-rounded students who have volunteer experience. Nearly every every college and university considers preparing students to be responsible citizens as part of their mission. What better way to fulfill that mission than by selecting those who've already given a year of their life to serve their country?

### A Year Off -- Or On?

AmeriCorps helps thousands of young people make a difference and figure out what they want to do before college. But it's also a very popular option for students already in college. About one-third of AmeriCorps members have a year or two of college under their belt, and are taking time off to serve their communities and explore different career paths.

Sara Potts had just finished her sophomore year at Truman State University in Missouri and had no idea what to major in. "I was involved in everything, but I just couldn't make up my mind." She heard about AmeriCorps and within months was tutoring in an elementary school. Potts believes this experience has changed her life. Not only has she changed majors, she even transferred colleges. Because of AmeriCorps, she now knows she wants to spend her life working with children.

There are increasing opportunities for college students to serve in AmeriCorps while they are in college. More and more universities are sponsoring AmeriCorps programs, often with part-time positions that allow students to continue taking classes while they serve. Most of these are in the area of education and childhood literacy.

AmeriCorps is in the forefront of America Reads, a national campaign launched by President Clinton in 1996 to ensure that every American child learns to read independently and well by the end of the third grade. AmeriCorps members are helping meet this goal by tutoring elementary students one-on-one and recruiting and mobilizing other volunteer tutors. In many cases, AmeriCorps members recruit college-work study students, who serve ten hours a week tutoring children instead of working on campus shelving books or washing dishes in the dining hall. In one program called JumpStart, college work- study students in Boston, New Haven and Washington, DC serve as AmeriCorps members tutoring children in Head Start centers.

History and common sense tells us the best way to make a lasting difference is to empower people to improve the conditions of their own lives. That's the key idea behind Volunteers in Service to America (VISTA), the national service program started in the 1960s which is now part of AmeriCorps. As an AmeriCorps*VISTA member, you might help start a youth center, establish a job bank, set up a literacy program or organize a domestic violence program. Whatever you do, you'll be be helping low-income communities help themselves to create long-term sustainable change. VISTA members must be at least 18 years old and usually have a bachelor's degree or three years of related work experience.

Many AmeriCorps*VISTA assignments are in cutting-edge fields such as microenterprise credit, business development and computer technology. For example, AmeriCorps members in the IBM Team Tech program help nonprofit organizations effectively use technology to increase the impact of their work.

In eleven cities, AmeriCorps VISTA Team Tech members offer computer hardware and software assistance, design websites and provide Internet training to nonprofit agencies. Members learn extremely valuable computer and training skills that can be transferred to other work in the nonprofit, government or private sectors.

In addition to AmeriCorps NCCC and VISTA, there are literally hundreds of national and local nonprofits that sponsor AmeriCorps members. They range from America's largest and most respected groups -- Habitat for Humanity, American Red Cross, Boys and Girls Clubs, Big Brothers Big Sisters -- to local homeless shelters, food banks and conservation corps. You can serve in your hometown or across the country; in a large city or rural hamlet; in teams or individually; whatever your interests and background, there's likely to be an AmeriCorps position right for you.

So whether you are in high school, have a few years of college, or are a college graduate, you can be a part of this national movement to get things done and bring communities together. The spirit of service runs deep in America. You can be part of that proud tradition. Call AmeriCorps today. You'd be surprised what a year of service could do for your community, your country, and your future.

> *I will get things done for America -- to make our people safer, smarter and healthier.*
> *I will bring Americans together to strengthen our communities.*
> *Faced with apathy, I will take action.*
> *Faced with conflict, I will seek common ground.*
> *I will carry this commitment with me this year and beyond.*
> *I am an AmeriCorps member, and I will get things done.*
> -- AmeriCorps Pledge:

To learn more about AmeriCorps, please call 1-800-942-2677
(TDD 1-800-833-3722),
or visit our website at www.americorps.org.

Editor's note: For a list of colleges offering AmeriCorps Matching Grants, get a copy of *Making A Difference Scholarship Guide*, available from SageWorks Press.

# COMMUNITY SERVICE:
## EXPERIENCE FOR A LIFETIME OF COMMITMENT,
## OF CITIZENSHIP, OF PARTICIPATION

### Elizabeth L. Hollander
### Campus Compact

When I was in college in the 1960's, my friends and I believed that it was our duty to be actively involved in shaping our nation's policy. We ventured outside our campus to the streets of Philadelphia, where we picketed stores that employed few minorities. In this way, we exercised our rights as citizens and called attention to civil rights.

Three decades later, college and university students all over the country have an incredible opportunity to get involved in their communities through the diverse array of community service programs offered through their schools. Opportunities for you to engage in tremendously challenging, important, and rewarding community service while you are in school are becoming available like never before. Whatever issue motivates you, whatever level of commitment you bring, whatever your personal style and unique talents, there is a place for you to contribute, to truly make a difference, to have a real impact in peoples' lives and in your own.

Better still, you will find that at many colleges and universities, community service is no longer limited to extracurricular activities that students undertake in their free time. Increasingly, faculty are incorporating service into their coursework, helping make the service more effective and the learning more profound. This powerful trend in education, called service learning, is breaking down the walls that separate campuses from communities, and is a major element in the national explosion of community service. Nearly 80 percent of Campus Compact member schools offer service learning courses.[1]

Service learning represents a merger of the movement for education reform, which holds among other things that education can be improved through combining active learning with the movement for responsible citizenship. These two movements agree that engaged citizenship in a democratic society is a learned behavior, a lifelong "habit of the heart" that can be acquired in part through service learning. Many of you may already be involved in service learning programs at your high school. More and more elementary, middle and high schools are building service into the educational experience, and several states and school districts now require service for graduation.

Perhaps the most exciting aspect of the student service movement is that it is largely led by students themselves. Today's students seek out quality service programs,and where programs do not exist, students are creating them. Students are indeed doing great things, and the nation has taken notice and is following their lead.

For instance, I work for Campus Compact, a national coalition of college and university presidents that was founded in 1985 to support students' community service efforts. The founding presidents saw college students actively involved in community service programs, and sought to encourage more students to get involved. The founders understood that service connects students to the community and to their lifelong civic responsibility to whatever community they live in. Additionally, the federal Corporation for National Service, created by President Clinton, funds and promotes national service programs such as AmeriCorps, Learn and Serve America, and National Service Scholars, a scholarship program for high school students engaged in community service.

Now, to the business at hand. There are a few things to consider as you set about selecting a school that is right for you. First, I would encourage you to look closely at the service programs offered at schools you consider, as the nature and quality of programs vary a great deal. Many of the schools in this guide have exceptionally strong service programs. You will find on some campuses that service programs are described in admissions materials and are well known by admissions staff. Some schools even offer scholarships for incoming students with service backgrounds. Catalogs are just a starting point. Although it may not always be easy to find out what is going on, you should make inquiries. Use the telephone or visit the college's web site. Try especially to talk with current undergraduates. Visit if you possibly can.

Second, find out who runs service programs. Programs are usually run by student organizations, by student life administrators, by the career office, or by academic departments. Programs run by students will challenge your organizing and leadership abilities, but may take time away from direct service, while programs run largely by faculty or administrators will allow you to devote more time directly to service, but with perhaps less influence in the direction of the project. So it depends on what you are looking for and where your talents lie.

Likewise, consider issues. If you have a passion for a particular issue, such as mentoring, the environment or literacy, you might want to look for schools with service programs that address your issue. Don't rule out a school if it doesn't have such a program; often, you will be able to create a program around a specific issue.

Finally, I suggest you inquire specifically whether a school offers service learning courses. Combining your service with learning will help you understand deeply the subtleties and relationships between the subjects you study, the problems that we face together, and the institutions we have created to address them.

Service will change the way you look at the world, and will give you experiences available nowhere else. "Behind the studies, the rhetoric, and the ideological struggles lies one simple fact: service works. Not only are trees planted, old people cared for, the hungry fed, but young people learn a new version of their familiar selves; they meet in themselves strong, resilient, reliable, demanding, determined, likable individuals who can change the world and change their own lives as well."[2] Good luck!

1. Judy Karasik, in a report for the John D. and Catherine T. Mac Arthur Foundation
2. ibid.

Elizabeth Hollander is the Director of Campus Compact, The Project for Public and Community Service. Campus Compact is a project of the Education Commission of the States.

# WELCOME TO THE MOVEMENT

## Lloyd Jacobson
### Campus Opportunity Outreach League (COOL)

Welcome to the movement. The fact that you are reading this book suggests that you are interested in joining a movement of people and ideas that is making college more about producing citizens, than just producing workers. This movement has many facets; some concentrating on issues of poverty and social disadvantage, some focusing on environmental issues, and some concerned primarily with peace and justice. What these facets all have in common though is a need for committed individuals dedicated to learning how to produce substantive and positive change in the world.

The schools you will find profiled in this book are true leaders in their field. They are taking on the challenge of expanding academic programs, or even creating new areas of study, that allow students to explore the real world. Students attending these schools are involved first-hand in work that makes learning come alive through service-learning, a teaching concept that encourages the gaining of knowledge not solely from books and lecture, but also through personal experience and observation in the community.

But just what has led these schools to become so different from all the others? In many cases these schools have distinguished themselves because of the initial efforts of an organized mass of students, just like you, who banded together to help create these programs. Starting in the mid-1980s, thousands of students across the country started to challenge themselves and their colleges to become involved in addressing our most pressing social and environmental problems through service and social action. Working with national organizations such as the Campus Outreach Opportunity League (COOL), the National Student Campaign Against Hunger and Homelessness, and the Student Environmental Action Committee, among many others, these students forged connections with the communities just outside their campus walls that in many cases never existed before. These connections took the form of community service partnerships with people in need, or involved getting students working directly to help save our threatened environment. Based on the ever expanding numbers of participants in these programs, and given the noticeable difference in these students learning levels, faculty on many campuses started to take an interest in promoting this kind of activity with even more students by integrating it into the curriculum. Thus these student service leaders had not merely helped change the face of their communities, but they were also helping change the face of higher education.

As you read this book and research campuses you should keep the importance of that student leadership role in mind. As someone interested in making a difference, you should not merely be considering a college based on its offering of degree programs, but also how you might be able to contribute to the on-going expansion of the movement on that campus. If you are lucky you will discover a campus with many of the same types of student groups that helped introduce service-learning in the first place. Many of these groups continue to be the source of the most innovative ideas for addressing community problems on today's college campuses, and they continue to influence the direction of their campuses own academic programs. Also these groups will many times offer you the best opportunity to practice and develop essential leadership, organizing, and advocacy skills which often can not be taught within the curriculum. In short, they will help you round out your interests in social change as well as help you supplement the skills you will learn in the classroom.

Even if you should end up not attending one of the schools profiled in this book, understanding the importance of this student role will be of tremendous help to you. If you truly committed to making a difference, recognize that you can still create, innovate and organize at that school for the benefit of yourself, the school and the community it shares. Even so, the book you hold in your hands will still be an excellent guide. The profiles enclosed can serve as a source of inspiration for you as well as a kind of road map to discover those schools, student groups, and national organizations that you can contact for helpful ideas in creating the kind of experience you want to bring to your own campus.

Over the past few years the number of students seeking a meaningful education has increased significantly. Over that same time the number of schools profiled in this book has grown steadfastly. Wherever you may end up choosing to attend college, I hope you take on the responsibility of helping to continue this growth. Once again, welcome to the movement.


Lloyd Jacobson is National Programs Director for COOL: Campus Outreach Opportunity League, the national student-lead organization  founded in 1984 to encourage, support and improve campus based service programs.

# COOL LEADERS

The COOL Leaders Program is a year-long intensive leadership training and development program for college students who are actively involved in campus-based community service and service-learning programs. Funded by a grant from the Corporation for National Service Learn & Serve America, the primary purpose of COOL Leaders is to help strengthen and expand service programs by providing increased training and support for emerging student leaders.

The COOL Leaders Program provides training for college students to develop and utilize their service and leadership skills. The goals of the program are to provide students with:

• Practical skills training that will make the student a more effective leader on campus and in the community.

• Exposure to a variety of other campus, regional and national organizations in the field of community service, heightening the opportunity for networking and learning.

• Resources and support to promote the improvement of service programming on their campuses.

COOL Leaders receive skills workshops, resource materials, on-going support, training from COOL staff and other service leaders 3 times per year, alumni mentoring, monthly mailings and a dedicated e-mail discussion group (list-serv) just for them.

Students interested in applying to the COOL Leaders Program must be active participants in an established campus-based service organization or service-learning program. The applicant should have at least one year of demonstrated student leadership involvement on campus.

Each school will be asked to sponsor the travel and registration cost for all training activities. COOL though will be responsible for all food and lodging costs during the summer and fall training components. A limited number of scholarships will also be available.

To get more information on the program and as well as a complete application packet please visit our web site at:

www.COOL2SERVE.org

(and then just follow the links from our "Programs" Page)
or go directly to our COOL Leaders Page at:
www.COOL2SERVE.org/COOLleaders.html

COOL
1531 P Street, NW, #LLa
Washington, DC 20005

# ENVIRONMENTAL LITERACY
## A GUIDE TO CONSTRUCTING
## AN UNDERGRADUATE EDUCATION
### THOMAS H. KELLY, PH.D
#### TUFTS ENVIRONMENTAL LITERACY INSTITUTE

Because all human activities are dependent upon and have repercussions within the environment, you have an opportunity to make a difference no matter what your interests. Whether you major in marketing, biology, mathematics or music and you spend your professional life in industry, government or journalism, your actions will have an environmental impact. So, remember whatever your major is, in a certain sense, it is an environmental one.

Ask yourself then, what kind of impact do you want to make? Where do you want to make it? How do you want to make it? These questions have important implications for deciding on the kind of college education you want. If you are concerned about the environment and want your education to reflect that concern and strengthen your capacity to assess, evaluate and judge where you fit into the environment, think about these questions. Independent of your ultimate career choice, what knowledge, skills and experiences do you want from your undergraduate education? If you are concerned about the Earth, yet do not wish to choose an environmental career, consider the notion of "environmental literacy."

An environmentally literate person understands the nature of the interdependence between human activities and the non-human world. With a modern education, so often career-oriented, if we are to graduate environmentally literate citizens, environmental concerns must be incorporated across the curriculum and even beyond the classroom. The prominence of the environment and an ecological perspective emphasizing systems such as the biosphere within the liberal arts education is relatively new. Many educators now seek to connect a broad range of disciplines in an effort to grasp complex, large-scale ecological problems. This is a tall order because there is a fundamental tension between the broad inclusive character of environment, and the practical significance of specialization to the job market or graduate school.

Moreover, recognition of the need to understand the social aspects of ecological problems has introduced questions of racism, equity, human rights, national sovereignty and national security into the environmental debate. These aspects of ecological problems are now widely acknowledged to be part and parcel of these issues. Internationally, the scientific, educational and governmental communities agree that segregation of the so-called "natural sciences" from "social sciences" is a significant obstacle to environmental education. Accordingly, calls for interdisciplinary and multidisciplinary educational programs are being heard from many quarters. Prospective undergraduates should be aware that while intuitively appealing, interdisciplinary and multidisciplinary education are interpreted differently by different schools. It is one thing to take a collection of courses from different disciplines; it is another to integrate and internalize their contents so that you can apply them to your personal and professional life.

When you are evaluating schools and deciding what kind of education you want, one consideration is the degree of disciplinary integration. Does a given program simply offer varying menus of courses from different disciplines? Or, does it offer an integrating mechanism such as a core curriculum or a culminating course or project specifically designed to aid your incorporation of the material into thinking and action? Is there a sufficient range of sciences in the curriculum to provide a graduate with a basic understanding of the materials, energy and processes within which human activity occurs? But beware of a scientific bias in course requirements; make sure adequate study of cultural, political and economic aspects of the environment are included. How integrated are environmental perspectives with the curriculum of other majors such as international relations, chemical engineering or theater? In addition to these types of general questions, you should also frame questions specific to your interests. For example, does the university offer semester abroad programs in developing countries? To what degree does the curriculum employ field work or problem-based learning?

While a general awareness of environmental issues has been prominent since the late 1960's, colleges and universities often change slowly. Therefore you should get the most specific information you can about the school you are considering before making a choice. The institutions in this book are among the nations strongest in environmental curricula.

But of equal importance, you will be well served in your search for the best education for you, if you begin by asking questions of yourself.

Thomas H. Kelly, Ph.D. is the Director of the Tufts Environmental Literacy Institute, Center for Environmental Management at Tufts University

# MAKING A DIFFERENCE IN THE WORLD
## HOWARD BERRY
### INTERNATIONAL PARTNERSHIP FOR SERVICE LEARNING

You want to help people. You want to go abroad.

A service program can be a semester or a year in a poor country, serving the needs of the hungry, the homeless, the ill or handicapped, the very young or very old. It can be construction and repair work or teaching literacy; caring for the sick, supervising recreation for troubled teens; conducting research or doing office work for an economic development or environmental agency or a museum.

Whatever your individual talents and goals, there is a point to consider carefully: the program should be based on mutuality -- giving and receiving. Obvious? Yes, but there are programs which are designed to give you a fine experience, but without reference to the host culture. And there are some which expect you to work hard but pay no attention to your own needs.

A service-learning experience is not easy, and shouldn't be. But if you approach it with flexibility, openness, and a willingness to learn - you too will encounter the host culture in a way not possible as a tourist or a traditional study abroad student, and you will be satisfied with your contribution to the people and society, and they with you.

Our agency, Partnership for Service Learning, is a not-for-profit consortium of colleges, universities, service agencies and related organizations united to foster and develop programs linking community service and academic study. Over 1,500 students from 180 colleges have participated for recognized academic credit in its programs.

Aaron Romano participated in a PSL project while a student at Bard College. A Jewish-American, he worked in a Christian-Jamaican church-based community center providing holistic (physical, mental and spiritual) services to people from low income neighborhoods. At first he felt uneasy, but he soon realized "our religious tenets shared the common principle that one who asks shall receive, and we were to assist in this process. Throughout the semester, I befriended doctors, nurses, teachers, priests, rabbis, and others leaders of the community who were involved in helping Jamaica keep it's head above water. I discovered the majority of Jamaicans are very concerned with the state of their country. Many are willing to devote their lifetimes to ameliorating the oppressive economic and social conditions. Never before have I encountered a place where people were willing to give so much and expect nothing in return. Here is where the essence of love is taught; and with love happiness soon follows."

Students often find that their ideas about what constitutes service are challenged by the values of their host culture. John Hathaway spent a semester in Ecuador and learned to face the differences between his notion of service and that community and the service agency. "The feelings and help of gringos come second in this organization. I realize now that that is how it should be."

Service learning addresses many of the complaints about higher education in this country. Concerns about its efficacy and value, doubts about the teachability of students coming into college who are alienated from the educational process, frustration about inability to find jobs upon graduation, and lack of education for increasing globalization beset education. Educators find it difficult to teach community in a world where the traditional ideas of community no longer work.

It is here that the concept of service-learning comes into the picture. Service learning involves far more than opportunities to work while pursuing studies. It is an integrating volunteer experience, often in another culture, designed to improve sense of values, to provide new knowledge, and to assist in the relief of human suffering. Service-learning is based on some quite simple premises. Learning is easier when rooted in practical experience. Service learning programs enrich both learning and experience by providing them with meaning. By linking formal study, formal evaluation and formal expectation with service, it is not an interlude in formal education but a part of it. That the best way to learn the values of sharing and service is by deriving them from concrete situations, where the human need to cooperate is absolutely clear. Volunteer work requires a willingness to put others before self, a willingness to give up something material in order to receive something spiritual in return. That the right way to learn self-worth is by observing one's ability to better the self-worth of others. Living in another culture is the best way to prepare young people for the multicultural and globalized world of today and tomorrow. Programs take place in other cultures to broaden students' horizons to the maximum, to teach them what is relative about their cultures, and to teach them to view their sense of self and their acquisition of knowledge through the values of another culture. That students who have been through such experiences are better able to deal with the world of work, more employable, more mature. Lastly, when all of this has gone on, there is something left behind and that something is good. A student who participates leaves a measurable improvement in the lives of others and hence in society.

International service-learning puts new life and vigor into liberal education for the 21st century, fights valuelessness and materialism, and that helps students go on to live more useful lives in the new multicultural, fragile, yet infinitely absorbing world that is before us.

Howard Berry is the President of The International Partnership for Service Learning. This essay draws heavily on an essay entitled *Service, Values, and a Liberal Education* by Dr. Humphrey Tonkin, President of Hartford University, and Chair of the Partnership for Service Learning Board of Trustees.

# WALKING IN BEAUTY

## Steven C. Rockefeller

If all life on earth is to flourish, education must include not only the larger context of nature, but be placed in within the context of reverence for nature. This edited version of a talk given at College of the Atlantic in 1994, by Steven Rockefeller, Professor of Religion at Middlebury College shows the cross-cultural historical and religious roots of this conviction.

A comprehensive program of environmental studies includes inquiry into environmental ethics and the religious dimension of life as well as the study of biology, chemistry, ecology, history, literature, political science, and other areas. The primary concern of this essay is exploration of the role of religious experience in deepening the interaction between people and nature and in shaping human attitudes toward nature. This topic can be approached through an initial brief discussion of environmental literacy and ethical values.

A good general definition of environmental literacy is found in a recent report of the National Commission on the Environment, which was formed by the World Wildlife Fund. In the Commission's report, environmental literacy is defined as involving "the knowledge, skills, and ethical values" that citizens need in order to cooperate in achieving sustainable development and environmental protection.[0]

This definition includes an understanding of ecology and related subjects. It involves practical competencies such as problem solving skills and the social and political skills required to get things done. In addition, an environmentally literate citizen needs a clear set of ethical values that begin with a basic respect for nature, a sense of intergenerational responsibility, and a commitment to live sustainably.

The formation of a social conscience governed by an informed sense of what constitutes responsible behavior in relation to the environment is of critical importance to any strategy for addressing the growing ecological ills that afflict the planet and our society. Human behavior is governed to a large extent by the attitudes of people and their values. Scientific knowledge, new technologies, government regulation, green taxes, and international agreements all contribute to the process of altering human behavior. However, ethical commitment and religious experience are also needed, if there is to be a social transformation that effects a major change in the way human beings view and treat the environment.

### The Nature and Significance of Religious Experience

In discussing what religious experience can contribute to development of an environmental social conscience, it is helpful to begin with the moral imperative that the World Conservation Union has made the first principle of its World Conservation Strategy (WCS): "Respect and care for the community of life."[1] The focus on "the community of life" in this fundamental principle gives the WCS a very important holistic and global perspective. Ethical values reflect what people judge to be good and bad in human behavior. In general, what people view as morally good is behavior that protects and sustains the community or communities to which they belong and upon which they are dependent for their survival and well-being. By referring to the whole community of life -- not just the human community -- the ethical principle underlying the WCS indicates that humanity is part of nature and that the community to which people belong embraces the whole biosphere. This expansion of the idea of community implies a dramatic extension in the scope of moral concern and responsibility.

The verbs "respect" and "care" are also important terms in this ethical imperative. At a minimum "respect" involves showing regard and consideration for its object. In the WCS it also connotes a sense of the intrinsic worth or value of the community of life. Just as respect for persons implies regard for their rights, so respect for the community of life implies acknowledgment that humanity has certain basic moral responsibilities for protecting the biosphere. In part these responsibilities grow out of the moral obligations people have to other people and future generations. However, if other life forms possess intrinsic value quite apart from their utilitarian value to people, then they may be said to have certain interests of their own which people should respect.

This leads to the concept of caring for the environment. The notion of caring for carries with it the connotation of vital concern and personal relationship. It also suggests protecting, nurturing, tending, and healing. These attitudes and values are essential if human beings are to halt the degradation of the environment and help with restoration of damaged ecosystems and protection of biodiversity.

These observations suggest that the imperative to "respect and care for the community of life" is a very good basis of environmental ethics and sustainable living. It can also be argued that religious experience is the ultimate source of the attitudes of respect and care for the community of life, which are the cornerstone of environmental ethics. Furthermore, religious experience may deepen the attitudes and feelings of respect and care in ways that have important ethical implications. Under the impact of religious experience, respect may become a reverence for life and care may become a strong sense of responsibility rooted in an attitude of compassion and love for all beings. For these reasons, living religious experience coupled with sound science constitutes the most secure foundation for an effective environmental movement.

What kind of religious experience has the power to generate respect and care for the larger community of life, and to deepen these attitudes into reverence and compassion? We will consider various forms of faith experience. However, it needs to be made clear that faith experience is not limited to the institutional religions, and this essay is concerned primarily with what may be called natural religious experience, that is, the kind of faith experiences that are a universal potential in people. The religions do not have a monopoly on the religious dimension of life. Institutional religions may help to awaken, nurture, and direct the natural religious sensitivities and sentiments in people, but religious experience can and does blossom quite apart from any institutional framework.

What is distinctive about religious experience is that it involves the deeper center of human personality, and it engages the whole person -- feeling, thought, and will. This deeper center is called the heart in the Bible and the heart-mind in much Asian thought. Furthermore, the awakening of faith is not so much the result of grasping intellectually some spiritual or moral truth as of being touched and grasped by the truth. In the act of faith the whole self is possessed by the object of faith in a fashion analogous to the way the beauty and wonder of the beloved possesses the heart of a lover. Writing about the experience that led him to his ethic of reverence for life, Albert Schweitzer states: "True knowledge consists in being gripped by the secret that everything is will-to-live...."[2] This "being gripped" is the nature of faith experience.

The thinking of Aldo Leopold, the early ecologist and founder of environmental ethics, was radically transformed by watching "a fierce green fire dying in [the] eyes" of a wolf that he had foolishly shot as a young forest ranger.[3] This was not primarily an intellectual experience. His whole being was gripped by a new awareness that led him to begin, as he put it, thinking like a mountain, that is, holistically. Leopold's experience with the wolf has a religious quality and power. It was in a sense a conversion to the earth. As described in the book *The Home Planet*, many of the astronauts also underwent a kind of conversion to the earth as a result of seeing our planet from outer space.

The experience of being grasped often strikes a person as an insight or revelation, but it is not knowledge in the strictly scientific sense. It may, however, be a direct realization of aspects of reality for which science is no substitute, just as a scientific understanding of a Mozart concerto is no substitute for the direct and immediate experience of enjoying Mozart's music. No amount of scientific information is a substitute for actually looking into the fierce green eyes of a wolf or seeing an Earth rise from the moon.[4]

Keeping these reflections in mind, it is possible to distinguish two general aspects of faith experience which are significant for environmental ethics. On the one hand there are direct appreciations and mystical intimations of the sacred and of belonging to the larger totality that awaken feelings of awe, wonder, gratitude, humility, trust, peace, courage, joy, and caring. On the other hand there is the moral aspect of religious experience -- the experience of being grasped by and committed to a unified vision of the moral ideal that deepens the sense of purpose and meaning in life and strengthens the sense of caring and responsibility. These two aspects of religious experience interconnect and overlap.

Regarding the mystical aspect of faith experience, many examples can be cited drawing on both Eastern and Western traditions. First of all, there is the direct realization of being a part of nature, involving a profound sense of belonging to the larger totality, which is the Earth and beyond that the great dynamic process that is the cosmos at large.

An ancient Navajo chant goes:

> The mountains, I become part of it . . .
> The herbs, the fir tree, I become part of it.
> The morning mists, the clouds, the gathering waters,
> I become part of it.
> The wilderness, the dew drops, the pollen . . .
> I become part of it.[5]

As Joseph Epes Brown points out, chants such as these are designed to bring the participant to the realization "I am the universe. We are not separate, but are one."[6] To live with this awareness in harmony with nature is the objective of Navajo spirituality. The Navajo call it nizhoni -- "walking in beauty."[7]

A Sioux prayer concludes:

> Grandfather Great Spirit
> Fill us with the Light.
> Give us the strength to understand,
> and the eyes to see.
> Teach us to walk the soft Earth as relatives
> to all that live.[8]

Living with this expanded sense of family involving a feeling of community with all life is "walking in beauty."

The sense of belonging to and community with the larger whole may be expressed in the form of what the American philosophers George Santayana and John Dewey called "piety toward nature." Santayana described piety as "reverent attachment to the sources of [humanity's] being," including family, ancestors, country, and the whole natural cosmos. Piety toward nature includes feelings of interdependence, respect, gratitude, and a high sense of responsibility to preserve the heritage of the past for future generations.

The Vietnamese Zen master Thich Nhat Hanh has an effective way of trying to awaken children to a sense of interdependence with nature leading to natural piety. He passes out tangerines or oranges. But before he permits the children to bite into the fruit, he asks them if they can see in the tangerine the tree on which the fruit grew, the sun that warmed the tree, the blue sky that held the sun, the rain that nourished the tree, the workers who picked the fruit, the truckers who shipped it to the market, etc. Then he invites the children to bite into their tangerines.[9] We are in the universe and the universe is in us. Thich Nhat Hanh wants us to feel this truth as well as think about it. Humanity and nature are interdependent and our destiny is to be sustained and sustaining members of the larger earth community as well as the human community. "Walking in beauty."

A second closely related theme concerns the way that the sense of belonging often leads to a liberating feeling of an expansion of the self. For example, the seventeenth century Japanese poet Bunan (1602-1676) writes:

The moon's the same old moon,
The flowers exactly as they were,
Yet I've become the thingness
Of all the things I see![10]

American philosopher John Dewey points out in Art as Experience that objects of aesthetic beauty are pervaded by a qualitative unity that has the power to awaken in people a heightened sense "of belonging to the larger, all-inclusive, whole which is the universe in which we live." This sense of unity, he argues, explains "the religious feeling that accompanies intense aesthetic perception." Dewey further explains:

We are, as it were, introduced into a world beyond this world which is nevertheless the deeper reality of the world in which we live in our ordinary experiences. We are carried out beyond ourselves to find ourselves. I can see no psychological ground for such properties of an experience save that, somehow, the work of art operates to deepen and to raise to great clarity that sense of an enveloping undefined whole that accompanies every normal experience. This whole is then felt as an expansion of ourselves.[11]

What Dewey has described is an experience of what some environmental philosophers like Joanna Macy call the ecological self.[12] There is no sharp separation of self and world from the ecological perspective. The truth is continuity, not dualism. The self is constituted by its relationships to its world. The self is in the world and the world is in the self. Each being is both a unique individual and also interrelated with the other beings that constitute its environment. This realization can lead to a profound sense of identification with the larger world as has been movingly expressed by the Australian conservationist John Seed. He writes:

As the implications of evolution and ecology are internalized there is an identification with all life... Alienation subsides... "I am protecting the rain forest" develops to "I am part of the rain forest protecting myself. I am that part of the rain forest recently emerged into thinking."[12]
"Walking in beauty"
Some environmental philosophers refer to the ecological self as the Great Self, and they also envision the entire world as one's extended body. The eleventh century Chinese Confucian philosopher Chang Tsai gave moving expression to this view in the following declaration of faith:

Heaven is my father and earth is my mother, and even such a small being as I finds an intimate place in their midst. Therefore, that which fills the universe I regard as my body and that which directs the universe I regard as my nature. All people are my brothers and sisters, and all things are my companions.[14]

In this statement one finds expressed many of the themes we have been discussing: a profound sense of belonging to nature, natural piety, and an expansion of self and sense of community with other beings.

Turning to another theme, for those in the Neo-Platonic tradition like the Romantic poets and American Transcendentalists, the experience of belonging to the whole is expressed in visions of nature as an organic unity pervaded by one great divine Spirit and in exquisite feelings of oneness with the infinite life of this organic totality. For example, the early nineteenth century English poet Wordsworth writes in *Tintern Abbey*:

> And I have felt
> A presence that disturbs me with joy
> Of devoted thoughts, a sense sublime
> Of something far more deeply interfused,
> Whose dwelling is the light of setting suns,
> And the round ocean and the living air,
> And the blue sky, and in the mind of man;
> A motion and a spirit, that impels
> All thinking things, all objects of all thought,
> And rolls through all things.

In the same spirit, Ralph Waldo Emerson wrote of the "Over-soul," the heart of the universe, within which all beings are contained and interconnected. Emerson asserts that: "We live in succession, in division, in parts, in particles. Meantime within man is the soul of the whole; the wise silence; the universal beauty, to which every part and particle is equally related; the eternal One."

The idea of nature as a living organic unity pervaded by intelligence and spirit has been revived today in scientific garb by the Gaia hypothesis. This theory, advanced initially by two scientists, James Lovelock and Lynn Margulis, proposes that the Earth functions like a single living being with its own consciousness and intelligence. Gaia was the name of the ancient Greek Earth Mother Goddess, and Lovelock and Margulis argue that the Earth is in fact an indivisible ecosystem that is a superbeing.

Such ideas regarding the Earth have been one reason for the revival of interest in ancient Goddess traditions, especially those which identify the Earth with the body of the Goddess and the mind and heart of the Goddess with the governing principle of the Earth. One leader of the contemporary Goddess movement, Starhawk, writes in a poetic vision:

> Earth mother, star mother,
> You who are called by
>         a thousand names,
> May all remember
>         we are cells in your body
>         and dance together.
> You are the grain
>         and the loaf
> That sustains us each day . . .
> You are the embrace that heartens
> And the freedom beyond fear . . .
> Within you we are born
>         we grow, live and die—
> You bring us around the circle

to rebirth,
Within us you dance
Forever.[15]

Another important aspect of the mystical side of faith is cosmic trust or a profound sense of the meaning and value of life coupled with inner peace. One finds this cosmic trust expressed in Starhawk's poem when she writes that the Goddess is "the embrace that heartens/and the freedom beyond fear." John Dewey found that his natural piety and mystical sense of belonging to the whole reconciled him to the tragic side of life. Paraphrasing the King James version of the Book of Job, he wrote: "We know that though the universe slay us still we may trust." Mystical faith includes the experience of the Great Yes to life arising in the human heart in spite of all the suffering and evil that can overwhelm the human spirit with fear and despair. It is precisely the letting go of egotism, the expansion of the self, and unification with the larger whole that sustains the great Yes to life and gives men and women courage, faith, and peace.

Finally, as some of the passages quoted indicate, when these various mystical intuitions and intimations are fully developed, they awaken a sense of the sacred, which is a distinctively religious awareness. The consciousness of the sacred is an awareness of a reality that is at once mysterious, awesome, and wonderful. It is not a thing or being among the other things that make up the universe. For this reason it defies objectification and conceptualization, and when we speak about it, we must use imaginative vision, poetic images, symbols, and metaphors. However, if we are prepared and open, it can touch and take possession of our hearts, making itself known. It can reveal itself in and through sunlight on water, in the night sky, and in the midst of intense struggle when we are faithful to the truth, or it can speak to us in the silent depths of our own being when we have withdrawn our attention from the busyness of the world to listen with inward concentration. The awareness of the sacred is a consciousness of the divine.

The sense of the sacred is especially important for environmental ethics insofar as nature or certain aspects of nature are viewed as sacred or directly related to the sacred. Underlying every ethical system there is an immediate sense of the presence of value, of some intrinsic good, some end in itself, which merits and commands respect, restraint, and care. This immediate sense of value is deepened by religious experience into the sense of sacred presence, that is, something mysterious, awesome, and wonderful before which a human being feels compelled to respond with reverence, humility, and gratitude. Some religious traditions have found the presence of the sacred in all life forms, and within many religions there are traditions that affirm the inherent goodness and sacredness of the entire creation. It is such traditions that provide a religious foundation for environmental ethics.

With respect to the kind of religious experiences that we have been considering, the sacred is often identified with the mysterious source of the universe, out of which it has emerged, within which it is contained, and by which it is sustained every moment. Even though it is transcendent in certain respects, it is also immanent. It surrounds us, and it is within us and all beings. It is in this connection that Albert Schweitzer's philosophy of religious experience and his ethic of reverence for life are especially important. Schweitzer found the sacred in the mystery of life wherever it appears. For Schweitzer to belong to nature is to be part of a great cosmic process pervaded by a sacred mystery that is manifest in the flowering of life in all its many forms.

### Moral Faith and Reverence for Life

The moral dimension of faith experience involves being grasped at the center of one's being by and committed to a unified vision of the moral ideal. When such a faith is so deep as to have the effect of unifying the self and creating a profound sense of harmony between self and world, it becomes religious in quality, generating a distinctively religious sense of meaning, purpose, and peace in the midst of life's busyness and turmoil.

The nature of the moral ideal changes and evolves with history. However, the attitudes of love and compassion have been a persistent universal theme for thousands of years in great religious moral visions. Much of the meaning of this ancient theme for life in the twenty-first century will be found by developing our understanding of democratic and environmental ethical values. Schweitzer's philosophy of reverence for life is a good place to begin on the environmental side.

For Schweitzer the discovery of the sacredness of life begins with inwardness and self-knowledge, with an encounter with the awesome and wonderful mystery of life within oneself.[16] When a person has been grasped by the sacredness of the spark of life that is his or her inmost being, Schweitzer contends, that he or she will spontaneously begin to feel sympathy for the suffering and struggle of other living beings. If, then, a person chooses to affirm and to nurture this impulse, a reverence for all life will begin to grow. What Schweitzer is describing is a deepening faith experience in which a person is grasped and committed to the ideal of reverence for life. As Schweitzer uses the term "reverence" it has the connotation of respect deepened by a sense of the sacred.

The miracle of life and of biodiversity in Schweitzer's view merits a response of reverence, and he envisions the ethical life as growing out of this reverence. He writes that "a [person] is ethical only when life, as such, is sacred to him, that of plants and animals as that of his fellow man, and when he devotes himself helpfully to all life that is in need of help."[17] For Schweitzer, then, a religious sense of the sacred is essential for the development of a moral faith for our time.

Schweitzer's faith in the ideal of reverence for life involves a profound realization of the intrinsic value and sacredness of all life quite apart from its utilitarian value for human beings. This awareness involves a powerful rejection of the anthropocentrism that has been so characteristic of Western ethics and modern civilization in favor of a more holistic and biocentric view. A sense of the sacredness of all life provides the strongest possible foundation for an expanded sense of community with all life and for faith in an environmental ethics of care for the Earth and protection of biodiversity.

Schweitzer formulated his philosophy of reverence for life as Europe was sliding into World War I, and he predicted that only an awakening to our identity as members of the whole community of life and to the ideal of reverence for all living beings would save European civilization from destroying itself. As the twentieth century draws to a close, one must conclude that he may well be absolutely right.

Charles Darwin, in The Descent of Man noted that humanity's sense of ethical concern and responsibility had gradually expanded over the centuries from families to tribes to nations and races and eventually to the whole species. He then speculated that humanity might eventually embrace a "disinterested love for all living creatures." Almost a century later Albert Einstein had a similar vision that summarizes much that we have been discussing. He writes:

> A human being is a part of the whole called by us universe, a part limited in time and space. He experiences himself, his thoughts and feelings as something separate from the rest, a kind of optical delusion of his consciousness. This delusion is a kind of prison for us, restricting us to our personal desires and to affection for a few persons nearest to us. Our task must be to free ourselves from this prison by widening our circle of compassion to embrace all living creatures and the whole of nature in its beauty.[18]

In order to free ourselves of the delusion of egotism, of which Einstein speaks, methods of growth and transformation are needed. Religious ritual, poetry and the arts, study, prayer, meditation, and psychotherapy can all help. However, in the final analysis the most effective form of spiritual practice is living a loving and compassionate life in our everyday lives. What Martin Buber called I-thou relations can open human beings up to the divine dimension of reality as no other practice. When caring and compassion spring from the heart, self-giving can become a profoundly liberating form of self-realization, the moral life can fuse with the mystical, and the secular can be integrated with the sacred.

The words of Father Zossima, a Russian Orthodox priest in Dostoevsky's The Brothers Karamazov, provide a fitting conclusion to these reflections. Zossima counsels:

> Love all God's creation, the whole and every grain of sand in it. Love every leaf, every ray of God's light. Love the animals, love the plants, love everything. If you love everything, you will perceive the divine mystery in things. Once you perceive it, you will begin to comprehend it better every day.[19]
> "Walking in beauty."

Steven Rockefeller is the author of John Dewey: Religious Faith and Democratic Humanism and co-editor of Spirit and Nature: Why the Environment is a Religious Issue. He recently served as a member of the National Commission on the Environment. He is also a member of the Governor's Council of Environmental Advisors in Vermont and of the Commission on Environmental Strategy and Planning of the International Union for the Conservation of Nature and Natural Resources.

# I'M CHANGING THE WORLD, I'M HAPPY, AND LOOK MOM, I'M EVEN EARNING A GOOD LIVING!

## Angela Curtes

### Education Director, Pacific Environment and Resources Center

It was very difficult for me to decide what path to take after high school. I had received a basketball scholarship from the University of Wisconsin, Parkside and that seemed to get my feet moving into a collegiate setting. I focused on the career of education -- maybe physical education, maybe science or English. But to my dismay I never found passion nor extreme interest in any of the topics a typical professor taught. Eventually, I transferred, left sports, left my identity in some ways, and most of all, was left with very little hope for my future. The University of Wisconsin at Madison which has a student population of over 55,000 was my next stop. In neither of these places did I feel I had made the contribution to the greater community of life that I was seeking to make.

The more I talked with teachers, and the more student teaching I did, the more disillusioned I gradually became about public school education. I wanted to choose a career that would sustain my aspirations for a life time. But the more I pondered this direction, the more I realized that I wanted to make a bigger difference in life than just teaching kids to read, write or dissect earthworms!

My love for the outdoors since childhood was really my only true passion. Fortunately, three and half months in the wilderness with the National Outdoor Leadership School introduced me to environmental education. During my youth the act of passionately caring for something outside of the self had been forever instilled in me through my encounters with nature. Until NOLS, I never imagined this love for the natural environment could be a career choice.

After 3 years of attending various colleges I finally enrolled at Prescott College in Arizona. It was here I discovered the beauty of experiential education, self-directed learning and in-depth self exploration. My dedication to studying the natural world and human relationships to it became my main focus, and has shaped my present reality. In my second year at Prescott, I signed up for its first community service course ever offered. I felt the class was long overdue. The students at this alternative, progressive college had no interaction with the conservative townspeople. I felt our knowledge needed to be shared with the greater community, and this class helped to bridge the gap. I served the Prescott community by organizing the town Earth Day Celebration in April 1991. This event took about four months to organize and became a central task in my life, in addition to being Co-president of the Student Union.

The many service oriented experiences throughout my years at Prescott College were in some ways like a profound spiritual ritual. Each of them challenged my perception of self and each of them dynamically contributed to the empowerment of the self. Every endeavor since graduating in 1992 has been successful and valuable for both myself and the endeavor.

Building strong relationships with others as well as the Earth is central to shaping a more positive and hopeful future. Overall, my experiences have reassured me of the resilience of the Earth and the pockets of true support and empathy that are woven through our communities. Until individuals learn to care for things outside of themselves, society will remain ignorant in its own temporary bliss. Shedding blinders enables others to be considered, respected, and even honored, but blindness only allows suffering to prevail. Service towards any moral cause is the beginning!

Presently, I work for a non-profit organization in the San Francisco Bay Area which strives for the protection of the natural environment through law advocacy, grassroots activism, and eduction. As the Environmental Education Director, I work to establish environmental awareness in youth, grades K-12 through interactive and experiential programs. Six program topics generate increased knowledge about global environmental issues as well as an understanding of the reverence for all life. Topics allow students to become aware of the impacts to the natural environment and how they are dynamically connected to the problems and the solutions.

Throughout the summer and fall I also co-direct a wilderness education program for women called Common Earth. As the co-founder of this program I strive to incorporate natural and cultural history, wilderness skills and safety, and empowerment of women from various cultural and socioeconomic backgrounds.

In addition to her work in environmental education,
Angela Curtes leads wilderness trips for women.

## JUDD WALSON
### Pre-Medical Student

Graduating from high school with a 2.70 GPA did not, as my parents put it, leave me many options. I remember the college application process well. While many of my friends were praying to get into this Ivy league or that Top 10 school, I was hoping to get accepted... well... anywhere.

Coming from the background that I did, I was expected to go to college. I was going for that reason alone. The worries and anxieties of my peers when they discussed futures in law, medicine or business seemed distant and foreign. I had no idea what I wished to do, but I did know that these options sounded far removed from what I wanted as my future.

I first heard about Pitzer College from my cousin, while I was looking for a school that might be suckered into admitting me. At my interview, learning that I had been a professional magician since age 12, the Pitzer admissions staff demanded a magic show, just like that, on the spur of the moment. They liked my show, and I was accepted.

At Pitzer the professors actually cared about what you thought, as long as you had a reason and were ready to discuss it. This was all part of the community awareness and service philosophy that Pitzer strives to impart to all of it's students. By the time I graduated, I had volunteered in a homeless shelter, helped serve food in a soup kitchen, worked with the Pomona Police Department, did research in an emergency room, and flown half-way around the world to Nepal.

The events that led to my decision to attend a post-baccalaureate pre-medical program, however, are all tied to my experiences in the last five years. One particular experience had a profound impact on my choice of careers.

The two women in front of me are wrinkled and look old, though they are probably only in their mid-thirties. I am in the middle of the Himalayas, the Kingdom of Nepal, seven days from the nearest road, light bulb, running water, or hospital. I know the women, they are friends of a Sherpa acquaintance of mine who is off trekking on an expedition in another part of Nepal. I have been living in Nepal for about a year and a half at this point, and my Nepali is good enough to communicate well with the women. They know that I am managing a small "health project" as an intern for Pitzer College. The women tell me that my friend's wife has been gored by a bull, she's not doing well, and that she is still a good two days walk from where I am. As if this were not enough, she is also eight months pregnant.

I was overcome by a tremendous feeling of helplessness. I was isolated from anyone who could be of help. I also had a tremendous feeling of inexcusable ignorance. Even if I could get to the woman, I was unsure of what I could do. For two days I trudged up the trail towards the woman's village. I had been told my friend's wife had been gored in the lower back, not reassuring, especially since she was pregnant. If the woman died, was I supposed to somehow try to save the baby? If there was an infection would the pregnancy prove more dangerous to the mother? As these thoughts ran through my mind, I began to contemplate the possibility of becoming a doctor.

When I finally did reach the woman, I discovered her wound was superficial, not in her back, but instead passing between her legs and tearing the skin of her buttocks and genitals. A health worker had already sutured her up, and I had only to clean her wound and give her antibiotics. Eventually she went to a hospital and had a healthy baby boy. The experience was an incredible lesson in the value of a medical education.

After finishing my internship I was hired as Marketing Manager by a Hong Kong pharmaceutical company to conduct various studies concerning Nepalese health care issues specifically related to pharmaceutical use. The position was offered to me because of my fluency in Nepali, my experiences in Nepal, and because I had worked to develop the trust of many people there.

Now I find myself back in the USA. I am currently working for the University of California, Office of the President, Division of Agriculture and Natural Resources. In a few months I will be entering medical school at Tufts University.

My college experiences in community service have made such a difference in everything about me including my future. They are undoubtably the reason that I was admitted into the medical program that I will be attending. To say that I did these things unselfishly would be a lie, yet this is perhaps the most important lesson I learned. I see so many people working so hard for personal achievement and status. So many people who base their happiness on material wealth. I wish that I could say that I am not driven by the same motivations, but I am. We are all striving to be happy and feel successful. I work in community service because by doing so I feel successful and worthwhile. I can go home at night and sleep comfortably, secure in the knowledge that I am doing what I need to be doing. Through community service I learned how wonderful it is to help others and to be helped by others. There is no one way street. In Nepal I took back far more than I could ever give. I have uncovered a wonderful secret, that the more I give of myself, the more I can receive, enabling me to gain far more than would by possible if I was working for myself alone.

During his semester in Nepal, Judd Walson worked at a health project, and found time to make friends.

# WORKING FOR A BETTER WORLD
# WHERE SCIENCE AND TECHNOLOGY ARE USED
# IN SOCIALLY RESPONSIBLE WAYS

## David Andersen
### Student Pugwash USA

Science majors spend countless hours in laboratories, peering into microscopes, designing experiments, and cleaning petri dishes. In the midst of endless assignments and tests it is easy to lose sight of the uses of the science we are doing. Rarely do we find time to think about how science and technology should be used in socially responsible ways. With the rapid pace of scientific and technological development, however, it is important to step back, examine the work that is being done, and ask tough questions about its applications. On college, university, and high school campuses across the United States, students are thinking critically about science, technology, global affairs, and social responsibility at Student Pugwash campus chapters.

Founded in 1979, Student Pugwash USA is the US student affiliate of the Pugwash Conferences on Science and World Affairs, recipients of the 1995 Nobel Peace Prize. With the advent of the hydrogen bomb as a humbling and frightening backdrop, Albert Einstein and Bertrand Russell co-authored a manifesto urging scientists to consider the social, moral, and ethical implications of weapons of mass destruction. This manifesto led to the first Pugwash Conference, held in Pugwash, Nova Scotia in 1957. The Pugwash spirit has always implied the need for scientists to broadly consider the ethical implications of their work, beyond the challenges raised by nuclear weapons.

The mission of Student Pugwash USA is to promote the socially responsible application of science and technology in the 21st century. As a student organization, Student Pugwash USA encourages young people to examine the ethical, social, and global implications of science and technology, and to make these concerns a guiding focus of their academic and professional endeavors. Student Pugwash USA offers educational programs that are interdisciplinary, intergenerational, and international in scope, reflecting a belief that all citizens share a responsibility to ensure that science and technology are utilized for the benefit of humankind. Student Pugwash is guided by respect for diverse perspectives, and as such does not adopt advocacy positions.

Student Pugwash USA chapters are always asking the tough questions, such as: What are the effects of science and technology on society and individuals? How can we responsibly manage science and technology? What is the role of the individual in examining these issues? What ethical questions should be considered when doing scientific research? In a given year, a single chapter of Student Pugwash USA might address issues ranging from the future of nuclear energy to the emerging trends in communications technology and from the international arms trade to the social consequences of the Human Genome Project. They do this by organizing events such as roundtable discussions, lectures, movie nights, and panels on their campus. In addition, the national office organizes national and international conferences, and regional events. Students from all over the country pile into cars, trains, and planes to travel to these events where they are able to listen to important leaders, learn valuable leadership skills, and meet like-minded "Puggers." Often conversations last late into the night and friendships are formed that last a life time.

Student Pugwash USA's national office also has resources to help you and your chapter. This includes a Chapter Organizing Guide which explains the A to Z of starting and running a chapter; Pugwatch, the monthly chapter newsletter; and mind•full: a brainsnack for future leaders with ethical appetites, a series of issue briefs.

Asking tough questions and organizing events that address those questions adds a new level to a student's education. Instead of passively taking classes, someone involved in a Student Pugwash USA chapter takes control of his or her education. A member of Student Pugwash USA is able to influence debate on campus and encourage discussions about critical issues that otherwise might never be addressed.

In addition to the chapter program, Student Pugwash USA encourages young people to take a pledge that commits them to work for a better world. On December 10, 1995, the Pugwash Conferences on Science and World Affairs and its then-president, Professor Joseph Rotblat, received the Nobel Peace Prize. In honor of the Nobel Peace Prize and inspired by Professor Rotblat's idea of a Hippocratic Oath for young scientists, Student Pugwash USA developed a pledge that advocates the responsible use of science and technology. The pledge campaign celebrates the work of the Pugwash Conferences and encourages students and young professionals to commit themselves to the high standards of Pugwash.

*I promise to work for a better world, where science and technology are used in socially responsible ways. I will not use my education for any purpose intended to harm human beings or the environment. Throughout my career, I will consider the ethical implications of my work before I take action. While the demands placed upon me may be great, I sign this declaration because I recognize that individual responsibility is the first step on the path to peace.*

The pledge embodies the ideals we promote at Student Pugwash USA, and is our way of saying that the time has come for young people to actively promote the kind of world in which they want to live. You can take the pledge at: www.spusa.org/pugwash/.

To get involved in Student Pugwash USA contact the national office in Washington, DC. The national chapter coordinator can send you a Chapter Organizing Guide and talk with you about what you can do to start a chapter on your campus. The pledge coordinator can help you initiate a pledge campaign on your campus or in your community. Contact them by email or through the www.

Student Pugwash USA

1-800-WOW-A-PUG     spusa@spusa.org     www.spusa.org/pugwash/
David Andersen is National Chapter Coordinator for Student Pugwash.

# GRADUATION PLEDGE OF ENVIRONMENTAL AND SOCIAL RESPONSIBILITY

**I, _____ pledge to explore and take into account the social and environmental consequences of any job opportunity I consider or any organization for which I work.**

Begun in 1987, the Graduation Pledge is intended to be taken by students and celebrated as a part of commencement ceremonies. Since its founding, dozens of schools around the country have instituted such an effort, and the Pledge has now gone international. The commitment is voluntary and allows students to determine for themselves what they consider to be socially and environmentally responsible.

Instituting the pledge gets at the heart of a good education and can benefit society as a whole. Not only does it remind students of the ethical implications of the knowledge and training they received, but it can help lead to a socially-conscious citizenry and a better world. The pledge can also serve as a focal point for further consciousness-raising around campus.

Each year more than one million American students enter the work force who might potentially influence the shape of corporate America, as well as other segments of society. Think of the impact if even a significant minority of applicants and job holders inquired about or questioned the ethical practices of their potential or current employers. And shouldn't a job represent more than just a paycheck -- a place where one can feel good about his/her own assignments and the general practice of the company?

We have learned of inspiring examples concerning student commitment to the pledge after graduation. "I told my boss of the pledge and my concerns. He understood and agreed, and the company did not pursue the (chemical warfare) project." Another supporter, "Now I make an effort to teach and think about social and environmental responsibility on a daily basis." Others have turned down potential jobs they did not feel comfortable with morally.

The pledge was founded at California's Humboldt State University and has been headquartered at Manchester College since 1996.

For more information concerning the pledge, visit the web site at
http://www.manchester.edu.
Go to the index and select "Graduation Pledge Alliance."
Or write: GPA, MC Box 135, Manchester College
604 E. College Ave., North Manchester, IN 46962.
Or send e-mail to: NJWollman@Manchester.edu.

# THE TALLOIRES DECLARATION
## ASSOCIATION OF UNIVERSITY LEADERS
## FOR A SUSTAINABLE FUTURE

The Association of University Leaders for a Sustainable Future (ULSF) is an international membership organization of academic leaders and institutions committed to the advancement of global environmental literacy and sustainability. ULSF supports members in their efforts to unite administration, faculty, staff, and students in a collaborative effort to create sustainable institutions. ULSF promotes the Talloires Declaration and maintains an international network, facilitating information exchange, providing technical support, and operating educational programs that build organizational and individual capacity to develop sustainable policies and practices.

The Talloires Declaration is an international consensus document created by a gathering of university leaders in 1990 in Talloires, France. This Declaration is a commitment to specific actions to realize higher education leadership for global environmental literacy and sustainable development. It is founded on the belief that institutions of higher learning must exercise leadership to promote and reinforce environmental responsibility by integrating the ethical, social, economic, and ecological values of environmentally sustainable development into institutional policies and practices. This leadership begins with each university's mission and expands into the community, the region, and the national and international spheres. As a signatory to the Talloires, an institution is making a commitment to providing this essential leadership and uniting with other institutions around the world in forwarding this agenda.

## Talloires Declaration 10 Point Action Plan

We, the presidents, rectors, and vice chancellors of universities from all regions of the world are deeply concerned about the unprecedented scale and speed of environmental pollution and degradation, and the depletion of natural resources.

Local, regional, and global air and water pollution; accumulation and distribution of toxic wastes; destruction and depletion of forests, soil, and water; depletion of the ozone layer and emission of "green house" gases threaten the survival of humans and thousands of other living species, the integrity of the earth and its biodiversity, the security of nations, and the heritage of future generations. These environmental changes are caused by inequitable and unsustainable production and consumption patterns that aggravate poverty in many regions of the world.

We believe that urgent actions are needed to address these fundamental problems and reverse the trends. Stabilization of human population, adoption of environmentally sound industrial and agricultural technologies, reforestation, and ecological restoration are crucial elements in creating an equitable and sustainable future for all humankind in harmony with nature.

Universities have a major role in the education, research, policy formation, and information exchange necessary to make these goals possible. Thus, university leaders must initiate and support mobilization of internal and external resources so that their institutions respond to this urgent challenge.

We, therefore, agree to take the following actions:

1. Increase Awareness of Environmentally Sustainable Development

   Use every opportunity to raise public, government, industry, foundation, and university awareness by openly addressing the urgent need to move toward an environmentally sustainable future.

2. Create an Institutional Culture of Sustainability

   Encourage all universities to engage in education, research, policy formation, and information exchange on population, environment, and development to move toward global sustainability.

3. Educate for Environmentally Responsible Citizenship

   Establish programs to produce expertise in environmental management, sustainable economic development, population, and related fields to ensure that all university graduates are environmentally literate and have the awareness and understanding to be ecologically responsible citizens.

4. Foster Environmental Literacy For All

   Create programs to develop the capability of university faculty to teach environmental literacy to all undergraduate, graduate, and professional students.

5. Practice Institutional Ecology

   Set an example of environmental responsibility by establishing institutional ecology policies and practices of resource conservation, recycling, waste reduction, and environmentally sound operations.

6. Involve All Stakeholders

   Encourage involvement of government, foundations, and industry in supporting interdisciplinary research, education, policy formation, and information exchange in environmentally sustainable development. Expand work with community and non-governmental organizations to assist in finding solutions to environmental problems.

7. Collaborate for Interdisciplinary Approaches

   Convene university faculty and administrators with environmental practitioners to develop interdisciplinary approaches to curricula, research initiatives, operations, and outreach activities that support an environmentally sustainable future.

8. Enhance Capacity of Primary and Secondary Schools

   Establish partnerships with primary and secondary schools to help develop the capacity for interdisciplinary teaching about population, environment, and sustainable development.

9. Broaden Service and Outreach Nationally and Internationally Work with national and international organizations to promote a worldwide university effort toward a sustainable future.

10. Maintain the Movement

    Establish a Secretariat and a steering committee to continue this momentum, and to inform and support each other's efforts in carrying out this declaration.

The list of US signatories can be found in the index.

University Leaders for a Sustainable Future can be reached at http://www.ulsf.org

# THE COLLEGE REPORT CARD:
## A TOOL FOR CHOOSING FROM AMONG
## YOUR TOP-CHOICE COLLEGES
### MARTIN NEMKO PH.D.

### Directions

There are 47 items on the Report Card. They are the major factors that affect students' success and happiness at college. Put a checkmark next to the 5-15 factors you consider most likely to affect your success and happiness.

Make a copy of the Report Card for each college you're considering.

Over the coming months, you'll have the chance to learn how each college measures up on your 5-15 factors: by reading college guides and materials from the colleges, talking with your counselor and college students home for vacation, asking questions at college nights, phoning college personnel and students, and making a campus visit. (See "How to Test Drive a College"). A primary source of information for each item is listed alongside it. Write what you learn in the margins of each college's Report Card.

*Important!!!* You can get information on most of the items by phone. For example, to talk with students, call the college's switchboard (the phone numbers are available from directory assistance and have the call transferred to a residence hall front desk, the student newspaper office, or the student government office.

By spring of your senior year, you'll have a wonderful basis for choosing your college. After you've finished recording what you learned, compare the report cards, then choose your college based on your gut feeling as to which one will best promote your intellectual, social, emotional, and ethical development.

# THE COLLEGE REPORT CARD
## FOR_____ COLLEGE/UNIVERSITY

### The Students

1. To what extent are you comfortable with the student body: intellectually, values, role of alcohol, work/play balance, etc.

### In the Classroom

2. What percentage of the typical first years class time is spent in classes of 30 or fewer students? (*Ask students.*)

3. What percentage of class time is spent in lecture versus active learning? (*Ask students.*)

Most educators agree that learning is often enhanced when students are active; for example, participating in discussions, case studies, field studies, hands-on activities. It's tough to achieve active learning in an auditorium. It's particularly important that first year classes be small because frosh are just getting used to college-level work. Students who might be tempted to space out or even play hooky in a large lecture class, should pay special attention to class size.

Many colleges report a misleading statistic about class size: the faculty/student ratio. This statistic typically ranges from 1:10 to 1:25, even at mega state universities, evoking images of classes of 10-25 students. The faculty/student ratio is deceptive because it often includes faculty that do research but never teach, or at least never teach undergraduates. The faculty/student ratio also includes courses that you're unlikely to take. What good is it that Medieval Horticulture has three students if Intro to Anything has 300? Hence, the previous two questions are important.

4. How easy is it to register for the classes you want; e.g., do students register by telephone? Are enough sections of classes offered? (*Ask students*)

5. If you are attending a large school, are there special programs that enable you to get into smaller classes: e.g., honors programs, college within-a-college, living-learning centers? How are students selected for these programs? (*Read college guides and admissions material.*)

6. What percentage of your instructors would you describe as inspirational? (*Ask students.*)

7. What letter grade would you give to the average instructor? (*Ask students.*)

8. Does the college make available to students a booklet summarizing student evaluations of faculty? (*Ask students.*)

Such a booklet makes it much easier to find good instructors. Also, its presence suggests that the college is more concerned about student rights as a consumer than it is about covering up professors' failings.

9. In a typical introductory social science or humanities course, how many pages of writing are typically assigned? In an advanced class? (*Ask students.*)

10. Does feedback on written work typically include detailed suggestions for improvement or just a letter grade with a few words of feedback? (*Ask students.*)

11. Must all assignments be done individually, or are there sufficient opportunities to do team projects? (*Ask students.*)

12. Is the institution strong in your major area of interest?

13. If you might want a self-designed major, is this a strong point at the school or an infrequently made exception. (*See catalog, ask students*)

14. Are there mechanisms for integrating different disciplines: interdisciplinary seminars, team teaching, internships, capstone classes? (*See catalog, ask admissions*)

**Intellectual life outside the classroom**

15. Describe and evaluate the advising you've received. (*Ask students.*)

16. How easy is it to get to work on a faculty member's research project? (*Ask students and faculty in your prospective major.*)

    Working under a professor's wing is an excellent opportunity for active learning, also when students become part of the research effort, they feel more like an member of the campus community.

17. To what extent do the viewpoints expressed on campus represent a true diversity of perspectives rather than, for example, just the liberal view or just the conservative stance? (*Ask students and faculty.*)

18. How frequently do faculty invite students to share a meal? (*Ask students.*)

19. How much does the typical student study between Friday dinner and Sunday dinner? (*Read college guides, ask students*)

20. Do faculty live in student residence halls? Does it encourage good faculty-student interaction? (*Call a residence hall front desk.*)

    **The remaining questions in this section can probably best be answered via a phone call or a visit to the academic affairs office.**

21. How does the institution assess a prospective faculty member's ability to teach?

    Ideally, undergraduate institutions should require prospective undergraduate faculty members to submit a teaching portfolio consisting of videotapes of undergraduate classes, student evaluations, syllabi, and conduct a demonstration class at the freshman level. Many colleges only require prospective faculty to do a demonstration of a graduate level seminar in their research area. That says little about their ability to teach undergraduates.

22. Recognizing that this will vary from department to department, how likely is it that a good teacher who publishes little will get tenure?

23. On your most recent student satisfaction survey, what was the average rating for academic life? For out-of-classroom life?

This is the equivalent of asking hundreds of students how they like their college. If they say that the institution doesn't conduct student satisfaction surveys, you've learned that the institution doesn't care enough to assess student satisfaction.

24. How much money per student is spent annually on helping faculty to improve their teaching? (not to include money for research-related sabbaticals and conventions.)

Colleges frequently espouse the importance of good teaching. The answer to this question lets you know if a college puts its money where its mouth is.

25. What is done to ensure that students receive high quality advising?

For example, does faculty get special training in how to advise students? Does advising count in faculty promotion decisions? Can students and advisors, via computer, see what courses the student has taken and yet must take?

**Co-Curricular Life**

26. Does the new-student orientation program extend beyond the traditional 1-3 days? (*Ask students, consult admissions brochure, and/or catalog.*)

27. What percentage of freshmen, sophomores, juniors, and seniors can obtain on-campus housing? This affects campus community. (*Consult admissions material, ask admissions or housing office.*)

28. Describe residence hall life. How close is it to the living-learning environment described in admission brochures? (*Ask students.*)

29. How attractive is student housing? (*Ask students. Tour facilities.*)

30. How well did you like your freshman roommate? This item assesses the quality of the college's roommate-matching procedure. (*Ask students.*)

31. Is the school's location a plus or minus. Why? (*Read college guides, ask students.*)

32. How many crimes were committed on or near campus last year? How admissions reps for the "crime pamphlet." (*Each school is required to provide one.*)

33. What is the quality of life for special constituencies; e.g., gay, adult, minority, or handicapped students? (*Read admission materials, ask students, phone the office that serves that constituency.*)

34. How strong is the sense of community and school spirit among the students? (*Read college guides, ask students.*)

35. In the dining hall, do students primarily eat in homogeneous groups: for example international, racial groups, etc. (*Ask students, observe first-hand.*)

36. How extensive are the opportunities for community service? What percentage of students participate in it? (*Ask students, the career center, service office.*)

### The "Real" World

37. How extensive are the internship opportunities?

    Internships embody active learning, allow students to bridge theory and practice, try out a career without penalty, and make job connections. (*Ask students, contact the career center.*)

38. How good are the career planning and placement services? (*Ask upperclass students*)

    Most colleges offer some career planning and placement, but the best ones offer critiques of videotaped mock interviews, the SIGI or Discover computer career guidance systems, video-interviewing with distant employees, extensive counseling, many job listings, on-campus employee interviews, and connections with alumni. (*Ask students and personnel at the career center.*)

39. In your field, what percentage of students get jobs or into graduate school? What percentage go into service-oriented careers? (*Ask students, faculty in your prospective major, ask at the career center.*)

### Overall Indicators of the Institution's Quality

40. What percentage of incoming freshmen return for the sophomore year? (*Consult college guides, ask admissions rep or call the office of institutional research.*)

41. What percentage of students graduate within four years? Five years? (*Consult college guides, ask admissions rep, or call the office of institutional research.*)

    Graduation rate depends in part on student quality: the better the students, the higher the college's graduation rate. But take note if two institutions with similar S.A.T. averages have very different graduation rates. The one with a higher graduation rate will generally have more satisfied students.

42. What should I know about the college that wouldn't appear in print? (*Ask everyone.*)

43. What's the best and worst thing about this college? (*Ask everyone.*)

44. In what ways is this college different from_____College? Ask about a similar institution that you're considering. (*Ask admissions rep, students, perhaps faculty.*)

45. What sorts of students are the perfect fit for this school? A poor fit? (*Read college guides, ask everyone.*)

46. What is the total cost of attending this college, taking into account your likely financial aid package? (*Ask the financial aid office.*)

47. What other information about the school could affect your decision? e.g., beauty of campus, food, a graduation requirements you object to, percent of students of your religious or ethnic group. (*Consult catalog, college guides, ask admissions rep.*)

# HOW TO TEST-DRIVE A COLLEGE
## Martin Nemko Ph.D.

College A or College B? A visit is the best key to deciding. You wouldn't even buy a jalopy without popping the hood and test-driving it. With a college, you're spending thousands of dollars and four or even six years of your life, so better take it for a good spin.

Trouble is, many students make a worse decision after a visit than they would have made without one. A college can feel so overwhelming that many students come away with little more than, "The campus was beautiful and the tour guide was nice."

Here's how to put a college through its paces.

### Preparing

Plan to visit when school is in session. Visiting a college when it isn't in session is like test-driving a car with the engine off.

Call ahead. Ask the admissions office if you can spend the night in a residence hall, perhaps with a student in your prospective major. If you think it might help, make an appointment for an interview. Get directions to campus, a campus map, and where to park. Also find out when and from where tours are given.

Reread the college guides. If you're just about to visit, that seemingly boring profile of Sonoma State may become fascinating. It can also raise questions, like, "The book describes Sonoma's Hutchins School of Liberal Studies as excellent. Is it?"

Review the questions on the College Report Card.

### The Visit

Write what you learn on the College Report Card. Especially if you're visiting more than one college, the differences between them can blur.

Here are the stops on my campus tour. If you're with parents, split up, at least for part of the time. Not only can you see more, but it's easier to ask questions like, "What's the social life like?"

### The Official Tour

Take the tour mainly to orient you to campus geography, not to help you pick your college. Tour guides are almost always enthusiastic, unless, of course, they're in a bad mood. The tour guide, however, is usually a knowledgeable student, so while walking to the next point of interest, you may want to ask some questions.

### Grab Students

I know it's scary, but grab approachable students in the plaza or student union and ask a question. Most love to talk about their school. You might start with, "Hi, I'm considering coming to this school. Are you happy here? What would you change about the school? What should I know about it that might not appear in print?"

In addition to students at random, consider dropping by a residence hall and talking with the student at the front desk. Or pay a visit to the student government or student newspaper office. Folks there know a lot about life on campus. While you're at the newspaper office, pick up a few copies of the student newspaper. What sorts of stories make the front page? What's in the letters to the editor? Athletes should query players on the team, oboeists should quiz orchestra members.

The key is: never leave a campus without talking with at least five people that the admissions director did not put in front of you. Don't just speak with who's paid by the school, speak with who's paying the school. Like at high school, some people love the school and others hate it, but talk with ten people, and you'll get the picture.

### A Dining Hall and/or the Student Union

Sample the food. Tasty nuggets or chicken tetrachloride? Are you a vegetarian? See if there's more than salad bar and cheese-drenched veggies.

While you're in the dining hall (or in the student union), eavesdrop on discussions. Can you see yourself happily involved in such conversations?

Most colleges claim to celebrate diversity. The dining hall is a great place to assess the reality because, there, integration is voluntary. Do people of different races break bread together?

Bulletin boards are windows to the soul of a college. Is the most frequent flyer, "Noted scholar speaks,"Political action rally" or "Semi-formal ball"?

### Sit In On A Class

Best choices are a class in your prospective major, a required class, or in a special class you're planning to enroll in, for example, an honors class.

At the break, or at the end of the class, stop a group of students and ask them questions. If it's a class in your prospective major, ask students how they like the major and what you should know about the major that might not appear in the catalog.

### How to Visit 10 Classes in Half an Hour

Rather than following the standard advice to "sit in on a class" which only lets you know about one class, ask a student for the name of a building with many undergraduate classes.

Walk down its halls and peek into open doors. What percentage of classes are alive and interactive? In what percentage is the professor droning on like a high schooler reciting the pledge of allegiance with the students looking as bored as career bureaucrats two days from retirement?

Some students say that they are too shy to peek into or sit in on classes, but it's worth conquering the shyness. Shouldn't you look at a sample of classes before committing to four years worth?

### A Night in the Dorm

It's an uncomfortable thought. "I'm a dippy high school kid. I'll feel weird spending a whole night with college students." Luckily, it usually ends up being fun as well as informative. A bunch of students will probably cluster around you, dying to reveal the inside dirt.

You'll also learn what the students are like: Too studious? Too raunchy? Too radical? Too preppy? At 10:30 P.M. on a weeknight, is the atmosphere "Animal House," an academic sweatshop, or a good balance?

Are the accommodations plush or spartan? One prospective student found a dorm crawling with roaches. You won't get that information on the official tour.

### Beware of Bias

We've already mentioned the peril of an overzealous tour guide. Here are other sources of bias in a college visit:

### Timing

You visited a college on Thursday at noon. That's when many colleges are at their best. Students are buzzing around amid folks hawking hand-crafted jewelry or urging you to join their clubs or causes, all perhaps accompanied by a rock band. But if you were to arrive at 4:30, even the most dynamic college won't seem as exciting.

### Weather

No matter how great the college, rain can't help but dampen enthusiasm for it.

### The Campus

Chant this 10,000 times: "Better good teachers in wooden buildings than wooden teachers in good buildings." As mentioned earlier, it's so easy to be overwhelmed by ivy-covered buildings, lush lawns, and chiming bell towers. A beautiful campus is nice, but don't let it overwhelm other factors.

Colleges begin to melt together after a while, however, so you might want to take photos of each campus.

### After the Visit

Finish recording what you've learned on the College Report Card immediately after leaving campus. Especially if you've visited a number of colleges, it's easy to confuse key features of one with another: "Was it North Carolina-Asheville or St. John's that had great vegetarian food?"

Probably, additional questions about each college will come to mind after you leave. Write them down and send them to your college interview as part of a thank you note which expresses your appreciation for the time spent and the advice you received.

**The Decision**

After you get home, ask yourself four questions:

- Would I be happy living and learning with these types of students for four years?
- Would I be happy being instructed by these professors for four years?
- Would I be happy living in this environment for four years?
- Will this college help me achieve my goals?
  If it's yes to all four, you may have found your new home.
  *Congratulations!*

Martin Nemko, Ph.D., co-author of *Cool Careers for Dummies* and author of *Your'e Gonna Love This College Guide* (Barron's) is an Oakland, California based consultant to families and colleges on undergraduate education.

# MAKING A DIFFERENCE CAREERS

**African-American Studies See Ethnic Studies**

**Agricultural Engineers** Design systems and strategies that preserve and protect our water and soil resources, regarding various engineering aspects of food and fiber production. Many work in developing countries helping with appropriate technology for increasing food production and quality while using human and natural resources responsibly.

**Agroecology** (The study of sustainable agriculture - more commonly known as 'organic farming') Graduates are in demand in farming, agribusiness, teaching, research and government.

**American Studies** Graduates find work as journalists, lawyers, government workers, teachers, business people, historical preservationists, and museum workers.

**Anthropology** Majors find work in federal, state, and local government, law, medicine, urban planning, business, and museums. They often go on to graduate work in anthropology as well, for a career in teaching.

**Atmospheric Science See Meteorology**

**Child Development** Careers as adoption counselors, child development specialists, educational consultants, working with handicapped children, hospital childlife specialists and go on to graduate work for Marriage & Family Counselor degrees. They work in crisis centers, hospitals, and both private and public agencies at both the local and national level.

**Civil Engineers** Conceive, plan, design, construct, operate and maintain dams, bridges, aqueducts, water treatment plants, sewage treatment plants, flood control works, and urban development programs. They are employed by governmental agencies at all levels and by engineering contractors, private consulting firms and in the areas of teaching, research, materials testing, city planning and administration fields.

**Community Health Educators** Work as school health educators, community health educators, family planning educators, environmental health specialists, occupational safety specialists, public health investigators, consumer safety investigators and OSHA inspectors.

**Conservation Law Enforcement** Graduates find work with state and federal governments as game wardens conservation officers, special agents for U.S. Fish & Wildlife, wildlife inspectors, border patrol agents, park rangers and state troopers

**Economics** Prepares students for careers both nationally and internationally in business labor, government, public service, or law.

**Entomologists** (Those who study insects) Work in the area of Integrated Pest Management which is essential part of organic farming. They work to understand the role of insects in the natural world and how they interact with man. They seek safe and effective solutions to insect problems in urban environments and agriculture.

**Environmental Education** Can lead to work in park and natural preserve administration, aquarium management, environmental advocacy organizations, nature writing, photography and documentation, teaching in elementary and secondary schools, and government work for environmental agencies.

**Environmental Engineers** Work in the areas of control of air & water pollution, industrial hygiene, noise & vibration control, and solid & hazardous waste management. Graduates find work in industry, consulting firms, and public agencies concerned with air and water pollution control, water treatment, and waste mgm't.

**Environmental and Forest Biology** Careers as animal ecologists, aquatic biologists, botanists, conservation biologists, consulting biologists, environmental assessment specialists, environmental conservation officers, fisheries biologists, natural resource specialists, ornithologists, park naturalists, plant and wetlands ecologists, public health specialists, sanctuary managers, soil conservationists, toxicologists, waterfowl biologists, wildlife biologists, game biologists, entomologists.

**Environmental Health Specialists** Work for state governments enforcing and administering laws governing water, food, and air contamination, noise, land use planning, occupational health hazards, and animal vectors of disease.

**Environmental Studies** Majors find a myriad of careers from cartographers, community resource development, cultural impact analysis, to environmental lobbyist, interpretive naturalist, park managers, recycled paper promoters, to wilderness survival instructors. Graduates also find work as pollution analysts, environmental journalists, air quality aides, transportation planners, pollution measurement technicians, environmental affairs directors, recycling co-ordinators, environmental educators, energy conservation specialists and legislative researchers.

**Environmental Toxicology** Those not going on to graduate study find work with government agencies, universities, industry and research and consulting firms in the areas of residue analysis, environmental monitoring, forensic toxicology, animal toxicology, environmental health and safety and pest control.

**Ethnic Studies** Graduates for work in community service organizations concerned with opportunities and problems of various ethnic and racial groups. They work as affirmative action officers, Equal Opportunity representatives, human relations specialists, peace officers, ombudsmen, urban specialists, diversity directors, educational specialists and lobbyists. Preparation for graduate work in the social sciences, law and humanities, and for work in municipal, state and federal government.

**Fisheries** Work in management, law enforcement and public information-education phases of fisheries work with national and international agencies as well as with regional, state and local government. Increasing opportunities are available with private industry interested in conservation, hydropower companies, and an expanding recreation business. Careers in research, administration, or teaching .

**Forest Engineers** Work in the areas of water resources (including water supply for urban areas and ground water aquifer protection) pollution abatement, and hazardous waste management. They design and plan collection systems to store and transport water, timber and energy structures, pollution abatement systems, and energy management. Careers as energy efficiency specialists, energy planning supervisors, environmental engineers, hydrologists, pollution control engineers, road engineers, survey party chief, water rights engineers, forest engineers, cartographers, ground water investigators, and natural resource engineers.

**Forestry** Graduates find work as foresters, arborists, environmental consultants, forest ecologists, timber buyers, urban foresters, land use specialists, forest economists, interpretive naturalists, consultants, environmental scientists, outdoor recreation, environmental conservation officers, naturalists, outdoor recreation, policy makers, forest protection work, including fire, insect and disease control. Managerial work planning timber crop rotations, and evaluating the economics of alternative forest management plans. Jobs far exceed the number of graduates each year.

**Forest Ranger** Graduates find work as county park rangers, environmental conservation officers, forest firefighters, forest rangers, forestry aides, survey party chiefs, engineer's aides, and forestry technicians. Jobs in forestry and surveying fields far exceed the number of graduates each year.

**Fuel Science** Graduates find work seeking to provide reliable energy sources without adverse environmental effects. They are employed by industry, government and utilities, as well as continuing on to graduate school.

**Geology** Geologists seek new resources, while insuring the most environmentally responsible means of doing do, ensure preservation of land and water quality, formulate plans for restoration of degraded lands. Career opportunities include industry, government and education. Many students continue on to graduate school in urban planning, engineering, environmental studies etc.

**Geography** Careers with environmental and resource management, location and resource decision-making, urban and regional planning and policy questions, and transportation in government, private, non-profit and international agencies.

**Gerontologists** Work in human service positions with the elderly or preparation for graduate school.

**Human Services** Work in advocacy, program development, management, direct service and case management in child-welfare agencies, drug and alcohol programs, crisis intervention settings, working in group homes for adolescents, community action programs, emergency housing programs, parole and probation. May provide case management, needs assessment, advocacy, crisis intervention and stabilization, and supportive task-oriented short term counseling.

**Integrated Health Studies** See Community Health

**International Agriculture Development** Careers in helping to solve hunger problems in Third World countries. This may involve working at the local level with government, private business, church or philanthropic organizations. Equally suitable for students with or without agricultural background.

**Labor and Industrial Relations** Graduates find employment in business, government, and labor organizations as labor relations specialists, personnel and human resource specialists, researchers, organizers, consultants and professionals in mediation and arbitration. The degree is also good preparation for graduate or law school.

**Landscape Architects** Work as city planners, coastal specialists, coastal zone resource specialists, community planners, environmental planners, land designers, land use planners, landscape architects and contractors, park landscape architects, regional, site, and transportation planners.

**Landscape Horticulture** See Urban Forestry

**Land Use Planners** Work with state or federal regulatory agencies, regional planning commissions, consulting firms and municipalities.

**Marine Biologists** Find careers in marine research, education and administration in marine industries and aquaculture, as well as further graduate study and research.

**Medical Anthropologists** (The study of the relationship between culture and health - a growing discipline for persons involved with the health needs of ethnically diverse populations.) Employment areas include local, state, federal and voluntary health agencies, and preparation for graduate programs.

**Meteorologists** (Study of the atmosphere) This field is important in environmental, energy, agricultural, oceanic and hydrological sciences. Graduates find careers with industry, private consulting firms, government, or continue on to graduate school.

**Native American Studies** Graduates teach social sciences, work in tribal governments and communities, and prepare for graduate work in anthropology, history, sociology, or professional training in law or business.

**Natural Resources Planning & Interpretation** Soil conservationist, environmental journalist, natural resources librarian, park ranger, rural county planner, environmental education leader, naturalist, hydrologist, information specialist.

**Natural Resources Management** Graduates work as public affairs specialists, soil technicians, wildlife biologist/ managers, plant curators, park ranger/managers, environmental planners, city planners, soil conservation planners, shellfish biologists, naturalists, and hazardous materials technicians. (See fisheries, forestry, wildlife...)

**Natural Resource Sciences** Careers in professional areas with a holistic perspective on resource management and research. Graduates are employed by all major public and private land management and wildlife organizations. They work as foresters, range conservationists, wildlife biologists, park managers, information specialists, game managers, consultants, researchers, and in developing countries.

**Oceanography** Graduates work as oceanographers, marine biologists, aquatic biologists, water pollution technicians, research assistants, earth scientists and environmental specialists.

**Outdoor Education & Interpretation** Careers in designing and administering recreation programs, guiding groups in wilderness adventures, counseling and working with diverse populations (troubled youth, handicapped people, senior citizens). Work with state, federal, private recreation departments, environmental education centers, camps, schools, groups such as Outward Bound.

**Paper & Science Engineering** Careers in recycling, paper making, and waste treatment, hazardous waste mgm't, oil spill prevention, environmental monitoring.

**Peace & Conflict** Careers in arms control and public policy, third world development and human rights, the faith community, Peace Corps, the United Nations, domestic social and economic justice, civil rights, mediation and conflict resolution. Preparation for law, journalism, education, government, and communications.

**Political Science** (The study of predicting, explaining, and evaluating political behavior, beliefs etc.) Graduates find socially relevant careers in public service, political analysis and teaching. They attend graduate school in areas such as law, teaching, social work, journalism, public administration and public policy.

**Public Administration** Graduates work in administrative positions, as well as personnel, budgeting, planning, and public relations, and in substantive policy areas ranging from health and human services and environmental protection to defense, criminal justice, transportation and taxation. Work in city and town management, regional planning commissions, the state budget office and administrative positions in education, national and international agencies.

**Public Health**  Careers as program analysts, mid-level administrators, technical staff persons, department heads in all areas of the health services delivery, and in the regulations field that require policy development, implementation, and evaluation.

**Range Management / Resource Science**  Careers are available as range conservationists, range managers, natural resource specialists, environmental specialists, soil scientists, park rangers, biological technicians, and agricultural inspectors.

**Science, Technology and Values**  See Technology and Society

**Sociologists**  Find work as consultants to business and government, as social change agents (such as community organizers,) politicians, educators and diplomats. They find careers as urban planners, youth counselors, employment counselors, public opinion analysts, social ecologists, industrial sociologists, correctional counselors, probation officers, health services consultants, and personnel management specialists.

**Social Workers**  Work in areas of health care, services to the elderly, community practice, rehabilitation, youth work, mental health, services to children and families, substance abuse, residential treatment, the developmentally disabled and employment services. They work in nursing homes, public schools, and probation offices.

**Soil Science**  Graduates work in conservation planning, wetland identification and delineation, land reclamation, sediment & erosion control, land use planning, site evaluations, waste management, soil fertility mgm't, computer modeling of nutrient and pesticide movement, and with international institutions and organizations.

**Technology and Society**  Employment is found with private industry, consulting companies, environmental foundations, and government in the areas of policy analysis and formulation, planning, risk analysis and environmental impact assessment.

**Urban Forestry & Landscape Horticulture**  Leads to careers in landscape design and contracting, urban forestry, park supervision, garden center management, arborists, and city foresters.

**Wildlife Studies**  Wildlife biologist, wildlife manager, fish & game warden, conservation officer, range conservationist, forestry technician, park ranger, soil scientists, naturalist, environmental planner, agricultural inspector, wildlife refuge manager, preserve manager, fisheries technician, and studying rare and endangered species. Work with state and federal environmental agencies and groups such as the Audubon Society and The Nature Conservancy.

**Women's Studies**  Is an asset to careers in such fields as education, social service, government, business, law, the ministry, journalism, counseling, health and child care. More specialized work is found in battered women's shelters, rape counseling services, and in displaced homemaker centers. Graduates also work as women's health care specialists, political advocates, psychologists, and teachers.

# MAKING A DIFFERENCE COLLEGES
. . .

· Please note, "Making A Difference Studies" include some minors.

# UNIVERSITY OF ALASKA, FAIRBANKS

3,900 Undergraduates    Fairbanks, Alaska

UAF students aren't afraid to be different. The University of Alaska Fairbanks isn't the right school for everyone, but if it is right for you, you can take advantage of small classes, first-rate faculty and access to hands' on research -- not to mention some of the most breathtaking scenery in the world. With a low student/faculty ration, students get lots of personal attention, more attention, in fact, than at almost any other public university in the country

The core curriculum provides students with a shared foundation of skills and knowledge. Among others, core experience achievements are expected to include:

- An intellectual comfort with the sciences -- including the objectivity of the scientific method, the frameworks which have nurtured scientific thought, the traditions of human inquiry, and the impact of technology on the world's ecosystems
- An appreciation of cultural diversity and its implications for individual and group values, aesthetics and social and political institutions
- An understanding of our global economic interdependence, sense of historical consciousness, and a more critical comprehension of literature and the arts
- A better understanding of one's own values, other value systems and the relationship between value systems and life choices.

Students in the College of Natural Sciences have one of the most exciting natural laboratories in which to learn. CNS has undergraduate programs in biology, geology, chemistry, physics, and wildlife management, all of which offers research opportunities. The college also offers two interdisciplinary programs in earth and general sciences, intended especially for those seeking teaching certificates. The research institutes associated with the college -- the Geophysical Institute, the Institute of Artic Biology (IAB,) the Alaska Cooperative Wildlife Research Unit -- are nationally and internationally recognized. IAB manages the Large Animal Research Station just north of campus, the home of musk oxen, caribou and reindeer.

In the College of Rural Alaska, the five departments of behavioral sciences and human services, education, general studies, rural development, and vocational education, all work to prepare students to be more sensitive to cross-cultural settings and diversity. Alaskan trained teachers and social workers are in demand in Alaska.

Although primarily a graduate institution, undergraduates in The School of Fisheries and Ocean Sciences are well prepared for graduate study or to enter management, law enforcement, and/or public information-education fields related to fisheries, and often are able to find summer field work opportunities through cooperating state and federal agencies. The school operates coastal facilities at Juneau, Kodiak, Seward and Kasistna Bay, and also the 133-foot oceanographic vessel R/V Alpha Helix for seagoing research and education.

With a population of more than 70,000, the Fairbanks area offers the conveniences of a big city, yet rolling hills and spectacular panorama are only minutes away. Literally millions of acres of wilderness surround Fairbanks. Whether the sport is canoeing, climbing, running, skiing, or fishing, nowhere else compares with Alaska.

# MAKING A DIFFERENCE STUDIES

## Natural Resources Mgm'.t  Tracks in Forestry, Plant, Animal & Soil Sciences

Forest Protection
Introduction to Conservation Biology
Introduction to Watershed Management
Alaskan Environmental Education
Environmental Policies

Natural Resource Legislation and Policy
Environmental Ethics and Actions
Natural Resources Conservation and Policy
Outdoor Recreation Planning
Ecological Anthropology

## Fisheries / Fisheries Management

The UAF location is advantageous for the study of interior Alaska aquatic streams & lakes.

Natural Resources Policies
Geography of Alaska
Magazine Article Writing
Wildlife Management Techniques
Alaska Native Politics

Natural Resources Legislation
Man and Nature
Congress and Public Policy
Wildlife Management--Forest & Tundra
Personnel Management

## Wildlife Management

Survey of Wildlife Science
Wildlife Policy and Administration
Wildlife Internships
Wildlife Diseases
Biotelemetry

Wildlife Management Principles
Grazing Ecology
Waterfowl & Wetlands Ecology & Mgm't
Nutrition & Physiological Ecology of Wildlife
Wildlife Populations and their Management

## Human Services / Human Service Technology A.A.

Interdisciplinary in approach, cross-cultural in content, and rural in orientation.

Rural Sociology
Human Behavior in the Artic
Substance Abuse Counseling
Sociology of Later Life
Helping Role in Child Abuse & Neglect
Family in Cross Cultural Perspective

Cross Cultural Psychology
Dev. Psych in Cross Cultural Perspectives
Alcoholism:Treatment and Prevention
Community Organization & Dev. Strategies
Group Dynamics & Therapeutic Activities
Ethics in Human Service

## Rural Development  Tracks in Land; Renewable Resources; Community Research and Documentation; Comm. Organization & Service; Local Gov't Administration.

Community Development in the North
Rural Alaska Land Issues
Resource Mgm't Research Techniques
Tribal People and Development
Cultural Impact Analysis
Narrative Art of Alaska Native Peoples

Issues in Alaskan Maritime Development
Perspectives on Subsistence in Alaska
Community Research Techniques
Rural Social Work
Women and Development
Knowledge of Native Elders

### Women's Studies    Northern Studies    Forestry 3/2 Northern AZ. U.

### Education    Social Work    Community Health Aide    Geology    Eskimo Studies

Student body: 89% state, 56% female, 44% male, 14% Alaska Native, 6% other minorities
Faculty: 74% male, 26% female, 9%minority
Costs: Residents $6,140   Non-residents $10,200     Apply By 8/1
• Prior Learning Credit   • Weekend & Evening Classes   • Independent Learning

Use form in back to contact: Office of Admissions and Records
University of Alaska, Fairbanks    Fairbanks, AK 99775-0060
(907) 474-7500   (800) 478-IUAF (Alaska only)
fyadmis@aurora.alaska.edu

# ALASKA PACIFIC UNIVERSITY

325 Students    Anchorage, Alaska

Alaska Pacific University is a liberal arts university that promotes the fullest development of its students in body, mind, character, and spirit so they can lead lives of personal fulfillment, rewarding employment, and effective service to the world - both human society and the natural environment. Through a model of student-centered education that extends respect, freedom, and responsibility to students, the university encourages the development of leadership abilities within each student so that they may lead good lives and make a difference in the world.

Alaska Pacific students draw inspiration from Alaska- - from its vast natural wilderness, from its cultural, linguistic, and geologic diversity, from its economic and professional vitality -- and often link their course of study to Alaska's remarkable attributes. How excited and involved students are with their education, how much they are learning, is first on the university's list of priorities.

The university's philosophy of education is founded on the premise that today's students need and deserve an active form of learning to prepare them for positions of leadership in a dynamic and rapidly changing world. It follows then that a modern university should teach students how to think for themselves, to set their own goals and accomplish them, to work creatively and effectively with, and on behalf of, others. Thus, the educational agenda at Alaska Pacific goes beyond the conventional classroom and the traditional format of lecture and examination, and instead emphasizes field-based learning, collaborative projects, internships, practica, and independent study.

Four-week "block" periods, during which students study a single subject intensively, provide opportunities for students to learn from direct experience, to take initiative, and to learn to be of service to others. For example, a group of environmental science students travelled to Borneo to study Tropical Rain Forest Ecology with an eminent biologist. A group of Outdoor Studies students travelled to Prince William Sound to collect data to be used by Alaska State Marine Parks in determining visitor preferences about potential management actions. One group of environmental science students went to the university's Rae Baxter Memorial Marine Laboratory, located on MacDonald Spit on the south side of Kachemak Bay accessible only by boat. The students used the laboratory's equipment and several-thousand volume library to study intertidal ecology in both soft bottom and hard bottom marine environments, examined nearby temperate rainforest and alpine environments, andstudied marine mammals, piscivorous birds, and a host of fish and marine invertebrates.

An education student who wants to teach in an Alaska Native village after graduating spends a month as a teacher's assistant in a village school, learning the basics of Yup'ik culture and language.

Opportunities for service to humanity and to the Earth are built into the undergraduate curriculum at Alaska Pacific. Annual directed studies allow students to make their education "hands-on," experiential, and relevant to real-world problem solving. One environmental science student recently participated in a joint study by the

United States Geological Survey and the Federal Aviation Administration designed to assess the level of risk that hazardous materials at numerous small airports in rural Alaska pose to nearby population centers. The student researched the level of contamination for several sites, assessed the risk to ground water supplies posed by the contaminants, and authored several summary reports which were used to prioritize sites for cleanup.

The activities of numerous student clubs and organizations are oriented towards service. The Environmental Club oversees the university's participation in the Green Star Program, a waste reduction, recycling, and energy conservation program, and organizes community-wide Earth Day activities. The Campus Women's Forum provides a platform for the discussion of issues relating to women, and sponsors an annual Feast or Famine event to raise awareness of world hunger. Shoshin Ryu Club members volunteer time as food servers at the Brother Francis Shelter. The International Students Organization educates the campus and the community about global issues, and is arranging to raise a Peace Pole on campus with the inscription "May Peace Prevail on Earth" in multiple languages. The Student Organization of Native Americans offers support services for Native Americans and Alaskan Natives, and organizes campus events for visiting Alaska Native high school students.

Outdoor recreation at Alaska Pacific mirrors the university's reverence for the natural world and its capacity to transform lives. The Outdoor Program challenges students to experience the vast wilderness of Alaska within a "leave no trace" philosophy. Monthly trips are designed to encourage shared responsibility and group decision-making. Past trips have included sea kayaking in Prince William Sound and the San Juan Islands (WA,) hiking on the Kenai Peninsula, ice climbing in the Talkeetna, Chugach and Alaska mountain ranges, climbing at Joshua Tree National Park (CA,) back country skiing in Denali State Park, and mountaineering on the Matanuska, Byron, and Eklutna glaciers.

The central campus in Anchorage is one of the most beautiful campuses in the United States, a serene and natural jewel set in the heart of a modern city, with the ever-changing Chugach Mountains rising up behind nearly 200 acres of lawns, woods, and University Lake. Moose are frequently seen on the campus in all seasons, as are a wide variety of other animals. Three miles of campus trials leads bikers, hikers, in-line skaters, skiers, and runners into an extensive regional trail system which stretches from the ocean waters of Cook Inlet, throughout the city, and into the mountains east. A world unto itself, with no through-roads or traffic, the campus has an atmosphere appropriate to the dynamic, student-centered, personal style of education for which the university is known.

# MAKING A DIFFERENCE STUDIES

## Environmental Science

Environmental Assessment and Audit
Resource Economics
Environmental Chemistry
Environmental Geology
Meteorology: Weather and Climate

Principles of Forest Management
Oceanography
Environmental Ethics
Winter Ecology & Cold Weather Physiology
Natural Resources Planning and Politics

- **Conservation Biology** An introduction to the science of preserving biological diversity, its principles, policy, and applications. Topics include extinction, ecological and genetic effects of habitat fragmentation, minimum viable population analysis, reserve design and management, the Endangered Species Act, and conflict mediation.

## Outdoor Studies

Wilderness First Responder
Program Design for Recreational Services
Intro to Wilderness Skills
Mountaineering
Search and Rescue

Outdoor Education and Interpretive Services
Log Cabin Construction & Wilderness Living
Expedition Sea Kayaking  Expedition
Outdoor Rec. Resources, Issues, &Trends
Adventure Programming & Leisure Services

- **Outdoor Leadership and Wilderness Education** Expedition format during May. Development, application, and evaluation of outdoor leadership skills. Students will plan, organize, and lead the expedition. Decision making, teaching techniques, expedition behavior, group dynamics, risk mgm't. and environmental ethics emphasized.

- Faculty Bio: **Roman Dial** (M.S., U of Alaska; Ph.D., Stanford U.) Dr. Dial's research has taken him from collecting field data in Caribbean rainforests and Borneo, to studying effects of habitat destruction on Alaskan mammals. A writer and photographer, Roman has contributed to Patagonia, Smithsonian, Outside, & Mountain Bike.

## Psychology and Human Services

Ecopsychology
Educational Psychology
Lifespan Human Development
Dynamics of Early Child Care
Intro to Counseling

Coping and Adjustment
Anthropological Psychology
Issues in Substance Abuse
Self Concept: Formation & Development
Group Process, Social Influence & Leadership

- **Applied Psychology: Intimacy, Relationships and Sexuality** What causes one human being to become attracted to another? How are expressions of love and sexuality related? What commitments and responsibilities are implicit in an intimate relationship? Sexual orientation, abortion, reproductive technologies, gender issues.

- Faculty Bio: **Dr. Ellen Cole's** interests include the psychology of women, refugees, and indigenous people; sex therapy; wilderness and adventure therapy; and ecopsychology. She is a licensed psychologist.

Student body: 70% State, 60% female, 40% male, 20% minority, 50% transfer
Faculty: 55% male, 45% female, 5% minority
Resident Costs: $14,100   Non-Resident: $15,300     Early Decision 12/1, Regular Decision 2/1
• Field Studies   • Life Experience Credit   • Interdisciplinary Classes
• All Seminar Format   • Team Teaching   • Individualized Majors

Use form in back to contact: Office of Admissions
Alaska Pacific University   4101 University Drive
Anchorage, AK 99508
(800) 252-7528
admissions@alaskapacific.edu   www.alaskapacific.edu

# ANTIOCH COLLEGE

600 Students    Yellow Springs, Ohio

Antioch College was founded in 1852 by educational reformer Horace Mann as a pioneering experiment in education which offered the first "separate but equal" curriculum to both men and women and stressed that there should be no bars for race, sex, or creed. Today, Antioch continues to dedicate itself to the ideas of equality, "whole-person" education, and community service.

Antioch students are expected to reach beyond conventional learning. They are encouraged to become courageous practitioners, intelligent experimenters, and creative thinkers. Both the faculty and the students strive towards the common goals of refinement and testing of ideas through experience, and of extensive student participation to mold both the campus and the community.

Antioch is committed to internationalization and to peace. The Headquarters of the International Peace Research Association, an association of peace researchers and educators from more than 70 countries, is located on campus. Antioch encourages its students to have a balanced respect for all of life -- for one's self, for others, for society, and for the Earth. Empowered by their education, students are encouraged to empower others.

To accomplish its mission of enhancing classroom education with hands-on experience, Antioch has one of the most challenging cooperative education programs in the nation. Just a few examples of positions which Antiochians continue to hold include environmental science jobs in Parana State, Brazil; The National Abortion Federation in Washington, DC; and the Peace Child Foundation in Fairfax, Virginia. Each academic year is composed of three trimesters. During the Fall and Spring trimester, students enroll in three to four courses per study term. The summer trimester consists of three 4-week blocks in which students participate in a single intensive course each month. Students will begin one of two divisions who alternate use of the college campus and off-campus work experiences. One division will begin in the summer trimester. All students study full-time on campus for a total of seven 14-week trimester. Students work full-time off campus, usually in paying jobs located throughout the country and the world, for a total of five 16-week trimesters.

The variety of experience this provides is substantial. One environmental science student, for instance, worked as an environmental education assistant on a sloop on the Hudson River, at a resource center in Minnesota, researched rare plants in Appalachia, cared for injured birds in a raptor rehabilitation project in St. Louis, and then traveled around studying issues of importance in the Northwest. The Co-op Faculty maintains a network of 300 employers who hire students on a regular basis. Advisers assist students in choosing, financing, and evaluating their co-ops, as well as dealing with unexpected problems.

During the study trimester, students take part in an academic program which relies on utilizing the strengths of each individual, a willingness to both speak and listen critically, and an international, multi-cultural focus. Professors apply their lessons to "the real world" by bringing politics, world events, and students' co-op experiences into discussions. Classes are offered in the morning, afternoon, and evening, and are evaluated not by grades, but with written evaluations. The performance of each individual in class is assessed both by the professor and the student.

Antioch recognizes that an important part of today's education involves the ability to live and work in the multinational and multicultural society of the 21st Century. In order that students learn about the geography, customs, and traditions of other peoples, the school mandates an in-depth experience of 3-12 months in a cross-cultural environment (either inside or outside of the U.S.) Students can take advantage of the Antioch Education Abroad program, which has included Buddhist Studies programs in Bodh, India, a Comparative Women's Studies Term in Europe, and a British Studies program in London.

Another integral part of Antioch campus life is Community Government. Decision-making councils contain students, faculty, and administrators who strive to consider the many views of the community regarding administrative policy, academic programs, curriculum, budget allocations, tenure, new programs, quality of campus life and matters such as publication standards and social activities etc.

A wide variety of independent groups, such as Survivors of Sexual Offense, Third World Alliance, and Women's Center, exist on the Yellow Springs campus, and visitors often lecture or hold workshops on issues ranging from the Los Angeles Poverty Department, to ritual abuse, to Japanese theater. With the community as small as it is, everybody knows, works, and studies with everybody else. With only 600 students and 62 full-time faculty, the College nurtures close-knit relationships between students, faculty, and administration. Because of this, a common sense of responsibility for the campus prevails. This responsibility manifests itself in an extensive recycling program, a student-authored sexual offense policy, an organic garden, and more.

The College's history of experimentation, its commitment to questioning traditional values and practices, and its willingness to act on its beliefs have had a profound impact on generations of Antioch students. Their achievements represent the living legacy of the Antioch educational experience. Antioch students approach their education, as well as their lives following graduation, with a serious resolve to tackle important issues, question the status quo, and work toward constructive change. Antioch's success carrying out its basic educational mission -- empowering students to make a worthwhile difference -- is its proudest and most enduring tradition.

Glen Helen, the College's 1000 acre nature preserve, a registered Natural Landmark complete with medicinal springs located right across from campus often serves as a laboratory for science-related courses. It also offers opportunities for hiking, horse-back riding, cross country skiing, canoeing, rock-climbing, rappelling and solitude.

With it's Little Arts Theater, a health food store, a town library, the tiny village of Yellow Springs is a safe haven where students can find the essentials. The town offers an array of restaurants and off-beat shops, as well as seasonal street fairs. Antioch alumni, staff, and faculty account for a sizable percentage of the village's population of 4,600 people.

# MAKING A DIFFERENCE STUDIES

## Environmental Studies

African Environments in Crisis
Tropical Environments
Water and Water Pollution
Evolution of Landforms
Soils and Civilization

Natural Resources and Environment
Environmental Botany
Field Botany
Introduction to Solar Energy
Wildlife Ecology

- **Plants & People** Plants of the world including economic, agricultural, medicinal, forest, and harmful plants, as they relate to and are used by people. How ethnic food preferences relate to available plants, economic and social basis for rain forest and other habitat destruction, and the herbal medicine tradition. Historical issues including the development of agriculture and its effects on societies.

## International Relations and Peace Studies

Majors learn a modern conception of the world that transcends the idea that international relations happens only between national governments and that peace is simply the absence of war. The major develops academic skills and sets up international and cross-cultural experiences that empower students as world citizens and encourage them to think globally and act locally. Includes both negative and positive peace, which relates to direct and indirect or structural violence, and multi-disciplinary peace theories of interpersonal, intergroup, and international relations. Peace Net, a global computerized peace information network, is in the library for student use.

Introduction to Peace Studies
The World as a Total System
Gandhi: Truth and Nonviolence

Global Peace Movements in Information Age
Self Realization East and West
Issues in International Politics

- **Prospects for Peace in the 21st Century: Alternative Futures** Considers probable and possible global peace developments in the 21st century. Issues include 21st century war, environmental conflict, cultural and ethnic conflict, human rights, poverty, community conflict and micro-violence as well as possibilities for zones of peace, world government, and the further development of non-violent relationships.

- Faculty Bio **Paul L. Smoker** (Lloyd Professor of Peace Studies and World Law; M.Sc and Ph.D., Lancaster University, England) Paul has taught Peace Studies and International Relations for more than 25 years at universities in Europe, North America and Asia. He is Secretary General of a world-wide association of peace researchers and educators. He has published books and more than eighty academic articles in journals, most recently *Trident Town: Action-Research and the Peace Movement*. Current research includes an international project on reconceptualizing security to include political, social, economic, ecological, cultural and technological dimensions; and work on increasing the effectiveness of global peace movements.

## Women's Studies

Women in Music
The Feminist Press
Feminist Theory
Poetry by Women
Contemporary Latin American Thought on Women

Non-Traditional Literature by Women
Women and Minorities in Management
Human Sexuality
Women in Cross-Cultural Perspective

## International/Cross-Cultural Studies/Anthropology

Program equips students with the scholarly and critical skills they need for personal and intellectual growth and for their social contribution. The systematic placement of human belief and behavior in society and culture; ways to compare and contrast their own cultural assumptions; the historical, geopolitical and social contexts of environmental, local and global human problems. Cross-cultural studies is unique in the college curriculum; it frames inquiry and proposes strategies for problem-solving in the 21st Century.

Cultural History of Latin America
Japanese Poetry
Spanish Readings and Conversation
The Aztec and Mayan Civilizations
Cultural Aspects of Perception
History of Traditional Japan Through Literature

Human Rights: Latin America
Tribalism, Ethnicity and the Nation State
Spanish Dramatics and Radio Workshop
Asian Theater Seminar
The Middle East: Its People and Culture

## African and African American Studies

Black Women in White America
Intro to Drum & Dance of W. Africa
Race, Class & Nationalism: S. Africa
Society Health and Disease in Africa
From Africa to the New World: Peoples and Cultures of the African Diaspora

Race and U.S. Law
Literature by Black Women
Field Project in Cross-Cultural Studies
African-American Intellectual Thought

- Faculty Bio **Joseph R. Jordan** Assoc. Prof. of African/American Studies (M.A., M.S., Ohio State Univ, Ph.D., Howard Univ.) Joseph has, throughout his professional life, sought to combine his intellectual pursuits with political and community activism. He has served as co-chair of the Southern Africa Support Project, and director of the Institute for African-American Writing. He has worked as a Senior Analyst in African Affairs at the Library of Congress and taught at Howard University. His research interests include current expressions of the African-American intellectual tradition and revisiting the idea of the Black aesthetic. He is interested in southern African liberation struggles and solidarity organizations.

## Social and Behavioral Sciences

Management of Non-Profit Organizations
Fascism
Environmental Economics
Politics and Change in the Middle East
Minority Group Relations

The Economics of Developing Countries
Women in Cross-Cultural Perspective
Political Change: Non-Western Societies
Sex, Gender and Identity
Development, Sociology and Social Policy

- **Women and Minorities in Management** Theoretical as well as practical issues concerning the expanding role of women and minorities in organizations, particularly in management positions. Diverse range of economic and organizations. Theories examined with respect to division of labor, authority-power relations, and gender/race. Career management, stereotyping, communicators, networking.

Student Body: 20% state, 59% female, 41% male, 13% minority
Faculty: 65% male, 35% female, 10% minority
Costs: $21,628     Apply by 3/1
• Field Studies    • Co-op Education    • Service Learning    • Interdisciplinary Classes
• Vegetarian Meals    • Study Abroad    • Individualized Majors

Use form in back to contact: Office of Admissions
Antioch College     Yellow Springs, Ohio 45387
(800) 543-9436
admissions@antioch-college.edu     http://college.antioch.edu

# BELOIT COLLEGE

1,297 Students     Beloit, Wisconsin

Beloit College prepares leaders for the 21st Century by emphasizing problem solving and critical thinking skills. The pace of the social and technological changes already taking place globally isn't going to slow down. It will be the citizens who know how to keep up with that pace, the ones who can deal with change effectively, and the ones who are unafraid to ask questions who will excel in the future. Life is the test Beloit College wants you to pass. The liberal arts structure provides a learning environment to lead you on a path to a life of productive and active citizenship.

The concept of active citizenship is so important at Beloit that it has now made community service a requirement for all of its first-year students. This is done through the "First-Year Initiatives Program," which links students from the day they arrive on campus to an experienced professor and a group of peers. The professor then teaches one of the first semester courses, and serve as academic advisor and mentor.

Rebuilding nature trails and serving breakfast to schoolchildren are just two of the FYI community service projects. For many at Beloit, FYI is just the beginning of volunteerism. Students have traveled to, among other places, Guatemala, the Netherlands, Alaska, and even Beloit, Alabama, doing such things as building schools, teaching school children, inventorying bird populations, and researching acid rain. Students may also participate in Beloit's nationally renowned Help Yourself Program, tutoring and mentoring disadvantahged youth as they shape their futures.

Pluralism, the idea of a society with numerous distinct, ethnic, religious, and cultural groups peacefully co-existing, is another concept Beloit stresses. At Beloit, students share their learning experiences with peers from 49 states and 54 countries. It's just as likely your roommate will be from Mississippi or Nevada, as it is that they're from Finland or Zaire. What they share is a kind of practical idealism, a deep respect for individuality and diversity, and a commitment to making diversity work. It's no wonder that in several recent years Beloit has had one of the highest proportion of graduates volunteering for the Peace Corps of any school in America.

There are more than 100 clubs and organizations that can help you find your cultural and social niche at Beloit, and students can always start their own club if one of those isn't what you're looking for. One of the most active clubs is the Outdoor Environmental Club which spearheads the campus' recycling program.

Finding one's own direction is far too personal an adventure to be standardized. At Beloit students can invent themselves; there is no lengthy list of requirements, no rigid formula for choosing a major, no mold in which one are expected to fit. Students are often encouraged to build a larger program of study through the interdisciplinary studies program. For example, if none of the regular minors meets your needs, you can explore a social interest through an interdisciplinary minor. There are literally hundreds of directions to go at Beloit. Students will have plenty of help, if they want it,but ultimately will make the decisions about their own future. Beloit's committed to providing students with the resources that will allow them to make critical and productive connections between thought and action in all aspects of their lives.

# MAKING A DIFFERENCE STUDIES

## Environmental Geology
This dep't is a member of the distinguished Keck Geology Consortium, providing majors outstanding opportunities to participate in summer research activities in US and overseas.

Enviro Geology and Geologic Hazards
Sedimentology
Natural History
Foundations of Economic Analysis
Geologic Field Methods

Mineralogy and Crystallography
Hydrology
Challenge of Global Change
Marine Biology
Field Excursion Seminar

## Biology  Tracks in Enviro, Behavioral, Mathematical, Medical, Molecular Biology
Botany
Behavioral Ecology
Comparative Physiology
Microbiology
Biological Issues

Environmental Biology
Population Biology
Zoology
Molecular Biology and Biotechnology
Developmental Biology

## Philosophy and Religion
Biomedical Ethics
Personal Freedom and Responsibility
Violence and Non-Violence
Hebrew Scriptures
Islam

Business Ethics
Philosophy of Science
Logic
Oriental Philosophy
20th Century Theology

## Government and International Relations
Women and Politics
Civil Liberties
Communist & Post-Communist Systems
Parties and Groups in American Politics
American Presidency

Principles of Government and Politics
The Politics of Developing Countries
Politics of Advanced Industrial Democracies
Theories of International Relations
American State Gov't. and Politics

- **International Organization and Law**  Political foundations of int'l institutions and law. Focus on transformation of the UN, the growth of specialized agencies and contemporary legal framework. Problems of int'l peace and security, arms control, economic development, social welfare and human rights in international organizations.

## Interdisciplinary Studies
Individually developed majors have included women, environment and change; choreography of the universe; set-design for educational TV, African studies; environmental design.

Energy Alternatives
Liberal Education and Entrepreneurship
Sense of Place: Regionalism in America
Circumstances of Agriculture in US
Photographic Images as Recorders of History and Social Change

Town and City in the Third World
Mass Communication in a Modern Society
Women, Feminism, and Science
Cultural Resource Management

### Sociology    Women's Studies    Health Care Studies

Student Body: 21% state, 55% female, 45% male, 11% minority, 12% int'l.,7% transfer
Faculty: 62% male, 38% female, 10% minority
Costs: $24,096   Rolling Applications   Apply by 3/1 for financial aid priority
- All Seminar Format  • Theme Housing  • Individualized Majors  • Vegetarian & Vegan Meals

Use form in back to contact: Admissions Office
Beloit College    700 College Street    Beloit, WI 53511
(608)363-2500    (800)356-0751
admiss@beloit.edu    www.beloit.edu

# BEMIDJI STATE UNIVERSITY

4,300 Undergraduates    Bemidji, Minnesota

Located on the shores Lake Bemidji and the headwaters of the Mississippi River, Bemidji State University has long been known as a college whose setting and sense of community are conducive to learning, living, and growing. As the only institution of higher education serving the baccalaureate needs of north-central Minnesota, Bemidji State recently completed its 75th anniversary by renewing its deep sense of commitment to the region, building a national reputation for quality programming, and enhancing the international perspective for its 4,300 students.

While large enough to offer more than 50 majors and 15 pre-professional programs, the university is small enough to earn its reputation as a friendly college. Understanding that all friendships require work, Bemidji State initiated a program called Responsible Men, Responsible Women, where students are exposed to concepts of civility and trust. In keeping with its philosophy of a caring campus, the university established the Service Learning Center to increase involvement in service learning as a critical component of the university curriculum.

Service is a value important to BSU students. A recent ACT study of new students planning to attend the university showed that nearly 50 percent fully expect to volunteer their time to help others on campus and throughout the community. There are ample opportunities to become involved on campus, with 84 clubs ready to satisfy any interest. These range from a very active Habitat for Humanity chapter to an Accounting Club that helps the elderly with income tax preparation. This volunteerism is officially recognized with students able to compile their work in a Student Service Transcript, which is made available to employers and others in a way similar to the normal academic record.

Situated between several major Native American reservations, the university also supports concepts of diversity and has the largest percentage of minority enrollment among the state universities in Minnesota. Bemidji State welcomes the challenge of global education. International students are actively recruited to study and live in Bemidji. At the same time, the university continues to expand its opportunities for study abroad.

Bemidji State was the first public college or university to offer single parent housing on campus. Part of the residential life complex. the one-, two- or three-bedroom apartments are dedicated to single parents with children of any age. The facility is adjacent to the campus daycare facilties and creates a ready network of single parents who trade baby-sitting services, share resources, and meet regularly to discuss common concerns.

Over the years, Bemidji State University has grown to be a comprehensive regional university offering both undergraduate and graduate degrees. Yet it's mission has remained constant over time. Founded on a sound liberal education, university programs educate students so that they may live as responsible, productive, and free citizens in a global society.

# MAKING A DIFFERENCE STUDIES

## Aquatic Biology
Preparing students for careers involving water quality and natural resource management.

Limnology
Organic Evolution
General Ecology

Fisheries Management
Methods of Water Analysis
Scientific Communication

## Environmental Studies
Defining and solving environmental problems caused by the actions of human beings.

Environmental Conservation
Ecosystems Studies
Environmental Economics

Environmental Politics
Waste Management
Society and Environment

## Indian Studies
Providing Ojibwe and other students with a viable academic area of study that is relevant to the heritage and diversity of Native Americans.

Ojibwe Culture
Elementary Ojibwe
Tribal Government
Contemporary Indian Issues

American Indian Literature
Contemporary Indian Issues
Federal Indian Law
Survey of American Indian Art

## Indian Studies & Minority Studies - Elementary Education
Presenting fields of emphases for educators on the Native American culture and other minority perspectives.

American Indian Literature
Ojibwe Language
History of the Ojibwe
Social Welfare Perspectives
Curriculum Development

Ethnic and Minority Group Relations
Cultural Anthropology
Education of the American Indian
Ojibwe Crafts
Native North Americans

## Health and Community Health
Investigating the intellectual, occupational, social, emotional, physical and spiritual factors of well being.

Health and the Consumer
Community Health
Nutrition
Family Violence
Physiology of Exercise

A Lifestyle for Wellness
Health and Drug Education
Human Sexuality
Neuromuscular Relaxation
Women's Issues

## Peace and Justice Studies
Focusing on ecological balance, economic well-being, sociopolitical justice, and nonviolent conflict management.

Global and Peace Justice Issues
Social Change
Philosophies of Nonviolence

Conflict Management
The Global Economy
Intercultural Communications

## Psychology and Applied Psychology
Exploring the science of behavior, cognition and affect.

Human Sexuality
Crisis Management
Lifespan Development
Human Responses to Death
Psychosocial Adjustment to Handicapping Conditions

Family Systems
Basic Counseling
Abnormal Psychology
Interpersonal Skills

## Social Work

Improving the quality of life for individuals, groups and communities.

| | |
|---|---|
| Social Work and the Law | Social Welfare Policy |
| Bureaucracy and Society | Chemical Use, Abuse and Dependency |
| Interpersonal Relations | Family Dynamics and Intervention |
| Human Relations | Psychology of Adjustment |

Chemical Dependency: Prevention & Intervention

## Women's Studies

Creating an academic extension of the women's movement.

| | |
|---|---|
| Women's Issues | Feminist Theories and Critiques |
| Women in Literature | Ideas About Women |
| Women and Philosophy | The Politics of Women's Health |

## International Studies

Promoting awareness, appreciation, and knowledge of the global community we all live in.

| | |
|---|---|
| The Global Economy | Comparative International Study |
| World Regional Geography | United Nations |
| Religion in the Modern World | Cultural Anthropology |
| International Conflict | Geography of Population & Settlements |

## Geography  Tracks in Regional and Land-Use Planning; Park and Recreation Planning; Geographic Information Systems.

| | |
|---|---|
| Human Geography | Conservation of Natural Lands |
| Economic Geography | Ecology |
| Public Administration | Land Use Analysis and Planning |
| Urban Geography | Environmental Conservation |
| Regional Planning Methods | Aerial Photography & Remote Sensing |

## Applied Public Policy

Acquiring a more sophisticated understanding of the laws, codes, social service programs and regulations that affect our daily lives.

| | |
|---|---|
| State and Local Politics | Introduction to American Politics |
| Public Economics | Markets and Resource Allocation |
| Benefit Cost Analysis | Public Administration |

### Environmental Ed Teaching Certificate   Minority Studies Teaching Certificate

### Pre-Law    Pre-Fisheries & Wildlife Mgm't    Pre-Forestry

Student Body: 90% state, 52% women, 48% men, 6% minority, 5% int'l, 13% transfer
Faculty: 69% male, 31% female, 8% minority
Costs: Residents $5,700 (includes ND, SD)   Non Residents $9,200   Rolling Admissions

Use form in back to contact: Admissions Office
Bemidji State University   Bemidji, MN 5660
(888) 345-1721
admissions@vax1.bemidji.msus.edu    www.bemidji.msus.edu

# BEREA COLLEGE

1500 students    Berea, Kentucky

Berea College, located in the foothills of the Cumberland Mountains, aims to fulfill its mission as a Christian school "primarily by contributing to the spiritual and material welfare of the mountain region of the South, according to young people of character and promise a thorough Christian education, with opportunities for manual labor as an assistance in self-support."

The seal of the College bears the inscription "God has made of one blood all peoples of the earth" which epitomizes Berea's belief in human-kind which should unite all people as children of God. It is hoped that men and women going out from Berea will further interracial understanding and that they will be courageous in opposing injustice and wrong.

Berea's distribution requirements for cultural area studies insures that each student will be able to demonstrate an understanding of some aspects of culture other than his or her own; a recognition of, and sensitivity to, similarities and differences in cultures; and an expanded perspective on a world of plurality of cultures. For Freshman Seminar all students select a series of courses designed to involve them in a critical study of the topic "Freedom and Justice" as it relates to the commitments of Berea College, to Appalachia, the Christian faith, the kinship of all people, or the dignity of labor. Similarly, students in the teacher education programs at Berea are asked to think deeply about the nature of teaching, learning, and schooling within the contest of the college's commitments: to able students who are economically disadvantaged; to the Christian ethic and to service; to the dignity of labor; to the promotion of the ideals of community democracy, interracial education, and gender equality; to simple living and concern for the welfare of others; and to service of the Appalachian region.

As an integral part of the educational program, each student is expected to perform some of the labor required in maintaining the institution, thus to gain an appreciation of the worth and dignity of all the labor needed in a common enterprise and to acquire some useful skill. The aim is to make available a sound education to students who are unable to meet usual college expenses, but who have the ability and character to use a liberal education for responsible, intelligent service to society.

Through the fellowship of meaningful work experiences, an atmosphere of democratic social living prevents social and economic distinctions and instills an awareness of social responsibility. Student industries include broomcraft, weaving, woodcraft and wrought iron work, the products of which are sold to the public from the student run giftshop, hotel, and catalog. Students also participate in running the college farm.

Berea's campus comprises 140 acres. Farm lands, including the experimental farms, piggery, and poultry farm cover 1400 acres. The college also owns a 7,000 acre forest.

Admission to Berea is limited to students whose families would have a difficult time financing a college education without assistance. Financial need is a requirement for admission.

# MAKING A DIFFERENCE STUDIES

## General Studies - Core Courses

Community Building

Freedom and Justice: The Third World

Housing: American Dream or Nightmare

Politics of Food

Immigrants and Minorities

Sacred Earth, Sacred Relationships

Health Decisions: Justice and Autonomy

Women, Society and Mental Health

Technology, Culture, Belief

Community and Spirituality

Values in Conflict

Labor, Learning and Leisure

- **One Blood, All Nations: Cultural Diversity & Environmentalism** Major issues concerning tensions between advocacy for cultural diversity and environmentalism, especially the environmental concept of a global commons. Achieve a deeper understanding of the issues contained within the concepts of kinship of all people and a way of life characterized by plain living; deeper understanding of the relatedness of these concepts; and understand how these concepts generate questions of freedom and justice.

## Black Culture

Introduction to Afro-American Studies

Slavery & Afro-American Culture

Afro-American Music: An Overview

Black Emancipation & Reform in the U.S.

Critical Issues of Black Americans in the Twentieth Century

Afro-American Literature

Contemporary Afro-American Experience

Race in America

Sub-Saharan Black African Art

## Appalachian Culture

Appalachian Literature

Appalachian Problems and Institutions

Appalachian Music

Appalachian Culture

Health in Appalachia

Appalachian Crafts

- **Community Analysis: The Appalachian Case** Study of history, demography, social structure and forces promoting social change in Appalachian rural communities. Sociological approach to understanding concept of community, its various systems, institutions and groups. Community problem-analysis orientation. American, European, and Third-World communities examined looking at content and method.

## Child and Family Studies

Principles of Food Science

Human Environments

Family Relations

The Exceptional Child

Contemporary Family Issues

Child Development

Advanced Child Development

Guidance of the Young Child

Cross Cultural Perspectives on Family

Family Resource Management

## Nursing     Agriculture     Sociology

Student Body: 80% from Southern Appalachia, 9% minority, 5% int'l.

All tuition costs are met by the college through endowment income and major fund-raising efforts.

Room and board, $3510 for which financial aid is available.

Rolling Admissions

• Field Studies   • Co-op Work Study   • Study Abroad

• Interdisciplinary Programs   • Individualized Majors

Use form in back to contact: Office of Admissions

Berea College     CPO 2344     Berea, Kentucky 40404

(606) 986-9341

# BETHEL COLLEGE

644 Students    North Newton, Kansas

Bethel is a liberal arts and sciences college affiliated with the General Conference Mennonite Church. Its 450-year-old Anabaptist heritage is the wellspring for a vibrant academic community with a tradition of combining academic excellence with a commitment to social justice, service to others, peacemaking and conflict resolution. Although Mennonite in character, there are 35 religious denominations on campus. Believing that authentic faith comes from free conviction and not from indoctrination or conformity, Bethel promotes freedom, openness, and voluntarism.

Bethel's distinctiveness, by heritage and conviction, includes a deeply-rooted commitment to peacemaking, service, and conflict-resolution. The urgency of this focus is self-evident in a nuclear world. Education has a special responsibility to seek ways to cope creatively and nonviolently with the human and environmental needs of our global community. The College seeks to study and practice ways of peacemaking and reconciliation in society both in its core curriculum and in special programs.

In a world of specialization and fragmentation the great need of our time is for coherences, to understand that we live in a world of linkages. Bethel seeks to provide an environment that integrates the worlds of faith, learning and work. In our world of finite resources, Bethel supports a conserving desire to accent the beauty of simplicity and to live more with less. Such a goal is also a more convincing witness to the developing nations of our world and to our understanding of Christian stewardship.

All Bethel students must meet a Global Awareness requirement to prepare them to live in a shrinking world of increasing complexity. Students take a global issues seminar or spend at least thirty days in a situation exposed to a culture significantly different from their home environment. Recent international placements include rural development and environmental health in Burkina Faso; with the Migrant Farm Workers Project in Missouri; in International Development with a center for hillside sustainable agriculture; and with a Mexican environmental education organization.

Bethel's Global Studies program integrates study of our environment, development (what we do in attempting to improve our lot within that abode,) peace and justice (how we react to unequal sharing of our planet's resources). The topics are inherently interwoven and international, hence multidisciplinary and cross-cultural.

Education student s are encouraged to student teach in schools of another culture or in a multicultural setting. Interested students are encouraged to student teach in inner-city schools, American Indian schools, or even overseas as the demand arises.

Convocation helps build community, broaden horizons, and allow exploration of basic value issues. Recent convocations included "Human Rights in the 1990's" with Bethel alumnus Curt Goering of Amnesty International, and "Housing for the Poor" with Millard Fuller, President of Habitat for Humanity International.

As a community Bethel expects its members to guard the dignity and worth, and to promote equality and empowerment of self and others, to value volunteerism, to work through conflicts without force, intimidation or retreat; to promote relationships free from sexual discrimination, coercion and exploitation; to keep the environment safe and clean; and to nurture the spiritual awareness and development.

# MAKING A DIFFERENCE STUDIES

## Global Environmental Studies

Introduction to Environmental Science
Ecology
Environmental Decision-Making
Environmental Biology
Environmental Monitoring & Management
Development Economics

- Faculty Bio **Dwight R. Platt,** Ph.D. has been Director of Sand Prairie National History Reservation. He taught at Sambalpur University in India, and was an Education Technician with the American Friends Service Committee there.

## Global Peace Studies

Conflict Resolution Theory & Practice
Peacemaking & International Conflict
Summer Peace Institute for Teachers
Christian Social Ethics
Majority/ Minority Relations
Theories & Strategies of Social Change
Just War in American History
Public Policy for Global Issues

- **Nonviolence Theory and Practice** Philosophical and religious foundation, theory and practice of nonviolence as a method of social change. Gandhi and M. L. King, Jr.

## Economics & Business

Development Economics
Public Policy & Finance
Comparative Economic Systems
Public Policy for Global Issues

- **Business Ethics & Social Responsibility** Theoretical and practical aspects of social responsibility of modern corporations as well as institutional values and goals. What role, if any, social responsibility plays in corporate activity an decision making.

## Global International Development

Seeks to prepare workers in International Development emphasizing cross-cultural understanding, an appreciation for the dignity of the poor and the complexity of their struggles.
Public Policy for Global Issues
Transcultural Seminar
Principles of Sustainable Agriculture
Development Economics
Relief, Development & Social Justice
Energy Issues & Appropriate Technology
International Health
Theories & Strategies of Social Change
Global Issues in Environment, Human Conflict and Development

- **Rural Development in Central America/Mexico** A hands-on field course about the problems and possibilities for rural development, social change, and conflict resolution. Food, population growth, urban migration and environmental degradation. Emphasis on hearing and understanding those who suffer with underdevelopment.

## Special Education Concentration

Strategies for Behavior Management
Consultation Skills for Special Educators
Handicapped Preschool Children Practicum
Characteristics of Adolescents with Handicap
Early Intervention for Handicapped Children
Education & Psych. of Exceptional Individuals

**Off Campus Study:** Biology/Anthropology Field Trip to Belize and Guatemala. Study of tropical marine, fresh water terrestrial biology, archaeological history and contemporary life.

Student Body: 68% state, 55% female, 45% male, 19% minority, 9% transfer
43% Mennonite    Faculty: 50% male, 50% female
Costs: $15,270    Apply by 8/15
• Life Experience Credit    • Team Teaching    • Non-resident Degree Program
• Nursing Outreach Program    • Co-op Work Study    • Service-Learning • Vegetarian Meals
Use form in back to contact: Admissions Office
Bethel College
300 East 27th Street    North Newton, KS 67117-9989
(800) 522-1887

# BREVARD COMMUNITY COLLEGE
14,925 Students     Cocoa, Florida

Brevard Community College is recognized as one of the leading community colleges in the United States in several areas including instructional excellence, equal opportunity, technology, distance learning, cooperative relationships, service to the community and service-learning. The college offers community and professional education opportunities, international/intercultural education, study abroad programs, independent study, telecourses and on-line courses, and an extensive experiential learning curricula.

The college, located in the heart of the nation's space capital on Florida's central-east coast, is known for its investment in social capital. An important part of Brevard's mission is to help students meet their civic responsibilities through service-learning. Brevard has immersed service throughout its curriculum and campuses. Maxwell C. King, President of Brevard Community College gives meaning to Brevard's priority for service to community when he states "Community service is an important part of our students' preparation for their role as truly educated and responsible citizens."

Brevard Community College has developed a continuum of service opportunity including: short term special projects; co-curricular community service; community related class assignments; direct service, advocacy, and leadership service opportunities; work-study/service placements; service-learning options in over 125 courses and 275 course sections; independent study service placements; introductory service-learning courses; in-depth service-learning courses; professional development workshops, seminars, courses for students, community organizations, and faculty; and a variety of immersion experiences including internships and international service-learning.

The college supports community service-learning for its students through an extensive infrastructure system, which includes a comprehensive Center for Service-Learning. The center recruits, places and assists over 2,000 students annually in meaningful service-learning experiences in over 250 community organizations and agencies in Brevard County including the following program areas: animal care, the arts, child care, community development, crisis care, drug prevention, environmental, family services, government, health care, historical, justice system, media related, mental health, physically challenged, recreation, senior services, special adults/children, subsistence services, and youth services. Students serve as mentors and tutors for school age youth and work extensively with people who have AIDS. There are numerous environmental projects in which students work with endangered species, native plant habitats and the fragile Florida ecosystem including the Atlantic Ocean and Indian River Lagoon. Many students have helped abused children and aided in the plight of many homeless and hungry people. Because of the inordinate amount of senior citizens in Brevard County, student volunteers fill a critical need in many elderly people's lives. Service-learners volunteer in crisis center intervention/care projects such as, ambulance service, hospice, domestic violence, and rape crisis.

Many students' lives have been changed personally, academically, civically, and occupationally through their involvement in service-learning. Several BCC students have been recognized for their service locally, statewide, and nationally. Some have been recipients of important national humanitarian awards and scholarships. The following student service-learning journal/questionnaire comments attest to the powerful impact of service-learning:

"Volunteering at the Hacienda Girls Ranch was one of the best experiences in my life. I learned so many things about children, abuse, myself, the effects it has on children and what I want to do to help them. It made me realize that there's more to life than just getting a job to pay bills."

"Riding on an ambulance as a volunteer is an enriching experience. I feel I am making a difference in other people's lives and my own. I can change someone's life just by being that hand to hold. It has changed the way I look at things in my life, and how I approach everyday life."

"Having completed my service-learning project, I have found a renewed interest in my major. Now I actually cannot wait to get my education rolling. I feel like knocking down class after class just to get closer to my degree and eventually off to medical school."

"In summary, I would say this was a learning experience. I learned I never paid enough attention to what was going on around me. I was never active in views and votes, but now I have chosen to be very active in these matters. I want to make a difference in some active way, but I need to open my eyes to the grays, not just to black and white."

"To say the least, this has been one of the best experiences of my life. I am very happy that you offered this assignment to us. For once in my life, I wrote a paper on something that I really enjoyed.

Recently the college has expanded its service-learning initiatives to include: international service-learning projects in India, an academic transcript notation for all community service hours; a 4th credit option in many courses; African-American history project; student leadership/coordination program, placement of service-learning in the general education program, and America Reads, a project to enhance the reading skills of children K-6. The college is promulgating a student Citizen Scholar program to involve and recognize students who significantly help in the community.

The Brevard International Education Program has gained worldwide respect as one of America's leading international education programs among community colleges. International education is a priority because we must learn to prosper in a global economy and learn to live peacefully with other nations. In the past 26 years, more than 2,200 BCC students have studied in foreign lands. Some have earned service-learning credits by volunteering in hospitals, at a blood bank, and at a Mother Teresa site for abandoned children. In 1997, BCC played a leadership role in bringing Catholics and Protestants from Ireland to America to foster religious harmony and economic development for Ireland. BCC offered an international business and multicultural education program for 24 students from the Republic of Ireland and Northern Ireland. They also shared leadership classes, field trips, practicums, internships, meals, lodging and entertainment.

# MAKING A DIFFERENCE STUDIES

Service-learning is an integral part of the total curriculum. Over 125 courses and 45 disciplines offer service-learning options for students. The strongest courses are in, psychology, mathematics, sociology, human services, social science, college success skills, environmental science, business, honors, world religions, criminal justice, communications, government, education, and humanities.

- Faculty Bio **Raj Ayyar** has been employed at Brevard Community College since 1981. He has been actively involved with service-learning since 1991. Mr. Ayyar has promulgated innovative methods for integrating service-learning in World Religion sand Humanities curricula. Raj is founder and faculty sponsor of the only service-learning club at the Melbourne Campus of BCC. He has integrated service with academic study in the humanities for the past six years. Raj has been a presenter and a participant at several Florida Campus Compact Conferences. He was a presenter at the 1996 National Campus Compact Conference.

## Social Work

Four stand-alone service-learning courses exist. Human Service Experience I, II, III, three one credit hour electives which provide students with a service-learning experience in a public/social service organization. Students complete at least 20 hours of volunteer work per semester and reflect critically on the experience through journals, seminars, and in-class debriefing methods.

- **Community Involvement** A general education core course, provides the student with a unique opportunity to examine community volunteerism, public service, and citizenship through practice and critical reflection. Thirty-two hours of volunteer work and 24 hours of seminars are required. The college also offers a version of this course for teacher recertification. Also, courses are offered in African-American history, multiculturalism, women's studies, study abroad, and international education.

- Faculty Bio **Linda Krupp** ( Ed.D in Educational Leadership, University of Florida) Dr. Linda Krupp has integrated service with academic study for eight years. She teaches stand-alone service-learning courses and has edited or written several service-learning publications, including a syllabi guide and handbook for agency supervisors of student service-learners. Linda has presented at several conferences and was a member of Brevard CC's team at the Institute on Integrating Service with Academic Study in Stanford University in 1991. She is very active in the community and with the college's service-learning program. Dr. Krupp has taught at Brevard since 1985 and teaches Community Involvement, Human Service Experience, education courses and College Success Skills.

## Human Services

| | |
|---|---|
| Introduction to the Human Services | Issues in Human Services |
| Basic Counseling Skills | Human Services Field Experience |
| Crisis Intervention | Drugs, Alcohol Crime |
| Counseling Techniques | Community Involvement |

## Education

| | |
|---|---|
| Introduction to Education | Teaching with Science Technology |
| Teaching with Computer Technology | Teaching Diverse Populations |

- **Applications of Service Learning** Provides opportunities to build competence in service-learning through personal participation in service and reflection. Examines service-learning as an instructional concept and method.

## Environmental Science/Studies

Of the 400 colleges and universities nationwide in 1996 wich were considered for outstanding science environmental education programs, Brevard's program was chosen as second best in the nation, second only to Harvard, for it's Florida Science Institute "Environmental Problem-Solving Through Water Monitoring" curriculum. Several student environmental organizations also recycle, beautify the campuses, test and improve its lake and waters and serve the surrounding communities. Courses in environmental studies, biology, and microbiology all integrate projects into coursework.

Introduction to Environmental Science
Florida Environmental Issues
Intro to Hazardous Materials Technology
Hazardous Materials Regulations I, II
Introduction to Industrial Hygiene
Contingency Planning

Emergency Response
Sampling and Analysis
Hazardous Materials Recovery and Disposal
Hazardous Materials Health Effects
Internship

## English Literature

Communications I, II
Honors Communications I, II
Creative Writing I, II
Contemporary Literature

Introduction to Shakespeare
Survey of British Literature I, II
Living Ideas in World Literature

- **Special Themes in Literature**  Intensive readings in a particular concept or topic of literacy appeal. Mystery fiction, Black writers, Latin American fiction, literature in the sixties, and women's literature

Student Body: 94% in state, 13% minority, 43% male, 57% female, 36% transfer
Faculty: 56% male, 44% female, 13%, minority
Avg. class size in 1st yr. 20    Avg. age 28
125 service-learning courses, over 20 majors with service-learning
Costs: Residents $39/credit hour in state, Non-Residents $140/credit hour

- Field Studies   • Service-Learning   • Non-Resident Degree Program   • Distance Learning
- Third World Service-Learning   • Interdisciplinary Classes   • Life Experience Credit
- Green Management Policies in Energy Conservation
- Outstanding Humanitarian Scholarship, Community Service &, Leadership/Service Scholarships
- Since 1988, over 550,000 hours of service performed by students!

Use form in back to contact: Admissions/Registration Office
Brevard Community College
Cocoa, FL 32922
(407) 632-1111 ext. 62720,

# BROWN UNIVERSITY
5,500 Undergraduates   Providence, Rhode Island

Very few centers of higher education can honestly claim to offer their students the best of both worlds: the breadth and depth of a university's resources, and the intimate experience of an undergraduate liberal arts college. Brown offers this rare balance. Recently implemented "University Courses" emphasize synthesis rather than survey, and focus on the methods, concepts, and values employed in understanding a particular topic or issue. Using a single discipline or interdisciplinary approach, they introduce students to distinctive ways of thinking, constructing, communicating, and discovering knowledge. This emphasis has spawned unusual interdepartmental concentrations and programs. For example, biomedical researchers have worked with the departments of Philosophy and Religion to create a concentration in Biomedical Ethics. The Health and Society concentration pulls together the fields of human biology, community health, economics, and the social and behavioral sciences to examine health care systems and address policy issues at the local, national, and international levels.

Collaborations between faculty and undergraduates in research, course development and teaching have resulted in research on the impact of TV advertising on election campaigns, developing mathematical models of predator-prey interactions in marine ecosystems, and cataloguing materials for the study of race relations in Brazil.

Brown students have designed and implemented a wink-controlled wheelchair for parapalegics, converted an unused carriage house into the University's Urban Environmental Laboratory, collaborated with engineering professors to build a "clean air" automobile, and worked at a missionary hospital in Kenya.

Brown President Vartan Gregorian noted "more than ever, we need to recover a sense of the wholeness of human life and to understand the human condition.... We need to admit questions of values to the arena of discussion and debate. The moral argument of a poem, the social implications of a political system, the ethical consequences of a scientific technique, and the human significance of our responsibilities should have a place in classrooms and dormitories. To deny that place is to relinquish any claims or any attempt to link thought and action, knowing and doing."

Brown's emphasis on civic and social responsibility, and on bridging the gap between academia and the world beyond, provides opportunities to integrate community work with their academic and career goals. The Center for Public Service coordinates its activities with various academic programs, including Public Policy, Health and Society, Urban Studies, and Environmental Studies. Students volunteer with educational, social service, health, government and cultural organizations. Faculty and staff serve too: the Taubman Center for Public Policy is working with the city of Providence to develop a comprehensive antipoverty program, and the Allan Shawn Feinstein World Hunger Program tackles the issue of starvation amid plenty.

With Brown's extraordinary array of religions, ethnicities, and nationalities, students tend to find common ground through academic, extracurricular, and social interests, as well as through cultural ties. Experiencing that diversity first-hand is, for many, one of the most rewarding aspects of the Brown experience.

# MAKING A DIFFERENCE STUDIES

## Public Policy and American Institutions
Ethics and Public Policy
Woman and Public Policy
Public Policy and Higher Education
Social Welfare Policy
Political Research Methods

Environmental Regulation
Education and Public Policy
Law and Public Policy
Housing & Community Development Policy
The Price System and Resource Allocation

## Development Studies
African History and Society
Slave Community
Culture and Health
Nuclear Weapons: Technology and Policy
Women & Health Care
Burden of Disease in Developing Countries

Population Growth and the Environment
Issues in Minority Health
Gender in 20th Century American Sport
Shaping of World Views
Anthropological Issues in World Population
Possibilities for Social Reconstruction

## Biology & Medicine Track in Community Health
Culture and Health
Research in Health Care
Economic Development
International Environmental Issues
Red, White & Black in the Americas
The Culture of Postcolonialism

Health Care in the U.S.
Ideology of Development
Comparative Sex Roles
Social Change in Modern India
Third World Political & Economic Issues
Comparative Policy and Politics: East Asia

## Biomedical Ethics
Ethical Issues in Field of Mental Health
Ethical Issues in Pediatric Medicine
Moral Problems
Religious Ethics and Moral Issues
Ethical Issues in Research and Use of Biomedical Technology

Ethical Issues in Preventive Medicine
The Aims of Medicine
Moral Theories
Sociology of Medicine

## Sociology
Economic Development & Social Change
The Family
Social Inequality
War and the Military
Environmental Sociology

American Heritage: Racism & Democracy
Population Growth and the Environment
Race, Class and Ethnicity: Modern World
Women in Socialist & Developing Countries
Social Structures & Personal Development

- **Industrialization, Democracy and Dictatorship** Examines the interrelations between economic development and political change. Does economic development encourage democratization in today's underdeveloped countries as it did in W. Europe? Does rapid economic change foster revolutionary movements? Does sustained economic growth require authoritarian rule? What is the impact of multinational corporations on political conditions in developing countries?

**Women's Studies    Environmental Studies    Aquatic Biology    Urban Studies**

**Afro-American Studies    Education    International Relations    Public Policy**

Student Body: 3% state, 51% female, 49% male, 26% minority, 9% int'l.
Comprehensive costs: $33,170    Apply By 1/1

Use form in back to contact: Director of Admission
Brown University    Providence, RI 02912
(401) 863-2378

# BRYN MAWR

## 1100 Students    Bryn Mawr, Pennsylvania

Bryn Mawr is a liberal arts college in both the modern and traditional senses. Its curriculum is modern in offering a full range of subjects in the arts, sciences, and social sciences, but the College is also traditional in its commitment to the original sense of "liberal arts" -- the studies of a free person.

Bryn Mawr believes in a broad education which prepares students to be free to question or advocate any idea without fear. This kind of education results in graduates who are determined to change society. Among Bryn Mawr graduates are the domestic policy adviser to Vice President Albert Gore; the deputy director of the U.S. Office of Management and Budget; the medical director of the only women's health clinic in Nairobi; federal judges, children's legal advocates, teachers at every level, and a much higher than usual percentage of women who are in positions to improve society — in this country and around the world.

Individual responsibility with a concern for the community are prime traits of Bryn Mawr students. The college believes that the pleasure of knowledge is insufficient if that knowledge does not lead to social action. Too many people act without knowing and too many highly educated people won't act on behalf of others. Bryn Mawr seeks students who wish to use their education, not merely for personal enrichment but to be fully contributing, responsible citizens of the world. Mary Sefranek is a good example of Bryn Mawr's philosophy in action. She was one of twenty USA Today All Academic Team winners for, among her many accomplishments, the work she has done with the Roberto Clemente Middle School in Philadelphia. Mary created a special program for this low-income, primarily Hispanic public school, including teams of Bryn Mawr student tutors and field trips. She is one of many Bryn Mawr students active in volunteer projects.

Bryn Mawr's students are from 48 states, Puerto Rico, D.C., and 51 other countries. American minorities make up 25% of the students. Several students from South Africa not only voted in the first free and open election in 300 years, they worked at the Philadelphia Absentee Ballot Center to help their compatriots vote. The unusually high percentage of foreign students means everyone learns first-hand about real world problems. Bryn Mawr is among a handful of private colleges which give financial aid to foreign students. A recent CBS Sunday Morning News show featured four Bryn Mawr students in a segment called "Women of the Revolution." Students from Kuwait, the People's Republic of China, Rumania, and South Africa talked about their hopes that their BM educations would be put to use for their people at home.

The Minority Coalition, an organization representing all of the minority student organizations, enables minority students to work together to increase the number of minority students and faculty, and to develop curricular and extra-curricular programs dealing with United States minority groups and non-Western peoples and cultures.

Bryn Mawr is one of the very few colleges and universities with an honor code- which characterizes a philosophy of mutual respect between students, faculty and administration.

86

# MAKING A DIFFERENCE MAJORS

## Geology

| | |
|---|---|
| Mineralogy and Mineral Paragensis | Stratigraphy/Sedimentation |
| Crystallography and Optical Mineralogy | Low Temperature Geochemistry |
| Principles of Economic Geology | Introduction to Geophysics |
| Tectonics | Structural Geology |

- **Environmental Geology** Issues affecting land use and management of the environment including natural geologic hazards, forces shaping the earth's surface, energy sources, waste disposal, and urban planning. Labs focus on local environmental issues.

## Peace Studies

| | |
|---|---|
| War and Cultural Difference | Nationalism in Europe |
| Social Inequality | Intransigent Conflict |
| Schools in American Cities | The Culture of the Cold War |
| Ethnic Group Politics | Great Powers and the Near East |
| Germany Since 1914 | Slavery and Emancipation: British & U.S. |

Conflict and Conflict Management: A Cross-cultural Approach

## Growth and Structure of Cities

This interdisciplinary major challenges students to understand the relationship of spatial organization and the built environment to politics, economics, culture and society. Students pursue their interests through classes in planning, art and architecture, archaeology, and in social and natural sciences including anthropology, economics, geology, sociology, and history.

| | |
|---|---|
| Urban Culture and Society | The Form of the City |
| Ancient Greek Cities and Sanctuaries | Comparative Urbanism |
| Latin American Urban Development | Topics in Urban Culture and Society |
| Modernization | Survey of Western Architecture |
| Topics in History of Modern Planning | Ethnic Group Politics |

Chinese Notions of Time and Space: Garden, House, and City

## Anthropology

| | |
|---|---|
| Sex, Culture and Society | Medical Anthropology |
| African Ethology: Urban Problems | Language in Social Context |
| Linguistic Anthropology | Cultural Ecology |
| Psychological Anthropology | Gender Differentiation |
| History of Cultural Theory | Traditional and Pre-Industrial Technology |
| Origins of Civilization and the State | Ethnography of South Asia |

## Feminist and Gender Studies

| | |
|---|---|
| Feminism and Philosophy | The Family in Social Context |
| Patterns in Feminist Spirituality | Topics in European Women's/Gender History |
| Studies in Prejudice | Women in Early Christianity |
| Women in Science | Gender, Class and Culture |

Women in Contemporary Society: Third World Women

Student Body: 14% state, 100% female, 25% minority, 10% int'l.
Faculty: 60% male, 40% female, 10% minority
Costs: $30,360   Apply By: 1/1

• Team Teaching  • Individualized Majors  • Multidisciplinary Classes  • Vegetarian Meals

Use form in back to contact: Office of Admissions
Bryn Mawr College    Bryn Mawr, PA 19010
(610) 526-5152
www.brynmawr.edu/college

# BURLINGTON COLLEGE

200 Undergraduates    Burlington, Vermont

The chief goals of the ideal college would be the discovery of identity,
and with it, the discovery of vocation.

-Abraham Maslow

"Burlington College is a small friendly school in a small friendly state. An alternative, liberal arts college in the Vermont tradition, this community of learners not only believes in the innate dignity of people, it believes that people should have a say in what matters most in their lives and in their education. And here they do!" Burlington College President Daniel Casey

Founded in 1997 as the Institute for Community Involvement, Burlington College continues its 26-year tradition of emphasizing individualized education and community action. The progressive liberal arts curriculum appeals to the broad interests of a highly diverse student body, while the small, intimate environment provides a level of support unparalleled on today's college campuses.

Above all, Burlington College treats students as individuals individuals with important contributions to make to the intellectual spirit of the college community. These contributions become the center of college life. Working in discussion-centered classes of between eight and twelve members, students come to know each other and themselves well. In a classroom atmosphere that balances academic rigor and mutual support, students are challenged to discover what truly matters to them.

The respect students are given is reflected in the College's non-grading evaluation system. In each course or other learning activity, students negotiate a learning contract for the semester with their instructor, and at the end, both provide written evaluations of progress toward the learning goals they set. The evaluation period is not, then, a time to cram for exams or to please an instructor to get a grade; it is a time for reflection on what one has learned.

Because Burlington College realizes that some forms of education are best learned in alternative settings, the College provides a wide range of learning modes. Students can complete their studies by combining campus classes, action and service learning, independent study, residential and outdoor workshops, and studies abroad. Students may also cross-register, attending classes at any of the 5 surrounding colleges to meet the needs of their particular course of study.

Burlington College seeks to admit students of diverse ages and backgrounds who are mature, independent thinkers and want to be actively involved in the planning of their learning. The College looks for students who strive to make a difference in their own lives and in the larger community, who are goal-oriented, and who have a strong desire to increase awareness, knowledge, and competency.

Rich in cultural and professional resources, the city of Burlington is our campus. The College is housed in a renovated, turn-of-the-century building located in Burlington's Old North End. It includes classrooms, a small library, an art studio and a community art gallery. Students also have borrowing privileges at nearby Trinity College's library.

# MAKING A DIFFERENCE STUDIES

## Interdisciplinary Studies

Students can design an individualized major with their academic advisor to meet their particular academic and career needs and goals. Recent individualized majors include: Communications and Graphic Design, Counseling in Women's Health, Arts in Community, Contemporary Spiritually, Dance Movement Therapy, Community Development, Educational Media Resources, and Environmental Design.

The City in History
In Search of American Identity
Film and Philosophy
Making a Documentary Film
Film and Psychology
The Unfinished Revolution: Racism in American History
Crossing Urban Boundaries: Geography of Class, Gender, and Ethnicity in Burlington, VT

Literature and Mythology
Spiritual Traditions and Practices
Individuality, Community, and Freedom
The Ethnic Experience: The Irish in America
Infinity

## Transpersonal Psychology, Psychology, and Human Services

Transpersonal Psychology is a relatively new discipline that rests upon the assumption that psychology needs both soul and spirit, and draws upon both Western Sciences and Eastern wisdom. Includes courses & workshops in tai chi, sacred art, mythology, aikido & more.

Community Development
Lifespan Development
Organizational Theory and Behavior
Death and Dying
Dreams and the Creative Imagination
Archetypal Psychology
Psychology of the Unconscious
Life Embodied: Experience in Wellness: Through the Mind/Body Connection

Aging Issues and Arguments
Theories of Personality
Buddhist Psychology
Social Psychology
Intro to Jungian Psychology
Archetypal Psychology
Addiction

## Gender Studies

Women and Film
Intro to Gender Studies
History of Women in North America
Psychology of Women

Theory and Construction of Gender
Gender Issues in American Society
Women's Literature
Men's Lives: Gender, Intimacy and Power

- **Partnership Studies** A study of the Goddess image throughout pre-history and recorded history, including a critical examination of how gylanic principles of partnership have been and can be manifested.

## Natural Sciences

Breeding Birds of Vermont
Visioning Science
Minerals: Brick of the Earth
River Ecology
Issues in Reproductive Health

Dynamics of the Earth's Atmosphere
Herbalism
Sustaining Agriculture in an Urban Setting
Society and Nature
Contemporary Ecological Issues

Student Body: 84%state, 57% Female, 43% Male, 60%Transfer
Costs $8650   No Housing   Rolling Admissions
• Prior Learning Credit   • External Degree Completion
Use form in back to contact: Admissions Office
Burlington College
95 North Avenue    Burlington, VT 05401
(800) 862-9619
admissions@burlcol.edu    www.burlcol.edu

# UNIVERSITY OF CALIFORNIA AT DAVIS

17,500 Undergraduates    Davis, California

With 5,200 acres, UC Davis ranks first in physical size of the nine campuses of the U of California. It has 24 undergraduate programs rated among the country's top 10, including the number one botany department. The Davis campus has undergraduate colleges of Agriculture and Environmental Sciences, Engineering, and Letters and Sciences.

Major programs in the College of Agricultural and Environmental Sciences highlight multiple connections among the environment, plant and animal systems, and human health and development, all within the larger context of the quality of life in the global economy. Broad study areas are Plant Sciences; Animal Biology; Human Health and Development; and Environmental and Resource Sciences and Policies with majors in Applied Behavioral Sciences, Atmospheric Science, Environmental and Resource Science, Landscape Architecture, Soil and Water Sciences.

The Davis branch of the California Agricultural Experiment Station includes 500 faculty. In addition to lab facilities, it has approximately 3,000 acres devoted to agricultural research in experimental crops, orchards, and animal facilities. Research emphasis is placed on resource conservation and management, water and soil pollution, and regional planning. The Jepson Prairie Reserve is used to study the effects of long-term grazing, to conduct fire ecology research, and to aid in the management of native grasslands.

The Student Experimental Farm, an innovative teaching and research facility located on 25 acres of University land, is the main focus of the Sustainable Agriculture Program. Since its inception, the Farm has provided students with unique opportunities to explore alternative agriculture technologies and philosophies through classes, internships, work study jobs and original research. Because the farm includes several acres of land that have been managed organically for over a decade, it provides researchers with a facility for conducting field research into sustainable agriculture.

The Education Abroad Program of the University of California offers a wide range of opportunities from university-based programs throughout Europe, Asia and Latin America, are options for studying ethnomusicology and Balinese dance in Indonesia; study and research in a tropical cloud forest in Costa Rica; and four weeks of field work in Togo.

Outdoorsy students can take advantage of Outdoor Adventures, which rents professional quality equipment to students, and whose library contains topographic maps, trail guides, and other materials. Classes, excursions and clinics in backpacking, rock-climbing techniques, white-water rafting, kayaking, sea kayaking, mountaineering and cross-country skiing are offered throughout the year.

Ecologically aware and socially innovative, the town of Davis has a small-town friendliness and spirit of volunteerism that distinguishes it from other cities of similar size. Students comprise nearly half of the city's population, making Davis one of the states' few remaining "college towns." With 50 miles of bike paths, and more bicycles per person than any other city in the nation, Davis has earned the title "City of Bicycles."

# MAKING A DIFFERENCE STUDIES

## Civil and Environmental Engineering / Transportation Planning

Transportation planning blends knowledge of the basic concepts of engineering, economics, and planning in the development of policies, programs, and projects.

Construction Principles
Intro to Transportation Planning
Transportation System Design
Energy Policy
Environmental Planning

Intro to Air Pollution
Transportation System Operations
Energy & Enviro. Aspects of Transportation
Methods of Environmental Policy Evaluation
Public Mechanisms for Controlling Land Use

## Plant Biology (Botany)

Plants, People and the Bioshpere
Plant Ecology
Biology of Weeds
Principles of Plant Biotechnology
Conservation of Plant Genetic Resources

California Floristics
Survey of Plant Communities of California
Mineral Nutrition of Plants
Developmental Plant Anatomy
Physiology of Environmental Stresses in Plants

## Agricultural Systems & Environment  Tracks in Sustainable Production Systems, Agricultural & Environmental Education, Agricultural Resource Management

Agricultural Systems and Environment
International Agriculture Development
Forage Crop Ecology
Introduction to Biological Control
Microclimate of Agricultural Systems
Environmental Law

Environmental Horticulture
Cereal Crops of the World
Greenhouse and Nursery Crop Production
Ecology and Economics
Conservation of Plant Genetic Sources
Enviro. & Occupational Epidemiology

## Atmospheric Sciences

Introduction to Air Pollution
Atmospheric Dynamics
Boundary Layer Meteorology
Severe and Unusual Weather

Weather Analysis and Forecasting
Computer Methods in Meteorology
Issues in Atmospheric Science
Radiation and Satellite Meteorology

## Avian (Bird) Sciences

Intro to Poultry Science
Captive Raptor Management
Fertility and Hatchability
Nutrition of Birds

Birds, Humans, and the Environment
Raptor Migration and Population Fluctuations
Patterns in Avian Biology
Raptor Biology

- **Management of Companion Birds**  Captive propagation of birds, including trade and smuggling. Emphasis on parrots and role of captive propagation in conservation.

## Environmental Toxicology

Toxicants in the Environment
Food Toxicology
Health Risk Assessments of Toxicants
Principles of Environmental Toxicology

Biological Effects of Toxicants
Air Pollutants and Inhalation Toxicology
Legal Aspects of Enviro Toxicology
Chromatography for Analytical Toxicology

### Chicana/o Studies    War and Peace    Women's Studies    Entomology
### Environmental Studies    Environmental and Resource Sciences

Estimated Costs $10,988   Non-residents $20,372   Apply by 11/30

Use form in back to contact: Office of Undergraduate Admissions
175 Mrak Hall   University of CA at Davis   Davis, CA 95616
(530) 752-2971

# UNIVERSITY OF CALIFORNIA AT SANTA CRUZ

10,100 Undergraduates    Santa Cruz, CA

Since it opened in 1965, UC Santa Cruz has won a distinctive position within the UC system as a collegiate university devoted to excellence in both undergraduate education and graduate studies and research. The residential college is an important part of the Santa Cruz experience. Every undergraduate student affiliates with one of the eight colleges while they participate in a campus wide academic program.

The theme of College Eight - Environment and Society - is an expression of concern for social, political, scientific and ethical issues within an environmental context. The fellows of College Eight are drawn from the environmental studies, community studies, biology, chemistry, psychology, and sociology. Fellowship in the college indicates the faculty's interest in the related issues of environmental quality and community development as they concern peace, justice, and human well-being. Both students and faculty develop courses, conferences and field projects. Experiential education in the form of internships and field studies offers a means bridging theory and action. These avenues provide students with the opportunity to act on their intellectual understanding under "real-world" conditions.

Kresge College is a center of innovative interdisciplinary, social, and cross-cultural programs, a place where diverse groups come together with the vision of communication across boundaries in an effort to spearhead social change. It's focus of Cultural Intersections emphasizes the create possibilities of inter-cultural exchange.

Merrill College seeks to expand its students' awareness of their own heritage and of the diversity of cultures around the world, past and present. Drawn largely from the social sciences, education, history, literature, and foreign languages, many Merrill faculty members specialize in social theory, international affairs, and social change. The college makes a special effort to be a home for students from different cultural backgrounds and for foreign students; it presents unusual opportunities to those who value multicultural perspectives.

The Agroecology Program is a research and educational group working toward the development of sustainable agricultural systems -- those that maintain environmental quality and provide employment, nutritious food, and an affordable way of lie while ensuring the same for future generations. The Program manages a 25 acre farm including research plots, raised-bed gardens, row crops, orchards and a solar green house and a 4 acre garden.

Other research programs include the Adlai E. Stevenson Program on Global Security, which stimulates research, education, and policy studies on issues related to global security, conflict, and cooperation. Interdisciplinary research includes nuclear weapons, proliferation, global environmental degradation, and international cooperation on the global environment.

About 400 acres of campus wildlands are designated as a Natural Reserve. Remarkably diverse, this reserve contains redwood forest, springs, a stream, vernal pools, secondary madrone/Douglas fir forest, and chaparral. The 4,000 acre Landels-Hill big Creek Reserve, a teaching and research facility on the Big Sur coast. includes undisturbed watershed containing numerous terrestrial and aquatic habitats.

# MAKING A DIFFERENCE STUDIES

**Environmental Studies   Tracks in Sustainable Agriculture & Agroecology; Policy, Planning & Public Values; Natural History & Wildland Conservation**

| | |
|---|---|
| Culture and Environment | Population, Community & Ecosystem Ecology |
| Natural History of Mammals | Natural History of Birds |
| Capitalism and Nature | Ecodevelopment |
| Integrated Pest Management | Principles of Sustainable Agriculture |
| Environmental Assessment | Environment, Culture and Perception |
| Conservation Practicum | National Environmental Policy |
| Energy Resource Assessment and Policy | Watershed Systems Restoration |

Political Economy of Sustainable Agriculture in Latin America

**Biology   Tracks in Marine Biology; Ecology, Evolution & Behavior; Plant Sciences**

| | |
|---|---|
| Kelp Forest Ecology | Intertidal Organisms |
| Biogeography | Biology of Marine Mammals |
| Biological Oceanography | Systematic Botany of Flowering Plants |
| Marine Botany | Infectious Diseases |
| Field Studies of Animal Behavior | Biology of Cancer |

## Community Studies

An opportunity for the student who is actively committed to social change to work on a full-time basis beyond the boundaries of the university. Each student designs their curriculum around a 6 month field study or internship with a community organization or agency.

| | |
|---|---|
| Social Documentation | Chicanos and Social Change |
| California: Edge of America | Mass Media and Community Alternatives |
| Introduction to the AIDS Epidemic | U.S. Regions & the Global Economy |
| Global Political Economy | Political Economy of U.S. Agriculture |
| U.S. - Mexico Border Region | Workers & Community in Industrializing Amer. |

Civil Rights Movement: Grassroots Change and American Society

## Social Psychology

| | |
|---|---|
| Health Psychology | Chicano Psychology |
| Social Psychology of Sex and Gender | Intergroup Relations |
| Social Psychology of Bilingualism | Social Influences |
| The Social Context | Psychology and Law |
| Gender and Power | Organizational Psychology |

## Sociology   Track in Institutional Analysis

| | |
|---|---|
| Key Issues in Race and Ethnic Analysis | Family and Society |
| Development, Inequality, and Ecology | Sociology of Health and Medicine |
| Communication and Mass Media | Sociology of Education |
| Drugs in Society | Sociology of Environmental Politics |

Sociology of Jury: Racial Disenfranchisement in the Jury and Jury Selection System

**Education   Earth Sciences   Latin American Studies   Economics
World Lit. & Cultural Studies   Women's Studies   Anthropology**

Student Body: 93% state, 61% female, 39% male, 36% minority
• Individualized Majors   • Field Studies   • Vegetarian Meals
Estimated Costs: Residents $10,871   Non-residents $19,855   Apply By: 11/30

Use form in back to contact: Office of Admissions
University of CA, Santa Cruz   Santa Cruz, CA 95064
(408) 459-4008

# CALIFORNIA INSTITUTE OF INTEGRAL STUDIES

80 Undergraduates     San Francisco, California

In a world of growing complexity no one culture or tradition can provide an education broad enough and deep enough to deal with the issues it presents. The California Institute of Integral Studies is an accredited institute of higher learning where intellect, intuition, and the ageless wisdom of diverse cultures converge. Integrating the intellectual and spiritual insights of Western and Eastern traditions, education at the California Institute of Integral Studies facilitates integration of body-mind-spirit, valuing equally the emotional, spiritual, intellectual, creative, somatic, and social dimensions of being human. Students are encouraged to take an interdisciplinary approach to learning by complementing their program of study with coursework in other departments and focus on the integration of their personal growth, scholarly work, and professional skills.

The Bachelor of Arts Completion (BAC) program aims to provide graduates with the skills to respond creatively and constructively to the rapid pace of change in the contemporary world. Distinctive qualities of the program include an opportunity to explore and understand a variety of cultural, historical, ecological, and personal forces that shape individual and social experience; an environment in which to discover and develop a mature sense of vocation; and the opportunity to acquire up to 45 quarter units for demonstrated learning based in work or life experience prior to enrollment (prior learning).

To carry forward the Institute's tradition of innovative approaches to education, students are encouraged to integrate and build on their life experiences and are challenged to broaden their perspectives and deepen their knowledge. The primary way in which students in the Bachelor of Arts Completion Program progress through the year is a "cohort," or learning community. Cohort members support one another and serve as an education resource for study that is both collaborative and individualized. The core curriculum is supplemented with Special Topics courses and seminars offered in the evenings and as weekend intensives. These specialized courses have included: The Politics of Female Reproduction, The African Experience, Morality and the Human Spirit, and Speaking Writing.

Building on self-assessment of strengths and needs, students collaborate with faculty and their cohorts to design a course of study relevant to their own passionate paths. All learners participate in core seminars and design and complete a Culminating Project. Depending on their needs and interests, learners can participate in specialized study groups designed mutually by faculty and students. By challenging existing paradigms and exploring new perspectives, the student enriches the base of knowledge in the area of study; all activities are intended to support one another in creating a unified experience.

# MAKING A DIFFERENCE STUDIES

Courses at CIIS change from year to year. The following course titles therefore are merely meant to be suggestive of the types of courses offered.

## Integrative Studies

These studies explore alternative worldviews that give shape to human experience and challenge participants to clarify their own values and assumptions through critical and experiential research and group interaction. Seminars address the following themes:

The Modern Condition
Earth Curriculum
Self and Society

Culture and Community
Transformative Learning

## Experience, Vocation, and the Development of the Self

This section of the curriculum focuses on individual reflective work, particularly autobiographical and journal writing. This process challenges students to examine their own underlying assumptions about themselves and the world in which they live, and to apply their new understanding in a practical way.

Culture and Community
Research Methods.

Learning from Community

## Learning and Change in Human Systems

These seminars begin with the assumption that individuals, groups, and institutions need to "learn their way out" of the dilemmas created on the planet and in the human community. The cohort becomes a laboratory for experimenting with ways of using learning strategies to enhance personal and group capacities, and for developing flexible and creative learning processes within individuals and groups.

Systems Theory
Social Ecology

Personal Responsibility
Social Change

- Faculty bio: **Linda Vance,** J.D., LL.M., has acted as an attorney for feminist, peace, and environmental groups in Vermont and New Mexico. Linda writes and lectures on ecofeminism and on the historical and philosophical dimensions of wilderness; she also conducts research on stream ecology.

- Faculty bio: **Mutombo Mpana,** Ph.D. is originally from Zaire. Mutombo has worked with international development agencies in several African countries for over 20 years. His areas of interest include environmental studies, international development, economics, technology impact assessment, environmental ethics, transportation systems, and ecological systems.

- Faculty bio: **Fabienne McPhail**, M.A., teaches women's studies and African American history and literature. She addresses racism and diversity issues in both business and educational settings, and sees making theory accessible to students as an important aspect of her teaching.

Student Body: 80% state, 63% female, 37% male, 7% minority, 100% transfer
• Interdisciplinary Classes • Non-Resident Degree Program • Team Teaching
• All Seminar Format • Life Experience Credit
100% of students do community service   Avg. 5 hours per week
Tuition: $9,230   No housing   Apply by: 6/1

Use form in back to contact: Office of Admissions
California Institute of Integral Studies
9 Peter Yorke Way   San Francisco, CA 94109
(415) 674-5500
www.ciis.edu

# CALIFORNIA UNIVERSITY OF PENNSYLVANIA

5,600 Undergraduates   California, Pennsylvania

California University of Pennsylvania is a state college that encourages students to take part in the life, not only of the university community, but the wider community as well. A number of successful programs provide an opportunity for students to learn and to grow both in and out of the classroom.

In 1995, CU created a Character Education Institute to foster critical discussion of ethical issues in the academic curriculum, in parental support classes, and to promote the timeless ideals of responsibility and respect. The institute activity promotes the core values espoused in the US Constitution such as honesty, human worth and dignity, justice, due process, and equality of opportunity. The CEI also serves as a resource for local school districts who want to examine the idea of values education.

Vulcan ll, the university's new research vessel, provides students with access to the Monongahela River and a variety of research opportunities. Faculty and students in the environmental sciences program are working on a three-year project integrating wildlife and agriculture funded by the PA Game Commission, the US fish and Wildlife service and a number of private conservation clubs. Another project involved researching acid deposition through small stream water quality analysis. For several years students in the Wildlife, Environmental and Biological Science Club (WEB) have been raising money for the purchase of acres of Colombian cloud forest to ensure preservation of that important resource.

Students in the College of Education and Human Services can choose from a variety of student teaching assignments. A special program, the Urban Teaching Center, allows participants to student teach in Pittsburgh urban schools and live in the city, too. The program stresses multicultural activities, providing students with special out-of-school cultural activities including dinners with neighborhood groups.

Other programs encourage student teachers to become involved with education reform through hands-on activities in local school districts. Student teachers have worked with their classes to create a living biome (a Pennsylvania pond,) a butterfly garden, tropical rain forest, and a prairie grassland. Other California U students worked with an area high school to create a local cultural and historical center.

Originally part of a pilot program, the successful SHARE program matches students in need of housing with senior citizens who are interested in sharing their home. Once the program identifies a likely match, the students and the elders work out the details of the living arrangements. SHARE is only one of a number of community outreach programs coordinated through the California Are Senior Center in cooperation with CU's Gerontology Department. The University's close ties with the Senior Center enables students to use the Center for an internship and/or practicum site for gerontology, social work, and even journalism or public relations.

Students volunteering to work with the California Area Senior Center also participate in the Friend to Friend program, where students make a commitment to visit with an elderly friend at least once a week. Others drop by the Center on a regular basis or help with the "meals on wheels" or other outreach programs.

# MAKING A DIFFERENCE STUDIES

## Teaching Credential / Environmental Studies
Man and His Environment
Ecosystems Ecology
Wildlife Techniques
Game and Habitat Management
Physical Geography

Environmental Biology
Man and His Physical World
Outdoor Activities
Recreation and Park Administration
Human Ecology

## Environmental Resources /Environmental Pollution
Contemporary Issues in Biology
Air Quality Monitoring
Environmental Regulations
Introduction to Oceanography
Solid Waste Management
Ecosystems Ecology

Earth Resources
Economic Geography
Climatology
Coastal Geomorphology & Marine Resources
Water and Wastewater Analysis
Environmental Research Problems

## Environmental Conservation
Principles of Biology
Wildlife Techniques
Plant Ecology
Water Pollution Biology
Biometry

Biotic Communities
Soil Science
Environmental Research Problems
Conservation of Biological Resources
Ornithology

## Wildlife Biology
General Zoology
Principles of Wildlife Management
Land Use Planning
Urban Planning
Principles of Biology

General Botany
Plant Taxonomy
Mammalogy
Ichthyology
Environmental Physiology

## Urban Studies
Survey of Urban Affairs
Political Economy
Urban Transportation
Housing and Housing Policy
History of Urban America
Urban Sociology

Municipal Government
Urban Geography
Recreation for Phys./Emotionally Handicapped
Practicum in Urban Affairs
Organizational & Administrative Behavior
Community Action & Neighborhood Gov't

### Social Work  Gerontology  Meteorology  Early Childhood Ed.
### Special Education: Community Services/Community Living Arrangements A.A.

Student Body: 82% state, 50% female, 50% male, 6% minority, 33% transfer
Faculty: 75% male, 25% female, 7% minority
Costs: Residents $8,580   Non-Residents $13,936    Rolling Admissions

• Team Teaching   • Evening Classes   • Field Studies   • Vegetarian Meals
• Over 100 Service Learning Courses   • Interdisciplinary Classes   • Life Experience Credit
90% of the students at CU do over 15 hours of community service annually.

Use form in back to contact: Director of Admissions
California University of PA.
250 University Ave.   California, PA 15419
(724) 938-4404

# CARLETON COLLEGE

1700 Students    Northfield, Minnesota

Carleton is one of the nation's most respected small liberal arts colleges, unusual for its location in the Midwest. Its vital intellectual community draws students from all fifty states and 20 other countries. Co-educational since its founding, Carleton has a long history of encouraging original thought and a sense of intellectual adventure through rigorous study of traditional academic disciplines, complemented by a wide offering of electives and interdisciplinary programs.

One such program, which appeals to students interested in environmental studies, is the Environment and Technology concentration which explores the implementation of emerging technology into public policy. Faculty in the program are drawn from several departments including economics, geology, and sociology. Other students interested in environmental studies, however, major in the natural sciences, taking advantage of one of the strongest undergraduate programs in the country.

Carleton's setting is distinct, with a 400-acre arboretum bordering the campus. The "Arb," as it is called by students, consists of a variety of habitats, including floodplain forest, wetlands, prairie, and a pine plantation. Used for both research and recreation, the arboretum is governed by students, who both decide what preservation projects are undertaken, and do the actual work themselves.

Students at Carleton have a long history of activism, involving themselves in over one hundred organizations on campus. Acting in the Community Together, or ACT, is one of the most popular. Through this umbrella volunteer organization, students administer over thirty separate community-based programs. Selected as the Minnesota hub campus for the national organization COOL (Campus Outreach Opportunity League,) ACT now serves as a consultant for other campus service programs.

Carleton encourages students to engage in honest discussions on issues of difference, whether based on gender, race, ethnicity, socio-economics, or political viewpoint. Through both informal discussion and coursework, the College aims to expose members of the community to perspectives that have developed outside of, in opposition to, or in ways only dimly visible to the dominant culture in which most of us have grown up and been educated. Before first-year students arrive at Carleton, they are invited to participate in a "Common Reading" of a book such as *July's People* by Nadine Gordimer or *Donald Duk* by Frank Chin. When they arrive on campus, the students meet with faculty and staff in their homes to discuss the book. In order to fulfill the "Recognition and Affirmation of Difference" requirement, students must take a course centrally concerned with another culture; with a country, art, or tradition from outside Europe and the US, or with issues of gender, class, race or ethnicity

With over 60% of its students participating in off-campus studies, Carleton operates one of the largest study abroad programs on any college campus. In an average year, Carleton students partake in 85 different programs. Whether it be in Nepal, Costa Rica, or Kenya, Carleton students gain not only an unusual academic experience, but also an invaluable personal one.

# MAKING A DIFFERENCE STUDIES

## Biology

Biology for the Humanist
Spring Flora
Marine Biology
Tropical Rainforest Ecology
Field Investigation in Tropical Rainforest Ecology (in Costa Rica)
Biology Field Studies and Research (in Australia/New Zealand)

Biology of Conservation
Introductory Botany
Ecology
Biology of Non-Vascular Plants

## Environment and Technology Studies

Information, Society and Democracy
Environmental Policy and Politics
Public Policy and the Human Fetus
Intro to Environmental Geology
Congress, Campaign Money & A National Energy Strategy

Technologies and Their Societies
Water and Western Economic Development
Environmental Chemistry
Technology Policy Project

## Sociology / Anthropology

Population and Food in Global System
Biography and Ethnography
Nationalism and Ethnicity
Islam and the Middle East
Explorations of Diaspora Populations
Conquest and Encounter: Europeans and Indigenous Peoples in the "New World"

Class, Power and Inequality in America
Economic Anthropology
Schooling and Opportunity in Amer. Society
Comparative Study of Developing Societies
Ethnology of Central America & Caribbean

## Political Science

Science, Technology and Politics
Parties, Interest Groups and Elections
Urban Politics
Political Theory of M. L. King, Jr.
International Conflict and War
Social Movements and Protest Politics

Liberal Democracy and Social Democracy
Feminist Political Theory
Urban Political Economy
Gender Discrimination & Constitutional Law
American Security and Arms Control
Urban Racial and Ethnic Politics

- **Poverty and Public Policy** Focus on the relationship between race, class, gender and poverty in the U.S. Students will analyze various explanations for the growth of the underclass and homelessness as well as public policy strategies for reducing poverty.

## Economics

Comparative Economic Systems
African Economic Development
Political Economy of Capitalism
Economics of the Public Sector
Environmental Health Economics
Economics of Poverty, Discrimination and the Distribution of Income

The Economics of Apartheid
Political Economy of the Third World
Economics of Human Resources
Economics of Natural Resources &
Economics of Poverty

**Educational Studies Concentration     Natural History Concentration
Women's Studies     African/African-American Studies**

Student Body: 24% state, 49% male, 51% female, 16% minority
Faculty: 68% male, 32% female, 9% minority
• Team teaching   • Individual majors   • All Seminar Format   • Vegetarian Meals
Comprehensive Costs: $27,195     Apply By: 1/15

Use form in back to contact: Dean of Admissions
Carleton College     Northfield, MN 55057
(507) 646-4190   (800) 995-2275

# CLARK UNIVERSITY

2,100 Undergraduates    Worcester, Mass.

For the spirited, independent, inspired learner, Clark University can offer the best of many worlds; combining the advantages of the intimate, liberal arts college and the distinctive, research university; prompting students to venture beyond classroom and laboratory into the community, across cultures, and even across the globe. Clark is dedicated to being a dynamic community of learners able to thrive in today's increasing interrelated societies.

The special strength of Clark's programs stems from a fruitful integration of teaching and research. Clark has attracted a faculty that is committed to excellence in teaching and original scholarship. Clark's academic community has long been distinguished by the pursuit of scientific inquiry and humanistic studies, enlivened by a concern for significant social issues. Clark especially contributes to understanding human development, assessing relationships between people and the environment, and managing risk in a technological society. In classrooms and laboratories, professors try out new ideas and recount their firsthand experiences with, for example, measuring Chernobyl's radioactive fallout in Europe, or helping villagers use resources more effectively to produce food in Kenya, Somalia, and Zimbabwe.

Clark was one of the first universities to offer an undergraduate major in the interdisciplinary field of Environment, and Society and Policy. E.S.P. is for students who hope to contribute to the solution of complex societal problems such as environmental protection, energy policy, technological hazards, and risk analysis. E.S.P. emphasizes a firm grounding in natural science coupled with considerable exposure to social science and public policy perspectives. Thirty problem-oriented and methodological courses and a variety of special projects are offered. Strong academic achievers are eligible for the BA/MA five-year program which is tuition free during the fifth year of study.

Clark's programs focusing on environmental change are among the very best in the country. Students are interested in helping alleviate acid rain, depletion of the ozone layer, drought, overdevelopment, and nuclear risk. New this year, Clark has opened an innovative Environmental School, offering an "alternative" liberal arts program built around the theme of human-environment relationships.

The International Development and Social Change program focuses on questions of equity, growth, and development at a time when developing countries are increasing their influence on the world's economic, political, and social systems. Clark recognizes that most problems transcend national boundaries, and the program emphasizes ways in which individuals can identify effective local action in the context of global change. The program serves students from developing nations as well as industrialized countries. Topics of particular interest include participation in local institutions, roles of women and community organizations, rural development, and geographic information systems.

Each year, 250 Clark students from every major take advantage of off-campus experiences earning one to four course credits, either paid or unpaid. One student recently interned at the UN, working in the office of the press secretary to the Secretary General. Others have interned at the US Dept of Health and Human Services, Planned Parenthood, the Audubon Society, and National Clean Air Coalition.

# MAKING A DIFFERENCE STUDIES

## Cultural Identity and Global Processes

Dramatic growth in transnational and global phenomena has led to the existence of a global community that has significantly contributed to the demise of the nation-state. Yet, at the same time there is a resurgence of cultural identities in both regional and local contexts.
Cultural Identities and Global Processes          Race, Migration, Gender and Ethnicity
The Creation of Nationalisms, Nationalist Cultures, and Symbols

- **Culture, Consumption, & Class in Local & Global Contexts** Focuses on consumption as it is culturally and ethnically determined, gendered, classes, and impacted upon politically by both individual consumers and capitalist producers. The ways in which consumption is linked to the identity values are explored. A central theme is the interplay between the forces of the world market and cultural identities, between local and global processes, and between consumption and cultural strategies.

## Cultural / Humanistic Geography

| | |
|---|---|
| American Land, American Mind | World Population |
| Culture Landscape | Cultural Ecology in Arid Lands |
| Agriculture in Third World Economics | The End of America: Los Angeles |
| Cultural and Political Ecology | Driving Forces of Global Change |
| Cultural Ecology in Humid Tropics | Race, Migration, Gender and Ethnicity |

Before and After Columbus: Ancient Middle America and Impact of the Conquest

## Regional / International Development / Political Economy

| | |
|---|---|
| Geography of the Third World | Economic Development and Policy Analysis |
| Political Economy of Underdevelopment | International Division of Labor |
| Development Problems | Dev. Theories and Philosophies of Change |
| Politics, People, and Pollution | Land & Development in Latin America |

Overcoming World Hunger - Agricultural Research and International Development
Money, Banking and Finance in Developing Countries

- **Gender, Space & Environment** How gender is reflected in the landscape, in our settlement and land use patterns, in environmental history, and in our present ecological science and practice from the global to the local level. Feminist and other alternative explanations of the gendered nature of knowledge, access, use, and control of space and resources in a variety of environments, past, present, and possible.

## Environment, Society and Policy

To enable individuals to deal with technical issues is a social and political context and to do so with an acute awareness of the short and long range limitations of the natural environment to respond to human interventions. Students are encouraged to obtain academic year internships or paid summer jobs. Placements have included the International Atomic Energy Agency in Vienna, the Mass. Energy Office, and the Mass. Office of Coastal Zone Mgm't. The program also offers an integrated B.A./M.A. option with a minimum of 5 years study.

| | |
|---|---|
| Introductory Case Studies | Introduction to the Global Environment |
| Economy and Environment | Technology and Social Change |
| Energy Systems, Economics & Policies | Environment and Society |
| Environmental Hazards | Limits of the Earth |
| Risk Perception | Decision Analysis for Environmental Mgm't. |
| Medical Ethics | Environmental Health |
| Conflict Resolution | Groundwater Resources |

## Environmental / Resource Management

The Global Environment
People, Ecology and Global Village
Gender, Resources and Development
Social Forestry and Development
Societal Responses to Global Change
Forest Hydrology Field Methods

Technology and Social Change
Locating Hazardous Facilities
Nature and Culture in the Ancient World
Management of Arid Lands
Environment and Society
Int'l & Comparative Resource Policies

## Physical Geography of Human Systems

Biogeography
Tropical Ecology
Earth Science and Development
Urban Ecology: Cities as Ecosystems
Environment and Disasters

Watershed Ecology
Land Degradation
Physical Environment of Arid Lands
Oceanic Islands: Geology and Ecology
Agriculture and Grazing

## Peace Studies

Peace Net international computer network access is available for student use

Introduction to Peace Studies
Arms Control
Development Problems
Global Capitalism
Social Movements

Politics of War and Peace
United States and the New Europe
Conflict Resolution
Local Action, Global Change
Race and American Society

## Philosophy

Personal Values
Social and Political Ethics
Legal Ethics
Politics and Human Nature
AIDS: Ethics and Public Policy

Medical Ethics
Business Ethics
Women and Philosophy
Feminist Theory
Idealism

## Women's Studies

Gender and Film
Women in Hispanic Literature
Women in Society
American Jewish Life

Gender, Resources and Development
History of American Women
Women and Social Change
History of African-American Women

Policies, Projects and Strategies for Change: A Focus on Gender
Women and Militarization in a Comparative Politics Perspective

### American Politics and Public Policy     Sociology

### Urban/Social & Economic/Planning     Psychology     Screen Studies

Student Body: 23% state, 55% female, 45% male, 9% minority, 15% int'l., 18% transfer
Costs: $26,767   Apply By 2/1
• Service Learning Programs   • Internships   • Interdisciplinary Classes
• Individualized Majors   • Team Teaching   • Vegetarian and Kosher Meals
• Opportunity for fifth year tuition free BA/MA programs in E.S.P. and International Development
More than 70% of classes have less than 20 students
Special interest houses include "global environment house"

Use form in back to contact: Dean of Admissions
Clark University   Admissions House
950 Main St.   Worcester, MA 01610
(508) 793-7431
www.clarku.edu

# COLLEGE OF THE ATLANTIC

250 Students     Bar Harbor, Maine

"A student is a light to be lighted, not a glass to be filled."

William H. Durry, Jr.

College of the Atlantic was created at a time when, for many students, it was becoming evident that conventional education was inadequate to prepare them for effective citizenship in an increasingly complex and technical society. The founders envisioned a pioneering institution dedicated to the interdisciplinary study of human ecology. Their goal was a college in which students could overcome the narrow points of view and integrate knowledge across traditional academic lines. COA's curriculum especially focuses on developing conceptual frameworks for the solution of human and ecological problems. As we approach the twenty-first century these problems include equitably addressing the use and distribution of global resources, preventing nuclear war, and developing a mechanism to insure lasting peace.

COA is a college for the environmentally and socially committed individual. Being willing to take a stand on an issue, to show compassion for others, to recognize and promote the interconnectedness of all species and systems - all are characteristics of many students who choose COA. The mission at COA is to equip students with the knowledge, understanding, enthusiasm, and sensitivity to solve complex environmental and social problems from a humanistic perspective. Truly interdisciplinary thinking requires new methods for synthesizing and utilizing knowledge. In an interdisciplinary academic culture the boundaries among disciplines are minimized. Scientific analysis joins with humanistic and aesthetic understanding. Insights from specialized knowledge are combined and contribute a fuller understanding of complicated issues.

Responsible citizenship also requires collaborative attitudes and skills. This is a central concept at COA and the main rationale for a commitment to participatory governance and consensus building. It is exemplified by creative ways to run meetings, resolve disputes, utilize computer technologies, or work partnerships with outside communities.

At COA, students work on real issues from the beginning of their studies rather than after they are "educated." Individual courses of study are created by students as they work together with faculty to expand their academic horizons and develop their sense of responsibility. The outcome is an education that builds competence and confidence for life-long learning and prepares effective citizens and leaders for the decades to come.

In order to remain interdisciplinary and help students see the connections between all academic disciplines, COA does not break down into academic departments. Courses are distinguished by three resource area: Arts and Design, Human Studies and Environmental Sciences. One facet of the Human Studies resource area is the innovative teacher certification program about which the Maine State board of Education noted "As a Board and as policy makers we have often talked about excellence... at College of the Atlantic we experienced excellence in education."

At College of the Atlantic each student is responsible, with the help of an advising team, for designing his/her own academic program. Upon entering the College, students are assigned an advising team with whom they meet to plan and evaluate their studies. At the end of the first academic year, students choose a permanent advising team, comprised of one faculty member, one student, and an optional third member of the COA community. Combining courses in Arts and Design, Environmental Sciences, and Human Studies, independent study courses, group tutorials, an internship, and a Senior Projects, each student tailors their education to their specific academic interest.

Internships are a required facet of the program at COA. Recent internships by students include work at Acadia National Park, Bimini Biological Field Station, Canadian Wildlife Foundation, Consumer Energy Council, Friends of the Earth, New Alchemy Institute, World Peace Camp and the Solar Energy Research Institute.

Another requirement of the COA degree is contribution of time and energy to the building of the college community. This obligation can be fulfilled by serving on an established or ad hoc committee, or with a community action group such as the Environmental Action Resource Network. Students can help with the production of a college publication, serving as an advisor, or helping to manage an essential system such as scheduling students or organizing a COA forum.

In 1995, COA opened a new campus residence hall. The building is designed to compliment both the new and historical buildings on campus. The new residence houses 56 students in 8-person suites. The opening of this dorm now allows COA to provide on-campus housing for 100 students. Interior fixtures and finishes are environmentally sensitive, emphasizing minimal environmental impact and maximum energy efficiency.

To introduce students both to outdoor recreational activities and to one another, the College coordinates optional outdoor orientation trips for entering students. Staff members and older students lead these trips which sharpen outdoor skills and encourage the development of friendships. Recent trips have included canoeing the Allagash, canoeing a series of Maine Lakes, hiking along the Appalachian Trail to Katahdin and bicycling through the Maritimes and coastal Maine.

The College itself is located in the town of Bar Harbor on Mount Desert Island, Maine, where Acadia National Park is also located. The large, scenic island is connected to the mainland by a causeway. Living on MDI introduces one to a preservation ethic—an ethic that encourages people to develop a sense of history and to value the buildings, gardens, parks, and open space in their community. COA's curriculum and the political-social climate of the island encourage students to join with residents in developing land-use policies to insure the islands uniqueness will be preserved.

The College's location enables students to participate in many outdoor activities. Nearby Acadia National Park has over 50 miles of carriage paths and 100 miles of open trails. Students regularly jog and bike, hike and rock climb, windsurf, canoe, and sail on the island lakes and in Frenchman Bay, and in the winter cross-country ski, snowshoe and skate. Students frequently participate in organized weekend camping trips to northern and western Maine and nearby New Hampshire.

# MAKING A DIFFERENCE STUDIES

## Environmental Sciences

Brings together the biological and physical sciences in exploration of the earth's systems by using the scientific method of identification and investigation, tracing ecological and evolutionary patterns, studying natural communities, and understanding the interactions of people and natural systems.

Animal Behavior
Biology of Fishes
Ecological Physiology
Gender and Science
Marine Ecology
Ornithology
Plant Taxonomy

Biology I and II;
Bio-Organic Chemistry
Conservation of Endangered Species
Geology
The Gulf of Maine
Plants and Humanity
Women in Science.

- **Marine Mammals** This course is primarily an introduction to the biology of whales, porpoises and seals, concentrating particularly on species that frequent New England waters, but also including other species or habitats as directed by current events and student interest. Practical work includes study of skeletal anatomy, study of prey species, visits to harbor seal ledges, visit to observe gray seals, evaluation of anew whale museum, and a whale watching trip to observe humpback whales feeding.

## Human Studies

By synthesizing the humanities with the social sciences, the human studies resource area provides students with a wide and diversified perspective on human nature. Through these courses students focus on aspects of the contemporary human condition and are challenged to blend ecological concerns with classical human studies.

Humans in Nature
Critical Theory to Feminist Theory
Environmental Law
International Environmental Law
International Peace In Theory and Practice
Literature and Ecology
Medicine and Culture
Philosophy of Nature
Use and Abuse of Our Public Lands
White Water and White Paper: Canoeing/Conservation

Technology and Culture
Environmental Journalism
History of American Reform Movements
Women and Men in Transition
Issues in Regional Resource Management
Literature of Third World Women
Outdoor Education and Leadership
Science and Society
Women's History and Literature

- **Environmental Education and Communication Lab: Using Media Arts in the Schools** This lab provides a theoretical and practical introduction to an environmental education methodology, which employs audiovisual media as documentary and artistic means of expression. The approach combines active, self-determined, and experiential learning with future oriented questioning aimed at identifying collective problems in the life-world of the learners and proposing solutions. The lab is carried out at a local school. Thematic issues may include local planning, place and community, and teenage issues on Mt. Desert island.

## Arts and Design

The curriculum not only fosters artistic development but also gives students the opportunity to immerse themselves in design problems and to find solutions to them by combining aesthetic theory with an understanding of ecological, economic, and energy constraints.

Architectural Survey
Art, Media, and Environmental Studio
Introduction to Video Production
Photography I and II
Projects in Theater Workshop

Design and Activism
Environmental Design
Presentation Skills
Primitive Art
Women in the Visual Arts.

- **Land Use Planning Studio** What are the key physical aspects that make Mount Desert Island so appealing to residents and visitors? What aspects are essential to retain the integrity of that landscape into the future? As the island towns and the national park develop their comprehensive plans, the answers to these questions should guide future growth and preservation/conservation. Students analyze the physical makeup in terms of types of development and the scenic, cultural and natural resources of a specific area on the island. The purpose of this analysis is to determine what defines the "quality of life" for residents as well as tourists.

## Teacher Certification K-12

Approximately 20 percent of COA graduates are engaged in graduate studies or employed in the field as naturalists, environmental educators, and classroom teachers.

Environmental Design: Learning Spaces
Perspectives on School and Society
Intro to Philosophy of Education
Qualitative Research in Schools
Mainstreaming the Exceptional Child
Curriculum and Instruction in the Secondary Schools
Practice Informed by Theory in the Integrated Curriculum
Environmental Education and Communication: Using Media Arts in the Schools

Art, Media, and the Practice of Learning
Mainstreaming the Exceptional Child
Learning Theory
Intellectual History of Schools

- Faculty Bio **Etta Mooser** (Ed.D. Columbia University) heads COA's innovative teacher certification program. Her specialty areas include curricular innovation, ethics in education, and learning and environment. She has recently been appointed to the Maine State Advisory Committee to the Office of Truancy, Dropout, and Alternative Education.

Student Body: 25% state, 60% female, 40% male, 1% minority, 35% transfer, 5% int'l.
Faculty: 56% male, 44% female
Average # of students in a first year classroom: 15
Costs: $23,550    Apply By 3/1, 4/15 for transfer
Dining arrangements are cooperative with students sharing housekeeping & food preparation duties. Many students choose to find their own housing in Bar Harbor or elsewhere on the island.

• Individualized Majors  • Interdisciplinary Classes  • Life Experience Credit
• All Seminar Format  • Team Teaching  • Field Studies  • Vegetarian Meals

Use form in back to contact: Admissions Office
College of the Atlantic    Bar Harbor, ME 04609
(207) 288-5015    (800) 528-0025
inquiry@ecology.coa.edu    www.coa.edu

# COLLEGE OF ENVIRONMENTAL SCIENCE & FORESTRY
## STATE UNIVERSITY OF NEW YORK

1,200 Undergraduate Students     Syracuse, New York

When the rest of the country celebrated the first Earth Day in 1970 it finally caught up with the College of Environmental Science and Forestry. Since 1911 when the College first opened its doors, ESF began preparing scientists, resource managers, and engineers to nurture the home planet, and to teach scientific principles and applications that would maintain and improve forest lands and support the wise use of natural resources. Today, ESF leads in the discovery of new knowledge and the use of new tools to deal with continuing, current, and future environmental challenges. Students in all programs at SUNY-ESF gain a coherent understanding of their natural environment and learn ways to improve its health and productivity. All students share an interest in the environment and science, design or engineering required to conserve resources and enhance the health of the Earth. SUNY-ESF has prepared people to sustain and improve the environment for almost a century.

ESF's mission is to be a world leader in instruction, research, and public service related to: understanding the structure and function of the world's ecosystems; developing, managing, and use of renewable natural resources; improving outdoor environments ranging from wilderness to managed forests to urban landscapes; and maintaining and enhancing biological diversity, environmental quality, and resource options.

As the 21st century looms and society becomes increasingly concerned about the environment, members of the ESF family have timing in their favor. The future of the world may be determined by those who have broad foresight and a balance of judgment in applying, scientific, technical, and sociological knowledge to guide environmental and human forces. Modern society with its compelling demands from industry and government needs people who think objectively and constructively, and act creatively and responsibly. Faculty and students are committed to resolving immediate environmental hazards, learning how to avoid future problems, and offering policy alternatives that will protect the environment and meet the needs of a global society.

Academic programs at ESF share a foundation of rigorous science and dedication to wise use of natural resources. The faculty's cutting-edge research becomes part of the classroom experience, and the classroom merges with the world beyond the campus. Paper science students at ESF earn real-world experience and paychecks through required summer work at leading paper companies.

Students participate in hands-on and laboratory work at the main campus and on the 25,000 acres of ESF campus outside Syracuse. The College's largest regional campus at Newcomb is located on the 15,000-acre Huntington Wildlife Forest. Faculty, undergraduates, and visiting scientists use the facility for general research and work related to forest management. The Wanakena campus is the site of the College's Forestry Technology Program. The summer session in field forestry, required of environmental and resource management majors and the dual option in environmental and forest biology and resource management, takes place at Wanakena. All locations are equipped with the latest technology.

# MAKING A DIFFERENCE STUDIES

## Dual Program in Environmental & Forest Biology and Resources Mmg't
Plant Ecology
Diversity of Plants
Wildlife Conservation
Principles of Animal Behavior
Ecology of Freshwaters

Ecology of Adirondack Fishes
Ecological Biogeochemistry
Principles of Forest Entomology
Wildlife Habitats and Populations
Wildlife Ecology & Management Practicum

## Environmental Studies
Environmental Geology
Intro to Environmental Impact Analysis
Natural Processes in Planning & Design
American Landscape History
Environmental Studies Internship

Environmental Communication
Decision Modeling for Environmental Mgm't.
Government and the Environment
Social Processes and the Environment
Technologies: Water & Wastewater Treatment

## Landscape Architecture
Intro to Landscape Arch. & Planning
Site Research & Analysis
Plant Materials
Comprehensive Land Planning
Community Land Planning Workshop

Fundamentals of City & Regional Planning
Natural Processes in Planning & Design
Selected Readings in Enviro Studies
Professional Practice in Landscape Arch.
Negotiating Environmental Disputes

## Forest Technology and Resource Management
Forest Ecology
Timber Harvesting
Soil and Water Measurements
Forest Influences
Soils
Forest and Resource Economics

Personnel Management
Elements of Wildlife Ecology
Structure and Growth of Trees
Silviculture
Forest Protection
Natural Resource & Environmental Policy

## Forest Engineering
Water Pollution Engineering
Harvest Systems Analysis
Soil Mechanics and Foundations

Resource Policy and Management
Air Pollution Engineering
Forest Engineering Planning and Design

## Forest Technology (Ranger School) AAS Degree
Forest Entomology
Forest Roads
Fire Management
Structure & Growth of Trees
Computer Applications

Aerial Photogrammetry
Forest Pathology
Personnel Management
Forest Recreation
Elements of Wildlife Ecology

## Accelerated 5-year BS/MS Plant Biotechnology

Student body: 81% state, 60% male, 40% female, 4% minority
Costs: Residents $10,760   Non-Residents  $15,660      Rolling Admissions
• Field Studies    • Housing at University of Syracuse    • Graduate Program

Use form in back to contact: Director of Admissions
SUNY College of Environmental Science and Forestry
1 Forestry Drive   Syracuse, NY 13210-2779
(315) 470-6600   (800) 7777 ESF

# UNIVERSITY OF COLORADO, BOULDER

19,640 Undergraduates   Boulder, Colorado

As the flagship institution of the four-campus University of Colorado system, CU-Boulder has a long tradition of teaching environmental and social responsibility to students. The campus has an international reputation for environmental education and research programs, which can be pursued through several avenues.

Environmental studies, for example -- a bachelor's degree program in place for more than 40 years -- features a comprehensive curricula in the basic sciences, economics, ethics, and policy that prepares students to make a difference in the real world. Its two academic tracks -- one in environmental sciences, one in society and policy -- allows undergraduates to specialize in areas ranging from environmental and natural resources to decision-making, planning, and public policy.

The University also offers a unique environmental studies program for undergraduates that offers course work and seminars within a residence hall setting. Courses in biology, economics, expository writing, geography, geology, mathematics and political science meet core requirements and are taught in classes of about 25 students.

All of the environmental programs on campus are buoyed by outstanding faculty members, some of whom are affiliated with internationally known campus institutes like the Cooperative Institute for Research in Environmental Science and the Institute of Artic and Alpine Research. The Mountain Research Station, located about 45 minutes from campus, features a long-term ecological study site, and hosts students and faculty from around the world.

The long tradition of volunteer service on campus is underscored by by the fact that CU-Boulder ranks second in the nation in the number of volunteers recruited by the Peace Corps. A total of 300 students have gone on to Peace Corps service over the past seven years, helping people in developing countries to help themselves. Since 1961, more than 1,400 CU graduates have served in the Peace Corps.

CU's International and National Volunteer Service Training (INVST) program combines academic training and fieldwork in how to start and run volunteer service organizations. During junior and senior years the 16-credit-hour INVST program features courses in global and community development, human ecology and social change. Participating students also learn about bookkeeping, office management, program evaluation techniques and how to gain access to global computing networks.

Students also can participate in the Farrand Program, an academic program set in a residence hall that emphasizes humanities studies. In addition to surveying western art and culture, the program offers contemporary subjects like global ecology, film and ethics that are taught by some of the finest University faculty and also provides a number of community outreach opportunities.

The new ethnic studies major promotes interdisciplinary research and teaching in Afro-American, American Indian, Asian American and Chicano studies, and cross cultural and comparative race and ethnic studies. The primary focus of this major is on people of color and indigenous peoples of the US, but the study of race and ethnic issues in terms of global interactions are also important.

# MAKING A DIFFERENCE STUDIES

## Environmental Conservation
Principles of Ecology
The Environment and Public Policy
Forest Geography: Principles & Dynamics
Environments and Peoples

Conservation Practice
Remote Sensing of the Environment
Water Resource & Management of Western US
Energy in a Technical Society

## Biology  Tracks in Environmental, Population and Organismic
Environmental Issues and Biology
Artic and Alpine Ecology
Ecosystem Ecology
Ecological Perspectives on Global Change

Global Ecology
Limnology (Water Ecology)
Medical Ecology & Environmental Health
Topics in Montane Ecology

## Geography
World Geographic Problems
Conservation Thought
World Agriculture
Nature and Properties of Soils
Mountain Geography

Natural Hazards
Migration, Urbanization and Development
Water Resources & Mgm't of Western US
Urban Geography
Geoecology of Alpine and Artic Regions

## International Affairs
Political Geography
International Conflict in a Nuclear Age
Alternative World Futures
Power: Anthropology of Politics

American Foreign Policy
International Relations
Comparative Politics: Dev. Political Systems
Cross-Cultural Aspects of Socioecon. Devlp't

## Sociology   Tracks in Population/Health; Medicine; Social Conflict; Sex/Gender
Sociology of Gender, Health and Aging
Population Control and Family Planning
Men and Masculinity
Nonviolence & Ethics of Social Action

Women, Development and Fertility
Folk Med. & Psychiatry: Chicano Communities
Social Issues in Mental Health
Sociology of Natural and Social Environments

## Anthropology
Hopi & Navajo, Cultures in Conflict
The Maya
North American Indian Acculturation
Medical Anthropology

Amazonian Tribal Peoples
Ethnography of Mexico & Central America
Analyzing Exotic Languages
Urban Anthropology

## Chicano Studies
The Mexican Revolution
The Contemporary Mexican American
Chicano Poetry
Barrio Issues

Hispanic & Native American Culture of SW
Latinos and the American Political System
Folklore, Mysticism & Myth of Hispanic SW
History of the Chicano in Amer. Labor Mvm't

## International and National Voluntary Service Training Certificate
Financial aid in return for 1-2 years of humanitarian service. 6 weeks of travel to a foreign country.
Democratic & Nonviolent Social Mvmts    Facilitating Peaceful Community Change
Global Human Ecology    Global Development

### Kinesiology    Peace & Conflict    Philosophy    Women's Studies

Student Body: 68% state, 47% female, 53% male, 14% minority
Faculty: 79% male, 21% female    30 Service-Learning Courses
Costs: Residents $7,439   Non-Residents $19,483   Apply By 2/15

Use form in back to contact: Office of Admissions
CPO 30    University of Colorado at Boulder    Boulder, CO 80309-0030
(303) 492-6301   apply@colorado.edu   www.colorado.edu

# COLORADO COLLEGE

1,900 students     Colorado Springs, Colorado

Students come to Colorado College knowing they will have the opportunity to explore their values and discover their place in society. Students find a community that listens and challenges, provides and delivers. Students interested in the people, cultures, and land of the American Southwest come to Colorado College for its distinguished Southwest Studies program. CC's location and programs are ideal for those whose wonder and concern for the natural world is integral to their education. The College encourages students to pursue their goals for serious independent research.

In 1970, Colorado College implemented a new schedule that allowed for indepth study, extended field trips, and ample opportunity for independent study. the Block Plan divides the academic year into eight three-and-a-half week segments called blocks. Students take one course during each block and faculty teach only one. Unrestricted by time and place, teachers can schedule class sessions to best suit the material. As a result, students learn through participation and "hands-on" exploration. Classes can spend entire days in the library or a museum gathering data for research projects; classes in geology, economics, and sociology can take prolonged field trips, studying their subject in the appropriate environment.

Because of its location and the interests of students and faculty, Colorado College has become a leader in the study of the American Southwest. Southwest Studies is interdisciplinary, asking students to understand the "big picture," to weave together various cultural and historical perspectives with the literature and language of the indigenous people and an understanding of the area's natural environment.

With a significant representation of Native American and Hispanic students , the campus is alive with a Southwest flavor. The Hulbert Center for Southwest Studies sponsors visiting scholars and events, such as the "Race, Immigration, and the Rise of Nativism in Late Twentieth Century America" and "Women of the West" lectures series. Southwest Studies classes often travel afield to visit Hispanic communities in Colorado, or to examine the Southwest terrain in the Four Corners region.

The interdisciplinary Environmental Science program is focused in the sciences while seeking the breadth in the humanities and the social sciences that is essential to a full understanding of environmental issues. Since 1971 nearly 100 students have bred, monitored, and studied falcons with Professor Jim Enderson, leader of the Western Peregrine Falcon Recovery Team for the U.S. Fish and Wildlife Service. Through their efforts, the Peregrine falcon is being considered for removal from the "endangered" and "threatened" list.

At Colorado College, students' environmental interests merge into a way of life. Almost every year, students band together to form an environmental theme house. The Outdoor Recreation Committee leads trips up mountains, down rivers, and through valleys -- focusing on student leadership and environmental reverence.

Students who want to get involved take advantage of the Block Plan's four-and-a-half day "mini-vacations" by traveling to places such as Denver, Chicago, or New Mexico to assist communities facing economic instability or work with Habitat for Humanity, providing decent, affordable housing for low-income families.

# MAKING A DIFFERENCE STUDIES

## War and Peace in the Nuclear Age
The Dawn of the Nuclear Age
War, Violence and the Humanities
Foundations of Nonviolence
Int'l Human Rights: Theory and Practice

The Non-Violent Tradition in Literature
Morality in War
Freedom and Authority
War & Peace in Nuclear Age

## Philosophy
History of Environmental Ethics
Science, Technology, and Values
History of Environmental Ethics
Business Ethics
Philosophy of Science

Philosophy of Feminism
Intro to Social and Political Philosophy
Philosophy of Education
Philosophy of Mind
Asian Philosophies of Feminism

## Southwest Studies
Geology and Ecology of the Southwest
Southwest American Indian Music
Ethnohistory of the Southwest
Arts and Cultures of the Southwest
Literature of the Southwest

Chicano Politics
History of SW Under Spain and Mexico
Southwestern Ecosystems
American SW: The Heritage and the Variety
History of the SW Since the Mexican War

## Economics and Business
Economics of Poverty
Business Ethics
Economics of Labor
Economic Development
Natural Resource Economics

Social Impact of Business
Legal Environment of Business
Political Economy of Defense in War & Peace
Economics of Discrimination
Economics of International Finance

## History
War and Society Since the Renaissance
Witchcraft & Witch Craze in Early Europe
History of 20th Century Europe
Black People in the U.S. Since Civil War

The Jews in Modern Europe
France & Italy: Fascism, War & Resistance
Women in America Before the Civil War
Women and Children in the Western Past

## Women's Studies
Gender and Science
Native American Women of the West
Feminist/Womanist Ethics
American Women in Industrial Society

Black Women, Fiction & Literary Tradition
Women, Literature and the Family
The Family Before Industrialization
Myth and Meaning

- **Ecofeminism** Ecofeminism explores the links between systems of domination such as sexism, racism, economic exploitation and the ecological crisis.

### Religion    Political Economy    Sociology    Ethnomusicology

Student Body: 26% state, 53% female, 47% male, 13% minority
Faculty: 64% male, 36% female    Costs: $26,208    Apply By 1/15
Avg # of students in first year class: 16    80% of students engaged in community service

- Individualized Majors    • Multidisciplinary Classes    • Study Abroad    • Field Studies
- Exclusive Seminar Format    • Team Teaching    • Vegetarian Meals    • Theme Housing

Use form in back to contact: Director of Admissions
Colorado College    14 E. Cache la Poudre
Colorado Springs, CO 80903
(800) 542-7214    (719) 389-6344
admissions@cc.colorado.edu    www.cc.colorado.edu

# COLORADO STATE UNIVERSITY

20,000 Undergraduates    Fort Collins, Colorado

Colorado State University has a unique mission in the State of Colorado. The land-grant concept of a balanced program of teaching, research, extension, and public service provides the foundation for the University teaching and research programs, Agricultural Experiment Station, and Colorado State Forest Service. In the land-grant tradition, the University emphasizes instruction and research in professional areas important to the state and nation.

The educational philosophy at CSU recognizes and respects people as individuals and as members of social groups. Because of this philosophical commitment, the University maintains programs to contribute to interpersonal, intercultural, and international understanding. Of equal importance, education at CSU emphasizes consideration of values, for knowledge without values leaves the learner ill-equipped to make critical choices in life.

The College of Forestry and Natural Resources offers studies and professional training in the management, administration, and scientific investigation of renewable and nonrenewable natural resources. Programs include the study of fish, forests, minerals, range, watershed, wildlife, and outdoor recreation areas - their environments, products, and services. The scope of the college's programs is more broadly based than most forestry or natural resources schools. Undergraduate curricula include fishery biology, forestry, geology, landscape architecture, watershed sciences and wildlife biology, some with specialized concentrations. International resources management is an increasingly important concern of the CFNR. Because it is desirable that students have the opportunity to study abroad, the college has agreements with colleges in Scotland, Australia, New Zealand, and South Africa.

The College of Agricultural Sciences majors include agronomy (the science of science of field crops and soils), animal science, farm and ranch management, and landscape horticulture. The International Agronomy concentration is designed to meet the need of developing nations. Graduates find jobs with the Peace Corps and other agencies working in demonstration and extension positions. As new crop varieties are developed or introduced into developing countries, appropriate agronomic practices may be designed, compatible with the farming systems which can succeed in those climatic and socioeconomic constraints.

The University offers an interdisciplinary (non-degree) concentration in Youth Agency Administration. This unusual program is designed to enhance a students academic readiness to enter a career position in the youth and human service fields through emphases in various areas of human services, organizational management, and administration in social services. Students who complete the program often find professional positions in service agencies such as Boy Scouts of America, Big Brothers/Big Sisters of America, 4-H, and the YMCA.

The Outdoor Adventure Program offers a variety of participatory programs for students and faculty. Some of the classes include wilderness survival, rock climbing, cross-country skiing, kayaking and cycling. An outdoor resources library and rental shop are additional dimensions of this curricular-learning program.

# MAKING A DIFFERENCE STUDIES

## Range Ecology / Land Rehabilitation Option

Rangeland Improvements
Surface Mining Rehabilitation
Soil Fertility Management
Range Ecosystem Planning
Agriculture Experimental Design

Natural Resource Ecology
Agriculture/Natural Resource Economics
Range Animal-Habitat Interactions
Range Plant Production and Decomposition
Land Use and Water Quality

## Natural Resources Journalism

Agric/Natural Resource Economics
Environmental Conservation
Principles of Wildlife Management
Public Speaking and Discussion
Economics of Energy Resources

Attributes of Living Systems
Photojournalism
Environmental Ethics
Media and Society
Economics of Urban and Regional Land Use

## Conservation Biology

Population Ecology
Maintenance of Biotic Diversity
Disturbed Lands
Environmental Toxicology
Range Ecogeography

Environmental Conservation
Population: Natural Resource & Environment
Ecology of Landscapes
Wildlife Ecology
Politics and Natural Resources

## Entomology

Beekeeping
Aquatic Insects
Population Ecology
Insects, Science & Society

Range and Livestock Insects
International Crop Protection
Insect Pest Management
Agricultural Pesticides

## Gerontology

Perspectives in Gerontology
Social Work with Social Gerontology
Nutrition and Aging
Death, Dying and Grief
Handicapped Individual in Society

Adult Development and Aging
Biology of Aging
Housing and Design: Special Populations
Philosophy of Aging
Family Financial Resources and Public Policy

## Nonprofit Agency Administration

Intro to Nonprofit Agency Administration
Nonprofit Agency Fund Raising & Mgm't
Accounting
Human Diversity Issues
Marketing/Public Relations

Volunteer Management & Service Leaning
Management Fundamentals
Human Development & Family Studies
Social Work
Community Dynamics and Development

## Economics

Issues in Environmental Economics
Economics of Natural Resources
Labor Economics
Economics of Energy Resources

Poverty and Income Distribution
Economics of Outdoor Recreation
Economics of Urban and Regional Land Use

**Teaching Endorsement/Natural Resources    Sociology    Landscape Architecture**

Student Body: 75% state, 50% female, 50% male, 10% minority, 3% int'l.
Approximate Costs: Residents $8,000   Non-Residents $15,500       Rolling Admissions

Use form in back to contact: Director of Admissions
Colorado State University     Fort Collins, CO 80523
(970) 491-6909

# CORNELL UNIVERSITY

12,750 Undergraduates    Ithaca, New York

Cornell combines both private and public education at their seven colleges. The private colleges include Engineering, the College of Arts and Sciences, and the College of Architecture, Art and Planning. The Colleges of Agriculture and Life Sciences, Human Ecology, and Industrial and Labor Relations are public institutions, and as such, their tuition is considerably lower than at the private college.

The School of Industrial and Labor Relations is a small school within a large university with about 650 undergraduates. Courses in the school are divided into six departments: Collective Bargaining, Labor Law and Labor History; Economic and Social Statistics; International and Comparative Labor Relations; Labor Economics; Organizational Behavior; and Personnel and Human Resource Studies.

The College of Agriculture and Life Sciences offers studies in Natural Resources; Entomology; Biological Sciences; Plant Sciences; Animal Sciences; Social Sciences; and Agricultural and Biological Engineering. Intercollege programs include Landscape Architecture; Science, Technology and Society; and Environmental Toxicology.

The College of Human Ecology seeks to understand and improve the relations of people to their environments. Faculty and students examine individuals in relation to their family, neighborhood, workplace, and community, seeking a balance between theory and practice that will improve the quality of every day life. Majors include Human Development and Family Studies, Human Service Studies, Nutritional Sciences, and an interdepartmental major in Policy Analysis.

The university-wide Program on Ethics and Public Life (EPL) is Cornell's initiative in the systematic study of the ethical dimension of public issues. In the economy we face questions of equity and justice and questions about the relation between prosperity, the environment, and the quality of individual lives. In constitutional law, we confront dilemmas about civil rights, freedom of speech, and abortion. In politics and government, we wrestle with questions about campaigning, character, and compromise. In international affairs, we encounter complexities of war and peace, human rights, multilateral aid, and climate change. EPL grew out of a conviction that these questions need something more than abstract philosophical discussion. Universities need to foster ways of thinking about the complex, uncertain, and urgent problems of the real world. EPL seeks to enhance and facilitate the discussion of ethical issues by students whose central educational interests lie elsewhere, but whose work and lives will nevertheless confront them with dilemmas and responsibilities for which a university eduction should prepare them.

The Center for the Environment is a campuswide center that promotes and coordinated interdisciplinary research, teaching, and outreach activities on environmental issues. An effort to "design, develop and demonstrate ecologically sustainable communities... and transfer this knowledge to the global community to guide land and resource development" is being explored. The Center for Religion, Ethics and Social Policy is building an EcoVillage on 176 acres located 31/2 miles from Cornell. The goal is to build a cooperative, environmentally sensitive community. Plans include energy-efficient healthy housing, passive solar design, and biological waste treatment.

# MAKING A DIFFERENCE STUDIES

## Agricultural and Biological Engineering

Soil & Water Management

Principles of Aquaculture

Enviro Systems Analysis

Biomass Conversion Processes for Energy & Chemicals

Treatment & Disposal of Agric. Wastes

Intro to Energy Technology

Bioenvironmental Engineering

## City and Regional Planning

Environment & Society: A Delicate Balance

Urban Economics

Environmental Politics

Progressive City

The Global City: People, Production, & Planning in the Third World

Intro to African Development

Gender Issues in Planning & Architecture

American Indians, Planners, & Public Policy

Urban Housing: Sheltered vs. Unsheltered Society

## Rural Sociology  Tracks in Development Sociology; Population, Environment & Society; Social Data & Policy Analysis

Human Fertility In Developing Nations

American Indian Tribal Governments

International Development

Technology and Society

Land Reform Old and New

Intro to Rural Sociology

Environment and Society

Gender and Society

Population Dynamics

Gender Relations, Ideologies, & Social Change

## Biology and Society

Religion, Ethics and the Environment

Living on the Land

Writing as a Naturalist

Ecosystems and Ego Systems

Land Resources Protection Law

Ethics and Health Care

Women and Nature

Ecology and Social Change

In the Company of Animals

The Politics of Technical Decisions

- **Global Climate & Global Justice**  Attempts to prevent changes in global climate have produced disputes between rich & poor states. What's fair when rich & poor cooperate to deal with a common threat? Liberal, communitarian, feminist, Third-World views.

## Economics

Economic Development

Economic Problems of Latin America

International Trade Theory and Policy

Business Mgm't of Worker Enterprises

Economics of Participation & Workers' Mgm't.

Practice & Implementation of Self-Mgm't.

Economics of Defense Spending

Public Finance: Resource Allocation, Fiscal Policy

- **Technological & Product Base of Worker Enterprises: Ecology & Solar Energy Applications**  Worker's self-mgm't. & cooperation through learning about & construction of simple energy-related technologies to be produced in workers enterprises.

## Africana Studies

Racism in American Society

Black Resistance: S Africa & N. America

Politics & Social Change in the Caribbean

Social & Psychological Effects of Colonialization & Racism

African Civilizations & Culture

African Socialism & Nation Building

Oppression & the Psych. of Black Social Mvm't

Women's Studies    Outdoor Education    Marine Science    Natural Resources

Int'l Agriculture    Policy Analysis    Near Eastern Studies    Human Services

Hispanic, Asian- American, American Indian Studies    Civil & Enviro Engineering

Student Body: 44% state, 43% female, 57% male, 23% minority, 4% int'l

Costs: Residents $17,369 - $30,429    Non-Residents $26,4090 - $30,429    Apply by 1/1

Use form in back to contact: Undergraduate Admissions Office

Cornell University    Ithaca, NY 14850-2488

(607) 255-5241    www.cornell.edu

# EARLHAM COLLEGE

## 1,050 Students   Richmond, Indiana

Earlham is a distinctive teaching and learning community in which students build an education that is principled, humane, global, and rigorous. Founded by Friends (Quakers) in 1846, Earlham continues as a non-sectarian college firmly rooted in the values and practices of Friends. At the heart of Earlham are commitments: to upholding the value and dignity of every person; to personal integrity and academic honesty of the highest degree; open inquiry in an interpersonally safe, but challenging, atmosphere; to increasing harmony in the world, both among humanity and between humanity and the natural environment in which we live.

President Dick Wood reflects on the Earlham experience in this way: "Earlham strives to be a special kind of learning community, one in which people are honest with others and themselves, a community in which people are encouraged to be friends, not rivals. We aspire to an academic integrity rooted in trust. Earlham's distinctive learning community rests also on another value important to Friends and, indeed, to the search for truth-- respect for other persons. None of us has a monopoly on the truth. There is open and honest argument about rival theories, but that argument does not degenerate into personal attacks. At Earlham we strive to keep the classroom and the residence hall discussion safe places for persons, but dangerous places for ideas, for it is by challenging ideas that we grow.

Earlham seeks a diversity of students and faculty. Diversity requires a heightened sensitivity of each of us in the way we listen and in how we speak to each other. We are all colleagues embarked on a shared journey to discover truth. Because we may find different paths, Earlham values individual freedom, but not at the expense of respect for those who are different or whose ideas we find disagreeable.

Earlham values social justice and peaceful resolution of conflicts. Students and faculty have many opportunities to work for justice and to give of themselves in service. Following the example of early Friends, Earlham seeks not only to avoid violence, but to remove the causes of violence. Community life at Earlham is based on the assumption that we are a community of adult learners, who can take responsibility for their lives and be supportive of others. Students, staff, and faculty share in governing the College through a system of joint committees. As much as possible, Earlham tries to reach decisions by consensus, by arriving at what Friends call a 'sense of the meeting' that is shared by all involved. The College combine the highest academic standards with a very supportive and cooperative environment. Community life is structured to draw out the best that is in each member of the community, in social as well as academic life. Earlham has high ideals; finding ways to live up to them is part of that adventure."

Earlham recognizes a responsibility for enabling students to grow in their knowledge and appreciation of American cultures, but also for challenging students through encounter with world cultures not familiar to them. Professor of English Anthony Bing says, "An Earlham education stresses the idea of global connectedness. A commitment to helping students see things from someone else's point of view. The other things compassion, understanding, humanity follow naturally."

Programs of study at Earlham are often unique and exciting. Students many times design their own majors, which have included Outdoor Education, Social Thought, and Museum Studies. Many students collaborate with professors on research and creative projects. Recent partnerships include: experiments in molecular biology focusing on the search for leukemia; a study of the responses of the American peace movement to conflict in the Middle East; and a research seminar on women, social movements, and temperance. Students frequently participate in field study research, whether in Puerto Rico, Kenya, the Galapagos Islands, nearby areas in Indiana to study bird migration, or Quaker Libraries to study Quaker Women. One-fifth of the students participate on research teams, gaining experience that applies directly to graduate school and careers. In addition, sixty percent of students participate in internships.

Earlham offers 25 off-campus study opportunities to 17 different countries including Martinique, Colombia, Kenya, China, Japan, and the Czech Republic. Students live with families in their homes and often work in social service agencies or alongside their hosts. Most students participate on at least one international study program.

Most Earlham students also participate in community service. Students tutor in high schools, participate in Big Brothers/Big Sisters, work with senior citizens, mentor young children, and volunteer at the YMCA and Girls Club. Last year they donated almost 20,000 hours of time to he local community.

Student life at Earlham is enriched by a 600-acre back campus of ponds, woods, and meadows which serves as a biological field station as well as the site for the College's observatory and farm, and where students may wander, run, or ride horses. Students also participate in a wide variety of campus opportunities in music, athletics, theater, religious fellowships, dance, and fitness/wellness activities. Earlham's 600 acre back campus of ponds, woods, and meadows .

## MAKING A DIFFERENCE STUDIES

### Conservation Biology
Students have designed and conducted projects in Puerto Rico on how spider populations have responded to environmental changes wrought by hurricanes; while others carry on long-term studies of turtle and iguana populations in the U.S., Mexico and the Bahamas.

| | |
|---|---|
| Ecological Biology | Biological Diversity |
| Ornithology | Field Botany |
| Population and Community Ecology | Tropical Biology Interterm |

Field Biology Training Program at Manomet Bird Observatory, Massachusetts

### Environmental Chemistry
Students are doing research on trace mercury in the environment using a new ultrasensitive technique available at only a few places in the nation. The Earlham Analytical Chemistry Lab, the only facility of its kind within an undergraduate institution provides water and wastewater analysis for local industries and other customers.

| | |
|---|---|
| Techniques of Water Analysis | Environmental Chemistry |
| Chemical Dynamics | Biochemistry |
| Instrumental Analysis | Quantum Chemistry |
| Organic Chemistry | Chemistry in Societal Context |

## Peace and Global Studies

War, the roots of violence, non-violent alternatives, conflict resolution, and social justice.

| | |
|---|---|
| Culture and Conflict | Introduction to Philosophy: Food Ethics |
| Politics of Global Problems | Methods of Peacemaking |
| Conflict Resolution | Theories of International Relations |
| International Law | Religious Responses to War and Violence |
| Moral Education | Technology and Arms Control |

- **Christian Ethics & Modern Moral Problems** Christian ethics in relation to other ethical alternatives and contemporary moral problems. Love, justice, sexuality, violence, pacifism, and medical ethics. Nature of moral self as it illuminates personal decisions.

## Human Development and Social Relations

| | |
|---|---|
| Theories of Human Development | Human Biology |
| Persons and Systems | Comparative Cultures |
| Social Science and Human Values | Institutions and Inequality |
| Field Study | Frontiers of Psychological Inquiry |
| Social Relations | Counseling & Psychotherapy |

## Management

Managers often make moral and ethical choices about how to interact with workers, and how to use the Earth's resources.

| | |
|---|---|
| Nonprofit Organization and Leadership | Conflict Resolution |
| Work and Culture | Health, Medicine and Society |
| Programming and Problem-Solving | Business Policy |
| Public Administration | Industrial Organization and Public Policy |
| Japanese Economic Development | Political & Econ. Development of Pacific Rim |

## Japanese Studies

Solid grounding in the language and culture of Japan. Combines study of Japanese language and civilization with extensive work in various disciplines, including history, political science, psychology, religion, economics, education, sociology/anthropology, and fine arts.

| | |
|---|---|
| Introduction to the Study of Japan | Super Japanese |
| Japanese Arts | Readings in Japan Culture |
| Religion of East Asia | Politics of Japan |
| Education and the Family in Japan | Senior Seminar |

## African/African-American Studies

| | |
|---|---|
| African-American Literature | African-American History |
| Southern African History | Intro to African/African-American Studies |
| History of Africa Before 1880 | History of Africa After 1880 |
| Institutions and Inequality | African-American Religious History |

**Environmental Geology      Women's Studies      Education**

**International Studies      Latin American Studies      Jewish Studies**

Student Body: 17% State, 55% female, 45% male, 12% minority, 10% transfer, 4% int'l.
Faculty: 55% male, 45% female, 10% minority      Average # of students in first year classroom: 18-20
Costs $24,008      Apply By 2/15

- Team Teaching  • Individualized Majors  • Service-Learning  • Study Abroad  • Field Studies
- Theme Housing  • Interdisciplinary Classes  • Vegetarian Meals  • Energy Conservation in effect

Use form in back to contact: Director of Admissions
Earlham College      Richmond, IN 47374
(800) 327-5426
admission@earlham.edu      www.earlham.edu

# EASTERN MENNONITE UNIVERSITY

1,000 Students    Harrisonburg, Virginia

Eastern Mennonite University places outstanding academics into the context of global awareness and active Christian involvement. The university's unique Global Village Curriculum builds on the belief that we are all interdependent in ways which can affect the survival or destruction of civilization. Eastern Mennonite educates students to use their talents to promote human transformation by working for peace, by creating just social structures, and by aiding access to basic human resources for life and dignity.

This educational perspective is rooted in the 450 year old Anabaptist-Mennonite tradition. EMU's particular theological principles include Jesus as the word of God incarnate, the Bible as the authoritative guide for faith and life, the church as a community of work and worship, and discipleship as the mark of an authentic life. Discipleship implies an active faith characterized by simplicity of life, peacebuilding (which expresses itself in nonviolence, reconciliation, active pursuit of justice and non-participation in the military,) evangelism and Christian service.

The cornerstone of this approach to learning is Eastern Mennonite's Cross Cultural Program, one of the strongest programs in international and cross cultural education in the country. EMU students study in a wide range of international and domestic locations such as Central America, the Middle East, Europe, China, Japan, Russia, Africa, Mexico, Los Angeles, New Orleans and American Indian reservations. On these cross-cultural study tours, led by EMU's faculty, students receive an education that reaches far beyond the classroom. The larger world serves as a laboratory for testing and refining knowledge, no matter what a student's major. Eastern Mennonite students have life-changing experiences which broaden their world view and give them expanded possibilities after graduation.

On campus, Eastern Mennonite is a vibrant community bringing together students from a rich variety of cultural and religious backgrounds. A large majority of faculty have lived and served abroad. This international perspective enters the classroom, as do the perspectives of the 14% of students who are international or American multiethnic. With about 1,000 students, EMU is a good size - large enough for a full range of quality programs and activities, but small enough so students are not lost in the crowd. Personal relationships with professors are part of every student's experience.

In addition to the college's strong theater, athletic, and music programs, students participate in a wide array of extracurricular clubs and events. These include community service opportunities coordinated by student organizations. Students quickly discover that at Eastern Mennonite success is measured not only by what they achieve after graduation, but how they have developed along the way. Development of the whole person is the goal at Eastern Mennonite University.

# MAKING A DIFFERENCE STUDIES

## Biology

Environmental Science
Ecology
Food and Population

Plant Pest Management
Soil Science
Biology as Inquiry

- **Agroecology** Explores agricultural ecosystems, especially in food deficit countries. Physical, biological, social, and economic bases of agroecology are examined using a variety of sources and case studies. Attempt is made to appreciate traditional agricultural rationality, and to investigate the effects of modification of existing agroecosystems.

## International Business (Interdisciplinary Approach)

Peace & Justice in Global Context
Development and Int'l. Economics
International Conflict and Peacemaking

International Marketing
Sociology of Development
International Business

- **Peace & Justice in Global Context** Religion, theology, economic perspectives, int'l organization, models for social change (development, revolution etc.) and missionary activity in creation, maintenance & change of social systems. Civil religion, Third World Theology, economic organization, and devp't as related to peace and justice.

## International Agriculture

Designed as a background for work in countries with food scarcities.

Anthropology and Social Change
Sociology of Development
Development & International Economics

Principles of Management
Plant Pest Management

## Peace and Justice

Conflict Resolution and Peacemaking
Anthropology and Christian Mission
Mediation and Conflict Transformation
Human Behavior & Social Environment

Peace and Justice in the American Context
Development and International Economics
International Conflict and Peacemaking
Sociology of Development

## Socio-Economic Development

Social Systems and Social Problems
Sociology of Development
Anthropology and Social Change
Food & Population

Conflict Resolution and Peacemaking
Peace and Justice in Global Context
Social Policy Analysis
Development and International Economics

## Camping, Recreation and Outdoor Ministries

Wilderness Experience Seminar
Backpacking
Camp Leadership
Environmental Science
Human Services Skills

Outdoor Living Skills
Technical Rock Climbing
Introduction to Youth Ministry
Camping, Recreation, Outdoor Ministries
Conflict and Peacemaking

Student Body: 37% state, 60% female, 40% male, 9% minority, 3% int'.l, 8% transfer
Faculty: 60% male, 40% female    Avg. # of students in 1st yr classroom: 25
Costs: $17,300    Apply By: 8/1
• Team Teaching    • Field Studies    • Interdisciplinary Classes
• Required Community Service    • Individualized Majors    • Vegetarian Meals
• Graduate Studies in Counseling, Education, Conflict Transformation
Use form in back to contact: Director of Admissions
Eastern Mennonite University    Harrisonburg, VA 22802
(540) 432-4118    (800) 368-2665
admiss@emu.edu    www.emu.edu

# EUGENE LANG COLLEGE
## NEW SCHOOL FOR SOCIAL RESEARCH

350 Undergraduates    New York, New York    Moderately Selective

Eugene Lang College offers a distinctive liberal arts education with an interdisciplinary focus designed for engaged and independent-minded students. The College is a vital intellectual community which aims to foster in its students a critical self-consciousness about the process and purpose of knowing. Students at Lang College are encouraged to participate in the creation and direction of their education.

Lang students are firmly grounded in the liberal arts. They work in depth in an area of their choosing, often doing original projects with an active faculty as a rich resource. The challenge of the experience produces graduates for whom critical thinking has become a way of life.

The liberal arts curriculum of Eugene Lang College is special. It is open and flexible; students design their own programs of study with their academic advisors. It is innovative and creative: many Lang courses explore topics that cross traditional academic boundaries and approach classic texts and traditional subjects from new perspectives. It is diverse and inclusive: Lang courses include works, voices, perspectives and ways of knowing of different peoples and different cultures. The curriculum is challenging and demanding; the small classes (15 students maximum) the emphasis on reading primary texts, the use of writing and revision as a way of learning - these hallmarks of the Lang educational program mean that students work hard and feel responsible for active participation in their classes. Most classes are conducted in seminar format. Seminars permit the most direct engagement of students with the material and the opportunity for close relationships with faculty.

Eugene Lang College offers students five broad areas of concentration, within which a student maps out an individual path. A student's particular course of study within the concentration consists of 8 to 10 courses leading to relatively advanced and specialized knowledge of an area of study. The concentrations are highly interdisciplinary, allowing students to make connections between varied modes of thought and different approaches to topics and ideas. These come under the broader headings of Cultural Studies; Mind, Nature and Values; Social Inquiry; Urban Studies; and Writing, Literature and the Arts.

Eugene Lang College believes that internships are central to undergraduate liberal education. Students earn college credit while contributing to the wider community and gaining a variety of skills available through hands-on work experience. Examples of internships include work with Madre, a women's aid organization raising money for health, prenatal and education programs in Central America and the Middle East; National Organization for Women; The Institute for the Development of Earth Awareness; the Interfaith Center on Corporate Responsibility; Homes for the Homeless; People Against Sexual Abuse; The Rainforest Alliance; The War Resisters League; and The Wetlands Preserve "New York City's only environmental nightclub".

Following is a general introduction to the areas of study offered at Eugene Lang:

- Social Inquiry  This concentration brings together a wide range of courses from such disciplines as history, political science, economics, anthropology, and sociology. Students interested in this area of study benefit from the New School's renowned Graduate Faculty of Political and Social Science. Students may take courses in the Graduate Faculty once they are advanced enough.

- Mind, Nature and Values  This concentration is the principal location for study in philosophy, religion, science and psychology, especially as the issues and questions from these disciplines exist in relation to each other and in specific social and historical contexts. Mind, Nature and Values takes as its starting point the central question: How do human beings know and live in the natural, spiritual and moral worlds they inhabit? Each of the fields of study constituting the area makes distinctive claims about how to address and answer this question.

- Cultural Studies  Whatever courses a Lang student chooses, no matter what the concentration, they will involve issues and perspectives of different peoples and different cultures, including those historically underrepresented in academic study. Cultural studies permits students to develop paths which focus directly on issues of the creation and representation of identity in social and historical contexts. In this concentration, the students take interdisciplinary approaches to theories of identity and difference and how they relate to political practice and to the practical, everyday experiences of individuals.

- Urban Studies  This concentration brings a multi-disciplinary focus to bear on the history, development, politics and problems of contemporary urban life. It is also directed to students who seek a more direct pathway to additional training and careers in the area of public policy. The concentration makes the city an object of study and uses New York City as an educational laboratory and resource. It unites theoretical inquiry with field experience, academic internships, and urban research.

- Writing, Literature and the Arts  This concentration enables students to pursue literary studies, the writing of prose and poetry, and the discipline of theater. At the same time it seeks to establish connections among these and other art forms that are usually studied in isolation. Students examine works  and traditions in a broad cultural context, framing political and aesthetic questions about issues such as the silencing and empowering of voice, or changing interpretations of artistic traditions.

Students may avail themselves of the University Tutorial Program, enabling advanced undergraduates to work with scholars located in other divisions of the University. Individually, or in groups of two or three, students construct a directed reading course in the area of the tutor's particular expertise and  interest.

Eugene Lang has school wide efforts (including hiring practices) to promote sensitivity and understanding about racial, religious and gender differences.

# MAKING A DIFFERENCE STUDIES

## First Year Studies

Feminist Focus on Men

The Economic Way of Thinking

Writing as Re-Vision

Approaches to Historical Inquiry

Physical Models of Reality

Conflict, Identity and the Written Voice

Sugar and Spice: Coming of Age and the Social Construction of Gender

Order Out of Chaos Gender and Culture in the Modern Western World

Political and Social Change in America; The 1960's

World Science and Social Change: Then and Now

Holistic Science: An Analysis of Science in Contemporary Society

- **Inventing Reality: What to Believe in What the Media Tells Us**  Examine the role the media plays in creating/inventing the reality about which it wants to or claims to be reporting. How business and government manipulate journalists and editors in order to advance political/economic agendas and ideologies and the extent to which journalists and editors willingly participate in that manipulation. The meaning of press freedom in a country where, as conservative critic James J. Kilpatrick has approvingly noted: "Freedom of the press belongs to anyone who owns one."

- **The Living City**  This course provides a cursory introduction to the ways of understanding the complexities of the city, but also offers an alternative to exploring the city in written form alone. This course attempts to integrate the ideas of urban theorists with a perspective of "the street." Students are sent throughout the semester into "the field" - specified neighborhoods in Lower Manhattan to work up projects on such topics as architecture and built environment, immigrants, deindustrialization and gentrification.

- Faculty Bio  **Sara Ruddick Ph.D.** (Harvard)  Sara Ruddick has taught at New School for Social Research, New York University and Haverford College. She is a consultant for Union Graduate School, on the editorial board of Peace and Justice, and a member of Network for Women in Development. Professor Ruddick received a Ford Foundation Grant for Faculty and Curricular Development in Women's Studies, and organized a conference on Simone de Beauvoir. She is a prolific writer and has been extensively published.

## Upper Level Studies

Gay and Lesbian Latino Voices

Fem. Critiques of Reason and Sexuality

Love, War and Work

Virtue and Politics

Feminist Inquiry

Feminist Psychology

Women in the City

Ecology and Politics

Little to X to Shabazz: A Hero for Daily Living

National Identity and Ethnicity in Latino/a Literature and Films

The Politics of Sexuality in African-American Literature

Social Experience of Men in Post-War America

Ecology in Perspective: Science, Technology and Power

Drugs, Ethnicity and Urban Communities

- **Global Boundaries: International Relations Beyond the State**  The recent emergence of a "global culture" coincides with the increasing globalization of vital issues such as poverty, health, identity, and the environment. Focus on issues such as: the global status of women, the representation of dominated peoples in the West, the power of global cities, the international circulation of knowledge, and the claims of the post-colonial societies and the individuals within them. Students will explore the ways identities, knowledge, images, people, and state power and capital circulate across national borders.

- **Holistic Science: An Analysis of Science in Contemporary Society** How and why is contemporary science becoming more interdisciplinary? What new discoveries have helped this process? What is chaos theory? Quantum physics? episodic evolution? dynamic biological systems? What are the philosophical, political, cultural, and economic consequences of these trends? We will explore these questions to become more informed about the political and cultural nature of scientific and technological thought and practice within world capitalism.

- Faculty Bio **Ann Snitow** A cultural critic, literary scholar, and feminist theorist and activist, Ann Snitow teaches a wide variety of courses in literature, gender, and cultural studies. Well known nationally and internationally, Ann Snitow is a leading example of the "public intellectual," whose work regularly appears in such places as *The Village Voice* and *Dissent*. She has most recently established The Network of East-West Women which has brought scholars and activists in the women's movements in Eastern Europe and the USA together for the first time.

## Joint BA/BFA Parsons School of Design Program - Architecture Program
Students in the architecture program have been developing mixed income housing projects for 3 sites in New York's depressed Lower East Side. The program was launched with a grant from Housing Opportunities for the Promotion of Equality, an organization that lends money to women and minority-owned companies. Community Access, a not-for-profit organization that develops housing, and the NY State Division of Housing and Community Renewal were involved in the project. The state initiated the project with the idea of creating useful, practical, architecturally interesting affordable housing.

Student Body: 30% state, 60% female, 40% male, 18% minority, 5% int'l.
Costs: $18,600    Apply by 2/1, 7/1 for transfers
Room & board only for students coming from beyond NYC $9,400
Average # of students in a first year classroom: 15
Eugene Lang has recycling and energy conservation policies in effect.

• Interdisciplinary Classes   • Individualized Majors
• Exclusive Seminar Format   • Kosher/ Vegetarian Meal Option   • Internships

Use form in back to contact: Director of Admissions
Eugene Lang College
65 West 11th Street    NY, NY 10011
(212) 229-5365

# THE EVERGREEN STATE COLLEGE

3,136 Undergraduates    Olympia, Washington

Evergreen is a challenging, high energy, continually evolving community founded on the values of cooperative learning, open inquiry and diversity. Evergreen has earned a national reputation as a pioneer in developing high quality innovative educational programs that bridge the gaps between academic disciplines. Students engage in the study of ideals, concepts and problems that are based on real-world issues and questions. From their freshmen to senior years, students work closely with faculty, who are all focused primarily on teaching and learning.

Evergreen's fundamental mission is to assist students in learning how to learn. The college prepares students to excel in a world where emerging technologies, new ideas, a changing economic climate and cultural shifts are altering the way we organize our communities, our public service agencies, our businesses and our governments. It emphasizes the fundamental skills of communication, critical thinking, problem solving, working effectively in teams, and working across differences.

Evergreen approaches its mission through the traditional academic areas of the humanities, arts, natural sciences and social sciences. However, the college's educational programs are transformed by a set of core beliefs that flow through everything the college does both inside and outside of the classroom. Evergreen believes:

- The main purpose of a college is to teach, and good teaching involves close interaction between faculty and students.

- Collaborative or shared learning is better than learning in isolation and in competition with others.

- Teaching across differences is critical to learning.

- Connected learning -- pulling together different ideas and concepts -- is better than learning separated bits of information.

- Active learning -- applying what's learned to projects and activities -- is better than passively receiving knowledge.

- The only way to thoroughly understand abstract theories is to apply them to real-world situations.

These beliefs are reflected in the way students learn at all levels of the curriculum. Instead of taking a series of courses on separate topics, Evergreen students typically enroll in a single program that draws together different academic subjects while exploring a central theme, idea or question. Program participants might, for example, study the theme of health care problems by exploring real-world issues from the points of view of biology, history, philosophy, sociology, drama, economics and literature.

Evergreen faculty love to teach. Their enthusiasm, their passion for teaching is infectious. The college's emphasis on students and educational innovation attracts some of the best teachers anywhere. They are hired and evaluated primarily on the quality of their teaching. Most faculty work with 23 to 25 students. Their goal is to be accessible, receptive and open to students and teaching is never delegated to teaching assistants. At Evergreen, faculty and students are all on a first-name basis.

Freshmen typically enroll in a single, full-time interdisciplinary program with 69 to 92 students and three to four faculty members who each represent a different academic discipline. Within this community of learners, students participate in lectures, discuss books they've read in 23 - to 25 member seminar groups, pursue projects with four or five students, work in labs or studios, and learn to navigate the library and other college resources. Students may stay together as a community for two quarters or an entire academic year.

More advanced students typically participate in smaller, more narrowly focused programs that strengthen skills in traditional areas of study -- but always drawing on other disciplines and exploring real-world themes. Or students may choose internships, enter into group contracts to work closely with one faculty member and a small group of students, or design independent study contracts.

Rather than signing up for a prefabricated major, Evergreen students have the flexibility to design academic pathways to concentrate on subject areas they are passionate about, within the range of expertise provided by faculty. These academic areas include biology, communications, computer science, energy systems, environmental studies, health and human services, humanities, language studies, management and business, marine studies, mathematics, Native American studies, performing arts, physical science, politics and economics, pre-law, pre-medicine and visual arts.

A majority of Evergreen students complete one or more internships by the time they graduate. One student worked as a river ranger with the U.S. Forest Service in the Grand Canyon guiding researchers working on an environmental impact statement, another as a marine mammal researcher documenting the travels of gray whales, while others have served as English tutors for refugees, as researchers in genetic laboratories, as support staff in shelters for abused women, the list goes on.

Evergreen's Organic Farm has received national recognition. Thirteen acres of bustling agricultural and academic activity are located on the west edge of campus.

Student representation is encouraged in all college task forces exploring college issues or new policies, and students participate in a wide variety of organizations that provide cultural, informational, social, recreational, spiritual and educational services and activities. Current organizations include the Asian/Pacific Isle Coalition, Bike Shop, Environmental Resource Center, American Indian Science & Engineering Society, Jewish Cultural Center, Women of Color Coalition, MEChA/Chicano Student Movement, Asian Solidarity in Action, Union of Students with Disabilities, and the Math and Science Network. Evergreen competes in the NCAA Division III conference in swimming, soccer, basketball and tennis.

Evergreen offers two undergraduate degrees, the Bachelor of Arts and Bachelor of Science, and three advanced degrees, Master of Environmental Studies, Master of Public Administration and Master in Teaching.

Evergreen graduates tend to carry their sense of involvement and social responsibility with them in their careers as educators, social workers, counselors, microbiologists, entertainers, lawyers, journalists, health care professionals, administrators, artists, entrepreneurs and a diversity of other occupations.

Evergreen's Tacoma Campus is located in an urban setting, and the college offers programs in four Native American communities.

# MAKING A DIFFERENCE STUDIES

**Core Studies for First Year Students** (48 credits each and team taught)

Love/Violence                             Making Modern America: 1820-1970

Politics and Ideologies from the Americas     Not by Bread Alone: The Elements of Life

Forests: Natural and Human Communities in the Pacific Northwest

- **Ordinary People, Extraordinary Lives: Making Meaning, Making a Difference**
  Many people today feel that social, economic, cultural and political problems are too big
  or complex to comprehend. They feel powerless to involve themselves. This program is
  founded on the premise that there are multiple ways individuals can address such problems, including artistic expression, religious or political activism and community service. The program will focus on the lives and work of individuals who have responded
  to the issues of their times.

### Environmental Studies

Biodiversity and Global Change (16 cr.)      Practice of Sustainable Agriculture (24-32 cr.)

Environmental Change and Community: Regional Policy and Politics (16 cr.)

Marine Life: Marine Organisms and their Environments (32 cr.)

Natural Histories: Botany, Biography and Community (48 cr.

- Faculty Bio **Nalini Nadkarni** (B.S., Brown University; Ph.D., College of Forest
  Resources, U. of Washington) Nationally renown for her work on rain forest ecology,
  Nadkarni is an enthusiastic, experiential, field-oriented teacher. Nadkarni's work has
  been featured in National Geographic, in and IMAX film, in several national maga-
  zines and a recent PBS special on rain forests.

### Culture, Text and Language

Japan Today (32 cr.)                    Take a Look: A Study in Perception (16 cr.)

The Meaning of History (16 cr.)

When Words Lose their Meaning: An Essay Writing Community (32 cr.)

Contested Realities: Power and Representation in Nations and Communities (48 cr.)

- **Victim Rhetoric: Chained, Choice, Change** (48 cr.) Are citizens who suffer from
  injustice and inequality victims of our political-economic system, our institutions or
  our public policies? Or could people be victims of their own irresponsibility? This
  program examines the debates that contain a range of rhetoric mounted by key players within welfare reform, family values, gambling and political campaigning.

### Scientific Inquiry

Matter and Motion (48 cr.)                 Evolutionary Biology (16 cr.)

Molecule to Organism (48 cr.)            Health and Human Development (48 cr.)

Computability and Cognition: The Scope and Limits of Formal Systems (48 cr.)

- Faculty Bio **Janet Ott** (B.S., St. Lawrence University; Ph.D., Biology, University of
  Southern California) Ott guides undergraduate research in the area of alternative
  healing methods, especially the mechanisms involved in acupuncture and acupres-
  sure.

### Expressive Arts

People of the Triangle (16 cr.)           The Empty Stage: Theater Intensive (48 cr.)

Horizon: Where Land Meets Sky (32 cr.)

Envisioning Home: Finding Your Place Through Art and Music (48 cr.

- **Images in Context** (48 cr.) This program examines artistic images in painting, literature, photography, and film within their social and historical contexts. It emphasizes
  the ways in which historical moments impact the images produced and the stories
  told within it.

## Social Sciences

Integrates anthropology, economics, history, law, political science, philosophy and sociology as a way of understanding the modern world, and as a set of tools for analyzing contemporary public problems, locally, nationally and globally.

Self and Community (48 cr.)                    Family, Community and Public Policy (48 cr.)
Psychological Theory and Practice (48 cr.)
Multicultural Psychological Counseling: A New Way to Integrate and Innovate
Political Economy and Social Change: The End of Prosperity (32 cr.)

- **Social Movements and Social Change: Theory and Practice in Comparative Perspectives** (32 cr.) Students will investigate social movements and social change and their relationship historically and in the late 20th century. Movements that will be examined include the North American and South Asian independence movements, various working class social movements, Hindu fundamentalism, the U.S. civil rights movement, and indigenous peoples' movements.

**Management and the Public Interest** (48 credits)
This program focuses on the private business sector, but also gives attention to public and not-for-profit sectors. Values, ethics and the public interest are addressed throughout the year. Special emphasis is placed on development of analytical and people skills.

## Native American Studies

The major goal is to provide an open alternative education opportunity through experiencing a Native American philosophy of education which promotes self-determination, individual research, goal setting, internal motivation and self-reliance. Designed to serve Native American students who are interested in enriching their unique cultural heritage and developing strategies for self-determination in a pluralistic society, and students interested in learning about their own traditional cultures and values including the dynamics of change in a pluralistic society.

- **Regeneration: A Celebration With the Land** Regeneration is a major concept in understanding the relationship indigenous people have to land, the politics of people and land and policies governing land use. The program will combine focused study of Native American culture (including an analysis of the effects of natural resource policies on nature and people, tribal and aboriginal rights) with project work and academic research.

## Science and Human Values    MA Enviro Studies    MA Public Administration

Student Body: 25% state, 58% female, 42% male, 16% minority, 60% transfer
Faculty: 59% male, 41% female, 41% minority      Apply By 3/1
Costs: Residents $7,167  Non-residents $13,860

- Team Teaching  • Interdisciplinary Majors   • Life Experience Credit  • Co-op Education
• Study Abroad  • Self-Designed Majors   • All Seminar Format
• Vegetarian & Vegan Meals  • Part-time Degree Program

Use form in back to contact: Office of Admissions
The Evergreen State College    Olympia, WA 98505
(360) 866-6000 x 6170
admissions@evergreen.edu    www.evergreen.edu

# GODDARD

150 Students · Plainfield, Vermont

Goddard is a small college in rural Vermont for plain living and hard thinking. Founded in 1863, Goddard is recognized for innovation in education. Its mission is to advance the theory and practice of learning by undertaking new experiments based upon the ideals of democracy, and the principles of progressive education first asserted by John Dewey. At Goddard, students are regarded as unique individuals who will take charge of their learning and collaborate with other students, staff, and faculty to build a strong community. Goddard encourages students to become creative, passionate, lifelong learners, working and living with an earnest concern for others and the welfare of the earth.

Progressive education is a transforming process. Goddard strives to help people change themselves and to help them work to change the world, with lifelong learning as the basic tool. College people talk about improving skills, developing a broad understanding of society, teaching disciplined thinking (and a discipline). But what about the heart, the spirit? Of what use is a mind packed with theory and method unless it is wedded to a knowledge of self, and a passionate involvement with life and the welfare of the planet? It is the whole person -- intellect, passion, heart, and spirit- whose needs are the starting point for a plan to learn, and whose purposes commit her or him to carrying out the plan. Within and outside the college Goddard students are asked to confront the issues of ignorance and prejudice that engender overpopulation, nationalism and war, alienating work, racism and sexism, homophobia, and poverty.

Never has there been a greater need for transformative education: learning that leads individuals to see the world in a new way- as a precious jewel, unique in the universe, facing socio-ecological issues created by the human species. Education must lead these people to search together for effective solutions, thinking globally and acting locally, recovering the true humanity of humankind.

Goddard's smallness has contributed to the success of its graduates: students know each other and their faculty closely; they learn how a community works. Like their Vermont neighbors, they learn to cope: to plan, to economize, to recycle, to make do, to take initiative, to create their own recreation. They learn that study and work, education and vocation -- a the work in the world that calls one to become part of it - are inseparable. North-central Vermont contributes to that learning. One learns that one is truly pat of, that one cannot live apart rom this web of life.

Progressive education has its own language. The emphasis is on learning as change. Individuals are important, but their individuality is understood in the context of interdependence. The words "whole" and "holistic" recur, emphasizing that persons and experiences cannot cannot be fragmented. Undergraduate campus study is centered around Group Studies, so named to emphasize the importance of collaboration in learning. Some group studies are called "Foundation" studies because their aim is to introduce a student to a particular way of looking and acting in the world- ecology or anthropology or literature and writing, for instance. The Goddard curriculum is different each semester, because student needs and the society change.

Examples of possible study at Goddard typically, though not always, fall under the following areas: Business, Leadership, and Community Organization; The Natural and Ecological Sciences; Psychology and Counseling; Feminist Studies; Multicultural Studies; Teacher Education; History and Social Inquiry; Writing and Literature; Performing Arts; Visual Arts; Media Studies and Communication.

The Work Program is a required part of the curriculum. Through it students help maintain and operate the college, at the same time reducing their tuition expenses. Two hours a week are spent on a meal team in the college dining room and kitchen; six hours a week on one of many jobs: shelving or signing out books in the library, assisting in one of many offices, operating the student bank, working in the college woods, and gardening. Work, in particular, and practical activity in general, have special value in progressive education. Values are involved, ethical judgements may need to be made, the social or moral worth of a product or process evaluated.

Students at Goddard also have several options for involvement in community service. They are encouraged to volunteer locally at one of the organizations in the Central Vermont area, or they can do their work program at a non-profit organization for one of their semesters. There are also new college grants for work study students enabling them to work in the community doing a variety of service projects. These have included tutoring adults through the adult basic education program, serving as a poet in residence at a local school, volunteering in the battered women's shelter, the local library or elementary school, or doing environmental research on the local river. Students may also do internships for credit which have a service emphasis, for example, they may work at the local health center, or teaching pre-school, or tutoring in high school. Or they can create field semester opportunities in which an internship or service activity is a key element in their time away from Goddard.

Goddard education may be described in analogies: a circle, a bridge, a door or window or gate, a dance. The Goddard learning process is circular: As the conclusion of one learning experience evokes the need for the next, the learning cycle begins again. In a more physical sense, Goddard group studies and other meetings are circles, students and faculty sitting around a room, all learning from what everyone has to contribute. Because the faculty emphasize collaborative learning and community involvement, the college can be a bridge from self centered individualism to contributing individuality. Many students discover Goddard to be a bridge from the passive learning of lectures and exams to active, participatory learning. Then there is the exciting bridge between ideas and actions, from the creative urges to the created products. These bridges lead to the most important bridge; that which a Goddard student builds between a changing self and a changing world. Goddard opens a door to one's inner self as the source of energy for learning. It opens many windows on the world, and helps students correlate what they see from varied perspectives.

Goddard College also has an off-campus study program. Students use campus facilities only during the week-long residencies that begin the Off-Campus semesters. They plan large scale independent study during the residencies, and carry out their study plans and keep in touch with their faculty mentors through correspondence. An additional 325 students pursue graduate and undergraduate study in the off campus mode.

# MAKING A DIFFERENCE STUDIES

Goddard "resource areas" are not "departments," and the studies listed for each often draw on resources from other areas. The Goddard curriculum is different each semester, because student needs and the society change. The "recent group studies" listed here under each area description are some of those offered during the past three years.

## Natural and Ecological Sciences

Holistic Health & Healing

Mind-Body Interaction

Global Issues & Ecology

Environmental Ed. in Elementary School

Ecology and Society

Botany for Sustainable Arts Living

Design & Construction: Solar Greenhouse

Gaia: the Earth as an Organism

Bio-ethics

Aquatic Ecology

- Faculty Bio: **Charles Woodward** (M.A. Goddard) Teaches environmental science. Mr. Woodward's interests include biological and environmental sciences, environmental management and restoration, and sustainable agriculture; environmental education.

## Business, Leadership, and Community Organization

How can people make a living and also make a life in socially responsible ways? Communities are places where both can happen, if there is acting on thinking: a socially responsible job, and a constructive and creative life.

Organizational Problem Solving

Grant Proposal Writing

Biographical Studies of Leaders for Social Change

How to Market Your Creativity Without Selling Out

Money & Power: Problematic Relationship

Group Dynamics for Middle Management

## Feminist Studies

Women, a majority rather than a minority, are challenged to invent a future qualitatively different from the historic (though not, perhaps, the prehistoric) past. The feminist perspective suggests the possibility of a world characterized by resistance to violence as a way of settling interpersonal and international disputes: by the rejection of exploitation of individuals, groups, cultures, and other life forms; and by a hope for a society based in life-giving wholeness, not life destroying fragmentation and competition. Feminist concerns are dealt with in every curriculum area.

Defining Feminism: Who We Are

Goddess Religion

Lesbian Ethics

The Gender of Language

Making Feminist Sense of World Politics

Refugee Voices: Women, Violence & Human Rights

From Victim to Hero: Women's Fiction, Women's Lives

History of Feminism

Women's Ways of Knowing

Women's Relationships

Women's Lives: Studies in Culture & Class

## History and Social Inquiry

Cultural, political, and social history are rich resources for understanding current world news. Especially relevant is "Modern" history - what has happened since the late 17th century. The current history of post-colonial cultures, including Native American history, is essential to an understanding of contemporary world tensions. Recent group studies include:

The Nature of Truth & Proof

Something About the Sixties

Who's Calling the Shots: Secret Government in America

History of Nature & Humanity's Relation To It

Technology & the Revolution of Consciousness

Global Political Economy

## Multicultural Studies and Cultural Anthropology

Development Problems in Third World      T'ai Chi & Kung Fu: Philosophy & Practice
Mayan Art      Intro to Navajo Culture (in Arizona)
Myths as Mirrors of Culture      Cross-Cultural Health & Healing
Religion & Spirituality in a Cross-Cultural Perspective
Rich Folks/Poor Folks: an Examination of Daily Life

- **Mayan Studies** A series of group studies related to the Mayan culture of Meso-America, culminating in a three- week study of the tour of the Maya lands in southern Mexico - including sites in Chiapas and Yucatan. We will meet with farmers, community leaders, government officials and development workers.

- Faculty Bio **Hong Yue Go** (Goddard, M.A. Beijing Teachers College) "A good education should not only help students with their academic progress, but also help them to discover themselves and the real meaning of their lives, help them to learn how to challenge themselves in their life journey. I feel life is a struggle, not a struggle with the world around us, but a struggle with our inner world, with weakness in our will. We must overcome this inner weakness in spirit before we can truly give to others."

## Education and Teaching

To earn a teaching license, you study human development, educational philosophy, social issues affecting education, and new as well as traditional teaching methods.

School and Society      Radical Ideas in Education
Do it for the Children      The Self and Others
Early Childhood Education

- **A Sense of Place; A Study of a Bio-Region** Students will learn to find a connection to a sense of place. We will look at many perspectives of what it means to live here and study this region's geography, history, and ecology. How did those factors shape both the people who first settled here and the people who live here today. Will provide a framework for those interested in integrating learning and teaching.

## Performing Arts

African & African American Music      Indonesian Gamelan: International Orchestra
The Life and Times of the Guitar      Improvisation/Dance Theatre Performance

Student Body: 10% state, 51% female, 49% male, 10% minority, 49% transfer
Faculty: 40% male, 60% female
Costs: $20,948    Rolling Admissions

- Exclusive Seminar Format • Team Teaching • Individualized Majors
- Non-Resident Degree Program • Life Experience Credit • Study Abroad
- Day care • Vegetarian/Vegan Meals

Use form in back to contact: Admissions Office
Goddard College    Rt.2    Plainfield, VT 05667
(800) 468-4888

# GOSHEN COLLEGE

1,000 students    Goshen, Indiana

With a Mission Statement that lists developing "informed, articulate, sensitive, responsible Christians" seeking to become "servant leaders for the church and the world" as its focus and a general education program that was the first in the nation to require international education, making a difference permeates everything about Goshen College. Owned and operated by the Mennonite Church, one of three historic "peace churches," the college has attracted attention as being a place where values are "lived as well as taught."

Central to that living out of values has been Goshen's international education requirement. Since 1968, about 85 percent of GC students have fulfilled the requirement by taking part in the internationally recognized Study-Service Term (SST) program. In the program, students spend a term in a culture significantly different from the United States, usually at the same cost as a term on campus. Students typically spend the first seven weeks of the term living and learning in a major city, studying the language and culture of the country. The second half of the term is spent in a service-learning assignment, usually in a rural setting and often related to the student's major. Education majors have taught in schools and nurses and pre-medicine students often work in clinics and other health-related settings. Goshen was instrumental in opening up the People's Republic of China to undergraduate students, developing the first exchange program between a U.S. college and the country. Currently, the school offers programs in Costa Rica, the Dominican Republic, the Ivory Coast and Germany. Goshen students traveled to Indonesia for the first time in 1994. Other SST sites have included Haiti, Honduras, Belize, Guadeloupe, Nicaragua, and Korea. Other students fulfill the international education requirement by taking part in other approved study-abroad programs or by taking on-campus courses focusing on intercultural studies.

But international education at Goshen isn't limited to a 13-week term in another country. Each year, around 70 students from more than 30 countries are part of the student body of 1,000. Most GC faculty leaders have lived and worked outside of the country and many bring their international experiences to the classroom. International education at Goshen also plays a significant role in the programming of the school's Multicultural Affairs Program.

Students minoring in environmental or related studies such as biology or environmental education can study at the college's nearby Merry Lea Environmental Learning Center, a 1,150-acre plot of bogs and meadow. Outdoor enthusiasts also find the center within easy riding distance by bicycle. Visitors can also spend the day hiking the trails of the facility, enjoying the hundreds of species of plant and animal life. Adjoining campus is Witmer Woods, another source of environmental study.

The college also offers a minor in peace studies. Activities around peace include the annual peace oratorical contest, the peace play, the C. Henry Smith lectureship, Students for Shalom, public lectures and conferences. Some courses are taught in "real-world" settings, including Guatemala, Ireland, Chicago and Washington, DC.

# MAKING A DIFFERENCE STUDIES

## Environmental Studies

General Ecology
Environmental Ethics
General Ecology
Geology
Water Resources
Field Botany

Agriculture in the Tropics
Marine Biology
Field Experience in Environmental Education
Land Resources
Ornithology

- **Conservation**  A study of the need for and the best methods of conservation of our national resources from an ecological approach. Emphasis on ecological principles related to populations, soil, water, forest, wild life pesticides, waste, pollution and energy. Includes first-hand study of natural areas, erosion, conservation practices, impact of humans and all-day field trips.

## Peace Studies

Prosocial Behavior
Issues in Peace Studies
Violence and Nonviolence
Peace Workshop
War and Peace Systems
Peace Studies Practicum

Third World Theologies
War, Peace and Nonresistance
Introduction to Economic Development
Contemporary Women's Issues
Seminar in Personal Violence

- **Doing Theology in a Latin American Setting**  The complex issues which face the Christian church in Guatemala. Anabaptist, Protestant and Roman Catholic approaches to missions and service activities in Guatemala examined. Mayan and Ladino cultures will be studied. Lectures, field trips, journaling, group Bible study and small group discussions provide an opportunity to investigate religious issues in Guatemala.

## Women's Studies

Marriage and Family
Liberation Theologies
Spiritual Writings of Women
Women's Growth and Development
Womanhood and the Cultures of the U.S.

The Bible and Sexuality
Social Problems
Contemporary Women's Issues
Women in Text and Image

## Intercultural Studies

Communication Across Cultures
Comparative Economic Systems
African Societies and Cultures
International Politics
Introduction to Linguistics
World Geography

Asian Religions
Race and Ethnic Relations
First/Third World History
International Literature
Community Development  ·
The Far East

Student Body: 44% state, 57 % women, 43 % men, 9% minority, 7% int'l.
Average # of students in a first year class: 16 students   Faculty: 61% male, 39% female
Costs: $16,310     Rolling Admissions
• Life Experience Credit   • Team Teaching   • Individualized Majors
• Vegetarian Meals   • Recycling and energy conservation policies in effect

Use form in back to contact: Admissions Office
Goshen College    Goshen, IN 46526
(800)348-7422     (219)535-7535

# GREEN MOUNTAIN COLLEGE

700 Students    Poultney, Vermont

Green Mountain College seeks to prepare students for productive, caring, and fulfilling lives in a rapidly changing world. Established in a setting of natural beauty, the College takes the environment as the unifying theme underlying the academic and social experience of the campus. As a four-year, coeducational residential institution, Green Mountain aspires to build a diverse and inclusive campus community. Through a broad range of liberal arts and career-focused majors and a vigorous, service-oriented student affairs program, the College aims to foster the ideals of environmental responsibility, public service, international understanding, and lifelong intellectual, physical, and spiritual development... Drawing on its rich and varied history, the College is committed to a spirit of adventure and leadership in undergraduate higher education.        - from the Green Mountain College Mission Statement

Founded in 1834, Green Mountain College is an independent, coeducational institution named for Vermont's famed evergreen hills. In recent years GMC has refocused its mission with the aim of educating the next generation of thinkers, teachers, and leaders who will help improve and protect the world's diverse environments. GMC defines itself as an environmental liberal arts college with an international focus. GMC offers a broad spectrum of liberal arts majors and pre-professional programs. Most students choose careers or graduate school programs in traditional fields such as management, English, teaching, the behavioral sciences, and the visual and performing arts, but enter these fields with an educated awareness of environmental issues and the responsibilities of global citizenship.

In their freshman, sophomore, and senior years, all GMC students take a three-course sequence entitled "Perspectives on the Environment." This core curriculum links disparate academic disciplines to a set of common environmental concerns facing our global community. Students in all twenty academic majors explore environmental issues together in these interdisciplinary courses. Each of the academic majors also contains courses that touch upon environmental themes, an approach GMC calls ecology across the curriculum. For example, a popular course within the English major examines the influence of nature on writers like Wordsworth and Thoreau.

*Perspectives on the Environment,* Green Mountain College's general education program, takes an interdisciplinary approach to the study of environmental issues and provides a common learning experience for all GMC students. Every student takes three core courses: Images of Nature, Dimensions of Nature and A Delicate Balance. Students select additional courses from four distribution categories -- Scientific Endeavor, Social Perspectives, Humanities, and Health and Well-Being Students who feel that their needs are not met by traditional majors can select the option of a self-designed major.

GMC's involvement with the environment is not merely academic. To complement ecology across the curriculum, GMC offers adventure across the co-curriculum. The adventure begins with new-student orientation and extends throughout campus life. In a special outdoor orientation called the Wilderness Challenge, new students choose from a variety of activities such as mountain biking, adventure camping, hiking the Long Trail, whitewater canoeing down the Battenkill River, rappelling, or sea kayaking on Lake Champlain. To sustain the spirit and momentum begun during the Wilderness Challenge, the college's campus activities office sponsors an ambitious series of weekend outdoor activities for the entire campus community throughout the academic year.

The "Greening Green Mountain" program encourages students, faculty, and the wider GMC family to enhance recycling efforts, waste management activities, and water or energy conservation measures. Student volunteers work in the college's organic garden and with a stream bank erosion project, design greenhouses, build cold frames, and plan special Earth Day celebrations. Students have renovated one residence hall into an experiment in sustainable living. An annual Environmental Expo held on campus helps educate visiting elementary school students and their families about environmental issues.

GMC sees itself as a laboratory for developing higher levels of environmental consciousness and performance. Lessons learned and habits transformed in campus life have an influence far beyond the college gates, as graduates carry tested environmental values into a world in urgent need of hope and balance.

GMC also maintains a strong commitment to international education and to the promotion of cross-cultural understanding. The campus community includes students from around the globe, and numerous opportunities exist for study abroad, including formal exchange agreements with colleges and universities in Korea, Wales, Japan and Mexico.

Internships and field experiences are vital components of most academic majors. This hands-on experience enables students to serve while they enhance skills, develop role models for success, and achieve a better understanding of career options. Students who feel their intellectual and career interests are not met through traditional academic majors can organize their own program through the self-designed major.

GMC challenges students to think about other people and larger causes, and offers financial aid programs that not only reward athletic and artistic accomplishment but also reward volunteer community or environmental service. Examples of service-learning projects undertaken by students are community recycling, youth intramurals, centers for aging, animal shelters, environmental education, and health care agencies.

GMC's location reinforces the college's commitment to ecology across the curriculum and adventure across the co-curriculum, offering easy access to Vermont's spectacular natural resources for both outdoor study and recreation. Students enjoy mountains for climbing, hiking, biking, skiing, and snowboarding, and lakes for skating, kayaking, canoeing, sailing, fishing, and swimming. Several major ski resorts -- Okemo, Killington, Pico, Bromley and Stratton Mountain -- are an easy drive from campus.

Sports teams -- soccer, basketball, volleyball, softball, tennis, golf, lacrosse, and alpine skiing -- consistently bring home banners and trophies. GMC also offers an active intramural program and a wide range of action and service organizations. Among the many clubs on campus are an Environmental Club, Mountain Bike Club, Outing Club, Rugby Club, Scuba Club, Do Everything Club and GMC Cares.

Recent GMC alumni have gone on to earn graduate degrees at such institutions as Columbia, Cal State, Drexel, the New School for Social Research, Syracuse, UNC-Chapel Hill and the University of Vermont. They can also be found navigating the waters of Alaska's Inside Passage, teaching English to students in Korea, running marketing agencies, painting watercolor portraits, coaching cross-country skiing, and making lives -- their own and others' -- more productive.

# MAKING A DIFFERENCE STUDIES

The Evolution Revolution
Simplicity and Sustainability
Nature in Music
Environmental Ethics

Contemporary Social Issues
Native American Perspectives
Utopias: Envisioning the Good Society
American Views of the Environment

## Environmental Studies

Introduces students to increasingly sophisticated studies in biology and ecology, with an emphasis on how these fields pertain to regional issues, and to the global implications of such issues as diminished biodiversity, ecosystem loss, and global warming. This interdisciplinary program is committed to developing not only scientific understanding, but also ethical, philosophical, and aesthetic approaches to the natural world.

- **The Northern Forest** A team-taught course with extensive field work, draws on the talents and expertise of five GMC professors to address issues from the perspectives of economics, ecology, education, and environmental philosophy. Students who enroll in The Northern Forest take only that 15-hour block course during the semester.

- Faculty Bio **William M. Throop** Environmental ethicist , chair of the Environmental Studies Committee, recently edited the Humanities Press anthology *Renewing Nature* and published articles in *Environmental Ethics* and in Roger Gottlieb's *The Ecological Community*, among other places. When not teaching, Dr. Throop enjoys hiking (he's hiked all 46 of the 4,000-foot peaks in the Adirondacks,) canoeing, and working on his family's farm.

## Adventure Recreation

is one of four majors, including Therapeutic Recreation, offered by the Department of Recreation and Leisure Studies. Through optional certification tracks, Adventure Recreation students can become certified whitewater canoe or kayak instructors, adventure program facilitators, open water dive instructors, mountain guides, or skiing and snowboarding instructors.

Fundamentals of Outdoor Living
Essentials of Mountaineering (or Paddling)

Leadership and Group Dynamics
Outdoor Emergency Care

- Faculty bio: **J. Thayer Raines**, widely published and the holder of numerous certifications, heads up the Adventure Recreation component of GMC's Recreation programs. In addition to his professional expertise in outdoor recreation and adventure programming, Dr. Raines is former national and current New England Ski-Archery Champion (recurve bow, classic ski).

Student Body: 7% state, 52% male, 48% female, 6% minority, 18% transfer
Faculty: 62% male, 38% female, 3% minority
Costs: $19,356   Rolling Admissions

- Field Studies  • Team Teaching  • Individualized Majors  • Interdisciplinary Majors
• Service-Learning  • Interdisciplinary Classes  • Environmental Housing
• SAT's may be optional  • Vegetarian/Vegan Meals

Use form in back to contact: Dean of Admissions
Green Mountain College   One College Circle   Poultney, VT 05764-1199
(802) 287-8000
admiss@greenmtn.edu   www.greenmtn.edu

# GRINNELL COLLEGE

1,327 Students     Grinnell, Iowa

Ask students, faculty, and staff what distinguishes Grinnell from other liberal arts colleges, and you will hear their agreement that Grinnell fosters a strong sense of community. At Grinnell, individuals are respected for who they are and what they believe, and differences can be expressed and appreciated. Grinnell is a place where great ideas and global issues are considered and debated. Faculty encourages debate over these significant issues in the classroom, and it continues throughout the campus, is carried into the community, and extends beyond Grinnell. Students leave Grinnell believing that they can and should make a difference in their careers and communities. The tone of the place is self-confident.

Grinnell is an institution informed by a pioneering spirit: a willingness to experiment and a commitment to community. Grinnell seeks and produces good students who are also concerned citizens, people who take an active part in the campus community and later in the world. The college has traditionally been a community with a conscience. Grinnell's pioneering past began in 1846, when New Englanders with strong Congregational, social-reformer backgrounds established the college. The college was named after abolitionist minister Josiah Bushnell Grinnell. Influenced by Grinnell's educational and social idealism, the college blended academic accomplishments with a sense of service to the world beyond the campus.

In 1959, Grinnell College established the Travel Service Scholarship Program, a precursor of the Peace Corps, which provided funds to send graduating Grinnell seniors to developing countries for a year to assist with language instruction, village work projects, or other special needs.

In 1989, Grinnell became the second college in the country to establish a Peace Corps Preparatory Program, a program of courses and experiential learning designed to prepare students for international volunteer service in the Peace Corps or other volunteer organizations.

"Grinnell stresses three qualities above all -- individualism, social commitment, and intellectual self-reliance. Our interest is not to produce undergraduate specialists devoted to narrow pursuits. We want to develop thinking individuals who continue the process of learning, caring, valuing, and questioning," stated President Emeritus Glenn Leggett.

Grinnell's pioneering present again links educational goals with society's realities. The college believes, as do leaders in business, government, and industry, that today any liberally-educated person must be able to analyze problems quantitatively and must be aware of the nature of technology and its impact on society. Corporations have taken note of a long-term AT&T study in which the best records for managerial progress and performance went to employees with humanities and social sciences degrees. Grinnell graduates not only join businesses -- they can be found in large numbers in the public sector -- the Peace Corps, political campaigns, public official staffs, environmental coalitions, and public and private education. For many, the social consciousness developed at Grinnell becomes a life-long commitment.

The interdepartmental General Science program allows students freedom to explore other areas of the curriculum as well and provides the broad background preferred in elementary-school teaching, interdisciplinary science fields such as psychobiology, and environmental science. A 365-acre environmental research area is also near campus.

Students who major in Chinese customarily spend the first two years on campus, the third year in the People's Republic of China, Taiwan, or Hong Kong, and return to Grinnell for the senior year. Grinnell is actively involved in Russian-American exchanges. The college annually hosts a visiting professor from Russia and offers four students from St. Petersburg the opportunity to study at Grinnell. The college sponsors its own interim study tour that allows 25 students and their instructors to visit Russia during winter break.

To introduce students to differing voices and ideas, Grinnell brings to campus many prominent thinkers. Lecturers have included civil rights leader Eleanor Holmes Norton, the founder of United Farm Works Cesar Chavez, former president of Costa Rica Oscar Arias, Ambassador George Moose '66, former U.S. Surgeon General C. Everett Koop, and former Soviet Foreign Minister Alexander Bessmertnykh. Recent symposia and conferences have focused on such topics as "Public Policy and Relative Environmental Risk," "Human Rights and Cultural Traditions," "Changing Visions of Public Service," and "Arab and Jew: The Psychology of Peace."

Grinnell students also join in campus and community life. As high school students, three-quarters did volunteer work. At Grinnell, they take part in student activities and organizations, including Environmental Action Group; Javanese Gamelan Ensemble; Students in Defense of Animals and the Environment, The Young, Gifted, and Black Gospel Choir; Amnesty International; and Model U.N. Also active on campus are the Juggling Club; Ultimate Frisbee; Stonewall Coalition; Concerned Black Students; Diversity Coalition; International Student Organization; Politically Active Feminist Alliance; Habitat for Humanity; Native American Students in Alliance; Poverty Action Now; Asian Students in Alliance; Student Organization of Latino/as; Chalutzim; Helping Hands and many more.

Many students keep one foot in the world beyond the campus by taking a part in the town of Grinnell and surrounding cities and towns -- including work with Head Start, Habitat for Humanity, the Native American Tutoring Project, local school systems, and church groups. A monthly newsletter published by the Community Service Center informs the campus community of volunteer activities and opportunities. The CSC welcomes student-initiated projects and encourages students to link service activities with academic interests and career exploration.

Outdoor activities are organized by the Grinnell Outdoor Recreation Program. Students decide on the group's activities: cross country skiing, backpacking, sailing, caving, whitewater canoeing and others. GORP provides training workshops and has equipment students can use at no charge. Campus members of the Environmental Action Group promote environmental awareness and engage in nature-oriented activities.

# MAKING A DIFFERENCE STUDIES

## Environmental Studies
Students may participate in off-campus study programs in Tropical Field Research in Costa Rica or at the ACM Wilderness Field Station.

Ecology

Human Ecology and Adaptation

Evolution and Ecology

Resource and Environmental Economics

- **International Politics of Land and Sea Resources**   Analysis of the international politics of the conflict between the developed nations of the north and the developing nations of the south for control of the world's resources and over a new economic order. The impact of national decision-making processes, international organizations, cartels, and multinational corporations. Case studies on fuel, mineral, and food crises, and law-of-the-sea negotiations.

## First Year Tutorials
Emotions

Food: Technologies and Ritual

The Rights of Minority Cultures

Mathematics and the Other Arts

Youth in Anthropological Perspective

Latinas and their Worlds

The Technological World

Music and Nature

Nuclear Technology: Fears, Facts, and Public Policy Health Care

Crisis, Liberation, Justice, and Leadership Human Behavior in Extreme Situations

## Technology Studies
Philosophy of Technology

Bridges, Towers, and Skyscrapers

Biotechnology and its Social Impact

Sociology of Health and Illness

Evolution of of Technology

Electronic Music

Solar Energy Technologies

Technology Assessment

## Latin American Studies
Latin American Cultures

State and Society in Latin America

International Economics

Political Economy of Developing Countries

Aztecs, Incas and Mayas

Economic Development

## Global Development Studies
African Cultures

Ecology

Gender in Cross-Cultural Perspective

Resource and Environmental Politics

Nations and the Global Environment

Int'l. Politics: Conflict and Cooperation

## Sociology
Dilemmas of Third World Development

Self and Society

The Black Community

Women, Men, and Society

Human Sexuality in the United States

Social Movements in the 20th Century

Social Inequality

Race and Ethnicity in America

The Family

Contemporary Sociological Theory

### Africana Studies    Gender and Women's Studies    Anthropology

Student Body: 13% State, 56% female, 44% male, 12% minority, 7% transfer, 8% int'l.
Faculty: 65% male, 35% female, 10% minority    35% of students engage in community service
Costs: $23,860    Early Decision 12/1   Regular Decision 2/1
• Individualized Majors   • Field Studies   • Interdisciplinary Concentrations   • Vegetarian Meals

Use form in back to contact: Office of Admission
Grinnell College    P.O. Box 805    Grinnell, Iowa  50112-0807
(800)247-0113    (515)269-3600
askgrin@admin.grin.edu   www.grinnell.edu

# GUILFORD COLLEGE

1,200 Students    Greensboro, North Carolina

"It takes a whole community to educate one person."

The African proverb has unique relevance for the kind of experiences you will have as a student at Guilford College. Here, learning is a cooperative effort shared by all members of the college community. Located in Greensboro, North Carolina and founded in 1837 by the Religious Society of Friends (Quakers,) Guilford College an independent college which offers a distinctive four year liberal arts and sciences education in the Quaker tradition. It is the third oldest coeducational colleges in the nation and the oldest in the South. Guildford's Quaker heritage stresses simplicity, integrity, compassion, tolerance, equality, hard work, enjoyment, spiritual receptivity and concern for social justice and world peace. Growing out of this heritage, the college emphasizes educational values which are embodied in a strong and lasting tradition of coeducation, a curriculum with intercultural and international dimensions, close individual relationships between students and faculty in the pursuit of knowledge, governance by consensus and a commitment to lifelong learning.

While embracing many traditional educational goals and methods, the college also promotes innovative approaches to teaching and learning. Both students and faculty are encouraged to pursue high levels of scholarly research and creativity in academic disciplines. Guilford particularly explores interdisciplinary and intercultural perspectives and to develop a capacity to reason effectively, to look beneath the surface of issues, to understand the presuppositions and implications of ideas, and to draw conclusions incisively, critically and with fairness to other points of view. The college desires to have a "community of seekers" comprised of individuals dedicated to shared and corporate search as an important part of their lives. Such a community can come about only when there is diversity throughout the institution including a diversity of racial and cultural backgrounds, a diversity of older and younger perspectives, a diversity of beliefs and value orientations. As a community, Guilford addresses questions of moral responsibility, explores issues which are deeply felt but difficult to articulate, supports modes of personal fulfillment and cultivates respect for all individuals.

Guilford students tend to be politically aware and concerned about campus and community issues. Guilford students are involved in campus decisions in ways that contribute to their personal growth. Student opinion is respected and valued at Guilford, and students have a voice in all major college decisions, including setting tuition, deciding budgets and assisting faculty and administrators with strategic planning.

Some Guilford students choose to live in theme housing with other students who share a common interest or concern. During the year, housemates discuss mutual interests and collaborate on activities and projects that increase awareness of issues in the community. In recent years, theme houses at Guilford have focused on awareness of handicapped children, gender awareness and equality, Habitat for Humanity, self esteem of young children, men against sexual assault, Greensboro Beautiful (Ecology,) Guilford Geology Workshops for Children, substance abuse awareness, recycling and environmental concerns.

It is estimated that Guilford students perform more than 40,000 hours in community service each year. Students who volunteer at community agencies and area schools believe these opportunities are an important part of their educational experience. Through the program Project Community, students work with several organizations, including Delancey Street, a nationally recognized two-year drug and alcohol rehabilitation program that serves as an alterative to the prison system; Turning Point, the rape crisis and child abuse agency of Greensboro; Gateway Center, a facility that educates the physically challenged. Students collaborated with faculty and three community service agencies to develop an interdisciplinary course on homelessness, which will be offered for the first time in the fall of 1996.

It has become tradition for Guilford students to spend their semester breaks traveling to communities across the United States helping people stricken by natural disasters or those who face the challenge of poverty. For many years, students have helped residents of Johns Island, South Carolina, with construction and renovation work on housing and area facilities. Other semester break work trips have brought Guilford students to the Cherokee Indian Reservation in North Carolina, to southern Florida to assist residents recover from the damage from Hurricane Andrew, and to Houston, Texas, to rebuild a community center.

One of the most important advantages of a Guilford education is that students have the opportunity to work directly with faculty. Faculty who are involved with research projects will often include their students in the project. To his courses in criminal justice, Barton Parks brings his own extensive experience of the judicial system. He helped start a successful dispute settlement center which mediates everything from neighborhood disagreements to criminal charges. Student interns are active participants in the operation of the center.

Psychology professor Richard Zweigenhaft, coauthor of *Jews in the Protestant Establishment and Blacks in the White Establishment?*, is also an avid basketball player and has developed a course on the psychology of sports. Zweigenhaft encourages students to undertake independent research projects. A recent collaboration between Zweigenhaft and student Michael Cody on *The Self-Monitoring of Black Students on a Predominantly White Campus* was published in the Journal of Social Psychology.

A collaborative program entitled Teaching in the Multicultural Classroom was developed by Guilford student Darlene Whitley and sociology/anthropology professor Vernie Davis. The program, presented to teachers and principals in the Guilford County, North Carolina public schools, presented anthropological concepts and examined cultural situations faced by teachers and administrators. The program encouraged teachers to use the multicultural makeup of a student body as a constructive resource.

# MAKING A DIFFERENCE STUDIES

## Geology

Physical Geography
Environmental Geology
Energy and Natural Resources
Crust of the Earth

Historical Geology
Marine Geology
Hydrology
Exploration Geophysics

- **Seminar West**   Summer course, including four weeks of camping and hiking, to study the American West. Geologic process of mountain building and erosion and their impact on man - history, prehistory, environment, literature and art.

## Justice and Policy Studies

Offers students study and participation in community service, focusing on the criminal justice system and related public service institutions, including community based organizations.

Intro to Criminal Justice
Trust and Violence
Conflict Resolution Strategies
Criminal Justice Policy and Practice
Public Administration

Youth in Trouble
Building Community
Ethics in Justice and Policy Studies
Media and Community Relations
Punishment and Corrections

- **Family Violence**   Wife abuse, child sexual abuse and rape/sexual assault. Causal factors, psychology of victim and offender, societal impact, treatment & intervention strategies.

## Religious Studies

Myth, Dream, Metaphor
Religion and Social Issues
Islam
Feminist Theology
Primitive Myth

History of Religion in America
Quakerism
Hebrew Bible
East Asian Religions
History of Christianity

## Peace and Conflict Studies

Peace, War and Justice
Community and Commitment
Conflict and Cooperation
Revolutionary Central America
International Politics

Nonviolence: Theories and Practice
Personal and Social Change
Women/Body/Voice
Personal and Social Change
International Economics

## Education Studies

Education Inquiry
Learning and Teaching
Processes of Elementary Teaching

Contemporary/Historical Issues in Education
Field Study in Cross-Cultural Education
Processes of Secondary & K-12 Teaching

**Sports Medicine    Women's Studies    3/2 Physician Ass't Training/ Wake Forest U.
Environmental Studies    3/2 Pre-forestry/ Duke    Economics    International Studies**

Student body: 30% state, 48% male, 52% female, 10% minority, 15% transfer
Faculty: 60% male, 40% female, 4% minority    Average number of students in first year class: 14
Costs: $21,000    Apply By 12/1 (early decision) 2/1 (regular decision)
• Individualized Majors  • Team Teaching  • Vegetarian Meals  • Eight Int'.l Programs
• Recycling policies in effect  • 50% of students engaged in community service  • Theme Housing
• Life Experience Credit  • Third-World Service Learning

Use form in back to contact: Director of Admission
Guilford College   5800 W. Friendly Ave.   Greensboro, NC 27410
(800) 992-7759    (336) 316-2100
admission@rascal.guilford.edu    www.guilford.edu

# HAMPSHIRE COLLEGE

1200 Students    Amherst, Massachusetts

In 1970, 200 students came to Amherst, Massachusetts to take part in an extraordinary new experiment in liberal arts education. Hampshire College has since grown to 1,200 students, and its position in higher education is secure. But true to Hampshire's original philosophy, an atmosphere of challenging accepted ideas, of intellectual and social ferment, still permeates the college.

Hampshire's innovations include the breaking down of barriers between academic disciplines, and fostering an integrated, dynamic view of knowledge; actively involving students in their own education; and connecting academic work to "real-world" issues and problems. All faculty and courses are organized into four Schools: Humanities and Arts, Social Science, Natural Science, and Communications and Cognitive Science. An anthropology professor daily rubs elbows with historians, psychologists, and political scientists. Faculty trained in different disciplines often "team up" and offer courses together. For instance "Women's Bodies, Women's Lives," was taught by a physiologist, a writer, and a sociologist.

Hampshire's founders were convinced that students would be better prepared for a rapidly changing society if they were also expected to carry out research and independent projects, and pursue internships and field studies. The student headed to law school works for a Congressional representative in Washington; a student concerned about the problems of refugees goes to SE Asia to work for the Red Cross.

Virtually all Hampshire students incorporate internships or other off-campus experiences into their academic programs. The Program in Public Service and Social Change assists students in finding placements in human service agencies or social action organizations. The college maintains close ties with all study and service programs in Third World Countries. Students are also required to perform community service, and to incorporate a non-Western or multicultural perspective into their work.

Students collaborate with faculty mentors to design an individualized program of study. Concentrations typically embrace several subjects; a student concentrating in environmental studies might take courses in biology, politics, Third World studies, even literature. She might work at a local conservation area, or conduct research on the effect of habitat destruction on local wildlife populations. In the absence of course requirements, students design programs that reflect their most passionate interests and concerns. The typical question, "What's your major?" might elicit "Well, I'm interested in health care in Third World countries, so I'm taking pre-med courses and studying African history and reading about the philosophy of medicine. Next term I'll be working in a rural clinic in Nigeria."

Some 85% of Hampshire students go on to graduate or professional school. Almost 20% run their own businesses, everything from restaurants to yogurt companies, to design-and-construction firms. Still others are working as physicians, writers, lawyers, college professors, scientists, school teachers and social workers. Having learned at Hampshire to take charge of their own lives, and to change the society around them, the college's alumni are engaged in doing just that.

# MAKING A DIFFERENCE STUDIES

## School of Natural Science  Programs in Agricultural Studies, Coastal & Marine Studies, and Women and Science

Agricultural program centers around facilities which include the Farm Center, bioshelter, a hydroponic labs, solar aquaculture, nitrogen fixation, and passive solar energy. Women and Science studies scientific theories about women and the impact of these theories on women's lives, health nutrition, and how women's participation in science might impact science.

| | |
|---|---|
| Marine Ecology | Pollution and Our Environment |
| Environmental Science and Politics | Sustainable Agriculture |
| Agroecology | The Science of Disarmament |
| Biology of Poverty | Health in America Before Columbus |
| Women's Bodies, Women's Lives | Land Degradation and Society |
| Agricultural Research &Technology in Developing Countries | |

## School of Social Science

Focuses on problem areas which reflect their interest in social institutions and social change.

| | |
|---|---|
| Culture, Gender, and Self | Poverty, Patriarchy, and Population |
| Poverty and Wealth | Politics of the Abortion Rights Movement |
| Third World Development | Psychology of Oppression |
| Land Degradation and Society | World Food Crisis |
| Inter-American Environmental Economics | Making Social Change |

## School of Humanities and Arts

| | |
|---|---|
| Art and Revolution | Women's Lives, Women's Stories |
| Technoculture | The Harlem Renaissance |
| Caribbean Crossing | Feminist Challenges to Art History |
| Chicano Narratives | Ethnic Expression in America |
| Latin America History Through Fiction | Gender, Race, and Class: U.S. History |

## School of Communications & Cognitive Science

| | |
|---|---|
| Culture Industries | Moral Theory |
| Producing Cable and Community TV | Culture and Human Development |
| Political Culture | Developmental Language & Learning Disorders |
| Moral Issues and the World of Work | Eurocentrism in Philosophy |

## Population and Development

How fertility, mortality, and migration issues are shaped by colonialism, gender inequality, the organization of economic production and international division of labor.

• Faculty Bio **Benjamin Wisner** has worked for 21 years in Africa, Asia, and Brazil with popular struggles to satisfy need for food, water and sanitation, health care, shelter, and education. Recent research has concerned socially appropriate technology for co-production of food and biomass energy, land reform, and refugee settlements.

## Education Studies    Food, Resources, & Int'l Policy    Third World Studies
## Feminist Studies    Peace & World Security    Civil Liberties & Public Policy

Student Body: 50% male, 50% female, 9% minority
Faculty: 50% female, 50% male, 14% minority
Costs: $30,715    Apply by 2/1
Hampshire College has 5000 sq. ft. of solar collectors for energy conservation.
• Required Community Service  • Team Teaching  • Individualized Majors  • Vegetarian Meals

Use form in back to contact: Director of Admissions
Hampshire College      Amherst, MA 01002
(413) 549-4600

# UNIVERSITY OF HAWAII AT MANOA

13,000 Undergraduates    Honolulu, Hawaii

The University of Hawaii at Manoa is located in Honolulu's lush green Manoa Valley. Much like Hawaiian cities, the mix of people from all over the world, bring with them the cultures and lifestyles of many lands, insuring a stimulating experience that goes beyond simple education. The cultural diversity of the student body insures an appetite for international culture, and the university community serves as the venue for year-round plays, concerts, dance and films.

Throughout it's history, the university has emphasized studies related to the distinctive geographical and cultural attributes of Hawaii. Geographical location generates interest in oceanography, marine sciences, Asian and Pacific studies, and interdisciplinary studies of tropical environments, problems, and resources. The physical characteristics of Hawaii focus academic attention in such areas as tsunami research, volcanology, astronomy, and astrophysics. The state's multi-ethnic culture and close ties to Asia create a favorable environment for the study of diverse cultural systems, including subjects such as linguistics, genetics, philosophy, and interracial relations.

Hawaii's incredible environment provides a focal point for much of the pioneering research done by the university's natural scientists. In the human realm, the university's social scientists are uniquely able to inquire deeply in the impact on people's knowledge of Hawaii's unique blending of cultures, heritage and the social life of these islands.

The Hawaii Institute of Marine Biology, a research institute within the School of Ocean and Earth Science and Technology, provides facilities and services for support of research and education in marine biology. Research into the life processes of marine plants, animals and microbes covers a broad range of topics, including coral reef biology and ecology, tropical aquaculture, behavior of reef animals, management of marine ecosystems, and coastal biogeochemical processes. HIMB is unique in its close proximity to a well-equipped laboratory, to a major university campus, and to sub-tropical environments.

The School of Hawaiian, Asian, and Pacific Studies, established in 1987, brings together nine research centers related to geographic regions in Asia and the Pacific, and is establishing new projects related to cross-cultural research topics. The centers for Chinese, Japanese, and Southeast Asian studies are the largest in the nation; the Center for the Soviet Union in the Pacific and Asian Region and the centers for Hawaiian, Pacific Islands, and Philippine studies are the only ones of their kind. SHAPS and its centers sponsor lectures, colloquia, conferences, film festivals, and special events, such as the Grand Kabuki, Chinese martial arts performances, and the SE Asian Studies Summer Institute.

The University of Hawaii at Manoa has made a commitment to the study of Asia far greater than any other university, in terms of numbers of languages taught, areas studied and faculty specialists employed. This provides a unique opportunity to students interested in Asia. Interdisciplinary programs draw upon the disciplines of anthropology, art, economics, geography, history, religion, sociology, theater and dance.

# MAKING A DIFFERENCE STUDIES

## Botany
Plants and Pollution
Plants in the Hawaiian Environment
Ethnobotany
Natural History of Hawaiian Islands
Hawaiian Ethnobotany

Resource Mgm't & Conservation in Hawaii
Ecology of Hawaiian Coastal Algae
Inside Tropical Rainforests
Vegetation Ecology
Plant Evolutionary Diversity

## General Science Enviro. Science; Island Environments; History & Nature of Science
Intro to Science: Hawaiian Environments
Technology and Ecology Forum
Endangered Species
Man and Energy in the Island Ecosystem
Natural Science as a Human Activity

Women and Genetics in Society
Environmental Issues
The Atoll
Human Role in Environmental Change
Island Ecosystems

## Geography  Tracks in Enviro. Studies & Policies; Resource Systems; Population, Urbanization & Regional Devlp't; Remote Sensing & Computer Applications
Resource Management in Asia-Pacific
Ecological Concepts and Planning
Tropical Agrarian Systems
Plants, People and Ecosystems
Conservation and Resource Management

Planning in Developing Countries of Asia
Atmospheric Pollution
Environment and Culture
Hazard and Human Decision
Energy Resources

## American Studies
Diversity in American Life
Filipino Americans
American Environments: Survey
Nonethnic Minorities
Race and Racism in America

Japanese-American Experience
Contemporary Hawaiian Issues
Television in American Life
American Ideas of Nature
Native America: Hawaiians & White Conflict

## Anthropology
Technology and Culture
Pacific Island Cultures
Ecological Anthropology
Polynesian Cultures
Pre-European Hawaii

Aggression, War and Peace
Ethnographic Field Techniques
Medical Anthropology
Micronesian Cultures
Melanesian Cultures

## Agronomy and Soil Sciences
This department is one of only a few in the nation with a special commitment to linkages with the developing world, and the only one fully dedicated to crops and soils of the tropics.

Agroforestry Systems
Soil, erosion and Conservation
Soil Physics
Lab Techniques in Microbial Ecology

Pasture Mgm't (tropical emphasis)
Soil Fertility
Farming Systems Research & Development
Techniques of Plant/Soil Analysis

**Civil Engineering     Hawaiian Studies     Entomology     Pacific Island Studies**
**Social Work     Peace Studies     Women's Studies     Zoology**

Student Body: 90% state, 57% female, 43% male, 58% Asian-Amer., 7% Native Amer., 10% int'l.
Faculty: 60% male, 40% female
Tuition: Residents $8,294   Non-Residents $14,724      Apply By 6/15

Use form in back to contact: Director of Admissions
University of Hawaii at Manoa       Honolulu, HI 96822
(808) 956-8975

# HOBART AND WILLIAM SMITH COLLEGES

Hobart 900 men    William Smith 950 women
Geneva, New York

Hobart College for men and William Smith College for women provide a distinguished liberal arts program within a co-ordinate system that establishes equality as the model for women and men, and offers a curriculum that promotes this model. Recognizing that psychological needs and socialization of women and men may differ in our culture, the methods employed to unite the social with the academic experiences will differ somewhat for women and men.

The history of H&WS is a record of bringing together the traditional and the innovative. The Colleges have been leaders in the development of general curricula, interdisciplinary teaching, and the interrelation between the rigorous pursuit of intellectual goals and reflection on their social consequences. Themes of gender awareness and global awareness span the curriculum, and inform the lives of students. All first-year students are required to attend acquaintance rape prevention workshops in single-sex settings. The men's workshops organized and facilitated by upper-class men are nationally recognized as a ground-breaking program.

The academic program of the Colleges stress the interconnections of knowledge and the dependence of one field upon another. Hobart and William Smith have sought professors whose interests span many fields. It is not unusual for professors to teach courses in two or more departments on a regular basis.

Most students of Hobart and William Smith Colleges will have had some kind of off-campus/international learning experience by the time they graduate. Whether the experience is teaching literacy skills to Native Americans in South Dakota, studying haiku in Tokyo, or living with a Russian family in Siberia, students at the colleges understand the value of "breaking away" to discover something about themselves and others. Students are also encouraged to look into the programs of Partnership for Service Learning, which offers terms in Jamaica, Ecuador and England. By enabling students to encounter the cultural differences between our own society and other parts of the country and the world, they become sensitized to major world issues and are encouraged to reflect on their own cultural identity

The outdoor recreation program provides both structured and unstructured recreational opportunities for outdoor enthusiasts. The program sponsors a combination of courses, clinics, and outings throughout the school year. Hiking and backpacking, orienteering, kayaking, winter camping, Nordic skiing, alpine skiing, horseback riding, canoeing, sailing, cycling and ice skating are available.

The Colleges maintains a 108 acre biological field station and preserve for ecological studies, with 40 ponds, a hardwood forest, swamps, marshes, and a large variety of wildlife. The HWS Explorer, is a 65 foot vessel for student and faculty research activities.

H&WS's Environmental Studies Summer Youth Institute is a 2 week interdisciplinary program for high school students. The program is an introduction to a variety of environmental issues and perspectives on nature. Students do in research on the Explorer and learn about a range of topics in environmental policy, economics and ethics.

# MAKING A DIFFERENCE STUDIES

## Environmental Studies

The Natural Science Perspective
Natural Resource and Energy Economics
Sociology of Environmental Issues
Population Crisis in the Third World
Natural & Agric. Ecosystems of Mexico

The Social Science Perspective
Senior Integrative Experience
Technology and Society
Environmental Geology
Philosophy of Natural Science

- **The Humanistic Perspective**  Examines ways in which theories of culture and the significance of cultural artifacts have been use to examine America attitudes toward the natural world. Designed to introduce the student of American culture to methods of cultural analysis. Provides a chronological overview of the evolution of American views of the natural world, touching on attitudes towards Native Americans, natural resources, gender and nature, human uses of animals and development of agribusiness.

## First Year Seminars

War and Society in America
Adolescence in Cross Cultural Perspective
Food Systems: Deciphering Food Systems at the Global, National, and Individual Levels
Resisting the Melting Pot: -Construction of Identities in the U.S.

Educational Opportunities: 40 Year Assessment
Prejudice, Discrimination and Responsibility

## American Studies

American Indian Texts and Testimonies
Sex and Power
African-American History

The Education of Minorities
Women in American History
Slavery in the Americas

Patterns: The Shaping of Natural and Human Realities in American Cultures

- **Discovery/Invasion: The Native American Experience of the European Colonization of N. America**  History of the Americas usually is examined from the perspective of the Europeans who invaded and conquered Native Americans, rather than from that of the indigenous people who were subjugated. Impact of European trade, disease, settlement, and warfare on the native populations of N. America, and policies of land acquisition and "Indian" removal developed by the U S government, and of the wars against the native peoples of the Great Plains. Special attention will be given to the ecological effects of these processes.

## Anthropology and Sociology

Feminist Social Theory
Sociology of Minorities
Action Anthropology

Environment and Culture: Cultural Ecology
Sex Roles: A Cross-Cultural Perspective
Third World Women & Political Mobilization

Pattern and Process in Ancient Mesoamerican Urbanism

- **Sociology of Environmental Issues**  Technological fix and social value definitions of environmental issues, how occupational and residence patterns are involved with the perception of and response to environmental issues, urban policies as aspects of environmental issues, stress involved with current life styles and occupations, the personal, group, and social responses to resolve environmental problems.

## Philosophy

Justice and Equality
Economic Justice
Facts and Values
Morality and Self-Interest
Philosophy of Medicine

Philosophy and Feminism
Environmental Ethics
Liberty and Community
Experience and Knowing
Critical Thinking & Argumentative Writing

## Economics

Environmental Economics

Women and International Development

Political Economy of Co-op Production

Environmental Policy

Women in the Economy

Natural Resource & Energy Economics

Political Economy of Race

The Political Economy of the Right

## Religious Studies

Religion and Class Struggle

Toward Inclusive Theology

New Heavens, New Earths

Therapy, Myth and Religion

History of East European Jewry 1648-1945

God, Gender, and the Unconscious

The Question of God/Goddess: Metaphoric and Philosophical Origins

- **Sacred Space** Comparative approach to explore the meaning, function, and structure of space for religious persons. "Wanderings" of the Australian aborigines, habitation modes of American Indians, the Peyote pilgrimage of the Huichol Indians of Mexico, the Hindu Temple, the Buddhist Stupa and the individual as cosmos in yoga.

## Off-Campus Study

**Geneva, Switzerland** The term focuses on issues that confront international organizations headquartered in Geneva, including UN agencies, and non-governmental agencies such as religious, human rights, women's, and youth groups.

The Struggle for Justice and Human Rights in a Global Perspective

- **Conflict, Conflict Resolution, and the Struggle for World Peace** The emphasis here is on public international law, on its reciprocal relationship to the U.N. structure, and on the problem of conflict regulation within the U.N. structure and outside of it. We look at the origins and current structure of public international law, at the U.N. structure, and at conflict-management techniques at the international level.

**Dominican Republic** Semester length program is designed to offer students interested in the Spanish-speaking Caribbean and Latin America the opportunity to study on site an Hispanic culture and a society of the Caribbean region from an interdisciplinary perspective.

The Dominican Economy                    Africana-Latino Studies: Social Problems - D.R.

- **An Education in the Dominican Republic** This seminar is conducted in Spanish, and is accompanied by a community workplace assignment to be chosen from teaching English as a second language; rural community development; teaching/recreation for street children; or work in a community health clinic.

### Education      Gay & Lesbian Studies      Geoscience      History

Student Body: 49% state, 52% female, 48% male, 14% minority, 2% int'l.

Faculty: 60% male, 40% female

Costs: $30,243      Apply by 2/1

• UN Semester   • Individualized Majors   • Study Abroad   • 21 Service Learning Courses

• Team Teaching   • Interdisciplinary Classes and Majors   • Theme Housing   • Vegetarian Meals

Use form in back to contact: Director of Admissions

Hobart College and William Smith Colleges

Geneva, NY 14456

Hobart (800) 852-2256      William Smith (800) 245-0100

hoadm@hws.edu      wsa@hws.edu

# HUMBOLDT STATE UNIVERSITY

6,675 Undergraduates    Arcata, California

Set between redwood groves and the Pacific Ocean 275 miles north of San Francisco, Humboldt State University is a campus of choice, not convenience. The northernmost institution in the California State University system, the campus tends to attract from afar students who are more adventurous and self-reliant. The intimate, natural setting and small class sizes foster friendliness and close faculty/student relationships. Undergraduates enjoy uncommon privileges: broad access to computers, equipment, and laboratories including the university forest, greenhouse, marine laboratory, and electron microscope. HSU is traditionally known for its sciences and natural resources programs such as forestry and wildlife

The intimacy of the campus mirrors the sense of community along California's North Coast. In the small-town atmosphere, students learn they can make a direct, positive difference in the lives of others. And they do, through programs for senior citizens, recycling, science outreach, legal counseling, health education, and other concerns. Many students acquire a long-lasting sense of social commitment, as evidenced by Humboldt's historically high proportion of graduates who enter the Peace Corps.

The University welcomes the challenges and opportunities of a diverse and rapidly changing society. To this end, it is a community striving to value diversity, to be inclusive, and to respect alternative paradigms of behavior and value systems. The mission of Humboldt State includes the development of a fundamental understanding of the interdependent web of life; and the cultivation of the capacity of individuals for self-initiative, self-fulfillment, and autonomous and responsible action.

Humboldt State has a remarkable array of resources. Students from fisheries, oceanography, geology, biology, and other majors get a chance to test experiments and work on research projects at the university's Marine Laboratory in the coastal town of Trinidad, not far from the main campus. The nearby bay and Pacific Ocean provide rocky and sandy intertidal and subtidal habitats for further study. HSU also has a seagoing vessel available for the primary purpose of providing instructional experiences on the ocean. Students also find instructional and research opportunities at a 300-acre Dunes Preserve, managed by HSU in behalf of the Nature Conservancy. The dunes, bounded by the Pacific and the River Slough, contain rare natural coastal habitats, where research can be conducted in a protected ecosystem. A recently acquired 4,500 acre ranch is being used by students in a wide variety of disciplines.

At the edge of Humboldt Bay is a 150 acre sanctuary which benefits students in botany, fisheries, environmental resources, engineering, biology, wildlife, and natural resources interpretation. Among the projects are a national model natural wastewater treatment process designed by a HSU professor; a co-generation system using methane digesters; and an aquaculture program devoted to rearing salmon, trout, and oysters in treated wastewater. Students interested in appropriate technology have a unique opportunity at the Campus Center for Appropriate Technology. Students combine theory and practice at the center, a live-in, working demonstration home, including photovoltaic and wind electric systems, a solar hot water system, a greenhouse passive heating system, a composting privy, a graywater system, and organic gardens.

# MAKING A DIFFERENCE STUDIES

## Environmental Resources Engineering
Principles of Ecology
Environmental Health Engineering
Environmental Impact Assessment
Solid Waste Management
Introduction to Design
Renewable Energy Power Systems
Solar Thermal Engineering
Air Quality Management

## Forestry  Track in Forest Resource Conservation
Wilderness Area Management
Forest Resources Protection
Natural Resource Management in Parks
Forest Ecosystems and People
Remote Sensing & Geographic Info. Systems
Advanced Forest Ecology
Forest Administration
The Forest Environment

## Oceanography
General Oceanography
Sampling Techniques and Field Studies
Estuarine Ecology
Beach & Nearshore Processes
Solid Earth Geophysics
Biological Oceanography
Physical Oceanography
Marine Primary Production
Zooplankton Ecology
Field Cruise

## Environmental Science  Track in Environmental Ethics
Environmental Ethics
Environmental Politics
Appropriate Technology
Case Studies in Environmental Ethics
Dispute Resolution
Water Pollution Biology
Technology and the Environment
Sociology of Wilderness
The Conservation Ethic

## Appropriate Technology Minor Especially useful for Peace Corps or overseas development work.
Whole Earth Engineering
Technology and the Environment
Politics of Appropriate Technology in the Third World
Appropriate Technology
Politics of Sustainable Society

## Natural Resources Tracks in Interpretation and Planning
Natural Resource Economics
Oral Interpretation
Natural Resources Public Relations
Intro. to Natural Resources Interpretation
Resource Planning in Rural Communities
Nature Writing
Intertidal Ecology
Interpretive Graphics
Natural Resources and Recreation
Environmental Impact Assessment

## Water Resource Policy
Forest and Range Soils Management
Systemic Geography
River Morphology
Watershed Management
Western Water Politics
Water Resource Development
Intro to Water Quality
Water Law

### Rangeland Resources  Peace & Conflict  Fisheries  Social Work  Wildlife  Enviro. Toxicology
### Indian Natural Resource, Science & Engineering  Indian Teacher & Ed. Personnel

Student Body: 96% state, 48% men, 52% female, 20% minority, 12% transfer

Faculty: 64% male, 36% female, 14% minority  Avg. 1st. year class size: 24

Costs: Residents $7,638  Non-resident tuition $246 add'l. per credit  Apply by 11/30

• Prior Learning Credit  • Individualized Majors  • Service-Learning  • Theme Housing

Use form in back to contact: Admissions and School Relations
Humboldt State University  Arcata, CA 95521
(707) 826-4402
www.humboldt.edu

# IONA COLLEGE

2,555 Undergraduates    New Rochelle, NY

Iona College takes its name from the isle of Iona located in the Inner Hebrides just off the west coast of Scotland. It was to this tiny island that the Irish monk Columba came in A.D. 563 to establish an abbey from which missionaries went forth to teach and evangelize. The island of Iona became a center of faith and culture that contributed significantly to the civilization of Western Europe. In 1940, the Congregation of Christian Brothers founded Iona College in New Rochelle, New York. The name Iona signifies the college's fundamental purpose; a synthesis of culture and faith and faith of life. Enriched by the cultural multiplicity within our society, the college further expresses this tradition in terms of action on behalf of justice and of participation in the transformation of the world.

There is a vision for Iona that its constituents be engaged in the task of building a concerned community. Iona believes that through this experience its members will be better prepared to work toward such a community within their families, places of employment, and neighborhoods, as well as in the nation and the world.

Iona has as its purpose the education of its students through intellectual discipline and a developing awareness of self, structured upon increasing understanding of their cultural, religious, and social heritage. Iona endeavors to develop informed, critical, and responsive individuals who are equipped to participate actively in culture and society.

Iona's Center for Campus Ministries offers vast opportunities for students in the areas of Peace and Justice Education and volunteer service activities. Iona has dedicated student groups such as Amnesty International, Project Earth, and Pax Christi that put a focus on helping to change the world today. As part of a unique commitment to creating positive change, there are on-campus activities such as environmental awareness, multicultural education and a Holocaust remembrance. Iona's commitment to assume a leadership role as an institution dedicated to Peace and Justice is evident every November as the college celebrates the "Week of the Peacemaker" recognizing the great works of peacemakers throughout history. The week-long celebration includes lectures, seminars, and performing arts events. Past visitors on this week include Mother Theresa, Coretta Scott King, the Dalai Lama, and geologian Thomas Berry.

Another natural way for students to express their faith is through service activities. Iona students serve communities locally at soup kitchens, Project S.W.A.P. (Stop Wasting Abandoned Property,) an inner-city rebuilding project; the Midnight Run, in which students bring food, clothing, and companionship to NYC's homeless; and the Lord's Pantry, which involves students delivering meals to homebound patients with AIDS. Students serve regionally as well, travelling during winter and spring breaks to Appalachia to assist in building homes in poor communities while learning about the history and culture of the Appalachian region. There is also a semester long program in Bonita Springs, Florida, where students work with migrant workers. Iona students even serve internationally and have travelled to El Salvador to live in community with the people of El Salvador while helping to build cinder block homes. There are service learning credit options for many of these programs.

# MAKING A DIFFERENCE STUDIES

## Biology Track in Ecology
The Department has a collaborative internship for students to do research with the Osborn Laboratories of Marine Sciences of the NY Zoological Society at the NY Aquarium.

Ecology
Oceanography
Invertebrate Zoology
The Life of Green Plants
Genetics

Microbiology
Microbial Ecology
Science, Technology and Society
Parasitology
Assessing the Environmental Future

## Peace and Justice
All faculty have made a commitment to directly address issues of peace and justice in a global and/or ecological perspective. Three week summer intensive courses in Ireland and with Native Americans of the Lakota tribe in South Dakota.

War and Peace in American Society
Sacred Cosmology
Ethics and Business
Contemporary Peacemakers
The Homeless of New York
Service Learning: Appalachia

Conflict Solving for Children
Race to Save the Planet
Health Care Ethics
Latin American Politics
Environmental Health
Service Learning: Urban Immersion

- **Iona Peace Institute in Ireland**   The opportunity to experience Ireland's social and political realities, its spirituality and cultural achievements in an integrated and lively way. Analysis of the roots of injustice, notably Ireland's "Great Famine" and "troubles," and exploration of possible routes to resolution of injustice and reconciliation.

## Economics
Health Economics
Economics of Labor
Urban Economics
Public Finance
Economics of Global Resources
Changing Role of Women in the Economic Development of the U.S.

Economics of the Arts: Performing & Visual
Economics of Poverty and Discrimination
Women in the Labor Market
Assessing the Energy Future
Environmental Econ. & Sustainable Develop't

## Political Science
American Political Thought
Politics and Criminal Justice
Politics and the Mass Media
Third World: Politics of Development
Soviet and E. European Systems

International Relations
Peace and Justice in the Contemporary World
Campaign Politics
Latin American Politics
Public Administration

### Social Work   Gerontology   Urban Studies
### Women's Studies   International Studies   Philosophy

Student Body: 88% state, 52% male, 48% female, 26% minority, 5% transfer
Faculty: 66% male, 34% female, 3% minority   Average # of students in first year class: 22
Costs: $18,330   Rolling Admissions
• Service-Learning Classes  • Life Experience Credit
• Team Teaching  • Vegetarian Meals  • Weekend/Evening Classes

Use form in back to contact: Office of Undergraduate Admissions
Iona College   715 North Ave.   New Rochelle, NY 10801
(800) 231-IONA
www.iona.edu/

# FRIENDS WORLD PROGRAM
## LONG ISLAND UNIVERSITY
250 in FWP    Southampton, New York

"While all life is being threatened by increasing military might and ecological ruin, a rising tide of quiet voices from all parts of the world reminds us that only knowledge inspired by justice and compassion has the power to save us and save the life sustaining power of the earth. We must listen to and learn from such farsighted scholars, professionals and others and search for those emerging concepts - globally applicable and globally acceptable - which can provide a basis for a saner future"
Morris Mitchell, First President, Friends World College

Very few colleges offer a program like Friends World; an experiential education by total immersion into other cultures. The program stands alone in two important aspects. The first is the faith in students. Friends World believes that intelligent young men and women have the ability, and the right to be deeply involved in determining their own educational plans. FW trusts them to be capable of gathering, absorbing, and synthesizing knowledge through their own experiences.

The second is Friends Worlds belief that all nations of the world need citizens who are educated to see beyond their own borders, and to recognize that individuals share in the responsibility for the future of the planet.

With eight centers and campuses around the world and a student body and faculty drawn from twenty-two countries, Friends World Program is uniquely international. The Program is designed for students who want to assume greater responsibility for their own lives and learning. The Program's worldwide facilities offer students the opportunity to live, study, and work in two or more foreign cultures while earning an accredited B.A. degree; to design individual programs of study based on their personal interests and goals; and to combine academic study with field experience and internships. While acquiring a balanced liberal arts education, including fluency in one or more foreign languages and an appreciation of the culture and values of several world regions, students have an opportunity to carry out in-depth study and gain practical experience in their chosen field. In addition, they develop a deeper understanding of and a broader perspective on current world issues.

In addition to the North American Center, located in Southampton, NY, there are centers in England, China, Japan, Kenya, Costa Rica, Israel, and India. The goal of Friends World is to encourage students to treat the entire world as a university, to take the most urgent human problems as the basis of their curriculum and, to seek designs together for a more human future.

While students do not have a major, in the traditional sense, they develop individual study plans in such areas as African-American studies, agriculture, animal behavior/wildlife studies, anthropology, archaeology, area studies (African, Asian, European, Latin American, and Middle Eastern,) communications (film, journalism, photography, and video,) community health, community organization and development, criminal justice and comparative legal systems, dance, economics, education, environmental studies/ecology, fine arts and crafts, holistic and natural healing, human services, Native American studies, nutrition, peace studies and conflict resolution, philosophy, psychology/counseling, rainforest ecology, religion, sociology, Third World development, United Nations studies, and women's studies.

The learning process is a carefully planned combination of academic study and field experience. The Program involves classroom study, immersion language training (often including homestays,) and independent fieldwork in at least two foreign countries. Under the guidance of an international faculty, students develop skills and competence in a major academic field by combining book research, hands-on experience, and analytical writing. Friends World students typically spend at least two years abroad working with center faculty to design and carry out field studies (such as internships, apprenticeships, and investigative research) in several cultural settings. For example, they have studied Gandhian nonviolence in India, desert agriculture in Israel, animal behavior in Kenya, and holistic healing and acupuncture in Japan. Students have worked with a feminist publishing cooperative in Paris, interned with a Congressman in Washington, researched agrarian economic development in Costa Rica, apprenticed with a modern dance company in Munich, worked with the United Nations in New York, and interned with a legal center in London. Many other projects range from anthropology to zoology.

Founded in 1965, sponsored by the New York Yearly Meeting of Friends (Quaker,) Friends World is non-sectarian. About 150 students are in the program. Students come from all over the U.S., and other countries and represent diverse ethnic and economic backgrounds. Each first year class contains between 40 and 60 students. FW accepts transfer students as well as students from other colleges who wish to study abroad for 1 or 2 terms; this is a popular option. FW also offers an associate program for non-degree seeking students who wish to study abroad.

As a record of their learning growth, students maintain portfolios of their work. The portfolio replaces the usual requirements of assignments and examinations in serving as a means of evaluating and awarding credits. Students do not receive grades, nor are they required to take traditional classes. Usually 15-18 credits are earned by successfully completing each semester's work.

On the New York campus dining facilities include a wide variety of choices for vegetarians. Outdoorsy types are drawn to the rural, seaside location on Long Island's East End. Recreation options include sailing, swimming, biking, camping, surfing, and enjoying some of the most beautiful beaches on the East Coast.

Environmental awareness is high on the Friends World Southampton Campus. Various groups in the Long Island area are active in land preservation and organic farming. The Shinnecock Indian Reservation is across the street from campus, offering students the ability to become involved with Native American issues. The campus is just two hours from New York city which provides access to museums, libraries, performances and international and social activist organizations.

# MAKING A DIFFERENCE STUDIES

**Experiential projects, field studies, seminars and workshops.**

Through the North American Center, students projects (15 credit) have included:

- Apprenticing in herbal medicine at The New Mexico Herbal Center, Santa Fe.
- Production assistant and actress at the avant-garde Nuyorican Poet's Cafe, N.Y. City
- Legal investigative assistant at Lawyer's Committee for Human Rights, Washington DC
- Creating a forum for patient-doctor dialogue at Albert Einstein Hospital, NYC
- Working with refugees at the Central Amer. Solidarity Association, Cambridge, MA
- Environmental activism with NY Rain forest alliance, NYC
- Photography apprenticeship at The International Center of Photography, NYC
- Student teaching at East Harlem school at Exodus House, NYC
- Woman's issues and reproductive rights with National Organization for Women, Boston
- At the **South Asian Center, Bangalore, India** students have worked in rural development and health education, conservation research with the World Wildlife Fund , studied dance, meditation, Ayurvedic medicine and taught Tibetan children in Nepal.
- At the **Latin American Center, San Jose, Costa Rica,** students have interned at a zoo, done rainforest botanical studies, participated in community health & nutrition programs in Nicaragua, and done biological field research in Guatemala.
- Through the **East African Center in Kenya,** students studied village development, worked promoting appropriate technology, studied the historical role of women in Somalia, and learned about community health and traditional medicine in Nairobi.
- Students interning at the **Middle East Center in Jerusalem, Israel** have been archaeological field assistants, done an anthropological study of Bedouin women in Sinai, and studied arid-zone agriculture in the Negev.
- At the **China Center in Hangzhou,** studies have included "Calligraphy and Politics", the Origins of Chinese Buddhism, The Chinese Writer as Social Activist, and Korean Nationality in Jilin Province.
- Through the **European Center in London,** projects have included film and video internships, an apprenticeship to an environmental publisher in Ireland, a study of the role of women in Portugal and the history of French feminism from 1860 to 1940.
- At the **East Asian Center in Kyoto, Japan** projects include the study of integration of Western and Eastern medical practice, US foreign policy in regard to Korea and Indonesia, and business mgm't and quality control in Japan, Taiwan and Singapore.

**Field Advisors** Friends World students have their education enriched by working with many leading professionals and specialists. They have included Dr. Helen Caldicott, founder of Physicians for Social Responsibility; Jenny Watson of Amnesty International; and Bernadette Valley, Friends of the Earth, London.

Student Body: 20% state, 55% female, 45% male, 10% minority.5% int'l.
Faculty: 60% female, 40% male, 85% int'l.
Costs: $23,000   Rolling Admissions
Avg. # of students in first year classroom: 15   • Community Service
• Individualized Majors  • Interdisciplinary Classes  • Service Learning  • Team Teaching
•All Seminar Format  • Vegetarian Meals  • Life Experience Credit  • On-Campus Recycling
Use form in back to contact: Friends World Program, Office of Admissions
Southampton Campus, LIU     Southampton, NY 11968
(516) 287-8465

# SOUTHAMPTON COLLEGE
## LONG ISLAND UNIVERSITY
1,200 Students    Southampton, New York

Southampton College's commitment to the environment began when it opened in 1963.The seacoast location was chosen in order to have access to a wide variety of marine environments to study. Located on the eastern tip of Long Island, the college is in one of the most ecologically beautiful and fragile areas of the country. Bordering on the Atlantic Ocean with miles of barrier beach, dunes, salt marshes, bays, pine barrens, endangered wildlife, and a fragile groundwater aquifer, the area is a kind of living environmental laboratory. The delicate relationship between water, wind and land has made environmental protection a priority here since early times. Local groups like the Peconic Land Trust and national groups like the nature Conservancy have long been active in this area. In the midst of such natural beauty and activist spirit, Southampton is ideally suited to preparing young environmentalists to undertake the research, plan the programs and create the policies that will make a difference in our world.

Four different environmental study programs are offered: Environmental science, Environmental Education, Environmental Studies and Marine Science. All are designed to prepare students for graduate study or a professional career in environmental work. The programs are interdisciplinary, combining courses from several academic areas. The college is one of only two in the country with a marine research station on campus.

The Environmental Science Program is designed to give students the experience and training to compete successfully for positions in the environmental field, one of the fastest growing employment areas in the country. The program offers a unique multidisciplinary curriculum developed by faculty in consultation with employers in the environmental field. Southampton prepares young scientists to deal with some of the world's most critical environmental issues. In Environmental Biology, problems may include the effects of harmful substances on ecosystems, the deforestation of tropical forests, the loss of biodiversity and protection of wildlife resources. In Environmental Chemistry, scientists study chemical species in water, soil and air, solid and hazardous waste management, acid rain, ozone depletion and global cycling of toxic substances. Environmental geologists explore such topics as pollution of surface and ground water, coastal processes, sedimentation and erosion.

Southampton is one of the few institutions in America that offers an undergraduate degree in Marine Science. In the past 23 years, the Marine Science Program has graduated 28 Fulbright Scholars, an extraordinary record for a small school. A fully equipped Marine Station on Shinnecock Bay houses aquaculture and water quality labs, teaching labs and classrooms, and research equipment. The 44-foot Paumanok is used for coastal research while the Shinnecock, a 35-foot platform craft, is used for bay and estuary work. Every winter a group of marine science students and professors travels to the South Pacific for a four-credit course in Tropical Marine Biology to study in some of the most pristine and exotic areas of the world including Australia's Great Barrier Reef and the Fiji Islands.

The Environmental Studies major is designed for students who wish to prepare for careers in environmental planing and policy. The course work and field experiences are aimed at helping students develop essential tools and skills in economic analysis and decision making, natural resource management and computing. Students are offered a variety of opportunities for "hands-on" work with Suffolk County environmental planning offices. Suffolk County has some of the most progressive planning and health requirements in the nation, and continues to be a region with vast public commitment to environmental protection. Students who choose to focus on alternative agriculture and energy sources may take internships on agricultural projects coordinated by the Friends World program centers in Kenya, Costa Rica, India and Israel, or they may participate in an experimental garden project on campus.

Environmental Education is a new concentration in the Biology major that emphasized natural history and is designed for students who love the out-of-doors. The program's main emphasis is interpretive naturalism -- how we explain the natural world to others and how we use the natural environment to teach scientific principles and aspects of environmental concern. A significant aspect of the program is an outdoor experiential component. All students participate in experiences that provide outdoor leadership skills and expose them to work in environmental education or to study in unusual and challenging environments.

"SEAmester," a unique program at Southampton, allows students not only to study the ocean environment, but to live it. For nine weeks they travel on board the *Spirit of Massachusetts,*a 125-foot schooner modeled after a turn of the century fishing schooner. Students earn up to 16 academic credits while undertaking responsibility of crewing the gaff-rigged schooner. SEAmester students sail almost 3,000 miles, stopping at ports of call to examine unique ecosystems, or "heave to" for oceanographic stations at sea while studying coastal ecology, navigation, and marine science. Field work includes studies of the finest reefs in the Caribbean to the mudflats of North Carolina. A coral reef becomes an intense experience when you dive from the ship to do a field laboratory on the reef front. Fish anatomy becomes unforgettable as you perform a megadisssection on a fresh 12 foot tiger shark.

Southampton has the largest concentration of undergraduate marine and environmental science faculty on the East Coast. They bring a diversity of backgrounds and interests to the Environmental Programs -- from environmental planning and management, to marine natural products, from energy conservation to beach processes, environmental law to marine mammals.

Experience counts, and at Southampton College students get it through cooperative education and internship placements with land use planners and leading scientists in prestigious institutions throughout the country. Southampton emphasizes field work, giving students valuable experience and helping them make contacts before they graduate. Students may earn up to 16 credits in off-campus work. Typical placements include The U.S. Environmental Protection Agency, New York City Aquarium, Woods Hole Oceanographic Institute, Outward Bound and the National Wildlife Federation.

# MAKING A DIFFERENCE STUDIES

**Marine Science**  Tracks in Marine Biology; Chemistry; Geology

Introduction to Cell Biology
Quantitative Chemical Analysis
Geochemistry
Marine Operations and Research
Physical Oceanography
Coastal Processes and Marine Geology

Plant Biology
Marine Ecology
Biology of Plankton
Evolution
Mineralogy

**Environmental Science**  Tracks in Biology, Chemistry, Geology

Ecology
Environmental Inventory
Physical Geology
Environmental Law
Technical/Scientific Writing

Microcomputer Analysis and Report Writing
Biochemistry
Hydrology
Environmental Impact Assessment
Chemical Oceanography

- **Environmental Chemistry**  A multidisciplinary study of the sources, reactions, transport, effects and fates of chemical species in water, soil, and the atmosphere and the influence of human activity on these chemicals. Biogeochemical cycles, water pollution and treatment processes, microbial transformations of pesticides in soils, trace metals, sources and reactions of atmospheric pollutants and their effects.

## Environmental Studies

Society and the Environment
Environmental Sociology
Regional Planning & Enviro. Protection
Alternate Agriculture and Society
Field Biology

Public Policy
World Population Problems
Environmental Psychology
Ethics
Coastal Zone Resources

- **Global Environment**  Study of international relations from an environmental perspective and an analysis of efforts by the UN in improving the human environment.

## Sociology

Society Through film
Social Problems
Community Field Service
Social Minorities

The Community
Contemporary Issues in Drug Abuse
The Sociology of Aging
Cross-Cultural Child Development

- **Science, Technology and Society**  Historical, ethical, ecological and social perspectives are used to define the broader context in which the practice of science and the adaptation of technology occur. value free science is discussed with reference to the Nazi doctors and development of the atomic bomb. Technological displacement of workers, social responses to "killer" diseases, high risk and nuclear technologies.

### Environmental Education      Biology      Psychobiology

Student Body: 70% state, 42% male, 58% female, 15% minority, 22% transfer
Faculty: 76% male, 24% female, 2% minority     Avg # of students in first year classroom: 20
Costs: $22,100     Rolling Admissions
• Field Studies   • Co-op Work Study   • Student Environmental Audits   • Interdisciplinary Classes
• Required Community Service   • Life Experience Credit   • Vegetarian Meals

Use form in back to contact: Office of Admissions
LIU, Southampton     Southampton, NY 11968
(800) 548-7526
scinfo@sand.liu.edu     www.southampton.liu.edu

# UNIVERSITY OF MAINE

10,000 Undergraduates   Orono, Maine

In the spirit of its land-grant heritage, the University of Maine is committed to the creation and dissemination of knowledge to improve the lives of its students and Maine citizens in their full social, economic, and cultural diversity. In 1980 the University was accorded Sea Grant College status by the Federal government.

The College of Forest Resources at the University of Maine is one of the oldest and strongest forest resources programs in the United States. Its strength comes from a commitment to quality education, research and public service. CFR is divided into three departments: Forest Biology, Forest Management and Wildlife. Faculty in these departments teach both graduate and undergraduate courses and serve as academic advisors. Bachelor of Science degrees are offered in Forest Engineering, Forestry, Recreation and Park Management, Wildlife Management and Wood Technology.

Maine offers diverse opportunities to study wildlife in a variety of natural environments ranging from the coast with its sea birds, marine mammals, and eagles, to the more mountainous northern boreal forest occupied by moose, loons and marten. Students in the University's Wildlife Management program are exposed to wildlife issues in national parks, wildlife refuges, state management areas, and small and large tracts of privately-owned land. Internships and cooperative education opportunities are available with state, federal, and private organizations.

The Darling Marine Center is the marine laboratory of the University of Maine system and functions as a research and teaching facility. Located on the ocean Gulf of Maine, its coastal habitats include rocky shores, march, beaches, and mudflats. The new 12,000 sq. ft. Flowing Seawater Laboratory serves as a multifunctional facility for culturing and experimenting with a wide variety of living marine organisms.

The Canadian Studies Program at UM offers a greater number and wider range of courses in this area than any other university in the country. Canadian Studies provides a valuable area of study for students entering fields of education, business, and government where knowledge of Canada is increasingly important and those specializing in international relations. For twenty years, students in the Canada Year Program have been sent to Canadian Universities such as Memorial University in Newfoundland, University of Prince Edward Island, Dalhousie University in Nova Scotia, McGill University in Quebec, and University of British Columbia.

The University recognizes the increasingly global context of economic, social, scientific, technological, and political issues, as well as the evolving multicultural dimensions of contemporary society. UM's Women in the Curriculum Program improves the quality of education for all students by helping to ensure that the experiences and perspectives of women are part of the University curriculum. It continues a long-standing effort toward revising existing courses so that they represent equally the experiences, values, contributions, and perspectives of both women and men and so that classroom climate in all courses is equally hospitable to both female and male students.

# MAKING A DIFFERENCE STUDIES

## Forest Biology—Five year Program

Forest Ecology

Conservation Biology

Tropical Deforestation

Forest Wildlife Management

Forest Protection

Artificial Regeneration

Wildlife Conservation

International Conservation

- **Sustainable Tropical Forestry** Strategies to produce and extract products from tropical forests in sustainable ways and to provide employment for indigenous people.

## Bio-Resource Engineering

Intro to Bio-Resource Engineering

Energy and Society

Energy Efficient Housing

Irrigation and Water Supply Design

Coastal Engineering

Water Supply and Waste Management

Engineering for Sustainable Agriculture

Soil and Water Resources Engineering

Plant Science

Aquatic Food Webs

## Natural Resources  Tracks in Resource/Enviro. Econ; Soil & Water; Marine Sciences

Natural Resource Economics and Policy

Public Finance and Fiscal Policy

Introduction to Public Policy

Shellfisheries Biology

Aquatic Food Webs

Resource Economics

Forest Economics

Marine Fisheries Management

Fundamentals of Environmental Engineering

Algae Growth and Seaweed Mariculture

## Sustainable Agriculture

Insect Pest Management

Engineering for a Sustainable Agriculture

Agricultural Ecology

Agricultural Pest Ecology

Soil Organic Matter and Fertility

Sustainable Animal Production

Pesticides and the Environment

Principles and Practices of Sustainable Agric.

## Public Administration

Foundations of Public Administration

Health Care and Human Services

Human Resource Management

Medical Anthropology

Ethical Issues in Health Care

Critical Analysis in Public Administration.

Urban Politics

Topics in City and Town Management

Industrial Workers in America

Public Organization and Management

## Recreation & Park Management/Interpretation Concentration

Conservation Biology

Environmental Interpretation

Wilderness and Wild River Management

Field Ornithology

Geology of Maine

Aspects of the Natural Environment

Visitor Behavior and Management

Field Natural History of Maine

Social Problems

Introduction to Forest Resources

## Peace Studies

Humanistic Economics

Hunger as an Issues in Social Welfare

Violence in the Family

Hunger in U.S. and the World

Race and Culture Conflict

Latin America: Reform and Revolution

Religion and Politics

International Conservation

Economic Development

Education for Intercultural Understanding

**Land Use Planning**  **Wildlife Mgm't.**  **Natural History & Ecology**

**Women's Studies**  **Forest Engineering**  **Recreation & Park Mgm't.**

Approx. Costs: Residents $10,000  Non-residents $16,000  Apply By 2/1

Use form in back to contact: Admissions Office

University of Maine  Orono, ME  04469-5713

(207) 581-1561

# MANCHESTER COLLEGE

1,050 Students     Manchester, Indiana

Manchester College has a long tradition of combining learning and values. Its goal, as presented in the mission statement, is "to graduate people who possess ability and conviction." Manchester recognizes that change cannot come from conviction alone, that those who ardently desire to build a better world need real world skills to accomplish those goals. At Manchester College, skills and abilities are developed through rigorous preparation in a student's academic major(s) and broad coursework in the liberal arts. Graduates leave well trained for graduate school or their first job.

Manchester's mission statement also speaks best to it's core values: "Within a long tradition of concern for peace and justice, Manchester College intends to develop an international consciousness, a respect for ethnic and cultural pluralism, and an appreciation for the infinite worth of every person. A central goal of the College community is to create an environment which nurtures a sense of self-identity, a strong personal faith, a dedication to the service of others, and an acceptance of the demands of responsible citizenship." Manchester College is an independent, co-educational college in the liberal arts tradition, and is committed to continue in the tradition of social concern which is a mark of the Church of the Brethren, its supporting denomination.

The learning environment at Manchester College emphasizes an open exchange of thoughts and ideas. Students are taught to ask tough questions and search for satisfying answers. The curriculum allows varied combinations of majors and minors, both in allied fields (history and political science) and across disciplines (physics and peace studies, music and gender studies). Students take advantage of travel opportunities through international studies programs (a semester or year at campuses in Brazil, China, France, Ecuador, England, Germany, Greece, Indonesia, Japan, Spain and Mexico) and during the three and a half week January Session. Recent January Session classes have gone to Spain, Morocco, Costa Rica, Mexico, Chicago, Egypt, England, Florida, India and Nicaragua, and students were involved in NASA research, health, fitness and wellness internships, field experiences in peace studies social work and psychology, and many other off campus opportunities.

Manchester's emphasis on developing abilities and convictions shapes the academic and extra curricular experiences of students in every major. Action-oriented student groups are open to all students. They include Amnesty International, the Environmental Group, Habitat for Humanity, prison visitation teams, Death Penalty Awareness, Women's Advocacy Group, and many others. Students also participate in the Peace Choir, retreats, coffee houses, concerts, lectures and discussion forums, and local and national conferences.

The Peace Studies Institute plans college-wide conferences featuring speakers, debates on issues of public policy, and workshops. Manchester also offers an unusually large number of scholarships to students majoring in Peace Studies.

Other special resources include the 100 acre Koinonia Environmental Center, including a 5 acre natural lake and woods, just 11 miles from campus. The retreat building provides class and seminar rooms and environmental laboratories. Koinonia has become a retreat and learning center for church and college groups.

# MAKING A DIFFERENCE STUDIES

## Environmental Studies  Tracks in Interpretation-Education and Technical Studies
Over 20 years old, this program was founded before "environmentalism" became popular.

Environmental Philosophy
Plant Taxonomy
Science and the Environment
Field Biology
Environmental Economics

Environmental Studies Practicum
Ecology
State and Local Politics
Environmental Science
Historical Geology

## Peace Studies  Tracks in Interpersonal and Intergroup Conflict, International and Global Studies, Religious and Philosophical Bases
The Peace Studies program, founded in 1951, was the first in the nation. Nearly all majors participate in a Peace Studies practicum, an internship, or a year of study abroad.

Current Issues in Peace and Justice
Religions and War
Philosophy of Civilization
International Politics
Confucian and Buddhist Worlds
Microeconomics

Literature of Nonviolence
Analysis of War and Peace
Environmental Philosophy
Conflict Resolution
The Brethren Heritage
Peace and Justice

## Social Work
The Social Work program has an excellent reputation among professionals in the region, resulting in strong placement rate for interns and graduates.

Introduction to Human Services
Social Service Policy
Social Welfare as an Institution
Juvenile Delinquency

Human Behavior and the Social Environment
Race and Minority Group Relations
Gerontology
Social Work Practice

## Psychology
Students interested in psychology and conflict resolution find an exceptional opportunity in Manchester's mediation program--the Reconciliation Service, one of only a few in the country where students are active participants in mediating disputes for students and outside groups.

Cross-Cultural Psychology
Psychology of Mediation and Conciliation
Psychology of Learning

Psychology of the Young Adult
Counseling Theory and Practice
Psychology of Childhood

## Gender Studies
Based on the theory that gender is a cultural construct, not a naturally given aspect of personality, Gender Studies calls on us to reflect on the role gender plays in our lives and in society.

Introduction to Gender Studies
Feminist and Womanist Theology
Self and Society
Women in European History

Women in Literature
Women in the Arts
Women in American History
Feminist Theory

Student Body: 85% state, 50% male, 50% female, 7% minority, 3% int'l, 18% transfer
Faculty: 60% male, 40% female   • Average # of students in a first year classroom: 20
Costs: $18,050     Rolling Admissions
• Service-Learning Programs   • Individualized Majors  •Interdisciplinary Classes & Majors
• Field Studies   • Theme Housing   • Vegetarian & Vegan Meals

Use form in back to contact:  Admissions Office
Manchester College    604 E. College Ave    N. Manchester, IN 46962
1(800) 852-3648    (219) 982-5055
admissionsinfo@manchester.edu    www.manchester.edu

# MARLBORO COLLEGE

275 Students    Marlboro, Vermont

"If we are to survive, it will take a combination of an objective mind and a humane spirit. Marlboro strives to develop both qualities and hence we leave prepared to confront these issues in a meaningful way."

Tadd Lazarus, M.D. '78, Spellman Center for HIV Related Disease

Founded in 1946 in the hills of southern Vermont, Marlboro College s goal is to teach students to think clearly, learn independently, develop a command of written language and aspire to academic excellence, all while participating in a self-governing community. Marlboro's insistence on independent thought, clearly expressed vision and responsibility toward others has produced compassionate and involved world citizens dedicated to making a difference in their own lives and in the world around them. Many Marlboro students begin college with boundless idealism. Marlboro encourages this idealism by helping each student build on his or her skills and experience to become more effective members of both the campus and global community.

Essential to a Marlboro education is the Plan of Concentration, within which students design a course of study tailored to their interests. The Plan is a two-year process in which juniors and seniors research and write an academic project; each Plan is as unique as the student who develops it.

Students study under the close guidance of one or two faculty members who suggest a coherent sequence of coursework in small classes (ranging in size from two or three students to 10 or 12) and one-to-one tutorials. However diverse, Plans share a common outcome. Every Marlboro graduate knows that he or she has gained the ability to define a problem, set clear limits on an area of inquiry, analyze the object of study within those parameters, evaluate the results of research or artistic production and report articulately on the outcome of a worthy project. These are very important and powerful skills in the arena of progressive change.

The world is becoming a more volatile place, threatened by exploding populations, dying ecosystems and a resurgence of ethnic hatred. Marlboro's World Studies Program, run in association with the School for International Training in Brattleboro, VT, works from the premise that we must develop an understanding, acceptance and celebration of the world s diversity through intercultural work and education.

The World Studies Program is designed to help motivated students acquire the cultural framework, practical skills and intellectual tools necessary to analyze global developments in the light of differing cultural values and traditions. Students study broadly within the liberal arts, focusing increasingly on a particular area of inquiry. They acquire foreign language proficiency and cross-cultural skills and in their junior years they experience living, working, and conducting research in a different culture.

Interns have traveled to over 30 different countries worldwide, from Russia to Bali, and return holding not only a broader global perspective but also increased insight and maturity. They complete their studies by producing a finished Plan of Concentration a work that fuses their academic and intercultural experience and in a world view, one which is often continued in their later work.

Outside the World Studies Program, students arrange study-abroad semesters or internships both in other countries and at other colleges and universities in the United States. Marlboro College's new academic partnership with Huron University in London will extend numerous exchanges and internship opportunities to students and faculty in all curricular areas.

The College also sponsors several field trips each year, including scientific expeditions to tropical, desert, or mountain environments; outdoor adventures in mountain climbing or white-water rafting; and a theater trip to England each winter. Those remaining on campus enjoy an annual intercultural lecture series, presentations from fellow students returning from internships and international nights that feature the food, music and films of different countries.

To the faculty at Marlboro, the term Environmental Science is synonymous with the term Human Ecology, that is, a study of the way that humans interact with their environment. Such a broad definition suggests that an interdisciplinary approach is warranted, and indeed, students should study the environmental sciences from the special perspective and knowledge of the arts, humanities, social sciences and natural sciences.

The integration of various disciplines into a coordinated approach to environmental questions is the challenge of this field. Each student majoring in environmental science must develop an in-depth familiarity with one or more approaches to solving problems. One cannot, for example, reasonably address the problems associated with acid rain without knowing something about biology and ecology, resource economics, public policy and political institutions, international relations, environmental chemistry and meteorology.

The interdisciplinary nature of Marlboro also allows great flexibility for students who wish to study gender issues. Students focus on women's studies throughout the curriculum, and, similar to work in environmental sciences, a broad perspective in all areas of the liberal arts coupled with a specific focus within a discipline or cross-discipline provide each student with multi-faceted and thus, more informed work.

Along with the academic challenge, Marlboro has a tradition of community service. To some degree this can be attributed to a highly distinctive aspect of Marlboro: the Town Meeting structure within which many college decisions are made. Town Meeting serves as a training ground for its members to participate in the democratic process and assume a considerable measure of personal responsibility for the health of the community, both at Marlboro and beyond.

Marlboro also offers a very active Outdoor Program, offering activities such as rock climbing, backpacking, spelunking, canoeing, cross-country skiing and winter camping, in places ranging from Vermont's Green Mountains to the Southwest deserts.

# MAKING A DIFFERENCE STUDIES

## Environmental Studies   Coursework & Tutorials*

Broad study develops an aesthetic sense in the arts, an appreciation of the foundations of civilization in the humanities, a view of the inner workings of past and present human societies in the social sciences, and a firm grounding in physical and biological principles in the natural sciences. Advanced students focus their studies to a specialized goal.

Environmental Policy
World Energy Issues
Global Environmental Issues
Public Policy & Endangered Species
God, Man, & Nature*
The Philosophy of Nature*
Solar Energy Building & Design
Climactic Change
Perception of the Environment
Effects of Pollutants on Ecosystems
Conservation Biology & Policy
Alternative Institutions & Communities

**Plans of Concentration in Environmental Studies:**

Coastal Zone Management Act
Wetland Policy and Protection in Vermont
Energy Policy Issues
Role of Wildlife in Community Development
Tropical Deforestation
Forest Practices and Management in the U.S.
Resource Management with focus on Solid Waste and Resource Recovery Strategies
Relation Between Range Management and Public Policy on Grazing of Public Land

- **Ethnobiology**   This course includes three distinct but interrelated segments: 1) an examination of how people in different cultures classify plants and animals; 2) a study of contemporary and historical events in the Americas in which resource consumption, environmental destruction and native land rights are linked; and 3) a brief survey of medical anthropology, the study of medical belief systems within particular cultural contexts.

## World Studies Program  Coursework & Tutorials

World Studies Program students are expected to gain a general education through the liberal arts and to develop skills as international citizens. These general goals include: an introductory knowledge of world history and cultures; an understanding of contemporary global issues; competence in cross-cultural communication, recognition of difference in cultural values and experience working and learning in another culture; proficiency in a second language; and, a basic knowledge of one world region (geography; economic and environmental systems; culture and history).

World Studies Colloquium
Central Africa Politics
Topics in Human Understanding
Southern African Politics
Professional Development
Economic Development
Mesoamerican Studies
Language in Culture
Third World Development
Russian and Soviet Studies
Seminar in Policy Studies
Inuit Healing Techniques

**Plans of Concentration in World Studies**

Gender and Healing in Tunisia
Cultural Responses to Development in Uganda
Tibetan Subcultures in Exile
History, Language,& Ethnic Identity in Ireland
Tourism and Tradition in Balinese Dance
Changing Roles of Women in East Africa

- **Twentieth Century World**  An introductory seminar for World Studies students. The course is designed to help students situate themselves in time and place, and begin to think historically, culturally, and geographically. Classes discuss concepts and issues relevant to the contemporary world and to historical experience, in global comparative contexts.

## Gender Studies

Gender Studies are conducted throughout the curriculum under the auspices of various disciplines, such as American studies, philosophy, world studies, art history, literature, sociology, psychology and the sciences. In almost all cases, gender studies are interdisciplinary.

Research in U.S. Women's History          African American Women Writers
Prostitution in America

**Plans of Concentration in Gender Studies:**

Working Women in the Progressive Era    A Feminist Critique of Philosophy of Science
Feminism and Drama                      Women, Science and Objectivity
Artistic Development of Modersohn-Becker, O'Keefe, and Virginia Woolf
Contemporary African-American Women & The Search for Identity
The Relationship between Women and Nature in Victorian Post-colonial Fiction

## Economics

Political Economy                       Organizations, Environments & Public Policy
Environmental Policy                    U. S. Capitalism
Politics of Deforestation               Economic Anthropology
The Soviet Economy                      Solid Waste Mgm't in Rural New England
Decision Making: Individual, Interactive, and Collective

- **Economic Justice** Considers the existing distribution of income and wealth, theories which attempt to explain this distribution, and programs which seek to change it.

- **James Tober** (B.A., UC Berkeley, M,Phil., Yale, Ph.D. Yale) Jim's doctoral dissertation was on Natural Resources for the Future. He was a Visiting Fellow and Research Scholar at Yale with the Program on Non-Profit Organizations, Institution for Social and Policy Studies, and was Co-director for two years of Marlboro's World Studies Program. Jim's long-term research on wildlife policy has led to two books: *Who Owns Wildlife* and *Wildlife and the Public Interest*.

## Biology

General Biology                         Plant Ecology
Plants of Vermont                       Conservation Biology
Plant Diversity                         Animal Behavior
Biogeography                            Community Ecology
Pollination Ecology                     Alpine Plant Ecology
Field Course in Tropical Biology (Mexico, Guatemala and Belize)

- **Biology of Deserts** A careful study of the biology of desert organisms. Emphasis will be placed on the physiological systems allowing existence in a hot, dry ecosystem and on community ecology. The original literature will be explored in a seminar format. An end-of-term trip will go to the U.S. Southwest

Student Body: 17% state, 45% male, 55% female, 3% minority, 3% int'l, 30% transfer
Faulty: 61% male, 39% female, 6% minority    Avg. # of students in a first year class: 8
Costs: $26,935   Apply by 3/1

- Team Teaching   - Individualized Majors   - Field Studies
- Study Abroad   - Interdisciplinary Classes & Majors   - Vegetarian & Vegan Meals
- Smoke-free, substance free dorms   - Graduate Programs
- Campus Wide Recycling Program   - Many buildings on campus are passive solar.

Use form in back to contact: Director of Admissions
Marlboro College   Marlboro, VT 05344-0300

(802) 257-4333

# UNIVERSITY OF MICHIGAN
## SCHOOL OF NATURAL RESOURCES AND ENVIRONMENT
417 Undergraduates    Ann Arbor, Michigan

Established in 1927, the University of Michigan School of Natural Resources and Environment (SNRE) is the first of its kind in the world. For seventy years, its mission has been to educate future leaders to be effective and innovative stewards of the environment. The School's academic program is interdisciplinary in scope, providing undergraduates with a background in liberal arts and sciences with an emphasis upon building analytical, problem-solving, and communication skills. With approximately 400 undergraduate students and 200 graduate students, SNRE provides a close knit community environment while at the same time being able to offer students the advantages of attending a large research institution. Teaching and building community are valued aspects of the school's program.

Most students pursue one of three academic concentrations: Resource Ecology and Management, Environmental Policy and Behavior, or Landscape Design and Planning. Individualized concentrations are also possible. The Resource Ecology and Management concentration is designed for students interested in pursuing field-oriented and science-oriented studies of natural resource systems, such as aquatic or terrestrial ecosystems, wildlife, remote sensing, and soils. Students in the Environmental Policy and Behavior concentration focus their study upon the human and societal aspects of natural resource and environmental problems. Landscape Design and Planning is intended for junior or senior students interested in becoming landscape architects, environmental planners or urban planners.

The Office of Academic Programs (OAP,) within the School of Natural Resources and Environment, coordinates academic advising and maintains a comprehensive Career Resource Center staffed by a professional career counselor. SNRE students will receive personal counseling on everything from academic program scheduling to career, internship, and scholarship opportunities. OAP receives over 1500 job postings per academic year which are related to environmental issues or concerns. Additionally, SNRE students have access to University of Michigan's Career Planning and Placement services and the largest alumni network of any college or university in the country.

There are over 600 extracurricular organizations for students attending the University of Michigan several of which are populated with SNRE students. Students Organized to Recycle and Reuse Organic Waste (SORROW,) SNRE Environmental Justice Group, Minorities in Agriculture and Natural Resources Related Sciences (MANNRS,) Environmental Action (ENACT,) the Rainforest Action Movement (RAM,) and a student chapter of the Wildlife and Conservation Society are among the most popular. SNRE students are also involved in campus service organizations such as Project SERVE, Alternative Spring Break, and Amnesty International

Many SNRE courses are taught with field or lab components. The Ann Arbor area features extensive wetland, inland lake, river, and forest ecosystems which provide unique opportunities for research. Near campus, the School of Natural Resources and Environment owns, manages, or uses several properties including the Matthaei Botanical Gardens, Nichols Arboretum, Stinchfield Woods and Saginaw Forest. Additionally, students may attend programs and classes held at the University of Michigan Biological Station in northern Michigan or they can go to Wyoming to participate in the University's Geology in the Rockies program. There are also many study abroad opportunities available jointly through SNRE and the School for Field Studies which enable students to pursue their studies in an international setting. Specific details about these programs may be obtained through SNRE's Office of Academic Programs.

SNRE students may participate in the University's Living Learning Community Programs which typically feature theme housing and exciting research opportunities in an environment more like that of many smaller schools. These provide an opportunity to develop leadership skills in a stimulating environment. The Lloyd Scholars, 21st Century, Undergraduate Research Opportunity, and Women in Science and Engineering Programs are among the most notable residential opportunities available at the University.

There are also academically non-residential programs available to all University of Michigan students such as the Comprehensive Studies Program and the University Mentorship Program.

## MAKING A DIFFERENCE STUDIES

### Environmental Policy and Behavior Concentration

| | |
|---|---|
| Environmental Law | Applications of Environmental Justice |
| Environmental Justice: Domestic & Int'l. | Environmental Ed. and Natural Resources |
| Environmental Politics and Policy | Women and Environment |
| International Environmental Policy | Natural Resource Internship Program |
| Senior Honors Seminar | Society and Environment |
| Undergraduate Experimental Course | Water Resource Policy |

Small Group Organization & Advocacy Planning
Conservation Behavior: Source Reduction and Recycling
Introduction to Environmental Policies: Race, Class, and Gender
Ecotourism for Ecodevelopment in National Parks and Protected Areas: Third World and Native American Perspectives

- **Environmental Thought and Activism** The course uses a race, class and gender approach to examine the history of American environmental activism (1850-present). It identifies the major period of environmental mobilization and significant forms of environmental activism among the white middle class, white working class and people of color. Examines the way in which a persons' social class, race, gender, and environmental, and labor market experiences influence their environmental perception and the kinds of environmental ideologies they develop. Examines the rise of major environmental paradigms and the factors that make them influential.

- **Environmental Ethics and Policy** This seminar critically examines selected issues in applied environmental ethics including: duties to future generations, animal rights, biocentrism, ecocentric "land ethics", and global environmental justice. The contributions of leading theories (deep ecology, social ecology, feminist ecology, economic rationality and ecological sustainability) are surveyed. Multicultural inspirations that might enrich western environmental ethics arising from Judeo-Christian, Hindu, Buddhist, Native American and Australian aborigine traditions are explored.

## Resource Ecology and Management Concentration

Advanced Forest Ecology
Aquaculture
Biology and Management of Insects
Ecological Restoration
Fluvial Ecosystems
Imaging Radar as a Remote Sensor
Insect Ecology
Optical Sensors and Instrumentation
Remote Sensing of Environment
Terrestrial Vertebrate Natural History
Wildlife Behavior and Ecology
Habitats & Organisms: Science of Interactions
Geographic Information Systems (GIS) Applications in Natural Resources

Agroforestry
Aquatic Entomology
Conservation of Biological Diversity
Ecology of Fishes
Human Resource Ecology
Multiple Use Forest Management
Introduction to Aquatic Ecosystems
Principles of Radiation for Remote Sensing
Senior Honors Seminar
Wetland Ecology
Woody Plants: Biology and Identification

- **Tropical Conservation & Resource Management**  Multidisciplinary course will examine the underlying problems of conservation and natural resource management in the tropics. Ecological, socio/political and economic aspects. Basic ecological principles, with an emphasis on how they relate to the conservation and management of renewable resources. Examine the complexity of social, political and economic factors that interact with environmental ones to limit, enhance, or somehow affect the conservation and management of resources. Tropical ecosystems, their ecology and management and the challenge that their conservation represents. Interactions between conservation and development and on the perspective of the people of the Third World, since most tropical countries are part of the Third World.

## Landscape Design and Planning

Construction Materials and Detailing
LA Design
Landscape Architecture History
Site Engineering

Elements and Principles
Landscape Architecture Design Theory
Plant Materials for Landscape
Visual Communications

## SNRE Electives

Culture, Adaptation, and Environment
Natural Resources Career Development
Our Common Future:  The Ecology, Economics, and Ethics of Sustainable Development

Introduction to Global Change
Natural Resources Mentoring Seminar

Student Body: 73% state, 43% male, 57% female, 12% minority, 4% int'l.
Faulty: 74% male, 26% female, 10% minority    Avg. # of students in a first year class: 85
Residents Costs: $11,444   Non-Residents: $24,010   Apply by 2/1

- Team Teaching   • Individualized Majors   • Field Studies
- Service-Learning   • Interdisciplinary Classes   • All Seminar Format
- Theme Housing   • Vegetarian Meals   • Graduate Programs

Use form in back to contact: Office of Undergraduate Admission
University of Michigan    1220 SAB/515 E. Jefferson
Ann Arbor, MI 48109/1316
(734) 764-1316
snre.help@umich.edu    www.snre.umich.edu

# MIDDLEBURY COLLEGE

2,000 Students    Middlebury, Vermont

Middlebury is well-known as one of New England's outstanding small, residential, liberal arts colleges of long tradition. It was founded in 1800 and in 1883 became one of the earliest co-educational institutions. Middlebury is distinguished for its long international and multicultural tradition. Middlebury seeks those who wish not only to learn about themselves and their own traditions, but those who wish to expand their vision, to see beyond the bounds of class, culture, region or nation. Indeed, it could be said that the central purpose of a Middlebury education is precisely this transcendence of oneself and one's own concerns.

Since World War 1, the College has operated internationally known language programs. Middlebury views languages both as a means of communication, and as ways to learn more about a culture or a discipline. Four out of ten Middlebury students spend at least one semester abroad, experiencing another culture first-hand and bringing their new perspectives back to campus.

At Middlebury, the New England tradition of the town meeting takes on an international dimension at many of our symposia. His Holiness, the Dalai Lama, the exiled spiritual and political leader of Tibet, spent a week on campus as part of a conference called "The Spirit and Nature Symposium." A symposium on South Africa had international speakers and a large audience: 140 stations of American Public Radio.

First Year Students at Middlebury are required to elect one of a number of seminars that are designed from a perspective which makes connections among a number of traditional academic disciplines. Recent topics have included Environmental Issues for the Nineties: Crises and Resolution; Thinking About War; and Cries of Injustice: Black Protest and the Civil Rights Movement.

Efforts are under way at Middlebury to "green" the campus. The college has decided it is important to incorporate what it teaches in it's daily workings. Everything from course work to meals to energy conservation is is being scrutinized.

Middlebury College has a very active volunteer service program. Over 600 students volunteer each year. One of the oldest programs is Community Friends, in which students choose individuals in need from the following groups: children between the ages of 6-12, the elderly, people with mental retardation and mental illness. Students also work reading to the blind, and in affordable housing renovation. Students take ungraded internships for credit in various areas, from a clinic for parasitology in Thailand to the office of a local attorney.

The College has a partnership with De Witt Clinton High School (Bronx, N.Y.) whose student population is 99% minority. De Witt Clinton teachers have participated in workshops with Middlebury faculty, and students have conducted teaching internships at the high school during winter term. Middlebury also has three regional "diversity task forces" designed to help recruit and retain students of color. In addition, a rural outreach program focuses on first-generation, college-bound students of modest financial means.

# MAKING A DIFFERENCE STUDIES

## First Year Seminars
Theory and Practice of Nonviolence
Stories About Women
Voices Across Social Groups: How Do We Talk To Each Other?
Women and World Politics: Questions About Gender

Social Class & Ethnic Relations in America
Moral and Ethical Decisions in Public Life

## Environmental Studies   Tracks in Conservation Biology; Enviro Geology; Enviro Economics; Geography; U.S. Enviro Policy; Environmental Perspectives in Literature & Writing; Philosophical & Comparative Perspectives; Human Ecology
Environmental Studies is one of the most popular majors at Middlebury.

Visions of Nature
Ethics and the Environment
Social Movement and Collective Action
Environmental Economics
Freedom, Faith and Ecology
Environmental Economics
Methods in Ecology

Environmental and Natural Resource Policy
Native Peoples of North America
Environmental Geology
Religion, Ethics and the Environment
Perspectives on the Environmental Movement
Natural Science and the Environment
Philosophy of Nature

## Geography
The Geography of Development
Population Geography
Surface Water Resource and Development
Energy Fuels and Mineral Development

Economic Geography
Geographic Perspectives on Middle East
Social Aspects of Environmental Issues
Women in the City

## Northern Studies
*Polar Biota: Flora
 Artic and Alpine Environments
*Northern Archaeology
 Public Policy in Circumpolar North
*Indigenous Cultures of Circumpolar North

*Political Economy Of Resource Mgm't.
 Northern Legal Issues
*Artic Policy Studies
 Northern Resource Conflicts
*Community Development in Circum.North

*These classes are offered at the Center for Northern Studies in Wolcott, VT

## Sociology/Anthropology   Concentrations in Social Inequality, Social Policy Issues, Health and Society
Women, Culture and Society
Indian Society
Sociology of Women
Social Movements and Collective Action
Medical Anthropology
Medical Sociology

Native Peoples of North America
American Community Studies
Women in Social Thought
Chinese Society and Culture
Sociology of Education
Race and Ethnicity

## Women's Studies          Third World Studies

Student Body: 5% state, 50% male, 50% female, 5% minority
Comprehensive Costs: $30,475    Apply by 1/ 15
• Internships   • Individualized Majors   • Field Studies
• Third World Study Abroad   • Mystic Seaport Program

Use form in back to contact: Admissions Office
Middlebury College    Middlebury, VT 05753-6002
(802) 443-3000

# UNIVERSITY OF MINNESOTA

28,000 Undergraduates    Minneapolis, Minnesota

At the University of Minnesota, students in the College of Liberal Arts integrate fields of knowledge through interdisciplinary and thematic courses. They have the opportunity to examine values, ethics, and social responsibility and learn about the cultural diversity of the world and U.S. society. Students also have opportunities for active learning, such as internships and study abroad. Carlson School of Management is known for its particular emphasis on socially responsible business practices.

The College provides a variety of programs to enhance or personalize chosen degree programs. Programs, such as the Honors Program, the Martin Luther King Program, and those offered through the Office of Special Learning Opportunities, the Foreign Studies Office, and the Career Development Office help students get the most from their undergraduate experience. Students earning a Bachelor of Individualized Studies (BIS) design their own program with three areas of concentration. The program must have a coherence based on stated academic objectives. Also available is an individually designed interdepartmental major; a unique program with an inter-disciplinary theme that meets the students individual academic interests. Established interdepartmental majors include African, American, East Asian, Jewish, Latin American, Middle Eastern, urban and women's studies, and international relations.

In order for students to transcend the boundaries set by major European and North American educational traditions, B.A. and B.I.S. degree students are asked to examine cultures substantially different from their own. At least two courses are required dealing with the cultures of Asia, Africa, Latin America or with traditional Native American cultures. Students are also required to take course in studying U.S. Cultural Pluralism, with a primary focus on social and cultural diversity, with special attention to race and ethnicity.

Field experience learning at UM is a form of study in which community resources are used to explore the questions and issues raised in the classroom. Students work in a paid or volunteer position, usually in a location such as a museum, social service agency, government office or community program. the fieldwork (sometimes called an internship or practicum) takes place of campus, but the study is carried out under the direction of a faculty member.

The College of Natural Resources seeks to increase the economic, social and environmental benefits of our most important renewable resources. The CNR offers six major curricular: Fisheries and Wildlife; Forest products; Forest Resources; Natural Resources and Environmental Studies, Recreation Resource Management; and Urban Forestry. Most majors are required to complete a 31/2 week summer term at Lake Itasca Forestry and Biological Station at the source of the Mississippi River. The college's Cloquet Forestry Center includes more than 3,700 acres of virgin and second-growth timber in a major forest products manufacturing areas. Forest Resources seniors spend their fall quarter at the center taking 18 credits of field-oriented instruction.

# MAKING A DIFFERENCE STUDIES

## Cultural Studies and Comparative Literature

The Body and Politics of Representation
Knowledge, Persuasion, and Power
Interpretation of Ritual
Architecture and Society
Political Discourse of Social Change

Text and Context
Humanities in the Modern World
Cinematic Discourse and Cultural Politics
Landscape and Ideology
Self-Realization in 20th Century Literature

## South Asian & Middle Eastern Languages & Cultures

The Religion of Islam
Women in India: Role and repression
Beginning/Colloquial Arabic
Folklore of India
Buddhism

The Qur'an as Literature
Islam and Communism
Persian Poetry in Translation
Tribal Peoples and Cultures of S. Asia
Gandhi and Non-violent Revolution

## Journalism and Mass Communication

Media in American History and Law
Public Affairs Reporting
Supervision of School Publications
Mass Media and Popular Culture
Communication & Public Opinion

Visual Communication
Community Newspaper
Racial Minorities & the Mass Media
Mass Media and Politic
Mass Communication & Public Health

## Urban Forestry

Urban Forest Management
Insect Pest Management
Nursery Management & Production
Plant Propagation
Forest Genetics

Forest Economics and Planning
Farm and Small Woodlands Forestry
Herbaceous Plant Materials
Landscape Management
Strategy and Tactics in Project Planning

## Paper Science & Engineering

Bio & Enviro Science of Pulp & Paper
Pulp and Paper Operations
Analysis of Production Systems

Analysis and Design of Wastewater Systems
Analysis and Design of Water Supply Systems
Renewable Nat. Resources/Developing Countries

## Resources and Environmental Protection

Land Economics
Pollution Impacts on Aquatic Systems
Organic and Pesticidal Residues
Environmental Policy
Technology and Western Civilization

Resource and Environmental Economics
Assessing the Ecological Effects of Pollution
Ethics and Values in Resource Management
Ecology & Mgm't of Fish & Wildlife Habitats
Resource Dev. & Environmental Economics

## Environmental Issues and Planning

Economic Dev. of American Agriculture
Energy Research Use
Recreation Land Policy
Politics, Planning and Decision Making
Politics of the Regulatory Process

Resource Dev. & Environmental Economics
Assessing the Ecological Effects of Pollution
Environmental Policy
Management of Recreational Lands
Impact Assessment and Enviro Mediation

Forest Biology/Harvesting/Resources    Fisheries & Wildlife    Waste Mgm't.
Water/Soil Resources   Int'l. Relations   Women's Studies    African-Amer. Studies
History of Science & Tech.   Sociology   Landscape Architecture    Philosophy

UM Student Body: 88% state, 49% female, 51% male, 14% minority, 2% int'l.
Tuition Only: Residents $4267  Non-residents $11,314    Rolling Admissions

Use form in back to contact: Office of Admissions
University of Minnesota      Minneapolis, MN 55455
(612) 625-2006    admissions@tc.umn.edu

# MONTEREY BAY

780 Students    Seaside, California

California State University, Monterey Bay is the California State University system's 21st campus for the 21st Century. Founded in 1994, CSUMB is located on the beautiful and historic Monterey Peninsula area on California's central coast. With its truly innovative curriculum, CSUMB is preparing students to become socially and professionally capable and well-rounded. CSUMB's academic programs are designed for people of diverse backgrounds who want to work hard at learning, have fun while learning, and consciously add value to their lives through the learning they do.

The vision for CSUMB includes a model, pluralistic, academic community where all learn and teach one another in an atmosphere of mutual respect and pursuit of excellence. Graduates will have an understanding of interdependence and global competence, distinctive technical and educational skills, the experience and abilities to contribute to a high-quality workforce, the critical thinking abilities to be productive citizens, and the social responsibility and skills to be community builders.

CSUMB's innovative curriculum is outcome based rather than "seat time" based; that is, students will be assessed in terms of what they actually know and what they can do rather than how many classes they have completed or how many tests they have passed. Graduates will have mastered seven learning outcomes which are:

- Effective and ethical communication in at least two diverse languages
- Cross-culturally competent citizenship in a pluralistic and global society
- Technological, aural, and visual literacy
- Creative expression in the service of transforming culture
- Ethics, social justice, and care for one another
- Scientific sophistication and value for the earth and earth systems
- Holistic and creative sense of self

The seven goals are achieved by demonstrating competency in 17 learning requirements that encompass the areas of technology, language, cross-cultural competence, and service to the community, as well as specific learning requirements in the 12 undergraduate programs offered. Service learning is an important and integral component of CSUMB's vision, philosophy, and educational programs. All students must complete two service learning courses. Service learning involves active learning drawing lessons from the experience of performing service work that meets community needs, as defined and determined by the communities. Typical courses include: Monterey Bay - A Case Study in Environmental Policy; Fieldwork in Multicultural Child Care; and Marine and Coastal Management- Integration of Science & Policy

At CSUMB, the class size is kept small and students work side by side with faculty to develop their unique learning paths. CSUMB has state-of-the-art technology and works with several high-tech industries right on campus. All students learn to utilize technology and communicate electronically on line with the campus community and the world.

It takes a special kind of pioneering student to succeed at CSUMB. Students must be adaptable, able to appreciate rigorous academic programs, and want to play an active part in a dynamic and diverse educational evolution.

# MAKING A DIFFERENCE STUDIES

## Human Communication

Emphasizes community building, peaceful co-existence, the development of individual and group potential, effective and ethical decision making, knowledge production, acquisition, and evaluation of other tools which are necessary to communicate effectively and ethically.

Communication, Culture and Conflict
Latina Life Stories
Communication and Gender
Critical Political Analysis in Everyday Life
Oral History and Community Memory

Communication Ethics
Free Speech and Responsibility
Linguistic Diversity and Language Barriers
History of Politics in the Americas
Linguistic Diversity and Language Barriers

## Global Studies

Encompasses issues of human well-being and survival, environmental degradation, persistent global poverty, racial and gender violence, and how various peoples interface with technology.

World Economy
Third World Issues & Cultures
Introduction to Global Studies

Changing Politics of Global Life
The Chicano Community
Global Organizations & the United Nations

## Earth Systems Science and Policy Tracks in Ecological Systems, Environmental Economics & Policy, and Marine Science

Teaches students to view the earth as a complex system of interacting components including the anthrosphere, atmosphere, biosphere, geosphere, and hydrosphere. A key factor in solving many of the serious challenges confronting our world (developing sustainable food and energy resources, reducing pollution, minimizing impact of natural disasters) is the ability to analyze and understand complex interactions between physical, biological, and socio-political processes.

Ecosystem Modeling
Environmental Chemistry
Ecosystem Hindcasting
Environmental Dispute Resolution
Advanced Watershed Systems

Water issues in California
Conservation Biology
Habitat Biodiversity
Environmental Politics
Ecological Economics

## Collaborative Human Service

As the program matures, it will offer courses with an emphasis of collaboration in the context of health services, criminal justice, mental health, and parks and recreation.

Civic Community
Women's Leadership Development
Public Policy Analysis
Empowering Communities

Personal Renewal & Organizational Develp't
Services and Support for Children & Youth
Systems Mgm't in Human Services Delivery
How to Develop a Full-Service Charter School

Reinventing Leadership: Facilitative Leveraging to Dissolve Barriers to Collaboration

Student Body: 98% state, 63% female, 37% male, 49% minority, 60% transfer, 1% int'l.
Faculty: 68% male, 32% female, 53% minority
Costs: Residents $6,110  Non-residents $14,380    Apply by: 11/30

• All majors have Service Learning    • Interdisciplinary Classes    • Exclusive Seminar Format
• Individualized Majors    • Team Teaching    • Field Studies
• Life Experience Credit    • Vegetarian Meals

Use form in back to contact: Student Information Center
CSU Monterey Bay    100 Campus Center
Seaside, CA 93955-8001
(408)582-3518
Student_Info_Center@monterey.edu    www.monterey.edu

# NAROPA INSTITUTE

275 Undergraduates    Boulder, Colorado

The Naropa Institute provides the unique educational environment that balances personal meaning and creative expression with academic excellence. The degree programs cultivate a spirit of openness, critical intellect and the development of effective action, while transmitting the principles of awareness and wisdom.

The Naropa Institute was founded in 1974 by Tibetan meditation master and scholar Chögyam Trungpa and is patterned after Nalanda University, an 11th century Indian university renowned for joining intellect and intuition and for its appreciation of various contemplative traditions. Naropa offers a full four-year undergraduate program in a wide range of majors, as well as M.A. and M.F.A degrees at the graduate level. An active Study Abroad program in both Bali and Nepal mixes academic study and experiential learning with the philosophy, music, painting, dance and traditional awareness practices of each country.

The Naropa Institute faculty is remarkable in its diversity and achievements. They are distinguished by a wealth of experience in the professional, artistic, and scholastic applications of their disciplines. They are committed to a heart-felt philosophy that brings out the individual insight and intelligence of each student. In addition to the outstanding core faculty, an international community of scholars and artists is consistently drawn to Naropa because of its strong vision and leadership in higher education. The faculty and student body at Naropa form a close-knit community, and this relationship between the students and faculty is a unique part of the educational experience. From the small class size, to the low teacher: student ratio, to the vibrant atmosphere of creative risk-taking, an integration of intellect and intuition is modeled and encouraged. Drawn from over 35 states and nearly 20 countries, Naropa students represent a wide range of life experiences, ages, cultures and backgrounds. Activism, altruism and community involvement are among the many notable characteristics of Naropa's unique student environment.

Naropa seeks students who have a strong appetite for learning, enjoy experiential education in an academic setting and who have demonstrated an ability to live independently. Non-traditional students and all those with a high school degree or GED are welcome to apply. The Office of Admissions reviews learning done outside the traditional college classroom (and CLEP scores,) in addition to academic transcripts. Naropa gladly accept international students, with certain language and financial requirements.

The Naropa Institute is nestled in the foothills of the majestic Rocky Mountains on 3.7 acres in the center of Boulder, Colorado. The campus and surrounding grounds include The Naropa Institute Performing Arts Center, a meditation hall, the Allen Ginsberg Library, Naropa Gallery, Naropa Cafe and Naropa's new North Boulder Campus. The City of Boulder, 25 miles northwest of Denver, is a town of 100,000 and was rated by Outside Magazine as one of the top ten places to live for health and outdoor recreation.

# MAKING A DIFFERENCE STUDIES

"When human beings lose their connection to nature, to heaven and earth, then they do not know how to nurture their environment. Healing our society goes hand in hand with healing our personal, elemental connection with the phenomenal world."

- Chogyam Trungpa Rinpoche

## Environmental Studies

Integrates science, spirit, and personal engagement in a broad and multidisciplinary environmental curriculum with specialization in Anthropology, Ecology, Horticulture, and Native American Studies.

| | |
|---|---|
| Small Farm Management | Ecology Practicum |
| Deep Ecology | Eco-Literature |
| Edible Plants and Survival Skills | Restoration Ecology and Changing Landscapes |
| Field Ecology | Field Botany |
| Vegetable Garden | Permaculture |
| Sustainable Communities | Ethnomedicine Seminar |

- **Nature, The Sacred and Contemplation.** The pure mindful experience of Nature often leads to a personal, emotional relationship, sometimes referred to as spiritual, sacred, or mystical. Individual, cultural, and contemplative dimensions of such a relationship. Integrates experiences and contemplation outdoors with teachings from contemplative traditions, ecological knowledge, and observations as a naturalist.

## Contemplative Psychology  Tracks in Buddhist & Western Psychology; Jungian Psych, Psychology of Health & Healing; Transpersonal & Humanistic Psych.

Prepares a student for any occupation requiring subtlety in interpersonal relationships, particularly in the helping professions.

| | |
|---|---|
| Psychology of Healing | Psychology of Meditation |
| Healing and Music | Psychology of Shamanism |
| Body Cosmology and Natural Healing | Dynamics of the Intimate Relationship |
| The Geshtalt Approach | Healing in Cross-Cultural Perspective |
| Archetypes and Collective Unconscious | Teaching Children in Contemplative Tradition |
| Tibetan Medicine | Buddhist Psychology: Maitri & Compassion |

## Early Childhood Education

Emphasizes personalized teacher education with teaching skills drawn from the holistic and spiritual traditions of Montessori, Waldorf, and Shambala. Graduates are preapproved by the state for certification as group leader qualified preschool teachers, directors of child care centers, and private kindergarten teachers.

| | |
|---|---|
| Buddhist Educational Psychology | Body Mind Centering |
| Cultural Anthropology & Social Change | Nourishing the Teacher |
| Teaching & Learning Styles | Child Development and Creativity |
| Contemplative Parenting | Educational Admin. of a Child Care Center |

- **Foundations of Contemplative Education**  Lays the ground for discovering the full-blown richness and dignity of ourselves and children. Study and practice the essentials of contemplative education psychology in order to apply its wisdom to teaching young children. Through an exploration of the traditional Shambala and Buddhist approaches to working with states of minds, you prepare for teaching with vigor, freshness, and openess. Encounter concepts and emotions directly, gently and creatively. Develop disciplines of mindfulness/awareness and contemplative educational observation, a natural extension of awareness practice. These practices enable you to perceive and bring forth children's true natures without prejudice and aggression.

## Inter-Arts Studies

Encourages students to practice their primary discipline while exploring other art forms and contemplative practices. The focus is on collaboration and the creative process. Four areas of concentration include: Dance/Movement, Dance Therapy, Music, and Theater Studies.

Body Mind Centering
The Dance of Haiti
Dance Therapy

The Dance of West Africa
Contact Improvisation
Contemplative Arts Practice

- **Dance Therapy 11**   Focus on developing movement relationships through empathic movement and verbal exchange. This discipline supports increasing intimacy, which is the ground of the healing relationship, and, eventually, participation in and support of another's process. Increased authenticity of presence and movement.

## Religious Studies

Major world religions as living traditions in both historical and contemporary perspectives.

Contemplative Christianity
Meditation Practicum
Contemplative Islam/Sufism
Buddhist Civilization
Women, Sufism, & Islam: Womanist Perspectives

Contemplative Religions of China and Japan
Tibetan
Contemplative Judaism: The Knowing Heart
Contemplative Hinduism

## Traditional Eastern Arts

The only degree program in the country offering training in the Traditional Eastern Arts of Aikido, T'ai-chi Ch'uan, and Yoga. Focus is integration of body, mind, and spirit through practices grounded in meditative awareness and physical acumen.

T'ai Chi Chu'an
T'ai Chi Ch'uan: Sword Form
Shambala Meditation Practicum
Ikebana: Japanese Flower Arranging
Bugaku: Japanese Court Dance

Aikido
Yoga
Kyudo: The Way of the Bow
Japanese Tea Ceremony

## Study Abroad: Nepal and Bali

Program provides a thorough introduction to the living traditions of meditation, philosophy, music, painting and dance presently flowering in both Nepal and Bali. Both programs infuse the cross-cultural educational experience with awareness of the personal journey.

Meditation Practicum
Balinese Gamelan Orchestra
Arts and Culture
Kathmandu Valley:Traditional Culture, Developing Nation

Buddhist Traditions
Balinese Dance
Independent Study and Travel

## Visual Arts

Eastern and Western art disciplines. Hands-on studio approach with studies in art history and portfolio/gallery presentations. Drawing, color theory, figure studies, watercolor, painting, calligraphy, brush stroke, thangka painting, and ceramics/sculpture.

Student Body: 30% state, 55% female, 45% male, 2% minority
90% transfers   75% over 25 years of age
Tuition: $11.358   No Housing   Rolling Admissions
- All Seminar Format  • Service-Learning  • Field Studies  • Individualized Majors
- Interdisciplinary Classes & Majors  • Life Experience Credit  • Required Community Service
- Graduate Programs  • Vegetarian& Vegan Meals  • Campus Recycling

Use form in back to contact: Director of Admissions
The Naropa Institute   2130 Arapahoe Ave.   Boulder, CO 80302
(303)444-0202
inquiry@naropa.edu   www.naropa.edu

# NEW COLLEGE OF CALIFORNIA

200 Undergraduates    San Francisco, California

New College is a place where students are intellectually challenged to make a difference – in an atmosphere that is, above all, personal. And New College encourages
people to see themselves not as isolated individuals, but as human beings who are part
of a community.

To be sure, the community is diverse, and not only in the usual aspects of ethnicity, class, and orientation. Diversity also means recognizing that we are all complex
beings who can nevertheless come together for a common purpose -- in this case,
embarking on a journey of academic exploration that mines the wisdom of the past in
order to raise the hope of a future that is more humane for everyone.

This unusual combination of concern for both the particularities of each individual and the welfare of the society as a whole -- mediated through real concern for the
situation of each person at the school -- makes New College the unique place it is.

If you choose to join this unusual community, one thing is certain: your life in its
many aspects - intellectual, spiritual, social, emotional - will never be the same.

And you will make a difference.

New College's School of Humanities - Weekday BA Program is committed to an
undergraduate education that fosters:

• Critical Thinking - This doesn't mean just questioning the facts or logic of an
argument. It means also understanding the social and cultural situations in which
knowledge is produced -- and grounding knowledge in ethical principles and application to daily life.

• Interdisciplinary Learning - Knowledge may need to be organized into distinct
areas or disciplines, but students should be able to move freely between them, using
the concepts of each to reveal what others leave out.

• Diversity - Individual experience is shaped - and society is divided-by income
and social class, race and ethnicity, gender and sexual orientation. New College is
committed to bringing this diversity into education, and building trust and solidarity
across social divisions by rediscovering shared needs and values.

• Activism - New College wants students to connect learning to life experience
and their current lives outside the classroom. It helps them create positive change in
society, both while in school and after graduation. All New College students do community internships or field studies.

• Community-Building - For New College, building community is both a means
and an end. Community is built in everyday interaction: in classroom dialogue and in
common projects. This community in turn enhances learning and helps envision, and
work for, the common good.

The curriculum is organized into three clusters: Community and Global Studies;
Cultural Studies; and Arts, Music, and Literature. Within each cluster are several
emphasis areas, but students can construct their own from courses offered by any cluster. The emphasis area is focused in a Senior Project. Learning options include the
tutorial, independent study, field study, and practicum.

The World Studies Project of New College is an academic field program whose mission is to facilitate communication and develop relationships between the New College community and friends and colleagues in other parts of the world.

The Semester Abroad Program enables students to immerse themselves fully in other cultures in in conjunction with a three to four week academic study tour. Undergraduate and graduate academic credit is available, but non-credit participants are also welcome.

Within this educational framework, the Project and its students search for community solutions to social and cultural conflicts by looking at the complex relationships between politics, economics, culture, geography, and spirituality.

The Project was created to enable students to take an active role in their education by connecting classroom learning with the outside world through field experience, while promoting an understanding of world cultures. The international community that grows out of these experiences fosters understanding through communication among peoples of varying social, economic, and cultural backgrounds. New College hopes to carry this vision of a truly global community into the twenty-first century.

The Weekend College Completion Program is an accelerated, upper-division course of study culminating in a BA in Humanities. Designed for self-motivated, disciplined working adults who have completed approximately 45 units of transferable college credit, or who can combine transferable units with credit awarded for earlier life experience and/or general subject matter testing through CLEP.

Twelve months of study divided into three 4-month trimesters combine interdisciplinary seminars one full weekend each month with supervised independent study and journal work. The cohort method creates learning groups that pass through the entire program together, providing a common context for concentration in either interdisciplinary humanities or individually-designed emphasis areas.

Culture, Environment, and Sustainable Community is also a Weekend BA Completion Program. Located just north of San Francisco in Santa Rosa, this one-year degree program is designed for people intellectually interested in the interdependence of culture, meaning, politics, ecology, and community --ß who want to use their knowledge to create sustainable alternative communities.

The focus is on developing a critical perspective on the history and present condition of modern society, learning new ways to conceptualize solutions to contemporary problems, while acquiring the skills to concretely solve them.

The three part program features a structured 12-month curriculum of core seminars; individualized research and study leading to an undergraduate thesis; and optional co-curricular activities including workshops, activist projects, community building rituals, and social gatherings.

Cohorts of up to 20 students will meet in the core seminars once a month, remaining in contact with each other throughout the program.

# MAKING A DIFFERENCE STUDIES

## Community & Global Studies

This cluster immerses students in the lives of communities anywhere -- from just around the block to halfway around the world. This program makes sense of the new global economy and its impact on culture, ecological problems and solutions, and social movements. Fieldwork and internship opportunities allow students to work for change while they prepare themselves for graduate school and/or socially relevant careers.

## Anthropology & Sociology

In this interdisciplinary approach, other cultures are studied in detail, while inquiry into our own is fundamental to responding creatively to our reality: global interdependence in a context of unequal power relations, and political, economic, and cultural struggle.

## Ecological Studies

Analyzes various areas of human interaction with the environment, while seeking ecologically-conscious alternatives. Students work in both the classroom and the community, learning through dialogue, creative problem-solving, and internships with local environmental groups.

| | |
|---|---|
| Nature as a Concept | Eco-Logics / Eco-Nomics |
| Eco-Literacy: Introduction to Ecology | Issues in Environmental Activism |

## Integrated Health Studies

The history and politics of health care - its ethical dilemmas, cultural, social, economic, and psychological dimensions, and role in the community -- as well as cross-cultural and alternative perspectives on health while doing practical, health-related work.

| | |
|---|---|
| Medical Anthropology | Political Economy of Health Care |
| Health Promotion and Awareness | Feminist Theory and Women's Health |
| Living Anatomy Through Movement | Health Studies: Strategies for Change |

Social and Psychological dimensions of Health and Medicine

## Media and Society

Blends a core curriculum examining the three "contexts" of the "global media society": theoretical, political-economic, and cultural- historical, with one-on-one mentorships covering media fields like film, TV, journalism, etc., and internships in local radio, newspapers, PR, advertising, etc. that provide hands-on experience. (www.newcollege.edu/media studies/)

## Cultural Studies

Culture represents the social production of meaning; it shapes both the self and the self's relation to society. This cluster provides critical tools for making sense of our relationship to the world we live in, and actively shaping both - drawing on history, aesthetics, psychology, economics, literature, religion, science, and theories of gender, sexuality, race and ethnicity.

## Cultural Histories

Some see culture as a form of social control, others as a field of resistance and play. Cultures are environments we inhabit: subcultures, microcultures, mass culture, popular culture, middlebrow and high cultures. How these work, where they came from, and where they're going.

## Psychology

To understand the mind, we must understand the social worlds in which minds are born and live. Foundation in development and therapy, and investigation of the unconscious aspects of social life. How does an ideology that justifies domination become anchored in the dominated? What lets people rape, torture, and kill other people designated as "the enemy"?

## Gender Studies

What is gender? How many genders are there? How many sexual orientations? Is gender different from sex? What roles do race and class play in all this? Feminist and queer theory as well as history, psychology, law, literature, sociology, anthropology, and media studies help us understand.

Creativity, Sexuality, and the Sacred     Queer Cultures, Queer Spaces
Cultural Notions of Self and Sexuality     AIDS and Society
Perspectives on Lesbian/Gay Experience     Fundamentalism & the Religious Right

## Politics & Society

Contemporary critical thinking challenges established versions of history and politics. Emerging movements demand accountability to women, queers, ethnic "minorities," working-class and poor people, and the biosphere. This emphasis area analyzes power relations, explores critiques of the status quo, and seeks viable alternatives.

Political Economy     Social Problems/Social Visions
Political History of San Francisco     Critical Moments in 20th Century US History
Global Political Economy     Schooling, Inequality, & Social Change

## Arts, Music, & Literature

Examine the history of art forms and media, their connection with society, and the ways they've been used to change people's attitudes and ways of knowing. In this context, "art"is not only for self-expression, but also social critique and communal celebration, political challenge and spiritual focus, training the senses and enlarging the imagination.

## Arts and Social Change

Acquire the skills to bring imagination to life through Performance, Movement/Dance, Video, and Visual Arts. Students learn to apply these skills in education, community organizing, therapy, and activism as well as personal art making. Simultaneously, they explore how other cultures have defined similar kinds of creative activity.

Arts and Learning     Arts and Social Change
Performance/Urban Ritual     Community Theater Making
Joy of Movement     Video Arts
Drama Therapy     Screenwriting and Propaganda

## Writing, Literature, & Publishing

Literature and its composition from an historical, social, and international perspective, exploring the role of the writer as witness, agitator, and activist. Letterpress printing and desk-top publishing are also taught.

Student Body: 55% female, 44% male, 36% minorities, 59% transfer
Faculty 53% male, 47% female, 40% minority
Tuition: $8,376 or $315 per unit P/T     No housing     Rolling Admissions

• Service Learning   • Weekend & Evening Classes   • Required Practicum   • Field Studies
• Team Teaching   • Individualized Majors   • All Seminar Format   • Life Experience Credit
• Interdisciplinary Classes & Majors   • Optional SAT's   • Graduate Program   • Distance Learning

Use form in back to contact: Office of Admissions
New College of California
741 Valencia St.    San Francisco, CA 94110
(415) 437-3460    (888) 437-3460
www.newcollege.edu

**Friends World Program** senior student on project site in Kenya with a traditional folk healer. He studied spirituality and healing in the U.S., India, China, Costa Rica and Kenya.

Natural Resources Management students at **Sterling College** work with draft horses even in Vermont's snowy winters.

A mother and her child in Cedar Apartments, a unique single parent housing complex on the **Bemidji State University** campus. Bemidji State was the first public college or university to offer single parent housing on campus.

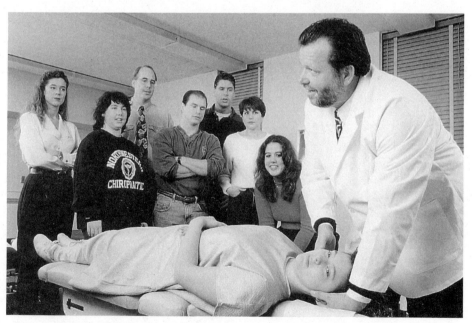

Students at **Northwestern Chiropractic** discuss a common neck adjustment technique with Dr. Jim Amundson in a neuromusculoskeletal systems lab. (See graduate school section.)

Work and community service are integral parts of student life at **Warren Wilson College**. Environmental studies majors often chose the organic garden work crew.

Students at **Brevard Community College** monitor water quality in a local pond. Brevard has one of the strongest service-learning programs of any college in the country.

**Goddard College** equally values internal knowing (through such practices as yoga) and external action in the world. Goddard is a place for hard thinking and plain living.

**Green Mountain College** attracts active learners interested in environmental issues. GMC takes an educational approach college officials call ecology across the curriculum and adventure across the co-curriculum.

# NORTHLAND COLLEGE

880 Students    Ashland, Wisconsin

The abundant natural beauty of the northern lakes and forests of Lake Superior country provide the perfect setting for a school like Northland. Over twenty five years ago the faculty of this one hundred and six year-old college committed themselves to a new vision; a liberal arts/environmental college. Since then, the idea that our natural and social worlds and that the knowledge they support are inextricably connected, has flourished and matured at Northland. A premise of Northland's educational mission is that we must strive to free ourselves from the alienating and self-destructive assumption that humans live in isolation from the natural environment. The essence of human existence is that we live in two worlds: the world we have created and the world that created us. We dwell simultaneously in the human realm of institutions, cultures, and ideas as well as in the life-giving realm of nature. As long as we separate these two realms, we can never feel completely at home, at peace with ourselves and our environment. In our quest for wholeness, we affirm our deepest humanistic values.

Northland is unique in that it does not restrict its study of the relationship between humanity and nature to a few courses in ecology or environmental studies. Almost a third of Northland's courses may be said to have some clear relevance to environmental issues. If the human and the natural world are as intimately interwoven as we believe, that relationship can be, and should be, analyzed and appreciated from all perspectives: scientific, political, anthropological, philosophical, literary, artistic, and recreational. A concern for the natural world around us runs throughout Northland's curriculum and co-curricular activities. Northland gained national recognition by receiving the Certificate of Environmental Achievement from Renew America in association with the National Environmental Awards Council. Northland has received national recognition for outstanding science and math programs.

As a liberal arts college, Northland strives to bring about the maximum intellectual, social, personal, and physical development of its students. In the long run, a liberal arts education is the most practical form of training. The world is quickly changing and tomorrow's problems cannot be anticipated. Success in the future will depend on the ability to cope with the unknown, to acquire new skills as the needs arise, and to gather knowledge about factual situations that could hardly have been imagined a decade earlier. A technical, overly specialized training prepares for today; a liberal arts education prepares for tomorrow.

A small college, Northland fosters an atmosphere in which there is a distinctive concern for both the individual human being and the natural world. Northland offers a value-sensitive education focusing on the liberal arts as a vehicle for understanding the disciplines, techniques and knowledge needed to function effectively in the modern world. Northland focuses on the study of our interactions with the environment, ranging from aesthetic and spiritual values derived from the great Northwoods and Lake Superior, to complex social and scientific issues. There is also emphasis on the study of human behaviors and interaction through traditional majors and interdisciplinary programs in such areas as environmental studies, outdoor education, cross-cultural and global understanding, education and business.

Emphasis is placed on individual relationships with faculty, field experience, internships, independent study, exposure to other cultures and travel abroad as well as cooperative and experiential experiences. The faculty is committed to including environmental subject matter or methodologies in their classes whenever appropriate. Several classes are team taught in a multidisciplinary approach. Northland's 4-4-1 calendar year offers many opportunities for travel to other countries.

Several environmental and social issue conscious groups are active on campus. The Sigurd Olson Environmental Institute is the environmental education outreach arm of the college. The Timber Wolf Alliance, and Loon Watch and the Bi-National Forum are among the sponsored programs. The Institute provides educational programs to increase public understanding of the Lake Superior Bio-region and environmental issues as well as in-service training in environmental education for teachers. The campus has adopted a goal of achieving zero-discharge for eliminating waste materials. A school wide recycling program and a pesticide policy was initiated at Northland ten years ago, and an environmental energy audit is done once a year. The Environmental Council, a college-wide task force, is designed to serve as the vanguard of environmental consciousness on campus.

In keeping with Northland's commitments to apply in practice what it teaches about environmental issues and ways to develop a sustainable future, the new The Environmental Living & Learning Center residence was designed with hundreds of environmental considerations in mind. Among the special features are a 20 kilowatt wind tower, three photovoltaic arrays, fourteen solar hot water panels, and composting waterless toilets. The apartments have passive solar design and share two greenhouses to be operated by the residents. Students joined architects and others on the campus committee to select the most environmentally friendly materials.

Lake Superior, the Apostle Islands, Chequamegon National Forest and dozens of freshwater lakes offer a natural setting for field studies. Outdoor Education majors may spend a full semester at the Audubon Center of the North Woods. Academic adventures abroad provide in-depth exposure to international culture and environments. Examples include the study of rainforest ecology in Costa Rica, tropical lowland ecology of Mexico, the mammals of Kenya, and natural history in the Galapagos.

Northland students have interned with the Fish and Wildlife Service, Department of Natural Resources, nature centers, U. S. Forest Service, Great Lakes Indian Fish and Wildlife Service, Olson Environmental Institute, businesses, as well as other organizations. Students started a volunteer service organization on campus to work with groups in Ashland as well as a service-learning program.

Northland also trains regional school teachers for expanded emphasis on the environment in Wisconsin classrooms, and the Apostle Island School, a cooperative educational venture with elementary and middle schools.

At Northland, students participate in many outdoor activities and excursions, from sea kayaking and biking to backpacking and cross country skiing. The outdoor orientation program for freshmen gives new students an opportunity to canoe, kayak, study native woodland skills, study wildlife on Stockton Island, or participate in small group outdoor experiences. Wild Careers is a special week-long summer program for high school students wanting to explore environmental careers.

# MAKING A DIFFERENCE STUDIES

## Teacher Certification in Environmental Studies &Education (Grs. 1-9, 6-12)
We also offer a Social Studies Teaching Major in Sociology/Native American studies.

Concepts of Biology
Environmental Public Policy
Sociology of the Environment
Ecology

Environmental Education Curriculum Review
Concepts of Earth Science
Environmental Law
Teaching Practicum

- **Environmental Citizenship**  Holistic investigation of what it might mean to live at peace with the earth, including philosophies, alternative lifestyles, and management skills necessary for participating in a democracy.

## Environmental Studies/Social Sciences
Sustainable Development
Environmental Ethics
Public Administration
Applied Problem Solving
Native Peoples and Rainforests

Environmental History
Expository Writing
Internship
Economics of Citizenship
Global Resource Issues

## Environmental Studies/Natural Sciences
Environmental Modeling
Land and Water Use Planning
Land Forms
Dendrology

Concepts of Biology
Populations
Remote Sensing
Pollution Biology

## Environmental Studies/Humanities
Humanity and the Environment
Environmental Policy Analysis
Artic Environments

Cultural Ecology
The Nature of Sound
Art in the Environment

## Native American Studies
Program includes student support and community education which provides credit and non-credit courses, workshops, and technical assistance to residents of reservation communities.

Introduction to Ojibway Language
Native American History to 1890
North American Indian Cultures
Native American Song and Dance
Native American World Views

Native American Cultures of Wisconsin
Native American History 1890 to Present
American Indian Literature
Native American Arts and Crafts
American Indian Law

- **Ethnobiology**  A study of native American beliefs and values in regard to the natural environment. Use of plants and animals to meet basic needs, i.e. food, shelter, clothing, medicines, etc. The course is oriented toward field work and projects incorporating the traditional lifestyle of Native American people.

## Government/Environmental Policy
Environmental Public Policy
Land and Water Use Planning
Sociology of the Environment
Environmental Ethics

Seminar in Environmental Law
Environmental Citizenship
Microeconomics
Policy Analysis Techniques

- **Global Resource Issues**  Analysis of growing human pressures on scarce resources and fragile ecosystems as a result of population increase and national and corporate policies with special view to the potential for human conflict generated by same: e.g. oil crisis, desertification, competition for minerals.

## Natural Resources   Concentrations in Resource Management, Land and Water Resources, and Wildlife and Fish Ecology

Natural Resource Field Study,
Woodland Plants
Environmental Impact Analysis
Land / Water Regulations
Wildlife Management
Intro to GIS
Aquatic Invertebrates

## Outdoor Education   Tracks in Natural History; Special Populations; Outdoor Ed/Native American; Recreation & Leisure Services; Adventure Education

Teaching Assistantships, Field Activities, Outdoor Education Practicums

Whitewater Canoeing
Orienteering
Group Process and Communication
Camp Counseling and Administration
Therapeutic Recreation Design
Basic Wilderness Skills
Rock Climbing
Introduction to Outdoor Education
Winter Exploration and Interpretation
Search and Rescue
Environmental Education Curriculum
Urban Ecology

Ecological Ecosystem Interpretation of Natural Science
Philosophy and Theory of Experiential Education

## Conflict and Peacemaking

Major has four components: Peace Strategies, Values & Ethics, Skills, and World Systems

War, Peace and Global Issues
Environmental Citizenship
Theory and Practice of Nonviolence
Human Relations Workshop
Global Resource Issues
Social Change and Social Movements
Nuclear Age
Exploring Alternative Futures
Conflict Resolution
Sociology of the Third World
Group Process and Communication
Conflict and Peacemaking

## Government/Social Welfare Policy

Economics of Labor
Social Problems
Nature of Inequality
Social Change & Movements
Microeconomics
Global Resource Issues
Conflict Resolution
Crime, Deviance and Criminal Justice
Sociology of the Community
Population
Issues in Political Thought
Introduction to Public Administration

## Sociology/Anthropology

Cultural Ecology
Sociology of Community
Sociology of the Third World
Group Process & Communication
The Nature of Social Inequality
Human Conflict
Sociology of the Environment
Exploring Alternative Futures
Modern Japanese Social Thought
Social Change and Social Movements

**Forestry Dual Degree/Michigan Tech U     Government     Education**

Student Body: 33% state, 53% female, 47% male, 10% minority, 25% transfer
Costs: $17,235     Apply By:5/1
Average number of students in a first year classroom: 25-30
• Student Environmental Audits  • Field Studies   • Individualized Majors
• Service-Learning   • Team Teaching  • Theme Housing  • Interdisciplinary Classes
• Optional SAT's   •Non-Resident Degree Program  • Vegetarian & Vegan Meals

Use form in back to contact: Director of Admissions
Northland College   1411 Ellis Ave.   Ashland, WI  54806
(715) 682-1224
admit@wakefield.northland.edu   www.northland.edu

# OBERLIN

2,823 Students　Oberlin, Ohio

As long as there has been an Oberlin, Oberlinians have been changing the world. As an institution and as a community, Oberlin is characterized by a heady spirit of idealism. Do Oberlinians arrive with the conviction that a single person's efforts can have far-reaching effects, or does Oberlin instill this idealism in them? Most likely it is a combination of the two, one reinforcing the other. Whatever its source, the results of this idealism are dramatic. It impels Oberlinians to be open to new perspectives, to rethink their positions when necessary, to speak their minds, to strive to make the world a better place. This spirit of idealism, this sense of conviction, unites the many different individuals in the Oberlin community. Students, faculty members, and alumni believe they can change the world.

What unifies this diverse and often opinionated group of students into a community of scholars? First, they are all extraordinarily committed to academic achievement. Second, their vision and progressive thinking - that Oberlin spirit of idealism - allows them to seize every opportunity as a learning experience. They educate one another on important issues, and they work to solve problems on campus, in the community, and in the world. Their ongoing debate is evidence of their willingness to confront issues that society often chooses to ignore. Oberlin students put their idealism to work on a variety of issues. Reflecting Oberlin's traditional concern for the betterment of humanity, about 30% of Oberlin graduates work in the field of education. Alumni also stay close to important social causes.

Oberlin was the first coeducational college in the country. Three women graduated in 1841, becoming the first women in America to receive bachelor's degrees. The admission of women caused Oberlin to be the center of controversy over coeducation for years.

Oberlin's decision to admit blacks in 1835 was in exchange for financial backing by two wealthy abolitionists. As a result of this decision, by 1900 nearly half of all the black college graduates in the country - 128 to be exact - had graduated from Oberlin. To put it in even greater historical perspective, in 1835, the state of Ohio was debating whether to allow blacks to attend elementary and secondary schools, and Southern states were drafting even stricter slave codes.

Once set on this progressive course, Oberlin became a center for abolitionism. The progressive impulse that inspired Oberlin's commitment to minorities and social justice in the 19th century and in the 20th century spurred innovations in academic and campus life. Programs focusing on cultural diversity have been part of Oberlin's new-student orientations since the early 1980's, and training sessions on similar topics are offered periodically to employees. While Oberlin has never been a utopia, neither has it been willing to give up its quest for perfection. Oberlin moves ahead in our changing world by continually reclaiming its proud legacy of dedication to social justice and inspiring all Oberlinians to change the world for the better. In 1991 Oberlin began requiring students to take at least nine credit hours in courses that deal with cultural diversity in order to graduate. Faculty members also are incorporating material on the environment, the experience of minorities and women, and other new areas into current courses, as well as developing new courses in these areas.

Freshman and sophomore colloquia are interdisciplinary, seminar style courses in which enrollment is limited to 10 first-year and five second-year students. This small size allows students to become familiar with the give-and-take nature of class discussions at the college level. Recent colloquia include "The Religious Thought of Mahatama Gandhi," "The Personal is Political: Representations of Activist Women in American History," "The Palestinian-Israeli Conflict" and "Explaining Social Power."

Students frequently work as research assistants for their professors. Biology students have assisted in research on the use of rock dust to remineralize soil and increase its fertility. Six students worked on a sociology survey investigating problems encountered by local low-income people.

In keeping with Oberlin's tradition of community service and social activism, Oberlin formed a chapter of the Bonner Scholars Program on campus in 1992. Bonner Scholars Program provides scholarship funds to first generation and low-income students by providing the equivalent of a full work-study award to students who complete ten hours of community service per week during the school year.

Off-campus study is quite popular, and by graduation about half of each class has spent at least one semester studying away from Oberlin. Nearly two dozen programs are available in countries such as Ireland, England, France, China, Kenya, Liberia, Nigeria, Sierra Leone, Japan, Costa Rica, Spain, India, and Scotland. The Mystic Seaport program, a wilderness program, and an urban planning and historic preservation program with Columbia university are among other options.

For members of the Oberlin Student Cooperative Association (OSCA,) cooperative houses and dining rooms are as much a statement of political conviction as they are place to live and eat. OSCA operates four room-and-board co-ops, and three board-only co-ops on campus. One co-op is kosher, and one is vegetarian. OSCA, a business with a $1 million operating budget, is operated almost exclusively by students. Members emphasize the democratic nature of decision making in each co-op and in the organization as a whole. On the average, co-op members devote five hours per week to work in the co-op. Working together also saves students money: in 1994-1995 the board fee charged by co-ops was 35% less than that charged in College dining halls, and the fee for a double room was 16% less. Co-ops purchase food from local family farms which to quote a student "is more ecologically conscious, healthier, and indicative of a more beneficial social theory." Co-opers also send work crews every week to help in harvesting on the farms.

Oberlin has more than 100 extra-curricular organizations. some of the most popular are the various community service, environmental, human rights, multi-cultural and Lesbian/Gay/Bi-sexual groups.

Oberlin's Experimental College is a student-run organization which sponsors courses (for limited academic credit) taught by members of the community - faculty, students, administrators, townspeople. Each year a very heterogeneous list of subjects is offered including crafts, special interests, community service, and academic subjects not found in the regular curriculum.

# MAKING A DIFFERENCE STUDIES

## Environmental Studies

Environment and Society
American Environmental History
Environmental Education Practicum
Environmental Economics
Organic Agriculture
Environment, Current Destitution, Future Generations and Moral Responsibility

American Environmental Policy
Ecology and the Environment
Energy Technology
Colloquium on Sustainable Agriculture
Conservation Biology

- **Oberlin and the Biosphere**   A seminar that will examine food, energy, water and materials flows, and waste management on the Oberlin campus; what enters and what leaves the campus community. Attention will be given to mines, wells, forest, farms, feedlots, dumps, smokestacks, outfall pipes, and to alternative technologies, and practices. Students participate in a joint research project.

## Black Studies

Practicum in Black Journalism
Education in the Black Community
African-American Drama
Pan-African Political Perspective
African-American Women's History

West African Dance Forms in Diaspora
Modern African Literature
Traditional African Cosmology
Cinema and Society: Racial Stereotyping
Langston Hughes and the Black Aesthetic

## Women's Studies

The Challenge of Gender and Race
Experiences of Religious Women
Issues in Language and Sexuality
Gender, Race and Rhetoric of Science
The Emergence of Feminist Thought
Feminist Theory and Challenge of Third World Feminisms

Turning Points in Women's History
Nature and Statue of Women
Paid & Unpaid Work: Sexual Division of Labor
Power and Marginality: Women & Develop't
Women in the Transition from Socialism

## Sociology

Community and Inequality
Urban Sociology
Gender Stratification
Race and Ethnic Relations
The City and Social Policy

Youth Subcultures, Movements & Politics
Revolution and Reform in Latin America
Sociology of the Black Community
State, Society & Social Change: Latin America
Social Change in Contemporary Societies

## Religion

Issues in Medical Ethics
Themes in Christian Ethics
Christian Social and Political Thought
Zen Buddhism
Mysticism in the West
Christian Utopias and Communitarian Movements

Islamic Spirituality and Mysticism
History of African-American Relig. Experience
Religion and the Experience of Women
Taoism
Selected Topics in Early Judaism

## History

Latinos in the U.S.
Roots of Feminist Analysis
Nourish or Punish? Ideologies of Poverty in 18th and 19th Century England
Caribbean History: Slaves and Slavery in the New World
Peasant Movements and the Agrarian Condition in Latin America

Race, Class and Gender in the Southwest
History of Vietnam

## Economics

| | |
|---|---|
| Poverty and Affluence | Public Sector Economics: Health Care Policy |
| Labor Economics | Environmental Economics |
| Economic Development in Latin America | Environmental & Resource Economics |
| Economics of Discrimination | Econ. of Land, Location & the Environment |

- **Introduction to Political Economy**  Economic problems of unemployment, inflation, the distribution of income & wealth, and the allocation of resources. The basic tools of analysis for studying these problems are developed and the role of public policy in securing economic objectives is explored.

## Politics

| | |
|---|---|
| Political Change in America | Federal Courts and the Environment |
| Government and Politics of Africa | Urban Politics |
| Public Policy in America | Third World Political Economics |
| Emergence of Feminist Thought | Nuclear Weapons and Arms Control |
| Political Economy of Women in Late Industrializing States | |

## Law & Society

| | |
|---|---|
| Philosophy and Values | Social & Political Philosophy |
| Christian Social & Political Thought | Deviance, Discord and Dismay |
| Economics, Ethics and Values | Reproductive Biology in the 80's |
| Equal Protection of the Law | Individual Responsibility |
| Moral Problems in Relig. Perspective | Turning Points: American Women's History |

## Latin American Studies

| | |
|---|---|
| Folklore and Culture of Latin America | Economic Development in Latin America |
| Dirty Wars and Democracy | State, Society and Social Change |
| Hispanics in American Politics | Int'l Political Economy / North-South Relations |
| Revolution and Reform in Latin Amer. | Female and Male in Latin American History |
| Latin American History: Conquest and Colonialization | |

## Anthropology

| | |
|---|---|
| Native American Literature | Engendering the Past |
| Immigration and Ethnicity in US | Ideology, Power and Prehistory |
| Immigration and Ethnicity in Israel | Jewish Society and Culture in Middle East |
| Ancient Civilizations of New World | Anthropology of Sub-Saharan Africa |

### Third World Studies        East Asian Studies

Student Body: 9% state, 56% female, 44 % male, 23% minority, 5% transfer, 6% int'l
Faculty: 71% male, 29% female, 13% minority
Comprehensive costs: $29,574     Apply By 1/15
50%+ of students engaged in community service     Average # of students in a first year classroom: 20

- Service Learning  • Field Studies  • Internships  • Interdisciplinary Classes
- Individualized Majors  • Recycling  • Student Environmental Audits  • Vegetarian Meals

Use form in back to contact: Admissions Office
Carnegie Building     Oberlin College     Oberlin, OH 44074
(440) 775-8411     (800) 622-OBIE
ad_mail@ocvaxc.cc.oberlin.edu     www.oberlin.edu

# OHIO WESLEYAN UNIVERSITY

1,850 Students    Delaware, Ohio

Ohio Wesleyan is a dynamic liberal arts university that seeks to prepare students for informed, ethical, productive and satisfying lives in the world community. The University strives to maintain an environment that both challenges and supports: that encourages individuals while it respects diverse opinion, that prizes excellence and applauds effort, that promotes personal growth and demands social responsibility, and that links today's learning with tomorrow's possibilities. The goal of Ohio Wesleyan is to prepare young men and women to know what they believe and why they believe it. Says one OWU professor: "The purpose of college is to figure out who you are, and how you can merge your personal and career goals as a caring citizen."

"I have been deeply impresses with the quality of education that takes place at Ohio Wesleyan: This is teaching and learning at its best." says the University's president, Dr. Thomas Courtice. "It is especially exciting to find this kind of academic excellence in an environment where students, faculty and staff all have a vested interest in contributing to the life of the college. Everyone at Ohio Wesleyan is eager to help address problems and develop solutions."

Since its founding in 1842, Ohio Wesleyan has been a leader in values-centered education, a place where public service and community leadership are the natural outcomes of an outstanding academic experience. At the core of the academic program are the professors: distinguished scholars, accomplished teachers, and dedicated mentors. Psychology Professor Harry Bahrick is a good example. Winner of the prestigious national Distinguished Teaching in Psychology Award for 1994, Dr. Bahrick has mentored dozens of students as research assistants while carrying out his internationally known studies of long-term memory. OWU professors are accessible and approachable, and they have a profound impact on the lives of their students. Philosophy Professor Bernard Murchland states: "Students worry a lot about jobs and how to make money. These are valid concerns. But a real problem in our society is not so much how to make money as how to spend it wisely. Values, decisions, freedom—that's what liberal education is all about."

The most distinctive aspect of an Ohio Wesleyan education is the way it links liberal arts learning with the civic arts of citizenship. The academic program and co-curricular life work together, fostering among students an awareness of their role as responsible citizens of society. As residents of Austin Manor, the nation's first inter-generational living unit on a college campus, OWU students learn from the life experiences of their neighbors, -- retired faculty and alumni. "National Colloquium" embodies the college's commitment to citizenship education within the curriculum. "NC," as the Colloquium is called, involves the entire community in a semester-long examination of a complex public issue. Past NC topics include racism, population and the environment, ethics and health care. The 1997-98 topic is "Was of the Words: Creativity, Censorship and Power."

Ohio Wesleyan's unusually broad curriculum blends traditional classroom learning with hands-on experience through research, independent study, internships, and off-campus experience. The University's 22 academic departments and four interdepartmental programs offer a total of 65 majors; four combined-degree (3/2) programs; and pre-professional programs in art therapy, dentistry, law, medicine, music therapy, public administration and veterinary medicine. Students may also design their own majors. The Center for Economics and Business and the Arneson Institute for Practical Politics further enrich academic life with seminars, guest speakers and special events such as the quadrennial Mock Political Convention.

Involvement is the theme of co-curricular life. From student political groups and media operations to athletics and intramurals, from the Environment and Wildlife Club to Amnesty International, from "improv" theater and modern dance to religious groups, and a respected Greek system that attracts about 40% of the student body, the campus hums with activity.

Public service is an Ohio Wesleyan tradition. Once known as "the West Point of Missions," the University continues its commitment to volunteerism as a key component of undergraduate learning. Each year, an extraordinary percentage of the student body participates in some form of community service. "Leadership for Tomorrow," a seven-week series of workshops, helps students develop and refine leadership skills in organizational and personal areas of their lives. Students volunteer at Global Village, drive for Meals on Wheels, train for the Helpline Hotline, and tutor Columbus City School students. House of Hope, a small living unit on campus, offers a unique residence for students who wish to focus on helping educate youth and adults.

Through participation in Habitat for Humanity, or a fraternity philanthropy project, or a mentoring program with adolescents, or any of a huge variety of service projects in the public schools, students try to "leave the woodpile a little higher than we found it." Most years, some students spend spring break working in health clinics in the Dominican Republic, learning about Third World poverty, neocolonial economics and health delivery systems. During the early years of the Peace Corps, Ohio Wesleyan sent more graduates per capita than any other college in the country. Recently Ohio Wesleyan was one of only 16 organizations in the country selected to host a Summer of Service project, in the Clinton administration's National Service Program.

Diversity characterizes the student body: 1,850 students from 44 states and 52 countries. Fully 18 percent of the students are either U.S. minorities or foreign students. This multicultural presence is a source of enrichment for all members of the community. OWU also participates in an exchange program with historically important, predominantly black Spelman College and Morehouse College in Georgia. Cross cultural understanding is further enhanced in the residential area. Among the "small living units" are the House of Black Culture, Women's House, Peace and Justice House, and the Creative Arts House.

Students graduate from Ohio Wesleyan with heightened awareness of world issues and a commitment to put their skills, insights, and concern for others to work in the world. Observes President Courtice, "Few other institutions so effectively combine quality, in their programs and people, with such a strong sense of community and commitment."

# MAKING A DIFFERENCE STUDIES

## Environmental Studies

Ecology and the Future of Man
Ornithology
Environmental Plant Biology
Economic Geography
The World's Cities
Animals and Their Environment

Plant Communities and Ecosystems
Environmental Chemistry
Biology and Tropical Nations
Technology & Environmental Ethics
Human Ecology
Marine Biology

- **Island Biology**  Characteristics of islands, and analysis of why island organisms provide superior examples for the study of evolutionary, ecological, and behavioral phenomena. This course includes a required trip to the Galapagos Islands.

- Faculty Bio **Edward Burtt**  Zoology Professor Jed Burtt's knowledge of birds is nearly matched by his commitment to recycling. Dr. Burtt and his family recently were named the most environmentally aware household in the county. He is an active environmentalist, a widely published zoologist, and a research ornithologist. He regularly attracts large enrollments in his ornithology class, inspiring science and non-science majors alike to attend pre-dawn bird-watching labs.

## Botany - Microbiology

Bacterial Physiology
Medical Microbiology
Genetics
Cytogenetics
Molecular Biology of Viruses

Biodiversity of Flowering Plants
Biology of the Fungi
Cell and Molecular Biology
Plant Physiology
Immunology

- Faculty Bio  **Gerald Goldstein** (Microbiology)  Because so few colleges teach virology (the study of viruses) to undergraduates, and even fewer teach it with a lab, Jerry Goldstein decided to write his own laboratory manual. Today, his book is used not only at Ohio Wesleyan, but in graduate-level courses at many other universities. Top OWU students work with Goldstein on research studying herpes simplex, vaccinis and adenovirus. Students also assisted in his landmark work on plasmid DNA isolated from bacteria discovered in intestinal remains of an 11,000 year-old mastodon.

## Politics and Government

Civil Rights and Liberties
Judicial Process and Policy-Making
International Politics
American Political Thought
The American Presidency
Political Parties
Public Opinion and Political Behavior
Global Issues: Human Rights, Terrorism, Arms & Arms Control

American Politics & The Mass Media
American Constitutional Law
Democracy & Its Critics
Congress and the Legislative Process
Public Administration
Equality and American Politics

## Psychology

Personality and Assessment
Abnormal Behavior
Psychology of the Exceptional Child
Adolescent Psychology
Community Psychology

Counseling & Psychotherapy of Women
Comparative Psychology
Organizational Behavior
Maturity and Age
Learning

- **Child Psychology**  The psychological and physiological development of the child from conception to 12 years. Effects of parents, school, and community practices on emotion, social and intellectual aspects of child behavior. Opportunities for direct observation of pre-school children.

## Sociology/Anthropology

Crime and Deviance
Race and Ethnicity
Peoples and Cultures of Japan and Asia
Health and Illness
The Family
Population Problems
Social Inequality

Peoples and Cultures of Africa
Peoples and Cultures of the Pacific
Science and Society
Gender in Cross-Cultural Perspective
Urban Society
Magic, Witchcraft and Religion
Self and Society

- Faculty Bio **Mary Howard** (Sociology/Anthropology and Women's Studies) Before joining the faculty in 1985, Dr. Howard spent 16 years as a counselor in the human services field. A scholar specializing in medical anthropology, her research has taken her into Amish communities, inner city shelters, and South African homes. For several years, she has coordinated OWU's Caribbean Seminar, which includes taking students to the Dominican Republic as volunteers in a health clinic for spring break.

## Economics

National Income and Business Cycles
Comparative Urban Economics
Economic Development
Intro. to Game Theory
Public Finance

Economic History
International Economics
Labor Economics and Problems
Monetary and Fiscal Economics
The Economic Growth of Modern Japan

## Women's Studies

Literary Perspectives on Women
Women Poets
Women in American History
Psychology of Women
Women in Antiquity

Gender and Identity
Gender in American Society
Philosophy and Feminism
Human Sexuality
Gender in Cross-Cultural Perspective

- **Sociology of Feminism** The diverse range of contemporary feminist social theories will be covered, including: Liberal Feminism, Radical Feminism, Socialist Feminism, Third World Feminism, and Lesbian Feminism. Topics such as (under) paid and unpaid labor, rape and violence against women, sexuality, women in the arts, the women's self-help movement.

## Urban Studies

A multidisciplinary program dealing with the character and evolution of complex urban systems, especially the city system of the USA. Introduces students to urban problem-solving, urban planning, and public policy formation.

Population Problems
Economic Geography
Contemporary Amer. Landscape Problems
Urban Society

Comparative Urban Economics
The World's Cities
Technology and Environmental Ethics
Judicial Process and Policy Making

- **Human Values & the Urban Process** An interdisciplinary orientation to the challenges of cities from a liberal arts perspective. Topics include urban structure, history, land use, planning, imageability, and future alternatives as they reflect human values.

Student Body: 49% state. 48% male, 52% female, 8% minority, 10% int'l.
Faculty 70% male, 30% female, 6% minority
Costs: $26,410   Apply by 3/1
• Internships • Study Abroad • Individualized Majors • Combined Degree Program

Use form in back to contact: Director of Admissions
Ohio Wesleyan University   Delaware, OH 43015
(800) 862-0612 (in Ohio)   (800) 922-8953 (outside Ohio)

Across the country students enjoy volunteering with Habitat for Humanity, helping to build affordable housing for low-income families.

With a strong emphasis on social responsibility, **Pitzer** encourages students to become involved in community activities and projects such as working with local youth groups.

**Audubon Expedition Institute's** unique field studies program takes students on extended bus tours to different regions of the country. (See travel section.)

**Sunbridge College** teacher training students in a third grade classroom at a nearby Waldorf school, at work on their "main lesson books" under the guidance of a master classroom teacher.

203

# UNIVERSITY OF OREGON

13, 765 Undergraduates   Eugene, Oregon

In the September/October 1996 issue of Mother Jones magazine, the University of Oregon ranked first in a list of activist campuses in the United States. Why? The UO produces more Peace Corps volunteers than any American university its size and ranks sixth overall in the nation. The UO was also the top school in the nation in voter registration for the 1996 presidential election. UO students are making a difference.

Recognized nationally and internationally as a research university committed to liberal arts and sciences education as well as professional preparation, the University of Oregon offers students more than 100 comprehensive programs, including professional schools of architecture, business, education, journalism and music. The UO's pioneering approach to interdisciplinary education allows students to combine majors in ways that best suit their needs and interests. Open discussion, exploration, questioning, and sharing information are what UO values. If you're curious, open-minded and willing to challenge yourself, you'll love it here.

The UO has developed innovative programs to ensure that its undergraduates have access to seminars, discussion groups, and other small-class settings, encouraging direct interaction with the institution's finest teachers and researchers. Freshman Interest Groups (FIGs,) for example, create social support groups based on academic interests by placing participating freshmen in small-class settings with students who have similar interests or majors. Freshman Seminars are small, discussion-oriented classes that allow freshmen to sample what's available academically at the University of Oregon—putting our most respected professors in touch with our newest students.

More than 250 student-run organizations and activities enhance students' educational experiences outside of the classroom. The Solar Information Center (SIC,) for example, promotes a higher awareness of the importance of conservation and renewable energy. SIC sponsors a quarterly lecture series on local, regional and global energy issues and publishes a quarterly newsletter. The Institute for a Sustainable Environment fosters research and education on environmental issues at the University of Oregon. The Institute's programs encompass environmental themes in the natural sciences, the social sciences, policy studies, humanities, and the professional fields. Because environmental problems are seldom adequately addressed by a single discipline, the Institute is particularly concerned with encouraging cross-disciplinary environmental research, education, and public service. Other student-run groups, such as OSPIRG (Oregon Student Public Interest Research Group); Students for Government Integrity; and the award-winning Student Recycling Program allow students to work together towards creating a better world.

Education continues beyond the borders of the Eugene campus. Students can participate in internships or community service experiences in the Eugene/Springfield community or travel overseas through one of the University's nearly 50 overseas study/international exchange programs. The University also has two off-campus facilities: the Pine Mountain Observatory and the Oregon Institute of Marine Biology

(OIMB,) which is situated on 107 acres of coastal property along Coos Bay. OIMB offers an interdisciplinary course encompassing marine ecology, marine mammals and birds, and biological oceanography as well as opportunities for individualized study.

University of Oregon's more than 170,000 graduates include leaders in business (Phil Knight of Nike,) journalism (Ann Curry, of NBC's "The Today Show," and Randy Shilts, author of And the Band Played On and Conduct Unbecoming,) education, science, and the arts (Ken Kesey, author of One Flew Over the Cuckoo's Nest). Three Pulitzer Prize winners, two Nobel Prize winners, six U.S. senators, and six Oregon governors are also among UO's distinguished alumni.

The University of Oregon is located in Eugene (pop. 126,500,) a city known for its commitment to individuality, in the heart of the Willamette Valley. Both the Willamette and McKenzie rivers run right through town, bordered by miles and miles of bike paths and running trails (100 in the city). The Pacific Ocean is one hour west; snow-covered peaks in the Cascade range are one hour east. The student-run Outdoor Program organizes trips to these and many other beautiful destinations between and beyond. Program activities include biking, hiking, kayaking, mountaineering, and windsurfing.

## MAKING A DIFFERENCE STUDIES

**Architecture   Includes tracks in Landscape and Interior Architecture.**
Five-year programs subscribing to the concepts of green architecture and sustainability.

| | |
|---|---|
| Architectural Form and Urban Quality | Housing in Society |
| Hydrology and Water Resources | Landscape Preservation |
| Natural Resource Policy | Preservation and Restoration Technology |
| Solar Heating | Urban Farm |
| Passive Cooling | Settlement Patterns: Japanese Vernacular |

**Planning, Public Policy & Management   Tracks in Planning & Community Dev'pt., Public Policy & Mgm't, Resource Dev'pt. & Enviro Mgm't, or Social Policy Dev.**

| | |
|---|---|
| Communities and Regional Development | Contemporary Housing Issues |
| Environmental Health | Planning in Developing Countries |
| Managing Fiscal Austerity | Managing Nonprofit Organizations |
| Energy Policy and Planning | Neighborhood and Community Revitalization |
| Planning & the Changing Family | Planning and Social Change |

**Environmental Studies**

| | |
|---|---|
| American Environmental History | Solar Heating |
| Conservation Biology | Architectural Form and Urban Quality |
| Environmental Politics | Community, Environment, and Society |
| Population Ecology | Gender and International Development |
| Urban Geography | |

**Ethnic Studies**

| | |
|---|---|
| Asian Americans and the Law | Chicanos and the Law |
| Intro to the Asian American Experience | Intro to the Chicano and Latino Experience |
| Intro to the Native American Experience | Minority Women: Issues and Concerns |

## Peace Studies

American Radicalism

Political Ideologies

Political Geography

Systems of War and Peace

## International Studies

Aid to Developing Countries

International Protection of Human Rights

Population and Global Resources

Global Ecology

International Community Development

Anthropological Perspectives on Health & Illness

Environmental Planning

Introduction to World Value Systems

Rich & Poor Nations: Conflict & Cooperation

Ethnology of Tribal Societies

## Education

Cultural Diversity in Human Services

Family Policy

Innovative Education

Mental Health

Self as Resource

Change in Educational and Social Systems

Community Organization and Social Planning

Interventions with Individuals and Families

Learning Environments for Diverse Students

Professional Communication & Collaboration

## Women's Studies

Global Feminisms

Lesbian and Gay Studies

Postcolonial Women Writers

Feminist Perspectives: Identity, Race, Culture

History and Development of Feminist Theory

Sexuality

## Human Services

Issues and Policies in Human Services

Mind and Society

Family Policy

Child Welfare Services

Cultural Diversity in Human Services

Innovative Education

Organizational Intervention

Mental Health

Prevention Strategies

Community Organization & Social Planning

## Journalism

The Mass Media and Society

Women, Minorities, and Media

Communications Law

Media Management and Economics

Cultural Approaches to Communication

Advertising as a Social Institution

Journalism and Public Opinion

Third World Development Communications

Mass Media Ethics

International Journalism

### Outdoor Pursuits Leadership    Burmese, Thai, Indonesian Languages

Student Body: 63% state, 51% female, 49% male, 13% minority, 90% int'l.
Faculty: 58% male, 42% female
Avg. # of students in a first year class: 28
Costs: Residents: $8.950    Nonresident: $17,700    Apply by 3/1

• Interdisciplinary Classes & Majors    • Internships    • Co-op Work Study    • Team Teaching
• Service Learning    • Student Environmental Audits    • Study Abroad
• Vegetarian & Vegan  Meals

Use form in back to contact: Office of Admissions
240 Oregon Hall    University of Oregon    Eugene, OR 97403
(541) 346-3201    1 (800) BE-A-DUCK
www.uoregon.edu/

# PENN STATE UNIVERSITY

59,700 undergraduates at 17 campuses    Rural Central PA.

Penn State, founded in 1855, designated Pennsylvania's land-grant university in 1863, was irrevocably dedicated to a threefold mission of teaching, research and public service. Even though the idea of the land-grant university -- higher education in service to the public good -- dates to Abraham Lincoln's time, Penn State and its sister institutions across the nation are constantly finding new ways to make land-grant ideals relevant in a constantly changing world. At Penn State, this idealism, rooted in practicality and the wisdom of experience, remains a great attraction to today's students.

Penn State's enrollment makes it one of America's 10 largest universities, but it was one of seventeen public institutions cited as attractive alternates to Ivy League schools for academic quality and ambience in Richard Moll's *Public Ivys*. One reason for this popularity is that teaching has remained central to the University's mission.

Penn State's University Scholars Program offers unusually flexible and rigorous courses of study for students at all Penn State locations and in all majors. Students have all the benefits of a small, selective, private college, and the resources of a major research university. The program believes that those with special talents have special obligations to others. The program offers seminars and workshops on topics of service and leadership, travel grants, and provides support for exemplary student-initiated projects that enhance communities and/or the moral ecology. Scholars may also take advantage of summer and service/learning programs that carry academic credit. These activities offer experiences in cultures around the world to students who are, at the same time, making a real contribution to local communities. Experiences include international work camps, helping a Mexican village build a basketball court at a community center, and projects organized in consultation with Native American organizations.

Beginning with a "Penn State-in-China" agricultural assistance program in 1911. the College of Agricultural Sciences is now involved in teaching and programs in such far-flung locations as Egypt, Kenya, Poland, Swaziland, and Ukraine. Students in INTAG, an interdisciplinary minor in international agriculture, gain an awareness and appreciation for the interrelationships and interdependence of the nations of the world, find out what resources are available to solve international problems, study the impact of technology transfer across cultures, and acquire skills in development work.

Shaver's Creek Environmental Center, offers environmental studies and an interpretation laboratory. The center promotes positive attitudes about the Earth; provides opportunities for experiential learning and research; and encourages individual and group development. It is the only center that holds both federal and state licenses to use birds of prey in its public education program.

Engineering education, one of Penn State's traditional strengths, is also more diverse than one might assume. The Minority Engineering Program, recruits and works to retain underrepresented minority students. Women in Engineering Program aids in recruiting and retaining women in engineering programs at Penn State, and assists in creating a more positive environment for women students.

# MAKING A DIFFERENCE STUDIES

## Human Development & Family Studies

Communities and Families
Family Development
Infant and Child Development
Biocultural Studies of Family Organization
Personal and Interpersonal Skills

The Helping Relationship
Observation with Pre-School Children
Adolescent Development
Policy and Planning for Human Development
Adult-Child Relationships

## Health Policy & Administration

Health Services Organization
Health Services Policy Issues
Health Systems Management
Principles of Public Health Administration
Field Experience in Health Planning

Intro to Environmental Health
Health Care & Medical Needs
Health Planning Methods
Population and Policy Issues
Comparative Health Systems

## Community Studies

Community Systems
Social and Behavioral Change
Environment, Energy & Society
Comparative Community Development
Issues in Community Physical Design

Youth and Societies
Housing Problems & Policies
Evaluation of Community Service Programs
Power, Conflict & Community Decision Making
Planning of Community Social Services

## Educational Theory and Policy

Education in American Society
Global Education
Education and Status of Women
Ethnic Minorities and Schools in U.S.
Intro to Philosophy of Education

Introduction to Comparative Education
Education in Socialist Societies
Education in Latin America and Caribbean
Anthropology of Education
Education in Africa

## Labor and Industrial Relations

Industrial Relations
Practice of Collective Bargaining
History of the American Worker
Collective Bargaining Trends
History of American Organized Labor

Employment Relationship: Law and Policy
Women, Minorities and Employment
Labor-Management Relations
Occupational Health: Policy and Practice
Industrial Psychology

## Public Service

Public Finance
Regional Economics
Urban Geography
Bureaucracy and Public Policy
Community Organization

Economics of Public Expenditures
Housing Problems and Policies
Planning and Public Policy
Public Management Technology
Urban Sociology

## Architectural Engineering

Solar Energy Building System Design
Environmental Systems in Building

Solar Passive Design & Energy Conservation.
Soils Engineering

**Enviro Ed. Teacher Certificate   Medical Anthro.   Forestry   Health Education**
**Rehabilitation Services   Agronomy   Wildlife & Fisheries   Science, Tech. & Society**

Student Body: 82% state, 45% female, 55% male, 9% minority, 3% int'l.
Est. Costs: Residents $5,466   Nonresidents $11,354      Rolling Admissions
Use form in back to contact: Undergraduate Admissions Office
201 Shields Building   Penn State University   University Park, PA 16802-1294
(814) 865-5471   admissions@psu.edu

# PITZER COLLEGE

875 Students    Claremont, California

Founded in 1963, Pitzer is a coeducational liberal arts college with a progressive educational philosophy. Enrolling approximately 875 men and women, Pitzer College is part of a uniquely stimulating higher education environment consisting of five schools known collectively as the Claremont Colleges. Together, these colleges bring a vast range of courses and facilities to Pitzer students. Indeed, students on this campus may have the best of two worlds: enjoying, on the one hand, a level of resources usually associated with mid-sized universities and, on the other hand, the close student-faculty relationships found within small, human-scale colleges.

Pitzer College offers no short cuts to intellectual discovery, no guarantees as to the kind of person you'll be when you graduate. It does, however, offer a setting rich in possibilities, and if Pitzer graduates are more creative, more independent of spirit, and more willing to seek new answers, then it could be that the opportunities unique to Pitzer helped to make them this way. Because of Pitzer's strengths in the social and behavioral sciences it tends to attract a student body that concerns itself with the critical social and political issues facing our world. Most students arrive at Pitzer already committed to various social or political issues. Once at the college, they're encouraged to develop these interests to a greater degree; to take them further and test them harder. But mostly, the ideals that bring people to Pitzer continue to guide them after graduation. A Pitzer graduate who becomes a lawyer is as likely to use those skills in the public defender's office as in a corporate law firm. The graduate who goes on to earn an M.B.A. may opt not to work on Wall Street, choosing instead to help run a foundation raising money to fight a deadly disease.

Pitzer presents a unique opportunity for self-exploration and for exploration of the world around us and our involvement in that world. The College believes that students should take an active part in formulating their individualized plans of study, bringing a spirit of inquiry and adventure to the process of academic planning. Rather than enforcing traditional requirements, Pitzer provides the following guidelines to students and faculty advisors in order that students will fulfill the College's educational goals:

- Breadth of Knowledge   By exploring broadly the programs in humanities and fine arts, natural sciences and mathematics, social and behavioral sciences, students develop an understanding of the nature of the human experience - its complexity, its diversity of expression, its continuities and discontinuities over space and time, and those conditions which limit and liberate it.
- Understanding in Depth   Through the study of a particular subject matter in depth, students experience the kind of mastery which makes informed, independent judgment possible.
- Critical Thinking, Formal Analysis, and Effective Expression   Through juxtaposing and evaluating the ideas of others, and through participation in various styles of research, Pitzer students develop their capacities for critical judgment. Through exploration of mathematical and other formal systems, students acquire the ability to think in abstract, symbolic ways. Through written and oral communication, students acquire the ability to express their ideas effectively.

- Interdisciplinary Perspective   Through bringing together the perspectives of several disciplines, students gain an understanding of the powers and limits of each discipline and of the kind of contribution each can make to an exploration of the significant issues. Pitzer wants its students to learn the differences and the connections between different disciplines, as well as the ability to look at a situation from different perspectives.
- Intercultural Understanding   Through learning about their own culture and placing it in comparative perspective, students come both to appreciate other cultures and to recognize the ways that their own thinking and actions are influenced by the culture in which they live.
- Concern with the Social Consequences and Ethical Implications of Knowledge and Action   Through examining the social consequences and ethical implications of the issues they explore, students learn to evaluate the effects of individual actions and social policies and to take responsibility for making the world in which we live a better place.

Because of the emphasis on classroom teaching and a student faculty ratio of 10 to1, students and teachers are colleagues in the educational process; faculty do not draw a hierarchical distinction between themselves and the students. The average class size is 18 students and, to facilitate discussion, is often taught seminar -- rather than lecture-style.

Pitzer has developed a variety of programs which offer opportunities to specially qualified groups of students as well as all students who participate in special courses, seminars, and programs beyond the regular course offerings. Among these are the New Resources program, designed for the special needs of the traditionally post-college-age students and PACE, designed to provide intensive English language training for international students.

Many students take advantage of Pitzer's interdisciplinary programs and courses in order to broaden their understanding of interpretations of the human experience. Interdisciplinary seminars include the New Resources Seminar: Strategies for Success. Students may take special programs and clusters in International/Intercultural Studies; Social Responsibility Studies; Critical Studies in Science and Technology; The Study of Education, and The Third World.

Internships are a popular way to apply theories to practical experience, and many Pitzer students have begun fulfilling careers through the internship program. Internships affirm Pitzer's commitment to connecting knowledge and action, and provide opportunities to link students to social issues in Los Angeles communities and thereby develop feelings of social responsibility. Independent study allows students to create a curriculum that meets their individual needs and goals. Through this program, students work individually with faculty to create a course and to work through the materials. External programs in over 100 locations throughout the U.S.A. and abroad have become a part of the curriculum for the majority of Pitzer students. With programs offered in China, Ecuador, Italy, Nepal, Turkey Venezuela, Wales and Zimbabwe, as well as am urban studies program in Ontario, California, Pitzer's External Studies program goes far beyond the traditional. The program provides students with opportunities for intensive language study, internships, independent research, homestays, and significant interaction with peoples of other cultures.

# MAKING A DIFFERENCE STUDIES

## Environmental Studies

Environmental Studies can provide an integrated, unifying perspective on life, as well as a program for radical change.

Chemistry and the Environment
Energy and the Environment
Environmental Ethics
Environmental Policy
Politics of Water
Perspectives on Environmental Justice

Ecology and Culture Change
Environment of Southern California
Enviro. Awareness& Responsible Action
Marine Ecology
Native Americans and Their Environments
Population and Society

Progress and Oppression: Ecology, Human Rights, and Development

- **Consciousness, Environment & Self: Multicultural Perspectives** How perception of the natural environment, self and society result in different ways of knowing the world. Notion of "consciousness" as reflected in diverse spiritual, social, and political forms and practices. How "western" & "eastern" perspectives differ, but also coalesce.

## Freshman Seminars

At Your Service
Identity and Community
Native California: Resistance and Revival

Youth Rebellion: Reggae, Rap and Beyond
Hand and Brain
Bridging East/West: China, Japan,& America

Science & Its Social Context: Galileo, Darwin, and Us
Los Angeles in the European Imagination: Los Angeles Constructed by Germanic Culture
Liberals, Radicals, Politics and Blacklists: Free Speech in California

## American Studies

African American History
Cars and Culture
Politics of Ecology
Rural and Urban Social Movements
Social Stratification
Women at Work

Asian American Experiences
Chicano Literature
Power and Participation in America
Slavery and Freedom in the New World
U.S. Labor History
Women of the Historic American West

## Asian Studies

Children and Families in South Asia
Culture and Power
The World of Buddhism

China and Japan: Economy and Society
Introduction to China, Tibet, and Nepal
Chinese Philosophy, Culture, Traditional Medicine

## Black Studies

African and Caribbean Literature
Blacks in American Politics
Race, Class, and Power
Survey in African American Fiction

Black Women, Feminism and Social Change
History of African American Women in U.S.
Pan-Africanism and Black Radical Traditions
The Politics of Race

Industrialization and Social Change in Southern Africa

## Chicano Studies

Chicano Literature
U.S. Immigration Policy
Latina Feminist Traditions
Chicano/a History
Chicanos in Higher Education

Regional Dances of Mexico
Latino Politics in the 90's
Contemporary Chicano Narrative
Chicano Bilingualism and Education
Rural and Urban Social Movements

## Science, Technology and Society

Alchemists, Magicians and Scientists
History and Systems of Psychology
Medieval Technology and Society
Technology and People
Archaeology, Prehistory, and Evolution of Technology

Economics of Technical Enterprise
Medicine in Historical Perspective
Science, Technology, and Politics
Theory of Knowledge

## Media Studies

Teaches the production, theory, history, and social context of the visual media including film, video, photography, and digital technologies, with emphasis on film and video as media for creativity, expression, social responsibility, and multicultural understanding.

American Politics in Media Age
Creative Writing: Screenwriting
Gender and Genre
Language of Film
Underground Film
The Individual and Society in 20th Century Literature and Film

Comedy in Film and Fiction
Film and the Novel
Harmony of Light and Sound
Representations of Vietnam

## Gender and Feminist Studies

Focuses on the relations of power which have produced gender inequality, analyzing it as a human construction subject to change, rather than an innate, ordained condition. Challenges conventional research that reflect heterogeneity of women's experience.

African American Women's History
Latina Feminist Traditions
Public Women, Private Lives
Theories of Gender and Sexuality
Women and Fiction of Moral Choice

Feminist Political Thought
Politics of Gender: The Humanities
Sociology of Gender
Third World Women Writers
Women in the Economy

## Organizational Studies

An interdisciplinary program which focuses on administrative, economic, political psychological, and sociological factors as they interact within complex social systems.

Economy and Society
Labor Economics
Organizational Theory
Technology and People
The Nature of Work

Bureaucracy and Complex Organizations
Organizational and Industrial Psychology
Small Group Processes
Social Responsibility and the Corporation
Women at Work

## Political Economy

Environmental Ethics
History of Economic Thought
Political Psychology
Social Indicators and Public Policy
Third World in Global Economy

Agricultural Development in the Third World
International Political Economy
Race, Class and Power
State and Development in Third World
Water Policy

Student Body: 58% state, 59% female, 41% male, 30% minority, 4% int'l., 8% transfer
Faculty: 66% Male, 44% Female, 10% Minority
Costs: $28,574    Apply By 2/1    Average # of students in first year classroom: 18
Full recycling and energy conservation programs in effect since founding of college in 1963
• All Seminar Format   • Individualized Majors   • Field Studies   • Study Abroad
• Team Teaching   • Multidisciplinary Classes   • Vegetarian Meals
Use form in back to contact: Office of Admission
Pitzer College   1050 North Mills Ave.   Claremont, CA 91711
(909) 621-8129
admission@pitzer.edu    www.pitzer.edu/

# PORTLAND STATE UNIVERSITY

10, 215 Undergraduates    Portland, Oregon

Portland State University (PSU) is Oregon's only urban public university and, as such, is defined by its relationship with the community. PSU is committed to the delivery of quality academic programs for undergraduates and graduates that are integrated with a campus-wide commitment to community service, and to collaborative strategies that link faculty and students in learning and research experiences that bear directly on the problems and opportunities of the community and state.

Portland State has won praise from scholars nationwide by replacing its traditional general education requirements with an inquiry-based interdisciplinary undergraduate program of study that meets the needs of today's students. The undergraduate experience at PSU offers many of the advantages found at small selective private schools, but at the price of a public university. The general education program, called University Studies, is designed to facilitate the acquisition of the knowledge, abilities, and attitudes which will form a foundation for lifelong learning among its students. This foundation includes the capacity and the propensity to engage in critical thinking, to use various forms of communication for learning and expression, to gain an awareness of the broader human experience and its environment, and to appreciate the responsibilities of persons to themselves, each other, and to their communities.

Freshmen and Sophomores enroll as small groups in interdisciplinary inquiry courses taught by teams of five faculty each, facilitated by peer mentors and supported by dedicated high tech classrooms and labs. Upper division students enroll in clusters of theme-related courses that offer in-depth learning as well as advanced skill development in communication, information technologies, group work, and research. Many of the inquiry and cluster courses contain elements of service learning. The general education program culminates in a two-term six-credit Senior Capstone course where students are organized in small interdisciplinary teams to apply and interpret their undergraduate learning experience in a community setting focused on a real-life issue. The capstone also offers an opportunity to connect to potential employers and gain work experience while addressing a priority need of the community.

Service learning is also integrated into many courses in the majors; more than 200 courses at PSU involve some aspect of community-based learning. One example is the Center for Columbia River History, which engages undergrads in history and related disciplines in research and educational programs to enhance understanding of River Basin history. Using folklore, geology, literature, history, economics etc, the project asks small communities to focus on changes since the big dams were built.

PSU offers thirty-two bachelor's degrees across Arts and Sciences, Business Administration, Education, Engineering and Applied Science, Fine and Performing Arts, Social work, Urban and Public Affairs, and Extended Studies.

Located around a tree-lined city park in downtown Portland, PSU offers access to jobs, shopping, sporting and cultural events, and relatively low-cost housing. The campus has strong connections with its immediate neighborhood, and the University District is becoming a model urban community with a blend of retail, business, housing, education, recreation and transportation services.

*213*

# MAKING A DIFFERENCE STUDIES

**Community Development    Tracks in Community Organization & Change/Housing & Economic Development**

One of only a few undergrad programs nationwide in the growing field of community development. Trains citizen activists and professionals empowered to take leadership roles in public affairs. Interdisciplinary approach includes anthropology, communications, cultural studies, ecology, environmental studies, history, political economy, social psychology and urban design.

| | |
|---|---|
| Methods of Community Development | Theory & Philosophy of Community Devlp't |
| Probability and Statistics | Sophomore Inquiry in Community Studies |
| Urban Economics | Downtown Revitalization |
| Housing Development | Neighborhood Conservation & Change |
| Communication in Groups | Afro-American Community Development |

**Environmental Studies    Tracks in Environmental Science & Enviro. Policy**

| | |
|---|---|
| Science and Policy Considerations | Environmental Risk Assessment |
| Institutions and Public Change | Environmental Economics |
| Environmental Ethics | Urbanism and Urbanization |
| Culture and Ecology | Groundwater Geology |
| Soils and Land Use | Epidemiology of Cancer |

**Child and Family Studies**

Collaboratively designed by faculty and professionals in cooperation with community agencies

| | |
|---|---|
| Child in Society | Family in Society |
| Anthropology of the Family | Admin. of Programs for Children & Families |
| Preparation for Early Intervention Settings | Health Promotion Programs: Children &Youth |
| Child Psychology | Survey of Exceptional Learners |
| Interdisciplinary Perspectives on Children & Families | |

**Geography**

| | |
|---|---|
| The Developing World | Geography of Portland |
| Urban Geography | Problem of World Population & Food Supply |
| Resource Management | Biogeography |
| Hydrology | Metropolitan Economic Geography |
| Water Resource Management | Cultural Geography |

**Health Education    Tracks in Community Health/Health & Fitness Promotion**

| | |
|---|---|
| Drug Education | Foundations of Health Education |
| Emotional Health | Epidemiology |
| Stress Management | Determinants of Health Behavior |
| Principles of Environmental Health | Planning & Evaluation: Health Educ. Programs |
| Communicable Diseases and Chronic Health Problems | |

**Environmental Engineering (Minor)    Women's Studies    International Studies
Anthropology    Psychology    Sociology**

Student Body: 83% state, 53% female, 47% male, 55% transfers, 17% minority
Tuition: Residents $3,360   Non-Residents $10,923   Room: Avg. $400 a month   Apply By: 6/1
• Interdisciplinary Classes   • Team Teaching   • Over 200 classes with service learning (all majors)

Use form in back to contact: Office of Admissions
POB 751   Portland State University   Portland, OR 97207-0751
(503) 725-3511
askadm@osa.pdx.edu   www.pdx.edu

# PRESCOTT COLLEGE

800 Students    Prescott, Arizona

It is the mission of Prescott College to educate students of diverse ages and backgrounds to understand, thrive in, and enhance our world community and environment. Reality and intelligence are culturally relative. Prescott College regards learning as a continuing process and strives to provide an education that will enable students to live productive lives while achieving a balance between self-fulfillment and service to others. Students are encouraged to think critically with a sensitivity to the human community and the ethics of the biosphere.

A liberal arts college with a very strong environmental component, the broad academic program utilizes classroom work, independent studies, library research, and field studies. Students are expected to demonstrate competence in individually designed study programs and possess two breadths of knowledge beyond their major area of study. Prescott's educational philosophy stresses experiential learning and self-direction within an interdisciplinary curriculum. Programs integrate philosophy, theory, and practice so that students synthesize knowledge and skills to confront important value issues and make personal commitments.

In addition, the College expects its graduates to demonstrate integration of the practical and theoretical aspects of human existence; integration of the spiritual, emotional and intellectual aspects of the human personality; sensitivity to and understanding of one's own and other cultures; commitment to responsible participation in the natural environment and human community.

Prescott College's programs and process are individualized in ways that reward the student personally and intellectually. Since learning takes place in different ways for different people, education at the College is self-directed. Prescott College wants its students to be problem solvers by the time they graduate; therefore, students are introduced to real, often original problems with all their accompanying complexity and frustration. The College also wants its students to know how to adapt in a changing world.

The Resident Degree Program begins with the 21-day Wilderness Orientation in which students backpack through the canyons and waterways of Arizona. Students are introduced to a variety of physical, social, and cultural conditions in which they learn the process of adaptation.

Following Wilderness Orientation, beginning students usually participate in introductory classes or structured field projects, working closely with faculty members and other students. Small classes promote participation and allow for flexibility to meet individual interests and needs. As students demonstrate their ability to assume increased responsibility, they pursue a broader range of learning experiences, and emphasis is placed on internships and independent studies. Students may work with faculty in apprentice relationships, often serving as assistant teachers, co-researchers, and expedition leaders.

Many of the courses at Prescott College have strong field components, and some are conducted entirely in the field. Students may live and study in a cultural context outside their normal experience. One-month blocks allow for intense immersion in one course, often entirely in the field, whether it be a fishing village in Mexico, the alpine meadows of Wyoming, or a local social service clinic.

Prescott College helps students become impassioned learners, sensitive listeners, practical idealists, and entrepreneurial leaders. The College believes that the following facets of education are crucial:

- A close relationship with faculty members in which learning is achieved through personal exchange, sharing, and commitment.
- Small classes that students participate in designing, in which teachers continually challenge students to articulate their beliefs in speech and writing.
- Independent studies and projects working with a supportive advisor to plan, accomplish, and evaluate a significant endeavor;
- An interdisciplinary approach to learning where students are challenged to construct complex understandings of real life situations, rather than simplistic, monolithic, rote understandings;
- Experiential, adventurous learning in the real world in which students also learn responsibility, appropriate risk-taking, group leadership, and collaborative skills.

Examples of independent studies completed by Prescott College students include: Ethnographic Field Study in Mexico, Deep Ecology Through Literature, Native Alaskan Cultural Studies, Multicultural Education, and Developing Sustainable Communities. Internships have included work with Woodswomen in Minnesota; working with the Arizona Nature Conservancy performing restoration ecology and conservation; working with the Caribbean Conservation Corps in Costa Rica; and doing mountain search and rescue in Denali National Park, Alaska.

Three off-campus field sites complement the Prescott facilities: the Rim Institute, Wolfberry Farm, and the Kino Bay Center. The Rim Institute is located on 24 forested acres in the Mogollon Rim area of the Tonto National Forest at an elevation of 6,300 feet. The College utilizes the Rim Institute to provide a viable, sustainable curriculum dedicated to the themes of personal growth, spiritual renewal, and planetary healing incorporating the arts, human development, and environmental education.

About 15 miles north of Prescott, the College has acquired 30 acres of land to develop a farm dedicated to education, demonstration, and research in Agroecology. Wolfberry Farm serves as the outdoor classroom for the summer program in Agroecology as well as a place where students can carry out independent studies and senior projects.

The Kino Bay Center is located in Kino Bay, Mexico, on the Sea of Cortez. This field station is used by a variety of classes such as Coastal and Cultural Ecology of Kino Bay, A Sense of Place, Field Methods for Intertidal Ecology, and Marine Conservation. It also serves as a launching point for sea kayaking courses as well as a meeting place for many Mexican and American researchers.

# MAKING A DIFFERENCE STUDIES

## Environmental Studies
Students have designed majors in Environmental Education, Natural History, Human Ecology, Environmental Conservation, Ecological Design and Agroecology.

Agroecosystems of the Southwest
Coastal Ecology of the Gulf of California
Ecological Design
Environmental Geology
Marine Invertebrate Ecology

Enviro. Restoration Thru Riparian Ecology
Colorado Plateau: Nature, Culture, Conservation
Issues of Global Food Production
Ecology and Natural History of the Southwest
Wetland Ecology and Management

- **Ecology and Natural History of the Southwest** Learn natural history skills such as field identification of organisms, use of dichotomous keys, record-keeping, basic sampling techniques, and the fundamentals of writing a scientific paper. Skills developed within the context of ecological principles such as natural selection and evolution, homeostasis, population dynamics and life-history patterns, community organization and structure, ecosystem functioning, and biogeographic concepts. Practice the art of thinking ecologically and consider how ecological principles can be applied.

## Adventure Education
Students have designed majors in Adventure Education, Outdoor Experiential Ed., Wilderness Leadership, Therapeutic Use of Wilderness and Outdoor Program Administration.

Aboriginal Living Skills
Avalanche Forecasting
Explorers and Geographers
Outdoor Education and Recreation
Wilderness Leadership

Alpine Mountaineering
Methods in Experiential Education
Expeditionary Kayaking
Outdoor Program Administration
Gender Responsible Adventure Education

- **Sea Kayaking and Marine Landscapes** Sea kayaking in the waters of Baja, California, learning basic techniques of sea kayaking, sea living, and sea safety. Studying and discussing basic concepts of marine, coastal, and desert ecology, geology, oceanography, and conservation issues. Interacting with the native people who work in and inhabit these areas. A large part of the activity time will include snorkeling while identifying, observing, and recording marine invertebrates.

- Faculty Bio: **Mark Riegner** Prior to teaching at Prescott, Mark taught ecology and related courses at Emerson College, a small interdisciplinary college in England. He has taught biological and field-oriented courses at alternative high schools in both England and the US. "By approaching nature with an open-minded attitude and by learning to recognize and formulate our own individual questions, we begin to develop the necessary tools to guide us through life."

## Integrative Studies
While all programs at Prescott College are interdisciplinary, what distinguishes the Integrative Studies program is the wide scope of subject areas it encompasses and seeks to integrate. These include many of the traditional areas of the Humanities or Liberal Arts as well as some which are new to college curricula. What ties these together is their focus on the human being. Cultivates the human arts and human sciences, from the individual, to social structures like the family and community, to the global: humanity within the ecosphere. Through Integrative Studies, students can look inside themselves, constructively criticize society, and carry out integrative study of various regions of the world. Integrative Studies also affords students many opportunities to travel to these regions and learn experientially.

Majors designed by students in recent years include Human Development, Psychology, Education, Religion & Philosophy, Peace Studies & Conflict Resolution, Cultural & Regional Studies and Sustainable Community Systems.

Addiction and Recovery
Counseling Theories
Expressive Arts Therapies
Human Rights Seminar
Latin American History

Christian Tradition: An Interpretation of Love
Dreamwork Intensive
Family Systems Theory
Interpersonal Communication
Nature and Psyche

- **Dreamwork Intensive** Students will be expected to do appropriate readings and research as well as keep an extensive dream log and learning portfolio, and work with their own dreams and symbolic language on a daily basis. Two-thirds of the class meetings will be devoted to the facilitation of a Jungian-Senoi style dream group in which the participants do work with a dream of their choice.

## Arts and Letters

The mission of the Arts & Letters program is to enhance students' abilities to think critically and creatively, to understand divergent perspectives, and to communicate powerfully through a variety of artistic mediums. Through experiential learning and the study and practice of art, language, and literature, students are able to integrate individualized study programs which emphasize personal creativity, with an historical appreciation of the rich tapestry of human experience. The Arts & Letters program not only helps students to become strong and flexible artists and writers, but also nourishes an aesthetic awareness and a creative response to the issues facing humanity. Self-designed majorshave included in Fine Arts, Photography, Performing Arts, Spanish, Writing and Literature

Alternative Processes of Photography
Bookmaking As Art
Intercultural Communication
Literary Journal Practicum
Reading & Writing About Natural History

African Inspired Arts & Drumming
Dance and Improvisation
Introduction to Fiction Writing
Movement Theater
Interpreting Nature Thru Art & Photography

- **Intercultural Communication** As the world rapidly becomes more interdependent, we find ourselves living with increasing complexity. Those who will take responsibility for guiding society must be knowledgeable, visionary, and skilled in intercultural communications. Explore applications and ramifications of interactions between cultures with different value orientations; examine specific cultures, including the non-dominant cultures of the U.S.; implications of global industrialization; ethics of overseas development; and current cultural issues in the U.S. Opportunities to pursue the specific aspects of intercultural communications of greatest personal relevance.

- Faculty Bio: **Wayne Regina** Wayne taught and administered at US International University for ten years, as well as designed curriculum and supervised graduate student training. His specialties include applying systems theory to family and social systems; life stage development and transitions; and integrating psychology, systems, and spirituality. He is a licensed psychologist with over ten years experience in treating individuals and families in transition.

Student Body: 3% state, 50% female, 50% male, 75% transfers, 5% minority
Estimated Tuition $11,500    No housing    Apply By: 2/1, 9/1

- Mentored Studies • Individualized Majors • Field Studies
- Adult Degree Program (520) 776-7116 • M.A. Program (520) 445-8048
- Center for Indian Bilingual Teacher Education (520) 776-5191

Use form in back to contact: RDP Admissions Office
Prescott College    220 Grove Ave.    Prescott, AZ 86301
800) 628-6364    (520) 776-5180
www.prescott.edu

# UNIVERSITY OF REDLANDS

1,500 Students    Redlands CA

The University of Redlands is one of the oldest and most respected liberal arts universities in the west, but it is not a college that dwells on its past. Comfortable with tradition but emboldened by experimentation, Redlands believes that a classical education in the arts, letters, and sciences is most powerfully applied to the world we inhabit when students are thoroughly invested in its creation. The University seeks to build a community of questioning, compassionate, and internationally aware students who can affect change in the world.

Redlands is an eclectic place with a broad range of backgrounds and lifestyles, and a place where diversity is defined in the broadest possible terms. This has created a rarity in higher education: a place where artists, business majors, feminists, evangelical Christians, activists, scientists, athletes, and others can find common ground amidst significantly differing belief systems. Redlands is not a utopian society-our diversity does not deny fundamental differences-but the University rejects the limitations imposed by both intolerance and political correctness.

The academic programs at Redlands reflect an interest in providing a wide-ranging and multi-disciplinary intellectual experience: the creative writing program, led by five full-time, working writers is one of the finest programs of its kind in the west; environmental studies utilizes state-of-the-art computer mapping technology and a thorough grounding in science, economics, and ethics to search for workable solutions to ecosystem degradation; communicative disorders provides theoretical and clinical experience within a liberal arts curriculum; and our strong government and international relations programs prepare leaders who will effectively shape public policy for years to come. These examples, in addition to 28 other academic majors, offer an uncommonly varied palette of courses and programs to choose from.

The University encourages each of its 1500 students to construct an educational course of study that engages their academic work with the local community and the world at large. This is done largely through ambitious foreign study and Community Service Learning programs. Students utilize one January term for a community service project that can take place in locations across the country and overseas. The University's Community Service Learning office coordinates hundreds of projects that have included work at a home for battered women, language translation in Bosnia, community relations work for the L.A. Police Department, construction of Habitat for Humanity homes, and AIDS education programs. From this experience, students discover a commitment to community building that extends well beyond their time in college.

To deepen students' cultural literacy and awareness, Redlands has assembled over 60 foreign study programs that help bring alive one's sense of what it means to be a world citizen in the modern age. By spending a semester as a "guest" of another culture, students learn first-hand the complexities and discomfort of cultural assimilation, the richness of newly appreciated intellectual traditions, and the simple joys of new friends, new food and new music. Redlands students have studied at the world's greatest universities in the U.K., Europe, and Asia where they have learned in educational environments quite different from U.S. They have also settled into cities and villages throughout Africa, Asia, and Latin America, discovering cultural, political, and artistic traditions largely unfamiliar to American students.

The most unusual aspect to the University of Redlands' innovative approach to education is The Johnston Center for Integrative Studies, home to 10 percent of the University's student population. Founded in 1969 at the peak of the experimental college movement in the U.S., Johnston is the most unorthodox expression of Redlands' approach to higher education. Johnston students have almost total freedom to handcraft their educational program by designing individually created classes and majors and they receive narrative evaluations for their courses rather than letter grades. Most Johnston students choose to live together in the Johnston Complex, where group decisions within the community are made using a weekly Quaker-style community meeting. Johnston students attempt to create an atmosphere of academic and social idealism, where ideas are vigorously debated and humanistic values are cherished.

Recent Johnston Center student-created majors include Religion and Transformation; Biochemistry and Neurobiology; Comparative Folklife Studies; Computer Science/Mystical Traditions & Ethics; World Development; Ecological Anthropology; Feminism and Politics; Education: Theory, Practice & Alternatives; Environmental Community Planning; and Psycholinguistics, Psychology and Healing.

Redlands is not an overtly political campus, but public activism is encouraged and supported. While a broad range of political perspective exists within the student body, activism on campus frequently originates from the left, with issues of animal rights and vegetarianism, environmentalism, and sexual politics currently on the forefront. Organizations like the Brotherhood of Rangi Ya Giza and Women of Many Shades are multi-racial groups dedicated to cultural awareness and solidarity and have been active on campus regarding issues of culture and race.

More traditional venues for involvement and leadership are available such as student government, the student newspaper, and a nationally competitive Division III NCAA athletic program.

The University is located in Redlands, California, a small, suburban, city of 70,000 people that was recently listed as one of southern California's "most livable cities". Just north of campus is the San Bernardino mountain range and to the east sits the highest peak in southern California, Mt. San Gorgonio (11,500') and three ski resorts. Joshua Tree National Park is just over the mountains and is home to some of the most beautiful scenery in the desert southwest.

The Redlands campus is considered one of the most beautiful in the west. Greek-revival and Spanish-influenced architecture predominates, and most residence halls border a 7-acre, tree-lined quadrangle. A modern student center is the hub of campus activity, and the University recently broke ground in May 1998 for Phase 1 of the Stauffer Center for Science and Mathematics, an $18 million Biology/Chemistry laboratory building and accompanying classroom.

# MAKING A DIFFERENCE STUDIES

## Government and International Relations
Slavery and the Constitution
Constitutional Law
Liberty and Authority: Women and Politics in Latin America
Political Philosophy: Power and Morality: Asian Politics and Development.

American Parties and Interest Groups
Modernization and the Politics of Ethnicity

## Environmental Studies
Environmental Design Studio
Issues in Ecology
Biosystems Modeling
Spatial Information System
Cultural Geography

Ethics and the Environment
Energy and the Environment
Urban and Environmental Economics
Global Environment

## Latin American Studies
Mexican-American Literature
Comparative Politics and Development
Brazil
Hispanic Poetry
Mediating Cultures

Women and Politics in Latin America
Latin American Civilization
Ways of Seeing: Art & Social Reality in Mexico
Power & Social Change in Global Economy
Latina Literature.

## Women's Studies
Women's Issues Across the Curriculum
Feminist Ethics
Women, Sexuality and Western Religion
Women in Collective Action.

Contemporary Feminist Theory
Economics of Race and Gender
Feminist and Womanist Theologies

## Race and Ethnic Studies
Eliminating Racism
Class and Inequality
African American Literature
Debating Change in the Modern West

Teaching Diverse Students in U.S. Schools
Urban Sociology
Economic Dynamism & Challenge for America
Columbus & Cowboys: Revisiting Frontier History

## Economics
Economic History
Industrial Organization and Public Policy
International Trade
Money, Banking and Financial Markets.

Economics of Race and Gender
Urban and Environmental Economics
Business Cycles and Economic Forecasting

## Sociology and Anthropology
African Society
Fieldwork and Ethnographic Methods
Sociology of Work and Family
Political Economy
Women and Collective Action

Classical Social Theory
Deviance; Crime and Delinquency
Social Movements
Community Social Change
Peoples of the American Southwest.

Student Body: 60% state, 53% female, 47% male, 32% minority, 15% transfer, 12% int'l.
Faculty: 55% male, 45% female, 5% minority
Costs: $26,164   Apply By: 12/1

• Interdisciplinary Classes   • Team Teaching   • All Seminar Format   • Theme Housing
• Field Studies   • Required Community Service   • Individualized Majors   • Graduate Programs
• Vegetarian & Vegan Meals   • Students do an average of 160 hours community service annually

Use form in back to contact: Office of Admissions
University of Redlands   1200 E. Colton Ave.   Redlands, CA 92374
(800) 455-5064
admissions@uor.edu   www.redlands.edu

# RUDOLF STEINER COLLEGE

## 250 Students    Fair Oaks, California

Rudolf Steiner College strives to provide a creative educational environment for men and women of diverse ages and backgrounds who seek a deeper understanding of the challenges of modern life and wish to develop new capacities as a basis for their life's work, for social service and cultural renewal.

Founded on the spiritual scientific work of Rudolf Steiner, the College has as its mission to provide programs that:

- Awaken independent thinking and healthy judgment about the deepest issues of human life;
- School powers of perception;
- Cultivate and enrich artistic faculties;
- Strengthen capacities for practical life.

The view of the human being as an individuality encompassing body, soul, and spirit is central to the programs of the College, along with emphasis on the cultivation of the inner life as a source of strength, creativity, and initiative. Programs strive to address the students' quest for the knowledge, insight, and moral imagination needed to bring balance and healing to human beings, communities, and the earth itself.

Rudolf Steiner College offers upper division and graduate level courses. Most students are between the ages of 22 and 45 with a few younger and a few older. Most have already earned at least one academic degree. The cosmopolitan community is comprised of students and faculty from many different countries. They have explored some of the world through travel, study, work and many are also raising families. They come seeking to make a difference.

Self-Development Through the Arts    Students seek to make a difference for the world through cultivating the imagination, insight and initiative required for addressing modern problems. The arts are studied as a basis for sensitivity, and to deepen perception, social awareness and balance of soul.

Waldorf Education    Making a difference for the next generations. Waldorf education (K-12 curriculum) seeks to cultivate balanced human beings by educating, head, heart and hand in harmonious interplay. People preparing to teach in Waldorf schools study human development based on the assumption that a human being is a spiritual being, curriculum appropriate to different age levels, and several arts. Waldorf education is the fastest growing independent education movement world wide. Upon graduation, teacher placement is 100%, with most getting multiple job offers.

Bio-Dynamic Gardening and Goethean Studies    Students seek to make a difference for the earth itself. Bio-dynamic gardening seeks to work with rather than against life forces in the growing of plants. Goethean Studies, initiated by scientist/artist Johan von Goethe, cultivates the powers of observation by bringing together outer and inner experiences.

# MAKING A DIFFERENCE STUDIES

## Foundation Program
One-year full-time and two-year weekend options. This speaks directly to the quest for deeper understanding of the human being, to a yearning for self-knowledge and higher wisdom of the world. It is designed to introduce and explore the insights and endeavors of Rudolf Steiner, as well as a focus on artistic development and personal growth. Evolution of consciousness in history, art and music. Personal biography and life cycles.

Introduction to Waldorf Education
Spiritual Streams in American Literature
Painting, Drawing, Sculpture
Movement and Spatial Dynamics
Karma and Reincarnation

Eurythmy (Movement)
Choral Singing
Parsifal: The Quest for the Holy Grail
World Evolution and Spiritual Development
Philosophy of Freedom

## Waldorf Teacher Education Programs
Full-time, part-time, certificate, B.A. and M.A. options. San Francisco weekend/summer option. Preparation for Early Childhood, Elementary, or High School teaching in a Waldorf school (over 600 schools in 46 countries). Practice in presenting subjects from fairy tales to mathematics in an artistic way.

Storytelling, Gardening
Learning and Development
Inner Work of the Waldorf Teacher
Painting, Drawing, Crafts
Psychology of Adolescence

Puppetry and Festivals for the Young Child
Speech, Eurythmy, Music
High School Curriculum Subjects
Teaching Science in the Elementary Grades
Working With Colleagues

Teaching Math, Science, Languages, History and Geography
Teaching Science in the Elementary Grades

## Arts Program
Watercolor painting: veil and wet-method. Use of these techniques in the Waldorf curriculum and art therapy. Supplemental studies of singing, eurythmy (movement) and clay sculpture.

## Biodynamic Gardening Course
Soil preparation, composting, Bio-dynamic preparations and sprays, crop rotation, Earthly and cosmic forces in plant growth. Pest management, seed saving.

## Goethean Studies Program
Goethe's theory of knowledge as a path to deepened perception and higher cognition. Botany, color study, meteorology, comparative morphology and study of sacred geometry, Gaia/Sophia and the alchemy of the soul. Exploration of science through artistic media.

Student Body: 20% international   Faculty: 80% female, 20% male
Tuition: $1,350 - $7,650   No housing   Rolling applications
• Part-time, Weekend, and Summer Study   • Vegetarian Lunch Program

Use form in back to contact: Admissions Counselor
Rudolf Steiner College
9200 Fair Oaks Blvd.   Fair Oaks, CA 95628
(916) 961-8727

# RUTGERS STATE UNIVERSITY OF NEW JERSEY
## COOK COLLEGE

3,285 Undergraduate Students    New Brunswick, N.J.

Cook College is one of four residential undergraduate colleges on the New Brunswick campus of Rutgers University. Although the college is a professional school offering B.S. degrees in programs in environmental sciences, food,nutrition, marine sciences and natural resources, the university's vast array of courses, student life programs, academic activities, and offerings in the arts is available and convenient.

Cook College was formerly known as Rutgers' College of Agriculture and Environmental Sciences, and it shares its campus with the New Jersey Agricultural Experiment Station, thus combining a rural setting on the outskirts of New Brunswick with state-of-the-art laboratory and research facilities in biotechnology, food science, bioremediation, geographic information systems, marine and coastal sciences, and sustainable agriculture.

Cook College has long been recognized as the national leader in land-grant college curriculum innovation. The Department of Environmental Sciences was the first of its kind in the nation, broadening the established land-grant agricultural mission to include its environmental effects and, ultimately, the environmental problems of urban and suburban development. The transition to Cook College, in 1973, reflected the faculty's commitment to a multidisciplinary, problem-oriented undergraduate program that includes the social, cultural, aesthetic, and ethical dimensions of problems in food, agriculture, natural resources, and the environment, in addition to the scientific and technical aspects that had been the focus of the land-grant colleges.

The current curriculum, which became effective for the Class of 1997, emphasizes the mastery of skills and competencies for lifelong learning, as well as the ability to apply them in the professions for which the college prepares its graduates. A required "Perspectives on Agriculture and the Environment" course introduces entering students to the mission of the college and the complexity of environmental problems, and a capstone "Junior-Senior Colloquium" requires students to work as a team, drawn from a variety of majors, to propose solutions to a well-defined "real world" problem. A stated goal of the new curriculums asserts that to sustain the integrity of our ecosystem, students should develop the ethical sensitivity and the analytical skills to address questions of social responsibility, environmental ethics, moral choices, and social equity.

Because of the complexity of environmental problems, all students, regardless of major, are required to master the basic concepts of biology, ecology, the physical sciences, economics, and domestic policy process. Students must also develop oral and written communication skills, an appreciation for the arts and modes of critical response, and an awareness of cultures other than their own. Requirements in quantitative methods, computer applications, professional ethics, and foreign languages are specified for the particular fields of study. Finally, all students are required to undertake a project in experience-based education -- preferably but not necessarily related to the major -- such as a Cooperative Education placement, independent research on-campus or off, or a community-service activity.

President Clinton launched Americorps at Rutgers because the university had in place the most ambitious community service program of any large, research-oriented state university. Although was originally intended for students in the liberal arts colleges, a number of Cook College majors are developing their own local community service activities under the auspices of this program.

The Cooperative Extension Service is an integral part of the land-grant college missions and, in New Jersey, is as involved in air and water resources, Youth-at-Risk programs, Urban Gardening projects, and nutrition programs for urban families as it has been traditionally devoted to the agricultural extension service and 4-H. The college's experiential-education requirement is intended to provide even more of our students with opportunities to work on projects throughout the state with extension faculty members.

Cook College offers traditional land-grant college programs in agricultural, animal, atmospheric, food, nutritional and plant sciences. Discipline-based programs in the natural sciences, journalism, communication and public health are offered in cooperation with other faculties of the university, but Cook students focus on the application of these disciplines to problems in the environment or human health. Nine multidisciplinary majors are open only to Cook students.

All minor programs of study offered in New Brunswick are open to all undergraduates. A Cook student, for example, could major in animal science and minor in women's studies, and a liberal arts student could major in history and minor in animal science at Cook. The nineteen minor and certificate programs offered by Cook College allow a journalism student, for example, to specialize in environmental risk communication, or a pre-med biochemistry major to focus on human nutrition.

Rutgers University offers eight Study Abroad programs in thirteen countries. Cook College has also established programs with Technion Institute in Israel, and the University of Reading in England, and the University of Natal in South Africa, which focus on agriculture and the environment. Regularly offered courses involve field work in Newfoundland, Alaska and Puerto Rico. The college also participates n a consortium of mid-Atlantic agriculture colleges.

An organic farm was established on campus in 1993, operated by students who remain in New Brunswick for the summer. The farm is a CSA (community-supported agriculture,) selling start-up shares to university faculty and staff. The shareholders and student farmers consume approximately 25% of the produce; the balance is donated to local soup kitchens and food banks, who are pleased to receive fresh, wholesome organic produce. Students, for their part, learn the fundamentals of organic gardening and the complexities of distributing fresh produce, skills which can be applied to backyards as well as possible sustainable commercial enterprises in the future.

# MAKING A DIFFERENCE STUDIES

## Environmental Planning & Design
Environmental Design Analysis
Legal Aspects of Conservation
Land Planning and Utilization
Conservation Vegetation

History of Landscape Architecture
Land Economics
Horticulture in the Residential Environment
Weather, Climate & Enviro. Design

## Bioenvironmental Engineering (5 year dual degree program)
Environmental Systems Analysis
Solid Waste Treatment Systems
Conservation Ecology
Applied Principles of Hydrology
Organic Crop Production

Air Pollution Engineering
Solar Energy
Energy Conversion for Biological Systems
Environmental Statement & Impact
Land & Water Resources Engineering

## U.S. or International Environmental Studies
Research Methods in Human Ecology
Population, Resources and Environment
Rural Communities
Environmental Teacher Education
International Environmental Policy

Environment & Development
Economics of World Food Problems
Social & Ecol. Aspects of Health & Disease
Rural Development
Economics of Peasant Agriculture

## Environmental Sciences
Solid Waste Management and Treatment
Soils and Their Management
Air Pollution Control
Environmental Health
Soil Ecology

Pollution in Int'l Perspective
Problems of Aquatic Environments
Hazardous Wastes
Water Resources-Water Quality
Pollution Microbiology

## Environmental Policy, Institutions & Behavior
Politics of Environmental Issues
Population, Resources and Environment
Human Ecology
Environment and Development
Social & Ecological Aspects of Health & Disease

Behavior and Environment
Energy and Society
Rural Communities
Global Environmental Processes & Institutions

## Natural Resources
Forest & Wildlife Conservation
Principles of Applied Ecology
Wetland Ecology
Natural Resource Administration

Field Ecology
Conservation Ecology
Environmental Law
Fishery Management

**Marine and Coastal Sciences    Integrated Pest Mgm't    Agroecology**

**Forest Resource Mgm't    Public Health    Fishery Science    Water Resources**

**Wildlife Science    Enviro. Health Science    Enviro. Journalism & Mass Media**

Student Body: 90% state, 50% male, 50% female, 28% minority    35% over age 22
Faculty: 71% male, 29% female, 13% minority
Costs: Residents $11.444   Non-Residents $116,338    Apply By 1/15, transfer 3/15

• Field Studies  • Team Teaching  • Individualized Majors  • Multidisciplinary Classes
• Service-Learning  • Vegetarian Meals

Use form in back to contact: Undergraduate Admissions
Rutgers University, Cook College      New Brunswick, NJ 08901
(732) 445-3770

# SAINT OLAF COLLEGE

## 3.000 Students   Northfield, Minnesota

St. Olaf provides an education committed to the liberal arts, rooted in the Christian Gospel, and incorporating a global perspective. In the conviction that life is more than a livelihood, a St. Olaf education focuses on what is ultimately worthwhile and fosters the development of the whole person in mind, body, and spirit.

St. Olaf College strives to be an inclusive community, respecting those of differing backgrounds and beliefs. Through its curriculum, campus life, and off-campus programs, it stimulates students critical thinking and heightens their moral sensitivity; it encourages them to be seekers of truth, leading lives of unselfish service to others; and it challenges them to be responsible and knowledgeable citizens of the world.

This liberal education cherishes a sense of continuity with the past, finding in the past not rigid, dead paradigms, but the vital wisdom of experience and the recognition of errors we should aspire not to repeat. Alive to change, this education celebrates the venturesome spirit of risk-taking ancestors who sought freedom, and it welcomes all who seek a similar adventure. It finds in this daring spirit of earlier generations the roots of compassion for others of diverse origins.

At St. Olaf, liberal education accepts the intriguing challenge of communication under the conditions symbolized by the destruction of the Tower of Babel, and the confusion of tongues. It accepts the responsibility to listen, study, and speak with all our brothers and sisters of every tongue and race. A cross-cultural component in the core curriculum insures that every St. Olaf student gains some insight into significant aspects of non-western culture or minority cultures of North America.

About 500 students participate in the St. Olaf International Studies Program each year. Typically, they study in Africa, Asia, Europe, Latin America, the Middle East, and the former USSR, with more than half of every graduating class having studied abroad at least once. Options include one month interim courses, semester, and year-long programs. All the programs add a cross-cultural dimension to a liberal arts education and aid in developing a global perspective.

Study/Service programs provide students with a challenging and independent study abroad experience. The aim is to provide an international experience combining academic study and active participation with nationals in rural and urban settings through local organizations. Programs provide enriched learning experiences through immersion in a local situation (in most cases Third World) and to make a direct contribution to the local community through a service project coordinated by the host institution.

St. Olaf students participate in numerous volunteer services, regularly visiting with juvenile offenders, with the physically and mentally impaired, visiting senior citizens in local hospitals and retirement centers, and as big brothers or sisters.

St. Olaf's Paracollege offers an alternative means of earning the B.A. degree. Paracollege students develop individualized plans for their education. Students implement their goals through a variety of educational options, especially tutorials, where they explore topics of their choice with the guidance of a faculty member, and seminars, which are small discussion courses frequently team-taught by professors from different disciplines.

# MAKING A DIFFERENCE STUDIES

## Environmental Studies

Introduction to Environmental Studies
Canyonlands Geology
Coastal Biology in California
Environmental Ethics
Ecological Principles

American Ecological History
Desert Ecology
Winter Ecology
Water Resources Management
The Land, American History and Culture

## Women's Studies

Women's Health
Women in the Visual Arts
Family and Economy
American Feminist Thought
Family & Gender in Cross-Cultural Perspective

Philosophy and Feminism
Dance, Gender and the Church
Women and Judeo-Christian Tradition
Women in America

## American Racial and Multicultural Studies

Introduction to ARM Studies
Native-American-White Relations
Race and Class in American Culture
Contemporary Native American Issues

From Wounded Knee to Red Power
Ethnic Music
Black American History
Dance in America

## Economics

Energy Economics
Entrepreneurship
Ethical Management
Labor Economics

Environmental Economics
Economics of Health Care
Economics of the Public Sector
Environmental Policies and Regulations

**Development Economics** The study of economic, political, and institutional requirements necessary to bring about relatively rapid and large-scale improvement in the
standards of living for Third World populations in Latin America, Asia,and Africa.
Major theories of economic development are employed to analyze specific problems
such as population growth, poverty and hunger, agricultural stagnation, industrialization, export-led growth and debt.

## Sociology

Men and Women in American Society
Social Problems and Social Change
Sociology of Global Interdependence
Encountering the "Primitive" Tribal and Peasant Societies
Forging a Latin American Culture: Indians, Conquerors and Revolutionaries

Contemporary Native American. Issues
Race and Class in American Culture
Culture, Conflict and Nonviolence

## Latin American/Latino Studies

The U.S. and Peoples of Latin America
Politics of Developing Nations
Problems in Political Development
Modern Mexico

Development Economics
Latin American Literature
Culture and Civilization of Latin America
Progress & Poverty: Modern Latin America

## Family Resources

"The family" as a focus for a discipline in higher education has increased in significance as
the well-being of individuals and families has become an area of major national concern.

Family Relationships
Child Development in the Family
Nutrition in the Community
Maternal and Child Nutrition

Lesbian and Gay Issues
Human Sexuality
Family Resource Management
Marriage

## Interim (January) Studies

Biomedical Ethics
Economic Justice: Government vs. Market
Women and Work in Africa
Wilderness in American Life
Human Relations in Cross-Cultural Perspective (abroad)

Public Policy and the Family
Liberation Theology
Freudian & Buddhist Psychology
Ethics, Animals & the Environment

## Paracollege Seminars:

Planning for the 21st Century
The Legacy of Columbus
Family, Gender and Economy
Feminism and Philosophy
Gender in the 1990's: New Women? New Men?
Saving Wild Places: The American Conservation Movement

Red, Black and White in American Religion
Religion, Theology and Ecology
Economics of Resource Depletion
Global Climate Change

## Interdisciplinary Courses

Values
Science, Technology and Values

Peace and Violence
Spain and Latin America from 1491 to 1992

## Around the World - The Global Semester

In cooperation with a St. Olaf coordinator at the American University in Cairo, Egypt, and with staff members from Bangalore, India; Taipei, Taiwan; and Kyoto, Japan, St. Olaf students may spend the fall semester and the Interim studying sociocultural developments in the non-western world.

- **India Studies** After an intensive ten-week orientation term, including language study, participants spend six months in Pune living with Indian families, and enroll at Tilak Maharashtra Vidyapeeth where they continue language instruction and other studies.

- **Biology in South India** Following a five week study and orientation session in Madras, students do independent study/internships in rural and/or urban health care, agriculture, fishing village, mountain ecology.

- **Indonesia** Students work as teaching assistants in the English Dep't at Nommensen University in Sumatra, and at Satya Wacana Christian University in Java.

- **New Guinea** Students work with English conversation programs or participate in local church activities such as religious education classes or alcohol abuse prevention. Ten weeks of course work are followed by ample time to visit villages.

### Africa and the African Diaspora    Hispanic Studies

### Social Work    Philosophy

Student Body: 57% state, 45% male, 55% female, 8% minority
Faculty: 60% male, 40% female, 13 minority    Avg. # of students in first year classroom: 21
Costs: $21,320    Apply By 3/1
Energy conservation and campus wide recycling policies are in effect at Saint Olaf

• Field Studies  • Internships  • Third World Study Abroad & Service-Learning
• Team Teaching  • Individualized Majors  • Evening Classes  • Vegetarian Meals

Use form in back to contact: Director of Admissions
St. Olaf College    Northfield, MN 55057-1098
(507) 646-3025
admiss@stolaf.edu

# SAN FRANCISCO STATE UNIVERSITY

20,725 Undergraduates    San Francisco, California

The society of the future is studying on San Francisco State University's campus today -- the broadest mix of race, ethnicity, culture, age and life experience likely to be found anywhere. Surrounded by one of the world's most ethnically rich cities, and with students enrolled from across the nation and more than 90 countries, SFSU helps prepare students with the skills and insight necessary to succeed in a pluralistic society and global economy.

A dynamic, cosmopolitan city, San Francisco is a global center of business, technology, and culture. As a laboratory for meaningful work-study and community involvement, for personal growth and recreation, San Francisco and the greater Bay Area help make SFSU an ideal place to live and to learn.

SFSU students consistently stand out as independent and creative thinkers and doers who contribute to their community and to the world. Because the University believes a multicultural, multiethnic community is the most productive environment for learning, students of all backgrounds will find San Francisco State a welcoming place. The campus reflects California with its various colors, lifestyles, and experiences.

"Diversity is to us a mission, a source of pride, and a source of strength," says SFSU President Robert A. Corrigan. "The efforts we have long made to build a truly diverse campus make us what we are."

Trained in the finest institutions in the country, SFSU professors are winning awards, doing cutting-edge research -- even discovering planets -- often while working side-by-side with their students. The faculty include winners of the Pulitzer Prize, the MacArthur 'genius" award, and Guggenheim Fellowships, among others. Excellent teaching is the faculty's highest priority. Like their students, faculty balance multiple demands, combining teaching with lively scholarship and creative work.

Opportunities for community involvement and service are many at San Francisco State University. The Community Involvement Center (CIC) is a service learning program which provides academic credit, training, supervision and support for students performing community service. This interdisciplinary program is based on reciprocal learning, sharing, and teaching and offers the opportunity for personal growth and career skills development. Students, regardless of major, may choose to learn through community service and may become involved working in such settings as the Rain Forest Action Network, Green Peace, Gray Panthers, and a variety of AIDS - related, health care, homeless, family service, legal and human rights agencies.

The NEXA program, started in 1975 with a grant from the National Endowment for the Humanities, is an established part of the curriculum that draws from the cooperative team teaching efforts of faculty from the Colleges of Creative Arts, Humanities, Science and Engineering, Ethnic Studies, Health and Human Services, and Behavioral and Social Sciences. NEXA courses are designed to bring convergent perspectives to bear upon the "two cultures" of science and humanities, and to investigate means for reconciling these domains of knowledge. The program is charged with maintaining a curriculum that demonstrates the historical, philosophical, and ethical interactions among humanities, arts, and the physical and social sciences.

230

The Romberg Tiburon Center for Environmental Studies, the University's off-campus marine and estuarine research and teaching facility, is the oldest and largest university-run research institute on San Francisco Bay. It is the site of continuing studies to maintain the Bay's health and ecology. Situated on a stunning, historically rich stretch of coastline in Tiburon, California, on one of the largest and most urbanized estuaries in the U.S. -- the San Francisco Bay -- RTC serves as an ideal laboratory for a broad range of environmental studies. Resident and visiting scientists, SFSU faculty, and students at RTC have contributed significantly to the body of knowledge of marine and estuarine environments, as well as to the future health of the Bay's waters and wetlands.

The University's International Relations Department and other related disciplines offer forums for the expression of the widest range of ideas about matters of international significance that place an emphasis on closing the gap between expert knowledge of world affairs and popular understanding. Students are able to interact with faculty, visiting experts and interested laymen to analyze, discuss, and understand the complicated patterns, processes, and institutions of international relations.

The Recycling Center, a student operated organization, is the driving force in waste management at SFSU. Since the founding of the center in 1987, it has expanded its collections to more than 350 recycling locations campus-wide. The latest addition has been the introduction of composting into the waste reduction plan. The center offers valuable working/education experience and employs approximately twenty students who gain job experience in management, operations, outreach, and research for recycling programs. The center also offers an extensive volunteer program for students who want experience in waste management and serves as a key resource to individuals who want to learn about environmental problems facing the world today. It maintains a library of resources about issues affecting the earth and how individuals can help to create change.

## MAKING A DIFFERENCE STUDIES

### NEXA Program - Science and Humanities: A Program For Convergence

| | |
|---|---|
| Science and Culture | Mythic and Scientific Thought |
| Business and Culture | The Feminist Revolution |
| The Nuclear Revolution | Explorations of the Future |
| Science as a Social Process | Computers in the Arts and Humanities |
| Animal Rights: Multidisciplinary Exploration | The City in Civilization |

- **Words, Culture and Change** How culture (including technology, social organization, religion, etc,) shapes and is shaped by language across the ages. Preliterate cultures.

### Labor Studies

| | |
|---|---|
| Know Your Work Rights | Women and Work |
| Union Structure and Administration | Affirmative Action |
| Organizing in the Workplace | Labor and Government |
| Collective Bargaining | Labor in an International Perspective |

## Urban Studies

Policy Analysis
Urban Growth Management
Urban Health Policy
Homelessness and Public Policy
Race, Poverty, and the Urban Environment

Urban Politics and Community Power
Politics, Law and the Urban Environment
Urban Housing
Urban Environmental Design
Alternative Urban Futures

## Holistic Health Minor

Gaining and optimizing health and preventing disease through holistic health concepts and practices derived from eastern and western perspectives. Body disfunctions as natural expressions of stress and lack of balance. Interdisciplinary systems perspective in which mind-body-consciousness interacts with physical, biological, and psychosocial environment.

Holistic Health: Western Perspectives
Holistic Health and Human Nature
Psychosomatics and Stress Management
Orthomolecular Dietary Therapy
Environmental Health
Ethics of Medicine

Holistic Health: Eastern Perspectives
Chinese Perspectives in Holistic Health
Chinese Body-Mind Energetics
Fd'ns. of Biofeedback & Self-Regulation
Healing Practices of the World
Traditional Sciences of Indian America

- **Psychobiology of Healing** Foundation, ramifications and practices of therapeutic touch and healee-healer interaction. Topical presentations of the healing process.

## Intercultural Skills Program

Cultural Awareness
Intercultural Communication
Culture and Personality
Language and Culture
Intracultural Communication

International Negotiation
Sociolinguistics
Kinship and Social Structure
Ethnic Relations: International Comparisons
Anthropology and Folklore

## Health Education

Health in Society
Women's Health--Problems and Issues
AIDS: Contemporary Health Crisis
Health Promotion in Ethnic Communities

Drugs and Society
Health Aspects of Aging
Environmental Health

## La Raza Studies

Oral History and Traditions
La Raza Community Organizing
La Raza Journalism
Acculturation Problems of La Raza
Central Americans in the U.S.

Socioeconomics of La Raza
La Raza Women
Latino Health Care Perspectives
Indigenismo
Community Mental Health

## Human Sexuality Studies

Psychology of Human Sexual Behavior
Research on Sexual Identity
Sex and Morality

Variations in Human Sexuality
Homosexuality as a Social Issue

**Non-Western/Cross-Cultural Musical Arts   Counseling   Marine Biology
Gerontology     Ecology    Amer. Indian, Asian American, Black, Jewish Studies**

Student Body: 93% state, 59% female, 41% male, 62% minority, 57% transfer
Faculty: 61% male, 39% female
Fees: Residents $1,982   Nonresidents $246 add'l. per unit   Apply during November

Use form in back to contact: Director of Admissions
San Francisco State University   1600 Holloway Ave.   San Francisco, CA 94132
(415) 338-1113

# SARAH LAWRENCE COLLEGE

1,050 Students    Bronxville, New York

Sarah Lawrence, a coeducational liberal arts college, offers a unique education to students who want to shape their own curriculum with the guidance of a talented faculty. Sarah Lawrence was the first college in the United States to propose that education should be shaped to fit individuals, with a sustained commitment to their needs and talents, and to realize that genuine learning engages the imagination as well as the intellect. Other innovations include:

- A seminar/conference system where students learn in small interactive classes (limited to 15 students) and private tutorials. The student/faculty ratio of 6:1 is one of the lowest in the country.
- Faculty advisers, called dons, with whom students work to design individuals program of study. The don also teaches the student's First Year Studies Seminar, meets weekly with first-year students and provides ongoing guidance throughout the undergraduate years.
- Written evaluations for coursework, with grades kept on file only for graduate school applications.
- No graduate assistants, instructors or adjunct lecturers. Each professor is fully a teacher, available to first-year through fourth-year students.

Sarah Lawrence endows students with the efficacy and will to make a difference in their own lives and in others. They are given the resources and support they need to study their areas of interest with intensity, and to explore the moral, social and political implications of the subjects they study.

The College was a pioneer in incorporating field work into its curriculum. Students can arrange to receive academic credit for interning at numerous social and political organizations if they work with a faculty member to explore and write about an academic aspect of their experience. Past field work sites include the NAACP Legal Defense Fund, the American Civil Liberties Union, the Landmark Preservation Commission and the Mount Sinai Center for Occupational and Environmental Medicine. Theater and dance students participate in outreach groups that work with area public schools.

In an expansion of its field work option, Sarah Lawrence recently initiated an effort to develop service/learning courses, in which all class participants do field work in a social service or public policy organization and their combined experiences are formally integrated into the course content.

Sarah Lawrence prepares students for global citizenship -- to meet the challenges of living and learning in a multicultural world. In recognition of this, the College has been named a member of the International 50, a select group of schools that graduates a disproportionately high number of people who enter careers in international affairs or in areas of government or academia with an international focus.

# MAKING A DIFFERENCE STUDIES

## Public Policy
Economics of the Environment
The Meaning of Work
Global Economic Development
Women, Families & Work
Changing Places: Social/Spatial Dimensions of Urbanization

Survival & Scarcity: Resources for the Future
Econ. Policy & the Environment of the Future
Science, Technology & Human Values
Ecological Principles: Science of Environment

## Political Science
African Politics
Politics of American Elections
Drugs, Trade, Immigration: U.S.-Mexico Relations in the Late 20th Century
Nuclear Weapons: Selected Explorations of their Impact on Modern Life
Is America a Democracy? Class, Race, Gender, & Political Participation
Politics & History: Conservative, Radical & Liberal

Politics & Government of Latin America
Perspectives on Politics & Society in 20th Cent

## Area Studies
Images of India
Islam, Flower in the Desert
Literature of Exile
Asian Religion
Middle East History & Politics
African Identities: Lives in Contemporary Sub-Saharan Africa

Culture & Society: Anthro Perspectives
Chinese & Japanese Literature & History
Tradition & Change in Modern China
Russian History, Literature & Politics
Latin American Literature & Politics

## Sociology
Crime & Deviance Theory
Contemporary Urban Lives
Social Movements & Social Change
Colonialism, Imperialism, Liberation: Third World Perspectives

Inequality: Social & Economic Perspectives
Social Theory: Class, Race, Gender & the State
African-Americans & Social Science Research

## Psychology
Education: Theory & Practice
Moral Development
Ethnicity, Race & Class: Psychosocial Perspectives
Ways of Knowing: Gender and Cultural Contexts
Deception & Self-Deception: The Place of Facts in a World of Propaganda

Social Development Research Seminar
Social Psychology

## Women's Studies
Equality & Gender
Mothers & Daughters in Literature
Daughters of Africa Circa 1992
The Female Vision: Women & Social Change in American History
Veiled Lives: Women & Resistance in the Muslim World
Theories & Methodology of Women's History & Feminism

Psychology of Women
Gender, Sexuality & Kinship
Women in Asian Religions

Student Body: 30% in-state, 70% female, 30% male, 20% minority, 5% int'l.
Tuition/room/board: $31,685    Apply by February 1
• Service Learning    • Individualized Programs    • Interdisciplinary Courses    • Field Studies
• Seminar/Conference Format    •Study Abroad    • Continuing Education    • Vegetarian Cafe

Use form in back to contact Office of Admissions
Sarah Lawrence College    Bronxville, New York 10708
(914) 395-2510    1(800) 888-2858
slcadmit@mail.slc.edu    www.slc.edu

# SEATTLE UNIVERSITY

3295 Undergraduates  Seattle, Washington

Seattle University, founded in 1891, is the largest independent university in the Northwest. It is a teaching institution and is one of the 28 Jesuit universities in the United States. The University's mission has four central themes: Teaching and Learning, Education for Values, Preparation for Service, and the Growth of Persons. These provide an intellectual environment promoting the growth of creative, ethically-aware individuals with the skills, values, and motivation to lead and serve their communities and professions.

Seattle University has been consistently ranked by U.S. News and World Report as one of the best comprehensive universities in the West. This is in part due to its developmental, unified Core Curriculum which embraces the unique tradition of Jesuit liberal education. The three phases to this Core Curriculum are: Foundation of Wisdom, Person in Society, and Responsibility and Service. Together they provide a developmental approach to educating students for a life of service, provide a foundation for questioning and learning, and give a common intellectual experience to all students.

Seattle University has a solid environmental institutional philosophy and culture. The University has a well-founded recycling, waste management and energy conservation program, recycling or composting more than 50% of its waste in 1995. Close monitoring of campus lighting, heating/cooling, and transportation uses makes Seattle U. a community leader in energy conservation. The campus is also certified as a Backyard Wildlife Sanctuary by Washington State. In 1981 Seattle U. was the first university to initiate Integrated Pest Management, which reduces the need for toxic pesticides by relying on alternative strategies which develop a balance of nature by allowing beneficial insects to control non beneficial insects.

Seattle U. was recently selected as one of five "lead institutions" as part of a national program, "Theological Education to Meet the Environmental Challenge", initiated by the Program on Ecology, Justice and Faith, and The Center for Respect of Life and the Environment. In response, Seattle University has been preparing its students for careers which maintain a clean natural environment while attaining a sustainable economic environment through three undergraduate environmental programs.

Seattle University's Bachelor of Arts in Ecological Studies is unique. Grounded in the concept of ecology, the study of one's home, it explores the complex web of human-nature relationships which constitute earth's many ecological systems. The fully integrated program focuses on earth (geological science,) life (biological science,) human (social science,) and spirit (humanities).

Program goals include developing sufficient ecological and scientific literacy to understand the function of natural ecological systems and the nature and complexity of human interactions with these systems. Students not only understand the historical context of ecological issues, but will develop a multi-perspective strategy for addressing them. The program considers local, national and global issues; students learn about local and regional ecosystems and the attitudes of human cultures towards these ecosystems. Coursework leads students into considering ecological dimensions of natural science, politics, history, philosophy, and religion. As part of Seattle University's Jesuit identity, students consider the importance of the spirituality of nature, and the critical role of spirituality and ethics to ecological issues.

Linkage of community service to classroom teaching broadens the learning experiences students receive because it enables them to test theories, gain first-hand practical experience and skills, and to network for jobs. Such opportunities also serve as an avenue for the community to share its collective experience, insight, wisdom, concerns and needs with the University; in this way the community and the University become partners in teaching and learning. Internships give students an opportunity to work on projects with leaders in the community while providing first-hand experience in issues and dynamics of environmental policies, organizations and agencies, advocacy, planning, and consulting.

The William J. Sullivan, SJ, Leadership Awards, named for the President of Seattle University, are renewable full-tuition scholarships and room grants to entering freshmen who demonstrate effective leadership.

Seattle University is located at the center of one of the most outstanding natural environments in North America. Few areas can match the majestic Cascade and Olympic Mountains, forested foothills, rain forests, pristine lakes and rivers, or the salt-water jewel, Puget Sound.

## MAKING A DIFFERENCE STUDIES

### Ecological Studies
An integral part of the program is the cultivation of collaborative relationships with the community and leaders in the environmental movement through four service-learning courses.

| | |
|---|---|
| Introduction to Geosystems | Introduction to Ecological Systems * |
| Human Ecology and Geography | Environmental History |
| Environmental Politics * | Environmental Philosophy * |
| Religion and Ecology * | Internship and Colloquium |
| Statistical Methods | *indicates service-learning* |

### Environmental Science Track/General Science Program
Provides a foundation to enter graduate programs and careers in wetlands research, forest mgm't, natural resource mgm't, watershed protection, fishery and oceanography research.

| | |
|---|---|
| General Biology | General Ecology |
| Invertebrate Zoology | Taxonomy of Flowering Plants |
| Marine Biology | Introduction to Geology |
| General Chemistry | Organic Chemistry |
| Quantitative Analysis | Microbiology |
| Calculus or Statistics &p Research Methods | Senior Synthesis Seminar |

### Psychology   Track in Addiction Studies

| | |
|---|---|
| Addiction: Law and Public Policy | Counseling - Alcohol and Drugs |
| Group Process in Treatment | Case Management and Record Keeping |
| Addiction and the Family | Ethics for Addiction Professionals |
| Intro to Alcohol and Drug Addiction | Pharmacology of Alcohol and Drugs |
| Field Experience | Intervention Techniques |

## Environmental Engineering
Provides a hands-on approach in preservation and protection of the natural environment. It combines a broad base of theory and basic sciences with exposure to the current engineering practices. Year long industry funded senior design projects in environmental, geotechnical, and water resources engineering provide unique team work experiences.

Engineering Geology
Soil Mechanics
Water Supply & Waste Water Engineering
Environmental Law and Impact Studies
Biological Principles for Environmental Engineers
Environmental Engineering Chemistry
Surface and Ground Water Hydrology
Solid and Hazardous Waste Engineering
Engineering Design Course Series

## Theology and Religious Studies
Spiritual Traditions: East and West
The Gospel of Jesus Christ
Church as Community
Biomedical Ethics
Contemporary Ethical Issues
Women and the Hebrew Bible
Women and Theology
Jesus and LIberation
Psychology and Religion
Religion and Ecology

- **Creation Spirituality**   The current Christian search for a holistic awareness of a God whose presence continues in an ongoing Creation and of human dynamic connectedness with and dependence on the natural world. Reflection on Chinese Taoism and Zen Buddhism, which contribute to environmental courtesy and personal harmony with the universe.

## Psychology   Track in Addiction Studies
Addiction: Law and Public Policy
Group Process in Treatment
Addiction and the Family
Intro to Alcohol and Drug Addiction
Field Experience
Counseling - Alcohol and Drugs
Case Management and Record Keeping
Ethics for Addiction Professionals
Pharmacology of Alcohol and Drugs
Intervention Techniques

## Political Science/Public Administration
Principles of Public Administration
Local and State Politics
Citizenship
Diversity and Change
Native American Politics and Protest
The Policy Process
Public Sector Analysis
Planning, Budgeting & Information Systems
Leadership in the Public Sector
Urban Politics and Public Policy

Students: 86% in-state, 25% minority, 43% male, 57% female, 47% transfer, 13% int'l.
Faculty: 59% male, 41% female, 13% minority
Costs: $20,255   Apply By: 3/1
Avg.# of students in first year classroom: 20     Average age: 24
33% of students engaged in community service

- Field Studies   • 20 Service-Learning Courses   • Third World Service-Learning
• Interdisciplinary Classes

For more information contact: Office of Undergraduate Admissions
Seattle University   900 Broadway   Seattle, WA 98122-4460
(206) 296-5800
admissions@seattleu.edu     www.seattleu.edu/

# SHELDON JACKSON COLLEGE

200 Students     Sitka, Alaska

Sheldon Jackson College is for the college student who chooses a decidedly different and bolder path through life. The campus of Sheldon Jackson is located on the western shore of Baranof Island in Southeast Alaska. Encircled by mountains and settled between ancient forests and the Pacific Ocean, it provides a vast wilderness classroom for education and discovery. Within walking distance of campus students can investigate tidelands, old-growth spruce and hemlock forests, observe freshwater estuaries, muskeg, high alpine meadows or kayak through Sitka Sound paddling past sea lions and humpback whales. Sheldon Jackson's campus borders on the 16.8 million acre Tongass National Forest, the largest temperate rain forest in North America.

While many colleges make commitments to the importance of ethnic diversity and cultural sensitivity in attempting to create a multicultural learning environment, Sheldon Jackson College provides the reality of such a community. Alaska Natives currently comprise twenty-eight percent of our student body. Some of these students come from villages in Alaska" where subsistence hunting, fishing and gathering are essential to survival, while other students celebrate their native heritage within a westernized society. The Annual Gathering of the People celebrates the heritage, culture and current experiences of Alaska's Native Peoples, complete with dancing and a potluck dinner in which traditional Native foods (seal, whale, herring eggs, moose and Eskimo ice cream) can be sampled along. This is a college of rich cultural and geographical diversity. Students come from 40 states and several foreign countries. At Sheldon Jackson diversity is something you encounter in the residence hall as well as in the classroom.

Sheldon Jackson believes that it is important for students to explore and develop the spiritual component of their lives, and to commit themselves in very practical ways to the application of that understanding in the profession of service. SJ is affiliated with the Presbyterian Church and provides an education in which the exploration of Christian faith and values is nurtured, while challenging students to develop a sensitivity to other faith traditions. The Community Service Program provides opportunities for students to volunteer while receiving tuition assistance for service.

The Environmental Awareness Team and Outdoor Recreation Program sponsor a very successful city-wide Spring Expo to celebrate Earth Day, complete with Intertribal Native drumming, an Eskimo blanket toss, sea kayaking, a river traverse, climbing wall session, snorkeling, tree planting and bald eagle release from the Alaska Raptor Rehabilitation Center.

The Wilderness Orientation Program allows new students to participate in a wilderness adventure which could include sea kayaking, a hike to the crater of Mt. Edgecumbe on nearby Kruzof Island, and a sampling of wild edibles. Opportunities abound for students to become involved as explorers and caretakers of the ancient forests and Pacific Ocean which surround Sheldon Jackson College. Sea kayaking, hiking, camping, scuba diving, hunting and fishing are all popular pastimes.

# MAKING A DIFFERENCE STUDIES

**Aquatic Resources** Emphases in Aquaculture, Fisheries, Marine Biology
Sheldon Jackson has the only college owned private salmon hatchery in the U.S. Hands-on work experience includes culturing shellfish and algae, taking eggs, and collecting samples

Salmonid Culture
Fish Health Management
Mariculture
Ecosystem Analysis
Marine Invertebrate Zoology

Marine Biology
Water/Genetics/Nutrition
Oceanography
Fish Ecology
Micro Economics

- **Fish Husbandry** Hydraulics and hatchery plumbing, fish rearing containers, carrying capacity calculations, programming of fish growth, fish nutrition, fish disease, marking and tagging of fish, and computer applications of fish husbandry.

## Natural Resource Management & Development

Surveying and Mapping
Field Studies in Resource Management
Native Perspectives on Resource Mgm't.
Natural Resource Policies and Law
Economic Considerations in Natural Resources

Forest Ecology
Forest/Range Soil
Photogrammetry
Wildlife Ecology and Management

## Outdoor Recreation

Outdoor Survival
Hiking
Sea Kayaking
Outdoor Leadership
Outdoor Recreation Planning

Small Business Management
Public Speaking
Environmental Interpretation
Rock Climbing and Mountaineering

## Business Administration

Prepares graduates for making intelligent business decisions based on analytical, moral, ethical and environmental decisions; making decisions from an international/global perspective; and conducting business in a manner that accommodates different cultural expectations.

Environmental Issues and Business
Personnel and Labor Relations
International Business

Ethics
Techniques Developing Creativity
Principles of Management

- **Native Issues in Business** Issues and problems important to Native Alaskans as they relate to business, society, and the physical environment. Topics include Alaska Native Corporations, cultural and environmental issues; accommodating-integrating Native perspectives and cultural sensitivity into business; multiculturalism; and the future of Native Alaskans in business.

### Education      Forestry Technology Certificate      Fish Husbandry Certificate

Student Body: 40% state, 55% female, 45% male, 30% minority (21% Alaska Natives,) 40% transfer
Faculty: 75% male, 25% female, 10% minority
Costs: $11,350     Rolling Applications
Average number of students in first year class: 10
• Service-Learning Programs   • Individualized Majors   • Required Community Service
• Interdisciplinary Classes and Majors   • Optional SAT's

Use form in back to contact: Director of Admissions
Sheldon Jackson College     801 Lincoln St.    Sitka, AK 99835
(800) 478-4556    (907) 747-5221

# SIMON'S ROCK COLLEGE

322 Students     Great Barrington, Massachusetts

Simon's Rock College of Bard is devoted solely to the academic acceleration and enrichment of the "younger scholar"; that is, the student who, after the tenth or eleventh grade, is ready to leave secondary school for serious undergraduate education. Elizabeth Blodgett Hall, the founder of Simon's Rock, understood the yearning of many younger American students to be taken seriously as thinkers and citizens. Her mission in founding Simon's Rock was to create a community where the habits and enthusiasms of scholarship and friendship could develop unfettered by preconceived age and grade level biases.

In 1979 Simon's Rock became part of Bard College. Through that affiliation, the college's resources were expanded and its mission was renewed and enhanced while the unique identity of Simon's Rock has been preserved. Both Simon's Rock and Bard share a strong commitment to quality undergraduate education and to innovation and reform of American secondary education.

Because students enter Simon's Rock after the tenth or eleventh grade, they differ in their preparation for college work. The first year curriculum embraces common intellectual enterprises while accommodating and strengthening the background and interests of each entering student. All students admitted to Simon's Rock enroll in the Associate in Arts degree program. During their first two years, they complete a coherent core curriculum that makes up approximately half of their total academic load.

Simon's Rock offers two options for completing a Bachelor in Arts (B.A.) degree Students eager to pursue their interests in several areas and those who wish to continue their ongoing work with Simon's Rock faculty may choose to pursue the interdisciplinary program at Simon's Rock. In this program, advanced course work is completed in a concentrations including Arts and Aesthetics; Environmental Studies; Intercultural Studies; Literary Studies; Natural Sciences; Social Sciences and Women's Studies, along with studies in one or more complimentary areas. Students are free to create individualized programs by combining advanced seminars, tutorials, and independent research projects under the guidance and support of the faculty. They may also supplement on-campus opportunities with study abroad programs, off-campus field projects, and internships, in order to satisfy their particular interests and goals.

Students may also select a major from a wider range of topics offered through a new joint B.A. program with Bard. The thesis, a requirement of both B.A. programs, is a year-long research or creative project that explores a substantive issue in depth.

The core faculty at Simon's Rock is active in feminist scholarship. Women's studies features speakers from around the country on topics such as feminist interpretation of education and sexual difference, and feminist challenges to objectivity.

Upperclass students in Environmental Studies are encouraged to enroll in at least one internship program. Recent internships have included the Massachusetts Audubon Society, the Center for Ecological Technology, and The School for Field Studies. Interns have been involved in assessment of wetlands, stream and lake alterations, and a study of the human perceptions of aesthetics in natural and built envi-

# MAKING A DIFFERENCE STUDIES

## Environmental Studies

| | |
|---|---|
| Environmental Studies | Principles of Ecology |
| Environmental Management | Ecological Methods |
| Aquatic Biology | Limnology |
| Nature and Literature | General Botany |
| Animal Behavior | Issues in Cultural Ecology |

- **Ethics and Environmental Issues** Examines ethical concepts and their implications for environmental problems. Students analyze environmental issues using ethical guidelines. By considering long and short term goals and courses of action and consequences, students gain expertise in decision making and communicating.

- Faculty Bio **Donald Roeder** Dr. Roeder was a consultant to the Canadian gov't. for an environmental-impact study of oil and gas pipelines in the Northwest Territories. He was Ass't. Director of the Environmental Studies Internship Program on Cyprus for the Cypriot government. He has done lake management studies in Massachusetts and New York and pollution studies of rivers in Boston and the Hudson Valley. He is an Associate Professor in the Graduate School of Environmental Studies at Bard College.

## Intercultural Studies

Recent senior theses include: The Element of the Sacred in the Folk Tales of the Peul: Revolutionary Change within the Indian Community of Guatemala; Alchemy East and West: A Path to the Self, the Other, the One; The Literature of Decolonialization.

| | |
|---|---|
| Latin America | The European Community |
| The Arab World | Music of India |
| Music of East Asia | Women Writers of Spanish America |
| Cultural Encounters | Issues in South African Development |
| Revolutionary Russia | Political Economy of the Middle East |

## Women's Studies

Women's' Studies is committed to the integration of theory and practice and grounded on the principle that the personal is political. Consequently, all students in the major undertake a practicum in a non-academic situation where issues they have considered theoretically may be addressed practically.

- Faculty Bio **Barbara Resnik**, Art History, Social Science, Women's Studies (B.A. Sarah Lawrence; J.D., Cardozo School of Law, Yeshiva University) Ms Resnik is an attorney, graphic designer, and printmaker. She has taught constitutional law, art history, and studio arts at Fairfield U. and Queens College. Her interests include issues of race, class, gender and the law; art and media in contemporary culture; and population policy and reproductive rights. She has served as exhibition designer for numerous galleries and institutions. Her work is included in many private collections.

Avg. age: 16    Apply by 7/1

20 full scholarships available to outstanding entering students.

Costs: $26,500

• Field Studies    • Team Teaching    • Interdisciplinary Classes    • Vegetarian Meals

Use form in back to contact: Admission Office

Simon's Rock College    84 Alford Rd    Great Barrington, MA 01230

(800) 235-7186

admit@simons-rock.edu    www.simons-rock.edu

# STANFORD UNIVERSITY

6,575 Undergraduates    Palo Alto, California

At Stanford, students are engaging in community service in growing numbers. Service has become part of student life in classrooms, in the residences and in extracurricular programs. According to recent senior surveys over 70% of undergraduates are involved in public service during their Stanford careers. Numerous student service organizations have taken root in the ethnic community centers, student residences, and religious organizations on campus. In addition, the Haas Center for Public Service serves as a focal point for public and community service locally, across the U.S. and overseas. By engaging students in the widest variety of service activities --through hands-on action, policy research, or community problem solving -- the Center enriches their education and inspires them to commit their lives to improving society.

The act of service is only the beginning for the Stanford-educated citizen who seeks to make an impact in society. Volunteer work does not end with the completion of a "service action;" rather, it provides an experiential foundation for intellectual work, including academic scholarship, that attempts to answer questions raised by the service experiences. The Haas Center serves as a hub for building study-service connections on campus and for linking Stanford with the outside community, by encouraging students to seek faculty sponsorship of service projects, supporting the creation of service-learning components in existing courses, and developing intensive study-service programs such as Stanford in Washington and the Public Service Scholars' Program.

Interest in study-service connections is growing among Stanford students and faculty. More than 50 courses integrate public service activity with study. Courses with service-learning components have been created in American Studies, Anthropology, Chicano Fellows, Children and Society, Communication, Earth Systems, Education, English, Feminist Studies, History, Human Biology, Linguistics, Native American Studies, Psychology, Public Policy, Sociology, and Urban Studies.

A few of the courses at Stanford with a service component include: The Process and Practice of Community Service; Aging: From Biology to Social Policy; Children and Society Program Internship; The State of Public Education in Urban Communities; Women in the African-American Freedom Struggle; The Impact of AIDS; The Meaning of Being Handicapped; HIV/AIDS Training Education; Policy Making at the Local and Regional Level; and an Urban Studies Community Organization Option.

Among the most intensive courses is History Professor Al Camarillo's colloquium, "Poverty and Homelessness," in which students gain an understanding of the nature of poverty and homelessness from readings and class discussions and from a two quarter experience working with homeless families or individuals at shelters. The most extensive venture is the Community Service Writing Project. Now in its seventh year, this joint project of the Haas Center and the Freshman English Program has involved over 1,000 freshmen, matching students with more than 100 community agencies that need newsletter articles, grant proposals, public education materials, and other kinds of writing. The project aims to give students a chance to write outside the academic setting, where their work will reach an audience beyond the teacher and will serve a purpose for its readers. More than 400 freshmen sign up for the program annually.

242

# MAKING A DIFFERENCE STUDIES

## Civil Engineering

Water Resources
Environmental Planning Methods
Ethical Issues in Civil Engineering
Building Energy Laboratory
Environmental Science & Technology

Building Systems
Small Scale Energy Systems
Environmental & Natural Resource Economics
Air Quality Management
Environmental Planning Methods

## Children and Society

The curriculum focuses on the study of children and society from diverse points of view. Emphasis is on public policy and includes research and field experiences.

American Education and Public Policy
Federal & State Policy: Educ. & Children
Current Trends in Policy Making
Adolescence
Communication and Children

Children, Civil Rights, & Public Policy in US
Understanding Research: Children & Schools
Children and Society
Urban Youth and Their Institutions
Language & Culture of Urban Youth

## Ethics in Society

Honors program open to majors in every field and may be taken in addition to a dep't major.

Introduction to Moral Theory
Medical Ethics
Distribution of Income and Wealth
Character and the Good Life
Contemporary Theories of Justice

The Ethics of Social Decisions
Economics and Public Policy
Computers, Ethics, and Social Responsibility
Ethics and the Built Environment
Ethics of Devlp't in the Global Environment

## Urban Studies   Tracks in Community Organization, Urban Planning, Arch./Urban Design

Urban Politics
The Multicultural City in Europe
Education of Immigrants in Cities
Gay and Lesbian Urban Youth
The Politics of Development

The Urban Underclass
Group Communication
Process & Practice of Community Service
Organizational Decision Making
Utopia & Reality in Modern Urban Planning

## Feminist Studies

Virgin Mary and Images of Power
Gender and Society
Gender, Power and Justice
Women and Technology
Harassment and Discrimination

Women, Sexuality, and Health
Women in the Health Care Debate
Women - Transition to Democracy: Latin Amer.
Women in Higher Education
Status, Expectations, and Rewards

## Anthropology

Ethnographic Film
Ecological Anthropology
Medical Anthropology
Sociocultural Studies of Biotechnology

Peasant Society, Economy & Environment
Conservation & Community Devp't: Latin Amer.
Cultural Approaches to Education & Devp't
Ethnography of Communication

- **Archaeology and Education at Zuni Pueblo**  Intensive experience in archaeological education in Zuni, N.M. Participants learn archaeology, current conditions of pueblo life, while living at pueblo and working as teachers and tutors for Zuni HS students.

Undergraduate Student Body: 40% state, 47% female, 53% male, 48% minority, 4% int'l.
Costs: $30,100   Apply by: 12/15

Use form in back to contact: Office of Undergraduate Admission
Old Union - 232   Stanford University   Stanford, CA 94305-3005
(650) 723-2091

# STERLING COLLEGE

90 Students    Craftsbury Common, Vermont

The rural beauty of Vermont's Northeast Kingdom surrounds Sterling College and the location enhances the focus of the curriculum: humans' relation to nature, and human relations within community. Sterling's mission statement states clearly that the college is a learning community cultivating the wisdom, skills, and values needed for sustainable living. Sterling has received national attention for blending environmental studies, hands-on skills, and outdoor group challenges into integrated learning experiences. Sterling College grants an Associate's and a new B.A. Degree. Sterling's program of studies includes experiential components, field studies, living and working in a community and challenge experiences as well as traditional academic coursework.

The nature of Sterling's curriculum makes it best suited to students who are willing to commit to full-time participation. Students living on campus are required to participate in the non-credit community work program. Students above the age of 21 have the option of locating off-campus housing after their first year of study. Exemptions to the on-campus housing requirement may be granted to first-year students. A request for exemption must be submitted to the Dean of Sterling College.

During the Associate's program, students enroll in a core curriculum and select electives in the areas of wildlife management, forestry, agriculture and outdoor leadership. Students study the scientific principles of nature in Ecology, the history and philosophy of human ideas in nature in Humans In The Environment, and current problems or conflicts over resource use in Resource Management. Practical hands-on skill development courses include Woodlot Practices, Farm Workshop and Organic Vegetable Production. In Practicum In Experiential Education students experience the importance of community, trust and effective communication through participation in group initiatives and personal challenge. Second-year students participate in a ten-week, off-campus internship. Interns typically work with federal land management agencies, sustainable farms, wildlife rehabilitation centers or outdoor leadership programs.

Students in their final two years of study select a concentration in the area of Wildlands Ecology and Management, Sustainable Agriculture, and Outdoor Education and Leadership. Bachelor's Degree candidates design a program of studies and a Senior Project. During the third year of studies, students will have the opportunity to enroll in Sterling College field programs such as the Southwest Field Program, study overseas in programs sponsored by Sterling College or other colleges, enroll as non-matriculated students or arrange an exchange semester at other colleges which offer relevant courses, and develop a second internship.

Fourth-year students spend their fall semester on campus in core courses largely determined by their concentrations while also finalizing plans for their Senior Projects. The Project is an integrated learning experience in which students develop theoretical knowledge necessary to tackle a real problem in their fields of study and then work on planning and implementation of solutions.

The fourth year concludes with the students presenting the results of their Senior Projects to the Sterling community and the public. This is a final exercise in synthesis and public speaking. Graduation concludes their Sterling College careers.

# MAKING A DIFFERENCE STUDIES

## Resource Management (First two years - A.A. Degree)

Study of the manipulation of resources to meet specific objectives. Investigates the relationship among resources and the short - and long-term effects of manipulation. Focuses include water, soil, fisheries, forage, forestry and wildlife resources.

| | |
|---|---|
| Writing And Speaking To The Issues | Elements Of Natural Science |
| Humans In The Environment | Practicum In Experiential Education |
| Tools And Their Applications | Ecology |
| A Reverence For Wood | Farm Workshop |
| Woodlot Practices | Resource Management: Watersheds |
| Exploring Alternative Agriculture | Animal Science And Lab |
| Fish And Wildlife Management | Vertebrate Natural History |
| Economics And The Environment | Triumphs Of The Human Spirit |
| Advanced Wilderness First Aid | Wilderness First Responder |

- **Practicum in Experiential Education (Bounder)**  Challenge activities to promote group problem-solving and individual initiative. Activities include a ropes and initiative course, preparation for winter camping and a four-day expedition, flat and whitewater canoeing and backcountry navigation. These activities promote a forum for understanding group interaction and reactions to challenge.

- Faculty Bio **Ann Ingerson** (B.A.,Williams College, M.Sc., Oxford University, John E. Moody Scholarship) Ann is interested in Ecological Economics, teaches Economics And The Environment, Practicum In Experiential Education, Plant And Soil Science, and supervises the college's organic garden.

## Bachelor of Arts  Tracks in Wildlands Ecology and Management, Outdoor Education and Leadership, Sustainable Agriculture

Senior Projects, a significant, integrated learning in the are done during the senior year.

| | |
|---|---|
| Land Use History And Planning | Field Ecology |
| Forgotten Arts | Southwest Field Program |
| Community Service Project | Systems Thinking |
| Psychology Of Groups | Practicum In Experiential Education |
| Outdoor Photography | Nature Writing |
| Human Nutrition | Natural Science And Lab |
| Desert Ecology And Geology | Southwest Literature |
| Draft Horse Management | Outdoor Leadership |

- **Faculty Bio**  Edward (Ned) Houston (A.B. summa cum laude Harvard University, Phi Beta Kappa, M.A., Social Ecology, Goddard College) Ned Houston is the Dean of Sterling and teaches Humans In The Environment, Literature Of The Rural Experience and Triumphs Of The Human Spirit. A teacher for twenty-eight years, Ned enjoys a particular interest in interdisciplinary learning and systems diagnosis.

Student Body: 17% state. 50% male, 50% female, 13% minority
Faculty: 55% male, 45% female
Costs: $17,900    Rolling Admissions
• Team Teaching   • Field Studies   • Service-Learning
• Required Community Service   • Optional SAT's   • Vegetarian & Vegan Meals Available

Use form in back to contact: Admissions Office
Sterling College    Craftsbury Common, VT 05287
(802) 586-7711    (800) 648-3591
www.sterlingcollege.org

# SUNBRIDGE COLLEGE

200 Undergraduates    Spring Valley, NY

Without question, a student's experience at Sunbridge is different than the form of learning one would find at most any other institution of higher learning. Seminar work is combined with artistic and practical activities to provide a new way for students to approach learning. Intense study expands out to movement, music, art, sculpture, etc. By virtue of the unique curriculum, students have a rare opportunity to meet themselves and their value systems in a fresh light.

An anthroposophical college chartered by the N.Y. State Education Dep't, Sunbridge is founded on the research and insights of Rudolf Steiner, the Austrian philosopher and scientist. Rudolf Steiner presented an image of the human being based on the physical, psychological and spiritual dimensions of human life. This threefold picture has inspired the Waldorf educational movement, as well as extensive work in, for example, curative education, social and economic development, agriculture, medicine, science and the arts. Anthroposophy, or spiritual science, holds at its core the needs and nature of human life as a whole.

Waldorf education, initiated by Steiner in 1919, is one of the largest and fastest growing independent educational movements in the world. It represents a long-practiced method which has deeply researched the meaning of a holistic approach to education. In Waldorf teacher training, a study of the nature of the whole human being, from birth to maturity, is part of the learning process. Related to this is the question of the teacher trainee's self-development, which is taken up in depth. A renewed understanding of human society, in terms of the totality of the arts, sciences and humanities is also undertaken, so that the child's faculties can be developed out of a complete experience of human life.

There are more than 600 Waldorf schools worldwide. Waldorf Teacher Training and Early Childhood Education program graduates find ready employment within the growing number of Waldorf schools (over 160) in North America. Others come to seek a new life direction in, for example, the realms of business, science and the arts. Sunbridge's student population spans several generations and hails from a wide variety of countries; students have the experience of meeting many different people who are also looking at the world and their places in it.

Sunbridge College is located 30 miles north of New York City. The location allows students to avail themselves of the City's many offerings while enjoying the natural surroundings of the College. Visitors to the college community find an established Waldorf school, a school of movement (eurythmy,) a center for the care of the elderly, a food co-op and a homeopathic pharmacy, all within walking distance. The social life for students revolves around Holder House, an attractive modern student residence. Many meals and other activities take place in the College's "Main House" dining facility. The College campus is also the venue for numerous lectures, workshops, stage performances and conferences of general and specialized interest during the course of the year.

# MAKING A DIFFERENCE STUDIES

## Orientation Year
A full-time program which gives a foundation in Rudolf Steiner's organic view of the world through intensive courses in spirituality, arts and sciences, and the humanities.

| | |
|---|---|
| Evolution of Consciousness | Astronomy |
| The Philosophy of Freedom | Eurythmy (art of movement) |
| Social Development | The Legend of Parzival |
| Projective Geometry | Human Development |
| Gardening | Music |
| Sculpture | Painting |

## Teacher Training (with option for Master's Degree)
A one-year, full-time program (Orientation Year or equivalent a prerequisite) which prepares the students for teaching in Waldorf Elementary or High Schools.

| | |
|---|---|
| Child Development and Learning | Language Arts |
| Painting | Remedial Education |
| Inner Development of the Teacher | Science |
| Practice Teaching | Curriculum Development |
| School Organization and Administration | Sculpture |

## Early Childhood Education (with option for Master's Degree)
A one-year, full-time program which is a preparation for teaching in Waldorf kindergartens. Students have also found it a valuable training and preparation for work with young children in nursing, social work, and daycare.

| | |
|---|---|
| Early Childhood Development | Practice Teaching |
| Language, Imagery and the Small Child | Puppetry |
| First Grade Readiness | Rhythmic Games |
| Music and the Young Child | Handwork |
| Festivals | Speech |

## Teacher Education (Three years)
Over the course of 6 weeks during each year, students experience a program that integrates studies in Steiner's spiritual science and Waldorf education for Elementary school. The program comprises three summer courses plus short, on-campus intensives, and continuing course work in the student's geographical area.

## Handwork, Woodwork, & Clay Modeling Program (3 yr. part time)

## Art of The Actor (1 yr. in N.Y.C.)     Master's Degree In Waldorf Education

## Non-Profit Administration & Community Development (2 yr. part time))

## Biodynamic Gardening and the Environment

Student body: 40% state, 35% int'l.    Avg. age: 30    Avg # of students in first year classroom: 35
Tuition $8,000 a year for full-time programs    Rolling Applications
• Evening programs in general studies & Waldorf education
• Summer Programs - educational & general topics  • Talks, Workshops & Conferences
• Center for Life Studies (family, parenting, adult development)
• Vegetarian Meals Available

Use form in back to contact: Sunbridge College

260 Hungry Hollow Rd    Spring Valley, NY 10977

(914) 425-0055

# SWARTHMORE COLLEGE

1,325 Students      Swarthmore, PA

If you want to make a difference in the world, Swarthmore College will encourage and support you all the way. Swarthmore is widely known for academic excellence; what insiders also know is that the academics serve a larger mission to train students to ask hard questions, to explore how things are, and then to act to improve their world. At Swarthmore, you'll get a philosophical and academic background that will prepare you for a life of service to your community.

And on a practical level, at Swarthmore you'll find scholarships for activists, funding for student-run social action projects, and a fully-staffed volunteer clearinghouse that matches students with organizations that need help. You can even choose a concentration such as Peace and Conflict Studies or Environmental Studies which will prepare you to make a profession of changing the world. Courses in social action combine academic study with classes spent actually tutoring poor children or working with residents of a housing project to improve access to medical care. There's nothing as powerful as the combination of theory and personal knowledge: students come away knowing their own power and how to use it effectively.

Swarthmore's campus is populated by people who believe not only that they can make a difference, but that they must. You'll meet professors who are involved in international struggles for peace and justice, and students who spend their breaks not in Aspen, but in Guatemala or Northern Ireland.

Swarthmore's academic atmosphere is as exhilarating as it is demanding, because every course is informed by the belief that things can change if one is willing to take risks and do the work. At Swarthmore, you'll find cynicism blessedly rare.

At Swarthmore there are many opportunities and support systems for idealism. Each year six entering students are awarded Lang Scholarships which give them up to $10,000 to support a social action project which they design and carry out themselves. For instance: a housing rehabilitation project started by a Lang Scholar over ten years ago is now carried forward by the people who were able to buy the houses at low cost through the project. (Students must apply for the Lang Scholarships when applying to the College.) Any student may apply to the Swarthmore Foundation for a grant up to $2,000 for a social service project of their own design.

CIVIC (Cooperative Involvement as Volunteers in Communities) a full time staffer supports students in volunteer work. CIVIC itself runs seven volunteer programs and puts students in touch with 200 other organizations that need volunteers, from soup kitchens to AIDS care. CIVIC also teaches the skills and sensitivities which volunteers need to be effective, and provides copiers, computers, paper, and experience to students who are working to make a difference.

There are many other opportunities at Swarthmore, and students can make of them what they will. Follow the lead of the student who has built her entire senior year around a project to make health care accessible in hard-hit housing projects. She is researching residents' needs and preferences, organizing care with a local hospital, identifying and training people who are willing to help their neighbors tap into the system, and writing reports and papers on her experience—all for credit.

248

# MAKING A DIFFERENCE STUDIES

## Environmental Studies
Students take related courses as diverse as religion and engineering, and conclude with a practical senior project. One recent project: building a prototype house of straw bales - strong, well-insulated, cheap, biodegradable, and not prone to fire, rats, or mildew.

Chemistry in the Human Environment
Water Quality and Pollution Control
Religion and Ecology
Swarthmore and the Biosphere
Food and Famine

Intro to Environmental Protection
Marine Biology
Solar Energy Systems
Economics of Environment & Nat. Resources
Problems in Energy Technology

## Peace and Conflict Studies
As a college founded by Quaker pacifists, Swarthmore has a strong tradition of pacifism, buttressed by a large and comprehensive peace library.

War and Cultural Difference
Power, Authority and Conflict
Race and Foreign Affairs
War and Peace
Nonviolence: Theory and Practice

Defense Policy
Nonviolence and Violence in Latin America
Comparative Politics: Comp Democratization
Peace Movement in the US: Women & Peace
Managing Conflict: Interpersonal to Int'l.

## History
The investigation, from various points of view, of those ideas and institutions -- political, religious, social, and economic -- by which people have endeavored to order their world.

European Revolutionary Tradition
Sex and Gender in Western Traditions
Nationalism and National Identity
Black Culture and Black Consciousness

Labor in Society and Culture
Revolution to Capitalism: Contemp. Russia
European Jewry's Encounter with Modernity
History of Manhood in America, 1750-1920

- **Murder in a Mill Town** Examines primary source documents concerning the trial of a Methodist minister for the 1833 murder of a female factory worker in Mass. Topics include gender, sexuality, industrialization, religious revivalism, and mental illness

## Sociology and Anthropology
Latin American Society and Culture
Explorations of Diaspora Populations
Social Inequality
Cultural Representations
Wisdom and the Healing Arts: A Multi-Cultural Study of Healing

Indigenous Resistance & Revolt in Latin Amer.
Language and Culture
Ecology, Peace, & Development in El Salvador
Psychological Anthropology

## Education
Educational Psychology
Environmental Education
Political Socialization and Schools
Political Economy of Education
Women and Education

Child Development and Social Policy
Ethnographic Perspectives in Education
Counseling: Principles and Practices
Urban Education
Arts as Community Service/Social Change

Student Body: 52% female, 48% male, 22% minority     Avg. # of students in first year class: 25
Faculty: 62% male, 38% female, 12% minority     Costs $30,740     Apply By 1/1
- Service Learning   - Individualized Majors   - Exclusive Seminar Format   - Study Abroad
- Team Teaching   - Interdisciplinary Classes   - Field Studies   - Vegetarian Meals

Use form in back to contact: Office of Admissions
Swarthmore College     Swarthmore, PA 19081
(610) 328-8300

# TRINITY UNIVERSITY

2,300 Undergraduates    San Antonio, Texas

Trinity University is a highly selective liberal arts and sciences institution that offers several professional programs nationally cited as models in their fields. Trinity offers its students a unique undergraduate experience; class sizes are small, averaging about 20, and contact with professors is frequent and personal (it is not unusual to be taken in for Thanksgiving dinner if "home" is too far away.) Trinity employs no graduate assistants and extraordinarily few part-time faculty. Trinity's $480 million endowment enables it to invest in state of the art equipment necessary for undergraduate research, an unusual opportunity. The 117-acre campus is known for its beauty and for its unique view of San Antonio, one of America's most interesting multicultural cities.

The development of intellectual insight, moral direction, and tolerance for diverse opinions is intrinsic to a Trinity education. In and outside the classroom, students are prepared for the lifelong quest for understanding themselves, their responsibilities in a changing world, and dedication to serving the larger community.

Trinity's dedication to its mission is evidenced through its students' activism and awareness. Trinity's largest student organization, the Trinity University Voluntary Action Center, involves 35% of students. Programs include AIDS and elderly visitation, mentoring at local schools, and Upward Bound, to name a very few. During spring break, groups of Trinity students participate in a variety of service projects nationwide which, in the past, have included work with Habitat for Humanity, Native American reservations, and troubled youth centers, among many others.

An important part of many students' experiences at Trinity is the opportunity to study abroad-increasingly in Latin America and Asia. Over 30% of students at Trinity take advantage of Trinity's extensive program list. Trinity recognizes the necessity of global awareness, and encourages its students to actively seek knowledge of other cultures in order to gain a better understanding of eve its and ideas worldwide.

A unique component of Trinity's contribution to its greater community is the acclaimed five-year dual degree program in education. Participants are granted a four-year degree in any given field, taking only 10-12 hours of undergraduate education courses, exhibiting Trinity's conviction that teachers be well educated before attempting to educate others. The fifth year is an intensive period of study combined with hands-on experience with a nine months of student teaching with a master teacher at a low-income school. The program is one of only six education reform programs recognized by The National Center for Restructuring Education, Schools, and Teaching.

All first-year students at Trinity take a First-Year Seminar class in which they and 10-12 other new students are assigned a topic to explore for the semester mainly through readings and discussion. Examples of topics include "Power and Authority," "Freedom and Responsibility," and "Self and Society."

Programs in environmental studies, urban studies, American intercultural studies, international studies, and women's studies involve many Trinity students, as do field studies in biology, geology, psychology, sociology and anthropology. Trinity is particularly strong in Latin American studies with faculty specialists (often several) in seven academic departments.

# MAKING A DIFFERENCE STUDIES:

## Economics
The World Economy
Study Tour of Eastern Europe
Urban Economics
Economic Development of Mexico
Economic History of the Atlantic World

Environmental Economics
Labor Economics and Labor Relations
Economic Growth and Development
Latin American Economic History
Comparative Economic Systems

## Education
School and Community
Growing up in America
Related Services for Handicapped student
Problems in Education

The Child in Society
Schooling in America
Biosocial Basis of Behavior and Emotion
School-Community Relations

## American Intercultural Studies
Contemporary Minorities
Mexican Americans in the US
Latin American Cultural Tradition
Civil Rights and Civil Liberties
Social Inequality

Jazz History and Styles
Political and Liberation Theology
Minorities in US Politics
Social Psychology
Religion in the US

## History
The Modern Middle East
The family in US. History
The Arab cultural tradition
Modern Brazil
Far East study tour incl. China, Greece & Italy or Eastern Europe including the former USSR

Value Conflicts in Contemp. American History
European social history
Latin American Economic History
Modern Mexico

## Religion
Contemporary Religious Thought
Judaism, Christianity, and Islam
The Hindu Tradition
The Christian Tradition
Mysticism in World Religions

Ethical Issues in Religious Perspective
Women, Religion, and Ethics
The Buddhist Tradition
The Islamic Tradition
Political and Liberation Theologies

## Sociology and Anthropology
Social Psychology
Contemporary Social Problems
Language, Culture and Society
Mind, Body and Society
Death and Dying

Sociology of Sex Roles
Contemporary Minorities
Field work in Ecuador
Intercultural Communication
The Anthropology of International Relations

## Urban Administration   Environmental Studies   Women's Studies   Int'l. Studies

Student Body: 69% state, 51% female, 49% male, 21% minority
Faculty: 75% male, 25% female, 7% minority
Costs $20,250    Apply By 2/1    Avg. # of students in first year class: 21
• Team Teaching    • Interdisciplinary Classes    • Field Studies    • Theme Housing
• Vegetarian Meals    • 35% of students engaged in community service    • Graduate Programs

Use form in back to contact: Office of Admissions
Trinity University    715 Stadium Drive    San Antonio, TX 78212-7200
(210) 736-7207
admissions@trinity.edu    www.trinity.edu

# TUFTS UNIVERSITY

4,550 Undergraduate Students    Medford, Mass.

"...[A] college works out abroad from itself, beyond the circle of its graduates, sending its energies forth through all other institutions, and down through all classes, even the most unlettered." *Hosea Ballou 2nd, First President of Tufts*

Since its founding in 1852, Tufts University's commitment to using knowledge, skills, and scholarship for active public leadership has broadened traditional definitions of service, citizenship and education. At Tufts, the responsibility of each individual to their local, national, and international communities is a basic tenet of the University's mission and philosophy.

Public service is promoted across the curriculum at Tufts. From the College of Engineering and the Sackler School of Biomedical Sciences to the College of Liberal Arts, Fletcher School of Law and Diplomacy, and the Urban and Environmental Policy Program, Tufts is a community of scholars dedicated to change through service.

Many courses and departments employ community service as a method of enhancing classroom learning and performance of service. Service learning courses can be found in Education and Child Study, as well as Mechanical Engineering and Chemistry. Courses that include service learning are a subset of a much wider group of courses that have public service content -- that explore, for example, different facets of public decision-making or the nature of community problems.

Tufts works to enhance public service education, research, and community outreach activities of students and faculty through the Lincoln Filene Center, Public Service Task Force, Center for Environmental Management, and many other organizations and disciplines dedicated to education for active citizenship. By sponsoring conferences and forums, courses, initiatives, and fellowship/internship opportunities, Tufts acts as a catalyst to connect people and resources in new ways and develop new approaches to public problems. Connections is a student initiative to expand the base of service learning courses offered to first-year students by incorporating a community service component.

Building on a tradition of service, today's students are also engaged in developing new initiatives for public service at Tufts. There are many organizations that not only participate in, but create venues for, community service. Tufts' largest and oldest community service organization is the Leonard Carmichael Society (LCS). Today, it has a core membership of 700 students that participate in 23 ongoing programs annually. Many cultural groups, such as the Pan-African Alliance and the Asian Community at Tufts, have long-standing service commitments to the various ethnic communities of Medford, Somerville, and Boston. Groups such as Environmental Consciousness Outreach and Oxfam Cafe also inform the student body on local, national, and international challenges to community and the environment.

Tufts' commitment to citizen education does not simply start with matriculation and end with graduation; through the Community Service Option, students may dedicate their minds, time, and energy to serving social needs before, during, and after their years at Tufts. Newly accepted and selected wait list students may defer admission for one year if they commit to a minimum of twenty-five hours of community service during that time. Current undergraduates may also postpone two academic semesters to do service as well, and upon graduation, are connected to a wide range of local, nation, and international service programs including Teach for America, Peace Corps, and Americorps/VISTA.

The Center for Interdisciplinary Studies brings together studies which are dedicated to "exploring critical, developing areas at the interfaces among and within disciplines". CIS is the umbrella organization for American Studies, Environmental Studies, World Civilizations, African and New World Studies, Women's Studies, Peace and Justice Studies, Community Health and the Experimental College.

Education for Public Inquiry and International Citizenship (EPIIC) is designed to offer Tufts undergraduates a unique challenge. Combining a seminar in the fall with a campus-wide international symposium in the spring, EPIIC strives to be both an intensive intellectual experience and a collaborative learning model that provides a highly participatory immersion in the world of global security studies. This year's topic is "Religion, Politics and Society."

John DiBiaggio, President of Tufts University and ardent supporter of community service learning within higher education, is committed to making public service a hallmark of a Tufts education: "We are using all the best educational innovations of this century to produce a corps of thinking, caring men and women dedicated to bettering their society."

## MAKING A DIFFERENCE STUDIES

### Civil and Environmental Engineering
While this has traditionally included buildings, bridges, and dams, C&E engineers now are engaged in research in environment-friendly construction materials, water resource management, and forecasting the impact of human activity on environmental quality.

Environmental Systems Engineering    Earth Support Systems
Water Quality Modeling    Environmental Toxicology
Public Health and Exposure Assessment.

### Environmental Health
Environmental Biology & Conservation    Environmental Systems Engineering
Introduction to Community Health    Wastewater Plant Design
Environmental Law    Hazardous Materials Safety
Public Health    Fate & Transport of Enviro Contaminants
Exposure Assessment    Public Administration

### Community Health
Multidisciplinary approach to health sciences and care. How anthropology, medicine, history, sociology, psychology, economics, ethics, political science, public health, and biology, affect communities' strategies to promote health and cope with disease. Analysis of factors that determine health and illness; the formation of health care policy with a comparative look at other countries; and institutions that plan, regulate, and deliver health care services.

Domestic Violence    Intro to Hazardous Materials Management
Cancer    Occupational and Environmental Health
Health and the Law    Addiction
Challenge of World Hunger    Contemporary Issues in Health Policy
Sexuality, Disease and Difference    Human Health and Risk Assessment

## Peace and Justice

An interdisciplinary structure for examining the obstacles, conditions, and paths to achieving a just global peace. Brings intellectual and experiential inquiry to the fundamental interrelationship of peace and justice. PJS nurtures an active responsibility for the human condition and examines practical activities for achieving a nonviolent and peaceful future.

Toward A Just World Order
Internship on Social Change
Contemporary Legal Problems of U.N.
Unions and Collective Bargaining
Racism and Social Inequality

Sociology of War and Peace
Peace, Justice and Global Change
United States and Vietnam
Sex and Gender in Society
Internships in Social Change Organizations

## Architecture / Social Focus

Introduction to the City
Urban and State Politics
Urban Sociology
Land Use and Planning Policy
Environmental Facilities for Children

Public Administration
Cognitive Psychology
Housing Theory
Urban & Environmental Planning & Design
Designing Educational & Therapeutic Enviro's

## Child Study

The Child and the Education Process
Personal-Social Development
Language and the New Immigrant
American Sign Language and the Deaf
Social Policy for Children and Families

Developmental Crises
Community Field Placement
Fostering Literacy Development
Child Advocacy Educational Rights
Rights of Children to Social Services

## Science, Technology, and Society

Chemistry in Art and Archaeology
Human Heredity
Technology as Culture
America in the Nuclear Age
Science, Magic & Society 1100-1700

Man and Nature
Principles of Systems
Environmental Geology
Biotech in Human Systems Design
Contemporary Biosocial Problems in America

## International Relations

Topics in International Development
Economics of Food & Nutrition Policy
International Global Human Rights
Cross Cultural Political Analysis
Cold War America

Natural Resources & Environmental Economics
Sociology of War and Peace
Political Economy of World Hunger
Non-Governmental Actors in Int'l Relations
African Politics

**Economics    Environmental Studies    Women's Studies    American Studies**

Student Body: state 31%, male 47%, female 53%, minority 21%, int'l. 8%,
Costs: $30,900  Apply by 11/ 15 Early Decision or 1/11 Regular Decision

- Internships   • Handicapped Programs and Accessibility   • Study Abroad
- Theme Housing    • Service Learning   • Adult Education program
- Individualized Majors    • Vegetarian Meals   • Interdisciplinary classes
- Early admissions programs to Fletcher School and School of Medicine

Use form in back to contact: Office of Undergraduate Admissions
Tufts University   Bendetson Hall
Medford, MA 02155-7057
(617) 627-3170
uadmiss/inquiry@infonet.tufts.edu    www.tufts.edu/as/uadmiss

# UNITY COLLEGE

### 525 Students   Unity, Maine

"We can never have enough of nature"

Henry David Thoreau

Unity College recognizes that we are custodians of a fragile planet. The College intends to graduate individuals with firm values, a sense of purpose, and an appreciation of the web of life. Unity graduates are professionally effective and environmentally responsive, recognizing their responsibilities as passengers on this fragile planet. They understand that as global citizens, they must assume a leadership role in the stewardship of the earth.

Unity College exists for the student whose love of the outdoors is reflected in career choices. Unity College students typically place a premium on jobs that do not require sitting behind a desk, thus Unity College combines academic rigor with equally demanding field experience. Education at Unity can be the first step to a position with a state park, wildlife refuge, nature education center, or wilderness recreation organization.

Unity students come from diverse backgrounds, but they share a spirit of independence and a love of nature. They are individuals who welcome the opportunity to participate actively in their own education and in life in a small college community.

To succeed at Unity College, students must bring with them a willingness to have their ideas questioned -- and possibly changed. Students must be prepared to accept new challenges that expand their limits. Climbing an ice-covered mountain demands courage and commitment. Waking up at 4 am. to go out in the field and conduct a small mammal survey requires determination.

Students learn from the core curriculum of liberal arts courses how to communicate, to reason, to think critically, to analyze and solve problems. In technical courses, the specific knowledge and skills needed to enter the job market are developed. Through the cooperative education program, students are able to apply in a professional setting what they have learned in the classroom. Students also have the opportunity to explore new interests and test leadership abilities by participating in a wide range of extracurricular activities.

Unity College has a special location. The mountains, lakes, and rocky coast of Maine offer innumerable opportunities to camp, hunt, hike, canoe, and fish. At Unity, students experience the personal growth that comes from awareness of the connections linking human beings with the natural environment. Nearby habitats as diverse as the ocean, mountains, freshwater wetlands, and lakes provide the opportunity for hands-on study of a variety of ecological systems.

The Learning Resource Center provides all students in need of academic improvement the support services necessary to succeed. The Learning Resource Center offers courses, tutoring, study skills workshops, and personal counseling. A learning disabilities specialist works with students who have specific cognitive disabilities that interfere with learning.

Students who demonstrate academic excellence are eligible to take part in Unity College's Mentor Program which provides an enriched educational experience. The program allows the student to work closely with a faculty member on projects such as research, teaching, or round table discussions.

Most Unity students gain work experience in their major field as part of their education. Students may choose credit-bearing internships, cooperative education work experiences, or summer employment to supplement classroom learning. Positions with state and federal agencies, business, or nonprofit organizations enable students to apply academic knowledge to real working situations. Typical internships by students participating in the Washington Semester have included work with the Environmental Defense Fund, the American Rivers Conservation Council, and the U.S. Environmental Protection Agency. Other internships have included Hurricane Island Outward Bound, Connecticut Audubon Society, Volunteers for Peace, and numerous nature centers and summer camps.

Unity College is the home of the College Conservation Corps of Maine, a partnership between the Maine Department of Labor and the College. Students enrolled in the 14-month program complete one semester of college coursework while providing 20 hours per week of conservation-related community service in the Unity area.

Unity students have a long history of participating in community service activities. The college is beginning to formalize its community service program by incorporating service-learning into its programs for first-year students and offering "learning to serve" programming and service opportunities for all students. Through these activities, the college builds closer ties to the community and fosters a tradition of service among the students, faculty and staff.

Unity's campus has a sense of open space that reflects the value Unity College places on the outdoors. Until the mid-1960's the land was occupied by a farm. Today, the 200-acre campus still retains an agrarian feel; in the warm months cows graze adjacent to the residence halls. Over 100 acres of campus land have been designated a tree farm used for educational and recreational purposes. In addition to its campus property, Unity owns more than 320 acres of land including frontage on Lake Winnecook, a Wetlands Research Area, and a 230-acre tree farm with a working sawmill.

Equally important to many Unity students, is the school's proximity to outdoor recreation areas. Hiking, backpacking, rock climbing, canoeing, sea kayaking, and cross-country and downhill skiing are all popular activities for Unity students.

Unity College acquired the old solar energy panels which used to adorn the White House under the Carter Administration. The panels have been installed at Unity as part of its continuing efforts as an environmentally conscious institution.

# MAKING A DIFFERENCE STUDIES

## Environmental Policy

| | |
|---|---|
| Environmental Pollution | Land & Water Law |
| Environmental Law | Geology of Environmental Problems |
| Natural Resource Policy | Freshwater Ecology/Limnology |
| Technical Writing | Social Problems |
| Soil Science | State & Local Government |

## Urban and Community Forestry

This program offers an understanding of how trees live and grow and interact with the living and non-living segments of their environment. Based on an understanding of the tree and how it grows in its natural environment, the environment of the park, backyard, and street are studied and contrasted. The concept of the "urban forest" is emphasized.

| | |
|---|---|
| Supervisory Management | General Ecology |
| Landscape Fundamentals | Urban Forest Management |
| Forest Tree Diseases & Insects | Arboriculture |
| Biology 1,11 | Conservation History |
| General Chemistry | Soil science |

## Aquaculture

Aquaculture is the science and practice of culturing aquatic organisms for providing food and pharmaceutical products or for supporting commercial and sport fishing.

| | |
|---|---|
| International Aquaculture | Fish Disease/Pathology |
| Applied Fish Physiology | Fish Disease/Diagnostic Techniques |
| Technical Writing | Gross/Microscopic Anatomy of Fish |
| Ichthyology | Freshwater Ecology/Limnology |
| General Genetics | Microbiology |

## Fisheries

| | |
|---|---|
| Biology | Marine Biology |
| Freshwater Ecology/Limnology | Ichthyology |
| General Genetics | Geology of Environmental Problems |
| Freshwater and Marine Fishes | Fisheries Science & Techniques |
| Analytical Chemistry | Population Ecology |

## Wildlife

Basic ecological principals and techniques, and management concepts used by professionals. Background in conservation & management of natural resources.

| | |
|---|---|
| Biology 1,1 | Systematic Botany |
| Forest Ecology | Ornithology |
| Environmental Plant Physiology | Wildlife Law Enforcement |
| Land and Water Law | Mammalogy |
| North American Wildlife | Wildlife Ecology & Management |

- **Wildlife Techniques** Scientific writing and research, public relations, bird and mammal capture techniques, sexing and aging, radiotelemetry, food habits analysis, habitat assessment and manipulation, home range, survival and population estimation.

## Outdoor Recreation Leadership

| | |
|---|---|
| Wilderness First Responder | Wilderness Skills & Techniques |
| Leadership | Program Planning |
| Group Process | Enviro Education: Methods & Materials |
| Cross Country Skiing | Canoeing |
| Adventure Ropes Course | Mountaineering |

## Conservation Law Enforcement

Introduction to Criminal Justice
Courtroom Procedures
Forest Fire Prevention & Control
Geology of Environmental Problems
Environmental Law
Ornithology

Conservation Law Enforcement
Firearms Training
North American Wildlife
Interpersonal Relations
Freshwater & Marine Fishes
Conservation Biology

- **Wildlife Law Enforcement** Career qualifications of the modern-day conservation officer. Conservation law history and levels of governmental jurisdiction, types of wildlife violations, search and seizure procedures, arrest tactics, evidence compilation, and court-room presentation. Laws governing use of boats & snowmobiles.

## Environmental Education (note - not a teaching credential)

Introduction to Outdoor Recreation
Conservation History
Environmental Ed: Methods & Materials
Group Process
Educational Psychology

Art Media Techniques
Ed. of Exceptional Youth
Instruction Practices & Curriculum Develp't.
Orienteering & Backpacking
Current Envir. Education Problems

## Ecology

We study the three major ecosystem types: terrestrial, freshwater, and marine.

General Ecology
Advanced Ecology
General Genetics
Ornithology
Microbiology

Marine Biology
Freshwater Ecology/Limnology
Forest Ecology
Environmental Plant Physiology
Political Economy of Environmental Issues

## Park Management

Park Planing, Design & Maintenance
Conservation Biology: Aquatic
Wildland Recreation Policy
Interpersonal Relations
Weather and Climate

Preprofessional Development in Park Mgm't.
Park Administration and Operations
Natural Resource Policy
Landscape Fundamentals
Geology for the Naturalist

## Environmental Studies -- Humanities & The Environment

Aesthetics
Ethics
Environmental History of the World
Survey of American Nature Writers

Conservation History
Ecophilosophy
Studies in Nature and Culture
Advanced Writing

### Forestry  Interdisciplinary Studies  Forest Mgm't Technology A.A.S.

Student Body: 33% state, 36% female, 64% male, 27% transfer
Faculty: 77% male, 23% female, 1% minority  Avg. # of students in first year classroom: 20
Costs: $16,490  Rolling Admissions
- Recycling and energy conservation policies in force.
Over 50% of students engaged in community service.  Avg. is 40 hours per year
- Team Teaching  • 35 Service Learning Classes -- available in all majors
- Field Studies  • Interdisciplinary Classes  • Individualized Majors  • Vegetarian Meals

Use form in back to contact: Dean of Admissions
Unity College  Unity, ME 04988-0532
(207) 948-3131

# UNIVERSITY OF VERMONT

8,000 Undergraduates    Burlington, Vermont

The University of Vermont and State Agricultural College blends the academic heritage of a private university with service missions in the land-grant tradition.

Environmental Studies is a University-wide undergraduate curricular option offering students several challenging academic programs. This option is one of UVM's most distinctive and popular academic programs -- unique nationally in its breadth and interdisciplinary nature. Program activities include undergraduate education, research, and community service programs dedicated to the study and improvement of the cultural and natural environments essential to the quality of life on earth.

The School of Natural Resources is actively committed to diversity; biodiversity in natural communities and cultural diversity in human communities. A major goal of the School is to develop men and women as leaders in the stewardship of renewable natural resources -- our forests, wildlife, fish, water, and land. An Honors Project, open to qualified juniors and seniors encourages original thought and creativity. The School includes academic programs in Environmental Studies, Forestry, Natural Resources, Natural Resources Planning, Recreation Management, Resource Economics, Water Resources, and Wildlife and Fisheries Biology, and provides a holistic framework that complements traditional natural resources curricula.

UVM recently reaffirmed its commitment to environmental values by hiring a full time coordinator for its Environmental Council. The council, a group of students, faculty, alumni and others, recommends ways the university can reduce environmental impacts and expand environmentally related research, education, and service. Current student projects include reducing junk mail, designing ecologically sound buildings, and socially responsible investing. The council is working on indicators of sustainability for the university, a campus arboretum, and hazardous materials in laboratories. A report is available at http://esf.uvm.edu/envcncl.

UVM's Center for Service-Learning provides structured experiential programs and volunteer placements within the context of public service. Through the Vermont Internship Program's service-learning internship, students get involved in the community by filling real needs and link their experience with a structured academic program. Typical placements include health and human services, law and justice, governmental, environmental and educational organizations.

The Community Service Program provides several ways for students to get involved as volunteers. They participate in a one-time events such as Hunger Clean Up or Into the Streets, work several hours per week at a local agency, or make a year-long commitment. The Alternative Spring Break Program allows students to increase their social awareness through service in an economically disadvantaged environment away from Vermont. Reflection and examination of the cultures and circumstances are built into the program. The Center also offers a Community Service Trek, a week-long experience for incoming first-year students prior to the first week of classes.

The Living/Learning Community Service Leadership Suite offers students the opportunity to live together while becoming involved in community service projects and to study the philosophical and practical aspects of service-learning.

259

# MAKING A DIFFERENCE STUDIES

## Agroecology (Sustainable Agriculture)
Agriculture & Resource Economics
Alternatives for Vermont Agriculture
Integrated Forest Protection
Conservation
Insect Pest Management
Agroecology

Agriculture in the Third World
Energy Alternatives
Biosphere (Gaia) EcologySoil Erosion &
Ecological Vegetable Production
Environmental Economics
Composting

## Agricultural & Resource Economics  Tracks in Int'l. Devlpm't. & Rural Economy
Comparative Economic Systems
Rural Planning
World Natural Environments
Intro to Urban & Regional Planning
Land Economics Issues

World Food, Population & Development
Agriculture, Planning & Project Dev.
Anthropology of Third World Development
Community Organization & Development
Rural Communities in Modern Society

## Natural Resources
Forest Ecology
Water as a Natural Resource
Int'l Problems in Natural Resource Mgm't.
Principles of Wildlife Management
Race & Culture in Natural Resources
Wilderness & Wilderness Management

Landscape Ecology
Environmental Policy
Assessing Environmental Impact
Ecological Aspects of Nat. Res. Conservation
Environmental Aesthetics & Planning
Effect of Human Activities on Lake Champlain

## Wildlife and Fisheries Biology
Wildlife Conservation
Fisheries Biology
Florida Ecology Field Trip
Uplands Wildlife Ecology

Ornithology
Wildlife Habitat & Population Measurements
Wetlands Ecology & Marsh Management
Marine Ecology

## Early Childhood and Human Development
Intro to Early Childhood & Human Dev.
Public Policy and Programs for Elders
Infancy
The Emerging Family
Adolescent Development

Contemporary Issues in Parenting
Family Ecosystems
Personal & Family Development in Later Life
Human Relationships and Sexuality
Creative Curriculum Activities

## Communication Science and Disorders
Voice and Articulation
Disorders of Language
Current Research in Language Acquisition
Audiological Assessment

Fundamentals of Hearing
Disorders of Speech
Physiological Phonetics
Habilitation of Hearing Impaired Children

## Women's Studies
Images of the Goddess
Women & Public Policy in Vermont
Feminist Theory
Women, Society & Culture
History of Women in US

Women & Society
Studies in Gender & Religion
Women in Develop't: Third World Countries
Psychology of Women
Women in the U.S. Economy

## Social Work    Environmental Studies    Teaching Credential: Enviro Studies (7-12)

Student Body: 50% state, 54% female, 46% male, 6% minority
Costs: Residents $13,228   Nonresidents $24,100    Apply by 2/1

Use form in back to contact: Director of Admissions
University of Vermont      Burlington, VT 05405
(802) 656-3370

# WARREN WILSON COLLEGE

650 Students    Asheville, North Carolina

Warren Wilson College is located on a beautiful 1100 acre campus in a mountain valley that the Native Americans called "Swannanoa -- Land of Beauty." It is a setting that throughout history has inspired community, creativity, learning and a sense of harmony with the environment. The mission of Warren Wilson College is to provide a liberal arts education combining study, participation in a campus wide work program, and required community service in an environment that promotes wisdom and understanding, spiritual growth, and contribution to the common good. Each component of this triad plays an important role in the education of a whole person.

The college invites to its educational community individuals who are dedicated to personal and social transformation and to stewardship of the natural environment. The core curriculum emphasizes how we learn and explores various "ways of knowing" in which humans have created or found meaning. A required freshman seminar such as "Thinking Globally, Acting Locally," "Cosmologies; War in the Modern World," and "Centering on the Creative Self" allows new students to explore various fields of study. The four-term calendar (students normally take two or three courses per term) allows concentration in a few subjects at a time. Classes are small (average class size of 12) and there are ample opportunities for independent tutorials.

Students have been the core work force for the college since its founding 100 years ago. Each student works 15 hours each week on one of 100 work crews that help run the campus, and the work compensates for approximately $2,472 toward school costs. The work crews give students experiential learning opportunities in their field of study: pre-vet students feed and medicate the pigs and cattle on the 300 acre college farm; education majors assist at the Early Learning Center where low-income families enroll their children in a Head Start nursery school, while others might provide support to the English Department or work in the campus computer center.

The work crew is not the only commitment Warren Wilson students make. Each student is also responsible for giving a minimum of 25 community service hours each year in the Asheville community, their home town, or in another country. The college believes that service to society enables students to make a difference in the world, understand the needs of others, and develops a moral perspective that benefits humankind. Examples of service projects include working at homeless shelters, rape-crisis centers, building homes with Habitat for Humanity, serving as Big Brothers and Sisters at juvenile jails, establishing tree plantations in Nicaragua, building one-room school houses in Indian villages, and developing water collection systems in Kenya.

In 1994 Warren Wilson was one of just ten colleges nationwide to have received a grant from the Council of Independent Colleges to incorporate it's community service program into a for-credit service learning program.

Warren Wilson's student body comes from 46 different states and 34 different countries. Because the college is a small community of 650 students, it is a natural environment for students and staff to learn about different cultures whether, it be a different part of the United States or an entirely different nation. Ninety percent of

Warren Wilson students and forty percent of the faculty and staff live on campus. Because students and staff live, work, and serve together, there is a strong sense of coherence and membership in the campus community.

The college is the perfect size for both students and staff to be involved and challenged with community leadership roles. The staff meets bi-weekly for a staff forum where issues, goals, and ideas are communicated and acted upon. The student government also plays an important role in the college's short and long term plans. They meet each week to discuss student concerns, plan events, communicate ideas and concerns to the administration, and make policy recommendations.

Community members meet often to address issues on sexism, diversity, the state of the world, peace issues, and other current local and global issues. The administrators are supportive of the community when communicating their feelings, reactions, and opinions. Students and staff are particularly sensitive to environmental issues. For more than ten years Warren Wilson has been recycling on campus. Student work crews are responsible for all aspects of the program, which includes curbside pickup for campus buildings and residences. The College also sponsors an annual clean-up of the Swannanoa River, which runs through the campus, and carefully maintains its 700 acre forest, 25 miles of hiking trails, and a Class II whitewater course. Additionally, students and faculty have participated for more than twenty years in an excavation of a pre-historic Indian village located on the campus.

Warren Wilson College is in partnership with the North Carolina Outward Bound program. In just four years, the new Outdoor Leadership major has become a very popular and well-respected program. The partnership with Outward Bound, the new major, and the Discovery Through Wilderness program have been received with enthusiasm from the greater Warren Wilson community.

Taking advantage of the special heritage of its Southern Appalachian location, Warren Wilson offers a program of Appalachian music, including instruction in the more common instruments used in the genre. Students and staff join together to create an Appalachian String Band which performs for campus activities.

Warren Wilson affirms a commitment to spiritual growth and social responsibility by emphasizing the practical application of Christian convictions, while respecting other religious faiths and secular perspectives. One applicant to the college wrote: "I'm lured to Warren Wilson College because of many things: the triad, the location, the classes, the cows, the kindness of the staff and students. I have found in my visit to the College a respect for life that coincides with my own. Very simply, I felt at home there, I felt that I had found an environment that would allow me to grow, that would unbiasedly witness a portion of the continuous evolving of my life."

On weekends, students stay on campus to enjoy a play, performance or music, see an art exhibit, go to dances, or create their own entertainment. The Outing Club, the largest club on campus, sponsors scheduled outdoor recreation trips each weekend with activities such as hiking, canoeing and rafting, rock climbing, mountain climbing, horse-back riding, cross-country skiing, and caving. The college's location just outside Asheville in the world famous Smoky Mountains provide many fascinating opportunities for students.

# MAKING A DIFFERENCE STUDIES

**Environmental Studies   Tracks in Environmental Analysis; Enviro. Ed.; Enviro. Policy; Forest Resource Conservation; Plant Biology & Horticulture; Wildlife Biology**

| | |
|---|---|
| Horticulture | Conservation of Natural Resources |
| Forest Biology | Aquatic Ecology and Water Pollution |
| Community and Regional Studies | Environmental Issues for the 90's |
| Wilderness: Past and Prospects | Introduction to Environmental Education |
| Environmental Impact Assessment | Environmental Policy |
| Thinking Globally, Acting Locally | Wildlife Management |
| Methods and Materials in Environmental Education | |

- **Discovery Through Wilderness**   Students in their junior year may register for this interdisciplinary learning experience that involves extensive study of a geographical area which is largely wilderness. The course challenges participants to explore their personal limits and to integrate knowledge from several academic disciplines. In the classroom, students study the history, geology, politics, culture, ecology, and the resources of the region. The class then travels to the region for a month of camping and backpacking. Past trips have visited New England, Atlantic Canada, the Pacific Northwest, and Caribbean islands.

- Faculty Bio: **Dr. Mark V. Brenner** (B.S.U of Wisconsin - Stevens Point, M.S. and Ph.D. U of Washington) is the chair of Environmental Studies Department. Mark's specialty is aquatic ecology and the ecological effects of pollution. He has assisted a number of students in doing research projects related to aquatic ecology and pollution. Currently Mark is working with waste recycling research, composting techniques, and waste from aqua-culture. For fun Mark plays on Warren Wilson's volleyball team and he also leads the Discovery Through Wilderness - Pacific NW trip.

## Biology

| | |
|---|---|
| Field Natural History | Ecology |
| Field Ornithology | Animal Behavior |
| Evolution | Immunology and Infectious Disease |
| Plant Morphology | Special Topics in Biology |

## Peace Studies

| | |
|---|---|
| Introduction to Peace & Conflict Studies | Special Topics in Peace Studies |
| Lifestyles of Nonviolence | Politics of Peace |
| Resolving Conflict: Global and Local | Current Issues of Peace and Justice: America |

## Social Work

| | |
|---|---|
| The Aged: Issues and Interventions | Substance Abuse: Issues and Interventions |
| Social Welfare as a Social Institution | Human Behavior in the Social Environment |
| Micro-Practice: Individuals | Micro-Practice: Groups and Families |
| Field Instruction | Social Work in the International Community |
| Macro-Practice: Communities, Organizations, and Policy Development | |

- Faculty Bio: **Dr. Deana Morrow** (B.A. Catawba College; MA Ed. Western Carolina U; MSW U of Georgia; Ph.D. North Carolina State) is a professor in the Social Work Department and is Director of the Social Work Program. Deanna's primary focus is teaching WWC students, but she also has a private counseling practice in the Asheville community. She volunteers with local community agencies as either a facilitator or board member. Deana's special passions are jogging and hiking.

## Intercultural Studies

Studies in this interdisciplinary field provide a foundation for further study and work in private or government international agencies, conflict resolution, and global development.

Economic Development
Mahatma Gandhi
Human Behavior in Social Environment
Global Issues
Intercultural Communication
Poverty and the American City

The Holocaust
Worlds of Change
Latin American Civilization
Social Work in the International Community
Development Agencies at Home & Abroad
Cross Cultural Field Study

- **International Development Practicum**   This course involves participation in a work-study service overseas field project of the international development program. Emphasizes providing a useful service to a local community program through use of appropriate skills.

## History and Political Science

The Holocaust
Civil War and Reconstruction
Poverty and the American City
American Immigrant Experience Thru Ethnic Literature
Mahatma Gandhi: Experiments With the Truth

Latin American Civilization
History of Black Experience in America.
Politics of Developing States

## Religion

Social Ethics in Story Theology
Religious America: Four Distinct Paths
Heaven on Earth: Religious Lifestyles in 19th Century America

Eastern Religions
Christ and Contemporary Culture

- **The Sacred/Secular Search**  This course explores fundamental questions concerning the nature of religion. Eastern and Western religions, and innovative as well as traditional examples of religious practice are examined. Particular attention is paid to the relationship between "religious" and "secular" claims upon one's time and energy; diverse rivals for our "ultimate concern" are studied, whether or not they bear overt religious labels.

## Appalachian Studies

Introduction to Appalachian Studies
Appalachian Folk Arts
Archaeological Field School
Southern Appalachian Term

Folk Tales and Storytelling
Appalachian Folk Medicine
Native Americans of the Southeast
Introductory Anthropology

### Outdoor Leadership     Human Studies     Philosophy     Psychology
### 3/2 Pre-Forestry with Duke University

Student Body: 28% state, 57% female, 43% male, 7% minority, 15% transfer, 6% int'l.
Faculty: 70% male, 30% female, 6% minority
Comprehensive fees: $14,728 (after deduction for work)     Apply By 3/15
Avg.# of students in a first year classroom: 15
• Work Program    • Service-Learning    • Core/Multidisciplinary Classes
• Required Community Service     • Individualized Majors    • Vegetarian & Vegan Meals
• Third World Service Learning

Use coupon in back to contact: Office of Admission
Warren Wilson College
P.O. Box 9000    Asheville, NC 28815
(828) 298-3325     (800) 934-3536
admissions@warren-wilson.edu    www.warren-wilson.edu

# UNIVERSITY OF WASHINGTON

20,500 Undergraduates    Seattle, Washington

The University of Washington has made pubic service one of it's top priorities. and has initiated intensified collaboration with city leaders, especially Seattle's public schools. The University is one of only three institutions invited to contribute to a Campus Compact publication on exemplary college service programs.

Students are actively involved in the community in a variety of meaningful ways, both within and alongside the curriculum. "This means that students are challenged to take an active role in constructing meaning and to recognize the ethical dimensions of making meaning" says Kim Johnson Bogart of the Carlson Leadership and Public Service Office. Many faculty have included community service in their courses, and more recently, others have joined them in providing service learning options in their courses. Service learning is incorporated in courses in philosophy, mathematics, Asian American studies and sociology, among others. A recently inaugurated interdisciplinary major in Community and Environmental Planning has community service as a principle strand of its two-year degree program.

The UW College of Forest Resources holds a position of national and international leadership in both instruction and research. Its location in one of the world's largest forest regions provides unique opportunities for field classes and research, actual management of forested lands, exposure to wood-based industries, and awareness of resource-use issues. About one hundred fifty undergraduates and two hundred graduate students are taught by more than fifty faculty members. Thus, students enjoy small classes and close association with faculty.

The Charles Lathrop Pack Demonstration Forest of approximately forty-two hundred acres, is located south of the University. This forested property is the focal point for on-the-ground academic work in forest management, resource science, and forest engineering. Research centers in the Cedar River watershed are utilized by the college for studies in forest hydrology and mineral cycling in the forest ecosystem.

The marine environment is a dominant factor in the Pacific Northwest. It is not surprising, therefore, that the University has a long tradition of commitment to teaching, research, and public service in the marine and freshwater area. The College of Ocean and Fishery Sciences is comprised of the School of Fisheries, Marine Affairs, Oceanography, Applied Physics and the Washington Sea Grant Program.

The School of Fisheries maintains joint programs with the College of Forest Resources, the School of Marine Affairs, the Institute of Environmental Studies, and the School of Oceanography. It searches for ways to use stocks of fish and shell fish more effectively, and culturing aquatic plants and animals. It is also concerned with impacts of pollution, industry, and human population pressures on the environment.

The College of Architecture and Urban Planning and the Department of Mechanical Engineering have jointly created facilities for studying energy usage in buildings. One facility contains direct-gain and Trombe wall passive-solar test bays, and tests alternative envelope insulation types. A second facility compares energy-efficiencies for houses build to various standards.

# MAKING A DIFFERENCE STUDIES
# COLLEGE OF FOREST RESOURCES

## Urban Forestry
Role of plants and ecosystems in urban environments; role of people in mgm't of urban forests.

Landscape Plant Recognition
Landscape Plant Selection
Computers in Enviro Design & Planning
Public Outreach in Urban Horticulture
Site Planning

Curatorial Practices in Public Gardens
Landscape Plant Management
Urban Plant Protection
Wetland Ecology & Management
Ecological Concepts & Urban Ecosystems

## Forest Resources Management
Forest Transportation
Forest Stand Dynamics
Wildlife Biology & Conservation
Forest Management & Economics
Forest Planning & Project Management

Forest Ecosystems
Intro to Forest Resources Management
Forest Protection
Wilderness Preservation and Management
Management of Wildland Recreation

- **Environmental Impact and Assessment and Regulation** Current environmental, forest resource, and land-use legislation affecting resource management. Selected case studies of prepared forest land use plans and environmental impact statements.

## Conservation of Wildland Resources
Introduction to Wildland Conservation
Forest Resources
Dendrology and Autecology
Forest Policy and Law
Economics of Forest Use

Wildlife Biology and Conservation
Social Functions of Forest Ecosystems
Physical Aspects of the Forest Environment
Wilderness Preservation and Management
Natural Resources Utilization & Public Policy

- **Global Change & Forest Biology** Ecological & Biological effects of atmospheric pollutants, acid precipitation, and climate change on forest trees and ecosystems. Potential climate changes are compared to current and historical climates.

## Wildlife Sciences
Wildlife Field Techniques
Wildlife Biology and Conservation
Wildlife Seminar
Social Functions of Forest Ecosystems
Plant Identification

Biology and Conservation of Birds
Range and Wildlife Habitat
Human Culture and Wildlife Conservation
Quant've Assessment of Wildlife Populations
Application of Computers to Nat. Res. Problems

## Forest Products & Engineering
Evaluate engineering, economic, biological, environmental, and social aspects of forest multiple use management, as affected by access, harvest, transportation and timber use.

Forest Surveying and Transportation
Creativity and Innovation
Snow Hydrology
Forest Harvesting
Hillslope Stability and Land Use

Timber Harvesting Management
Introduction to Soil Mechanics
Wildland Hydrology
Microclimatology
Hillslope Hydrology

Student Body: 90% state, 48% women, 52% men, 23% minority
Costs: Residents: $8,265   Non-Residents: $6,287   Apply By 2/1

Use form in back to contact: Director of Admissions
University of Washington   Seattle, WA 98195
(206) 543-5150

# WASHINGTON STATE UNIVERSITY

16,000 Students at four campuses    Pullman, Washington

Founded by the Legislature in 1890 as the state's land-grant university, Washington Sate University is today a four-campus university with a growing national reputation. WSU offers a liberal arts education balanced with practical instruction in professional and technical fields. Quality teaching and a special student experience in and out of the classroom are hallmarks of a WSU education.

The University includes the historic home campus in Pullman, a pleasant college town of 24,000 in the agriculturally rich Palouse region of southeast Washington, and three new campuses in Spokane, the Tri-Cities and Vancouver.

WSU has a number of unique programs that prepare students to make a difference in society. For example, the university offers:

- The nation's most comprehensive educational program in pollution prevention. Students learn to assess business and industrial practices to identify ways to keep pollution from occurring;
- A speech and hearing program aimed at training native American students to work with their own people who have communication disorders at 5 to 15 times more often than the general population;
- Sustainable agriculture and integrated pest management;
- The Extended Degree Program, using various teaching technologies, that allows Washington residents in the rural areas of 16 counties to take junior and senior year courses to complete a bachelor's degree in social sciences.

One of the state's two public research universities, WSU is known for teaching and research that makes a difference in people's lives, and the state's industries and professions. Current studies range from cancer prevention to analog-digital computer chips, disease-resistant crops to qualities of successful marriages, education reform to animal health. WSU faculty work in an array of developing countries on agricultural, animal health and educational projects to improve the quality of life.

International elements can be seen in many of WSU's academic programs. They are part of a comprehensive effort to increase student understanding of diverse cultures, economies, political systems and environments. A pair of world civilization courses, required for undergraduates students, is at the heart of WSU's nationally recognized core curriculum. WSU is one of the top universities in funding from the Agency for International Development.

Highly regarded academic programs include the famous Edward R. Murrow School of Communications with one of the country's top broadcasting programs; the biological sciences, especially biochemistry; the College of Veterinary Medicine, known for a commitment to animal well being; and sociology.

267

# MAKING A DIFFERENCE STUDIES

**Environmental Science & Regional Planning   Tracks in Agric., Human or Cultural Ecology; Enviro.Ed; Enviro. Quality Control; Natural Resource Mgm't & Transportation**

Topics in Radiation Safety
Environmental Impact Statement Analysis
Environmental Ethics
Environmental Policy
Environment and Human Life

Natural Resource Policy & Administration
Hazardous Waste Management
Human Issues in International Development
Econ. Development & Underdevelopment
Advanced Resource Economics

**Bio-Agricultural Engineering -- Five year program**

Conservation Engineering
Irrigation Engineering
Agricultural Processing and Environment
Drainage System Design

Global Agricultural Engineering
Soil and Water Engineering
Hydrology
Irrigation Water Requirement

**Soil Resources & Land Use  Tracks in Soil Conservation & Sustainable Agriculture**

Soil Conservation
Botany
Remote Sensing:Terrain Evaluation
General Ecology
Soil Microbial Ecology

World Agricultural Systems
Soil & Water Conservation and Management
Soil Analysis
Forestry Application /Airphoto Interpretation
Soil-Plant Relationships in Mineral Nutrition

**Entomology -- Integrated Pest Management**

Pest Management Internship
Insects and People
Toxicology of Pesticides
Urban Entomology
Pesticides and the Environment

Urban Entomology
Beekeeping
Systems of Integrated Pest Management
Insect Ecology
Biological Control: Arthropod Pests & Weeds

**History**

History of Medicine
Native Peoples of Canada
History of Cuba & the Caribbean
History of Women in American West

North American Indian History
History of the Pacific Northwest
Politics of Developing Nations
Gandhi & 20th Century India

**Comparative American Cultures/Native Amer., Asian & African-Amer., Chicano**

Ethnic Diversity
Civil Rights Movement in America
Indians of the Northwest
Native Peoples of North America
Chicano-Latino Politics

Black Politics
America Before Columbus
East Asian Culture
Contemporary Native Peoples of the Americas
Intersections of Race, Class and Gender

**Child/Consumer/Family Studies**

Patterns of Chicano Families
Family Housing Decisions
Families in Crises
Perspectives on Aging
Management Experiences With Families

Guidance of Young Children
The Child and Family in Poverty
Women in Management
Curriculum for Young Children's Programs
Adolescent and Early Adult Development

**Enviro. Engineering   Peace Studies   Women's Studies   Geology
Natural Resources Mgm't. in Wildlife; Range; Forestry; Wildland Recreation**

Student Body: 77% state, 47% female, 11% minority   Faculty: 69% male, 31% female, 10% minority
Costs: Residents $12,442   Non resident $19,600    Apply by 8/1
• Co-op Education   • Service-Learning   • Team Teaching   • Individual Majors   • Veg. Meals

Contact: Director of Admissions
Washington State University     Pullman, WA 99164
(509) 335-5586

# WELLESLEY

## 2150 Women Students    Wellesley, Mass.

Wellesley College is an independent, residential, liberal arts college for women with an enrollment of 2150 students. Since opening its doors in 1875, Wellesley has been a community of scholars rich in cultural, religious and ethnic differences. Wellesley is a college for the serious student, one who has high aspirations. Understanding, respecting and learning from one another's heritage enriches the Wellesley student's experience. The Wellesley education is founded on the conviction that women can do anything. As a Wellesley senior put it, "To celebrate our diversity, to learn from our difference; that is the Wellesley legacy."

Wellesley has distinguished itself as a community where faculty and students feel a collegial link often lacking in larger institutions. The College's student-faculty ratio of 10 to 1 enables students to participate in research, in the preparation of professional papers and in similar academic experiences normally reserved for graduate students at other colleges. Wellesley's diversity is reflected strongly in the curriculum. Students may choose from more than 125 courses that fulfill the multicultural distribution requirement introduced by the College in 1990. The emphasis on concentrated, small-group learning, even in the first and second years maximizes student involvement and faculty attention. The enduring strength of a Wellesley education resides in the expansive foundation it establishes, the critical skills it

One of things that Wellesley can provide is an active community of role models, people who have met the challenges that are particular to women, Part of what draws and keeps the Wellesley community together is a graceful blend of tradition and contemporary life which characterizes the College in every aspect from academics to architecture. In addition to offering a strong liberal arts foundation, the College helps prepare women to succeed in an increasingly global society. Opportunities for career exploration are offered through the Shadow Program, volunteer/community service experiences and over 1,500 internship listings.

The Center for Research on Women was established in 1974. The Center's policy-oriented studies focus on women's education, employment, and family life. Extensive research is conducted on gender equity, curriculum change, childcare, mother/infant bonding, the effects of economic and social policies on women of all races and social classes, and women in the sciences.

At Wellesley, the possibilities are abundant for cultural and intellectual exchange, athletic activities, performance in the arts, political activism, religious observance, social service -- and, of course, casual conversation, relaxation and fun. Cultural diversity provides an essential context for knowing oneself and understanding others. Most important of all, though, is the relationship that students develop with themselves at Wellesley. The academic journey they embark upon here allows students to find the very center of themselves, to define themselves in an atmosphere where their ideas are important, where women are significant role models, where each individual's gifts-are revealed and cherished.

# MAKING A DIFFERENCE STUDIES

## Peace Studies

Anthropology of Law and Justice
Urban Poverty
Politics of the World Food System
Human Rights
Gender, Culture and Political Change

Politics of Race Domination in South Africa
Contemplation and Action
Liberation Theology
European Resistance Movements in WW 11
Technology and Society in Third World

## Women's Studies

Feminism and the Environment
Women, Social Policy and the State
The Body Politic
The Virgin Mary

Women's Lives Through Oral History
Asian Women in America
The Politics of Caring
Women in the Civil Rights Movement

Women and the African Quest for Modernization and Liberation

- **Women, Peace & Protest: Cross-Cultural Visions of Women's Actions** Women's participation in the movements of nuclear disarmament, human rights and social and economic justice. Under what circumstances gender becomes a central force in the development of these movements. Why and in what ways have women been central to the European peace movement; how has the involvement of women helped to define the human rights movement in Latin America?

## First Year Cluster - Construction of Self: Gender, Reproduction, Sexuality (changes annually)

Develops a sense of the relationship between materials and methods of different disciplines.

Visual Arts: Gender and Genre
Spanish: Sexual and Literary Identity

Psychological: Perspectives on Sex & Gender
Biology: Technology of Human Reproduction

Sociology:Fertility and Infertility: Importance of Children to Women in America
Women's: The Intersection of Sexuality, Gender and Culture

## Political Science

Mass Media in American Democracy
Political Economy of the Welfare State
Gender, Culture, and Political Change
Politics of Health Care
Women, the Family and the State

Political Economy of Dev. & Underdevelopment
The Military in Politics
Politics of the World Food System
Human Rights
Politics of Minority Groups in US

- **Ethics and Politics** Ethical issues in politics, public policy and the press. Is it permissible to lie? Does it matter who your friends are? Do some purposes justify deception, violence or torture? Proper role of journalists in upholding ethical standards.

## Chinese Studies

Diverse Cultures of China
Introduction to Asian Religions
Buddhist Thought and Practice
Images of Women in Chinese Literature
Politics of East-West Relations

The Cultural Revolution in China
Political Economy of E. Asian Development
Democracy Movements in East Asia
China on Film
Tienanmen as History

Student Body: 16% state, 100% female, 33% minority, 6% int'l.
Faculty: 55% female, 45% male, 17% minority     Avg. # of students in a first year classroom: 20
Costs: $28,500     Apply By 1/15
• Internships  • Study Abroad  • Individualized Majors

Use form in back to contact: Director of Admissions
Wellesley College     Wellesley, MA 02181
(617) 235-0320

# WESLEYAN UNIVERSITY

2,775 Students   Middletown, Connecticut

Wesleyan has long been known as an institution committed to preparing students with such a diverse education that they are poised to make a difference upon graduation. Nationally known for its long-standing commitment to a multicultural student body, Wesleyan's students also boast a diversity of ideas, interests, and viewpoints, as well as diverse socio-economic, geographic, and international backgrounds. The interaction of these factors on a small campus, coupled with top-notch academic departments, enables Wesleyan students to understand "the big picture". Wesleyan graduates are involved at all levels of public and private service, education, community organization, and academia.

The Center for Afro-American Studies (CAAS) sponsors a wide range of academic, social, and cultural events open to the entire university community. Established in 1974, the Center's annual roster of events includes a lecture series, jazz concerts, dance performances, art exhibits, a spring film series, and a Fellows Program designed to encourage students and faculty members to meet informally.

The Mansfield Freeman Center for East Asian Studies presents a continuing program of interesting exhibitions, concerts, courses, lectures, and special events. The Center is a place to meet distinguished visitors and faculty and to learn from first-hand observers about current political and cultural events, from the repercussions of Tiananmen Square to contemporary theater and philosophical trends. Majors in East Asian Studies are able to have a concentration on either China or Japan, but the societies and cultures of both countries are treated as an interrelated field of study. Most majors study abroad during their junior year, making it especially important to begin required language and history courses as early as possible.

Wesleyan's Science in Society curriculum has been designed to help students explore systematically the interrelations between scientific knowledge, society, and the quality of human life. The Earth and Environmental Science department emphasizes field work on the coast and inlands of Connecticut, and is known for the cohesiveness that field experiments help create. Faculty have taken students to Central America, Newfoundland, Montana, Greece, Italy and elsewhere.

Students have been involved in a broad range of internships in hospitals, museums, television stations, architectural firms, publishing companies, and educational institutions. The College Venture Program places students for 3-6 months in positions such as advocate for the homeless, research assistant, and teaching.

All students are encouraged to become involved with the local community and to use the Office of Community Service as a resource for volunteer opportunities. The OCS supports for student-run tutoring programs, and offers mini-grants to students who create programs for local children, and sponsors service projects. In 1997, for the first time, community service was a voluntary option for entering students and 40% of the class of 2001 elected to participate in over 15 community service projects in Middletown.

# MAKING A DIFFERENCE STUDIES

## Earth and Environmental Science
Physical Geology: Our Dynamic Earth
Geology of Connecticut
Coastal and Estuarine Environments
Invertebrate Paleontology
Water Resources
Introductory Oceanography
Environmental Geology Seminar
Principles of Geobiology
Coral Reef Ecology & Geology (in Belize)
Global Change

## Science in Society
Philosophy of Science
Sociology of Health and Illness
Policy Implementation
Sociology of Science and Technology
History of Scientific Though to 1700
Myths and Paradigms
Cultural Studies of Scientific Knowledge
Public Policy Analysis
Discourse, Text and Gender: A Feminist Methodology?

## Women's Studies
Areas of study include Women and History, Gender in Cross-Cultural Context, Gender and Society, Gender and Representation, and Science and Gender.
Feminist Ethics
Women in History and Memoir
Domesticity & Gender-Mid 19th Century
Modernity, Gender and War
The Newest Minority
Feminism in Global Perspective
Women, Health and Technology
Women and Political Power
Psychology of Gender: Cultural and Historical Perspective

## Government
The Moral Basis of Politics
Unheavenly Cities
Educational Policy
Caring, Rights, and Welfare
Conflict in the Middle East
Urban Politics
Strategies of Political Mobilization
Expert Knowledge & Political Accountability
Comp. Welfare States in Europe & America
Arms Control and Global Security

## Afro-American Studies
Interdisciplinary major offers broad knowledge of the life of blacks in US & Caribbean
Education and the Urban Poor
Making the Underclass
Black Politics in Urban America
Toni Morrison
Power and Poverty in Postindustrial Cities
Religions of Afro-American Peoples
Women of Color and Identity
Race, Gender and Ethnicity in America
Other than Black and White
Education and the Urban Poor

## East Asian Studies
Introduction to East Asian Music
Traditional China
Taoism: Visionaries and Interpreters
Salvation and Doubt
Japanese Film & Japanese Society
Japanese Literature 1700-1945
Tibetan Buddhism
Twentieth Century Japan
Women in Buddhist Literature
Politics & Political Development in China

Student Body: 8% state, 50% female, 50% male, 29% minority, 6% int'l.
Faculty: 70% male, 30% female, 10% minority
Costs: $28,020    Apply by 1/1
• Individualized Majors    • Interdisciplinary Majors & Classes    • Co-op Studies
• Theme Housing    • Vegetarian & Vegan Meals    • Graduate Programs

Use form in back to contact: Dean of Admissions
Wesleyan University    Middletown, CT 06457
(203) 685-3000
admissions@wesleyan.edu    www.admiss.wesleyan.edu

# WESTERN WASHINGTON UNIVERSITY
## FAIRHAVEN COLLEGE
400 Students    Bellingham, Washington

Fairhaven, begun in 1967 as an experimental college within Western Washington University, exists today as an undergraduate learning community defined by four attributes: (1) inter- disciplinary study, (2) student designed studies and evaluation of learning, (3) examination of issues arising from a diverse society, and (4) development of leadership and a sense of social responsibility.

Fairhaven's interdisciplinary curriculum is centered on the process of inquiry as well as on the development of knowledge. Classes are small and most are held in a seminar format where the use of primary sources and student participation is essential. Each class examines a central theme or content area from more than one disciplinary perspective. Classes are often problem focused, and students use the methods and the research tools of those disciplines to examine these problems. Narrative assessments, and written responses from faculty, replace letter grades encouraging students to take risks and explore new ideas. Students learn to engage respectfully in discussion, to value and respect different world views, and to appreciate multiple voices reflecting the diversity of experience in our society.

Fairhaven students are encouraged to develop a self-designed interdisciplinary concentration (major) integrating the contributions of several disciplines to a central problem, issue or theme, or to choose an established major in another college within WWU. The self-designed concentration process allows students to develop plans of study -- including independent study projects, internships and/or apprenticeships.

Cultural pluralism is an important part of Fairhaven's curricular focus -- a positive learning environment embraces difference. The College recognizes that survival requires diversity - that difference is essential, and is in the best interest of the planet. Courses and other learning experiences examine the impacts, contemporary and historical roots of race, class and gender relations. Social issues such as homophobia, ageism, and internalized oppression are examined along with strategies for conflict resolution.

Students are encouraged to find their connection with the world, to understand relationships of thought and action, theory and experience, to cultivate opportunities to apply what they learn, and to develop a strong sense of themselves as individuals in a community, including the benefits and responsibilities that come from membership in it.

The Fairhaven Concentration allows maximum flexibility in designing a program to meet academic and personal goals. Interdisciplinary in nature, it places responsibility for its design and development in student hands. A sampling of recent titles includes: Latin American Studies; Video/Photographic Documentaries; Wetlands: Assessment and Policy; Somatic Psychology; Studies in Power: Women, Law and Policy; Contemporary Political and Economic Issues in Native America.

Independent Study projects enable students to take responsibility for the direction and content of their education. Sample Independent Studies include: Multicultural Women's Literature; Writing for Children; Philosophy of Science; Grant Writing; Wilderness First Aid; Wetlands Restoration; Ethnobotany; Creative Expression; Woodworking; and Video Documentary.

Elective seminars allow the study many different ideas and issues, and to reflect on current changes in the world. Recent seminars include: Pacific Rim Studies; Mediation Across Cultures; Awareness Through the Body; Regional Ecologies; Art and the Environment; Death and Dying; Scriptwriting; and Organic Gardening.

Fairhaven offers alternatives for students seeking more responsibility for their educations. The college seeks to help students learn in a collaborative and non-competitive way, examining the new and different while avoiding new dogmas and conformities.

# MAKING A DIFFERENCE STUDIES

Note: Fairhaven resource areas are not "departments," and the studies listed for each often draw on resources from the other areas.

## Law and Diversity
A rigorous two year program aimed at developing skills and knowledge necessary for law school. Open to any student interested in law, social justice and legal assistance for diverse populations, particularly students with potential for becoming leaders and role models in ethnic and other communities under-represented in the legal profession.

| | |
|---|---|
| American Legal System | Critical Thinking |
| Gender & Law | Government Power Under the Constitution |
| Politics of Inequality | Political Economy, and Society |
| Law and Morality | |

## History, Culture and Society

| | |
|---|---|
| Television and Media: A Critique | Third World Women & Econ. Development |
| Political Economy and Status of Women | The Philosophy of Nonviolence |
| The US in Central America | Hispano/a American Experience |

Curers, Clients and Culture: Cross-Cultural Perspectives on Health & Illness
Women, Ideas and Change: A History of Feminist Thoughts and Actions

## Nature, Science and the Environment

| | |
|---|---|
| Organic Gardening | Patterns in Nature |
| Current Environmental Topics | Feminist Science |
| Regional Ecologies | Frontiers |
| Alternative Futures | Applied Human Ecology: Living Sustainably |

## Human Development, Personal Identity and Socialization

| | |
|---|---|
| Awareness Through the Body | Personal Empowerment |
| Death and Dying | Men and Identity |
| Psychology of Women | Theories of Moral Development |
| The Art of Play | Adult Devlp't in Women: Choices & Conflict |

## Arts, Self-Expression & Creativity

| | |
|---|---|
| Dreams, Imagination and Creativity | Symbols in Art, Culture, & the Unconscious |
| American Culture in the Video Age | Art and Society |
| Art in the Environment | Doing Theater |

Fairhaven Student Body: 80% state, 61% female, 39% male, 17% minority, transfer 60%
Faculty: 54% female, 46% male, 27% minority
Avg # of students in a first year class: 15   Avg. age: 25   Apply by: 3/1 first year, 4/1 transfer
Costs: Residents $7,225   Non-residents $13,2000
• Service Learning   • Exclusive Seminar Format   • Individualized Majors
• Field Studies   • Team Teaching   • Vegetarian Meals
See Huxley College at WWU for address

# WESTERN WASHINGTON UNIVERSITY
## HUXLEY COLLEGE OF ENVIRONMENTAL STUDIES

As we approach the beginning of the 21st century, it is clear that one of the responsibilities of colleges and universities is to help society become aware of environmental problems and issues. A new synthesis of knowledge is needed that's global in its frame of reference, interdisciplinary in its character and experimental in its work.

Huxley College contends that the more people know about their environment in its interdependent detail, the better they will be able to make decisions relative to a quality of life that depends on the environment. To this end the College teaches and researches, in an interdisciplinary and systematic way, the complex issues and problems of the natural environment and its social overlay. Huxley is a gathering place and focus for those genuinely concerned about environmental well-being of the earth.

Environmental studies at Huxley centers on three academic majors: environmental science, environmental policy and assessment, and environmental education. Studies in these areas allow students to pursue specialization or breadth, to acquire a synthesis of environmental knowledge and to develop skills applicable to careers or further advanced study.

At Huxley, faculty staff and students alike work to create a teaching-learning environment that reflects the ideals and values of personal communication, independent learning, new approaches to education and a sense of community. Students often attend faculty meetings, co-sponsor seminars with faculty members, and work with faculty and staff on decision-making college committees.

Huxley College was created in 1968 to develop programs of environmental studies that reflect a broad view of man in a physical, biological, social and cultural world. Most of Huxley's courses are at the junior and senior levels. Lower-division preparation may be completed at WWU or at another institution. Huxley courses and seminars are open to all students at WWU, admission is through WWU.

Huxley's common requirements consist of five core courses; Huxley seminars, and the choice of a senior thesis, a senior project or an internship. The core courses provide a common background of environmental concepts, knowledge and perspectives. Recent seminars include: Bioregionalism: Cultural Approaches to Environmental Problems; The U.S. High-Level Radioactive Waste Program; and The Media and the Environment. The Senior Project may be a creative or community project such as writing of a children's book on ecology or the establishment of an interpreted nature trail. Recent examples of internships include work with Olympic National Forest, Wolf Hollow Wildlife Rehabilitation Center, Environmental Resource Services, State Legislatures, and National Parks.

The Institute for Environmental Toxicology and Chemistry provides opportunities for research and education of the effects of toxic substances on aquatic and terrestrial species, and the Institute for Watershed Studies provides opportunity and specialized equipment for freshwater and watershed studies. The Leona M. Sundquist Marine Laboratory on Fidalgo Island, within easy traveling distance of the campus, provides facilities for marine students.

# MAKING A DIFFERENCE STUDIES

## Environmental Studies

Environmental Systems
Human Ecology
Environmental Decision-Making
Current Forest Practices in Washington
Bioregionalism: Cultural Approaches to Environmental Problems

Environmental Pollution
Environmental Ethics
Coastal Ecosystems Management
U.S. High-Level Radioactive Waste Program

## Environmental Science

Ecology
Environmental Physiology & Biochemistry
Air Pollution
Water Quality Lab

Introduction to Environmental Toxicology
Energy & Energy Resources
Environmental Impact Assessment
Conservation of Biological Diversity

## Environmental Policy and Assessment

Leaders of politico-economic systems, awakening to world-wide dangers as resource depletion, desertification, climate change, population growth, urban blight and congestion are realizing that great political and economic reforms may have to be made soon.

Alternative Energy Sources and Systems
Social Impact Assessment
Environmental Impact Assessment
Environmental Risk Management
Conflict Resolution of Current Issues

Modeling Alternative Futures
Environmental Design: Processes & Problems
Effects of Global Climate Change
Comparative & Int'l Environmental Policies
The History of Conservation in America

## Outdoor Education and Interpretation

Environmental Education
Environmental Interpretation ·
Adventure Programming and Leadership
The Writings of American Naturalists

The Environmental Education Curriculum
Outdoor Education
Experiential Learning in Environmental Ed
History of the Concept of Nature

## Environmental Studies/Economics

Resource Economics
Economics, The Environment, & Nat. Res.
Environmental Ethics
Environmental Impact Assessment

Environmental Economics
US Environmental Policy
Comparative & Int'l Environmental Policies
Environmental Risk Management

- **Multinational Corporations and Global Ecology** The character, functions and values of multinational corporations. Assessment of impacts of such companies on Third World economies and environments and the economy of the U.S.

- **Dr. Marie Eaton** (M.A., Ph.D., U of WA) Dean of Fairhaven, Dr. Eaton also teaches courses in alternative education models, learning theory, death and dying, and grant writing. She is published widely in the areas of gifted and learning disabled students, creativity and risk, and narrative self-assessment. She is also a folksinger and guitarist.

### Marine Biology    Mass Communication & Environmental Education
### Education/Environmental Studies (Elementary)

Student Body: 94% state, 61% female, 39% male, 16% minority
Fairhaven faculty: 53% female, 47% male, 24% minority
Costs: Residents $8,285  Non-Residents $14,978    Apply By: 3/1

Use form in back to contact: Director of Admissions, Huxley College
Western Washington University    Bellingham, WA
(206) 650-3682

# UNIVERSITY OF WISCONSIN, STEVENS POINT
## COLLEGE OF NATURAL RESOURCES

1,500 CNR Students    Stevens Point, Wisconsin

The College of Natural Resources (CNR) is widely regarded as the leading under-graduate program in natural resources in the United States. It began in 1946 with the nation's first conservation education major. The conservation education program provided a broad background in natural resources management, ethics and philosophy for high school teachers. In 1970, the College was formally established and is now the largest undergraduate program in North America, with over 60 faculty and staff, 1600 undergraduates and 70 graduate students. The strength of the program is the interdisciplinary education of its students. All students take coursework in forestry, wildlife, water resources and soils before focusing on their major.

All of CNR's faculty are committed to undergraduate education with over one fourth receiving the coveted excellence in teaching recognition at UW Stevens Point.

UWSP is located on the north edge of Sevens Point in Portage County, the geographic center of Wisconsin. Portage County is located within an ecological "tension zone" that separates northern plant and animal communities from those in the south. As a result, the county has a rich diversity of flora and fauna. A general inventory of the county includes: 160,000 aces of forest land, 32,000 acres of wetlands, 31,000 acres of public lands within a 20 mile radius of campus, 64 streams and 135 lakes.

Students at CNR are are involved. The CNR has 16 student professional organizations with over 650 active members. Student organization members gain skills and experience in leadership development, communications, public relations and practical application of their knowledge. Over 150 students hold paying internship positions earning in excess of $300,000 annually, with 56 state, federal and private agencies throughout the United States.

The CNR emphasizes field experience in all curricula. The College operates three field stations. Treehaven is a 1,200 acre field station near Tomahawk, Wisconsin that serves as a year round conference center as well as a base for our summer camp and short courses. All CNR students participate in a six week summer camp field experience at Treehaven or attend a similar program in Europe. The Central Wisconsin Environmental Station (CWES) is a 500 acre facility on Sunset Lake, 17 miles east of Stevens Point. CWES is a year-round conference and education center. The Schmeeckle Reserve is a 200 acre nature preserve, adjacent to the UWSP campus, that provides a field laboratory for many UWSP classes as well as an extension of the city park program.

CNR international programs allow students to gain a global perspective on resource management. The three international programs coordinated by the CNR are: the European Environmental Studies program in Poland and Germany for 6 weeks; a semester abroad in Australia, New Zealand & the Fiji Islands; and an interim trip to study rain forest ecology in Costa Rica for 3 weeks.

Graduates of the CNR are in great demand. Students have many job offers and overall, 80 -100% either go to graduate school or find jobs in their fields.

# MAKING A DIFFERENCE STUDIES

## Wildlife

Wildlife Ecology
Wildlife and Society: Contemporary Issues
Wildlife Diseases
Wildlife Population Dynamics
Human Dimensions of Wildlife and Fisheries Management

Wildlife Forum
Principles of Captive Wildlife Management
Management of Wildlife Habitat
Nonconsumptive Uses of Wildlife

## International Resource Management

International Resources Management
Processes of Sociocultural Change
Peoples of Central & South America
World Populations & Resources
United Nations At Work

Internship
International Economics
Latin American Development
Introduction to Environmental Study
Environmental Psychology

## Resource Management (Conservation)

Foundations of Enviro Education
Environmental Policy
American Environmental History

## Secondary Teaching Certification

Resource Economics
Population Problems
Environmental Degradation: World Survey

## Environmental Education  Elementary & Middle School

Intro to Enviro Study & Enviro Education
Environmental Field Studies
General Ecology

Environmental Field Studies
Environmental Ethics
Physical Environment Under Stress

## Captive Wildlife Management

Animal Physiology
Wildlife Diseases
Animal Behavior
Museum Methods

Principles of Captive Wildlife Management
Techniques of Captive Wildlife Management
Wildlife Economics
Animal Parasitology

## Environmental Communication

Natural Resources and Public Relations
Interpretive Publications
Planning for Interpretation
Interpersonal Communication
Film Laboratory

Interpretive Signs, Trails and Waysides
Interpretation for Visitor Centers
Oral Interpretation Methods
Basic Broadcasting Laboratory
Local Production of Media

## Natural Resources: Tracks in Enviro. Education & Interpretation; Land Use Planning; Youth Programming & Camp Mgm't. & General Resource Mgm't.

Environmental Interpretation Practicum
International Resource Mgm't
Integrated Resources Management
Environmental Law Enforcement
Park Interpretation

Citizen Action in Environmental Education
Resource Economics
Environmental Issues Investigation
Natural Resource and Public Relations
Soil Conservation & Watershed Inventory

| Urban Forestry Mgm't | Soil Science | Aquatic Toxicology |
| Groundwater Mgm't | Water Chemistry | Fisheries |

Estimated costs: Residents $6,400   Non-residents $13,200   Rolling Admissions

Use form in back to contact: College Of Natural Resources
University Of Wisconsin - Stevens Point     Stevens Point, WI 54481
(715) 346-2441

# YALE UNIVERSITY

5,200 Undergraduates    New Haven, Connecticut

At Yale, education is achieved by dialogue -- between roommates and classmates, between students, teachers and texts, and between the university and the city in which it is located. The richness of this dialogue reflects the richness of the Yale community, which attracts talented students from all over North America and the world. Everyone at Yale encounters difference and is challenged in his or her assumptions and beliefs. At the same time, the student body of 5,200 undergraduates is large and heterogenous enough that all students can find the support they need to develop and articulate their concerns.

One such support is the residential college system. Every student belongs to one of 12 residential colleges throughout his or her years at Yale. Students live and eat in the residential college community, which draws from a cross-section of Yale's diverse undergraduate population which is small enough to be familiar and close-knit.

Students at Yale also learn about being part of a larger community, and that community extends beyond the campus to include New Haven, a city whose roots stretch back to the 1600's. More than 50 percent of the student body is involved in volunteer work in the community, whether it is addressing critical social issues, tutoring at a local school, or volunteering at a soup kitchen. Dwight Hall, the umbrella organization for undergraduate community service groups, is the largest such organization on any college campus in the US.

In more than 200 undergraduate social, political, and cultural groups, and in more than 30 publications, students are able to voice opinions about campus, national, and international issues. Among these organizations are cultural houses for Yale's minority communities, single-issue groups like the Student Environmental Coalition, the Yale Hunger and Homelessness Action Project, and the Yale Journal for Human Rights.

Among major universities Yale is distinctive for the number of courses with comparatively small enrollments. Of its 2,000 courses, 85 percent have fewer than twenty-five students. Equally important, professors at Yale are dedicated to undergraduate teaching. Widely respected senior professors and young aspiring scholars share their passion and knowledge in classes and in one-on-one conversations during office hours. Quality student-faculty relationships are often cited as one of Yale's most important strengths.

Every student's course of study is self-selected and unique. Without requiring specific courses, each student takes a broad sampling in humanities, arts, sciences, and social sciences. Yale's extensive array of academic resources offers undergraduates unparalleled opportunities to explore and learn. With its combination of breadth and depth, Yale starts students on a path of learning that lasts throughout their lives.

Yale stays abreast of new philosophies of education and recognizes that, in a complex world, people need to develop a broad cultural and ethical awareness. Interdisciplinary majors respond to these and other issues: International Studies focuses on global socioeconomic, environmental, and political change; Ethics, Politics, and Economics examines the institutions, practices, and politics that shape our world. Within many majors there are "tracks" for students interested in special subtopics, such as the new track in Geology -- Earth, Environment, and Resources.

# MAKING A DIFFERENCE STUDIES

## Ethics, Politics and Economics

Constructive responses to natural and social hazards, allocation of limited social resources (medical care,) or morally sensitive political issues (affirmative action,) require close knowledge of their political, economic, and social dimensions, and a capacity to think rigorously about the basic questions they raise.

Classics of Ethics, Politics & Economics
Culture and Social Criticism
Enviro. & Development in Third World
Comparative Political-Economic Systems
Welfare Economics, Social Choice and Political Theory

Liberalism and It's Critics
Ethics in International Relations
Gender, Race, and the State in America
The Politics of Parental Authority

## Economics

Labor Economics
Economics of Developing Countries
The Economics of Population
Int'l Trade, Development & Environment
Economic Problems of Latin America

Health & Social Consequences of Econ. Devlp't
Economics of Natural Resources
Topics in Labor Economics
Corporation & State in 20th Cent. Capitalism
From Plan to Market in Russia & Eastern Europe

## History

War and Society in the U.S.
American Labor in the 20th Century
The Balkan Lands and Peoples
Colonial Latin America
The U.S. in Viet Nam
Excellence & Equity: Competing Goals in American Education

China in Western Minds
The Holocaust in Historical Perspective
Amer. Missionaries & W. African Christianity
New Deal Liberalism and It's Critics
Suburbanization of America: Social History

## Literature

Identity & the Landscape in Literature
Science and Literature
Self-Representation and Technology
Art and Ideology
Postcolonial Literatures

Modern French Feminisms
Cultural Perspectives in Chinese Literature
The Problem of Evil
The Writing of History After the Holocaust
Problems in Cultural Criticism

- **Totalitarian Humanity: Literature & History** Ideological-totalitarian regimes of the twentieth century in which intellectuals and artists played a visible role both of support and of defiance. Focus on Soviet terror and the Jewish Holocaust as well as on Yugoslavia. Nationalism, linguistic culture, utopian ideologies, terror and resistance.

## Political Science

Multinationals and the State
Ethics in International Relations
Public Opinion
Politics of National Security and Law
Political Economy of East Asian Newly Industrialized Countries

Intelligence and Covert Operations
Environment & Development in Third World
The U. N. & Maintenance of Int'l Security
Religion & Politics in Comparative Perspective

### Women's Studies    Anthropology    Psychology    Geology & Geophysics

Student Body: 10% state, 48% female, 52% male, 32% minority, 5% int'l.
Costs: $29,950    Apply by 12/31
• Individualized Majors  • Multidisciplinary Classes  • Team Teaching  •Vegetarian/Vegan Meals

Use form in back to contact: Office of Undergraduate Admissions
Yale University    POB 208234    New Haven, CT 06520-8234
(203) 432-9300

# MAKING
## A
# DIFFERENCE

• • •

## FIELD STUDIES

• • •

## SUMMER INSTITUTES

• • •

## TRAVEL PROGRAMS

• • •

# ARAVA INSTITUTE FOR ENVIRONMENTAL STUDIES

Kibbutz Ketura, Israel

The Arava Institute for Environmental Studies offers a year or semester of intensive hands-on learning on the grounds of Kibbutz Ketura in the scenic Arava Valley of southern Israel. Situated near the Jordanian and Egyptian borders, AIES serves as a regional center for conservation and environmental protection activities, developing ties between Middle Eastern and International university students. Students at the Arava Institute receive transcripts from the Overseas School of Tel Aviv University.

Arava Institute is the foremost environmental studies program in Israel and the Middle East. The Institute is based at Kibbutz Ketura, an agricultural settlement situated in the Arava desert along the Syrio-African rift. Ketura is 50 kilometers from Eilat, Israel's Red Sea resort, and Aqaba, the adjacent Jordanian port city.

The Institute's curriculum is divided into three main tracks: environmental policy, environmental sciences, and environmental ethics. Students are required to take basic courses in each of these areas. They also select from a series of related electives. While the Institute prefers students to complete a two-semester program, it is possible to attend for one semester only. Taught in English, AIES courses are designed to provide university students with the technical literacy, familiarity with public policy, and comprehension of philosophical concepts necessary to participate actively and effectively in environmental matters. Academic credits are given through internationally-recognized Tel Aviv University Overseas School.

Specific projects and training include areas such as wildlife captive breeding and repatriation, coral preservation, sustainable agriculture, and environmental activism and advocacy, contributing to a holistic educational experience. The Institute's location allows it to focus on issues surrounding desertification, water conservation, sustainable architecture, wastewater treatment and reuse in agriculture, and marine environment preservation.

Students in the program examine regional environmental issues from an interdisciplinary perspective with a diverse group of students from Israel, the Palestinian National Authority, Jordan, Egypt, and nations outside the Middle East including the US, Canada, Sweden, and China. They participate in multi-day trips exploring natural and cultural sites in Israel and the Middle East, with a focus on environment and development issues. A recent trip focused on regional water issues, and included a visit with Shimon Peres, former Israeli Prime Minister.

Opportunities abound to learn about the challenging and growing environmental movement in the Middle East through classes, trips and a bi-weekly Speakers Forum.

The AIES faculty is comprised of academics and practicing professionals who offer students a solid theoretical grounding in environmental studies, as well as practical skills required for conservation activities. In addition, leading experts from the Arab world are integrated into the teaching program, offering supplementary seminars and lectures during the semester.

"I really like the location, the combination of people, and the fact that you can choose your courses and your projects... AIES is good for people to explore what they really want to do; you are exposed to so many different areas. It helps you decide what you want to do, or helps you think about different topics. You learn to accept every individual on the basis of their own personality and behavior, not on culture or nationality or religion." Arnold Yezarski, Israel

"The Arava Institute has been a new experience for me... to be on a Kibbutz, and to deal with Israeli people -- especially Jewish people. I discover something new every day about the Jewish community, the way they deal with each other, and with Muslims. I have made new friends in the program, dealt with different cultures, different people, and different beliefs." Firas Alawneh, Jordan

"On the first day Firas arrived, there was a group filming a movie on the kibbutz. They had Firas and I sit next to each other. They asked us what are your dreams and hopes in coming to the Arava Institute? I said that I want to be able to visit new friends in new places which I wouldn't be able to visit otherwise. I would definitely say that this is becoming a reality " Inbar Telem, Israel

"My most positive experience here was when we went to Tayseer's (a Palestinian AIES student) wedding outside of Hebron. It was a traditional Arab wedding and it was an opportunity to experience something that in normal situations I wouldn't get to see. I felt the amazement of taking part in a cultural ceremony so different from my own... the villagers were very welcoming, and treated us like guests of honor. The family made us part of the wedding, not just observers." Karen Goldenberg, Canada

For more information you can speak with an Alumni Representatives in the United States, and/or email the Arava Institute at the email address below.

Costs: Semester $7,500, Year $13,500 + airfare

Use form in back to contact:
The American Friends of Tel Aviv University
New York, NY
(800) 665-9828
TAUOAA@aol.com
or
The Arava Institute for Environmental Studies
Kibbutz Ketura, Israel
tel: 927-7-635-6618
fax: 927-7-635-6465
ketura-aies@ketura.ardom.co.il
www.ardom.co.il/heilot/ketura/aies

# AUDUBON EXPEDITION INSTITUTE
## National Audubon Society
### 100 Students    Based in Belfast, Maine

The Audubon Expedition Institute offers an extraordinary educational journey. AEI's philosophy comes directly from years of creating and living in our unique educational environment - North America. The journey, which began as an educational experiment twenty five years ago, has become a sought after educational model.

Nature has always been and continues to be our best teacher. The places we have visited, and the people who inhabit them, have guided our curriculum. AEI has changed and grown as environmental and student needs have changed. The lessons have been transforming, and through our experiences we have created an academic program that speaks to the environmental and educational needs of today.

AEI offers an opportunity to actively experience nature and people as parts of a whole. The Institute's program fosters a thorough understanding of the world of plant, animal, air, earth, and spirit - the world where community, relationships, and life are of primary importance.

Through small community living, AEI challenges students to experience and examine life. By using the school community as a microcosm of larger systems, students learn to apply fresh insights and skills from their lives both to the political and social structure of society, and to the workings of natural systems.

AEI believes in open and honest communication as a route to personal growth. We foster the development of clear and honest written and verbal communication, as well as a healing and open relationship with ourselves and others, in order to promote interpersonal understanding.

Audubon's program promotes educational excellence through structured, self-directed field studies, hands-on experience, and traditional academics. AEI integrates challenging outlooks with progressive ways of learning in nature to encourage the evolution of independent thinking, self-discovery, and scholastic competency.

Each student is encouraged to cultivate individual, spiritual growth. Developing a spiritual relationship with the environment is of primary importance in understanding the inherent connections between people, nature and culture. AEI encourages a lifestyle that leads to the integration of humanity and nature. By providing ethical, philosophical, and practical skill development in ecological studies, we prepare the individual for a life of service as a global citizen. AEI invites students to consider that their physical, emotional, intellectual and spiritual well-being can lead to global health. The Institute encourage students to approach their relationship to the Earth with the care and reciprocity that allows all persons to seek their fullest potential.

Participation in AEI's Bachelor's degree program is an exciting opportunity for a student to broaden his or her experience in preparing for careers in education, public policy, conservation, small and non-profit business, industry or other science, or environmental work. The environment becomes your educator as you immerse yourself in the study of culture and nature. Students develop skills in such diverse subjects as ecology, geology, English, psychology, history and anthropology melding the sciences with the humanities to bring a holistic overview to each student's journey in education. The faculty members guide students in expanding their communication skills and broadening their environmental outlook. Each student's vision is cultivated through direct contact with diverse cultural groups, studies in nature, idea exchanges among students and faculty, and analysis of expedition experiences.

Undergraduate students may participate in the field program for one semester, a full year, (two semesters), three semesters, or two years (four semesters). AEI's Quest Program described below is an individually designed Independent Study/Internship that takes place during a student's third year. Students may wish to participate with Audubon Expedition Institute immediately following high school as a post-graduate year instead of taking a year off before college. Credits taken with AEI can generally be applied towards a student's undergraduate degree. Many students come as sophomores or juniors in order to enhance their classroom experiences. Most colleges accept credit either directly from AEI or from Lesley College in Cambridge, Massachusetts with which our program is affiliated.

Students can receive a Bachelor of Science degree in Environmental Studies from AEI and Lesley College. The undergraduate program sequence of 64 AEI credits (equivalent of four traveling semesters), plus 64 additional liberal arts credits can be arranged in several ways. Up to 3 semesters taken with AEI may be applied to the following degrees granted by Lesley College: B.S. in Education, B.S. in Human Services, B.A. in Liberal Studies, B.S. in Self-Designed majors, or an A.A. in Liberal Arts.

Quest is a student-designed, junior or senior year personal "expedition" to seek educational and career settings that complement the Audubon/Lesley B.S. degree. Quest may take the form of an internship, an apprenticeship, an independent study project or a combination of these during the third year.

A limited number of Advanced Placement high school students may also enroll in the AEI program. Students are given the opportunity to challenge themselves academically in a supportive, experiential setting while earning both their final high school credits as well as Lesley College credits. Students take the combination of high school and college courses while traveling and participating fully as Expedition members. They are involved in every aspect of the educational process, from selecting and planning activities to carrying them out and evaluating them. The Advanced Placement program is only offered during students final semester of high school.

Audubon Expedition Institute also has a 2 year fully accredited graduate program offering a Master of Science in Environmental Education.

# MAKING A DIFFERENCE STUDIES

Following is a sample of AEI programs and regions visited. While no one bus visits all of these places in the course of a year, nor does each bus necessarily have all the experiences listed, this list gives a brief glimpse of the scope of the program.

- **Pacific Northwest Semester**  Southwestern British Columbia, Washington, Oregon, Northern California. Explore strikingly different ecosystems including the Sierra Mountains, the Hoh Rain Forest, and Mount Saint Helens. Listen to a Makah Indian story teller recite legends in her traditional tongue, investigate highly controversial logging practices, study sea lions on the Oregon coast, and hike on trails through old-growth redwoods.
- **Southwest Semester**  Arizona, New Mexico, Southern Utah, Southern Colorado. Backpack, explore, and ski cross-country among the canyons, buttes, mesas, and desert ecosystems of the Four Corners area. Discover and explore ancient Anasazi cliff dwellings, then experience the ceremonies of their descendants, the Hopi Indians. Water scarcity, grazing, and mining are major environmental struggles in the Southwest.
- **Southeast Semester**  Florida, Georgia, Louisiana, South and North Carolina, Tennessee. From wading through the Everglades in search of unusual birds, to West Virginia hiking in the Smoky Mountains during the spring wildflower extravaganza, the Southeast provides a rich tapestry of folklore and natural history. Talk with old-time musicians, wrestle with development issues, visit a citrus plantation and work to protect endangered wildlife.
- **Mountain/Plains Semester**  Wyoming, Colorado, Montana, South Dakota. Rocky Mountain geology, grassland ecology, national park mgm't, water issues, and endangered species are the academic backdrop for this semester. Discover the difference between the Lakota-Sioux Indian and European/American influence upon this bioregion and explore some of North America's best known parks.
- **Canadian Maritime/New England Semester**  Newfoundland, New Brunswick, Nova Scotia, Maine, New Hampshire, Vermont, Massachusetts. Glacial geology, coastal and tundra ecology, and forest biology accent this semester. Spend a day with an old-time fisherman, canoe in the northern Maine woods, and be immersed in a tidepool during a day of estuarine ecology. Issues surrounding forest management, acid rain, and hydro-electric projects are highlighted.

These experiences translate into course work in the following manner:

### First Year Courses

Ecology of Place

People, Land and Traditions

Learning Communities

English as a Means of Self-Expression

Physical Education: Camp & Outdoor Ed.

Physical Education: Health and Wellness

- **Ecology of Place**  Survey the biomes, ecosystems, microsystems and geological features which comprise the bioregion. The ability to visualize and conceptualize geologic processes and principles which have shaped the earth and its life are emphasized. An understanding of the interrelationships of all life as well as humanity's position in the natural world is stressed. This course will examine natural systems with a deep ecological perspective in addition to a more traditional scientific approach.

## Second Year Courses

Applied Ecology
Practicum in Environmental Education
Human Diversity
Methods of Independent Learning & Self-Directed Study

Eco-Philosophy
Special Topic in Ecology

- **Eco-Philosophy**--Our post-industrial society is in the midst of a transition, with the outcome still unknown. This course offers students an opportunity to personally explore a newly-emerging ecological world view which pursues wisdom and is spiritually alive, life-oriented, socially-concerned and environmentally-sensible. At the core of this philosophical journey is the art of asking questions that open hearts and minds to a healthy dialogue. In this time of deep personal and social change, such questions encourage us to expand our ecological consciousness and increase our reverence for natural wisdom.

## Third Year "Quest" Courses

Voice of Nature
Survey of Personal Growth

Environment As Educator
Internship

- **Life Systems Communication** Examines the functioning of earth's ecosystems on a global scale. Based on the Gaian hypothesis that the planet Earth is alive and that all life has a common interest in self-preservation, this course identifies the basic communication processes between critical ecological and geological systems. Earth communication is compared to the various means by which people communicate.

- Faculty Bio **Susan Klimczak** (M.S. Environmental Ed., Lesley College) Susan worked for nine years as an engineer specializing in communications. Her work includes community organizing around feminist issues, renovating shelters for the inner city homeless, volunteering in a prison and living on a permaculture demonstration farm. A published writer, she is enthusiastic about Environmental Justice, sustainable agriculture, multi-cultural education as well as Quaker and Eastern philosophy.

- Faculty Bio **Hank Colletto** (M.S. Environmental Ed., Lesley College) Hank has been part of a consensus-run community land trust where he built a solar, earth-bermed home, and was active in grassroots environmental organizations. As an energy conservation consultant, Hank presented workshops on photovoltaics, superinsulation, solar construction techniques and solar heating. His work as an environmental education trip leader adds to the foundation of his teaching career. Hank's humor and storytelling are an integral part of the bus experience and he finds particular joy in guiding students on a transformative journey in search of their dormant inner wildness.

Student Body: 10%, state, 50% male, 50% female, 2% int'l.     Avg. age: 19
Faculty: 50% male, 50% female
Fall semester and full year apply by:Early Decision - January 1, Preferred Admission - March 1
Spring semester applications Early Decision - September 1, Preferred Admissions - November 1
Costs: $9,487one semester, $16,170 for full year    Rolling Admissions
Add'l $2,080 per semester credit fee if arranged through Lesley College.

- Team teaching  • Individualized majors  • Exclusive seminar format
- Vegetarian meals  • Service-learning  • Student environmental audits
100% of students do community service.

Use form in back to contact: National Audubon Society Expedition Institute
P.O.Box 365    Belfast, Maine 04915
(207) 338-5859
AEI@audubon.org    www.audubon.org/audubon/aei.

# BIOSPHERE 2 CENTER
## COLUMBIA UNIVERSITY SUMMER PROGRAMS
60 - 75 students - Arizona        14 students - Baja California, Mexico

Columbia University Biosphere 2 Center programs offer students a variety of ways to learn about the environment and planetary stewardship. Students design and run experiments inside Biosphere 2 itself. They work side-by-side with internationally noted researchers studying one of the most critical issues of the future. Students explore the desert Southwest from the Grand Canyon to the Gulf of California.

In the mid-1980's Space Biosphere Ventures purchased constructed an award-winning set of research facilities in the foothills of the Santa Catalina Mountains, focused on exploring the dynamics of life in closed systems. These facilities included the world-renowned Biosphere 2. Biosphere 2 is a 3.15 acre research facility with seven biomes focusing on those environmental regions found at 30 degrees north and south of the equator. It houses a tropical rainforest, million gallon ocean with living coral reef, a desert, savannah, marshland, human habitat and intensive agricultural area. Cutting edge research and education programs on the effects of global warming and greenhouse gasses have been the focus of the facility since Columbia took over management in 1996.

The programs at Biosphere 2 are interdisciplinary in their approach. This means that while you study biology and geology and botany and political science and history and economics you don't take different courses for each of these topics. Instead, you will study an environmental issue from the perspective of each of these disciplines at the same time. This teaches you about the intersections between subjects, and it also teaches you how to respect and understand the complexities of opposing viewpoints.

The programs focus on team-based projects giving students the opportunity to learn how to create successful working groups -- an invaluable skill for college and beyond. Students utilize the latest in computer technology and complex systems management theory to problem-solve. The goal is not to make each person an environmental scientist, rather to provide each student with the tools to approach decision-making with a critical eye and to understand the impact of their actions on all members of planet Earth.

Student life programs help students discover the unique and interesting cultures and natural wonders of the desert Southwest. Programs include social, cultural and athletic activities. Each class is unique in its personality and help to shape the list and mix of activities. Weekend shuttle service is provided for the students. Special events have included Native American heritage celebrations, astronomy, Latin dance lessons, canyon and mountain hiking trips and lots more.

Biosphere 2 programs welcome and are designed to work best with a diversity of students. Students from around the United States and the world have participated in each of our programs. Students come from schools representing all areas of the U.S. and from such countries as Nepal, Sri Lanka, Austria, Bulgaria, Mexico and Canada.

# MAKING A DIFFERENCE STUDIES

Students may choose to participate in either the semester-long (fifteen weeks) program or a summer programs ranging in length from two-weeks to six weeks.

### The Earth Semester

A comprehensive, interdisciplinary study abroad experience. Explore the desert Southwest on field trips, interpret data from your own original research, participate in team-based projects on the future of planetary stewardship and study the history of planet Earth. This program is open to students who have completed at least the first semester of college.(16 credits from Columbia University)

### Island Conservation and Biogeography in the Sea of Cortez (2 weeks)

Program takes place aboard a ship and on the islands of the Southern Baja peninsula in Mexico. Study islands as models of the impact humans have on environments. This program is open to students who have completed at least their junior year in high school. (2 credits) Mid-June

### Earth Systems Field School, Session 2 (Planetary Stewardship - 4 weeks)

This is a management course which teaches students the basics of environmental science from a whole Earth perspective while teaching them to be good managers of the planet and their lives. This course focuses on the tools necessary to be good managers giving skills which will be useful to students regardless of their career aspirations. Open to students who have completed at least their junior year in H.S.. (4 credits) Mid-July to mid-August

### Earth Systems Field School (6 weeks)

Session 1 (Earth Camp) is a field geology and ecology course which studies how the Earth and environment has evolved to its current state especially looking at the impact of humans. Students explore the desert Southwest from the Grand Canyon to the Gulf of California and the Biosphere 2 research facility. Open to students who have completed at least their sophomore year in college. (6 credits) Beginning of June to mid-July )

Hiking is required in each of the programs, sometimes up to 15 miles each day in high heat and altitude conditions. Each student is strongly encouraged to discuss the program with his/her family physician prior to program participation.

Costs vary by program depending upon length and number of college credits awarded.
1998 semester program is approximately $14,000. Summer program $2600 to $7000.
Includes tuition, room, board, books and recreation. Travel not included.
Financial assistance is available. Scholarships from $500 to full-tuition .
Rolling Admissions. Apply Early.

Use form in back to contact: Office of Student Affairs
Columbia University's Biosphere 2 Center
32540 S. Biosphere Road
Oracle, AZ  85623
(800) 992-4603
admissions@bio2.edu
www.bio2.edu

# CENTER FOR GLOBAL EDUCATION

A Program of Augsburg College, Minnesota

The Center for Global Education at Augsburg College offers six undergraduate academic programs abroad for students from many diverse colleges and universities throughout the U.S. and Canada. These unique study programs bring you face-to-face with people struggling for justice, give you hands-on opportunities to meet and discuss current issues with people at the grassroots level, expand your worldview and challenge your perceptions about global justice and human liberation, and provide you with a life-changing experience and the foundation for a job that can make a difference in the world.

These six programs are currently available for sophomores, juniors and seniors at any college or university in the U.S. or Canada. The Center has exchange agreements with many colleges and universities, allowing you to participate in its programs without changing schools.

What Makes Global Education's Study Abroad Programs Unique?

- Experiential Education - Integrate solid academic work with real-life experiences.
- Diverse Resource People - Learn directly from local people involved in some of the most important issues of our time.
- Living/Learning Community - Reflect on your learning experience in a community of students interested in similar issues.
- Family Stay - Spend several days to several weeks living with local families and participate in their daily life/activities.
- Regional Travel - Broaden your perspective on the cultural history and current social and political struggles in the region through group travel experiences.

Programs are open to sophomores, juniors and seniors at any college or university.

Programs in Mexico and Central America require one previous college-level course in Spanish or its equivalent. Students from over 170 colleges and universities in the U.S. and Canada have participated in CGE's academic programs abroad. The Center also coordinates numerous one to three-week programs to Mexico, Central America, Southern Africa, and the Asia/Pacific Region.

What have previous students said about the programs?

"A person who is sincere about ... questioning himself/herself has everything to gain from this experience. It has deepened my understanding and widened my perspective on the world immeasurably. A wonderful, deeply gratifying experience."

"This was an adventure in empowerment -- being confronted with so many other realities made me look so much more critically into my own. Thanks!"

"My experience in Mexico with this program will always be remembered in a positive light and it has influenced the directions I have pursued professionally. Thanks for running the program and giving such a great experience to so many."

"Keep up the tremendous work! I owe the Center my focus and my career path."

"I think this experience was the most important part of my college career. I highly recommend it to anyone interested."

# MAKING A DIFFERENCE STUDIES

## Mexico/Central America

### Women and Development: Latin American Perspectives    Fall Semester
Learn about the experience of women in Latin America, focusing on their roles in economic development and social change strategies. Explore connections women are drawing among issues of gender, race, class and global economics. Based in Cuernavaca, Mexico with travel to Chiapas and Guatemala. Orientation at US/Mexico border.

### Gender and the Environment: Latin American Perspectives    Spring Semester
Explore socio-economic and political issues with a focus on the impact of environmental policies on the lives of women and men from varying economic classes and ethnic groups in Mexico and Central America. Based in Cuernavaca, Mexico with travel to El Salvador and Costa Rica.

## Guatemala, El Salvador & Nicaragua

### Sustainable Development & Social Change in Central America  Fall& Spring
Explore the life and culture of the people of Guatemala, El Salvador and Nicaragua. Improve Spanish language skills while living with families in the Guatemalan highlands. Study the role of the church and social injustice in El Salvador. Examine economic development and the impact of social change movements in Nicaragua.

## Namibia/South Africa

### Multicultural Societies in Transition: Southern African Perspectives    Fall Semester
Examine the reconciliation process to end an era of apartheid. Explore the rich mosaic of cultures in Namibia. Challenge yourself to confront your own attitudes toward race and class. Based in Windhoek, Namibia with travel to South Africa.

### Women/Gender and Development: Southern African Perspectives    Spring Semester
Learn about the central issues facing Southern Africa with special emphasis on the unique struggle faced by women. Reflect critically on issues of development, hunger, injustice, and human rights. Based in Windhoek, Namibia with travel to South Africa.

## Courses Include:

| | |
|---|---|
| The Development Process | Internship |
| Environmental Theology and Ethics | The Church and Social Change |
| Women in Comparative Politics | Topics in Latin Amer. Politics – Dev't. Issues |
| Sustainable Economic Development | Contemp. Social Movements in Central Amer. |

Political and Social Change in Namibia: A Comparative Perspective
Family Systems and Social Policy in Southern Africa
Social Stratification: Gender, Class and Ethnicity
Namibia and South Africa: A Historical Perspective

Average group size: 20 students
Costs roughly comparable to a semester at a private university    Financial aid usually applies
Rolling admissions through 4/1    Scholarshps available

Use form in back to contact: Center for Global Education
Augsburg College    2211 Riverside Avenue
Minneapolis, MN  55454
(800) 299-8889
e-mail: globaled@augsburg.edu    www.augsburg.edu/global/

# GEOCOMMONS COLLEGE YEAR
## GAIA EDUCATION OUTREACH INSTITUTE & UNH
### 12-16 Students   Temple, New Hampshire

Gaia Education Outreach Institute was founded out of three main questions:

- What would an education look like that helps people study, experience, and practice the highest ideals of humankind around love, peace, beauty, and compassionate service?
- How can education build more sustainable, harmonious, human-Earth relations that work for the interbeing and well-being of all species and environments?
- Can we create learning communities that will inspire and train people to see with mindful awareness how everything one does and every place one lives are essential parts of one's lifelong curriculum, so that daily living and formal education become integrated?

In 1991 GEO formed the Geocommons College Year (GCY) as a kind of "sustainable lab school" for addressing these questions. The first step was to seek inspiring small communities working towards sustainability and arrange for GCY students to study, work, and participate in these "intentional" communities. The next step was to build an enlivening, innovative curriculum around ecology, sustainability, and mindful living and to find a university to collaborate with the GCY program. And finally, to attract students with a program that meets their natural idealism and yearning to develop compassionate, empowered selves in service to a healthy Earth Community.

GCY was successful in achieving these objectives and, through spring '98, has run six, semester-long programs to sustainable communities in Europe and India plus three summer institutes in sustainable living. Students may choose 1-3 of the following programs: International Communities Semesters in India or Israel; North American Foundation Semester; Summer Institute in Sustainable Living in New Hampshire. 12-16 students from diverse backgrounds, ages, and academic pursuits join with faculty to study, do service internships, and share in community living. Students immerse themselves in sustainable studies, ecological design, community development, globalization issues, and cross-cultural experiences. The University of New Hampshire gives 12, graded credits for each semester program, and UNH professors help in reviewing students' work. Credits are readily transferable to other schools.

At GCY "sustainability" becomes a word that is lived out in a rich variety of life-transforming ways -- intellectual, emotional, spiritual. If one looks deeply into sustainability, one encounters questions about the origins, duration, and meaning of life. Sustainability is about relationships, ecology, and interbeing with the other creatures and places of this Earth. It calls upon one's fullest capacities to live life as an experiment in truth. It asks us to slow down, to be mindful and grateful for living in this present moment. It brings us into the midst of nature, to honor, enjoy, protect, and celebrate its presence. And throughout the Geocommons journey, sustainability calls one to the practical action of "making things work and last," of supporting healthy environments, food, shelter, technologies, livelihoods, consumption, economics, governance, and social interaction.

# MAKING A DIFFERENCE STUDIES

A typical day at GCY begins at 7 a.m. and includes group yoga stretches, mindfulness meditation, check-ins, seminars, service internships, field site visits, lectures, student presentations, base group meetings, study, journal-writing, exercise/recreation, chores, free time, and evening cultural activities. Community agreements help everyone maintain coursework, clear communication, and healthy, balanced lifestyles without alcohol, tobacco, and drugs.

## University of New Hampshire Courses

Int'l and N. American semesters require separate but parallel sets of three, 4-credit courses :

- Studies in Sustainable Community Design: sustainable models, indicators, and ecological design; analysis of field communities—the physical, social, economic, political, ethical, and spiritual elements; applications to students' own communities.

- Problems in Human Relations to their Environment: state of the world, ecological footprint, limits to growth, local place studies, eco-literacy, systems analysis, mindful awareness, cultural contexts, lifestyles and worldviews.

- Internship in Sustainable Development: cross-cultural learning challenges; history, methods, and controversies around sustainable development and globalization; selecting, implementing, and reporting on an internship project.

- Ecological Worldview Education: a fourth, required, non credit course that explores worldview, self, and culture through deep ecology, new science, bioregionalism, eco-feminism, indigenous wisdom, voluntary simplicity, and mindfulness.

## North American Foundation Semester (fall semester)

Studies, community living, and physical work at the NH farm campus alternate with local community service, wilderness experience, and two, three-week field trips to sustainable and Native American communities. Students and faculty share in academics, personal studies, cooking, gardening, building, arts, meditation, exercise, celebrations, and reflection time.

## International Communities Semesters:

### India (fall/spring) or Green Kibbutzim (spring)

Students are immersed in cross-cultural, community, and world environmental issues. The India Semester includes: 12-day orientation in NH; 10 days at Plum Village in France, a mindfulness training community led by Thich Nhat Hanh; 10 weeks in Auroville, South India, a diverse community of 1,300 people from 35 nations whose goal is to "realize human unity;" 2 weeks in Kerala at Mitraniketan, a Gandhi inspired training and village empowerment center. Green Kibbutzim Semester includes 10 weeks at Kibbutz Gezer plus 5 weeks visiting other green kibbutzim while meeting leaders of Israel's growing sustainability network.

## Summer Institute in Sustainable Living (dates vary, 2-4 weeks long)

In the summer beauty of New England, students and faculty explore sustainability and ecological design through the lens of permaculture. A major goal is to add to the ongoing plans for a future educational ecovillage on the GCY, 115-acre, hilltop site at Derbyshire Farm in southern NH. Internship in Sustainable Living is the optional, four-credit course that includes study and hands-on practice with ecological and permaculture design in site mapping, food production, shelter, energy systems, and cooperative community processes.

1998-99 semester fees for tuition, room, board, travel: ICS $9,400; NAFS $7,800.

Some scholarships available. Rolling admissions, but apply early.

Use form in back to contact: Geocommons College Year

RR2 Box 793, Derbyshire Farm, Temple, NH 03084

(603) 654-6705    geo@ic.org.    www.ic.org/geo

# INSTITUTE FOR SOCIAL ECOLOGY

Plainfield, Vermont

"What is nature? What is humanity's place in nature? And what is the relationship of society to the natural world? In an era of ecological breakdown, these have become searing questions of momentous importance for our everyday lives and for the future that we and other life-forms face. They are not abstract philosophical questions that should be relegated to a remote, airy world of metaphysical speculation. Nor can we answer them in an offhanded way, with poetic metaphors or with visceral, unthinking reactions. The definitions and ethical standards with which we respond to these questions may ultimately decide whether human society will creatively foster natural evolution or whether we will render the planet uninhabitable for all complex life-forms, including our own."     Murray Bookchin, *The Philosophy of Social Ecology*
Co-Founder, Director Emeritus, and faculty member of the ISE

The Institute for Social Ecology was established in 1974 at Goddard College and incorporated in 1981 as an independent institution of higher education for the purpose of research, education and outreach in the field of social ecology. The Institute incorporates principles drawn from nature: mutualism, unity through diversity, cooperative action, and non-hierarchical organizational forms into the structure, content and intent of it's educational programs. The Institute uses local communities as a framework for examining problems which have global implications. This educational approach integrates study, critique, and creative action into a holistic process which fosters self-understanding, cultural knowledge, and a deeper sense of people's relationship to nature.

The mission of the Institute for Social Ecology is the creation of educational programs that enhance people's understanding of their relationship to the natural world and to each other. That understanding, by necessity, involves the Institute in programs that deepen a student's awareness of self and others, helps her or him to think critically and to expand her or his perception of creative potentialities for human action.

ISE's focus on people's relationship to the natural world integrates studies in the Social Sciences, Arts, Humanities, and the Natural Sciences. The purpose of ISE programs is the preparation of well-rounded students who can work effectively as constructive participants in the process of ecological reconstruction. ISE is committed to making out programs financially accessible to a diverse student body.

The Institute's programs reflect it's commitment to the idea that creative human enterprise can foster a more ecological future. Toward that end, the Institute offers both community education and academic programs, sponsors research projects and community activities, and produces educational materials and publications. A unique aspect of the Institute for Social Ecology is this integrated approach.

The learning goals of the Institute for Social Ecology are:

- The development of a student's understanding of how the principles of social ecology - mutualism, cooperation, unity through diversity, feminism and egalitarianism - incorporate into the student's life.
- The development of a student's analytical abilities - the skills of critical thinking.
- The development of a student's ability to act creatively to affect positive change in both the cultural and natural environments.
- The development of the student's ability to communicate effectively - the ability to articulate ideas clearly in spoken and written form.
- The development of a student's understanding of self and the world through the exploration of the holistic perspective of social ecology and specialized knowledge in at least one of it's component fields.

The Institute for Social Ecology offers the following programs:

Ecology and Community is a four week, intensive educational experience which includes courses,workshops, colloquia and lectures. College credits are available. The Ecology and Community Program is also the starting point for those who wish to embark upon the non-residential Master of Arts in Social Ecology, which combines on-campus work, a practicum, independent research and ongoing graduate seminars to gain a theoretical grounding and practical experience in the field of social ecology.

A series of three colloquia will be offered as part of the Ecology and Community Program. This year they are: New Currents in Ecological Activism; Environmental Racism; and Radical Democracy and Our Future: A Call to Action. During the week following Ecology and Community students can also participate in From Theory to Practice: Focus on Organizing, in which students will examine approaches to implementation of social change. Finally, Social Perspectives on Women and Ecology is a five day colloquium for students, teachers, activists and newcomers to ecofeminism to come together to map out future directions for this steadily emerging movement.

The Institute for Social Ecology draws an international group of students annually whose ages range from 17 - 70, with the average age being 24. Many participants in these programs are activists who do not attend for academic purposes, however, quite a few people transfer credit to other institutions. Credit transfer can also be arranged through Goddard College for an additional fee. ISE programs are held at Goddard on 250 acres of woodlands and meadows. Goddard's facilities include a library, an organic vegetable garden, a solar greenhouse and a community radio station.

The ISE's programs are best suited to mature, self-directed students who are capable of independently pacing themselves. The programs are often extremely intensive and offer a total immersion in the field of social ecology. ISE attempts to build a community of learners and social ecologists during our time together. ISE often receives comments to the effect of "This month (the Ecology and Community program) has been the single most intense and exciting educational experience I've ever had. I only wish that it were not limited to one month each summer" and "I have made more intellectual gains in these four weeks than I have over my past three years at U. of..."

The ISE is involved in several projects, such as publication of a bi-annual newsletter and Society and Nature: the International Journal of Political Ecology an annual conference on social ecology, and the Social Ecology Network.

# MAKING A DIFFERENCE STUDIES

## Ecology and Community

Community and Development
Community Cultural Work
Agriculture and Food Systems Issues
Reconstructive Anthropology

Feminism and Ecology
Health Perspectives: From Personal to Global
Perspectives on Social Ecology
Third World Development&Ecological Issues

- **Ecological Technology: Architecture and Society** Examines technological issues in community development, planning, and design in the context of the following questions: How can we create a regionally adapted architecture that supports and enriches our damaged ecosystems? How can we integrate the principles of preventive and holistic health into the disciplines of architecture and urban design? How can architecture best express and serve decentralized and democratic communities?

- Faculty Bio: **Louis Mannie Lionni** (B.S. Arch, MIT) Mr. Lionni has taught architecture at Pratt Institute and City University of NY. He currently serves on the planning board and practices in Burlington, Vermont with a focus on housing and community facilities in low and moderate income areas.

## Lectures

American Radicalism and Social Ecology
Ecology and Society
Native American Perspectives,
Cooperatives and Building an Ecological Democracy

Anarchist Education
Ecology and Spiritual Renewal
Lessons From The Past

## Workshops

Biological Agriculture

Appropriate Tech: Design & Dissemination

## Colloquia

The first three colloquia will be offered as a part of the Ecology and Community program. Those unable to attend the full four week program may participate in selected colloquia.
New Currents in Ecological Activism
Social Perspectives on Women & Ecology
Radical Democracy and Our Future: A Call to Action

Environmental Racism
From Theory to Practice: Focus on Organizing

**MA Social Ecology     Advanced Studies in Social Ecology**

Comprehensive costs: $2395     Rolling Admissions
Average age: 24    Vegetarian Meals

Use form in back to contact: Institute for Social Ecology
P.O. Box 89     Plainfield, VT 05667
(802) 454-8493
ise@igc.apc.org
www.tao.ca/~ise/

# INTERNATIONAL HONORS

30 Students

"I will never forget the many people who unselfishly shared their lives with me this year, and I hope that parts of me will also live on with my new friends and host families in different countries. They have given me the most beautiful gifts of all: the strength to face the challenges that lie ahead, the courage to find my own limits and to push them further, the hope that I can help to make the world a better place, and the determination to really make a difference."

Laura Sessions, IHP '95, Oberlin College '96

Founded in 1958, the International Honors Program offered in cooperation with Bard College offers a small group of 30 students per year the opportunity to study and travel around the world, working with an international faculty and living with families in most locations. IHP has two study/travel programs; Global Ecology and the newly added Cities in the 21st Century. The itinerary for the 1998-99 Global Ecology program is: Boston, England, Tanzania, India, the Philippines, Mexico and Washington DC. This year's program will combine academic study in the areas of ecology, biology, cultural anthropology and sociology with on-site examination of governmental policies and independent projects concerned with ecological balance, the environment and indigenous cultures. The Cities in the 21st Century semester long program will travel to New York, Bombay, Johannesburg, Rio de Janeiro and Curtiba, Brazil and Washington, D.C. In this semester long program students will study political science, urban planning, anthropology and environmental issues in these mega-cities.

The two semester 1998-99 Global Ecology program will be the ninth with guidance from Edward Goldsmith, publisher of The Ecologist magazine, activists, author, winner of the Right Livelihood Award (alternative Nobel Prize); biologist Brian Goodwin, author, former chair of the biology department at England's Open University and ecologist Jim Kettler, from Bard College Graduate School of Environmental Studies. Joining the faculty for the first time this year is cultural anthropologist Wendy Walker, from Johns Hopkins University. IHP leadership will be provided by at least two professors in each country with contributions from local academics, environmental experts and activists, including Peter Bunyard in England, Fatma Alloo in Tanzania, Smitu Kothari in the Philippines and Gustavo Esteva in Mexico.

The one semester 1998-99 Cities in the 21st Century program will be under the leadership of Janice Perlman, founder and president of the Mega-Cities Project, Inc. a non-profit organization dedicated to finding innovative solutions to the problems of the world's largest cities; Lisa Peattie, Senior Lecturer in Anthropology at MIT and Hans Spiegel, professor in Urban Affairs and Planning at Hunter College and CUNY; and Damon Smith, junior faculty who earned his MA in Urban in Regional Planning.

Each program is composed of approximately 75 percent undergraduates, and 25 percent recent graduates, mid-career professionals, and occasionally teachers on sabbatical. Although course work is at the undergraduate level, several students have obtained partial graduate credit for their work with IHP. Students come from a mix of academic backgrounds; while many are majoring in ecology-related or urban studies related fields, recent IHP students have also brought to the program an interest and expertise in anthropology, art, philosophy, architecture, engineering, politics, music and history.

# MAKING A DIFFERENCE STUDIES

### Global Ecology (Two Semesters)

### Science, Technology and Culture
Genetics, development population biology and evolution, with readings by Dawkins, Goodwin, Margulis, Gould, Lewontin...

### Ecology and Ecosystems
Through visits to key habitats in each country, study first-hand the ecology, threats to survival and conservation and land-use management issues. Fieldwork-based projects in habitats to be visited -- including salt marshes, mangroves, tropical forest and aquatic systems -- are an important component.

### The Environmental Crisis
Energy use, both historical & contemporary; agricultural & industrial activities; global climate change and atmospheric chemistry; politics of over-population, consumerism and distribution of natural resources; health issues and diseases of the environment; environmental resilience and the loss of biological & cultural diversity; ecological world view, environmental ethics and deep ecology.

### Economic Development and Sustainability
Considers the concept of development as related to ideas of scientific, technological; and industrial progress, and whether present development strategies are truly sustainable. Review such key events as Bretton Woods, establishment of the World Bank, GATT, and analyze the "politics of aid" and effect of development on agriculture, water development projects, and forestry. Readings by Redclift, Daly, Goodland, Sachs, Shiva, Esteva.

### Society, Culture and Ecology
The course focuses on the relationships between individuals and larger socioeconomic conditions, and the utilization of natural resources, examining inequalities and conflict as well as cooperation and possibilities for change at this convergence. A wide variety of societies and cultures will be examined, including farming, fishing, nomadic and urban industrial communities.

### Global Ecology Itinerary (September 1998 - May 1999)
- **Boston (1 week)**  Get started, meet students, first homestays, first assignments! Classes with lecturers from BU, MIT, Harvard. Half-day Outward Bound Program.
- **England (6 weeks)**  Study in Cornwall at Wadebridge Ecological Center, and in Cambridge. Meet with James Lovelock, originator of the Gaia Hypothesis, Helena Norberg-Hodge, and other activists.

- **Tanzania (4 weeks)** Explore the fragile island ecosystem of Zanzibar, home to mangrove swamps and endangered species. Meet with leaders of Tanzania's strong environmental movement. On the mainland in Dar es Salaam examine development issues of a major port city. Assess game preserve ecology and land management issues.

- **India (9 weeks)** Spend 2 weeks in the Himalayas, 1 week in Delhi and remaining time in South India, confronting firsthand the problems of population, health issues, energy and development. View eco-restoration initiatives, sustainable agriculture projects, and biodiversity conservation programs.

- **The Philippines (6 weeks)** Study with Nicanor Perlas, founder of the Center for Alternative Development Initiatives and study ecological soundness, associative economics, social justice, cultural sensitivity, holistic science and deep sustainability. Visit Ajuy on Panay Island to plant mangrove seedlings and visit Zambales to see large scale ecological planning.

- **Mexico (5 weeks** Live and work in Oaxaca, exploring ecology of the surrounding valley, learning about culture of local Mixtec and Zapotec communities. Meet local environmental and political leaders.

- **Washington DC** (1 week) Opportunity to meet with government officials as well as representatives of environmental advocacy organizations such as Friends of the Earth, Worldwatch Institute and Development Gap.

## Cities in the 21st Century (one semester)

### Urban Politics: How decisions are made

The course focuses on the political process, and in particular group interests. Who exercises power in cities? What are the sources of their power? Specific topics of study will include government structures; relationship between city and regional institutions; role of NGOs and the private sector; approaches to government funding and project financing.

### Culture and Society in World Cities

How do people identify and bound various social groupings? What places in the city are of symbolic importance to people? What are the celebrations and festivities? Who participates in them? The course will examine how these elements combine to form the rich layers of multicultural urban society.

### Sustainable Urban Environment and Global Ecology

This course examines service delivery and public policy. What is the potential for making these processes of transformation more efficient and less polluting? What are the relative contributions to waste and pollution of industries, public transport, private automobiles, and private individuals and families? You will look a which groups are working to solve these problems.

### Urban Planning: Guiding the Development of Cities

This course introduces students to the basic elements of urban studies. You will focus on the history of cities, worldwide urbanization, urban design and planning basics, the role and impact of urban architecture, elements of a livable city, patterns of urban industrialization, metropolitan growth and the relationship between urbanization and poverty.

## Society, Culture and Ecology

The course focuses on the relationships between individuals and larger socioeconomic conditions, and the utilization of natural resources, examining inequalities and conflict as well as cooperation and possibilities for change at this convergence. A wide variety of societies and cultures will be examined, including farming, fishing, nomadic and urban industrial communities.

## Cities in the 21st Century Itinerary (January 1999 - May 1999)

- New York (1 week): Get started in one of the earliest mega-cities and a global hub of information, art, capital, labor and transportation. Explore the city's diverse neighborhoods, markets and housing. Meet classmates and faculty, undertake first assignments and experience first homestays.

- Bombay, (Mumbai) India (5 weeks): By 2015, it may be the second largest city in the world. Meet with ecological and social activists, including spokespersons for the Hindu Nationalists Movement and organizers of pavement dwellers.

- Johannesburg, South Africa (4 weeks): Students will meet urban policy leaders who a few years ago were in prison or were political refugees. Meet government representatives; business and religious leaders. Field trips to Soweto, Pretoria and nearby wildlife reserves.

- **Rio de Janeiro and Curitiba, Brazil (6 weeks)** In Rio you will explore the workings of the First Lady's Community Solidarity Program as well as the historic city center renovation in progress. Meet with community leaders from different NGOs. In Curitiba you will study an exemplary example of urban planning. Spend time at the Open University of the Environment, and meet the creative individuals who designed such innovations as Theater in the Quarry and Light House Schools.

- **Washington, D.C. (1 week)** Wrap up meeting policy makers in Congress, the World Bank, USAID and other agencies, as well as Washington based advocates who work on urban sustainability issues at home and abroad.

IHP encourages and supports an active network of alumni, and in 1994 established a formal mentoring program to connect recent graduates with students from the past 35 years of IHP. Alumni and incoming students have access to a private online conference on the Internet where information is shared and many practical questions are answered.

Student Body: 50% male, 50% female, 10% int'l.

Faculty 50% male, 50% female

Costs:  Global Ecology:$21,300    Cities in the 21st Century: $12,100

Airfare $3,900

Deadlines: Global Ecology: Rolling until March 15, 1998

Cities in the 21st Century: Rolling until October 1, 1998

• Field Studies    • Team Teaching    •Full Academic Credit

Use form in back to contact: International Honors Program

19 Braddock Park    Boston, MA 02116

(617)267-0026    FAX (617)262-9299

info@ihp.edu    www.ihp.edu

# RAINFOREST CONSERVATION

The Rainforest Conservation Fund, Inc. (non-profit) has organized high quality/low cost Rainforest and Marine Biology Workshops in Belize, Costa Rica and Ecuador. Each is approximately two weeks in length and hosted by highly respected non-profit organizations in each country.

During these Workshops you will spend most of your time in the field with local guides and biologists studying rainforest ecology, wildlife, biodiversity, medicinal uses of native plants, natural history, rainforest conservation, land management, local cultures, archaeology, geology and much more. One week of the Belize Workshop is devoted to Marine Biology and Reef Ecology. Future trips include Panama, Honduras and Peru.

Your participation in these valuable experiences helps support a variety of rainforest conservation projects in Latin America.

Rainforest Conservation Fund Workshops have been designed to create a better understanding of the many complex issues surrounding the conservation of precious tropical resources. You will return home enlightened and hopefully even more committed to conservation, not only in the tropics, but in your part of the world as well.

The trips are not designed solely for students, but academic credit is offered through Aquinas College in Grand Rapids, MI. Future trips include Panama, Honduras and Peru and Alaska.

## MAKING A DIFFERENCE STUDIES

**Belize: Rainforest Ecology /Marine Biology /Mayan Archaeology** (2 weeks)
Our Belize Workshop is hosted by Possum Point Biological Station and their experienced staff of biologists and guides. Located in a beautiful jungle setting along the Sittee River, Possum Point offers easy access to lowland tropical forests, a variety of rainforest communities, vast coastal mangrove and lagoon environments. The area is teeming with wildlife including parrots, howler monkeys, coatimundis, anteaters, jungle cats, and numerous amphibian species.
Activities include trips to riverine ecosystems in hopes of spotting iguanas, and crocodiles; visits to local Creole and Garifuna communities, where you interact with residents and learn about their unique cultures, medicinal uses of local plants and sample some of their ethnic food. You'll travel to Cockscomb Basin Wildlife Sanctuary and the world's only Jaguar Preserve to study rainforest ecology. Other activities include night hikes to observe nocturnal animals; and talks about subjects such as including Mayan archaeology, conservation vs. economics in a developing country and conflicts between ecology and Belize's citrus industry.
The second week the focus changes to Marine Biology as the group travels by skiff to Wee Wee Caye (WWC), a small mangrove island located ten miles off the coast of Belize. The pristine waters support a variety of marine ecosystems including-tide pools, turtlegrass beds,and mangroves. Participants will be taught how to snorkel to explore these habitats. The Barrier Reef, largest in the Western Hemisphere will also be investigated. The variety of marine life found here is incredible- countless species of coral, anemones, starfish, spectacular fish and dolphins.

**Costa Rica: Rainforest Ecology / Geology / Conservation** (12 days - June, July, Aug))
Workshop participants will study rainforest ecology, conservation, land management and geology. You will visit the Quaker community of Monteverde and surrounding Cloud Forest Reserve. Characterized by cool climate and lush vegetation, Monteverde is home to three species of monkeys, sloths, coatimundis, kinkajous, the spectacular resplendent quetzal, red-eyed tree frogs, and blue morpho butterflies. The group will also visit the village of Santa Elena to discuss conservation and reforestation projects with members of the community.

You'll travel to Arenal Volcano, the most active in the Western Hemisphere, and visit Palo Verde National Park, which has one of the largest concentrations of waterfowl and shore-birds in Central America. At Palo Verde you'll boat down the Tempisque to observe croco-diles, iguanas, howler monkeys and a wide variety of birds. Then to Santa Rosa National Park which protects the largest remaining stand of tropical dry forest in Central America. Other activities include a coffee plantation tour ; mist netting of bats; a guided night hike in the rainforest and evening presentations on topics including medicinal uses of rainforest plants, sustainable uses of rainforests and reforestation projects.

**Ecuador:Rainforest Ecology /Quichua Indian Village** (2 weeks- June, July, Aug.)
In Quito you'll visit the National Herbarium and Vivarium, where rainforest plants are identified and stored. This will be followed with a spectacular eight hour bus ride across the continental divide at an elevation of 13,000 feet, and then down into the upper Amazon basin to the Jatun Sacha Biological Station. At Jatun Sacha you'll study insects, amphib-ians, reptile, birds and plants. Many consider the surrounding region as the most biological-ly diverse in the world with 520 bird species, 750 kinds of butterflies and more than 100 species of orchids.
Your group will also learn about rainforest ecology; take part in a reforestation project; have a "solo" experience in the rainforest and learn about the medicinal uses of rainforest plants from a local Shaman. The latter will include a visit to the Shaman's home and nursery, where many of these herbal remedies are grown. A highlight in Ecuador will be your hike to a Quichua Indian village where you'll spend two days observing how the Quichua live in harmony with the rainforest. Indian guides, using interpreters, will explain how they hunt, fish and garden. Your stay will include evening story telling, listening to Indian music and sampling local food. Back to Jatun Sacha by dugout canoe, and to Quito through the famous "avenue of the volcanoes" with spectacular canyon scenery, waterfalls and rivers.

All costs are under $1,000 plus international airfare.
Apply by April 15

Use form in back to contact: Rainforest Conservation Fund
29 Prospect NE Suite #8
Grand Rapids, Michigan 49503
(616) 776-5928
rainforest@mail.org

# THE SCHOOL FOR FIELD STUDIES

The School for Field Studies provides motivated young people - from secondary schools, colleges and universities nationwide, and from a variety of academic backgrounds - with an action-oriented, experience-based education in environmental issues. At the same time, students are able to make immediate and real contributions toward sustainable management of natural resources. In doing so, SFS seeks to make tomorrow's leaders more environmentally literate, aware and able to recognize the environmental effects of how they choose to live.

Since its inception in 1980, SFS have given more than 5,000 students a unique opportunity to conduct hands-on field studies and research addressing some of the most critical environmental issues facing the world. SFS is the largest private educational institution exclusively offering courses and fieldwork for undergraduates in the increasingly important fields of research management and conservation biology.

In an SFS program, students are face-to-face with the issues. SFS takes you to the best possible laboratories for environmental studies, the actual ecosystems were where problems are occurring. This provides dramatic real-life illustrations of the issues that can only be imagined through lectures and textbooks. SFS provides an educational experience which fully integrates theory and practice.

Rainforests don't fit under a microscope. Giraffes don't graze in a test tube. SFS teams range from 15 students and two faculty on a month-long course to 30 students and three to four faculty for semester programs. As an SFS team member, students are actively involved in all aspects of research and day-to day living. This team approach to learning and problem solving is at the heart of the SFS educational philosophy and it is one of its greatest strengths.

SFS semester programs require successful completion of one college level ecology or biology course. Applicants to semester programs must be at least 18 years of age and should have completed at least one semester at a college or university. Since a 15 week semester is compressed into 13 weeks (by working on weekends among other methods), be prepared for an intensive learning process.

Of course, all students will receive college credit. Full semester credit for SFS participation was accepted or awarded by over 150 colleges and universities during the past year. Financial assistance is available to qualified students based on need and comes in the form of scholarships and/or interest-free loans.

SFS operates seven Centers where students can participate in 13-14 week semester programs with a 21 quarter credit course load. These Centers also offer one or two month-long summer courses. Summer courses are offered at the college introductory. level. SFS's low student to faculty ratio and interactive teaching approach allows SFS to adjust course pace and content to suit the needs of the team. Summer participants must be at least 16 years of age and have completed the junior year of high school.

# MAKING A DIFFERENCE STUDIES

## The Center for Island Management Studies in the Republic of Palau
**Semester Program**: **Island Management Studies** (16 semester credits)
• Summer Program: Mgm't of Tropical Island Resources (8 weeks/8 semester credits)
Tropical Ecology & Sustainable Dev.          Directed Research
Principles of Resource Management          Env. Policy and Socioeconomic Values

## The Center for Coastal Studies on Vancouver Island, British Columbia
**Semester Program: Coastal Rainforests & Marine Resources** (16 semester credits)
• Summer Program: Conserving Marine Resources & Coastal Rainforests (1 month/4 credits)
Coastal Ecology          Directed Research
Principles of Resource Management          Economic & Ethical Issues in Sust. Dev.

## The Center for Rainforest Studies in Australia
**Semester Program: Tropical Rainforest Management** (16 semester credits)
• Summer Program: Tropical Reforestation (8 weeks/8 semester credits)
Rainforest Ecology          Principles Of Forest Management
Ecological Anthropology          Directed Research

## The Center for Marine Resource Studies in the Caribbean
**Semester Program: Marine Resource Management** (16 semester credits)
• Summer Program: Marine Parks Management (1 month/4 semester credits)
Tropical Marine Ecology          Directed Research
Principles of Resource Management          Enviro. Policy and Socioeconomic Values

## The Center for Wildlife Management Studies in Kenya
**Semester Program: Wildlife Ecology and Management** (16 semester credits)
• Summer Program: Community Wildlife Management (1 month/4 semester credits)
Techniques of Wildlife Management          Wildlife Ecology
Enviro Policy & Socioeconomic Values          Directed Research

## The Center for Sustainable Development in Costa Rica
**Semester Program: Studies in Sustainable Development** (16 semester credits)
• Summer Program: Alternative Strategies for Preserving Tropical Ecosystems (1 month/4 cr.)
Tropical Ecology & Sustainable Devel.          Economic & Ethical Issues in Sust. Devel.
Socio-Political Systems & Sust. Devel.          Directed Research

## The Center for Wetlands Studies, Magdalena, Baja, Mexico
**Semester Program: Wetlands Mgm't:Preserving an Ecosystem, an Economy, & a Community**
• Summer Program: Wetlands Management
Coastal Ecology          Principles of Resource Management
Directed Research          Economic & Ethical Issues in Sustainable Devl't

Tuition for semester programs: $11,350-$11,750 (plus transportation)
Average tuition for summer courses: $2,870 - $3,450 (plus transportation)
Use form in back to contact: School for Field Studies
16 Broadway     Beverly, MA 01915-4499
(508) 927-7777

# SIERRA INSTITUTE
## UNIVERSITY OF CALIFORNIA EXTENSION, SANTA CRUZ

At the end of his sophomore year the young John Muir left the University of Wisconsin of what he called the "university of the wilderness". He traveled to the Sierra Nevada mountains in California and began a lifelong adventure in learning directly from nature. It is that first-hand contact with the natural world that Sierra Institute programs seek to provide.

The Sierra Institute offers academic field courses taught entirely in wildlands -- students never enter a campus classroom. For up to a full academic quarter, students from around the country join with instructors to form small traveling field schools, backpacking throughout bioregions in the western U.S. and Central and South America.

Program coursework is diverse, interdisciplinary, and always focused on specific places. You can study field ecology and natural history in Utah's canyonlands, California's Sierra Nevada, or the rainforests of Belize and Guatemala. Unlike classes on campus, the plants, animals, and ecosystems of these bioregions are always available to you because you are living among them. If you study environmental ethics and philosophy in the Sierra, you will read John Muir and Gary Snyder while following in their footsteps through the mountains. In the Pacific Northwest you will experience old growth forests, northern spotted owls, clearcuts, and conservation biology while studying public lands management.

Whether studying natural science or nature philosophy, Sierra Institute students all share a common experience -- their classroom is alive. There is an immediacy to coursework that enhances and supplements the educational process. Academic and experiential learning combine to create a richness rarely found on campus. The direct knowledge of the rhythms of the natural world that students get through learning outside also fosters a deep sense of place. Accordingly, personal growth is often an important part of the learning experience.

Along with the outdoor classroom, all Sierra Institute programs share several academic and logistical themes. All instructors have advanced degrees and are skilled wilderness leaders with appropriate first aid training. Programs offered by the Sierra Institute are first approved by the Environmental Studies Board at the University of California, Santa Cruz. Courses are generally at the lower-division undergraduate level; there are no prerequisites. The application process can be somewhat competitive depending on how many people apply for a given program by the application deadline.

Group size is limited to 12-13 students. Academic materials (books, papers, journals) are packed into the backcountry by the group. All instruction takes place outdoors, usually on a series of backpack hikes ranging from 4-14 days long. Yet the physical pace is slow, allowing participants to sink into the place and come to know it well. (No prior backpacking experience is necessary.) Groups commonly hike to base camps, conduct classes, take day hikes to explore the area, then move to a new location. Because of the small group size, daily lectures and discussions are usually lively and always intimate. Students use many of the same academic tools that they are

305

familiar with from campus including seminar discussions, field journal assignments, lectures, required readings and papers.

How are academics integrated into the wildlands classroom? Using the Desert Field Studies program (see description under Spring) as an example, a few days on the trail might look like this: A four mile hike to a new base camp might occupy the morning. After camp is set up and lunch is eaten, students pair off along a mile of canyon bottom and search for different species of returning spring birds. They are asked to take notes on diagnostic marks, behavior, and habitat. After a few hours the group gathers to share observations and an overview of the avian community begins to emerge. Field marks, observation techniques, and record keeping are stressed. A paper in the course reader by a contemporary nature writer on canyon birds is assigned for the following day. After dinner as the evening falls, the group visits a nearby Anasazi site for an encounter with prehistory. Later they will be asked to write about the ecological limitations that the Anasazi must have encountered living in the desert.

The following day is devoted to geology. After a short day hike, the group reaches an inspiring classroom on top of the slickrock. It is a perfect place to unravel sandstone, joints and faults, bedding planes, and geologic time. Returning to camp, the afternoon is reserved for catching up on reading and journal assignments and swimming. After supper, everyone gathers by candlelight to share discoveries, ideas, hassles, and sore muscles.

Over the following days as their academic knowledge deepens, students gain insight into desert spring windstorms, heavy packs, and problem solving with a group of peers. Though living and studying outdoors for an entire season, academic and experiential education intermingle. The body is connected to the mind by a backpack full of books.

A Sierra Institute experience may serve as a powerful springboard back into university life that surrounds and increasingly threatens the backcountry. Many students upon returning to campus are inspired to work on the environmental problems facing society. John Muir said, "I went out and found that I was coming home." One recent student remarked that "until Sierra Institute I had thought environmental issues were not worth discussing because they were hopelessly unsolvable. Now I know there exist positive solutions and that change is possible".

University-level wildlands programs work best when they combine critical perspectives with profound personal experience. The Sierra Institute seeks to combine these two and to stimulate an overall ecological literacy in participants. Ecological literacy asks of students to both understand the ecology of their place and work toward sustainable living in school and beyond. In an urban culture that continues to separate itself from its wild roots, we need educational opportunities that reconnect culture with nature. It is just these bonds that Sierra Institute programs foster.

# MAKING A DIFFERENCE STUDIES

Sierra Institute field programs can vary from year to year. The following is a sample of recent offerings.

## SUMMER (application deadline April)

**Mountain Ecology: The High Sierra** (June-July)  This 8-week program explores the ecology and natural history of John Muir's high Sierra. Most of the hiking routes and classrooms are in forests and meadows above 9000 feet in Yosemite and the north-central Sierra. This program was created for students in love with natural history and wild mountains.

**Spirit in the Mountains: Idaho Wild** (June-August)  There are rich bonds between humans, creativity, and nature -- this program explores these key interrelationships while hiking in Idaho's spectacular Sawtooth Mountains.  Methods include the cross cultural analysis of myth and poetry, environmental ethics, and the art of journal writing. Focus on the contemporary ecofeminism and deep ecology movements.

**Wilderness At Risk**  This is a special hands-on field course in conservation biology and ecosystem management in the North Cascades of Washington. Hiking on both sides of the Cascades, you will encounter owls and ancient forests, public lands managers, grassroots activists, and more. The two courses are: Ecosystem Management and Wilderness Education.

Other Sierra Institute summer offerings include studying environmental ethics in the Olympic Mountains, public lands politics in Montana, and natural history and ecology in northern California.


## FALL (application deadline mid-July)

**Mountains, Canyons, Mesas: Southern Rockies Field Studies** (Sept.-Oct.)
From the peaks of the Colorado Rockies to Mesa Verde and the canyons of the Four Corners country, this program explores southwestern field ecology and environmental issues. If you want a broad introduction to the natural history and resource conflicts of this fascinating region, this program is for you. The three courses are: Introduction to Natural Ecosystems, Contemporary Environmental Issues, and Wilderness Education.

**Sierra Field Studies: The Mountains of California** (Sept.-Oct).  This is Sierra Institute's longest running field program and the reason for it's popularity is clear -- Wild California. From the Sierra to the Big Sur coast students follow a fascinating ecological transect of the state. The focus is on introducing students to biodiversity and natural history from the mountains to the sea. The three courses are: Introduction to Natural Ecosystems, Sierra Nevada Natural History, and Wilderness Education.

**California Wilderness: Nature Philosophy and Religion** (Sept.-Oct)  California's landscapes are diverse  -- the desert of Death Valley, the High Sierra, the Big Sur coast, and secret ranges in the north. These are the places that help spark the exploration of nature's influence on American philosophy, religion, ethics, and literature. This program affords provocative reflection at the boundary of nature and culture. The three classes are: Perspectives On Nature, American Nature Philosophers, and Wilderness Education.

**WINTER** (application deadline early November)

Sierra Institute international winter programs in Central and South America are unique and very popular. Unlike other field programs abroad, you are not be based out of a field station. Instead, you immerse yourself in the natural and cultural landscapes of our neighbors to the south. You travel with the locals on public transportation, live and work with villagers, and backpack in the bush far from any tourist routes.

**Rainforest Field Studies: Guatemala and Belize** (Jan.-March)   The natural history and ecology of Guatemala and Belize are the focuses of this field program. With your instructors you live and work with Maya villagers in the Guatemala highlands, explore the temples and forests of Tikal National Park, visit an agoforestry research station, backpack in Belize's wildest mountains, and camp on a Caribbean coral reef caye. The protection of tropical ecosystems and human cultural adaptations past and present are emphasized in academic work. The three courses are: Evolution and Conservation of Neotropical Diversity, Natural and Cultural History of Central American Rainforests, and Wilderness Education.

**Endangered Wildlife: Chile** (Jan.-March)   Enter into the fascinating world of ecosystem planning and international conservation politics through study of the huemul and it's habitat. The secretive huemul deer serves as Chile's national animal as well as one of the country's most endangered species. You will backpack into several mid-elevation study sites in the Andes and search for remnant huemul populations, meet will Chilean campesinos, foresters, and conservationists, and contribute to ongoing research that seeks to protect Chile's wild places from development. The three courses are: Wildlife Conservation in Chile, Ecosystem Management in Chile, and Wilderness Education.

**SPRING** (application deadline early January)

**Desert Field Studies: The Canyons of Time** (April-May)   Natural history and nature writing are combined in this program that explores the slickrock country of pinyon pine and juniper, Ed Abbey and Terry Tempest Williams. The combination of ecological observation and exploration of landscape and self through writing is powerful. The field journal from both the naturalist's and nature writer's perspective is emphasized. The three courses are: Natural History of the Colorado Plateau, Introduction to Nature Writing, and Wilderness Education.

**Nature and Culture** (April-May)   This program explores the interconnections between human cultures and landscapes from Death Valley to Mount Shasta and wild southern Oregon's Siskyou Mountains. Using interdisciplinary studies from ecology, environmental history, literature, and anthropology, the role of wild nature in shaping people and their world views comes alive. The three courses are: Cultural Ecology, Contemporary Environmental Issues, and Wilderness Education.

Other Sierra Institute spring offerings include Sierra Field Studies: The Mountains of California and California Wilderness: Nature Philosophy and Religion. (See Fall descriptions.)

Student Body: 79% state, 60% female, 40% male, 10% minority, 5% int'l.
Faculty 65% male 35% female
Costs: Residents $1,400 per quarter, Non-residents $1.600
• Field Studies   • Team Teaching   • Multidisciplinary Classes   • Vegetarian & Vegan Meals

Use form in back to contact: Sierra Institute
UC Extension   740 Front St.   Box C
Santa Cruz, CA 95060
(408) 427-6618      sierrai@cats.ucsc.edu

# WILDLANDS STUDIES PROGRAM
## SAN FRANCISCO STATE UNIVERSITY

Wildlands Studies, a unit of San Francisco State University's College of Extended Learning, invites you to join field teams in a search for answers to important environmental problems affecting endangered wildlife and threatened wildland ecosystems. Now entering its 18th year, Wildlands Studies offers onsite field research projects throughout the US and around the world. This year you can choose among 34 wildlife, wildland, and wildwater projects in the US Mountain West, Alaska, Hawaií, New Zealand, Canada, Belize, Thailand or Nepal.

Wildlands Studies projects are exciting and challenging opportunities for which previous fieldwork experience is not required. In backcountry settings, you acquire and directly apply field study skills while examining firsthand issues in wildlife preservation, resource management, conservation ecology, and cultural sustainability.

Your fellow team members will come from diverse US and Canadian locations, and bring with them a variety of college interests, a mix that provides ample substance for trailside conversations, and new networks of friendship. Teams are small in size. In most cases there will be no more than 9-14 team members working with the project faculty. Small teams are best suited for sharing energies, responsibilities and discoveries.

Wildlands Studies projects occur entirely in the field, and while there is time for solitude and relaxation, they are not simply vacations. Fieldwork sometimes means long days and uphill trails in not always ideal weather, but it is also a rare and fascinating opportunity to explore wildland firsthand, while striving toward shared goals with experienced researchers and new friends. Students earn 3-12 upper division semester units per project. Units earned are transferable to both semester and quarter system colleges throughout North America.

As concerned students you can join a wildlands team, and help in the effort to solve critical problems facing wildlands and wildlife populations. Wildlands Studies programs afford a rare chance to gain an intimate introduction to the ecology of fascinating and remote ecosystems, while taking part in field studies of significance to the region's future. All necessary skills of data acquisition and analysis will be taught onsite.

Wildlands programs will expose you to a stunning flux of new information. In the field, you will discover how boundaries that separate subjects like wildlife behavior, biogeography, conservation biology and cultural ecology tend to dissolve, and information appears as a richly integrated text. A primary goal of wildlands studies is to teach you to read this text in critical and meaningful ways.

A cooperative, experiential approach is at the heart of WS's educational philosophy. Education is most effective when students are involved in the learning with all their faculties. As a participant, expect to become an active member of a small community, learning from all aspects of your daily life. The way in which learning occurs is as important as the content of any particular discipline. Questions, and the thoughts and processes behind the answers, may be as valuable as the answers themselves. Wildlands approaches field studies the same way you might approach a glacier, a fern, or a friend: first with direct experience and observation. Then study can ask how the conclusions drawn tie into personal and global conditions.

Using an interdisciplinary approach of rigorous ecosystem/wildlife observation and experimental field investigation, students consider the complex network of inter-related biological, ecological, and social processes which shape wildernesses and the wildlife populations they support. Throughout, students develop and sharpen their skills in creative and critical thinking. While considering wildlands and wildlife from a variety of perspectives, students integrate what they are learning about a particular landscape into a wider framework of social, ecological, and educational concerns.

Developing self-confidence in new and challenging environments is an important part of Wildland's programs. Expect to arrive excited and prepared for a rewarding academic, social and physical experience.

## MAKING A DIFFERENCE STUDIES

Wildlands Studies field programs take place year round from approximately 3 weeks during the summer to a full academic or summer term.

### Canadian Corridor Project

Two field teams will participate in an extensive search for elusive and endangered gray wolf populations, one of the west's rarest predators now recolonizing western US mountain ecosystems. Students gain onsite instruction and direct participation in key field research activities including howling surveys, wolf habitat examination, prey base investigation and wolf sign identification as they strive to document wolf presence and assess wildland habitats for their ability to support wolves.

### Yellowstone Endangered Species

Another field study will combine a firsthand field observation and evaluation of the ecological relationships and habitat needs for recoveryl in the wildlands of the Greater Yellowstone Ecosystem: Gray Wolf, Grizzly Bear, Bald Eagle and Peregrine Falcon.

Working in the largest essentially intact ecosystem in the temperate zones of the earth, team members will gain a firsthand understanding of the ecological parameters and wildlife management complexities surrounding efforts to recover Yellowstone's endangered wildlife.

### Thailand Ecosystems and Cultures

Students take part in a rare onsite examination of Thailand's wild ecosystems and the environmental challenges they face. Working onsite, the Wildlands Studies team will use several of Thailand's National Parks as models to investigate the biological ecology of Southeast Asia and how the Thai people's interaction with wild nature shapes emerging conservation strategies. The goal during ten weeks in Thailand is to explore how the people of Southeast Asia might hope to balance economic development, biological conservation and cultural survival.

**Himalayan Ecosystems    Big Sur Wildlands    North Cascades Wilderness    New Zealand
Birds of Prey & Bighorn Sheep    NY Adirondacks    American Wildwaters    Belize**

Academic costs range from $425 to $1900 depending on the length
and location of the field study. There are no additional out-of-state fees.

Use form in back to contact:  Wildlands Studies
3 Mosswood Circle    Cazadero, CA 95421
(707) 632-5665
wildlnds@sonic.net    www.wildlandsstudies.com/ws

# MAKING
# A
# DIFFERENCE
### • • •
# GRADUATE
# PROGRAMS

# GRADUATE STUDY

The graduate programs listed on the following pages are an eclectic smorgasbord. There are sections on health (from acupuncture to community-based medicine,) programs from the Peace Corps - for people planning service therein and folks who have already returned, there are "consciousness" programs and lots of green and social change/social improvement programs. Quite a few of these are really singular - and many of them are hard to categorize, so rather than try to do so, the programs are mostly listed alphabetically. You are invited to journey through these pages with an adventurous spirit.

As you may have already learned, investigating graduate programs can be arduous. Had even half the programs I contacted responded with information, this section would be a separate book. This also accounts for the apparent over-representation of some institutions, and conspicuous absence of others. You will, however, find a very special and rich mix of programs on the following pages.

I haven't included much of the data you typically find in a graduate guide - I'd rather tell you about the content of the program. If you find it interesting, you'll contact the program and get the data from them.

It should be noted that many graduate programs, rather than sending us a profile, gave us permission to edit materials from their websites.

A look at the resources section in the back will point you to some more specific guides to help you focus your search further. If in your search for a graduate program you find one or more which you think fits the guide, please send along the information to us. We're all in this together.

Miriam Weinstein
SageWorks
P.O.Box 441
Fairfax, CA 94978

sageworks@igc.apc.org
www.sageworks.net

# AGRICULTURAL & BIOLOGICAL ENGINEERING
## CORNELL UNIVERSITY

A diversity of interests and an integration of engineering, physical and biological sciences characterize graduate study and research in agricultural and biological engineering at Cornell. Courses are taken in several colleges and numerous departments. Graduate theses typically blend analytical and experimental work and draw on Cornell's strong programs in physical, biological and engineering sciences. Theses reflect the variety of faculty strengths and interests, and the talent of the graduate student group we are fortunate to attract.

One of the professors has International Agriculture and Food Processing interests, so many of his students look at helping those in lesser developed countries find ways to store their post-harvest crops before taking them to market for sale. (i.e which type of small structure set up near the fields will keep freshly picked fruits/vegetables fresher or cooler in the hot weather).

Cornell University has also just recently signed a degree program certification with Dr. Mark Gearan (US Peace Corps Director). We now offer a Masters of Professional Studies (Peace Corps) in which students do a year of course work followed by 2 years of service.

Graduate study at Cornell is organized into 94 major fields, independent of traditional colleges and department units; Agricultural and Biological Engineering is one of these fields. Members of the Department of Agricultural and Biological Engineering, and other departments may be elected to membership in the Graduate Field of Agricultural and Biological Engineering as appropriate to their interests.

Within the Field of Agricultural and Biological Engineering there are nine research specialization areas: Biological Engineering, Energy, Environmental Engineering, Environmental Management (MPS only,) Food Processing Engineering, International Agriculture, Local Roads, Machine Systems, Soil and Water Engineering, Structures and Environment

Within the Field of Agricultural and Biological Engineering there are four degree options. These are the Master of Science, the Doctor of Philosophy, the Master of Engineering (Agricultural and Biological,) and the Master of Professional Studies (Agriculture) programs. All programs require full-time enrollment for timely completion of the degree.

Contact: Graduate Student Coordinator
Agricultural and Biological Engineering
207 Riley-Robb Hall
Cornell University
Ithaca, NY 14853
(607) 255-2173
abengradfield@cornell.edu
www.cals.cornell.edu/dept/aben

# BIOLOGY / CONSERVATION
## UNIVERSITY OF SOUTHWESTERN LOUISIANA

Conservation Biology students can pursue studies in biodiversity, systematics, environmental toxicology, wetland restoration, coastal ecology, organismal evolution, behavioral ecology, and conservation genetics through the Department of Biology at University of Southwestern Louisiana. The department offers a M.S. in Biology and a Ph.D. in Environmental and Evolutionary Biology. The department consists of 30 faculty members, including a very active Research Faculty, 60 graduate students, and 7 support staff members. Research scope and possibilities are expanded by diverse Adjunct Faculty.

Adjunct faculty serve as both major professors and committee members. The adjuncts are largely associated with the USGS National Wetlands Research Center (NWRC), located on campus, and the Louisiana Universities Marine Consortium Marine Laboratory (LUMCON), located in Cocodrie, Louisiana.

Facilities on campus are augmented by the new 50-acre Environmental Research Annex located about 6 miles from the main campus. Several vehicles and small boats are available for field research. Large marine research vessels are available at the LUMCON Marine Laboratory.

USL is located in Lafayette, the heart of Acadiana, the area of southern Louisiana settled by "Cajun" French exiles from Nova Scotia. Within a short drive of campus, students can work in the Atchafalaya Basin and Delta (the largest bottomland hardwood forest in the Mississippi Drainage,) coastal marshes and prairies, beaches and barrier islands, and upland pine forests.

James B. Grace  Plant ecology and conservation, exotic species, wetland and prairie ecology, plant life histories, statistical models of natural communities.

Clinton W. Jeske  Waterfowl and shorebird biology, avian and reptile physiological ecology, migration ecology, international avian conservation.

Paul Klerks  Environmental toxicology, long-term effects of environmental pollutants, adaptation to environmental changes, detoxification mechanisms, ecology of zebra mussels and other invading species, biology of fishes and oligochaetes.

Mark Konikoff  Aquaculture of fishes and crustaceans, life history and ecology of fish, water quality analysis.

Paul L. Leberg  Ecology and evolution of vertebrates, population viability and extinction, genetic diversity, habitat disturbance and management, conservation genetics of bats and poeciliid fish, statistics, simulation modeling, introductions and translocations, migration and breeding ecology of seabirds and songbirds.

Contact: Dr. Karl Hasenstein, Graduate Coordinator
Department of Biology
P.O. Box 42451 Lafayette, Louisiana 70504
(318) 482-6750
hasenstein@usl.edu
www.usl.edu/~khh6430/

# BOTANY
## UNIVERSITY OF HAWAII AT MANOA

Hawaii's location provides the best opportunity in the nation for hands-on botanical exploration of both marine and terrestrial tropical ecosystems. Moreover, the isolation and geology of the islands has produced a unique flora and a context to probe questions of systematic, evolutionary, and ecological diversity that are unmatched by any other location on earth. The interaction of Hawaiian and introduced species provides a rich assemblage of conservation problems and offers many opportunities to study resource management, restoration, and preservation.

The Botanical Sciences Graduate Program in the College of Arts and Sciences offers MS and PhD degrees in Botanical Sciences. The Botany Graduate Program offers training in a wide range of botanical specialties, although emphasis is placed on terrestrial and marine plant ecology, evolution, and systematics. The Hawaiian Islands are home to many rare, endemic plant species, and the Hawaiian Islands provide a unique environment for studies of island evolution, conservation biology, ethno-botany, tropical plant ecology, and alien plant invasions.

A wide range of taxa are studied by faculty and students in the Botany Graduate Program, including marine and terrestrial angiosperms, algae, fungi, and ferns. The Hawaiian Islands provide excellent opportunities to study physiological ecology, adaptation, and genetic differentiation. Many students learn and apply techniques for DNA analysis to address questions relating to plant ecology, population genetics, evolution or species hybridization.

The program in affiliated with the National Parks Service, the Harold L. Lyon Arboretum, the Kewalo Marine Laboratory and the Hawaii Institute of Marine Biology. Further arrangements can be made with the National Tropical Botanical Gardens and the Volcanoes and Haleakala National Parks among others.

The Botany Department offers a variety of facilities for general use in graduate research, including greenhouse space, growth chambers, an electron microscopy suite, dark rooms, an herbarium, and on site computers for data processing, graphics, word processing, and email.

Separate graduate programs in Plant Molecular Physiology and Plant Pathology are offered through the College of Tropical Agriculture. Programs in ecology, evolution and conservation biology are offered through the Ecology, Evolution and Conservation Biology Graduate Specialization Program.

Contact: Dr. George Wong
Graduate Program Chair
Department of Botany, St. John 101
University of Hawai'i
3190 Maile Way
Honolulu, HI 96822
(808) 956-8369
gwong@hawaii.edu
www2.hawaii.edu/graduate/

# CHIROPRACTIC
# NORTHWESTERN COLLEGE OF CHIROPRACTIC

NWCC was founded in 1941 as a single purpose institution offering education and training for the doctor of chiropractic career. Graduates of NWCC serve as primary care providers who are highly trained and confident in diagnosis and chiropractic case management. Further, these clinicians possess special expertise in the prevention, diagnosis, and management of neuromusculoskeletal conditions and their manifestations. Northwestern graduates practice quality chiropractic and collaborative care based upon the highest levels of empirical and scientific evidence. NWCC strives to instill the values of service to mankind, ethical behavior, preparedness to manage successful health care practices, and participation in the affairs of the profession and public community.

Northwestern maintains a limited enrollment of about 650 students per academic term. The doctor of chiropractic program consists of ten trimesters (3 terms per year) with equivalent foundations in basic sciences, chiropractic methods, and clinical (patient care) experience. Of particular interest is the College's Interdisciplinary Program, a clinic experience in which students interact with neurologists, physiatrists, orthopedists, and other health care specialists. The complete array of clinic opportunities is unmatched in chiropractic education. The promotion of integrated health care and the conduct of interdisciplinary research are additional unique features of Northwestern.

In the public clinics of the College, an 8:1 student to faculty ratio is maintained thereby ensuring individualized attention for all students. Northwestern's five public teaching clinics provide a rich experience for the intern in caring for patients who are suffering from a great variety of health problems. The number and diversity of patient populations of the clinics are a unique strength of the College. The newest outpatient clinics is located in the Institute for Low Back Care, a facility physically linked with Abbott-Northwestern, a major urban hospital in Minneapolis.

A typical student entering NWCC will have completed 3-4 years of preprofessional education and have a grade point average above 2.50 (4.00 scale.) Completion of a bachelors degree prior to entry is encouraged but that degree must also include certain specific science requirements.

Employment in health care fields which emphasize preventative, wellness, conservative, and holistic principles are projected to increase faster than average for all occupations. This is due to the rapid growth of the senior population and their increased health care needs as well as the need to find less expensive answers to increasing national health care expenditure. Graduates are eligible for examination before licensing boards in 50 states and all foreign countries. Some states or countries may impose requirements in addition to a D.C. degree. Students should be familiar with the licensure policy where they intend to practice.

# MAKING A DIFFERENCE STUDIES

**Trimesters 1 and 2**

Biochemistry
Embryology
Skeletal Radiology
Principles and Philosophy
Spine and Pelvis

Gross Anatomy
Histology
Professional Issues
Introduction to Chiropractic
Universal Precautions

**Trimesters 3 and 4**

Physiology
Central Nervous System
Pathology
Critical Thinking
Neuromusculoskeletal

Microbiology
Physiological Therapeutics
Physical Diagnosis
Organ Systems:
Chiropractic Methods

**Trimesters 5 and 6**

Community Health
Physiological Therapeutics
Cardiovascular System
Clinic Internship
Gastrointestinal System

Infectious Diseases
Patient Interviewing
Endocrine System
Clinical Nutrition
Genitourinary System

**Trimesters 7 and 8**

Pediatrics
Practice Management
Dermatology
Legal Aspects of Chiropractic Practice
Radiographic Technology

Geriatrics
Mental Health
Obstetrics
Emergency Procedures
Clinical Nutrition 2

**Trimesters 9 and 10**

Clinic Internships
Clinical Case Studies
Research

Legal Aspects of Chiropractic
Occupational Health

**Electives Include:**

Acupuncture
Sports Care

Applied Biochemistry & Nutrition
Occupational Health & Industrial Chiro.

- **The Mind/Body Connection to Health and Disease**  Correlation of the physical, emotional and spiritual aspects of health and disease. The role of chiropractors as holistically oriented health care physicians, helping patients to appreciate how thoughts, feelings, attitudes and beliefs affect their health. Discussion of recent literature related to psychoneuroimmunology.

Contact: Admissions Office
Northwestern College of Chiropractic
2501 W. 84th St.    Minneapolis, MN 55431
(800) 888-4777
admit@nwchiro.edu
www.nwchiro.edu

# CONTEMPLATIVE STUDIES
## THE NAROPA INSTITUTE

For general information about Naropa,
please see the profile in the undergraduate section.

Contemplative Psychotherapy is a pioneering program that combines the wisdom traditions of Buddhism and Shambhala with Western, humanistic psychotherapy. Academic study, meditation and community participation are combined in an intellectual and experiential environment in which students are prepared to work in clinical settings.

Somatic Psychology trains students in the clinical practice of body-centered psychotherapy, offering degrees in both Body Psychotherapy and Dance/Movement Therapy. The Dance/ Movement Therapy program is designed in accordance with the training guidelines of The American Dance Therapy Association (ADTA).

Transpersonal Counseling Psychology offers training in therapeutic skills, knowledge, and awareness based on the integration of psychology and spirituality. Areas of concentration in Art Therapy (in accordance with the American Art Therapy Association for ATR training), Music Therapy (approved by the American Association for Music Therapy) and Counseling Psychology.

Buddhist Studies combines thorough scholarship and study of classical texts with disciplined meditation practice and provides the opportunity for in-depth study of Buddhism as a literary, religious and cultural tradition. Concentrations include Contemplative Religion, Engaged Buddhism and Tibetan or Sanskrit Language.

Environmental Leadership, an integrated, transdisciplinary program, explores a contemplative study of ecosystems, sustainable communities, Native American environmental wisdom, horticulture and ecology. Community-based leadership training emphasizes compassionate engagement in environmental issues.

Gerontology and Long-Term Care Management, an educational and caregiving community providing creative and compassionate approaches to elder care. The program leads to licensure for employment as a nursing home administrator and is useful for other types of long-term facilities and elder-care services.

Graduates of all MA Psychology programs at The Naropa Institute meet the academic requirements for the Licensed Professional Counselor (LPC) credential examination in the state of Colorado.

Master Of Fine Arts in Writing and Poetics, the creative composition of poetry and prose fiction is balanced with literature courses in a supportive and vital writing community. Concentrations include poetry and prose, with coursework in translation, letterpress printing, participation in public readings, and community outreach.

Contact: Director of Admissions
The Naropa Institute
2130 Arapahoe St.
Boulder, CO 80302-6697
(303) 444-0202
admissions@naropa.edu    www/naropa.edu

# CREATION SPIRITUALITY
## UNIVERSITY OF CREATION SPIRITUALITY

"UCS has sprung from the hope of our time: to awaken awareness of the sacred in our work and everyday lives. At its core are cosmology, deep ecumenism, Earth awareness and the emerging consciousness of women and indigenous peoples. It is from this broad source that faculty, students and staff will find the heart of their work and efforts to build community... People often ask: 'What does one do with a degree in spirituality?' I answer: Everything. You can do everything better when the Source of your life comes together with you living of it. You can become a better parent, a better spouse, a better citizen, a better human being, a better business person, secretary, artist, athlete, theologian, therapist, educator, politician -- a better warrior on behalf of social and environmental justice, on behalf of the young, the old and the future. "                              Matthew Fox, President

Creation Spirituality integrates the wisdom of western spirituality and global indigenous cultures with the emerging scientific understanding of the universe and the passionate creativity of art. It is the earliest tradition of the Hebrew Bible and was celebrated by the mystics of medieval Europe. Creation Spirituality provides a solid foundation and holistic perspective from which to address the critical issues of our times, including the revitalization of religion and culture, the honoring of women's wisdom, the celebration of hope in today's youth, the wisdom to be learned from deep ecumenism and the spiritual traditions of the world's religions and the promotion of social and ecological justice. Creation spirituality is concerned with developing theologies and practices within religion and culture which promote personal wholeness, planetary survival, and universal interdependence.

This liberal arts Master's degree requires 32 credits of study either in the full-time 9 month program or a 2 year Weekend of the Spirit which allows students to complete the degree in 2 or more years of weekend courses. The Doctor of Ministry degree program is for professionals, so that they can return to their ministries as leaders in the transformation of society, bringing work and the sacred together. The D.Min. program is flexibly structured for people working in a wide variety of ministries. People active in all areas of spirituality and religion may apply, as well as therapists, social workers, educators, physicians, lawyers, artists, business people, people reinventing retirement, and others. Credit is through New College of California.

Courses include: Intensive in Creation Spirituality; The New Cosmology; Reinventing Work; Dancing Sacred Texts; Men's Rites of Passage; Tai Chi and Art; Perspectives from Ecofeminism and Ecopsychology, and Sustainable Communities.

Contact: Admissions Coordinator
University of Creation Spirituality
2141 Broadway
Oakland, CA 94612
(510) 835-8404
www.netser.com/ucs

# DEVELOPMENT /COMMUNITY AND ECONOMIC
## NEW HAMPSHIRE COLLEGE

The CED program enables CED practitioners from across the United States and around the globe to work together in applying economic principles for building sustainable, socially concerned programs. The program provides education and training in the field of CED and provides technical assistance and develops new models of CED through the affiliated Institute for Cooperative Community Development.

Community Economic Development is viewed as a strategy for people to develop the economy of their community by benefiting the greatest number of its residents; a systematic and planned intervention promoting economic self-reliance, focusing on issues of local ownership and capacity of local people; a program for helping consumers become producers, users become providers and employees become owners of economic enterprises; a method of building efficient, self sustaining locally controlled initiatives that support both profitable ventures and effective social programs; and a commitment to working within the context of a community's social, cultural and political values.

New Hampshire's program is an alternative to the orthodox models of development. It believes that social and economic institutions must operate so as to guarantee an equitable allocation of opportunities and resources for all people in society. That equitable institutions can only be achieved and maintained through community participants and awareness, and that social and economic development programs are most effective when they address the needs of the community as articulated by a representative membership of that community. Concern and care for the environment is a key element of the development process.

Examples of CED developed programs include worker-owned businesses; producer and consumer cooperatives; revolving loan funds and other financial strategies; micro-enterprise development programs; community-managed health delivery; parent-owned child care centers and neighborhood redevelopment land trusts.

The CED Program emphasizes a learner centered model in its approach to education. Participants visit a variety of community economic development projects throughout the New England area as well as attend conferences and workshops covering related topics. This one-year residential program leads to a Masters of Science in CED with a specialization in International Development. A one weekend a month program is also offered for non-local students.

| | |
|---|---|
| Training of Trainers | Appropriate Technology and Development |
| Housing and Land Use | History and Philosophy of Development |
| Economics and Development | Health Planning and Policy for Development |
| Micro Enterprise Development | Development as a Tool for Conflict Resolution |

Contact: Michael Swack
CED Program   New Hampshire College
2500 North River Road
Manchester, NH 03106
(603) 3130

# DEVELOPMENT / INTERNATIONAL
## UNIVERSITY OF DENVER

The faculty of the Graduate School of International Studies accepts the notion that "development" is a broad and somewhat ambiguous concept and thus presents a program that is both interdisciplinary and cross paradigmatic. As a result, the program allows a high degree of flexibility both in terms of the pursuit of individual interests and the variety of courses offered. Congruent with the realities of international life, courses depict the very nature of a complex, interdependent world, incorporating sociological, anthropological, historical, political, economic, and ethical perspectives on problems of development.

Development focuses on political, economic, and social problems that face developing countries and provides students with a basic understanding of their interrelated features. Each student pursuing a concentration in development must begin their course work by completing Introduction to Development. This course evaluates the meaning of development and presents alternative interpretations that incorporate problems of power and the environment. Modernization theory, dependency theories and theories of imperialism are presented, and issues of growth and reform are examined. Thus, this course imparts the basics of development and is the foundation from which students can build their own concentration.

Other fields and concentrations complement work conducted in development studies. A student is free to choose to work extensively in international economics, comparative politics, international technology management, human rights, international security, or in some specific geographic region of the world. While seminars are constructed so as to provide necessary methodological skills and research techniques to analyze more general issue-oriented problems, the student is encouraged to apply these skills to their own particular intellectual concerns.

Additionally, the visiting speaker's series, international student body, and the faculty and student exchanges arranged with several universities around the world significantly enlivens the atmosphere at GSIS.

Flexibility is the cornerstone of the development concentration at GSIS. The development program at GSIS is unique because of its flexibility and interdisciplinary nature. The greatest advantage of the development concentration at GSIS is its flexibility, thus GSIS encourages students interested in development to explore interrelated fields and concentrations.

Contact: Jeffrey Judge
Admissions Counselor
Graduate School of International Studies University of Denver
Denver, CO 80208
(303) 871-2989

# DEVELOPMENT / SOCIAL CHANGE
## JOHNS HOPKINS UNIVERSITY

In stressing the primacy of local initiative, the Johns Hopkins Program on Social Change and Development (SC&D) affirms the importance of community. The community provides the framework within which individuals develop their abilities and modern interest groups compete. Relationships depend upon the moral responsibility of community members and the internal sanctions of accountability, complemented by a public life that rejects paternalism. Locally-initiated development stresses the knowledge, leadership, and creativity of the poor themselves, many of whom are often suspicious of development directed by centralized government or by outsiders.

The SC&D Program hopes to contribute to the process by which development practitioners learn from those whom they would serve. SC&D seeks to provide a holistic comprehension of society, culture, and the challenges of low-income families. Many in the field of development welcome new emphases on the market economy as these accentuate initiative, spontaneity, diversity, and even consumerism.

Many individuals working in development and academia share these "participatory" values, but few academic programs have risked placing them up front, as their credo. One factor encouraging the SC&D Program to do so is the exciting community of alternative-paradigm doers and thinkers in Washington.

The SC&D community interacts with people coming from the local level in developing countries and with leaders of innovative neighborhood initiatives in inner-city Washington. Out of this interaction comes a rich flow of "best practice" cases, evaluations, and self-reflections about "participation" and "empowerment." There are few other places in the world in which so many innovations in development are being discussed by people who are also trying them out.

To encourage focused career preparation, the program helps each student develop a theoretical or functional concentration in his or her studies at SAIS, frequently deepening an interest acquired in grassroots work before entering the program. Many students define their functional fields broadly, choosing such areas as primary and secondary education, the rural - urban interface, the informal economy, or maternal and child health, while some have focused on concerns that affect only certain countries, concentrating on refugee work, for instance, or the particular challenges of small nations.

Entrepreneurship & Development           Cross-Cultural Perspectives on Social Org.
Theories of Social Change and Continuity  Management Principles of NGOs.
Assisting Refugees-Values, Issues & Practical Matters
Health Problems and Practices in Developing Countries

Contact: Margaret Frondorf
SC&D Assistant Director
Paul H. Nitze School of Advanced International Studies
1740 Massachusetts Ave. N.W.
Washington DC 20036
(202) 663-5691

# EARTH LITERACY
## SAINT MARY-OF-THE-WOODS COLLEGE

Earth Literacy is interdisciplinary learning that fosters the capacity to understand the natural world in order to ensure sustainability of the planet as a habitat for life. The 36-hour master's degree program grounds participants in the theory and practice needed in order to effectively work toward a just Earth Community. The curriculum includes 24 hours of team-taught courses that explore Earth Literacy using the perspectives of the natural and social sciences, the humanities, the arts and spirituality. Twelve hours are devoted to internships and practica which provide the experience and skills needed within the person's area of interest.

The Program format uses distance learning. Each of 6 required courses has a 5-day campus residency to build community among participants and to utilize the campus as a learning resource; preliminary and follow-up work are completed at home.

The programs goal is to understand the world as a web of elegant, complex and integrated systems, to develop skills in identifying and solving problems, to formulate effective strategies for change, to foster development of a personal world view which integrates the individual into the web of life, to experience and celebrate the beauty, mystery, and wonder inherent in the Universe, and to recognize community as a sustaining force for transformation.

The learning outcomes are to understand the foundations and principles of natural and socio-cultural communities and the systems by which they function, understand the connection between long-term sustainability of the planet and just systems and practices, understand the natural world as primary referent in which humans are derivative, apply analytical, evaluative, and integrative/synthetic skills, gather, analyze, interpret, and use relevant data, demonstrate problem-solving and negotiating skills, deepen a biospiritual integration which gives expression to the relationships of self to, with, and in the world leading to unity of being and doing, effectively communicate values and concepts which are transformative through the arts, humanities, and sciences, initiate, implement, and evaluate just and holistic strategies for change, and develop personal strategies for sustaining the change agent role.

The 1200 acre campus includes trails, varied natural habitats, the White Violet Eco-Justice Center and ecologically managed farmlands, orchards and gardens.

Course titles include Concepts of Earth Literacy, Principles of Evolution and Change, Nature and Cultures, Justice and the Earth, and Healing Earth.

Faculty include Dr. Sharon Ammen, Theater and Literature, Dr. Constance Bauer, Anthropology, Dr. Rebecca Goff, Biology, and Dr. Paul Salstrom, History.

Contact: Mary Lou Dolan CSJ
Earth Literacy Program
Saint Mary-of-the-Woods College
Saint Mary-of-the-Woods, IN 47876
812-535-5160
mldolan@woods.smwc.edu

# EDUCATION / EXPERIENTIAL
## MANKATO STATE UNIVERSITY

The basic tenet of experiential education is that when learning is integrated with the activities of everyday life that learning becomes more effective and engaging. Persons interested in the service-learning movement will find this program of particular value.

The Master of Science degree program in Experiential Education at Mankato State University is the oldest graduate degree program in experiential education in the United States. Originally started in 1971 as a joint venture between Mankato State University and Voyageur Outward Bound School, the Master's program is now housed in the Department of Educational Leadership and has expended its vision and developed an ever-increasing number of options for graduate students. Although there is a strong and still viable tradition of involvement in outdoor oriented activities, the department is committed to the idea that experiential education is much broader than wilderness programming.

The first fundamental assumption of the Master's program is that there is more to the knowing process than much of the traditional education assumes. Graduate students in the program are encouraged, even required, to leave the classroom and develop meaningful learning experiences for themselves. Whether their interest is outdoor programming, classroom teaching, administration, psychological interventions or others, the program gives students academic credit for testing ideas. The program is designed for strongly self-directed individuals who want to experiment with new educational ideas.

The other fundamental assumption of the Master's degree program in Experiential Education is that raw, direct experience must be complemented with careful thought and reason. In this light, the core seminars are oriented toward the analysis and questioning about the fundamental theory of experiential education. In addition to the core seminars, students can develop their reasoning abilities by taking graduate level elective courses of the student's own choosing. The goal of the program is to unite practical skills with scholarly abilities in the interests of the individual student.

The MSEE enables students to learn how to use experience as a means of instruction. The program promotes direct participation and involvement in a number of activities, followed by periods of reflection and analysis, a process based on the assumption that experience needs to be interpreted and internalized in order to have value.

Contact: Educational Leadership Department
MSU 52
POB 8400
Mankato State University
Mankato, MN 56002
(507) 389-1116
www.mankato.msus.edu/dept/edlead

# HIGHER EDUCATION & SOCIAL CHANGE
## WESTERN INSTITUTE FOR SOCIAL RESEARCH

This interdisciplinary PhD program provides advanced, individualized learning and professional training for educators, community service professionals, community activists, and other adults concerned with the relations among social change. education, and community service or development in everyday practice. Examples of specific objectives are (I ) the preparation of teachers for innovative college and university programs, (2) assisting the personal and intellectual growth of leaders In community service organizations. (3) helping to advance knowledge of ways to meet the needs of low-income and ethnic-minority communities, and (4) contributing to the education and knowledge of professionals in such fields as education, community services, and counseling. Students in the PhD program critically examine existing programs and institutions; innovative models and practices; the social/cultural/political forces that influence institutions and programs, local communities, and professional practices; and the creative potential of new kinds of learning and teaching processes-

Examples of areas of concern to PhD students are multicultural education, community-based adult literacy programs, health education, the educational effectiveness and social impact and self-help groups, the professional education of counselors concerned with creative practices that consider the larger social context, and the educational practices in formal school and college settings.

This PhD program enrolls very mature and capable adults who are able to do creative, specialized work in one or more areas pertaining to the education of adults for social change. Ph.D. students at WISR learn how to create useful knowledge for educators, community-based professionals and leaders, and lay people who are interested in using educational processes to address social problems.

Some examples of the individually designed student coursework include: Action-Research Theories and Methods; Theories of Social Analysis and Change; Multicultural Education; Social Change through Cross-Cultural Contact; Educational Theories and Metaphors; Adult and Continuing Education; Gender Roles and Culture; African Philosophy; American Indian Cultural Perspectives; Trauma Education and Men, Women and War.

For a more in-depth look at Western Institute for Social Research, see their profile under that name.

Contact: Western Institute for Social Research
3220 Sacramento St.
Berkeley, CA 94702
(510) 655-2830

# INTERNATIONAL EDUCATION
## BILINGUAL/BICULTURAL EDUCATION
## PEACE EDUCATION / FAMILY & COMMUNITY
## TEACHERS COLLEGE -- COLUMBIA UNIVERSITY

Teachers College offers interdisciplinary degree programs in Comparative and International Education/International Educational Development with emphases in Bilingual/Bicultural Education, Economics and Education, Family and Community, Language and Literacy, Peace Education, Comparative and International Education and International Educational Development.

The programs in International Educational Development and Comparative and International Education offer advanced preparation for professional careers in a wide range of teaching, policy and evaluation, administrative and research roles. In the Bilingual/Bicultural Emphasis special attention is directed to the role of bilingualism as a major resource in education for democratic pluralism and intercultural understanding.

The Family and Community Education program examines issues in basic processes of education with families such as the social construction of family memories, the mediation of television and other forms of technology by families, and the changing configurations of education in community settings. When extensive immigration and transnational migration are taking place, as in many areas of the world today, the connections between global culture and the cultural resources of families and communities come to be of critical importance for educators and policymakers.

Outdoor Educational Programs
Comparative Education
Postcolonial Studies of Education
Education for Global Security
Issues and Institutions in Int'l. Educational Development
Preparation of Instructional Materials for Developing Countries
Educational Planning in Int'l. Education Dev.: Ethnicity, Gender, Human Rights
International Education and the United Nations

The Family and Television
Education in Community Settings
Education & Development of Nations
Education for Global security

Contact: International Education
Teachers College
New York, NY 10027
(212) 678-3710
tc.info@columbia.edu

327

# EDUCATION / WALDORF TEACHER
## RUDOLF STEINER COLLEGE

For a more general idea about Waldorf education,
read the undergraduate profile for Steiner College.

Rudolf Steiner College offers a 30-semester-hour Master of Arts in Waldorf Education. An applicant must qualify for the Waldorf Teacher Education diploma program at Rudolf Steiner College and have already earned a B.A. degree. Upon successful completion of the diploma, an additional 3-week summer session plus a thesis or artistic project completes the M.A. requirements. Summer courses deepen the student's understanding of Waldorf Education and mainstream education; further develop powers of perception; give advanced experience in an artistic discipline; and prepare the student for education-related research, including the use of computers.

A qualified student who has completed a Waldorf Teacher Education diploma at another institution may satisfy the Rudolf Steiner College M.A. program requirements by completing three 3-week summer sessions and the thesis or project.

The best way to take advantage of this advanced program in Waldorf Education is to enroll after having several years of Waldorf teaching experience.

The conversation among teachers and experienced teacher-students allows profound insights to arise for all the participants. In this field of education, sharing with others engaged in similar striving gives support to each for truly making a difference. (Experienced Waldorf teachers may enroll in individual summer courses without applying for M.A. candidacy.)

Interested persons might also look into the work of Professor Douglas Sloan at Teachers College/Columbia University.

Contact: Admissions Counselor
Rudolf Steiner College
9200 Fair Oaks Blvd.
Fair Oaks, CA 95628
(916) 961-8727

# EDUCATION / TEACHER
## SCHOOL FOR INTERNATIONAL TRAINING

With a focus on applied classroom practice, the academic program that leads to the Master of Teaching (M.A.T.) degree is designed to prepare graduates for a successful career in language education. Concentrations offered are English to speakers of other languages (ESOL), French, and Spanish. The program can be completed as a one-academic-year program or in a two-summer format specifically designed for working teachers. In the one-year program, students may choose either single or double language concentrations.

The teaching internship, supervised by program faculty members during the winter quarter, is a period of rapid professional growth as the student is called upon to put theory into practice in the classroom and to make individual choices regarding teaching styles and approaches. Internship sites in the U.S. are located primarily in New England. Overseas sites used in recent years include Mexico, Singapore, El Salvador, Morocco, and South Africa. The practical focus of the program serves to equip graduates to achieve a high professional standing in their field.

During course work, interactive seminars, and small group projects, students listen, share, debate, and challenge their learning. In the field, during the teaching internship or professional practicum, they test and refine their classroom learning, developing the practical experience to contribute successfully as professionals. All programs combine on-campus study with a professional practicum.

Students in the academic-year format are eligible for public school certification after a second teaching internship during the fall following the course work. There is also an optional endorsement in bilingual-multicultural education (BME) available. The Summer M.A.T. Program consists of two 8-week sessions in consecutive summers, with the teaching practicum supervised by program faculty members during the interim year. The format brings together experienced ESOL, French, and Spanish teachers from all over the world who can earn the M.A.T degree with out having to take time off from their jobs.

"We ask our students to add a political or social dimension to their work -- to think about what it means to go into another person's culture and teach a foreign language "        Diane Larsen-Freeman, SIT Faculty

For a more in-depth look at the School for International Training, see their listing under International and Intercultural Management

Contact: Admissions
School for International Training
PO Box 676; Kipling Road
Brattleboro, VT 05302
(802)258-3282

# ETHNOBOTANY
## WASHINGTON UNIVERSITY

Doctor's Walter and Memory Elvin-Lewis in the Biology Department at Washington University specialize in Ethnobotany. In collaboration with the laboratory of Dr. Walter Lewis, studies among the Amazonian Jivaro and other adjacent mestizo and Indian groups that still successfully practice ethnomedicine have been underway since 1982. Whenever in vitro and in vivo studies were applied to validate their pharmacopeia it became evident that their preferences continued to identify pharmaceutically active plants e.g., in the use of potentially stimulating beverages, to prevent tooth decay, remove teeth, promote parturition, treat skin infections, malaria, hepatitis B, delta hepatitis and to significantly enhance wound healing. Of interest to this laboratory is the use of biodirected anti-infective assays to isolate potentially therapeutic anti-viral, anti-bacterial and other anti-infective agents. Studies begin in the field by developing an inventory of candidate plant species, conducting appropriate surveys to identify those most valued, and whenever possible by correlating these with therapeutic observations made by collaborating clinicians. Selected species are then studied in order to isolate the active principles in collaboration with natural product, organic and synthetic chemists and others expert in various aspects of diagnostic or molecular virology and microbiology.

Empirical selection continues to be an important factor in identifying plants with potential therapeutic value. Prioritizing preferred plants by epidemiological methods has invariably shown that the most popular are also the most efficacious. The concept of ethnomedical/dental focusing, evolved in this laboratory, has been applied to understanding the therapeutic value of plants used in folk dentistry and medicine, worldwide.

The Program in Plant Biology at Washington University has made outstanding contributions to the plant sciences. The research areas of the member laboratories span the breadth of plant biology. A major emphasis is placed on using plants as an experimental system for the molecular genetic dissection of key processes, including photosynthesis, plant growth regulator action, environmental response, transcriptional control and DNA modification.

Contact: Prof's Lewis
Program in Plant Biology
110A Busch Laboratory Box 1137
Washington University
St. Louis, MO. 63130
elvin@wustlb.wustl.edu

# ENVIRONMENTAL ANTHROPOLOGY
## UNIVERSITY OF WASHINGTON

Environmental Anthropology is an interdisciplinary graduate program based in the Department of Anthropology. Its purpose is to provide a coherent framework for graduate students wishing to study environmental issues from an anthropological perspective, while building and maintaining strong interdisciplinary connections. Like other graduate programs in the department, study in Environmental Anthropology will lead to M.A. and Ph.D. degrees in Anthropology.

The program in Environmental Anthropology (EA) considers human-environment interactions across the full range of sociocultural variation, and from the earliest human societies to the contemporary global system. It endeavors to understand environmental problems and knowledge not only from a western scientific standpoint, but also from the multiple and often conflicting perspectives of members of various local or indigenous cultural systems. These goals require familiarity with concepts and methods in various sciences: social, biological, and physical; hence EA is inherently interdisciplinary.

While environmental problems are widely recognized as matters of great public and scholarly concern, far more attention has been focused on physical and biological dimensions of these problems than on social, cultural, and historical dimensions. A primary aim of EA is to redress this imbalance. Since sociocultural and environmental phenomena shape each other through a process of mutual influence, EA fosters an integrated analysis of their interaction. The primary areas of interest within this EA Program include:

- indigenous environmental knowledge (e.g., ethnobiology),
- social and cultural causes & consequences of environmental modification
- environmental conservation and sustainability
- culturally-appropriate environmental economics
- political ecology of economic and environmental change

Depending on their particular interests or backgrounds, students in the program may focus on ethnographic or archaeological contexts for the study of human environment interaction; and they may work in any region of the world. The present EA core faculty (see below) focus their research on (Native) North America, Mesoamerica, the South Pacific, and (paleolithic) Europe. The University of Washington has long been a premier center of environmental studies, and offers a particularly rich array of faculty and courses in this area.

Contact: Eric Smith
Graduate Program in Environmental Anthroplogy
Box 353100
University of Washington
Seattle, WA 98195
(206) 543-5240
easmith@u.washington.edu

# ENVIRONMENTAL MANAGEMENT
## UNIVERSITY OF TENNESSEE

University of Tennessee at Knoxville's MBA Strategic Environmental Management concentration was developed by strategic management faculty (Iain Clelland, Tom Dean, Jerry Fryxell, Bill Judge, and Alex Miller) and consists of a team-taught course in the College of Business Administration (CBA) and two related courses taught by other departments or schools (e.g., Economics Dept. & Engineering and Law Schools). The course is also open to graduate students in other disciplines and qualified business undergraduates. Earlier this year, Environmental and Natural Resources Management was identified by the Academic Program Evaluation Committee as one of eight areas of scholarly strength at UTK. University and CBA resources such as the Center for Industrial Services and the Energy, Environment Resources Center (http://eerc.ra.utk.edu/) have enabled the strategic management faculty to conduct research and further develop the curriculum. A number of environmental and business publications and grants have been garnered by the faculty.

The World Resources Institute's (WRI) 1997-98 Survey of Business School Faculty recently rated UTK's Environmental Management Program and MBA Concentration as one of the top ten in the nation among both public and private universities. The survey of nearly 100 business school faculty who have been associated with WRI's Business-Environment Learning & Leadership (BELL) program indicated that UTK's program in the (CBA) is on the forefront of business & natural environment pedagogy.

Contact: Strategic Environmental Management
College of Business Administration
University of Tennessee--Knoxville
527 Stokely Management Center
Knoxville, TN 37996-0552
(423) 974-5033

To see the syllabus of the MBA course, visit Starfish site at:
http://www.2nature.org/programs/starfish/ courses.nsf/
and search by my name or institution (UT).

# ENVIRONMENTAL RESTORATION
## NORTHERN ARIZONA UNIVERSITY

Academic study, research, and practical ecological restoration projects are brought together in an innovative program newly created by Northern Arizona University (NAU). Students can incorporate a restoration emphasis into their undergraduate and graduate programs. A unique undergraduate research or fieldwork opportunity complements the coursework, allowing students to gain solid work experience in conjunction with an independent project to investigate and apply restoration principles on the ground.

"Northern Arizona is an ideal natural setting for ecological restoration," said Dr. Wally Covington, program director. "We are surrounded by ecosystems of outstanding beauty and tremendous natural and cultural value, like the Grand Canyon and the forests and grasslands of the Colorado Plateau. But many of these landscapes have been severely degraded over the past century as a consequence of livestock grazing, old-growth tree harvesting, and exclusion of the natural frequent fire regime. Our goal is to bring together managers, scientists, and all people concerned with the management of these ecosystems to build a consensus on appropriate methods for restoring and sustaining ecosystem health."

Among the projects currently underway are collaborations with the Bureau of Land Management, National Park Service, Forest Service, and the Arizona National Guard. A central theme is the integration of science and management. Ecological restoration treatments are designed as landscape-scale experiments. As treatments are put in place, the effects on grasses, trees, wildflowers, animals, and soils are carefully monitored. Results from initial treatments are applied to refine the next set of restoration prescriptions. This adaptive approach to wildland management holds promise for dealing with urgent environmental problems in a rational and open way.

The new university program will support student researchers to investigate a broader range of questions. For example, "herbaceous plants and shrubs make up the greatest species diversity and wildlife habitat resources in southwestern forests. As they decline, we see ecosystems become less complex and more fragile, but far too little is known about how to restore these diverse and productive communities," said Dr. Margaret Moore, ecology professor. A great variety of issues, ranging from conservation genetics to the sociology of public policy making, are open for motivated students to explore. Funding comes from the state of Arizona and outside research grants, with strong backing from the School of Forestry and the College of Ecosystem Science and Management.

Contact: Program in Environmental Restoration
Northern Arizona University. Box 15016
Flagstaff, AZ 86011
(520) 523-9011
www.nau.edu

# ENVIRONMENTAL SCIENCE & ENGINEERING
# ECOSYSTEM MANAGEMENT & RESTORATION
## THE OREGON GRADUATE INSTITUTE

The Oregon Graduate Institute is a private, graduate-only technical university dedicated to contemporary scientific research and education. The department of Environmental Science and Engineering offers interdisciplinary graduate study leading to the degrees of Master of Science (nonthesis and thesis) and Doctor of Philosophy. The nonthesis and thesis M.S. programs can be completed in 1 year and 2 years, respectively. The Ph.D. program takes 4 to 5 years to complete.

The department's low student-faculty ratio allows for close interactions with faculty. The coursework is highly relevant to modern environmental science and engineering. The 18-month Environmental Systems Management program combines training in environmental science with innovative instruction in the management of technology. The Ecosystem Management and Restoration program integrates rigorous environmental science principles, laboratory and field applications, risk assessment, project management, and policy/regulation into a cohesive curriculum.

The faculty members are active in grant-supported research and have expertise in groundwater hydrology and geochemistry, aquatic chemistry of organic and inorganic pollutants, estuarine and coastal hydrodynamics, trace organic analysis of air and water, and nutrient cycling in watersheds.

Graduates are prepared for work in industry, government, or for the pursuit of further work in academia. M.S. graduates work at the various major environmental firms throughout the country and at government agencies. The Ph.D. graduates are now faculty, scientists at laboratories of the Environmental Protection Agency, U.S. Geological Survey, and Department of Energy, or are environmental program managers at private, state, federal, and international agencies.

M.S. applications are considered year-round, and Ph.D. applications should be received by February 15.

Contact: Dr. Patty Tuccalina
Department of Environmental Science & Engineering
Oregon Graduate Institute of Science & Technology
POB 9100
Portland, OR 97291-1000
(800) 685-2423 (503) 690-1086
admissions@admin.ogi.edu
www.ese.ogi.edu

# ENVIRONMENTAL SCIENCES AND ENGINEERING
# IN THE SCHOOL OF PUBLIC HEALTH
## UNIVERSITY OF NORTH CAROLINA AT CHAPEL HILL

The Department of Environmental Sciences and Engineering (ESE) was founded in 1921 as a program of instruction and research in sanitary and civil engineering. Since that time, it has become one of the largest graduate environmental education and research programs in the United States. Faculty and student body represent a broad range of disciplinary backgrounds, including specialties within biology, chemistry, economics, engineering, mathematics, microbiology, physics, policy and toxicology.

ESE is one of the few degree-granting units at a research university that integrates environmental science, engineering, and policy analysis. ESE also collaborates with units in UNC's School of Public Health; School of Medicine; School of Business; departments of Biology, Chemistry, City and Regional Planning, Economics, Geology; and curricula in Ecology, Marine Sciences, Public Policy Analysis, and Toxicology.

The Master of Science in Public Health is designed to develop the science base of the field of public health with specialization in one or more of the areas in environmental sciences and engineering. The Master of Public Health is designed to provide professionals in the health care and health-related areas with a broad base of knowledge of the field of environmental science and engineering, and an understanding of its relationship to public health. Emphasis is placed on understanding of the scientific principles underlying environmental health.

The Master of Science in Environmental Engineering develops the engineering skills and technical knowledge base for entry into professional engineering. The PhD in Environmental Sciences and Engineering is granted by the Graduate School, and the curriculum of study is individualized according to each candidate's interest area.

Research and teaching in ESE has steadily expanded to encompass the chemical, biological, toxicological, and physical aspects of environmental and engineered processes, as well as social, political, and legal considerations of managing the quality of our water, soil, and air resources. Faculty hold advanced degrees in fields ranging from chemistry, microbiology, and engineering to economics, planning, and public administration. Research is conducted individually, jointly, and interdisciplinarily.

The department is organized into six administrative program areas which define and administer the curricula. They are: Air, Radiation, and Industrial Hygiene, Aquatic and Atmospheric Sciences, Environmental Health Sciences, Environmental Management and Policy, Water Resources Engineering, and Environmental Modeling

Contact: Student Services
Department of Environmental Sciences and Engineering School of Public Health
The University of North Carolina at Chapel Hill CB #7400
Chapel Hill, NC 27599-7400
(919) 966-3844
web: http://www.sph.unc.edu/envr

# ENVIRONMENTAL STUDIES
## INSTITUTE FOR ENVIRONMENTAL STUDIES
## UNIVERSITY OF WISCONSIN-MADISON

The University of Wisconsin-Madison's excellent academic reputation and progressive political climate have attracted many social and scientific innovators, including some of America's leading environmentalists.

Here, John Muir studied more than a century ago before departing for the mountains of California, where he founded the Sierra Club and lobbied successfully for creation of the national park system. Here, Aldo Leopold established the first wildlife management department at any university and penned his conservation classic: *A Sand County Almanac*. Here, Gaylord Nelson earned a law degree en route to becoming one of the U.S. Senate's leading environmental advocates and the "father" of Earth Day.

The university today is home to hundreds of professors with environmental expertise of one kind or another. About 150 of them, representing 50-plus academic disciplines, converge in the Institute for Environmental Studies (IES,) which promotes interdisciplinary environmental instruction, research, and outreach programs.

The institute offers more than 80 graduate-level courses with the university's academic departments. It also offers Master's Degrees in Conservation Biology and Sustainable Development, and Water Resources Management; Master's and Doctoral Degrees in Environmental Monitoring, and Land Resources; a "dual degree" (with the UW Law School) combining any of these degrees with a law degree; and graduate-level certificates in air resources management, and energy analysis and policy.

IES's 200-plus graduate students hail from throughout the United States and around the world. Many come not only with outstanding academic backgrounds but with years of professional experience. More than 1,100 people have earned graduate degrees or certificates through IES since its creation in 1970. The majority of the institute's alumni work in government (30 percent), business and industry (21 percent), or academia (15 percent); others work for citizen organizations and international agencies.

The university offers a growing number of opportunities for students to lead and/or participate in innovative on-campus demonstrations of ecological restoration, resource reuse and recycling, and other "environmentally friendly" projects.

U Wisconsin-Madison's foreign-student population is second or third largest in the U.S., and the university is strongly oriented toward international and global concerns.

Contact: Senior Student Services Coordinator
Institute for Environmental Studies
University of Wisconsin-Madison
70 Science Hall, 550 N. Park St.
Madison, WI 53706-1491
(608) 262-0651

# GEOGRAPHY AND URBAN STUDIES
## TEMPLE UNIVERSITY

Temple University's Department of Geography and Urban Studies (GUS) offers the M.A., as well as an interdisciplinary Ph.D. linked with Anthropology, History, Political Science, or Sociology. GUS graduates find careers in community service, planning and public administration, environmental management, geographic information systems management, and social change efforts.

Key features of the program include diverse students and faculty, close personal attention, an issue-oriented curriculum that provides exposure to practice-based learning, and opportunities for funded research, internships, and international study. GUS has linkages with African-American Studies, Asian Studies, Environmental Studies, Latin American Studies, and Womens Studies.

Students are afforded opportunities to work with individuals and resources of the Geographic information Systems and Cartography Laboratories, Institute for Public Policy Studies, Paley Library Urban Archives, and Social Science Data Library.

The program has had 40 graduates in the last five years, with a current enrollment of 34 students in the master's program, and 3 in the Ph.D. program. Recent graduates have had a 95% employment rate within six months of graduation.

Sanjoy Chakravorty: Development theory, third world urban and regional development, inequality, GIS and spatial analysis

Robert J. Mason: Environmental management, land use planning, non-governmental organizations, Japan

Michele Masucci: Water resources management, GIS and society, information technologies, planning theory

Contact: Chair
Graduate Admissions Committee
Department of Geography and Urban Studies
309 Gladfelter Hall
Temple University
Philadelphia, PA 19122-6089
(215) 204-7692
www.temple.edu/gus

# GEOGRAPHY / RURAL
## NORTHERN ARIZONA UNIVERSITY

The Department of Geography and Public Planning at Northern Arizona University offers a graduate program in Rural Geography. The Master of Arts in Rural Geography provides an advanced degree for geographers who will work in the area of rural, environmental, and small town analysis. The strength of the program and the faculty in the areas of:

- Rural, small town and Native American planning and development
- Natural Resource development in rural areas
- Tools of spatial analysis specifically appropriate for conducting research and solving problems in rural areas (including geographic information systems,computer cartography, and remote sensing)
- Climate and geomorphology of arid lands and mountain regions
- Recreation and tourism geography
- Areas studies: West and Southwest US, Colorado Plateau, Pacific Rim (Latin America, East and Southeast Asia).

There is a growing need for professionals with skills that are particularly applicable to the needs of small towns, rural and natural areas and Native American reservations. The Department has close working relationships with local, city and county planning agencies and Native American reservations in Arizona. Paid internship positions with these agencies are often possible. Opportunities also exist for cooperative projects with the USGS facilities located in Flagstaff and the numerous National Park Service facilities located throughout northern Arizona.

Northern Arizona University, with over 14, 000 students on the Flagstaff campus is situated within one of the largest ponderosa pine forests in the world. Located at 7,000 feet, atop the scenic and historic Colorado Plateau, it is 15 miles to the Arizona Snowbowl Ski area and 80 miles to the Grand Canyon. The Navajo and Hopi reservations are but two of the many Native American communities within easy driving distance. This setting offers students a rich variety of opportunities to study environmental, rural and small town problems and practices. Flagstaff, the Verde Valley communities to the south, the Native American reservations are all dynamic and growing places. These combined with the diverse recreational and resource opportunities in the surrounding national forests and parks provide many issues for rural geography students and classes to explore.

Contact: Leland Dexter
Program in Rural Geography
Northern Arizona University. Box 15016
Flagstaff, AZ 86011
(520) 523-6535
lrd@alpine.for.nau.edu
www.nau.edu

# GLOBAL POLITICAL ECONOMY
## UNIVERSITY OF DENVER

Global Political Economy examines pressing problems relating to global economic integration by focusing on the interconnections between economics and politics. Theoretical debates in political economy are investigated through such issues as social and economic development, the debt crisis, and globalization of trade, production and investment.

Faculty have research interests involving the interconnection of economics and politics, specifically in the areas of finance, trade, development, the environment, economic justice, and economic integration.

The Global Political Economy concentration offers numerous and diverse courses which explain these connections between economic and political systems. Some courses explore the theoretical approaches to understanding the relations between these two vital systems. Other courses may examine global economic integration in the postwar period, the "new international division of labor," and the status of national sovereignty/policy autonomy in an integrated world economy. Courses offered include Theories of Political Economy, Global Political Economy, Japan and the World Economy, Debt Crisis, Trade and Development, Global Competitiveness, and International Environmental Economics. These are a just a few of the topics explored in the global political economy concentration

Contact: Jeffrey Judge
Admissions Counselor
Graduate School of International Studies University of Denver
Denver, CO 80208
(303) 871-2989

# COMMITMENT TO UNDERSERVED PEOPLE
## COLLEGE OF MEDICINE, UNIVERSITY OF ARIZONA

The University of Arizona College of Medicine in Tucson, Arizona provides a unique opportunity for the medical students at this college; the CUP program, which stands for Commitment to Underserved People. The University of Arizona College of Medicine only accepts students who are residents of the state of Arizona or WAMI students. Students have mentioned the CUP program as one of the primary reasons they elected to attend The University of Arizona College of Medicine.

CUP is truly a student run student directed program. Students decide if there is a need to change or update a program and the responsibility for the development and success or failure of the program lies with the students. The College of Medicine, through the CUP administrative staff, provides technical, educational and programmatic support for all the programs. Student coordinators lead each CUP program. Training sessions are held to provide the students with program specifics, technical skills and background knowledge. The second year students who have worked in leadership in these programs conduct training with faculty and staff assistance.

New programs developed by students are based on their desire to work with a particular population. Students learn to establish connections with community organizations, set meetings and timelines, and the 'how to' of program development.

The CUP programs are grouped into two categories: clinical and educational. The clinical programs all require faculty attending physicians to be involved. CUP staff and faculty provide administrative support to the students, such as ordering supplies, receiving faxes from laboratories and referral physicians, printing materials and support in curricular development. Students in who select into leadership positions begin to be mentored by the preceding year's leaders in late fall, so that generally by mid January, leadership has been passed from one class to the other.

The Refugee Clinic is one of the largest and most complex CUP programs. Medical students, under the supervision of a volunteer attending physician, administer and staff a weekly medical clinic for refugees, primarily from Central America. The patients are case-managed through a local church program which provides the only medical care for this population. The patients have many medical problems caused by years of absent or poor medical care. In addition, many have been victims of torture and have had harrowing trips from their country of origin. The resulting psychological problems take a toll on the refugees' mental and physical health. On top of this, the refugees face legal issues and obstacles as they attempt to gain asylum status in the United States.

Staffed primarily by first and second year students, they draw blood for labs, give immunizations (we have a better record than the Family Practice clinic here!), provide patient intake, maintain medical records and perform translation services. Supervised by attending physicians, fourth year students, and teams of third years who have had some clinical clerkships see the patients and provide medical care. Volunteer physical therapists and psychologists also provide services for this population. Pharmaceutical support is available from Pharm D. students,.

Since 1993, medical students travel with residents and an attending nurse practitioner to a local shelter for homeless men, to provide care and triage to men in the shelter system. The nurse practitioners who supervise the residents and medical students work with the El Rio Community Health Center, which sees the men for follow-up care. Students solicit donations of over-the-counter medications, and personal care products to provide for the homeless men.

Begun in 1996 after six months of student planning, CUP students provide care to the women and children staying at a local domestic violence shelter. The psychosocial aspects of caring for an abused population helps sensitize the students to working with abused women. The women would otherwise not receive health care, as all are displaced and many are without insurance or the means to pay.

One of the most recently developed CUP programs is the Guadalupe Clinic. Through this program medical students work with Dr. John Molina, a former CUP student. This clinic provides healthcare to the Yaqui Indians. When Dr. Molina was a student involved in CUP, he expressed desire to serve his home community when he had completed his training. After his residency in obstetrics and gynecology, and while working for the Indian Health Service, Dr. Molina began seeing patients in the economically depressed community in which he spent his childhood. Now Dr. Molina's program has received nonprofit status, has received some grants to help supply the operating expenses, and is seeing patients several days a week. Medical students see patients under the direct supervision of a volunteer attending physician, and performing various lab and intake duties. Through Dr. Molina, medical students are able to see how CUP experiences can impact on a medical career.

In the Medical Students Educating Teens program, medical students provide health education at a local teen shelter system and to young women in a halfway house emerging from substance abuse treatment. Subjects include contraception, STDs, HIV, nutrition and decision-making. MedSET students have expanded this program to include outreach to other at-risk populations who need this health education. CUP members also provided smoking prevention teaching in several elementary schools located in a poor, urban part of the community.

Contact: Carol Galper
University of Arizona College of Medicine
Program in Community Responsive Medicine
1247 N. Warren
Tucson, AZ 85724
(520) 626-2351

# HEALTH AND HOUSING

## BOSTON UNIVERSITY SCHOOL OF PUBLIC HEALTH
## JOHNS HOPKINS UNIVERSITY SCHOOL OF NURSING

The mission of the AmeriCorps Health and Housing Fellows Program is to provide an opportunity for Returned Peace Corps Volunteers to continue their commitment to service while training for the health professions. The program's distinct objectives are to:

- Develop and refine a service-learning model for students of public health and community nursing; to directly serve populations at risk;
- Provide public health and nursing students with first-hand experience of the everyday lives of the people they serve; and
- Establish permanent and working linkages between community agencies and health professions schools.

A long-term objective of the program is to attract RPCVs to careers in community health. This program represents a collaboration among a number of institutions including Boston University School of Public Health (BUSPH), Johns Hopkins University School of Nursing (JHUSoN), the Peace Corps, and AmeriCorps. The schools recruit RPCVs and others with extensive community service experience and provide them with training and education for a career in public health and community nursing. Fellows work on community-identified projects during graduate study.

At BUSPH, RPCVs are assigned to public housing authorities where they live in family or elderly developments and organize residents around health strategies for improving nutrition, the prevention of drug and alcohol abuse, teen pregnancy, violence, and HIV/STD infection. Fellows at JHUSoN work at transitional housing projects in inner-city Baltimore where they provide a variety of health and social support services to previously homeless families.

BU has nine public housing authorities which provide the Fellows with a rent-free living unit and a stipend. JHUSoN Fellows work in groups at three transitional housing sites with nursing faculty supervision. All Fellows receive educational awards from AmeriCorps and each institution provides partial tuition assistance.

Both sites have seen a considerable amount of success in the two-plus years they have been operating. Some of these successes include: 1785 hepatitis 13 vaccinations given in Baltimore city schools; 894 people screened for blood pressure 744 for blood sugar at the Hollander Ridge Transitional Housing site as part of ongoing health sessions; and 7 tenant resource centers established at public housing authorities.

Contact: Sarah Dowley
Boston University School of Public Health
80 East Concord St.
Boston, MA 02118
(617) 638-5036
scd@bu.edu
See editor's note in Returned Peace Corps Fellows Programs, page 397.

# HOMELESS AND INDIGENT POPULATION HEALTH OUTREACH PROJECT
## UMDNJ-ROBERT WOOD JOHNSON MEDICAL SCHOOL

HIPHOP (the Homeless and Indigent Population Health Outreach Project) is a student run organization at UMDNJ-Robert Wood Johnson Medical School involving over 120 medical and physician assistant students, faculty/staff, and community representatives. HIPHOP provides a variety of health outreach services to an underserved population and fosters responsible citizenship while encouraging a lifelong commitment to community service.

The major components of HIPHOP (Clinic/Home Visit, Health Workshops Project, MOMS Project) link student learning objectives with the health related needs of the community. The Clinic/Home Visit Project increases access to health care during evening hours while enabling students to gain clinical experience and exposure to primary care and community health. The Health Workshops Project, consists of two educational programs: SHARRP (the Student Health Awareness and Risk Reduction Project) and STATS (Students Teaching AIDS To Students). Through these programs, HIPHOP tries to reach the youth of the New Brunswick community and promote healthy living and responsible behavior. The MOMS project pairs medical students with expectant mothers. The student is encouraged to attend all of the mother' s clinic visits while serving as a source of support and friendship to the mother.

Currently, HIPHOP offers two credit electives (SHARRP and Clinic/Home Visit) and three non-credit electives (STATS, MOMS, HCOA-Health Care Organization and Administration). HIPHOP works to provide ongoing service with the local soup kitchens and family shelters. Monthly Grand Rounds seminars are given in which distinguished faculty and speakers are invited to address issues important to the practice of community oriented primary and preventive medicine in an underserved population. In addition, HIPHOP helps to coordinate World AIDS Day activities and local community health fairs and is teaming up with the Cancer Institute of New Jersey. Everyone is encouraged to provide service to the members of New Brunswick and neighboring communities.

HIPHOP, the Homeless and Indigent Population Health Outreach Project, is entering its six year in existence at Robert Wood Johnson Medical School-UMDNJ Piscataway Campus. HIPHOP is a student driven organization administered by a Steering Committee.

Contact: Regina Gandica or Juana Canela<br>
HIPHOP<br>
RWJMS - Dep't. ECM<br>
675 Hoes Lane<br>
Piscataway, NJ 08854<br>
(732) 235-4198<br>
hiphop@umdnj.edu<br>
www2.umdnj.edu/hhopweb

# HEALTH / INTERNATIONAL & DEVELOPMENT
## LOMA LINDA UNIVERSITY

This program prepares graduates to fill leadership roles in governmental and non-governmental agencies that are active in the field of public health and development. Applicants will have a master's degree in public health or a related field, at least two years of experience in professional public health practice, appropriate career goals and prospects.

Professionals in the field of international health are employed by a variety of agencies and organizations working in the field of development and health care. These include government agencies -- both host country and donor government agencies, non-government organizations, intergovernmental and church related entities. Roles include planning and management of health and development programs, education of health care professionals, communication support to health care services and research.

Students prove their ability to apply their learning in a "real world" setting during a ten-week field practicum, during which they demonstrate their ability to function as a public health professional in a cross cultural setting.

Programs are designed to meet the needs of professionals working in developing countries or for international agencies. Curricula are based on a recognition of the need for technology and organization that is appropriate to cultural and economic realities. Interdisciplinary programs combine public health knowledge with competence in techniques applicable to the developing country context and/or to medically underserved communities and social groups within developed countries.

Cross-Cultural Health Education
Agriculture in Development
Population Dynamics
Delivering Primary Health Care Services
Integrated Community Development
Health and Behavior Change
Refugee Health
Violence: Global Public Health Perspective
Evaluation of International Health and Development Programs
Grant and Contract Proposal Writing
Program Planning and Evaluation

Advanced Seminar in International Health
Issues and Programs in Family Planning
Epidemiology of Infectious Disease
Dynamics of Sociocultural Change
Principles of Environmental Health
Women in Development
Methods of Cross-Cultural Communication
Comparative Health & Development Systems

HIV/AIDS: Implications for Public Health
Interventions for High-risk Infants & Children

Program in International Health
School of Public Health
Loma Linda University
Nichol Hall, Rm 1511
Loma Linda, CA 92350
(909) 824-4575
www.llu.edu

# HOLISTIC STUDIES
## GRADUATE SCHOOL FOR HOLISTIC STUDIES
## JOHN F. KENNEDY UNIVERSITY

J.F. Kennedy University is a community of educators, practitioners and students who share a vision of personal and societal transformation. The programs and courses are designed to provide a balance between academic learning and experiential understanding. The intention is to honor all aspects of consciousness and to promote a fuller integration of body, mind and spirit. Collectively, students use the structure of an academic setting to learn the skills that will prepare them to seek new career paths while profoundly deepening their self-knowledge.

The school has four departments: transpersonal psychology, holistic health, arts and consciousness and consciousness studies. While each department has its own focus, all share a holistic approach to the understanding, expansion and expression of consciousness. This perspective binds them together in a shared appreciation of the interrelatedness of all things, an understanding that every element is part of a larger whole, a concern for the flows and patterns, and an awareness of our connection to the larger community and its very pressing needs.

All students in the school take core courses that challenge the belief systems through which they see themselves, other human beings and the nature of reality itself. Students explore the shift from a linear, mechanistic world-view to one that is more holistic and systems-oriented. The implications of such a paradigm shift for understanding human behavior are examined, as is the need for a deeper involvement in the life of the community. Students examine the principles of holism and mind-body-spirit interaction and explore the power of art and the role of body-oriented disciplines in the transformation of consciousness.

Contact:
The Graduate School for Holistic Studies
John F. Kennedy University
Orinda CA 94563
(925) 254-0105
www.jfku.edu.

# HUMAN RIGHTS & HUMANITARIAN AFFAIRS
## COLUMBIA UNIVERSITY

Responding to the need to prepare personnel and institutions to deal with all forms of violence and social conflict, the Human Rights and Humanitarian Affairs (HRHA) concentration focuses on both research and advocacy skills. The curriculum prepares students for different advocacy professions, particularly law, monitoring and reporting, policy analysis, NGO development and the protection of refugees and displaced persons, especially women and children. Degrees are in Master in International Affairs and Master of Public Affairs.

The HRHA concentration offers a broad range of approaches to human rights, including advocacy in its various forms, as well as reporting and empirical research. Courses also offer training in the new range of skills needed to address recent problems of refugees and displaced persons, conflict resolution, peace-making, and democracy-building. HRHA offers the most extensive array of human rights courses of any university in the world.

Students are encouraged to accept internships with the many human rights-related organizations based in New York, and to seek additional field experience overseas during summers. Funding for summer internships is available through both the Human Rights Center and SIPA. Recent local placements have included Human Rights Watch, the Lawyers Committee for Human Rights and the Open Society Institute. Overseas, many of the placements are with human rights organizations in countries such as Argentina, Brazil, Colombia, Mali, Nepal, Peru, South Africa, Thailand and Zimbabwe.

Students are encouraged to specialize in their chosen interest and to develop the necessary skills such as monitoring; research and documentation; fundraising; lobbying; public relations; human rights education and training; communication technology; policy-making and policy analysis.

Courses are taught by internationally recognized scholars in the field, by experienced advocates for human rights organizations such as Human Rights Watch, The Lawyers Committee for Human Rights and the United Nations.

Graduates find work in human rights monitoring, refugee advocacy, disaster relief, peacekeeping, women's issues, child welfare, and development work.

| | |
|---|---|
| Refugees and Displaced Persons | International Affairs |
| UN Peacekeeping: Case Studies | International Law |
| Human Rights & International Affairs | Women and Human Rights |
| Report Writing for Human Rights | Human Rights and Social Justice |

Contact: Patrick Bohan, Admissions Director
International Affairs Building 408
420 W. 118th St.
Columbia University
New York, NY 10027
(212) 854-2479
pb3@columbia.edu

# HUMAN RIGHTS
## UNIVERSITY OF DENVER

The study of Human Rights at the Graduate School of International Studies is designed to provide the student in depth consideration of the rights of both individuals and collectives within the context of international relations. Students have the opportunity to analyze specific policies of countries and to investigate international regimes designed for the protection of human rights.

GSIS offers a unique program to understand conflicting perspectives in human rights as a field of study. Though many would agree that human rights abuses challenge the "New World Order" championed at the end of the Cold War, there is still no consensus regarding what constitutes human rights and how they should be implemented. A clear understanding of human rights is thus vital to develop a comprehensive human rights agenda for the twenty-first century. To meet this need, GSIS has developed an interdisciplinary program to examine human rights from economic, sociological, anthropological, historical, political, and cultural perspectives. Our courses are designed to provide the student with foundations to examine rigorously and critically several topics of your choice: legal and organizational aspects of human rights; human rights issues of particular countries and regions; various themes of contemporary relevance considered from a human rights perspective-- e.g., immigration, refugees, genocide, nationalism; and more theoretical issues, such as the affinity, if any, between, for example, human rights and democracy, social justice and the market, or Realism and democracy.

Specialization in Human Rights may be acquired at two different levels: first, by completing a trilogy of required courses of the concentration; or, second, by completing an additional four courses beyond the required trilogy which enables the student to receive a Certificate in Human Rights.

Additionally, the Center on Rights Development enlivens the atmosphere at GSIS by housing a Documentation Center; running a speakers' series; publishing the journal Global Justice, as well as monographs and books; and offering fellowships and internships to graduate students pursuing human rights activities and research.
Our program offers many advantages specifically, we offer a highly flexible program with none of the rigidity of a specialized degree- flexibility congruent with the ever-changing needs of a dynamic international environment.

The Human Rights program has grown into a versatile, lively and serious course of study for those interested in pursuing a career in monitoring and promoting human rights. The Consortium on Rights Development links GSIS, the College of Law and the Iliff School of Theology in an effort to promote the study of Human Rights.

Contact: Jeffrey Judge
Admissions Counselor
Graduate School of International Studies University of Denver
Denver, CO 80208
(303) 871-2989

# INTERNATIONAL & INTERCULTURAL MGM'T
## SCHOOL FOR INTERNATIONAL TRAINING

"Leadership and learning are indispensable to each other"
John Fitzgerald Kennedy
Remarks prepared for delivery at the Trade Mart in Dallas, November 22, 1963

Three years before President Kennedy wrote these words, he made a dream come true and called it the U.S. Peace Corps. The Experiment in International Living became part of that dream -- putting to use its years of experience in language and cross-cultural training preparing volunteers for service abroad. In 1964 the Experiment took this expertise to new, more challenging levels. Thus was born the School for International Training (SIT).

Students at SIT are true partners in determining the course and success of their learning. By the time they come to SIT, many students have lived and worked with cultures and in countries other than their own, and many speak a second language. SIT graduates are entrepreneurial by nature, culturally-sensitive and well-prepared to make a difference in their fields, communities, and the world.

The experiential educational approach often utilized in the classroom offers students the opportunity to both act and react, and to make connections between theory and practice. Because the programs require students to take responsibility for their own learning, SIT appeals to mature, experienced learners, regardless of age. Students learn how to construct and progressively build upon their own experience. In addition to the body of knowledge typically acquired in a classroom or laboratory setting, graduates master a set of applicable competencies appropriate to their career goals in a supportive and goal-oriented environment with a low faculty to student ratio.

The academic program that leads to the Master of International and Intercultural Management degree develops the intercultural, managerial, and training skills necessary for careers in international and intercultural professions. The program is based on the college's philosophy of learning through experience and combines on-campus academic study and a minimum six-month professional-level practicum with an organization appropriate to the student's area of interest. Students write a professional paper and present their work to their colleagues and program faculty. Course work focuses on project management, development administration, training and organizational development, intercultural communication, and leadership and managerial skills. There are three areas of concentration: international education, training and human resource development, and sustainable development. Alumni work in such fields as sustainable development, community development, exchange management, global education, international student advising, cross-cultural training, and refugee relief. They work with organizations such as CARE, NAFSA, Oxfam, the United Nations, and the American Field Service International.

Contact: Admissions
School for International Training
PO Box 676; Kipling Road
Brattleboro, VT 05302
(802)258-3282

348

# INTERNATIONAL SECURITY POLICY
## COLUMBIA UNIVERSITY

· An interdisciplinary program of courses and professional internships that prepares students to analyze a broad range of political, military, and economic problems in security. The Master of International Affairs in International Security provides a solid conceptual foundation for dealing with military strategy and technology, defense economics, regional conflicts, multilateral peacekeeping arms control, and diplomatic alternatives to the use of force. The program designed to prepare students for the rapidly expanding agenda of problems that have evolved since the end of the Cold War.

Most ISP courses are taught by the members of Columbia University's Political Science department, many of whom are associated with the Institute of War and Peace Studies. Others are associated with SIPA's regional institutes.

Additional courses are offered by university research scholars, faculty from other universities, and practitioners from Washington and New York who have served in the State Department, Pentagon, National Security Council, congressional staffs, United Nations, and elsewhere.

There is one field trip each year, alternating between a combination of U.S. military installation in one year, and government offices in Washington D.C. in the other. Students have a chance to see something of both operational and policy-making aspects of U.S. national security policy. Past trips have included Fort Bragg, NATO headquarters in Brussels, the House Armed Services Committee, the Bosnia Task Force, International Security Affairs, and the Arms Control and Disarmament Agency.

Graduates have been hired by the U.S. Departments of State and Defense, Arms Control and Disarmament Agency, intelligence agencies, the United Nations, public interest organizations and other areas.

| | |
|---|---|
| Conflict & Cooperation | Security Issues in South Asia |
| General Problems in Int'l. Security | Military Force |
| Weapons, Strategy War | Countries and Regions |
| American Strategies in World Politics | Politics UN Peacekeeping |
| Causes of War | Diplomacy & International Bargaining |
| Third World Security Issues | War & Alliance in the Third World |
| Political Economy of National Security | Nationalism & Contemporary World |
| War, Peace, & Strategy in the 20th Century | Limited War & Low Intensity Conflict |
| Nuclear Weapons, Strategy, & Arms Control | |

Contact: International Security Policy
School of International and Public Affairs
Columbia University
420 W. 118th St.
New York, NY 10027
(212) 854-7325

# INTERNATIONAL SECURITY
## UNIVERSITY OF DENVER

Just a few years ago, many believed that the end of the Cold War and the heralding of a "New World Order" would result in a sharp reduction in global conflict and, consequently, a decline in the importance of and interest in security studies. Instead, a variety of troubling cases has presented major new challenges to scholars and policymakers in the field of security.

Desert Storm demonstrated the continuing danger of major interstate conflict. The diminishing U.S. presence in Asia and Europe, coupled with the instability of the former Soviet Union, raised new concerns over security in those regions. Savage ethnic conflicts posed dilemmas regarding the viability and costs of humanitarian intervention. The long-standing problem of proliferation-- of both conventional weapons and weapons of mass destruction-- received belated recognition as an ominous and growing global threat. Finally, increasing disparities between rich and poor states and regions, the ongoing population explosion, environmental degradation, and the surge in communicable diseases inspired calls to expand security studies to encompass the spectrum of global threats.

The International Security concentration at GSIS has been designed to meet these challenges and further explore the central issues of instability and revolution, repression and other forms of violence, international conflict and war, the danger of nuclear holocaust, great-power intervention and the promotion of domestic and international peace and justice. The program is highly flexible. Within the international security studies program, diverse courses are offered which cater to the interests of all students. These courses cover the spectrum of international security studies, from traditional courses such as U.S. National Security policy to non-traditional courses such as Human Rights and International Security, Future Issues in Security and Nationalism and Ethnic Conflict.

The program offers many advantages specifically, we offer a highly flexible program with none of the rigidity of a specialized degree -- flexibility congruent with the ever-changing threats emerging in a dynamic international environment. The flexibility of our program encourages students to explore theoretical and topical issues, which influence the emerging international system. The relaxed educational atmosphere at GSIS encourages active student participation and lively debate.

There is no greater challenge at the end of this century than to understand and resolve these conflicts. The Security Concentration has been designed to provide indepth understanding of the nature of current security problems and evolving approaches to addressing and (hopefully) resolving them. Interdisciplinary inquiry is designed to stimulate research into alternative approaches into the field.

Contact:Admissions Counselor
Graduate School of International Studies University of Denver
Denver, CO 80208
(303) 871-2989

# INTERNATIONAL & PUBLIC SERVICE MANAGEMENT
## DePaul University

As of 1997, a new master's degree in International Public Service Management, "a practical alternative for people whose business isn't just business" is being offered at DePaul University. The program combines a liberal arts education in international studies with hands-on training in the technical skills necessary for public service management. Students who devote their careers to public service are discovering that need has no borders in a DePaul University program that trains future leaders of non-profit programs with international missions.

Graduates of the program could work as program officers and administrators for large nonprofit public service organizations that operate across borders, such as the International Red Cross, or smaller, transnational agencies focusing on local issues.

"In the tradition of St. Vincent de Paul, our first responsibility is to our students and graduates and all who benefit from or are served by them -- their clients, co-workers and citizens in our urban and international society. We respect the dignity and recognize the merit of each person as we work in partnership to build a multira-cial, multicultural and international community among us."

The Public Services Graduate Program prepares graduates for effective manage-ment of nonprofit organizations and government agencies, and fosters development of sound public policies affecting the delivery of social services. Programs of instruc-tion, research, and community involvement prepare adult learners to pursue adminis-trative careers in a broad range of public service organizations. Following the tradi-tion of St. Vincent de Paul, the Public Services Graduate Program devotes special attention to policies and practices that promote social equity through delivery of affordable, quality services to those in greatest need.

Degree and certificate programs are interdisciplinary, drawing primarily upon the knowledge bases of sociology, economics, political science, law and the human-ser-vice professions. The curriculum balances theoretical and applied approaches to con-temporary challenges of administration and policy analysis.

Contact: Public Services Graduate Program
DePaul University
243 S. Wabash, Room 600
Chicago, IL 60604-2304
(312) 362-8441
pubserv@wppost.depaul.edu

# INTERNATIONAL SERVICE
## UNIVERSITY OF SURREY, ENGLAND

The International Partnership for Service Learning, in cooperation with it's affiliated universities in Britain, Mexico and Jamaica, sponsors a one-year program leading to the British Master's Degree in International Service. Combine rigorous academic study and substantive community service in 2 nations for 1 year and receive a British Master's Degree.

The studies and resulting degree prepare participants for work and careers with international, non-profit, private and voluntary organizations, as well as governmental and inter-governmental agencies in areas such as development, relief, education and social services. Combining academic studies and community service, the program gives future professionals both the practical knowledge which comes from working in service agencies at the grass roots level and also the theoretical framework and analytical skills developed from formal academic study. Degree recipients are able to develop informed programs and policies and provide leadership in international and local service and educational organizations.

Students select to study and serve in either Jamaica or Mexico, where they serve in a community agency and earn 16 hours of credit through their academic study. In January, all students go to England where they continue their studies, earning 16 hours of credit, serve in a London-based agency, and begin work on the Master's thesis.

A final period of time in England (June, July) is spent in the preparation of a Master's thesis, using experiences, observations and research from the semesters of service and learning. The thesis, takes the form of a proposal to a development, relief, educational or policy-making body, in which a social /cultural/economic problem, a budget, and evaluation procedures described.

The thesis, along with the course work and the service experience, are evaluated by an international panel of Partnership practitioners and academics. The degree is awarded by Roehampton Institute, University of Surrey, England. The Affiliated Universities are distinguished and fully-recognized institutions of higher education, validated to award graduate degrees by their respective governments and Ministries of Education. All have a long history with and commitment to community service and to the study of social administration.

Contact: The International Partnership For Service Learning
815 Second Avenue, Suite 315
New York, NY 10017-4594
(212) 986-0989
pslny@aol.com

# LANDSCAPE ARCHITECTURE
## UNIVERSITY OF MICHIGAN
## SCHOOL OF NATURAL RESOURCES & ENVIRONMENT

Landscape Architecture (LA) at the University of Michigan is offered as a graduate specializing within the School of Natural Resources and Environment (SNRE). The master provides a first professional degree to students with or without prior design training and an advanced degree to students with previous training from undergraduate programs in Landscape Architecture. The Master's of Landscape Architecture is unique for its strong emphasis on an ecological approach to design and planning at all scales, in addition to its attention to a broad range of professional skills and knowledge. It is distinctive for its location within the context of a professional school of natural resources and environment. The emphasis of the program is on design and planning based on a clear understanding of environmental and cultural factors and direct integration of ecological and socio-behavioral sciences.

All master's students are required to complete a master's opus as their capstone experience. Some students elect to write a thesis which explores their particular research in the Resource Ecology and Management concentration (REM). Resource Policy and Behavior (RPB) and LA students work together on projects in teams of 6-8 students to address resource problems for real-world clients. This is a terrific opportunity for SNRE students to apply their knowledge and skills to particular environmental problems or situations. The third option, a practicum, is available primarily for two-year LA students for whom LA is a 2nd professional degree (e.g., they have received a bachelor's degree.)

Students can develop dual degree programs in combination with many university departments including, Urban Planning, Architecture, and Resource Planning at the School of Natural Resources and Environment.

LA students draw from a range of courses including, Plant Materials for Landscapes, History of Western Landscape Architecture, Woody Plants: Biology and Identification, Land Use Planning and Design, Site Planning and Engineering, Master Planning and Design for Parks and Recreation, and Landscape Design Theory.

Graduates of the School find work with at local, state, national, and international levels; non-profit organizations; colleges and universities; and the private sector. Examples of positions held by recent graduates include Landscape Architect, Urban Planner, Vice President, Associate Professor and Environmental Planner.

Contact: Graduate Admissions Team
1024 Dana, SNRE-OAP
University of Michigan
Ann Arbor, MI 48109-1115
(734) 764-5453
snre.gradteam.@umich.edu
www.wnre.umich.edu/

353

# LAW / ENVIRONMENTAL
## VERMONT LAW SCHOOL

Vermont Law School's environmental law specialty has consistently been ranked one of the best in the country by a survey of law school environmental faculty. VLS offers the traditional core legal curriculum and a series of experiential programs, in addition to an emphasis on environmental and public interest law, which prepare students for practice in any locale and legal environment. It's location in a small Vermont town encourages an unusual balance between academic rigor and the sense of community and strong ethical values for which Vermont is noted.

The mission of the Environmental Law Center is to educate for stewardship, to teach an awareness of underlying environmental issues and values, to provide a solid knowledge of environmental law, and to develop skills to administer and improve environmental policy. Environmental law and policy are often about change, and since change can be threatening to those who benefit from the status quo, it is no surprise that consensus on environmental issues is difficult to achieve. For that reason, environmental professionals understand that sound environmental policy must be formed at the intersection of politics, law, science, economics, and ethics.

"The Environmental Law Center combines the core strengths of the School with the talent and expertise of leading environmental practitioners and scholars to provide an unmatched interdisciplinary training for lawyers and other professionals who seek to serve in the field of environmental law and policy." -- Dean L. Kinvin Wroth

The goal of the Master of Studies in Environmental Law. is to educate leaders who will fashion and carry out environmental policy grounded on the stewardship ethic. Specifically the M.S.E.L. aims to:

- develop knowledge of the environmental goals and standards embodied in U.S. law, and of the legal mechanisms used to achieve those goals
- develop an understanding of the political, economic, cultural, institutional, and scientific mechanisms by which environmental policy is shaped
- explore the ethical bases for environmental policy
- provide a basic understanding of ecological concepts that govern the relationship of living organisms within the biosphere
- introduce students to international environmental issues such as ozone depletion, global warming and conservation of biodiversity
- examine the concepts of hazard, risk, and uncertainty and their role in and effect upon environmental policy.

In addition to its regular curriculum, the MSEL Programs offers courses which are of specific interest to First Nations Members, as well as a special fellowship.

Contact: Vermont Law School
Chelsea Street
South Royalton, VT 05068
(800) 227-1395
admiss@vermontlaw.edu
www.vermontlaw.edu

# LAW / PUBLIC INTEREST
## NEW COLLEGE OF CALIFORNIA SCHOOL OF LAW

New College of California School of Law is the oldest public interest law school in the country. From its inception 25 years ago, New College has been a leader in the effort to link law and social justice using critical legal analysis, apprenticeships, clinical electives, and a supportive environment to help students of different races, income levels, and social backgrounds succeed. The desire at New College has been to provide an outstanding legal education to people who plan to use their legal knowledge to redress injustice, and to change the status quo.

In addition to providing excellent and rigorous preparation for the bar exam, our aim is to make sure that every student receives the practical skills training needed to become an effective public-interest attorney. While New College places great emphasis on teaching the intricacies of existing legal rules and doctrines, it also supplements these standard elements of legal education with readings and discussions that seek to offer a critical perspective on the moral and ethical assumptions of existing law and on the role of law in achieving social change.

The overall goal is to provide students with a thorough grasp of both the analytical and practical skills required of any good lawyer, while also enabling them to learn to challenge the assumptions embedded in the law where they should be challenged and to assist in developing their own moral vision of how the law should serve others.

The Law School is ideally located for the study of law. It is within easy walking distance of San Francisco City Hall, and various California and federal courts. Major libraries, government offices, the State Bar of California, and various law firms where our students apprentice, are nearby.

San Francisco's progressive legal community provides ample opportunity for law students to become involved in a variety of public interest pursuits, from providing legal services to the poor and criminal defense work to environmental protection advocacy and advising socially conscious small businesses. In addition, the diverse neighborhoods of San Francisco provide students with unique and exciting opportunities beyond the walls of the classroom.

New College offers an innovative and refreshing educational program. It has an inspiring legacy and a motivated community of students, professors, administrators, alumni, and friends. New College strives to keep the flame burning for justice, equality, and human understanding while sensitive, talented, and principled legal professionals. The College knows that public interest lawyers need to be creative and resourceful in finding ways to accomplish their client's goals.

Contact: Director of Admissions
New College School of Law
50 Fell St.
San Francisco, CA 94102
(415) 241-1300 x314

# NATURAL RESOURCES
## THE SCHOOL OF FORESTRY
## THE UNIVERSITY OF MONTANA

The School of Forestry at The University of Montana offers a broad set of pro-grams in renewable natural resources. Graduate degrees offered are Master of Science, Master of Ecosystem Management, and Doctor of Philosophy. Primary areas of study are Forestry (nearly all natural resource management emphases,) Recreation Management, Resource Conservation, and Fish and Wildlife Biology. Approximately 115 graduate students are enrolled in the School with one-third doctoral students. Fellowships and teaching and research assistantships are available, and most graduate students are funded through some or all of their graduate study.

Field work characterizes much of the course and thesis research work. Research is carried out through the Montana Forest and Conservation Experiment Station. The Station operates a 28,000 acre experimental forest and a 3,400 acre experimental ranch within about 30 and 50 miles, respectively from the Missoula campus. The Station also has access to an additional 6,000 acre ranch along the east face of the Rocky Mountains just south of Glacier National Park.

A joint degree program is offered with the Fish and Wildlife Biology program at Montana State University.

The University of Montana, located in Missoula, is known for outstanding pro-grams in natural resources and environment, creative writing, avian biology, legal practice, and Native American Law. Missoula has about 90,000 people (including the surrounding area) and is surrounded by mountains and wilderness areas and with a river running through it. It is a major natural resources center with a region-al office of the USDA Forest Service, numerous offices of other federal and state agencies, and national and regional offices of many non-profit natural resource and environment organizations.

Contact: Dr. Donald Potts
Associate Dean
School of Forestry
University of Montana
Missoula, MT 59812
(406) 243-5521
request@forestry.umt.edu
www.forestry.umt.edu

# NATUROPATHY
## BASTYR UNIVERSITY

"The ordinary doctor is interested mostly in the study of disease. The nature curist is interested more in the study of health. His real interest begins where that of the ordinary doctor ends."                                             Gandhi

Founded in 1978 as the John Bastyr College of Naturopathic Medicine, Bastyr University is the first accredited school of natural healing in the United States. The College trains naturopathic physicians, and offers baccalaureate degrees in nutrition, University medicine and applied behavioral sciences, graduate degrees in nutrition, Acupuncture, and certificates in Midwifery and traditional Chinese herbal medicine.

The College's philosophical orientation honors and reflects the unique and worldwide traditions of natural medicine: the treatment of the whole person, prevention of disease, teaching patients how to take responsibility for their own health, working with each individual's inherent healing ability and using natural, non-toxic therapies. Its curriculum recognizes and utilizes the enormous amount of information that scientific research brings to the understanding of health and disease. The Natural Health Sciences Programs at Bastyr provide unique two-year upper division programs that lead to the Bachelor of Science degree.

There is a growing recognition of the importance of traditional and natural health care practices throughout the world. Midwifery, acupuncture, and botanical medicines are a few of the practices that are recognized and supported by the World Health Organization. Bastyr believes that effective solutions to the "health care crisis" being experienced in many of the developed countries must include the principles and practices of natural medicine. Bastyr College is a leader in the effort to create an international, intercultural understanding of and commitment to education in natural health care. In addition, Bastyr has been recognized by the United Nations Educational, Scientific and Cultural Organization (UNESCO).

Bastyr College is playing a pioneering role in the development of science-based natural medicine in the United States. The College's mission includes the pursuit of scientific research on the use of natural therapies in the management and treatment of health care problems and in the prevention of chronic disease. Students are engaged in primary clinical research at the college's outpatient teaching clinic. Faculty members from Bastyr College are participating in a number national agencies, such as the Office of Alternative Medicine at the National Institutes of Health, the Office of Technology Assistance and the Task Force on Health Care Reform.

The new Department of Spirituality, Health and Medicine's purpose is to create a rich mix of educational offerings and experiences in areas related to spirituality, health, and medicine. The vision is to develop a faculty of the nation's leading experts and scholars in the area of spirituality and medicine - not only to create new programs but also to enhance Bastyr's existing ones. The BA in Oriental Medicine is the first half of a three year program that leads to the MS in Acupuncture.

Botanical Medicine is a program of study for naturopathic medical students dealing with medicinal use of plants, fungi and extracts of both. Research projects in botanical medicine and a reference source. Naturopaths are the only licensed physicians in the U.S. specifically trained in the medical use of medicinal herbs.

Psychology with a Health Concentration encourages the integration of mind, body and spirit and emphasizes interdisciplinary studies in the field of the natural health sciences as related to psychology. Focus is on critical thinking and research methodology within psychology as it relates to principles of health and healing.

The Spirituality, Health and Medicine Certificate is dedicated to integrating spirituality into the processes of health and wholeness. Treating the whole person and enhancing the individual's inherent healing ability. Increases practitioners' competency in bringing the spiritual dimension into their work in medical, ministerial and related settings. Balances rigorous academic work with experiential education and self-discovery. Develops personal growth of practitioners through transpersonal work, self-exploration, and integration of a form of spirituality that is meaningful to them.

Holistic Relationships & Communication
Personal and Professional Identity
Measuring the Mystery
Religion, Science and Medicine
Major Religious and Faith Traditions: Their Relationship to Health

Disease and Death
Religion, Science and Medicine I
Values and Ethical Practice
Walking the Talk

## Oriental Medicine
Meridians & Points
Traditional Chinese Medicine Diagnosis
Traditional Chinese Medicine Pathology
Fund'l Principles: Chinese Medicine
Counseling
Psychology & Treatment of Addiction
Acupuncture Therapeutics

Anatomy & Physiology
Tui Na
Acupuncture Techniques
Clinical Observation
Traditional Chinese Medicine Herbology
TCM Prepared Medicines
Disease Processes

## Naturopathic Medicine
Addictions & Disorders
Normal Pregnancy & Birth
Public Health
Naturopathic Manipulation
Psychological Assessment
Naturopathic Counseling

Botanical Medicine
Therapeutic Nutrition
Environmental Health
Naturopathic Philosophy
Pediatrics
Family Medicine

Contact: Director of Admissions
Bastyr College
14500 Juanita Dr. NE
Bothell WA 98011-4966
(425) 602-3102
admiss@bastyr.edu
www.bastyr.edu

# NON-PROFIT MANAGEMENT
## UNIVERSITY OF JUDAISM

Combining leadership and learning, the University of Judaism's mission is to educate men and women who are destined to take part in shaping the future of society. The University of Judaism (UJ) offers fully accredited undergraduate and professional graduate degree programs. UJ's liberal arts college has been selected by U.S. News and World Report as one of the leading institutions of its type. The University offers four graduate degrees: the Masters in Education, the Masters in Behavioral Psychology, the Masters in Hebrew Letters (Conservative Rabbinical Ordination,) and the Masters of Business Administration (MBA) in Non-Profit Management. Gifted students and distinguished scholars from around the world are attracted to programming that is designed to stimulate and nourish a passion for intellectual excellence, scholarly inquiry, meaningful spiritual growth, and vital engagement with the arts.

The Lieber School of Graduate Studies of the University of Judaism offers a MBA geared specifically to students planning careers in the non-profit world. This service sector is the economy's fastest growing segment, and with more than 1.2 million not-for- profit organizations in the U.S. there is a tremendous demand for well-trained managers. The MBA is designed to meet this growing need by training professionals for middle and upper management positions in cultural, educational, religious, social service, and health care organizations. Courses in finance, ethics, accounting, fundraising, marketing, human resource management, organizational and individual behavior, and public relations blend traditional business management with training in areas unique to the not-for- profit sector. The program focuses on the ethical, managerial, and humanistic issues of non-profit organizations.

MBA students may also complete a Certificate in Jewish Communal Studies. The program emphasizes the historical, social, and moral principles vital to the contemporary Jewish community. Most courses are offered in the late afternoon and evening to provide time during the day for students to gain hands-on experience and to accommodate working students. In addition, students complete a a 600-hour internship, and a thesis. Recent internship placements have included: The World Recreation Center for the Deaf, Big Brothers, the Jewish Federation, and the Tree People.

For managers already holding a master's level degree or higher who want to enter the non-profit sector, the University of Judaism also offers a 10-course program focusing on management skills and theory. Generous financial subsidies and fellowships are available for all UJ academic programs. The University of Judaism is open to students regardless of race, religion, nationality, or ethnic background.

Contact: Richard Scaffidi
Dean of Admissions and Financial Aid
University of Judaism
15600 Mulholland Drive
Bel Air, California 90077
(310) 476-9777 888/UJ-FOR-ME
admissions@uj.edu    www.uj.edu

# NONPROFIT MANAGEMENT
## NEW SCHOOL UNIVERSITY
### (NEW SCHOOL FOR SOCIAL RESEARCH)

The Master of Science (M.S.) Degree Program in Nonprofit Management at the New School prepares students to assume increasingly important positions of leadership in the nonprofit sector. The program combines theory with practice, providing students with knowledge and skills in areas such as nonprofit governance, general management, fund raising and development strategic planning, program development, financial and human resources management, policy analysis and problem solving, ethics, and marketing.

There are more than 30 nonprofit management courses to choose from as well as courses in the Milano School's other masters programs in Human Resources Management, Health Services Management and Policy, and Urban Policy Analysis and Management. Courses may be also taken on a non-degree basis.

This program/school is outstanding because the courses are specialized and applied. The program is distinctive because very few nonprofit management programs in the country offer a full M.S. in Nonprofit Management. The nonprofit management program is not a concentration of courses in an MBA or MPA program, but rather a "stand alone" degree in nonprofit management. This program is the only one of its kind in the New York metropolitan area. Students have opportunities within the context of the courses to work with nonprofit organizations.

Religious Nonprofit Organizations and their Role in Community Building
| | |
|---|---|
| Social Movements and Advocacy | The Role of Nonprofit Organizations |
| International Nonprofit Sector | Community Health Programs |
| Women and Health: Past and Present. | Race and Public Policy |
| Community Development | Children, Youth. and Family Policy |
| Techniques of Counselling. | Group Processes: Facilitation & Intervention |

Dr. Pier Camille Rogers has conducted studies of the representation of people of color in nonprofit leadership and management in the U.S., and on diversity and nonprofit boards

Dr. Dennis Derryck has thirty years experience in both research and executive management positions. His expertise includes economic andß community development, institutional strategic planning; and program development

Contact: Nonprofit Management Program
Robert J. Milano Graduate School of Management and Urban Policy
New School University
80 Fifth Avenue, Suite 405
New York NY 10011
(212) 229-5950
www.newschool.edu/academic/gs

# PHILANTHROPY
## INDIANA UNIVERSITY

The Indiana University Center on Philanthropy offers the Master of Arts in Philanthropic Studies that focuses on the history, culture and values of philanthropy. While other programs focus on the "how" of nonprofit management, this program focuses on the "why" -- the social, cultural, political and economic roles played by philanthropy and nonprofit organizations in both contemporary and historical settings. Students in this program investigate the broader theoretical issues of philanthropy from a variety of perspectives. The 64 faculty members come from history, public administration, economics, American studies, religious studies, and many other departments for a truly interdisciplinary program.

The M.A. in Philanthropic Studies is a 36-credit-hour graduate program, which includes core courses, electives, an internship, and a thesis. Dual degrees exist with nonprofit management, economics, history, and nursing. Several scholarships and assistantships are awarded each year to incoming students. Also, there are two minority fellowships for persons underrepresented in the field of philanthropy.

The Executive M.A. program allows individuals who cannot come to Indiana University for the traditional program the opportunity to earn the full master's degree. Students in this program correspond electronically with their instructors and classmates and come to the campus one week per summer for each course they take. Scholarships are also available to incoming students in the executive program.

Approximately 70 students are currently pursuing the Master of Arts in Philanthropic Studies. Individuals from at least 25 different states and several foreign countries have ventured to Indianapolis to study philanthropy. Some are early-career students who come directly from college, but many are mid-career students who come with several years of relevant work experience. There is also great diversity in the undergraduate backgrounds and future goals of the students because of the interdisciplinary nature of philanthropy.

Contact: Melissa Grider
Center on Philanthropy
Indiana University
550 W. North St.
Indianapolis, IN 46202-3162
(800) 854-1612
maphil@iupui.edu
www.philanthropy.iupui.edu

# PSYCHOLOGY
## ANTIOCH UNIVERSITY, LOS ANGELES

Antioch University's model of clinical education brings the real world into the classroom. The MA in Clinical Psychology (MAP) prepares students for a variety of professional roles in today's emerging systems of mental health service delivery. Students receive training in short term therapy, groups and individual and family therapy.

Antioch's socially aware and ethically sensitive education focuses on the development of each student as an individual. Eclectic in orientation and pragmatic in spirit, the program prepares students for licensure as a Marriage, Family and Child Counselor.

If a student wishes to pursue an MA in Psychology, but is not interested in MFCC licensure in California, Antioch offers the flexible individualized MA in Psychology. Students design an individualized degree plan of learning activities in concert with a faculty advisor. Some take courses in Graduate Management to combine psychological practice and organizational management. Recent concentrations include: domestic violence, parenting education, substance abuse counseling, conflict resolution for children, death and dying, children's creativity, existential psychology, counseling African-American elders, career counseling and transpersonal psychology.

Antioch helps students develop as professionals through continuing education workshops, professional development seminars, and mentoring with experienced clinicians. Clinical training placements are considered an integral part of educational and professional development. Antioch's Clinical Training Office finds, evaluates, authorizes and lists potential clinical training placement for Antioch students. Clinical skills are developed through hands-on experience with expert supervision in Antioch's more than 200 clinical placement settings. Clinical Training and Career Resource Day provides students and alumni the opportunity to network with job sites and receive the latest information on future job opportunities in a rapidly changing marketplace.

The Antioch University Counseling Center, a nonprofit mental health center since 1974 is a training site for selected students in the MA in Clinical Psychology Program. Group workshops, career counseling and testing are available.

Antioch's 72-unit MAP is designed for working adults, and provides education meaningful for your personal development. It can be completed in 18 months or more slowly by part-time enrollment, and offers flexible scheduling with choices of day and evening classes. Written narrative evaluations are used instead of grades.

In the one-day-a-week program, students complete all required courses in six consecutive quarters of full-time study with classes typically scheduled from 8:30 a.m. to 6:30 p.m., one day per week. Remaining requirements for clinical training, personal psychotherapy and electives, are scheduled individually by students.

Contact: Office of Admissions
Antioch University, Los Angeles
13274 Fiji Way
Marina del Rey, CA 90292
(310) 578-1080
admissions@antiochla.edu    www.antiochla.edu

# PSYCHOLOGY
## SONOMA STATE

The Psychology Department at Sonoma State University, working in conjunction with Extended Education, offers Master of Arts degrees in several areas of psychology.

With Creative Arts Therapy, a range of subjects in the creative arts therapies are taught primarily through small-group learning experiences and supervised field work. Completes the first part of the credential process with the American Art Therapy Association.

Depth Psychology is a new structured two-year curriculum which explores Jungian and archetypal psychology through work with cross-cultural symbolism, mythology, art, religion, ritual and dreams. It combines core classes with independent supervised Master's thesis work.

The Organization Development program is a two-year evening program that combines theory with practical field experience. This special focus M.A. emphasizes development of competence in emerging models of leadership, consultation and change. Designed for a small group of mid-career individuals who move through the two-year curriculum together, students develop the personal awareness, interpersonal competence and conceptual understanding required for effective practice in organization development.

In the Mentor/Portfolio Model for Humanistic/Transpersonal Psychology concentration, students work closely with a mentor to design individual programs that combine core courses, individual and small-group learning experiences, and opportunities for teaching, internships and workshops that focus on a selected interest area. Faculty are qualified to guide students in many areas, and successful application depends upon the availability of a qualified mentor to share the applicant's interest.

This M.A. does not prepare students for the MFCC license in California.

Contact: Sally Tomlinson
Graduate Admissions Coordinator
Psychology Department
Sonoma State University
Rohnert Park, CA 94928
(707) 664-2682
www.sonoma.edu/psychology/

# PUBLIC POLICY AND MANAGEMENT
## H. JOHN HEINZ III SCHOOL
## CARNEGIE MELLON UNIVERSITY

The H. John Heinz III School of Public Policy and Management at Carnegie Mellon University provides a Ph.D. program in Public Policy and Management and masters programs in Arts Management, Public Policy and Management, Health Care Policy and Management, Information Systems, and a mid career masters program in Public Management. The programs offered at the Heinz School provide students with an opportunity to gain strong analytical and quantitative skills while specializing in particular policy areas including: Economic Development, Financial Analysis, Sustainable Economic Development, Environmental Policy, Information Systems, to name a few. The programs combine the interdisciplinary structure of Carnegie Mellon university and provides students with an opportunity to gain practical skills through required internships for majority of the masters programs.

Alfred Blumstein: Professor of Operations Research, Criminal Justice Systems and Policy and Director of the National Consortium of Violence Research

Richard Florida: Professor of Regional Economic Development (with research interest in economic transformation of advanced industrial societies) and Director of the Center of Economic Development

Linda Babcock: Associate Professor of Economics (with research interest in collective bargaining and dispute resolution, labor economics, behavioral economics).

Dan Martin: Associate Professor of Arts Management and Director of the Arts Management Program. Area of research include not-for-profit organizational structure and the practical application of information and computer technology in the arts management process.

Ramayya Krishnan: Professor of Management Science and Information Systems with research interest in information networking and decision support systems, electronic commerce, and data privacy.

Contact: Ms. Sandra Day
The H. John Heinz III School of Public Policy and Management
Carnegie Mellon University
5000 Forbes Ave.
Pittsburgh, PA 15213
(412) 268-2164
www.heinz.cmu.edu

# RESOURCE ECOLOGY AND MANAGEMENT
## UNIVERSITY OF MICHIGAN
## SCHOOL OF NATURAL RESOURCES & ENVIRONMENT

Human populations have dramatically altered most ecosystems on earth, yet continue to rely on these ecosystems for food, water, fiber and recreation. Managing our ecosystems for multiple use creates an ever-increasing demand for scientists trained in the sustainable management of natural resources. Such scientists may focus on particular resources, such as forests, fisheries, wildlife, but also must understand interactions between these organisms and the environment, including natural and human influences. The Resource Ecology and Management (REM) graduate concentration in the School of Natural Resources and Environment is a national leader in research and teaching on such complex issues of sustainable resource and ecosystem management.

The REM program at the U Michigan is unique in that it pays attention to issues of large scale, integrating physical, biological, and social concepts into the understanding of natural resource problems. The Resource Ecology and Management concentration is an outstanding choice for making a difference in the conservation of biological resources for future generations. The program uses the latest ecological theory, field observations, and management practice to provide an education that allows scientists to integrate biological and social components of resource management into actions that are significant, large scale, and sustainable for future generations.

All master's students are required to complete a master's opus as their capstone experience. Some students elect to write a thesis which explores their particular research -- REM. Landscape Architecture (LA) and Resource Policy and Behavior (RPB) students work together on projects in teams of 6-8 students to address resource problems for real-world clients.

Students in concentrating in REM further specialize in aquatic or terrestrial ecosystems. REM graduate students might further focus on conservation biology and ecosystem management. An aquatic ecosystems course of study might include fluvial ecology, ichthyology, the ecology of fishes, aquatic invertebrates, water resource policy, and fishery management. Students in the terrestrial ecosystem plan might expect to study forest ecology, soil properties and processes, forest hydrology and watershed management, conservation biology, wildlife behavior and ecology, tropical conservation, or the biology and management of insects.

Graduates of the School are employed at the local, state, national, and international levels; non-profit organizations; colleges and universities; and the private sector. Positions held by recent graduates include: Aquatic Ecologist; Environmental Scientist; Fisheries Research Biologist; Project Scientist and Assistant Professor.

Contact: Graduate Admissions Team
1024 Dana, SNRE-OAP
University of Michigan
Ann Arbor, MI 48109-1115
(734) 764-5453
snre.gradteam.@umich.edu   www.wnre.umich.edu/

# RESOURCE POLICY AND BEHAVIOR
## UNIVERSITY OF MICHIGAN
## SCHOOL OF NATURAL RESOURCES & ENVIRONMENT

The Resource Policy and Behavior (RPB) concentration draws from economic, political, psychological, anthropological, and other social models of human behavior to enable students to understand the social dimensions of resource controversies and to devise and analyze strategies to intervene in these issues. In other words, its focus is two fold: understand human behavior at all levels of social organization and then mobilize to change that behavior.

Intelligent decision-making and informed applied research must be grounded solidly in the social and natural sciences. Since RPB is housed in the School of Natural Resources at the U Michigan, the program is distinctive in that it allows students the ability to study policy and behavior within a scientific framework. The multidisciplinary setting provided by SNRE and the depth of social science and professional schools at the U Michigan provide fertile ground for learning about real-world problems, and help to provide students with the professional skills to make a difference.

All master's students are required to complete a master's opus as their capstone experience. Ecology and Management concentration (REM), Landscape Architecture and RPB students work together on projects in teams of 6-8 students to address resource problems for real-world clients.

Students concentrating in RPB can choose an emphasis on either policy or behavior. Those pursuing environmental policy further specialize in resource policy or resource planning. Those concentrating in behavior emphasize advocacy, behavior, or environmental education. RPB concentrators might further specialize in conservation biology and ecosystem management or environmental justice issues.

RPB has formal joint degree programs with the Center for Russian and East European Studies, Corporate Environmental Management Program with the U Michigan Business School, and Environmental Law with the U Michigan Law School. Many other possibilities for dual programs exist, as well.

A resource policy/planning course of study might include courses in resource policy administration, aquatic ecosystems, conservation biology, negotiation skills, environmental law, water resource economics, and water resource policy. Students focusing on human behavior in an environmental context might study research methods in environment and behavior, conflict management, conservation behavior, social impact assessment, environmental education, and small groups and advocacy planning.

Examples of positions held by recent graduates include: Legislative Aide; Project Manager; Attorney; Endangered Species Lobbyist; Policy Analyst and Associate Professor.

Contact: Graduate Admissions Team
1024 Dana, SNRE-OAP
University of Michigan
Ann Arbor, MI 48109-1115
(734) 764-5453
snre.gradteam.@umich.edu www.wnre.umich.edu/

# SCIENCE / HOLISTIC
## SCHUMACHER COLLEGE, ENGLAND

Schumacher College, in partnership with the University of Plymouth, is launching the first postgraduate program in the world to offer an M.Sc. in Holistic Science. The program's goal is to provide an integrated framework of study and research that recognizes the changes occurring in science as it goes beyond interdisciplinarity to the understanding of complex wholes and their emergent properties at the levels of organisms, communities, ecosystems and the biosphere. These changes are also responses to the limitations of conventional science in dealing with crises in the state of the environment, in food production, health, community structure, and quality of life.

It has become evident that basic assumptions need to be re-examined so that values and ethics become integral to scientific practice, instead of add-ons. Holistic science includes qualities as well as quantities in our understanding of nature, our relationship to it and to each other. We are moving from a science of manipulation to one of participation in natural processes which are too complex to be controlled but which we can influence, for better or for worse.

Schumacher College is focusing its attention on ecological economics and development issues; the links between philosophy, psychology and ecology; and the new understandings arising out of recent scientific discoveries.

Schumacher College was founded in 1991 upon the twin convictions that the world view which has dominated Western civilization has serious limitations, and that a new vision is needed for human society, its values and its relationship to the earth. The College explores innovative forms of learning for sustainable living with distinguished thinkers and scientists such as Fritjof Capra, James Lovelock, Vandana Shiva, James Hillman and Theodore Rozsak.

The College offers rigorous enquiry to uncover the roots of the prevailing world view; it explores ecological approaches which value holistic rather than reductionist perspectives and spiritual rather than consumerist values. It also offers a learning experience that is consistent with a holistic philosophy.

A significant component of study and research at Schumacher College will be participation in the communal life of the College. This provides an opportunity for teamwork and experiential learning through interaction with the diversity of highly motivated, informed and talented people who attend the short courses. This will complement and extend the emphasis on participation and cooperative enquiry that is an integral aspect of holistic science.

Contact: The Administrator
Schumacher College
The Old Postern, Dartington
Devon TQ9 6EA, UK.
+44 (0)1803 865934
schumcoll@gn.apc.org

# SOCIAL POLICY
## HELLER GRADUATE SCHOOL
## BRANDEIS UNIVERSITY

Brandeis University's Heller Graduate School is a school for social policy that offers three degree options that bridge the gap between theory and practice.

The Heller School's Master's Program is at the intersection of cutting-edge management and social policy. The Master's Program prepares managers for leadership positions in a range of health and human service, non-profit, public, and private organizations. Students in the Master's Program can choose a formal management concentration in health care or child, youth and family services, or self-design a concentration from one of our other policy specialties.

Students in the Heller School's Doctoral Program pursue a course of study that provides intensive scholarly preparation in general and specialized social policy areas, honed research skills, and a strong working knowledge of various social science disciplines. Doctoral Program educate students for careers in: teaching, research, social planning, administration, and policy analysis.

The Heller School's policy specialties include: aging; children, youth and families; disabilities; health; mental health; international and community development; substance abuse; and work, inequality and social change.

Since its founding in 1959, the Heller Graduate School for Advanced Studies in Social Welfare has been committed to developing new knowledge and insights in the field of social policy and health and human services management. Faculty members and students actively engage in examining policies and programs that respond to the changing needs of individuals and social groups in society. Heller and its nationally renowned research centers have pioneered in a variety of policy areas including health; children, youth, and families; aging; workforce and community development; mental retardation and developmental disabilities; and social change. The faculty represents many social science disciplines and includes both scholars and practitioners. The School offers educational programs designed explicitly to bridge the gap between theory and practice: a Ph.D. in Social Policy, a Master of Management (M.M.), and a Master of Business Administration in Human Services.

The Heller School's Master's Program (M.M. and M.B.A. degrees) trains leaders who manage a wide range of health and human services organizations. The curriculum uniquely combines social policy with cutting-edge management education, cross-training students not only to identify the issues and needs of disadvantaged groups but to address those needs through effective and efficient program design and management within the complex and changing environment of health and human services. The Master's Program offers the option of two specialized tracks -- health care and child, youth and family services -- allowing students interested in careers in a specific area of human services to pursue a course of study that emphasizes both management and policy in that field. A final team consulting project allows students to apply management and analytical skills in a real-life context. The full-time, accelerated program takes fifteen months, beginning in June and finishing in August of the following year. Part-time and evening study are available for the M.M.

Students in the Heller School's Doctoral Program pursue a course of study that provides intensive scholarly preparation in general and specialized social policy areas, honed research skills, and a strong working knowledge of various social science disciplines. The course of study is interdisciplinary, based on economics, sociology, and political science. Courses in social welfare, policy analysis, and research methods combine with those in substantive areas of interest for an integrative approach to social policy. Students must complete fifteen courses and a comprehensive paper in the social sciences as well as successfully defend, both orally and in writing, a policy research dissertation. The Doctoral Program educates students for careers in teaching, research, social planning, administration, and policy analysis.

Students benefit from association with an expert research staff in six policy centers conducting nationally significant projects in a wide range of areas. Heller course offerings reflect the work of the Institute for Health Policy, The policy Center on Aging, the Center for Human Resources, the Family and Children's Policy Center, the Center for Social Change, and the Nathan and Toby Starr Center for Mental Retardation. In addition to the work at the six centers, active research is conducted in mental health, substance abuse, and long-term care.

Former Secretary of Labor Robert B. Reich; University Professor and Maurice B. Hexter Professor of Social and Economic Policy; J.D., Yale. Work and inequality.

Stuart Altman, Sol C. Chaiken Professor of National Health Policy; Ph.D., UCLA. Health-care policy.

Andrew B. Hahn, Research Professor and Associate Dean for University Relations: Ph.D., Brandeis. Labor Market Studies

David G. Gil, Professor of Social Policy; D.S.W., Pennsylvania. Social Welfare, inequality.

Constance W. Williams, Associate Professor and Director of the Ph.D. in Social Policy Program; Ph.D., Brandeis. Family and children, race, class, culture.

Jack P. Shonkoff, Professor of Social Policy and Dean; M.D., NYU. Pediatrics, child and family policy.

Full-time students complete the Master's Program in fifteen months, a considerable advantage in cost and time over equivalent two-year programs. Part-time students finish in two-three years. Evening students typically take two courses per semester and finish in three to four years.

Contact: Office of Admissions

The Heller Graduate School/MS 035

Brandeis University

Waltham, MA 02254-9110

(781) 736-3820

hamlin@binah.cc.brandeis.edu

www.brandeis.edu/heller

# SOCIAL WORK
## BOSTON UNIVERSITY

The Boston University School of Social Work is committed to education that furthers social and economic justice in the urban environment and strives to incorporate this commitment into its curriculum, programs, and activities. There is particular concern with empowerment of all oppressed groups.

The primary aim of the School of Social Work is to educate professional social workers who will become leaders in a complex multicultural society. They will possess the knowledge and skills to address the needs and potential of individuals, families, groups, organizations, and communities. The School of Social Work offers an integrated program of study, including clinical and macro social work methods. The School of Social Work offers full-time and part-time programs leading to the Master of Social Work, Joint degrees with the School of Public Health (M. S.W./M.P.H.), The School of Theology (M.S.W./M.T.S. or M.S.W./M.Div.), and the School of Education (M. S.W./M.Ed or M. S.W.Ed.D.) Also are available to students. The School of Social Work has an advanced standing program for graduates of an undergraduate social work program accredited by the Council of Social Work Education ad accepts students transferring from other graduate social work programs.

In both classroom and field, professional education is divided into four broad categories of instruction: human behavior in the social environment, social welfare policy, social work research, and methods used in social work practice. The School of Social Work's multimethod social work practice program offers the opportunity to concentrate in clinical social work practice (with individuals, families, and groups) and macro social work practice (community organization, management, and planning).

Maryann Amodeo, Clinical Associate Professor, M.S.W., Syracuse; Ph.D., Brandeis. Substance abuse identification and intervention skills.

Melvin Delgado, Professor; M.S., Columbia; Ph.D., Brandeis. Social welfare, issues of populations of color, cross-cultural practice.

Lena Lundgren-Gaveras, Assistant Professor; M.S.W., Ph.D., Chicago. Public welfare dependency, urban poverty, unemployment policy.

Susan Stern, Associate Professor; M.S.W., Michigan; Ph.D., Chicago. Family and marital conflict, childhood aggression, child abuse, adolescent mental health and delinquency.

Contact: Boston University School of Social Work

264 Bay State Road

Boston, MA 02215

(617) 353-3765

busswad@bu.edu web.bu.edu/ssw/

# SUSTAINABLE COMMUNITY / CULTURE, ECOLOGY
## NEW COLLEGE OF CALIFORNIA

The 12 month program at the New College campus in Santa Rosa focuses on creating alternatives - a "parallel universe" of sustainable agriculture, community currencies, cooperative businesses, natural building techniques, appropriate technology and holistic health, where students sill still the the traditional activist skills necessary to deal with corporate globalization and greed.

Students develop a critical perspective on the history and present condition of modern society, learn new ways to conceptualize solutions to modern problems, and acquire skills to build a sustainable future. Students design a program of study that suits their own particular interests and needs.

Students seeking a Master's degree integrate the Santa Rosa curriculum with the MA Program in Humanities and Leadership based in San Francisco. Students attend seminars with local grassroots and nationally prominent leaders in the field including Helena Norberg Hodge, winner of the "alternative Nobel Prize" for her work in Ladakh, and Helen Caldicott, founder of Physicians for Social Responsibility.

Although most students are from the North Bay region, students can live at a distance from Santa Rosa while conducting the necessary independent research or activist project to complete their degree in their home communities. Currently there are students in the program from Santa Cruz to Mendocino and into the Sierras.

Seminars include Environment, Civilization and Development; Sustainable Community and Cultural Renewal; Politics, Culture and Society.

Contact: Michael McAvoy

New College of California

Weekend Program in Culture, Ecology & Sustainable Community

99 Sixth Street

Santa Rosa, CA 95401-6200

(707) 568-0112

www.newcollege.edu

# SUSTAINABLE SOCIETIES
## NORTHERN ARIZONA UNIVERSITY

The Master of Liberal Studies in Visions of Good and Sustainable Societies is an interdisciplinary program for people seeking to create models of community for the twenty-first century. The program is offered to adult learners who seek a broad and integrated perspective on the complex issues of contemporary society. The degree program is organized around the curricular them - Visions of Good and Sustainable Societies - that cuts across many academic areas, including anthropology, the arts, business, economics, environmental science, gerontology, psychology, sociology, religion, technology, and women's studies.

Students work with a faculty advisor to develop an emphasis appropriate to their interests. For example, some students have emphasized ethics and leadership, spirituality and health, women's studies, or aging - all in relationship to strengthening community life. A 6 hour final integrative project can be a traditional research thesis, a creative work, or an applied research project in your community.

As part of a community of learners that respects the experiences and insights of mature students, you can study models of communities as well as environmental and social issues of immediate importance to regional, national, and international communities. The program is appropriate for students who are committed to the connection between thought and action. Secondary school teachers working in the humanities and social and natural sciences also find this program particularly appealing.

The program is tailored to students who with to pursue graduate study on a part-time basis. Courses are offered on a flexible schedule - including summers, evenings and weekends.

Northern Arizona University is one of a small group of colleges in the Historically Black Colleges and Universities/Minority Institutions Environmental Technology Consortium that are making a concerted effort to green their education, and to particularly reach out to native and minority populations in the process.

Contact: Dr. Sandra Lubarsky
Master of Liberal Studies Office
Northern Arizona University
Flagstaff, AZ 86011-6031
(520) 523-9359
Sandra.Lubarsky@nau.edu

# SUSTAINABLE SYSTEMS
## SLIPPERY ROCK UNIVERSITY

The Master of Science in Sustainable Systems (MS3) Program at Slippery Rock University was established in 1990 and charged with preparing students to face the pressing economic and environmental challenges of the future by considering sustainability as the underlying framework for action. In the 37-hour Program, students study and practice sustainability through the integration of agriculture, natural resource management, and the built environment with particular attention focused on the design of productive systems that reflect the diversity and resilience of natural systems. The program embraces the human element in the landscape, searching for sustainable ways to satisfy food, energy, shelter and other material and non-material human needs.

An on-campus homestead, the Macoskey Center, integrates the three focal areas of the Program and provides a host of research, outreach, and experiential learning opportunities for MS3 students and the wider Slippery Rock Community. The homestead building itself has been renovated for energy conservation, utilizing alternative energy technologies, allergy free/non-toxic design techniques and material recycling. Sustainable farming and natural resource management is also practiced on site within the 84-acre property.

Three full-time faculty are currently dedicated to the Program with areas of expertise in agroecology/sustainable agriculture, the built environment/green architecture, and natural resources/forestry management. The Program has attracted a broad spectrum of students with graduates working in mostly the private sector.

Contact: Dr. Karen Kainer
101 Eisenberg Classroom Building
Slippery Rock University
Slippery Rock, PA 16057-1328
(724) 738-2622
karen.kainer@sru.edu

# URBAN AND ENVIRONMENTAL SCIENCE
## TUFTS UNIVERSITY

The graduate Department of Urban and Environmental Science at Tufts University offers a two-year master's degree to prepare public-spirited individuals for challenging careers in government, nonprofit organizations, citizen advocacy groups, and the private sector. The mission of the department is to educate a new generation of leaders, "practical visionaries" to face complex problems in public policy. Distinctive features include an interdisciplinary approach; an emphasis on values, democratic principles, and citizen initiatives in setting a public agenda; an appreciation of the centrality of nonprofit organizations in implementing programs; and a concern for the local and distributive aspects of public policy.

Students receive a Master's Degree in Public Policy with a concentration in Environmental Policy (natural resource management; pollution prevention; chemicals, health and the environment; or international environmental policy) or in Urban and Social Policy (community development and housing; social welfare policy; or child and family policy). Students also have the option of developing individually tailored specializations in consultation with their advisers. The program normally takes the equivalent of two years of full-time study, although it is possible to be enrolled in the program on a part-time basis.

The curriculum emphasizes practice as well as theory, linking academic instruction with policy issues defined by communities and public agencies. Practical planning and research experience is provided to students through their participation in field projects. Students work in teams for clients from a variety of organizations including government, community, or non-government agencies to evaluate existing initiatives and to formulate alternative policy approaches to actual problems. A required internship gives students additional experience working in a professional setting.

Students may be enrolled exclusively in UEP, in a joint degree program with the Departments of Civil and Environmental Engineering, Biology, Economics, or Child Development, or in a three-year dual degree program with the Fletcher School of Law and Diplomacy. The department also has a collaborative master's degree in agriculture, food and environment with the School of Nutrition, science and policy.

Tufts is located in the Boston area.

Contact: Ann Urosevich
Urban and Environmental Policy
Tufts Unversity
97 Talbot Ave.
Medford, MA
(617) 627-3394

# WESTERN INSTITUTE FOR SOCIAL RESEARCH

Since 1975, the Western Institute for Social Research has offered mature adults opportunities to design their own individualized B.A., M.A. and Ph.D. programs. Dedicated to social change, students and faculty are people committed to changing today's oppressive patterns of race and gender relations, of wealth and poverty, of extreme power and powerlessness, in peaceful and constructive ways.

WISR combines theory and practice, demonstrating that high quality, academic study and full-time work on community problems can go together -- that each, in fact, enhances the other. All students do active reading, writing, thinking, and discussing while they continue wrestling with specific, practical problems in their work and/or other community involvements, with the guidance and support of faculty and their fellow students. Each student builds a personal learning plan and works with a few faculty, other students, and community resource people on problems he/she deeply cares about.

WISR is a small, multicultural learning community. Students, faculty and Board members are engaged in a living experiment in cooperation among people of different races, cultural, and personal backgrounds. People know each other personally, and procedures are human-scaled. Active collaboration with others, not competition and distance, lend richness and interest to each person's learning process.

Not many universities or colleges combine these kinds of commitments and ways of learning and teaching. The founders of WISR were people who had worked in other "innovative" colleges, and who got together to fill some gaps they saw being left open. The result after 23 years is a vital, changing, and deeply involved group of people who are helping each other to operate a living laboratory for multicultural education and social change.

Students meet regularly with faculty to design and receive feedback about their academic projects -- readings, written papers, jobs, internships, and community involvement. The majority of WISR students are working full-time. While most live in the San Francisco Bay Area, a few students live in other parts of California, and even occasionally outside of California and in foreign countries.

In 1997-98, 40 graduate and undergraduate students were enrolled at WISR, ranging in age from 20 to over 60. Students at WISR are all strongly motivated, mature people who are actively engaged in the work of the communities where they live, as well as in their own personal growth. WISR graduates are very successful in going forward in such careers as directors of non-profit agencies, college professors, licensed counselors, and self-employed writers and activists.

Program areas include masters degrees in Psychology, Human Services and Community Development, Social Sciences, Education and a Ph.D. in Higher Education and Social Change.

Contact: Western Institute for Social Research
3220 Sacramento St.
Berkeley, CA 94702
(510) 655-2830

# PEACE CORPS
# MASTER'S
# INTERNATIONALIST

♦ ♦ ♦

# RETURNED
# PEACE CORPS
# FELLOWS
# GRADUATE PROGRAMS
## (CHECK THEM OUT!)

♦ ♦ ♦

# PEACE CORPS
# MASTER'S INTERNATIONALIST PROGRAMS

For more than ten years, the Peace Corps has joined forces with colleges and universities across the United States to provide a unique academic experience through the Master's International Program (MI Program). First established at Rutgers University in 1987, the MI Program has provided hundreds of students the opportunity to incorporate Peace Corps Volunteer service into a Master's degree program. These "Student-Volunteers" forward their own professional and personal goals and develop technical expertise that is valued by people in developing nations throughout the world.

The Peace Corps collaborates with 23 colleges and universities to offer the MI Program in 27 different degree programs. Students may pursue studies in public health, forestry, agriculture, English teaching, business, non-profit management, or urban planning. They are placed in Peace Corps assignments overseas where they are able to apply theoretical knowledge learned in the classroom to practical, real-life settings.

Participating in the MI Program is demanding, but the rewards -- both to you and to the people you serve -- are great. We encourage you to consider the MI Program as you look to build your professional career.

Mark D. Gearan

Director

### Deciding between Peace Corps and Graduate School?

Since 1987, the Master's International Program has made this decision easier for hundreds of prospective students and Peace Corps Volunteers. A cooperative partnership between the Peace Corps and colleges and universities, the Master's International Program provides a unique opportunity to incorporate Peace Corps service into a graduate degree program. The program combines a minimum of one year on-campus study with the training and field experience for which the Peace Corps is renowned. Upon completion of the program, Master's International (MI) graduates possess both excellent academic credentials and international field experience -- an attractive combination for prospective employers.

The MI Program is offered in disciplines where the Peace Corps can provide relevant field assignments. The specific degree(s) offered by each school will vary.

### Master's International students as Peace Corps Volunteers

Since the Peace Corps' inception in 1961, its mission has remained unchanged:

- To provide Volunteers who contribute to the social and economic development of interested countries;
- To promote a better understanding of Americans among the people whom Volunteers serve;

- To strengthen Americans' understanding about the world and its peoples -- to bring the world back home.

More than 145,000 Americans have joined the Peace Corps since the agency was established. They work for two years, sharing their technical expertise, creativity, flexibility, and dedication with people all over the world. Peace Corps Volunteers live and work in local communities, encouraging small enterprise, protecting the local environment, improving agricultural production, promoting sound health and sanitation practices, and teaching English to students who recognize the language as a means to economic and educational opportunity. Master's International students bring a strong knowledge base to their overseas assignment, making them highly valued by the people with whom they work. MI students also enjoy the benefit of having a faculty advisor in the United States who can provide technical support and advice. Over the last 35 years, the needs of Peace Corps' host countries have evolved, and requests for Peace Corps Volunteers with strong technical skills have increased. Host countries are increasingly requesting Volunteers skilled in forestry, agriculture, business and non-profit management, English teaching, public health and urban planning.

### What will I do as a Peace Corps Volunteer?

MI students are placed in projects relevant to their course of study. Some of the many projects in which MI students have worked are:

A public health project in Madagascar to introduce improved nutrition and hygiene practices to school children and their mothers;

An agricultural project in Nepal introducing more efficient crop production, pest management, seed production and storage techniques in order to increase both food production and income;

A forestry project in Albania to promote the integration of forestry with current agricultural practices, working with farmers to help increase farm income and conserve local natural resources;

A business project in Kenya to assist entrepreneurs in gaining practical business skills, including inventory management, accounting, marketing, and accessing credit;

A project in Kyrgyzstan to teach English to secondary students and to introduce new teaching methodologies to local English teachers.

### What are the benefits of being a Master's International Student?

In addition to receiving excellent training and practical experience, Master's International students receive a number of benefits from the Peace Corps, including:
- Transportation to and from the country of service
- Living and housing expenses
- Full medical and dental care
- Vacation time and allowance
- Cancellation or deferment of certain government-backed educational loans
- $5,400 readjustment allowance upon completion of 27 months of service
- Career counseling and support
- Non-competitive eligibility for Federal government jobs upon completion of full term of service

Most participating Master's International schools offer academic credit for Peace Corps service. In addition, several schools provide scholarships or tuition waivers for these credits. Depending on their availability at specific universities, Master's International students may also compete for research or teaching assistantships.

### How do I apply to the Master's International Program?

Master's International students must apply and be accepted to both the Peace Corps and at least one of the participating Master's International schools. The Peace Corps application will be evaluated based on the agency's selection criteria for Volunteers, including medical and legal clearances. The application to the school will be evaluated based on the school's own admission requirements.

To be eligible for Peace Corps service, you must be a U.S. citizen, in good general health, and at least 18 years of age. Married couples without dependent children may be accepted, but both spouses must qualify for a Volunteer assignment.

We recommend that your Peace Corps application and the application for admission to the MI school be submitted simultaneously, using the admission deadline of the school as a guide. This allows enough time for the necessary medical, legal, and other clearances from Peace Corps to be completed.

### When will I receive my Peace Corps assignment?

While you are completing your course work, your Peace Corps application will be kept active with the Peace Corps Office of Placement which is responsible for assessing and placing applicants. Peace Corps' host countries submit requests for Volunteers approximately six months prior to the scheduled start date of training.

### How is this different than entering graduate school and Peace Corps separately?

As a MI student, you earn academic credit for your Peace Corps service. In many cases, the school will waive the cost of these credits. You will have the benefit of your faculty advisor's technical expertise and support as you identify and address areas of need overseas. In addition, you will return to the United States with two years of professional, international experience incorporated into your graduate degree.

### Does the Peace Corps provide financial support to MI students?

The Peace Corps does not provide scholarships to MI students. However, some student loans can be deferred or cancelled, and all costs associated with your Peace Corps experience are covered by the Peace Corps, including transport, medical care and living expenses. In addition, the Peace Corps provides a $5,400 readjustment allowance which is paid to you at the end of your assignment. Most schools provide students with an opportunity for research or teaching assistantships, scholarships, or a tuition waiver for the cost of credits earned while in the Peace Corps.

Peace Corps Recruitment
Washington, DC 20526
(800) 424-8580, option '2," x2226
eparker@peacecorps.gov

# AGRIBUSINESS
## ARIZONA STATE UNIVERSITY EAST

The School of Agribusiness and Resource Management and the Center for Agribusiness Policy offers a Master of Science degree in Agribusiness. The Master's International program consist of 33 credits, six of which may be earned for Peace Corps Volunteer service. The program is designed to prepare student participants for assignments in agribusiness management and for Volunteer and development activities generally. Courses will cover issues such as: advanced agribusiness marketing, management and finance, food management, international agricultural techniques, world agricultural development, and advanced agribusiness policy. Depending on the nature of their assignment and their particular interests, students will register for internship, independent study, and/or research credits.

Benefits: Students may earn up to six credits for their Peace Corps service.

Contact:

Dr. Eric Thor
Director
(602) 727-1583
Center for Agribusiness Policy Studies

Dr. Julie Stanton
Assistant Professor
(602) 727-1126
Agribusiness Resource Mgm't..

ASU East, Mail code 0180
6001 S. Power Road, Bldg. 765
Mesa, AZ 85206
idept@asuvm.inre.asu.edu

• • • • •

# AGRICULTURE
## COLORADO STATE UNIVERSITY

Colorado State University offers Master's Degree programs through the College of Agricultural Sciences. To complete the program, three semesters of course work must be taken on the CSU campus. During the final semester on campus, candidates are required to write a professional paper integrating issues relating the field experience with their area of academic experience. The program of study is individually designed within departmental parameters to meet your needs, taking into consideration the needs of the Peace Corps and the host countries. Students can specialize in one of five Departments within the College of Agricultural Sciences: Animal Sciences, Bio-Agricultural Science and Pest Management, Agriculture and Resources Economics, Horticulture, and Soil and Crop Sciences.

Benefits: Between eight and ten credits can be earned for Peace Corps service; competitively based scholarships, research and teaching assistantships may be available through the academic departments.

Contact: Dr. Jack Fenwick
Dept. of Soil and Crop Sciences
College of Agricultural Sciences
Colorado State University
Fort Collins, CO 80523-1170
(970) 491-6907
jfenwick@ceres.agsci.colostate.edu

* * * * *

# INTERNATIONAL AGRICULTURE
## CORNELL UNIVERSITY

The MPS/Agriculture program has an emphasis on conservation of natural resources, sustainable farming systems, and various aspects of international development such as population, nutrition, planning, policy or agriculture. The program prepares students, through a combination of academic studies and application of analytical skills, to assume a leadership position in development programs, in government and non-government organizations, or in the private sector. The MPS/Agriculture combined with a Peace Corps tour will require satisfactory completion of 30 credit hours related to the candidate's professional interest. Twenty four of the 30 credit hours will be earned at Cornell prior to entering the Peace Corps. After two semesters of academic work, the student will undertake his/her Peace Corps assignment. Following the 27- month Peace Corps field experience, the candidate will prepare and submit a problem-solving project paper that will draw upon and systematize their field experience as a Peace Corps volunteer. Students are highly encouraged to enroll for one additional semester of study at Cornell University following their Peace Corps service for further extension and refinement of their learning.

Benefits: During Peace Corps service, students are not required to pay full tuition. They will, however, be required to pay an absentia tuition of $200 per semester. Up to six credit hours may be earned during Peace Corps service through the completion and acceptance of the MPS project paper.

Contact: James Haldeman
Box 14, Kennedy Hall
Ithaca NY, 14853
(607) 255-3037
JEH5@cornell.edu

* * * * *

# AGRICULTURE
## PURDUE UNIVERSITY

The Purdue University School of Agriculture offers a Master of Science Degree in Entomology with special emphasis in crop extension, crop protection, and integrated pest management. The program will provide students with working knowledge of crop production, integrated pest management principles and practices, agricultural extension (philosophy and methodology), and economic aspects of international agricultural development. There are no specific course requirements for this degree. The program is tailored to student's interests, background, and career goals. Students will pursue a non-thesis master's option in the Department of Entomology. However, the Purdue MI curriculum involves nearly all of the academic disciplines in the School of Agriculture thus providing the student with a broad educational base in agriculture, natural resources, and the food system.

Benefits: No credits are earned for Peace Corps service, but part of the requirement for the M.S. option in Entomology is a "creative project" which will be based on work done while overseas; a 1/4 to 1/2 time assistantship is available to MI students on a competitive basis, administered through the Entomology department.

Contact:

Dr. David Sammons
Assoc. Dean, Int'l.. Programs in Ag.
Agriculture Admin. Bldg., Room #26
Purdue University
West Lafayette, IN 47907
(317) 494-8466
DJS@admin.agad.purdue.edu

Dr. Chris Oseto
Department of Entomology
Purdue University
West Lafayette, IN 47907
(317) 494-4554
chris_oseto@mailhost.ntm.purdue.edu

♦ ♦ ♦ ♦ ♦

# AGRIBUSINESS
## SANTA CLARA UNIVERSITY

The Leavey School of Business and Administration as Santa Clara University offers a Master of Business Administration (MBA) with a specialization in agribusiness. The program is designed to prepare students for careers in the food and agribusiness industry and to contribute to more effective Volunteer service in the scarce skills areas of agriculture economics/farm management and advanced business development. Depending on the course work already completed by the student prior to admission, the agribusiness MBA program requires a minimum of 15 courses and a maximum of 24 courses. The on-campus course work is complemented by three enrichment programs: a mentor program, internships, and international study tours. The Leavey School of Business at Santa Clara University is the only nationally-ranked business school that offers a degree in agribusiness management.

Benefits: Full and partial scholarships are available through the Institute of Agribusiness. Assistantships and loans are available through the University. Students can earn six (6) quarter units for their Peace Corps service through two consecutive internships or through an internship followed by an independent study. Participants will work with their advisors to determine the best course of study.

Contact: S. Andrew Starbird, Ph.D.
Director, Institute of Agribusiness
Leavey School of Business Administration
Santa Clara University
Santa Clara, CA 95053
(408) 554-4086
agribusiness@scu.edu

♦ ♦ ♦ ♦ ♦

# AGRICULTURE
# WASHINGTON STATE UNIVERSITY

Washington State University (WSU) offers the Master's International Degree option in Agricultural Education, Agronomy, Horticulture, and other agricultural disciplines. Students who enroll in the program must complete a year of graduate course work at the University prior to their Peace Corps assignment. In most cases, students will return to WSU for a semester after two years abroad in the Peace Corps to write their thesis or project report. All departments participating in the program offer both thesis and non-thesis options.

Benefits: Three to six credits are granted for Peace Corps service; no guaranteed financial aid, although some fellowships and assistantships may be available on a competitive basis.

Contact: Sally M. Burkhart
Assistant to the Director
International Programs
French Administration 328
Washington State University
Pullman, WA 99164-1034
(509) 335-2541
sburkhar@wsu.edu

♦ ♦ ♦ ♦ ♦

# INT'L. BUSINESS ADMINISTRATION
## MONTEREY INSTITUTE OF INTERNATIONAL STUDIES

The Fisher Graduate School of International Management (GSIM) at the Monterey Institute of International Studies offers an International Master of Business Administration (MBA) degree that prepares Peace Corps Volunteers for international business development. Master's International students begin study in June or September and spend two semesters in Monterey. During this time, they learn International Business Planning and may intern at the Institute's Small Business Institute (SBI) or the Business and Economic Development Center (BEDC.) The program prepares students for a future Peace Corps assignment working with businesses in an advisory capacity. Peace Corps Volunteers use their experiences as the core for a final project or case study during their final semester in Monterey. Three semesters and 42 semester credits of course work are required for an MBA.

Benefits: Students satisfy the language component of their degree program while in the Peace Corps, but do not earn actual credits; half tuition scholarships are available for the final semester of study following Peace Corps service.

Contact: Dean, Fisher
Graduate School of International Management
Monterey Institute of International Studies
Dr. William Pendergast
425 Van Buren Street
Monterey, CA 93940
(408) 647-4140
wpendergast@miis.edu

◆ ◆ ◆ ◆ ◆

# FORESTRY/NATURAL RESOURCES MGM'T
## COLORADO STATE UNIVERSITY

Colorado State University (CSU) offers Master of Science programs through the College of Natural Resources. Thirty semester-credits are required to complete the program. Candidates are required to write a professional paper integrating issues relating the field experience with their area of academic experience. The program of study is individually designed to meet the student's professional/research objectives, taking into consideration the needs of the Peace Corps and the host country. Students can apply to one of five departments: Earth Resources (Watershed Management,) Fishery and Wildlife Biology, Rangeland Ecosystem Science, and Natural Resources Recreation and Tourism

Benefits: Eight semester credits may be earned for the Peace Corps internship; competitively based scholarships, research and teaching assistantships may be available through the academic departments.

Contact: Dr. Freeman M. Smith
Peace Corps/MI Liaison
International School of Natural Resources
Colorado State University
Ft. Collins CO 80523-1401
(970) 491-5678
freeman@cnr.colostate.edu

* * * * *

# FORESTRY/NATURAL RESOURCES MANAGEMENT
## MICHIGAN TECHNOLOGICAL UNIVERSITY

The Michigan Technological University (MTU) School of Forestry and Wood Products has designed a MI Program for students with an interest in forestry and Peace Corps service. Students with or without a forestry, environmental studies, or natural resources background are encouraged to apply. The program is designed for students who have liberal arts degrees. However, adjustments are made for students with natural resources, forestry, and environmental studies backgrounds. Students spend one academic quarter at the 4000+ acre Ford Forestry Center, learning fundamental forestry skills. Two more quarters are spent at the main campus of MTU completing course work involving traditional forestry, general ecology, and international forestry. Thesis, project, and course work degree options are available.

Benefits: Students can earn up to nine graduate quarter credits for Peace Corps service; $500 work study allowance for first year MI students; no specific financial aid is available through MTU, though students can apply for Stafford loans and Federal Aid; FAFSA application is recommended before the January 31 deadline.

Contact: Dr. Blair Orr
School of Forestry
Michigan Technological University
1400 Townsend Drive
Houghton, MI 49931-1295
(906) 487-2291
bdorr@mtu.edu
http://forestry.mtu.edu/peacecorps

♦ ♦ ♦ ♦ ♦

# FORESTRY/NATURAL RESOURCES MANAGEMENT
# UNIVERSITY OF MINNESOTA

The University of Minnesota College of Natural Resources offers a Master of Science (MS) Degree in Forestry. The degree program requires a minimum of 44 graduate credits. Students entering the program without natural resource backgrounds may need additional courses to achieve the necessary background. Participants spend three quarters on campus prior to Peace Corps service and take a full course load of 10-15 credits per quarter. Four to eight credits are awarded for the Peace Corps assignment and for a research activity that will be conducted during service. After completion of the Peace Corps assignment, students will return to the University for one or two quarters to complete the degree requirements.

Benefits: Between four and eight credits are awarded for Peace Corps service; tuition fellowships and partial grants are available on a competitive basis.

Contact: Dr. Kenneth Brooks
Professor and Director of Graduate Studies in Forestry
College of Natural Resources
University of Minnesota
235 Natural Resources Administration building
2003 Upper Buford Circle  St. Paul, MN 55108-6146
(612) 624-2774
kbrooks@forestry.umn.edu

♦ ♦ ♦ ♦ ♦

# FORESTRY/NATURAL RESOURCES MANAGEMENT
# UNIVERSITY OF MONTANA

The School of Forestry offers students interested in international conservation and resource management, the opportunity to combine academic course work with a Peace Corps experience. Students may earn a Master's Degree (thesis or non-thesis option) in Forestry (Forestry, Resource Conservation, Recreation Management) or Wildlife Biology. A total of 36 credits are required to complete a master's non-thesis option and 30 credits for a master's with thesis option. Academic credit is granted for the Peace Corps assignment. Candidates in the program usually attend school for at least one year prior to two years of service in the Peace Corps. The course of study specifically designed for MI students includes courses in ecology, tropical forest management, development sociology, international resource management, and statistics.

Benefits: Four to six credits can be earned for Peace Corps service; teaching assistantships are available.

Contact: Dr. Steven Siebert
School of Forestry
University of Montana
Missoula, MT 59812
(406) 243-4661
siebert@selway.umt.edu

♦ ♦ ♦ ♦ ♦

# FORESTRY/NATURAL RESOURCES MANAGEMENT
# NORTH CAROLINA STATE UNIVERSITY

Graduate students enrolled in the College of Forest Resources, Department of Forestry will be able to pursue a Master of Forestry, Master of Natural Resources, or a Master of Science degree in Forestry or Natural Resources. The MIP will consist of a minimum of 36 semester hours of academic study for the Master of Natural Resources or the Master of Forestry, or 30 semester hours of academic study for the Master of Science. The program is designed to prepare students for Peace Corps assignments in forestry (primarily agroforestry) and/or natural resources management with an emphasis on environmental education, and for Volunteer and development activities generally.

Benefits: Each of the three degree programs will include 6 units of independent study related to the students' Peace Corps Volunteer service. Research assistantships are available on a competitive basis to students pursuing research-based Master of Science degrees.

Contact: Erin Sills
Department of Forestry
Box 8008
North Carolina State University
Raleigh, NC 27695
(919) 515-7784
SILLS@cfr.cfr.ncsu.edu

* * * * *

# FORESTRY/NATURAL RESOURCES MANAGEMENT
# WASHINGTON STATE UNIVERSITY

Washington State University (WSU) offers the Master's International degree option in Environmental Science, Natural Resources Sciences and Regional Planning with emphasis on Environmental Management. Students who enroll in the program must complete a year of graduate course work at the University prior to their Peace Corps assignment. In most cases, students will return to WSU for a semester after two years abroad in the Peace Corps to write their thesis or project report. All departments participating in the program offer both thesis and non-thesis options.

Benefits: Three to six credits are granted for Peace Corps service; no guaranteed financial aid, although some fellowships and assistantships may be available on a competitive basis.

Contact: Sally M. Burkhart
Assistant to the Director
International Programs
French Administration 328
Washington State University
Pullman, WA 99164-1034
(509) 335-2541
sburkhar@wsu.edu

* * * * *

## FORESTRY/NATURAL RESOURCES MANAGEMENT
## UNIVERSITY OF WISCONSIN AT STEVENS POINT

The College of Natural Resources offers a Master's International Program in Forestry/Natural Resources. The program combines a minimum of one year of advanced training in forestry/natural resource management, with two subsequent years of Peace Corps service. Both thesis and non-thesis options are offered, the former preparing more for careers in research, the latter for careers in management. A thesis is the final requirement for the thesis option; the non-thesis option will require one or more projects such as a management plan, diary, seminar, publication(s), or other measurable evaluation demonstrating the candidate's professional growth during their Peace Corps experience. Additionally, MI students may transfer up to one semester of course work taken at the University of Hawaii-Manoa.

Benefits: Six credits hours are earned for Peace Corps service; occasional part- or full-time scholarships are available for which MI students compete with other graduate students.

Contact: Dr. Hans G. Schabel
Professor of Forestry
College of Natural Resources
University of Wisconsin
Stevens Point, WI 54481
(715) 346-4230
hschabel@uwsp.edu

* * * * *

# PUBLIC HEALTH/NUTRITION
## UNIVERSITY OF ALABAMA AT BIRMINGHAM

Participants in this cooperative program may enter either Master of Science in Public Health or Master of Public Health degree tracks which require 46 to 60 credit hours of core, specialty, field experience and research. Students choose electives of importance in international health such as nutrition, infectious disease control, program planning and evaluation, and family health. Nine hours of field experience and research are required, which can be met through Peace Corps service. The program is focused on public health issues in developing countries and encourages the recruitment of minorities. Completion of the MI Program requires 12 to 18 months at UAB plus Peace Corps service. Students do not have to return to campus residency after service, but are required to register for the term in which they are graduated, and to present a summary of their field experience and research to the department.

Benefits: Nine credit hours are earned for Peace Corps service; students can compete for the School of Public Health funds when they apply for UAB financial aid.

Contact: Dr. Walter Mason
School of Public Health
University of Alabama at Birmingham
315 Tidwell Hall   720 20th Street, South
Birmingham, AL 35294-0008
(205) 934-8647

♦ ♦ ♦ ♦ ♦

# PUBLIC HEALTH/NUTRITION
## BOSTON UNIVERSITY

The program at Boston University is flexible as MI students can complete two or three semesters of MPH course work prior to Peace Corps service in public health (the MPH degree can be completed in three full-time semesters). There are six concentrations to choose from: International Health (IH), Epidemiology and Biostatistics, Environmental Health, Health Services, Health Law and Health Behavior, Health Promotion, and Disease Prevention. The IH concentration courses are designed to provide skills that are practical and relevant to the environment of a developing country. MI students will meet many mid-career professionals from developing countries in this concentration and through the IH Department's certificate programs which offer credit towards the degree.

Benefits: Up to eight credits for Peace Corps service; favorable loan terms are available; priority access to Perkins Loans. Certificate courses are offered at a reduced tuition rate.

Contact: Michael Devlin
Associate Director for International Programs
Boston University
80 East Concord Street, A-310
Boston, MA 02118
(617) 638-5234
cih@bu.edu

* * * * *

## PUBLIC HEALTH/NUTRITION
## UNIVERSITY OF CALIFORNIA AT BERKELEY

University of California-Berkeley offers a Master's in Public Health with emphasis in Community Health Education, Public Health Nutrition, Maternal and Child Health (MCH) and Epidemiology. In a typical four-semester academic program, the first three semesters will be spent on the Berkeley campus. In the winter of the second year, the student will begin their two-year Peace Corps service. After their assignment, students return to the School of Public Health for a fourth semester, integrating the international experience with final course work.

Benefits: No credits can be earned for Peace Corps service; financial aid is available, including fellowships, scholarships, and loans.

Contact: Rick Love
School of Public Health
University of California - Berkeley
Berkeley, CA 94720
(510) 643-8452
ricklove@uclink2.berkeley.edu

* * * * *

## PUBLIC HEALTH/NUTRITION
## THE GEORGE WASHINGTON UNIVERSITY

The Department of Health Care Sciences hosts a Master's of Public Health Program (MPH) which offers several tracks of special interest to Volunteers including Health Promotion / Disease Prevention and International Health. Program completion will require 33-36 credit hours and will take 10 to 12 months. The MPH Program benefits enormously from the Washington, D.C. metropolitan area's vast cultural, professional, and educational offerings. Lecturers and guest speakers come from a wide array of professional organizations representing public health, the health sciences, and health services at their best.

Benefits: A supervised Peace Corps Special Project generally satisfies two to three required credits toward the MPH degree. Partial scholarships, Federal traineeship support, Federal Loans, and work-study are available to MI students; financial aid applications should be submitted by March 15.

Contact: Joy Panagides
GW School of Public Health and Health Services
2150 Pennsylvania Avenue  Floor 2B
Washington, DC 20037
(202) 994-8901
joy@hcs.gwumc.edu

♦ ♦ ♦ ♦ ♦

## PUBLIC HEALTH/NUTRITION
## LOMA LINDA UNIVERSITY

Loma Linda University School of Public Health offers a Master's in Public Health through the Department of International Health. The curriculum is based upon the recognition of the need for technology and organization that is appropriate to cultural and economic realities. The program combines public health knowledge with competence in techniques applicable to the developing country context. Students complete five quarters of academic work for a total of 55 quarter credits. The first four quarters are completed at LLU; the last quarter is a field practicum that participants will satisfy by completing two years of Peace Corps service. Students can also work as teaching assistants during their time on the LLU campus.

Benefits: Twelve quarter credits can be earned for the field practicum component of Peace Corps service; tuition waiver by the University for the field practicum; Federal Aid including Perkins and Stafford Loans, work-study, and grants are available.

Contact: Dr. Barbara Frye
Associate Professor
Department of International Health
Loma Linda University
Loma Linda, CA 92350
(909) 824-4902 or (800) 422-4558
bfrye@sph.llu.edu

♦ ♦ ♦ ♦ ♦

# PUBLIC HEALTH/NUTRITION
## UNIVERSITY OF NORTH CAROLINA AT CHAPEL HILL

The School of Public Health (SPH) offers Master's Degrees in the area of Maternal and Child Health, Nutrition, Nursing and Health Administration. The program involves an alliance of four SPH departments, as follows: the Department of Health Policy and Administration (HPAA) offers a Master's of Healthcare Aadministration and a Master's of Science in Public Health; the Department of Maternal and Child Health (MCH) offers a Master's in Public Health; the Department of Nutrition offers a Master's in Public Health in Nutrition; and the Department of Public Nursing offers a Master's of Science in Nursing.

Benefits: Six credits for Peace Corps service, traineeships and graduate assistantships available; tuition remission for out-of-state students; full academic year tuition and fees scholarships available on a limited basis for North Carolina residents.

Contact: Pam McDonald
Department of Health Policy & Administration
School of Public Health
1102-A McGavran-Greenberg Building, CB #7400
University of North Carolina at Chapel Hill
Chapel Hill, NC 27599-7400
(919) 966-7391

♦ ♦ ♦ ♦ ♦

# PUBLIC HEALTH/NUTRITION
## OKLAHOMA STATE UNIVERSITY

The Department of Nutritional Sciences offers a master of science degree, requiring the completion of 34 credit hours. A basic nutrition course is a prerequisite of the program. Academic course work begins during the summer; students are eligible for Peace Corps service following twelve months of study. Four credit hours are earned for Peace Corps service, but enrollment in the research credit hours occurs after the student returns to OSU. During the final semester at OSU, students complete the thesis requirements and the final two credit hours.

Benefits: Up to four credit hours can be earned for Peace Corps service; competitive assistantships are available.

Contact: Dr. Barbara Stoecker
Department of Nutritional Sciences Room 425
Oklahoma State University
Stillwater, OK 74078-0337
(405) 744-5040
chrom@okway.okstate.edu

# PUBLIC HEALTH/NUTRITION
## TULANE UNIVERSITY

The School of Public Health and Tropical Medicine offers a Master's International Program leading to a Master's in Public Health or a Master's of Science in Public Health. A unique aspect of Tulane's program links MI students with Returned Peace Corps Volunteers through a series of activities such as community service projects, guest lecturers, and social events. The degree requires 40 credits (36 for Tropical Medicine), after which students will begin their Peace Corps assignments.

Benefits: Five credit hours are waived for Peace Corps service; students receive a Dean's Grant of $3500 during the second semester of their course work, contingent upon Peace Corps service.

Contact: Tara Sullivan
MI Coordinator
Tulane University Admissions Office
1501 Canal Street, Ste.700
New Orleans, LA 70112
(504) 588-5387
tsulliv1@mailhost.tcs.tulane.edu

* * * * *

# PUBLIC HEALTH/NUTRITION
## WASHINGTON STATE UNIVERSITY

Washington State University (WSU) offers a Master of Science Degree in Nutrition. Students who enroll in the Master's International Program must complete a year of graduate course work at the University prior to their Peace Corps service. Program offers both thesis and non-thesis options. Students will return to WSU for a semester after their Peace Corps assignment to write their thesis or project report.

Benefits: Three to six credits are granted for Peace Corps service; no guaranteed financial aid, although some fellowships and assistantships may be available .

Contact: Sally M. Burkhart, Assistant to the Director
International Programs
French Administration 328
Washington State University
Pullman, WA 99164-1034
(509) 335-2541
sburkhar@wsu.edu

* * * * *

# PUBLIC POLICY AND ADMINISTRATION
## NON-PROFIT MANAGEMENT
### RUTGERS UNIVERSITY AT CAMDEN

Rutgers University offers a Master's Degree in Public Administration (MPA), with a concentration in International Development Administration. Students in will spend two semesters and one winter term studying at the University, then complete six graduate internship credits and three directed study credits for while serving abroad with the Peace Corps. MPA students receive training in the formation, implementation and evaluation of public policy and administration. Special course work focuses on international development. Students may choose to emphasize course work in particular areas, including non-profit/NGO management and development, international community development, and international municipal management.

Benefits: Students receive nine credits for Peace Corps service; assistantships and financial aid are available on a limited and competitive basis.

Contact: Dr. Jennifer Coston, Program Director
Graduate Department of Public Policy and Administration
Rutgers University-Camden
401 Cooper Street
Camden, NJ 08102
(609) 225-6353
jmcoston@crab.rutgers.edu

# TEACHING ENGLISH TO SPEAKERS OF OTHER LANGUAGES (TESOL)
## SACRAMENTO STATE

The Department of English at CSUS offers a master of arts in teaching English to speakers of other languages (TESOL) for MI students. Program consists of 27 units of course requirements, six units of elective courses, and a thesis option. MI students complete 18 units before their Peace Corps service. When overseas, participants will complete several projects, to be designed in consultation with the program's advisor. Volunteer service will serve as an elective for the degree. Upon returning to the campus, students' final semester will consist of nine units of coursework.

Benefits: Six credit hours can be earned for Peace Corps service; financial aid is available for all MI students, including assistantships, grants, loans, and work-study positions; CSUS will assist MI participants with job placement during their graduate program and following graduation.

Contact: Dr. Dana Ferris
English Department, CSUS
6000 'J" Street
Sacramento, CA 95819-6075
(916) 278-5394
ferrisd@csus.edu

## TESOL
## MONTEREY INSTITUTE OF INTERNATIONAL STUDIES

The Graduate School of Language and Educational Linguistics (GSLEL) at the Monterey Institute offers a master of arts in teaching English to speakers of other languages (MATESOL). Participants begin studies in early September, allowing them to finish their first two semesters by May, when the Peace Corps will place them as English teachers overseas. In order to receive the MATESOL, students must complete 37 units: 26 units are completed during the first two semesters at MIIS, and 11 units during the third semester at MIIS following Peace Corps service. MI TESOL students are not charged for eight of the 12 units during the final semester; and four of those units are for directed study units completed during Peace Corps service.

Contact: Dr. Ruth Larimer, Dean
GSLEL
Monterey Institute of International Studies
425 Van Buren Street
Monterey, CA 93940
(408) 647-4185
rlarimer@miis.edu

# TESOL
## SCHOOL FOR INTERNATIONAL TRAINING

The teaching program offers a curriculum which leads to a Master of Arts in Teaching English to Speakers of Other Languages with optional public school certification. The degree candidate will earn between 35 and 44 credits in one academic year. The Peace Corps serves as a second internship. A thesis, which can be done while overseas, is required to complete the degree. The program focuses on applied classroom practice and features a supervised off-campus, two-month teaching internship. Many of SIT's staff and faculty are former Peace Corps Volunteers or former Peace Corps staff and trainers. This degree program also has an outstanding worldwide reputation and consequently, an excellent job placement record for graduates.

Benefits: Students can earn up to 12 credits for Peace Corps service, six for the second teaching internship and six for completion of a thesis; no tuition charge for credits earned during Peace Corps service; $1000 SIT grant, work study, scholarships.

Contact: SIT Admissions
P.O. Box 676 Kipling Road
Brattleboro, VT 05302
(802) 258-3270
fiona.cook@worldlearning.org

♦ ♦ ♦ ♦ ♦

# URBAN PLANNING
## FLORIDA STATE UNIVERSITY

The Department of Urban and Regional Planning offers a professional Master's degree in planning with opportunities to specialize in planning for developing areas, housing and community development, transportation, comprehensive land use, environment, and health. MI participants will specialize in planning for developing areas, but may take electives from the other specialization areas. The typical MI program will take 48 semester hours over two years, including an internship and 21 hours in the core curriculum. All MI participants will complete their degree prior to Peace Corps training due to requirements of countries requesting Urban Planners.

Benefits: Up to three credit hours can be earned as intern credit for Peace Corps service; scholarships, and grants are available for MI students who demonstrate need.

Contact: Dr. Peter L. Doan
Department of Urban and Regional Planning, R-117
Florida State University
Tallahassee, FL 32306
(904) 644-4510
pdoan@coss.fsu.edu

# RETURNED PEACE CORPS
# FELLOWS/USA PROGRAM

Editor's note: On the following pages you will find a sample of the Peace Corps Fellow/USA graduate programs. Although they are offered especially to returned Peace Corps volunteers, some of the program offer a comparable educational experience for non-Peace Corps students. If you find one of interest to you, contact the program and enquire further. These are very rich, experiential programs. There are many more teacher training programs not listed here. You may get a list of all the programs by contacting the program at the address below.

Are you interested in a graduate degree or certificate program that will provide hands-on practical experience? Is the cost of graduate school a concern? Would you like to apply your Peace Corps skills to assist underserved U.S. communities?

If the answer to any of these questions is "yes," then consider the Peace Corps Fellows /USA Program. As a Returned Peace Corps Volunteer (RPCV), you have the opportunity to continue your professional development and fulfill the "third goal" of the Peace Corps through the Fellows/ USA Program. For two years, you lived and worked in places unknown to many Americans. The "third goal" of the Peace Corps to bring the world back home" and put your Peace Corps experience to work in the United States. The legacy of your Peace Corps service is not confined to your country of service. It is enhanced through you Interaction with neighbors, students and colleagues in the United States. Additionally, as a Peace Corps Fellow, you will receive financial assistance or reduced tuition for coursework while applying the lessons learned as a Peace Corps volunteer

The Fellows Program can help you take what you have learned overseas and use it to build a better future rather than storing it away as a memory of a once-in-a-lifetime experience. Whether you are still overseas, recently returned home, or thinking about a career change, examine the benefits of the Peace Corps Fellows Program.

In exchange for a two-year commitment to work in a community that needs your help, you can earn a master's degree and establish your career. A local university, with financial support from foundations, government agencies, corporations, and individual donors, will assist you in this process. You may receive any number of benefits such as tuition assistance, yearly stipends, housing, paid employment, and health benefits. The exact nature of the award varies with each university. In addition, through the Fellows Program you can form personal and professional relationships and expand your understanding of the United States and the world. There is no better way to bring home your Peace Corps experience and to make a difference -- for your community and yourself -- than through the Peace Corps Fellows/USA Program.

Peace Corps Fellows/USA Program
1990 K St. N.W., Room 9500
Washington, DC 20526
(800) 424-8580, press "2", then ext. 2259
fellows@peace corps.gov

# BUSINESS ADMINISTRATION / SOCIAL & PUBLIC POLICY
## DUQUESNE UNIVERSITY

The A. J. Palumbo School of Business Administration awards a MBA to RPCV's. Fellows work in community and economic development organizations associated with Duquesne's University-Community Collaborative Project. Fellows find their own community placements with the coordinator's guidance and support. Fellows have worked with Conservation Consultants, the Green Building Project, and the North Side Civic Development Corporation on program development, proposal writing, and management of housing, business development, and environmental programs.

The McAnulty Graduate School of Liberal Arts participates in the same program offering a MA in Social and Public Policy, with concentrations in policy analysis and administration or conflict resolution and peace studies.

Benefits: Stipends to Fellows working 20 hours per week as graduate assistants assigned to a community organization. Partial or full tuition scholarships.

Contact:

Dr. William D. Presutti, Associate Dean
A.J. Palumbo School of
Business Administration
704 Rockwell Hall
Pittsburgh, PA 15282
(412) 396-6269(-
presutti@duq2.cc.duq.edu

Dr. G. Evan Stoddard, Director
Center for Social & Public Policy
215 College Hall
Duquesne University
Pittsburgh, PA 15282
(412) 396-5179
stoddard@duq2.cc.duq.edu

♦ ♦ ♦ ♦ ♦

# BUSINESS ADMINISTRATION
## LOYOLA MARYMOUNT UNIVERSITY

Fellows work in public housing communities in the greater Los Angeles area assisting residents with small business development, tutoring programs, and other community initiatives. The university works directly with local public housing authorities on new and existing projects. Examples of economic development efforts have included job placement, grant writing, creation of a computer lab, and leadership workshops in the community.

Benefits: All tuition and fees associated with attending the MBA program at LMU, not including books; stipends may be available, but are not guaranteed.

Contact: Dr. Rachelle Katz, Assistant Dean
College of Business Administration, Dep't. of Management
Peace Corps Fellows Program
Loyola Marymount University
Loyola Boulevard at West 80th Street
Los Angeles, CA 90045
(310) 338-5196
rkatz@lmumail.lmu.edu

# COMMUNITY AND REGIONAL PLANNING
## UNIVERSITY OF OREGON

RPCVs are invited to participate in Resource Assistance for Rural Communities (RARE). Qualified applicants live and work in a rural community for one year helping to improve environmental and economic conditions. This is a Learn & Serve Higher Education demonstration program. RPCVs may apply for RARE placement prior to enrollment in a University program, part-way through, or upon completion of a master's program. The RARE program is expected to continue to grow and require skills characteristic of RPCVs.

Benefits: RPCVs accepted to the Learn & Serve Program receive a S1,000 per month stipend and in educational award of $4,275 for completing 1,700 hours of service, nine credit hours toward a degree in Community and Regional Planning, and qualify for in-state tuition. Benefits available only to those who have completed one year of service in the RARE program.

Contact: Professor David Povev, Director RARE
(541) 346-3812
or Scott Craig, Assistant Director RARE
(541) 346-3889
RARE Opportunities, PPPM Hendricks Hall
University of Oregon
Eugene, OR 97403
darkwing.uoregon.edu—cpw//rare/rare.html
dpovey@oregon.uoregon.edu

♦ ♦ ♦ ♦ ♦

# MANAGEMENT AND URBAN POLICY
## NEW SCHOOL UNIVERSITY

The Milano Graduate School offers MS Degrees in four concentrations: Urban Policy Analysis and Management, Nonprofit Management, Health Services Management and Policy, and Human Resources Management. Fellows work for clients as part of several courses. The School recently established a partnership with the New York City Housing Authority that will enable students to work on projects of high priority to the nation's largest housing authority. Projects at NYCHA will be integrated throughout the curriculum, and will also involve a paid summer internship. Potential topics include welfare reform, economic development, youth services, crime prevention, and transportation.

Benefits: RPCVs receive special consideration for admission and tuition assistance (which includes grants, loans, and college work study.) Students meet their education expenses through student aid and loan programs.

Contact: Susan Morris
Assistant Dean for Student Services
Robert J. Milano Graduate School of Mgm't. and Urban Policy
New School Univeristy
66 Fifth Ave.
New York, NY 10011
(212) 229-5388
smorris@newschool.edu

♦ ♦ ♦ ♦ ♦

# PUBLIC MANAGEMENT
## CARNEGIE MELLON UNIVERSITY

The H. John Heinz 111 School of Public Policy and Management offers a Master of Public Management Degree. Fellows work in public housing communities in the City of Pittsburgh assisting residents in designing and implementing an economic development plan, initiating programs to reduce crime and violence in the communities, and building a computer-based Neighborhood Information Network. Fellows are assisted by city officials and faculty from the Heinz School. Classes are conducted in the evening, allowing Fellows to work at their projects during normal working hours.

Benefits: Scholarships toward tuition and fees are available. Stipends are provided by the Pittsburgh Public Housing Agency.

Contact: Dr. Harry Faulk, Associate Dean
The Heinz School
Carnegie Mellon University
5000 Forbes Ave.
Pittsburgh, PA 15213-3890
(412) 268-2195
hf0c@andrew.cmu.edu

♦ ♦ ♦ ♦ ♦

# PUBLIC SERVICE/ PUBLIC ADMINISTRATION
## (ECONOMICS AND POLITICAL SCIENCE)
### ILLINOIS STATE UNIVERSITY

The two-year program provides training in Community and Economic Development, including field experience in rural communities in Illinois and across the United States. Fellows earn a Master's Degree by completing two to three semesters of coursework and applied workshops, as well as 11 months of hands-on work in development projects in mainly high poverty rural and urban areas.

Benefits: Full tuition waiver and graduate assistantships during the first year; full tuition waiver and a monthly stipend during the second year (year of community work).

Contact: Michael Kelleher, Director
PC Fellows Program
Department of Economics
Box 4200
Illinois State University
Normal, Illinois 61790-4200
(309) 438-8685
www.econ.ilstu.edu/Peace-Corps/PCorps.html
frnkelle@ilstu.edu

• • • • •
## RURAL AFFAIRS
### WESTERN ILLINOIS UNIVERSITY

Master's degree in Economics, Geography (Regional and Rural Planning,) Business Administration (MBA,) or Recreation, Parks, and Tourism Administration, and Gerontology are awarded through the program. In two years, Fellows complete a master's degree in one of the above fields and obtain specialized training and experience in community development. The program is coordinated by the Illinois Institute for Rural Affairs (IIRA). IIRA works closely with other economic development programs, transportation assistance, community planning, and small business support organizations. Peace Corps Fellows have access to the scope of IIRA services and resources.

During the first year, Fellows complete courses within their specific academic department, as well as core Courses in community development. For their graduate assistantship, Fellows gain experience working in development projects coordinated through the IIRA. In the second year, Fellows serve a paid internship in a rural community, providing hands-on assistance and leadership to local development projects.

Benefits: Full tuition waiver and graduate assistantships during the first year; full tuition waiver and internship salary during the second year. Educational award upon completion of community service.

Contact: Dr. John Gruidl
Illinois Institute for Rural Affairs
Western Illinois University
518 Stipes Hall
Macomb, 1161455
(800) 526-9943 or
(309) 298-2237
John-Gruidl@ccmail.wiu.edu

\* \* \* \* \*

# NURSING
## JOHNS HOPKINS UNIVERSITY

The School of Nursing offers a B.S. degree in Nursing, a M.S. in Nursing - Community Health Nursing, Nurse Practitioner, and dual degrees in Nursing and Public Health, and Nursing and Business. Fellows work at the Johns Hopkins Hospital and community health clinics in a variety of roles. A concentration in Family and Community Health Nursing is offered to Fellows who are committed to working with underserved populations. Fellows at the School of Nursing will be placed in sites such as the Rutland Transitional Housing Program in Baltimore where they will work with the residents to improve their health and social status through intensive case management, health education, and parenting education. Fellows also work in clinics and schools at other community sites. The curriculum is adapted to prepare Fellows for practice in underserved communities.

Benefits: RPCV's are given special consideration for admission, tuition assistance, which includes scholarships, grants, loans, and college work study; Peace Corps Fellows Scholarship, which covers a portion of tuition costs.

Contact: Mary O'Rorke, Director of Admissions
Johns Hopkins University School of Nursing
525 N. Wolfe St.
Baltimore, MD 21205
(410) 955-7549
ororke@son.jhmi.edu

\* \* \* \* \*

# THE SHRIVER PEACEWORKER PROGRAM
## UNIVERSITY OF MARYLAND

Various degrees are awarded with focus on four areas of social concern: education, economic and community development, juvenile justice and health. The Peaceworker Program is a two-year program integrating graduate study, community service, and ethical reflection which enables Fellows to adapt their experience as Peace Corps volunteers to solving problems confronting America's cities. Participants develop (1) an intellectual framework that enables them to identify and respond to the ethical and spiritual dimensions of urban problems, and (2) the leadership and facilitation skills necessary for effective work in e program and the community. To become Fellows in the Peaceworker Program, applicants seek admission to full time graduate study at UMBC or another member of The Shriver Center Higher Education Consortium. Graduate study in the humanities, sciences and professional schools is available. Fellows are then placed in part-time community service positions correlated as closely as possible with their graduate study.

Benefits: Peaceworkers are funded at the level of graduate assistants as UMBC: full tuition, stipend ($13,000) and health care.

Contact: Dr. James R. Price lll, Director
Shriver Peaceworker Program
The Shriver Center at UMBC
1000 Hilltop Circle
Baltimore, MD 21250
(410) 455-2493
jprice@umbc.edu

✦ ✦ ✦ ✦ ✦

# TEACHING
## UNIVERSITY OF NEW MEXICO

Education Areas available: Elementary Education; Secondary Education: Language Arts, Mathematics, Science; Bilingual Education/ ESL, Special Education. Fellows teach full-time while pursuing a Master's Degree and New Mexico Teacher Certification. Most schools in the program are located within or adjacent to the Navajo Nation. During the academic year, teacher education classes are offered at branch campuses, 150 miles west of the University of New Mexico main campus, to support the Fellows in the Gallup McKinley County Public School System. Summer classes, as well as a spring and summer pre-service preparation, take place in Albuquerque. These include classroom and in-the-field experiential learning opportunities focus on Native American, Hispanic, and Anglo history, culture in the Southwest, and multicultural pedagogical methods relevant to teaching in New Mexico.

Benefits: 30% of tuition is provided by the DeWitt Wallace-Reader's Digest fund.

Contact: Dr. Paul S. Miko, Program Coordinator
UNM/COE Peace Corps Fellows/ USA Program
University of New Mexico
Johnson Center, Room 112C
Albuquerque, NM 87131-1251
(Initial inquiries by mail only please)

♦ ♦ ♦ ♦ ♦

# TEACHING
## PACIFIC OAKS COLLEGE

A Quaker-founded institution, the college philosophy states in part that each person has a unique identity and human potential which they contribute to the lives of all those with whom they come in contact. Experiential learning is emphasized. Portfolios and personalized evaluations replace tests. The Internship Program is a 14-month, summer-to-summer program which provides field supervision and teacher support. Fellows may continue at Pacific Oaks to receive a MA in human development.

Areas offered: Elementary and Bilingual Education; teaching credentials in multiple subjects; master of arts in human development

Benefits: Approximately $8,000 tuition scholarship; regular financial aid; placement assistance for full-time salaried teaching positions

Contact: Ramona Young
Teacher Education and Credentials Program
Pacific Oaks College
5&6 Westmoreland Place
Pasadena, CA 91103
(626) 397-1334

# SCHOOL OF COMMUNITY SERVICE
## UNIVERSITY OF NORTH TEXAS

The Center for Public Service at the University of North Texas operates several sustainable healthy neighborhood programs in the Dallas/Fort Worth Metroplex. Field placement and scholarships are available with links to the regional office of the Environmental Alliance for Senior Involvement, and the Educational Consortium for Volunteerism. The Department of Sociology offers a Ph.D. program in community development.

Master of Science (M.S.) in Applied Economics, Sociology, Criminal Justice, Applied Gerontology, Behavioral Analysis and Rehabilitation, Social Work, and Addictions; Master of Public Administration; M.S. in Interdisciplinary Studies in Sustainable Communities, or Volunteer and Resource Management are available.

Benefits: RPCV's are given special consideration for admission; tuition assistance, which includes MS scholarships from the School of Community Service, grants, loans, and college work-study. Peace Corps Fellowships are also available from local developers and local agencies.

Contact: Dr. Martin Jaeckel, Director (940) 565-4630
mjaeck@scs.unt.edu
Sustainable Communities Studies
Cathy Davidson, Coordinator (904) 565-3474
davidson@scs.unt.edu
Peace Corps Fellows Program
The University of North Texas
Center for Public Service
P.O. Box 13438
Denton, TX 76203-6438

◆ ◆ ◆ ◆ ◆

# URBAN STUDIES
## MICHIGAN STATE UNIVERSITY

Joint MA, MS and PhD degrees are awarded in Urban Studies with over 15 academic programs including: Urban Planning, Resource Development, Social Work, Sociology, and Criminal Justice. Fellows work with residents and resident-based organizations in public housing to identify community concerns and develop effective responses to urban problems. RPCVs with community and economic development experience are strongly encouraged to apply.

Benefits: Graduate assistantship for one or more semesters; in-state-tuition; tuition waiver for six credit hours per semester, monthly stipend.

Contact: Dr. Rex LaMore
State Director, Center for Urban Affairs
Michigan State University
1801 West Main St.
Lansing, MI 48915-1097
(517) 353-9555
lamore@pilot.msu.edu

♦ ♦ ♦ ♦ ♦

# RESOURCES

**Au Sable Institute of Environmental Studies** promotes the care and keeping of the whole Creation, through summer and intersession college-level courses and programs in restoration ecology, conservation biology, field studies, environmental science, environmental ethics and land stewardship. Operates as a community based on Christian teachings and practice. Surrounded by forest, lakes and rivers, participants develop practical tools for environmental stewardship. ASI, 7526 Sunset Trail NE, Mancelona, MI 49659 (818) 567-8888

**Campus Ecology - A Guide To Assessing Environmental Quality & Creating Strategies For Change** A guidebook from the country's leading student environmental organization for learning practical environmental management skills and greening your campus. April Smith and Student Environmental Action Coalition. Living Planet Press 1993

**Campus Favorites - Vegetarian Recipe Collection** Dieticians in College and University Food Service, American Dietetic Association, 605 S. Madison St., Lancaster, WI 58313

**Colleges That Change Lives - 40 Schools You Should Know About Even if You're Not A Straight A Student** Worth reading. Many of the same colleges as in this guide, many different. A critical look at standard thinking about colleges. Loren Pope, Penguin 1996

**Community-Campus Partnerships for Health - A Guide for Developing Community-Responsive Models in Health Professions Education** An excellent source of newly emergent models of health education. Profiles programs in medicine, dentistry, nursing. Sarena Seifer and Kara Connors UCSF Center for the Health Professions 1997 (415) 476-8181

**ECO - The Environmental Careers Organization** a non-profit organization offering paid, short-term environmental positions for undergraduates and other entry-level environmental job seekers. They sponsor environmental career conferences, workshops and advising through their Environmental Career Services. They publish *The New Complete Guide to Environmental Careers* Island Press, an important resource for environmental job hunting.

**Earth In Mind - On Education, Environment, and the Human Prospect** A collection of insightful essays from Oberlin Professor David Orr on the implications of typical current higher education practices, and thought provoking suggestions on better ways to go. Highly recommended for parents!!! Island Press 1994

**EarthSave** Non-profit organization founded by John Robbins - author of *Diet for A New America*. EarthSave educates the public about the relationship between how they eat and environmental and health impacts. Santa Cruz, CA (408) 423-4069

**Ecodemia - Campus Environmental Stewardship at the Turn of the 21st Century, Lessons in Smart Management from Administrators, Staff and Students.** Innovative green management practices at universities across the country. Much information can be easily extrapolated. Julian Keniry, National Wildlife Federation, 1995 (800) 432-6564

**EcoNet** Online? Check out EcoNet - a non-profit unionized service provider for people networking around the globe in the areas of the environment, peace, and labor, and women's issues. The Institute for Global Communications (415) 561-1600 www.igc.apc.org

**Education for Action - Undergraduate and Graduate Programs that Focus on Social Change** Small but valuable for the graduate programs. Sean Brooks and Allison Knowles, Food First Books 1995

**Education For an Ecologically Sustainable Culture - Rethinking Moral Education, Creativity, Intelligence, and Other Modern Orthodoxies** Deep reading. Bowers, C.A. State University of New York Press, 1995

**Educational and Career Opportunities in Alternative Medicine - All You Need to Find Your Calling in the Healing Professions.** Rosemary Jones, Prima Publishing 1998

**Green Corps, Field School for Environmental Organizing** Trains college students who have an interest in organizing as a career. Training includes advocacy organizing, case studies of organizing problems, skills and training clinics, working case study, campaign trainings and lectures. 1109 Walnut St, 4th fl, Philadelphia, PA 19107 (215) 829-1760

**Guide to Careers and Graduate Education in Peace Studies** PAWSS, Hampshire College, Amherst, MA 01002

**Guide to Graduate Education in Public Affairs and Public Administration, NASPAA Directory of Programs** Craig Donovan, National Association of Schools of Public Affairs and Administration 1997 (202) 628-8965 naspaa@naspaa.org

**Guide to Graduate Environmental Programs** Over 150 green graduate programs - long on data, short on information about the actual studies. Student Conservation Association Island Press 1997

**The International Partnership for Service-Learning** The original experts in international service-learning - excellent programs all across the world. IPSL, 815 Second Avenue, Suite 315, New York, NY 10017-4594 (212) 986-0989

**Making a Difference While Making a Living** Excellent book for those seeking "right livelihood." Wide range of sectors from business to government to non-profits. Melissa Everett, Bantam Books, 1995

**Student Conservation Association** Helps college students find volunteer positions as professional assistants in national and state parks, nat'l forest and wildlife refuges. Work for 3-4 months and gain valuable training and field experience. Provides funds to cover travel and food expenses plus free housing. Publishes *Earth Work*, a monthly magazine for folks seeking conservation employment. PO Box 550, Charlestown, NH 03603 (603) 826-4301

**Student Pugwash** Provides college and select high school students with programs to better understand the social and ethical implications of science and technology. Chapters at over 25 colleges. They publish *Jobs You Can Live With*, have alternative job fairs, and promote mentor relationships with concerned professionals. 1638 R St. NW, Ste 32, Washington, D.C. 20009 (800) WOW-A-PUG

**Volunteers for Peace International** Publish the *International Work Camp Directory*, the ultimate for 900 inexpensive (under $200) international work camps primarily in Europe. Restore medieval villages, work with refugee children, learn bio-dynamic gardening, work at music festivals... A great prelude to college. VFP (802) 259-2759 vfp@vfp.org www.vfp.org

Footnotes: *What is Education for?*

1 Elie Wiesel, "Global Education," Speech before the Global Forum Moscow, USSR (Jan 1990)

2 Barry Lopez, "American Geographies," *Origin* (September 1989)

3 Page Smith, *Killing the Spirit* (New York: Viking Press, 1990)

4 Loran Eiseley, The Star Thrower (New York: Harcourt, Brace, Jovanovich, 1985), p. 284.

5 Thomas Merton, *Love and Living* (New York: Harcourt, Brace, Jovanovich, 1985), p. 11.

6 Ron Miller, "Editorial," *Holistic Education Review* (Spring 1990)

Footnotes: *Walking in Beauty*

0 *Choosing A Sustainable Future: The Report of the National Commision on the Environment* (Covelo, CA: Island press, 1993), p. 33

1. Published in Partnership by IUCN (the World Conservation Union), UNEP (Uited Nations Environment Programme), and WWF (World Wide Fund for Nature), *Caring for the Earth: A Strategy for Sustainable Living* (Covelo, CA: Island Press, 1991)

2 Albert Schweitzer, *The Philosophy of Civilization*, trans. C.T. Campion (Buffalo, NY: Prometheus Books, 1987), p. 325. italics added.

3 Aldo Leopold, *Sand County Almanac* (New York: Ballantine Books, 1966), p. 137.

 Kevin W. Kelly, ed. *The Home Planet* (New York: Addison-Wesley Publishing Company, 1988).

4 See also Alfred North Whitehead, *Science and the Modern World* (New York: Free Press, 1967), p. 199.

5 Cited in Elizabeth Roberts and Elias Amidon, eds. *Earth Prayers From Around The World* (San Francisco: HarperSanFrancisco, 1991), p. 5.

6 Joseph Epes Brown, "I Become Part of It," in D.M. Dooling and Paul Gordon-Smith, *I Become Part of It* (New York: Parabola Books, 1989), p. 20.

7 "Navajo, Surgeon, Pioneer," in *New York Times*, February 17, 1994, Section C, p. 1.

8 *Earth Prayers From Around The World*, p. 184.

9 Thich Nhat Hanh, *Peace is Every Step; the Path of Mindfulness in Everyday Life* (New York: Bantam Books, 1991), pp. 21-22. *Present Moment, Wonderful Moment: Mindfulness Verses for Daily Living* (Berkeley, CA: Parallax Press, 1990) p. 48,51.

10 Lucien Stryk and Takashi Ikemoto, ed. and trans., *The Penguin Book of Zen Poetry* (Chicago: Swallow Press, 1977), p. 76.

11 John Dewey, Art as Experience, in *John Dewey: The Later Works, 1925-1953* (Carbondale: Southern Illinois University Press, 1987), Vol. 10, 198-99.

12 See Joanna Macy, *World As Lover; World as Self* (Berkeley, CA: Parallax Press, 1991), ch. 17.

13 John Seed, as quoted in J. Baird Callicott, "The Metaphysical Implications of Ecology," in J. Baird Callicott and Roger T. Ames, eds. *Nature in Asian Traditions of Thought*, (Albany: SUNY, 1989), p. 64.

14 As quoted in Tu Wei-Ming,"The Continuity of Being: Chinese Visions of Nature," in Callicott and Ames, eds. *Nature in Asian Traditions of Thought*, pp. 73-74.

 *The Complete Poetical Works of Wordsworth* (Boston: Houghton Mifflin Company, 1932), p. 91.

 Ralph Waldo Emerson, "The Over-Soul," in *Essays: First and Second Series* (Mount Vernon, N.Y.: Peter Pauper Press, n.d.), p. 138.

15 Starhawk, as quoted in *Earth Prayers From Around The World*, p. 14.

 Dewey, *Experience and Nature*, in *The Later Works*, Vol. 1, 313-14.

16 Albert Schweitzer, *Out of My Life and Thought: An Autobiography*, trans. C.T. Campion (New York: Henry Holt and Company, 1933, 1949), p. 157.

17 *Ibid.*, pp. 158-60.

 As quoted in Roderick Frazier Nash, *The Rights of Nature: A History of Environmental Ethics* (Madison, Wis.: University of Wisconsin Press, 1989), p. 44.

18 As quoted in Roger Walsh, "The Ecological Imperative," in *ReVision: A Journal of Consciousness and Transformation* Fall 1993, Volume 16, Number 2, p. 51.

19 Fyodor Dostoevsky, *The Brothers Karamazov*, trans. Constance Garnett and ed. Ralph E. Matlaw (New York: Norton, 1976), p. 298.

# COLLEGE INDEX

**Field Studies, Summer & Travel Programs**

# GRADUATE PROGRAM INDEX

## PEACE CORPS MASTER'S INTERNATIONALIST PROGRAMS

## RETURNED PEACE CORPS FELLOWS PROGRAM

# STATE BY STATE INDEX UNDERGRADUATE

**Alaska**
Alaska Pacific University
Sheldon Jackson College
University of Alaska at Fairbanks
**Arizona**
Prescott College
**California**
California Institute of Integral Studies
CSU Monterey Bay
Humboldt State University
New College of California - World College Inst.
Pitzer College
Rudolf Steiner Institute
San Francisco State
Stanford University
University of CA, Davis
University of CA, Santa Cruz
University of Redlands
**Colorado**
Colorado College
Colorado State University
Naropa Institute
University of Colorado at Boulder
**Connecticut**
Wesleyan University
Yale University
**Florida**
Brevard Community College
**Hawaii**
University of Hawaii at Manoa
**Indiana**
Earlham College
Goshen College
Manchester College
**Iowa**
Grinnell College
**Kansas**
Bethel College
**Kentucky**
Berea College
**Maine**
College of the Atlantic
University of Maine at Orono
**Massachusetts**
Clark University
Hampshire College
Simon's Rock College
Tufts University
Wellesley College
**Michigan**
Univ. of Michigan School of Natural Resources
**Minnesota**
Bemidji State University
Carleton College
St. Olaf College
University of Minnesota at Minneapolis
**New Jersey**
Rutgers State - Cook College

**New York**
College of Environmental Science & Forestry
Cornell University
Eugene Lang College
Hobart & William Smith College
Iona College
Long Island U --Friends World / Southampton
Sarah Lawrence
Sunbridge College
**North Carolina**
Guilford College
Warren Wilson College
**Ohio**
Antioch College
Oberlin College
Ohio Wesleyan University
**Oregon**
University of Oregon at Eugene
Portland State Unversity
**Pennsylvania**
Bryn Mawr
California Univ. of Pennsylvania
Penn State University
Swarthmore College
**Rhode Island**
Brown University
**Texas**
Trinity University
**Vermont**
Burlington College
Goddard College
Green Mountain
Marlboro College
Sterling College
University of Vermont
**Virginia**
Eastern Mennonite College
**Washington**
The Evergreen State College
Seattle University
University of Washington
Washington State University
Western Washington U - Fairhaven / Huxley
**Wisconsin**
Beloit
Northland College
University of Wisconsin --Stevens Point
**Field, Travel, Summer Programs**
Arava Institute
Audubon Expedition Institute
Biosphere 2 - Columbia University
Center for Global Education
GAIA / Geocommons Program
International Honors
Institute for Social Ecology
Rainforest Consevation
School for Field Studies
Sierra Institute
Wildlands Studies - San Francisco State

# United States Signatories of the Talloires Declaration

Alaska Pacific University, Alaska

Blue Ridge Community College, Virginia

Bowling Green State University, Ohio

Brown University, Rhode Island

Cape Cod Community College, MA

Christopher Newport College, Virginia

Clark University, Massachusetts

Clemson University, South Carolina

Clinch Valley College, Virginia

College of the Atlantic, Maine

College of William & Mary, Virginia

Connecticut College, Connecticut

Hampden-Sydney College, Virginia

George Mason University, Virginia

George Washington U, Washington, DC

James Madison University, Virginia

Longwood College, Virginia

Mary Washington College, Virginia

Merrimack College, Massachusetts

Middlebury College, Vermont

Muhlenburg College, Pennsylvania

Norfolk State University, Virginia

Northern Arizona University, Arizona

Northern Virginia Comm. College, VA

Old Dominion University, Virginia

Patrick Henry Comm. College, Virginia

Philadelphia College of Textiles & Science, PA

Piedmont Community College, Virginia

Radford University, Virginia

Randolph Macon College, Virginia

Rice University, Texas

Richard Bland College, Virginia

Rutgers University, New Jersey

Southern University and A&M College, LA

Sterling College, Vermont

Tri-County Technical College, So. Carolina

Tufts University, Massachusetts

University of Arizona, Arizona

University of California-Santa Barbara

University of Colorado, Boulder

University of Florida

University of Georgia

University of Hawaii

University of Massachusetts at Boston

University of Nevada

University of New Hampshire

University of North Carolina

University of Northern Iowa

University of Pittsburgh, Pennsylvania

University of Rhode Island

University of Virginia

University of Wisconsin-Madison

Utah State University

Virginia Commonwealth University

Virginia Military Institute

Virginia State University

Virginia Western Community College

Xavier University of Louisiana

## *YES, I WANT TO MAKE A DIFFERENCE*

Please send me more information about your school. I am interested in:

❐  Academic programs in _____
   _____

❐  Sevice or Extracurricular activities in _____
   _____

❐  Other _____
❐  I will be entering _____  ❐  I am a transfer student
Name_____
Address _____
City State Zip _____

---

## *YES, I WANT TO MAKE A DIFFERENCE*

Please send me more information about your school. I am interested in:

❐  Academic programs in _____
   _____

❐  Sevice or Extracurricular activities in _____
   _____

❐  Other _____
❐  I will be entering _____  ❐  I am a transfer student
Name_____
Address _____
City State Zip _____

---

## *YES, I WANT TO MAKE A DIFFERENCE*

Please send me more information about your school. I am interested in:

❐  Academic programs in _____
   _____

❐  Sevice or Extracurricular activities in _____
   _____

❐  Other _____
❐  I will be entering _____  ❐  I am a transfer student
Name_____
Address _____
City State Zip _____

## ABOUT THE EDITOR

Miriam Weinstein lives with a fluctuating number of her four children in San Anselmo, California. She has an avid interest in education and has studied many philosophies of education from elementary level through college. She has been active in environmental and social causes since her early teens. She was the director of the Eco Design & Builders Guild, a "green" building network she founded in the San Francisco Bay Area. An award-winning photographer, Miriam is an educated tree-hugging vegetarian who recycles conscientiously, and a graduate of New College of California.

# ORDER FORM

Please send me __ copy (ies) of

❑ **Making A Difference College & Graduate Guide.**
Enclose $18 per copy,  plus $3.00 for shipping for first copy,
$1.50 shipping for each additional copy.

Please send me __ copy (ies) of

❑ **Making A Difference Scholarships
Awards, Fellowships, Social Entrepreneur Funds,
Community Service Project Funding
To Help Make A Better World**
Enclose $13 per copy,  plus $2.50 for shipping for first copy,
$1.00 shipping for each additional copy.

❑ Please bill my Mastercard/Visa account # _____

Signature_____ Exp. Date_____

Name_____ PO#_____

Address_____

City, State, Zip _____

Telephone_____

Please send the person named below information about your books.
Name_____

Address_____

City, State, Zip _____

### Make checks payable to:

SageWorks Press
POB 441
Fairfax, CA 94978-0441

## or call (800) 218-GAIA
## www.sageworks.net